D0723699

WITHDRAWN

KENTUCKY

THERESA DOWELL BLACKINTON

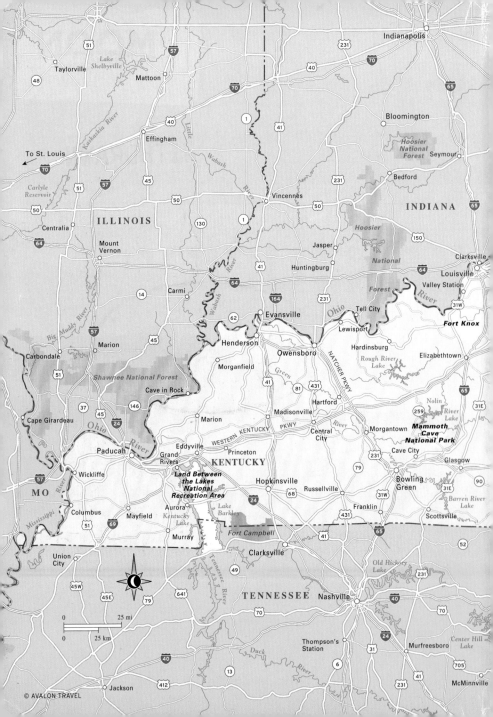

Contents

DISCOVER
Kentucky

To put Kentucky into words is hard, because Kentucky is more than a collection of places. It's more than thoroughbred horses grazing on rich limestone-fed land in the rolling hills around Lexington. It's more than the blazing colors of Appalachia, lit on fire by autumn days. It's more than the bustling downtown streets of Louisville, where new enterprise lives in historic buildings. It's more than weathered tobacco barns, bourbon distilleries, record-length caves, and bluegrass festivals. Kentucky is a feeling, like sunshine in the winter or rain on a warm spring day.

Kentucky is home to cave miners and environmental activists, farmers and country music stars, doctors and artists. It's home to people who register Democrat and vote Republican, people who think basketball is religion, people who consider the first Saturday in May to be a holiday. It's a place of contradictions that somehow draws people in—those who have lived in the Bluegrass State their entire lives and those who show up as transplants, but become, just like bluegrass itself, practically native. Governor A.B. "Happy" Chandler once said, "I've never met a Kentuckian who wasn't coming home," and he was right. Even those of us Kentuckians who are displaced still consider Kentucky

home. It's the place we all want to end up, the place where people not only know you, but know your momma, your daddy, and your grandparents, too.

Kentucky is a place of warm hospitality, where people treat neighbors like family, and are never too busy to sit on the porch for a glass of sweet tea and some gossip. But to assume that Kentucky is all country roads and simple pleasures would be wrong. The state has big urban areas, with top-ranked hospitals, innovative art galleries, award-winning restaurants, and first-rate universities. The birthplace of bluegrass music and home to the first integrated college in the south, Kentucky is at once traditional and progressive.

Although people say statistics don't lie, the truth about Kentucky is found in the spaces between. Too often stereotyped and misunderstood, Kentucky will blow you away if you only give it a chance. Just be aware that once you arrive, you may not want to leave. But hey, that's okay. Kentucky welcomes you to stay just as long as you'd like.

Planning Your Trip

Where to Go

Louisville

Louisville is Kentucky's biggest city, offering the most museums, historic sites, and other tourist attractions, as well as hosting the biggest restaurant, nightlife, and art scenes in the state. Home of the Kentucky Derby, Louisville packs people in on the first weekend of May, but with unique offerings like the Louisville Slugger Museum and Muhammad Ali Center, and the fantastic downtown hotels and Old Louisville B&Bs, it makes for a wonderful visit any time of year. After a few days in Louisville, it's easy to head off to destinations throughout the state.

Bardstown, the Bourbon Trail, and Frankfort

Kentucky's spirit comes to life in this central section of the state. Travel along the famed Bourbon Trail and you'll get to taste more than the nation's only native liquor. Thomas Merton's Gethsemani and the Basilica of St. Joseph speak to Kentucky's religious heritage, while Abraham Lincoln's Birthplace captures Kentucky's pioneering past. From My Old Kentucky Home in Bardstown to the Capitol in Frankfort, this region attracts those interested in Kentucky tradition and history.

Lexington and Horse Country

Quintessentially Kentucky, Lexington and Horse Country almost seem like a stereotype. On gentle fields enclosed by fences, thoroughbreds are bred into champion racehorses. Visit a horse farm to see just how it's done. Opening day at Keeneland is a tradition unlike any other, except perhaps UK basketball in Rupp Arena. In the area surrounding this Southern belle of a city, you'll find historic sites with critical connections to the state's founding.

Northern Kentucky and Covered Bridge Country

Bordered by the Ohio River, Northern Kentucky bears the influence of its northern neighbors, but retains a distinct Southern sensibility. Covington and Newport are high entertainment destinations, especially with Cincinnati just across the river. The Newport Aquarium is a must. Farther east, quaint towns interrupt sprawling farmland. Covered bridges, barn quilts, and bright green fields of tobacco are characteristic of the area.

Appalachia

Remarkable natural beauty, a tradition of folk art and music, and a history filled with legendary characters are the earmarks of Appalachia in far eastern Kentucky. Catch a concert along the Country Music Highway. Watch artisans at work in Berea. See a

IF YOU HAVE . . .

- **A WEEKEND:** Pick either Louisville or Lexington and fill your days with visits to museums, historic sites, and horse-related attractions.

- **FIVE DAYS:** Add the Bourbon Trail. Pick it up at either end and travel from Louisville to Lexington or vice-versa while enjoying sips of bourbon and sites along the way.

- **A WEEK:** Add some outdoor adventure to your itinerary. Visit a cave, go to the lake, take a hike, or just relax at one of the state parks.

- **TEN DAYS:** Get cultured. Explore the art scene in Berea or Paducah, seek out a barbecue or bluegrass festival, or catch the beat on the Country Music Highway.

© AVALON TRAVEL

moonbow at Cumberland Falls. Hike among sandstone arches in Red River Gorge. Take a tour of a coal camp in Stearns or a coal mine in Lynch. Attend a barn jamboree in Renfro Valley. Follow Daniel Boone's Wilderness Road at Cumberland Gap. The diversity of Appalachia and the kindness of the people will surprise and delight you.

Bowling Green, Cave Country, and South-Central Lakes

Adventure lovers are drawn to south-central Kentucky, where many of the state's best lakes are concentrated. State parks offer hiking, golfing, and wildlife-watching opportunities. Others prefer to escape the sun while exploring Kentucky's many

Bluegrass was born in Rosine.

natural beauty at the state parks

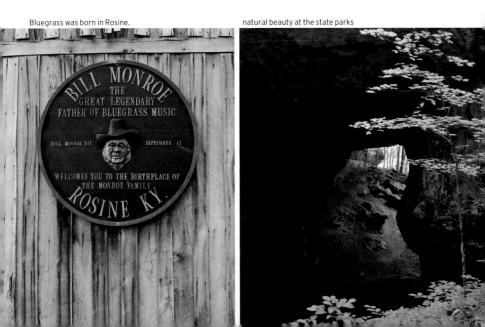

caves, including Mammoth Cave, the longest cave system in the world. If your idea of adventure involves speed, Bowling Green's Corvette Assembly Plant and National Corvette Museum will get your motor running.

Owensboro, Paducah, and Land Between the Lakes

Western Kentucky is a celebration of Americana. Owensboro, where there's a festival nearly every weekend, is the home of Kentucky-style barbecue, which is built around burgoo and mutton. Nearby Rosine is home to Bill Monroe, the father of bluegrass music. Stop by on Friday when musicians gather to play at the Rosine Barn Jamboree. Paducah is a small town with a big spirit and a huge focus on art. For fans of the great outdoors, the Land Between the Lakes area just might be heaven. Thousands of acres of water and shoreline make it paradise for sports of every sort.

When to Go

Kentucky is a year-round destination, but the most popular time for visiting is May-October.

Spring brings warm days without the summer's humidity. Attractions that are closed in the low season begin to reopen and other year-round attractions extend their hours. It's a great time to get outdoors, although pollen can be a problem for those with allergies. Spring is also Derby time. The Run for the Roses is held on the first Saturday in May, with the Derby Festival occupying the two weeks leading up to the race. It's a celebratory and fun time to visit, although you'll have to deal with soaring hotel and flight prices as well as crowds in Louisville and surrounding areas.

For those who don't mind heat and humidity, summer is the peak season for travel. The state's lakes and waterways are popular destinations this time of year, and the parks are also busy. Festivals and other cultural events mark most weekends, providing lots of day-trip opportunities.

Many people declare fall their favorite season in Kentucky, and it's hard to argue. Temperatures are mild, the trees burst into color, and crowds are down. This might be the best time of year to tour the state's parks or head to the mountains. It's also the season for farm visits.

Winter is a quiet time in Kentucky. Some parks close for the season, and other attractions, especially in small towns, operate on reduced schedules, but it's a fine time to visit museums and other indoor attractions.

The Best of the Bluegrass State

Let's be honest: The trip outlined here is a bit crazy. It's an ambitious attempt to get you to see the best of Kentucky in just two weeks. What you really need is a month, or better yet, a lifetime, but most people just don't have that amount of time. So consider this your sampler platter, your chance to savor the best of the best. You're not going to see everything—not in the state, and not even in each destination—but you'll get a taste of what Kentucky has to offer, so next time you can dive in deeper.

Day 1

Start in Louisville with a day of museum-hopping. Begin downtown with a visit to the Louisville Slugger Museum & Factory to immerse yourself in all things baseball, then head to the Muhammad Ali Center to air box with The Greatest. If history is more your thing, swap the Ali Center for the Frazier International History Museum to see their remarkable collection of artifacts. In the afternoon, head south to the Kentucky Derby Museum, where you'll get to pop in at historic Churchill Downs. Grab dinner in NuLu—maybe at Decca or Rye—and then splurge for a room at 21C Museum Hotel or enjoy the atmosphere at one of Old Louisville's B&Bs.

Day 2

A lot of driving awaits, so wake up early and travel to Paducah in far western Kentucky. Art is at the heart of Paducah, so make sure the National Quilt Museum and the Lower Town Arts District both make it onto your itinerary. Enjoy dinner at Cynthia's and then have sweet dreams in one of the enormous suites at Fox Briar Inn.

Day 3

Start your journey back east with a short drive to Land Between the Lakes. Stop at Kentucky Dam Village State Resort Park and rent a boat, and go for a morning cruise on beautiful Kentucky Lake, the largest man-made lake east of the Mississippi. Dedicate your afternoon to exploring Land Between the Lakes National Recreation Area. You can go for a hike or a horseback ride, or visit the Nature Station or The Homeplace. Sit down to a plate of fried fish at Catfish Kitchen, then pitch a tent and sleep under the stars at one of the many campgrounds.

Louisville skyline

Get Wild

Outdoor and adventure lovers are in luck in Kentucky, where there are literally hundreds of opportunities to engage in active pursuits. From state and national parks to nature preserves and federal recreation areas, you have your pick of places to engage in heart-pumping activities that will get your adrenaline flowing. True adventurers will want to put the following activities at the top of their to-do list:

- **Bike** the **Horsey Hundred** in Lexington, a 26-100-mile bike ride that lets you enjoy horse country from your bike saddle.

- Cast a line at **Kentucky Lake,** an **angler's paradise** and the largest lake east of the Mississippi by surface area.

- Get off-road on your **ATV** in **Harlan,** exploring the landscape of FX's *Justified* on a four-wheeler.

- Hang out on a **houseboat** on **Lake Cumberland,** joining the throngs who come to party every summer.

- **Hike** the **Pine Mountain Trail,** where the wilderness seems just as wild as it did when Daniel Boone first blazed through.

- **Raft** the **Russell Fork River,** where the rapids rage in October when the dam is opened.

- **Ride horses** on **Land Between the Lakes,** trotting along the trails of this national recreation area.

- **Rock climb** in **Red River Gorge,** home to some of the best climbing in the eastern United States.

- **Scuba dive** the **Blue Springs quarry** in Hopkinsville, where an inland location is no challenge to underwater fun.

- **Spelunk** at **Mammoth Cave,** getting up close and personal with the world's longest cave system.

- Watch for **elk** in **eastern Kentucky,** where they were reintroduced in 1997 and now number nearly 10,000.

- **Zip-line** over the forests of **Cave Country,** getting an aerial view of an area more known for its below-ground activities.

elk in eastern Kentucky

Day 4

Continue east to Bowling Green to admire the hot rods at the National Corvette Museum. In the afternoon, hop on I-65 and drive north to Cave Country to explore Mammoth Cave or the cave of your choice. The national park is a good place to have a picnic dinner before making your way north past Munfordville to Country Girl at Heart Farm Bed and Breakfast, where you can get a peaceful night's sleep.

Day 5

After breakfast, make your way to Bardstown to say hello to My Old Kentucky Home and then get started on the Bourbon Trail. You have your choice of distilleries, but stop at Maker's Mark in Loretto if you have

National Corvette Museum

time for only one. After your tour, continue on to Harrodsburg, where the Beaumont Inn is the place to go for both dinner and a room.

Day 6

Try to be at Shaker Village when it opens so that you have time to peek into the many buildings and watch the demonstrations. If you wish, have lunch there before continuing north to Frankfort, Kentucky's capital city. With little time in Frankfort, make the Center for Kentucky History your destination. Plan for dinner at Rick's White Light Diner and then see if a room is available at The Meeting House Bed and Breakfast.

Day 7

From Frankfort, it's on to Northern Kentucky, where the Newport Aquarium is a must. Between Newport and Covington, you have a slew of dining and hotel options, so let your mood guide you. In the evening, enjoy a view of both the Northern Kentucky and Cincinnati skylines while on a cruise with BB Riverboats. End the night with a stein of beer at the Hofbräuhaus Newport.

Day 8

Put on your hiking boots this morning, as today is going to be an outdoor adventure. Travel south to Red River Gorge, a nature lover's paradise in the Daniel Boone National Forest. You can hike to sandstone arches and waterfalls, paddle down the Red River, or try your hand at rock climbing on some of the east's best routes. Rent a cabin in the gorge or book a room at Natural Bridge State Resort Park.

Day 9

Drive an hour east from Red River Gorge to Paintsville, located on the Country Music Highway in Kentucky's Appalachians. See if Herman is available to give you a tour of Butcher Hollow, the birthplace of Loretta Lynn, then explore Mountain HomePlace. In the evening, head south to Jenny Wiley State Resort Park in Prestonsburg, where you'll spend the night. Try to catch a show at either the Mountain Arts Center or the Jenny Wiley Theatre.

Day 10

Put on some country music as you continue down the highway to Pikeville, where you can spend your morning on the Hatfield-McCoy

Feud Driving Tour or getting back to nature at Breaks Interstate Park. In the afternoon, head west to the coal company towns of Benham and Lynch, where you'll want to make time for a tour of Portal 31 and a visit to the Kentucky Coal Mining Museum. The Benham School House Inn welcomes you to overnight in a former school.

Day 11

Rise and shine early to see if you can spot any black bears at Kingdom Come State Park before continuing west to Middlesboro and Cumberland Gap National Historical Park. Sign up for the trip to the Hensley Settlement, where you'll get a taste of Appalachian homestead life. In the evening, watch the sunset from the Pinnacle Overlook. You'll sleep well at Cumberland Manor Bed and Breakfast.

Day 12

Make it to Stearns in time for the morning departure of the Big South Fork Scenic Railway, which chugs its way through scenic forest to the Blue Heron Coal Mining Camp, which is interpreted by the National Park Service. Really immerse yourself in the region's coal mining history with an afternoon visit to Barthell Coal Mining Camp, a perfect

reconstruction of the former camp. For a unique experience, overnight in one of the miner's cabins.

Day 13

Cruise north to the town of Berea, Kentucky's folk arts and crafts capital, passing Cumberland Falls State Resort Park on your way. Spend your day in Berea hopping between the galleries and workshops of the town's studio artists, where you can watch them at work and do a bit of shopping. Try for an early dinner reservation at Boone Tavern, where you'll also spend the night. For evening entertainment, backtrack to Renfro Valley to catch one of their jamborees.

Day 14

Your tour of Kentucky ends in Lexington, where horses will be the theme. Sign up for a tour of a horse farm and then spend a few hours at the Kentucky Horse Park. If the Keeneland meets are going on, abandon all plans and go to the races. You'll have a hard time choosing among the many fine restaurants in the region, but if you can get a reservation at Holly Hill Inn in nearby Midway, take it. With wonderful B&B options, Midway or Versailles is a good place to spend the night.

The Cumberland River cuts through the mountains of Appalachia.

Fall Foliage

Fall in Kentucky is a sensory experience, marked by crisp and cool mornings, pumpkin-flavored everything, the smell of bonfires, and, perhaps above all else, the colors of the changing leaves. Together, these beautiful trees—the bright reds and oranges of sugar maples; the plum purple of ash; the yellow of poplars, birches, and willows; and the dark red of dogwoods, redwoods, and sassafras—paint the landscape. Although one's mind naturally goes to the mountains when it's leaf-peeping time, every region of the state has wonderful sites for taking in the colors of fall.

LOUISVILLE
Within the city, head to the **Olmsted Parks.** The summit of **Iroquois Park** is hard to beat, but the view from Hogan's Fountain at **Cherokee Park** is also nice. If you're willing to go a bit further afield, hike through the colorful forests of **Otter Creek Outdoor Recreation Area.**

BARDSTOWN, THE BOURBON TRAIL, AND FRANKFORT
Bernheim Arboretum is a prime choice for fall beauty, especially if you venture out onto the Canopy Tree Walk. The trails at **Salato Wildlife Education Center** should also satisfy any need to have leaves crunching underfoot.

LEXINGTON AND HORSE COUNTRY
For an in-city escape in Lexington, take a stroll through the **University of Kentucky Arboretum,** where color abounds. In nearby Winchester, seek out **Lower Howard's Creek Nature & Heritage Preserve.** A bike ride from Midway to Versailles, past tree- and fence-lined horse farms, is sure to wow.

NORTHERN KENTUCKY AND COVERED BRIDGE COUNTRY
The trip out to **Rabbit Hash** is certain to please those looking for a perfect fall drive. Add the trails at **Boone County Cliffs State Nature Preserve** and **Dinsmore Woods State Nature Preserve** for a full day of leaf-peeping excitement.

APPALACHIA
You'll find excellent fall colors throughout Appalachia, but the area's parks are the place to be. Take the colors in while rafting at **Breaks** or **Cumberland Falls,** climbing in **Red River Gorge,** hiking at **Pine Mountain,** or elk watching at **Jenny Wiley.**

BOWLING GREEN, CAVE COUNTRY, AND SOUTH-CENTRAL LAKES
Enjoy autumn from the water while **paddling the Green River,** or take in a bird's-eye view of the trees on a zip-lining trip with **Mammoth Cave Adventures.** The shoreline view from a houseboat on **Dale Hollow Lake** or **Lake Cumberland** is also mighty nice.

OWENSBORO, PADUCAH, AND LAND BETWEEN THE LAKES
Land Between the Lakes is a kaleidoscope of color in fall. A drive down the length of the natural recreation area via The Trace will provide plenty of views, but to really absorb it all, consider saddling up and seeing it on horseback or doing a multi-day backpacking trip.

Horsin' Around

When people think Kentucky, they think horses, and honestly, that's only fair. Horses are big business (and big fun) here. For horse lovers, Kentucky is a dream destination, with enough equine attractions to fill an entire itinerary. October is an ideal time to do this trip, at least if you want to see live racing at Kentucky's two major tracks.

Day 1

Start in Lexington, the horse capital of the world, where the Kentucky Horse Park should be your first destination. The shows, demonstrations, and museums will easily fill an entire morning. In the afternoon, head north to Georgetown for a visit to Old Friends, a retirement farm for racehorses, followed by horseback riding with Whispering Woods Riding Stable. Return to Lexington in the evening for dinner and an overnight stay.

Day 2

If it's not April or October, rise early to catch morning workouts at Keeneland and to have breakfast at the Track Kitchen with jockeys and trainers. If one of the meets is going on, you have the option of attending the races at Keeneland, one of the most beautiful tracks in the world, or touring horse farms. Claiborne Farm in Paris, the final resting place of famed Secretariat, is a top choice for farm tours. Of course, you can also add an extra day to the itinerary and do both. Again, overnight in Lexington or one of the surrounding communities, such as Versailles or Midway.

Day 3

Depart Lexington for Shelbyville, which sits between Lexington and Louisville. Although often overlooked, Shelbyville is the saddlebred capital of the world. (Saddlebreds are Kentucky's only native breed of horse.) Tours of Shelbyville horse farms can be arranged through the local tourism bureau. After a morning tour, have lunch at Claudia Sanders Dinner House and then continue east to Louisville. Spend the night in Old Louisville for easy access to the next day's attractions.

Derby Traditions

To fully partake in Derby, to completely understand what it is about a two-minute horse race that makes a city go mad, you have to do more than attend the Kentucky Derby and the many officially sanctioned Derby Festival events going on around town. You must also live, breathe, eat, and talk Derby for at least the two weeks leading up to it and the day itself (the first Saturday in May).

You must also plan in advance because it's difficult to find accommodations around Louisville at Derby time or to get tickets to the Derby itself. For tickets, you could enter the lottery through the **Churchill Downs** website (www.churchilldowns.com), shop around on www.stubhub.com or http://craigslist.com, or just content yourself with general admission tickets to the infield that can be bought at the gate. For accommodations, start calling the hotels and bed-and-breakfasts as soon as you know you're going, with your fingers crossed that a room is open. If not, keep calling back to check for cancellations. The other option, which is pricier but much easier, is to opt for a ticket package, such as that offered by **Derby Experiences** (http://derbyexperiences.com). They'll set you up with tickets, a hotel room, and certain niceties, depending on what package you opt for. The earlier you plan, the more options you'll have.

Regardless of where you stay or where you find yourself on Derby Day—Millionaires Row or the third turn of the infield—to truly immerse yourself in the Derby experience, add these traditional activities to your to-do list.

Eat Derby Pie. Created by Kern's Kitchen, the only company with the rights to the name, Derby Pie is a gooey confection of chocolate chips, walnuts, and other ingredients that Kern's considers top secret. You can purchase an entire pie at locations around town or have a slice served to you at the Brown Hotel's J. Graham's Café. Other restaurants and bakeries serve up their own version of "Kentucky pie," sometimes with a hint of bourbon, sometimes without.

Sip a mint julep. Although it's just a simple mix of bourbon, mint, sugar, and water, it takes a good bartender to make a mint julep just right—not too sweet, not too minty, and with the proper amount of warmth from the bourbon. Seek out a good one at one of downtown's bourbon bars. The official drink of the Kentucky Derby is served in an official keepsake glass at Churchill Downs, in an old-fashioned or highball glass at most bars, and in a silver julep cup at any proper Southern home.

Don a hat. The hats at the Kentucky Derby get almost as much attention as the horses, so make the right statement with a proper topper. Those with reserved seats should seek a look that is stylish and elegant. Decorated wide-brimmed hats are most common. If you're headed for the infield, the more ridiculous the hat, the more attention you'll get. Let your imagination run wild.

Gawk at celebrities. Security isn't going to let you anywhere near Millionaires Row on Derby Day, so to see your favorite celebrities, you have to join your fellow fans outside the home of Patricia Barnstable Brown on Derby Eve. The yearly themed gala, hosted by the former Doublemint Twin and with proceeds benefiting diabetes research, draws in big names from Hollywood, New York, and the sports world, many of whom happily chat with fans as they arrive.

See the garland of roses as it's made. The evening before Derby at a local Kroger grocery store, dozens of employee volunteers sew together the blanket of more than 400 red roses that becomes the 40-pound garland of roses awarded to the winning Derby horse. A different Kroger is given the honor each year, but all of them welcome you to come and watch as this Derby icon is assembled.

Enjoy dawn at the Downs. Take your breakfast at a seat in Churchill Downs's Millionaires Row while watching Derby and Oaks contenders work out during Derby week. You can enjoy the view from up high, then go trackside for a closer look. It's a quiet, intimate experience far from the madness of Derby Day.

Day 4

Spend your morning at the Kentucky Derby Museum, which not only celebrates the Derby, but also the entire sport of horse racing. For lunch, try Wagner's Pharmacy, where track regulars and horse industry insiders like to dine. Then it's time for a full schedule of racing at Churchill Downs, the famed home of the Kentucky Derby. Visit the paddock, place a few bets, take a photo under the twin spires, and call your trip through horse heaven a success.

Traveling the Bourbon Trail

Although there are plenty of worthwhile non-bourbon-related sites in Kentucky's bourbon country, many travelers descend upon this section of the Bluegrass State with nothing but bourbon on their minds. If that's you, use this itinerary to pack as many bourbon sites into your visit as possible.

Bourbon tourists should keep a few things in mind. Some tours require participants to wear closed-toe shoes, and with all the walking involved, it's a good idea to pack athletic shoes for this trip. Tour times vary by day of the week; check each distillery's schedule before finalizing your plans. The final tour at most distilleries departs one hour prior to the posted closing time. Don't assume you can show up at the end of the day and get on a tour. The distilleries shut down production during the high heat of summer, so plan to visit at a different time of year if you want to see bourbon being made. Spring and fall are the best seasons for bourbon tours. Finally, don't drink and drive. Samples are small, but the cumulative effect of many samples can be an impairment, and the roads between distilleries are often windy and can be dangerous. Don't assume you'll be fine. Have a designated driver or opt for a tour. Mint Julep Tours (www.mintjuleptours.com) offers a selection of Bourbon Trail tours.

Day 1

Start your tour of Kentucky's bourbon country in Louisville at the Evan Williams

Bourbon aging at Buffalo Trace Distillery

Sing Me One More Song

Impromptu jam sessions are a way of life in Kentucky.

As the birthplace of bluegrass and the home state of many big names in country music, Kentucky prides itself on its musical heritage and works hard to preserve the old-time music that has inspired generations. From front porches to concert halls, there are many places throughout the state where you can hear music. Here are a few favorites.

RENFRO VALLEY ENTERTAINMENT CENTER

Since 1921, Saturday night's Renfro Valley Barn Dance has been pleasing crowds with its combination of bluegrass, gospel, and country music. Sunday morning's Renfro Valley Gatherin' is a good way to start your day on a harmonious note.

ROSINE BARN JAMBOREE

Witness how deep the talent for bluegrass runs in the birthplace of Bill Monroe, father of the genre, at Friday night's free jamboree. If you've got talent of your own, bring your instrument and join in the pickin.'

BILLIE JEAN OSBORNE'S KENTUCKY OPRY

This resident group at the Mountain Arts Center in Prestonsburg puts on a good-time show that's heavy on country, bluegrass, and gospel.

PICKIN' ON THE PORCH

A tribute to the tradition of families and friends gathering on a porch to sing and play, Pickin' on the Porch events take place all over the state. Among the most popular are the program at the Country Music Highway Museum in Paintsville and the program at the Berea Welcome Center, both of which occur on Thursday nights.

BLUEGRASS FESTIVALS

Kentucky has more than its share of bluegrass festivals, so you ought to be able to catch at least one of them. The Festival of the Bluegrass is held in Lexington in early June, the River of Music Party (ROMP) is held in Owensboro in late June, the Mandolin Farm Bluegrass Festival is held in Flemingsburg in early September, the Poppy Mountain Bluegrass Festival is held in Morehead in mid-September, and the Jerusalem Ridge Festival is held in Rosine in October.

Bourbon Experience, located in an old Whiskey Row building. Then jump on I-65 and cruise down to Clermont for a tour of the Jim Beam American Stillhouse in Clermont. If you planned in advance, you could also visit the nearby Four Roses warehouses. From Clermont, follow KY 245 to Bardstown, where you might still have time to jump on the 4pm tour at Willet Distilling Company, a craft distillery that bottles four boutique bourbons. End your evening with a bourbon-focused dinner at Kentucky Bourbon House.

Day 2

Spend your second day touring the remaining two distilleries in Bardstown, Barton 1792 Distillery and Heaven Hill. Give yourself extra time to enjoy the Heritage Center at Heaven Hill. Tours completed, head to the Oscar Getz Museum of Whiskey History. You could spend a second night in Bardstown or get a head start on your next day by pointing your car toward Lebanon, stopping in Springfield for the night at Maple Hill Manor.

Day 3

Rise early to continue your way through the countryside to Lebanon to see bourbon barrels being made on the 9:30am tour of the Kentucky Cooperage. If you don't dillydally, you should then be able to drive to Maker's Mark in time for their 10:30am tour. Retreat to Lebanon for lunch and a quick stop at Limestone Branch Distillery, where you can taste moonshine if the bourbon's not yet ready. From Lebanon, head on to Lawrenceburg, where you can spend the night at the Lawrenceburg Bed & Breakfast.

Day 4

Get up and moving so that you can tour both Wild Turkey Distillery and Four Roses Distillery before lunch. Then grab a sandwich at Heavens to Betsy before driving on to Frankfort to do some sampling at Buffalo Trace Distillery. If you get a chance, try the bourbon balls at Rebecca Ruth Candy before dinner at Serafini, where at least one of the nearly 90 bourbons on offer ought to satisfy.

Day 5

Head east to Versailles to continue your trip with a visit to Woodford Reserve. You can have lunch in the café at the distillery before making the drive to Lexington, where you'll end your tour. Once there, make your way first to Barrel House Distillery before sipping your last sample of Kentucky bourbon at Lexington Brewing and Distilling Co.

Kentucky's Scenic Byways

Kentucky is truly one of America's prettiest states. You are, of course, entitled to your opinion, but before you give it, why don't you take a drive through the landscape of the Bluegrass State? Enjoy the mountains and the hollows, the rolling hills and the open meadows, the lakes and the forests, and you'll see what I mean. Beyond scenery, you'll also get a taste of Kentucky's interesting history.

For more information about scenic drives in Kentucky, visit www.byways.org.

Country Music Highway

Located in far eastern Kentucky in the hills of Appalachia, the heart of the Country Music Highway (U.S. 23) runs from Ashland in the north to Whitesburg in the south. You'll pass right through the mountains and will have opportunities to stop at coal mining sites, country music heritage sites, and multiple state parks. Butcher Hollow, Jenny Wiley Theatre, elk viewing, and a plate of soup beans and cornbread are musts. Try to plan your trip for the fall, when the mountains are

A narrow set of rock stairs leads to the top of Natural Bridge.

Constitution Square in Danville, where Kentucky gained statehood

on fire with color. And be sure to get off of the highway once in a while to see what life is like in the hollows.

Lincoln Heritage Scenic Highway

Abraham Lincoln, one of the greatest presidents the United States has known, was born in a tiny cabin in the knobs of Central Kentucky. This driving tour, which takes you on U.S. 31E and U.S. 150, begins in Hodgenville, where you can visit the Abraham Lincoln Birthplace and Boyhood Home and the Lincoln Museum. You'll then pass through Bardstown, where you can stop at the Civil War Museum or have a sip of bourbon at one of three distilleries. The highway continues to Springfield, home of Lincoln Homestead State Park; Perryville, site of Kentucky's biggest Civil War battle; and Danville, where Kentucky statehood was negotiated.

Red River Gorge Scenic Byway

For downright beauty, nothing beats the Red River Gorge Scenic Byway. This 46-mile drive, while short, can easily fill an entire day. You'll pass through the very cool Nada Tunnel as you enter Red River Gorge Geological Area, and then you'll spend most of your day pulled over at hiking trailheads and viewpoints. Make sure your hiking shoes are in the trunk, because you'll want to visit Sky Bridge and Angel Windows, which are accessible by a short walk. You may also want to paddle Red River or take the sky lift at Natural Bridge State Resort Park.

Wilderness Road Heritage Highway

This highway, which leads from Middlesboro to Berea, allows you to follow in the footsteps of Kentucky's earliest pioneers. Begin at Cumberland Gap National Historical Park to see where Daniel Boone carved his Wilderness Road. Then head north, passing Pine Mountain State Resort Park with its lush hemlocks and rhododendrons; Levi

A Taste of Kentucky

Kentuckians don't need a reason to celebrate their culinary heritage, but that doesn't mean that they don't enjoy throwing a festival every now and then as a tribute to a favorite food.

September is Kentucky's favored month for feasting. Kick things off with Berea's **Spoonbread Festival** (www.spoonbread-festival.com), which celebrates the sweet bread made with cornmeal. If spoonbread makes you thirsty, travel west to Bardstown for the **Kentucky Bourbon Festival** (www.kybourbonfestival.com), which runs for an entire week in mid-September. Fried chicken is next on the menu, celebrated at the **World Chicken Festival** (http://chickenfestival.com) in London in late September. During the four-day event, fried chicken is prepared in the world's biggest skillet. The last weekend in September is busy with two food festivals in towns that aren't too far apart. Lebanon invites you to help eat more than 6,000 pounds of country ham during **Marion County Country Ham Days** (www.marioncountykychamber.com), while Lawrenceburg welcomes you to sample as much burgoo—a type of barbecue stew—as you can handle at the **Anderson County Burgoo Festival** (www.kentuckyburgoo.com).

A few events earlier in the summer help you warm up for September's eating extravaganza. Owensboro, Kentucky's barbecue capital, hosts the **International Bar-B-Q Festival** (www.bbqfest.com) on the second weekend in May, allowing you to judge for yourself who makes the best chicken, ribs, and mutton. On the second weekend in June, the **Beer Cheese Festival** (www.beercheesefestival.com) is celebrated in Winchester, the home of this tasty spread. Taste the creations of professionals or enter your own concoction in the amateur division. For a sample of something you'll have a hard time finding anywhere else, head to Newport on the first weekend in August for **Goetta Fest** (www.goettafest.com). A sausage-type food made of ground meat and oats, goetta is a popular breakfast food in the region, but during the festival is served on everything from pizza to ice cream.

Jackson Wilderness Road State Park, home to a re-created pioneer village; and Renfro Valley Entertainment Center, the best place to see an old-time music show. End in Berea, where you can immerse yourself in arts and crafts.

Woodlands Trace

Running the length of Land Between the Lakes National Recreation Area, The Trace takes you through wooded scenery, with connections to lakeside drives. Along the way you can make detours to the Nature Station, Elk and Bison Prairie, Golden Pond Planetarium and Observatory, waterfront picnic areas, and The Homeplace. Opportunities for hiking, horseback riding, and camping abound.

LOUISVILLE

Louisville (pronounce it LUH-vul if you want to sound like a local) is where the Fortune 500 meet the nation's largest high school football game, where the first Saturday in May is marked by designer duds and ostentatious hats as well as cut-off shorts and bikini tops, and where the country's best Victorian-era preservation district gets along neighborly with striking modern architecture.

Even to those who call it home, Louisville is a conundrum and a contradiction. It's a big city, the biggest in Kentucky, but it's also city of neighborhoods where everyone is connected by far less than six degrees of separation. A hint of Midwestern modesty and Northern sensibility season the city's personality, thanks to its location at the falls of the Ohio River, but Southern hospitality is still the prevailing ingredient.

Built on the backs of Irish, German, and other European immigrants as well as enslaved Africans, Louisville has also been influenced by Hispanic culture, as well as the traditions of more recent immigrants and refugees from Eastern Europe and Asia. In a state that paints itself red every election season, Louisville remains a solid dot of blue.

On paper, Louisville might not make sense, but hey, neither does love, and that's exactly what residents and visitors alike feel for the city. For some, the passion stems from Louisville's big-city amenities. The Derby City is home to a performing arts scene that supports one of the nation's most respected theater festivals, so many art galleries as to require two monthly trolley hops, research hospitals that perform groundbreaking work like the first hand

© THERESA DOWELL BLACKINTON

HIGHLIGHTS

◖ **Louisville Slugger Museum & Factory:** Witness the transformation of a piece of ash wood into an iconic Louisville Slugger baseball bat on the factory tour, then relive magical moments in the history of America's pastime in the museum (page 31).

◖ **Muhammad Ali Center:** Far beyond a simple celebration of the boxing prowess of the self-proclaimed "Greatest," this multimedia museum explores Ali's controversial struggles as well as his humanitarian acts. It is a must whether you're a boxing fan or not (page 35).

◖ **Old Louisville Tours:** The nation's best preserved Victorian neighborhood, Old Louisville brims with houses that will make your jaw drop. Take a tour to really dive into the history and architecture of the area, or spend the night in one of the neighborhood's grand B&Bs (page 37).

◖ **Kentucky Derby Museum and Churchill Downs:** Churchill Downs brims with atmosphere as the most historic thoroughbred racetrack in the world, and the adjoining Kentucky Derby Museum lets you experience the thrill of the races even when the track is dark (page 39).

◖ **Louisville Zoo:** An award-winning gorilla exhibit brought the Louisville Zoo to the forefront for animal lovers, but the new arctic animals exhibit and the much loved Islands exhibit mean the gorillas have to share the spotlight (page 45).

◖ **First Friday Trolley Hop:** Downtown's Main and Market Streets are home to an ever-expanding population of art galleries, all of which can be explored via trolley on the first Friday of the month, when many galleries host openings, offer snacks and drinks, and make artists available for conversation (page 51).

◖ **Kentucky Derby Festival:** The most exciting two minutes in sports (also known as the Kentucky Derby) cap off not only a day of glamour, madness, and myth at Churchill Downs, but also a two-week party that takes over the entire city (page 52).

◖ **Kentucky State Fair:** This annual August event draws people from all over the state to celebrate what makes Kentucky special, featuring everything from agricultural exhibits to arts and crafts competitions. Shows, concerts, midway rides, and more food than you can eat are all part of the tradition (page 55).

◖ **Olmsted Park System:** In a city full of green spaces, the parks designed by Frederick Law Olmsted stand out as hometown favorites. Follow the parkways from the open fields of Cherokee Park to the formal gardens of Shawnee Park to the forested hills of Iroquois Park (page 58).

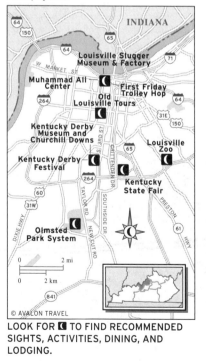

© AVALON TRAVEL

LOOK FOR ◖ TO FIND RECOMMENDED SIGHTS, ACTIVITIES, DINING, AND LODGING.

transplant and first artificial heart transplant, more good restaurants than one could possibly hope to visit, and the headquarters of major corporations like Yum! Brands and UPS.

For others, their affection for Louisville relates to its small-town charm and its ability to maintain a strong identity even as the city grows. They love that the first question Louisvillians ask when they meet each other is "Where did you go to high school?", that the city supports its college sports teams with the same gusto as other cities support professional teams, that Heine Brothers is more popular than Starbucks, that downtown's golden-era hotels and Old Louisville's Victorian mansions are as revered as any new development, and that the best museums celebrate local goodness like the Louisville Slugger and Muhammad Ali.

As for what puts Louisville on the world's map—well, it's a little thing really, just a two-minute spectacle. Run every first Saturday in May, the Kentucky Derby and the accompanying two-week festival are the city's pride and joy and the state's largest tourism event. Put it on your calendar, because it's a spectacle that everyone should see at least once.

Whatever your tastes, Louisville will win you over. The old dame's no one-hit wonder, and her charm is guaranteed to bring you back time and again.

PLANNING YOUR TIME

Louisville tourism spikes in late April and early May, and for good reason. Many visitors plan their trips around the Kentucky Derby, which is always run on the first Saturday in May, and the Kentucky Derby Festival, which kicks off two weeks before Derby Day. It's a great time to visit. With a little luck, the weather is beautiful, with robin-egg blue skies, pleasantly warm days, and spring flowers painting the city with color. With everything spit-polished and shined, the city is prepared to win over the world. But beware, the weather doesn't always cooperate (both

© THERESA DOWELL BLACKINTON

Louisville's skyline, as seen from the Big 4 Bridge

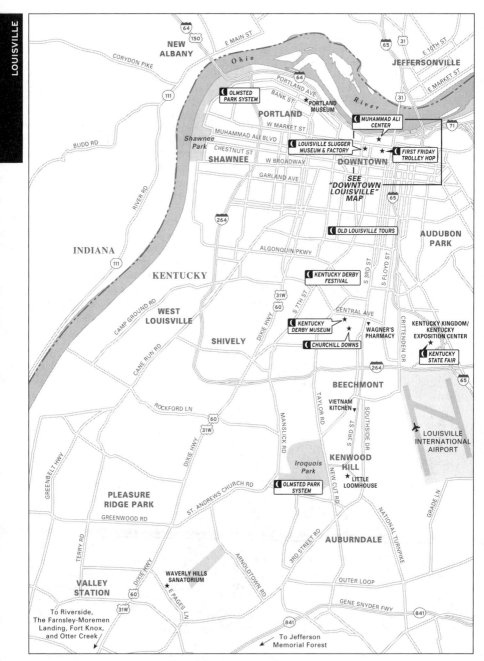

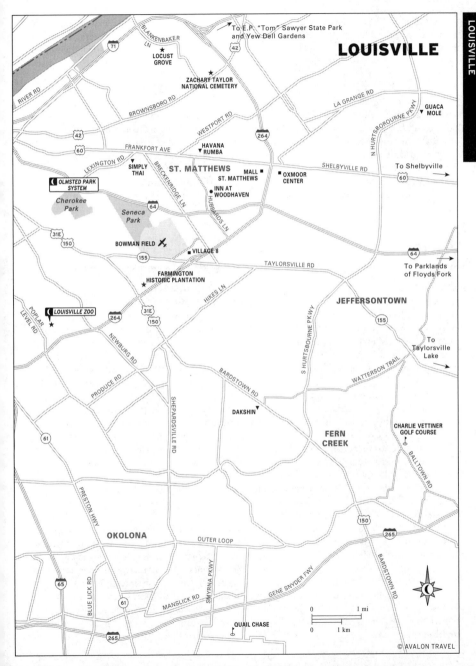

LOUISVILLE

To E.P. "Tom" Sawyer State Park
and Yew Dell Gardens

71

BLANKENBAKER LN

★ LOCUST
GROVE

★ ZACHARY TAYLOR
NATIONAL CEMETERY

RIVER RD

BROWNSBORO RD

LA GRANGE RD

N HURTSBOROURNE PKWY

▼ GUACA
MOLE

42

WESTPORT RD

264

42
60

FRANKFORT AVE

LEXINGTON RD

▼ SIMPLY
THAI

▼ HAVANA
RUMBA

ST. MATTHEWS

BRECKENRIDGE LN

■ MALL
ST. MATTHEWS

● INN AT
WOODHAVEN

HUBBARDS LN

SHELBYVILLE RD

To Shelbyville

60

■ OXMOOR
CENTER

☾ OLMSTED PARK
SYSTEM

Cherokee
Park

Seneca
Park

64

31E
150

155

BOWMAN FIELD ✈

■ VILLAGE 8

TAYLORSVILLE RD

64

To Parklands
of Floyds Fork

★ FARMINGTON
HISTORIC PLANTATION

HIKES LN

JEFFERSONTOWN

155

S HURTSBOURNE PKWY

To
Taylorsville
Lake

☾ LOUISVILLE ZOO
★

POPLAR LEVEL RD

264

31E
150

NEWBURG RD

WATTERSON TRAIL

PRODUCE RD

61

SHEPARDSVILLE RD

BARDSTOWN RD

▼ DAKSHIN

FERN
CREEK

CHARLIE VETTINER
GOLF COURSE
⛳

BALLTOWN RD

PRESTON HWY

OKOLONA

OUTER LOOP

150

265

BARDSTOWN RD

65

BLUE LICK RD

61

MANSLICK RD

SMYRNA PKWY

GENE SNYDER FWY

265

QUAIL CHASE

0   1 mi
0   1 km

N

© AVALON TRAVEL

snowstorms and heat waves have been known to hit on Derby Day), hotel prices will be through the roof (if you can manage to secure a reservation at all), and restaurants will have long waits (show up well before you're hungry).

If you're not set on attending the Derby, choose another time to visit. Weather-wise, spring and fall are the most pleasant. Winters usually aren't too bad, although the city does get socked with a major storm every few years. Summers are hot and humid, but they're packed with things to do.

As for how long to stay, aim for a long weekend. You'll be able to cover most of the city's museums and sights all while enjoying leisurely meals at Louisville's fine restaurants as well as evenings out on the town. If you're interested in visiting any of the surrounding areas, such as Fort Knox or Shelbyville, tack an extra day onto your itinerary.

Most visitors will want to set themselves up in downtown or Old Louisville, where you'll find the city's best accommodations and restaurants as well as have easy access to most attractions. If you're looking to explore more of the state, Louisville makes an excellent jumping-off point, with day trips to Lexington, Frankfort, and the Bourbon Trail distilleries easy possibilities.

Sights

DOWNTOWN

Over the past two decades, Louisville's downtown has regained its title as the heart of the city. West Main Street's **Museum Row** (known as Whiskey Row in the early 1900s), stretching the four blocks from 5th to 9th Streets, can easily keep you busy for a weekend, if not a full week, and the **NuLu** area (New Louisville, or the East Market District) is the hot place to be these days, especially for eating, nightlife, and shopping. Adding oomph to the downtown experience is the city's notable architecture, as well as the lively waterfront scene.

If you plan to hit a lot of the museums, consider purchasing the **Main Ticket,** available online (www.gotolouisville.com/main-ticket) or at the **Louisville Visitors Center** (301 S. 4th St., 10am-5pm Mon.-Sat., noon-5pm Sun.). This ticket, which costs $29.99 for adults and $23.99 for youth 6-12, is good for one year and allows for admission to the Frazier International History Museum, the Louisville Slugger Museum & Factory, the Louisville Science Center, Kentucky Museum of Art & Craft, the Muhammad Ali Center, and KentuckyShow!

Frazier International History Museum

On the far western end of Museum Row, the **Frazier International History Museum** (829 W. Main St., 502/753-5663, www.fraziermuseum.org, 9am-5pm Mon.-Sat., noon-5pm Sun., $10.50 adults, $8.50 seniors, $7.50 students 14-17 and college students with ID, $6 youth 5-13) bears the honor of being the only place outside the United Kingdom to house a permanent exhibition of items from the Royal Armoury, the U.K.'s prized national collection of many centuries' worth of arms and armor. The museum's collections go far beyond the Armoury pieces, however, with Teddy Roosevelt's "Big Stick," Geronimo's bow, the Daniel Boone family bible, Lewis and Clark artifacts, and Frank and Jesse James's letters all finding homes at the Frazier. As impressive as the collections are, for many visitors they're overshadowed by the museum's 80 historical interpretations performed by a full-time staff of actor-historians. The 1,000-plus years of history on display at the Frazier come to life as Annie Oakley, Abraham Lincoln, Joan of Arc, and other historical figures make appearances

JUST ACROSS THE BRIDGE: INDIANA SIGHTS

Cross the Ohio River, and you'll find yourself in southern Indiana, which is for all intents and purposes a suburb of Louisville. A handful of interesting sights make a trip across the state line worthwhile.

Falls of the Ohio State Park & Interpretive Center (201 Riverside Dr., Clarksville, IN, 812/280-9970, www.fallsoftheohio.org, 9am-5pm Mon.-Sat., 1pm-5pm Sun., $5 adults, $2 youth) welcomes visitors to wander among 386-million-year-old fossil beds and search the 220 acres for signs of life from the Devonian period. The Interpretive Center hosts 100 different exhibits focusing on paleontology, geology, and history. A 14-minute movie, aquarium with fish found in the Ohio River, and a full-size mammoth skeleton are visitor favorites. If you just want to wander among the fossils or have a picnic at the river's edge, the park itself is open 7am-11pm, and you must pay a $2 parking fee.

Enjoy a night out at **Derby Dinner Playhouse** (525 Marriott Dr., Clarksville, IN, 812/288-8281, www.derbydinner.com), a dinner theater that specializes in productions of Broadway musicals, having put on all 50 of the top musicals of all time. There are no bad seats at the in-the-square theater, and a vocal ensemble entertains you as you enjoy your buffet dinner. Performances are held Tuesday-Sunday evenings with matinees on Wednesday and Sunday. Ticket prices range $35-44.

The **Howard Steamboat Museum** (1101 E. Market St., Jeffersonville, IN, 812/283-3728, www.steamboatmuseum.org, 10am-4pm Tues.-Sat., 1pm-4pm Sun., $6 adults, $5 seniors, $3.50 students) invites you to return to the golden era of steamboat travel on a tour through the 1894 mansion of the steamboat magnate Howard family. Models of steamboats, photographs, and artifacts are found throughout the grand house.

The **Carnegie Center for Art & History** (201 E. Spring St., New Albany, IN, 812/944-7336, www.carnegiecenter.org, 10am-5:30pm Tues.-Sat., free) features an award-winning exhibit on the Underground Railroad as well as a smile-inducing collection of hand-carved, mechanized dioramas depicting rural life at the end of the 19th century. Each year the center also hosts a juried art quilt exhibition, drawing entries from contemporary fiber artists across the country.

A visit to **Huber's Orchard, Winery & Vineyards** (19816 Huber Rd., Starlight, IN, 812/923-9463, www.huberwinery.com, 10am-6pm Mon.-Sat., noon-6pm Sun., extended hours May-Oct.) is an annual tradition for many locals, especially during apple- and pumpkin-picking seasons. Year-round you can take a complimentary wine tour with tasting (11am, 2pm, and 4pm Mon.-Sat., 2pm and 4pm Sun.), purchase produce at the farm market, and enjoy a hearty farm meal at the Starlight Café. A Farm Park ($6) with mountain slides, pedal karts, rope mazes, and mini-tractor rides welcomes kids.

on the 1st floor stage or in the 3rd floor Tournament Ring.

◖ Louisville Slugger Museum & Factory

Louisville might not have a Major League Baseball team, but America's pastime wouldn't be the same if it weren't for the Louisville Slugger, the official baseball bat of MLB. On a tour of the **Louisville Slugger Museum & Factory** (800 W. Main St., 877/775-8443, www.sluggermuseum.org, 9am-5pm Mon.-Sat., 11am-5pm Sun., $12 adults, $11 seniors, $7 youth 6-12), visitors can learn how the history of baseball and the Louisville Slugger go hand in hand, take a practice swing with bats used by favorite players of the past and present, and tour the factory where each bat is made with as much love and care as in 1884, the year the Louisville Slugger was born. At the end of the tour, each participant receives a free miniature Louisville Slugger. Take it home with you

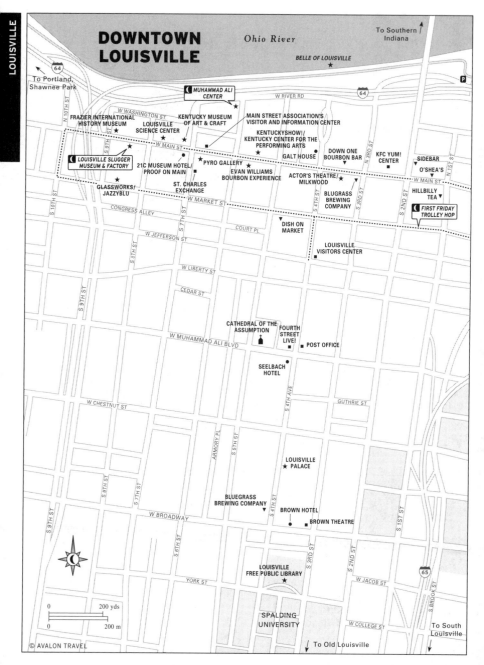

DOWNTOWN LOUISVILLE

Ohio River

BELLE OF LOUISVILLE ★

To Southern Indiana

To Portland, Shawnee Park

W RIVER RD

MUHAMMAD ALI CENTER

FRAZIER INTERNATIONAL HISTORY MUSEUM

W WASHINGTON ST

KENTUCKY MUSEUM OF ART & CRAFT

MAIN STREET ASSOCIATION'S VISITOR AND INFORMATION CENTER

LOUISVILLE SCIENCE CENTER

KENTUCKYSHOW!/ KENTUCKY CENTER FOR THE PERFORMING ARTS

W MAIN ST

DOWN ONE BOURBON BAR

KFC YUM! CENTER

SIDEBAR

O'SHEA'S

LOUISVILLE SLUGGER MUSEUM & FACTORY

21C MUSEUM HOTEL/ PROOF ON MAIN

PYRO GALLERY

GALT HOUSE

EVAN WILLIAMS BOURBON EXPERIENCE

ACTOR'S THEATRE/ MILKWOOD

W MAIN ST

HILLBILLY TEA

GLASSWORKS/ JAZZYBLU

ST. CHARLES EXCHANGE

BLUGRASS BREWING COMPANY

FIRST FRIDAY TROLLEY HOP

W MARKET ST

CONGRESS ALLEY

DISH ON MARKET

W JEFFERSON ST

COURT PL

LOUISVILLE VISITORS CENTER

W LIBERTY ST

CEDAR ST

CATHEDRAL OF THE ASSUMPTION

FOURTH STREET LIVE!

W MUHAMMAD ALI BLVD

POST OFFICE

SEELBACH HOTEL

W CHESTNUT ST

GUTHRIE ST

ARMORY PL

LOUISVILLE PALACE

BLUEGRASS BREWING COMPANY

BROWN HOTEL

W BROADWAY

BROWN THEATRE

LOUISVILLE FREE PUBLIC LIBRARY

YORK ST

W JACOB ST

SPALDING UNIVERSITY

W COLLEGE ST

To South Louisville

To Old Louisville

0   200 yds
0   200 m

© AVALON TRAVEL

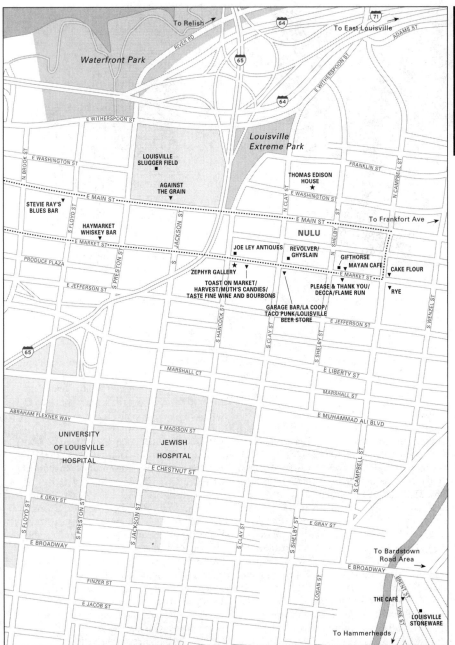

It takes more than two sets of arms to encircle the bat at the Louisville Slugger Museum.

© THERESA DOWELL BLACKINTON

(though only in your checked luggage!) after first posing with it in front of the world's largest bat, a 120-foot-tall, 68,000-pound steel replica of a Babe Ruth bat that greets everyone walking past the museum.

Louisville Science Center

More than a field-trip destination where you can see a mummy and be enclosed in a bubble, the **Louisville Science Center** (727 W. Main St., 800/591-2203, www.louisvillescience.org, 9:30am-5pm Sun.-Thurs., 9:30am-9pm Fri.-Sat., $13 adults, $11 youth 2-12) is an all-ages destination where science education meets hands-on fun. For the little ones under age seven, KidZone offers age-appropriate excitement, including exploration of occupations via dress-up and a table of wet and wild construction fun. Older children will enjoy the more than 150 learning stations in the museum's three permanent exhibitions—The World We Create, The World Within Us, and The World Around Us. The crawl-through cave and climb-aboard Gemini trainer space capsule are just a few of the favorites that encourage visitors to engage with the exhibits. Special exhibitions are rolled out every 3-4 months and often appeal to adults, as do many of the standing exhibits, such as the ones on healthy living. An IMAX theater ($7) with a four-story screen completes the museum.

Kentucky Museum of Art & Craft

In a restored cast-iron building with cork floors and exposed beams, the **Kentucky Museum of Art & Craft** (715 W. Main St., 502/589-0102, www.kentuckyarts.org, 10am-5pm Tues.-Sat., 11am-5pm Sun., $8 adults, $5 seniors, $4 youth 13-17 and college students, $2 youth 6-12) celebrates the wealth of artistic talent and creativity found throughout the state. The museum's three galleries offer permanent and rotating exhibits featuring woodwork, textiles, ceramics, jewelry, photography, painting, and more. You'll likely find something you've never seen anywhere else and just have to have. Lucky for you, some items on display are also for sale, and there's a gift shop next to the galleries.

21C Museum

Occupying the reception area and lower atrium of the hotel of the same name, the **21C Museum** (700 W. Main St., 502/217-6300, www.21cmuseum.org, free) exhibits cutting-edge artwork from living artists. Exhibits change every six months, and the museum also offers a full program of film screenings, poetry readings, artist talks, and concert series. Pop in often, and don't forget to check out the elevator lobby as well as the restrooms—art isn't restricted to the galleries here; it's an integral part of the entire building.

◖ Muhammad Ali Center

While most museums beg you to keep your hands off the exhibits, the **Muhammad Ali Center** (144 N. 6th St., 502/584-9254, www.alicenter.org, 9:30am-5pm Tues.-Sat., noon-5pm Sun., $9 adults, $8 seniors, $5 students, $4 youth 6-12) repeatedly asks you to "Please touch." This hands-on, full-sensory, multimedia-heavy museum is a look at the life and times of The Greatest, a tribute to a hometown hero who became a universal icon. Far from one-sided, the Center depicts Ali the boxer, Ali the poet, and Ali the humanitarian, and it doesn't shy away from controversy, depicting Ali's losses alongside his wins, his radical comments alongside his inspirational quotes, his contentious choices alongside his universally celebrated moments. On the three floors of exhibition space, you can view a five-screen orientation film, test your boxing skills with punching bags and in a shadowboxing ring, watch your choice of Ali's 15 most famous fights, and check out memorabilia from Ali's life and career.

Evan Williams Bourbon Experience

When it opened in early 2014, the **Evan Williams Bourbon Experience** (528 W. Main St., 502/585-3923, www.evanwilliamsbourbonexperience.com, 10am-5pm Mon.-Sat., 1pm-5pm Sun.) became the first official Bourbon Trail site to be located in Louisville. Honoring Evan Williams, Kentucky's first distiller, and located in a Whiskey Row building across the street from the 18th-century Evan Williams distillery, the Experience immerses visitors in bourbon history, taking them back to 1783 on a guided tour through this artisanal distillery with museum-style exhibits. A tasting is included with the tour ($12 adults 21 and over, $9 youth 10-20).

KentuckyShow!

Want to get a taste of everything the great state of Kentucky has to offer before you dive into any deeper exploration? Then grab a seat at **KentuckyShow!** (501 W. Main St., 502/562-7800, www.kentuckyshow.com, $7 adults, $5 seniors and youth), a 30-minute multimedia production shown at the Kentucky Center for the Arts. Narrated by Kentuckian Ashley Judd, KentuckyShow! provides a moving look at Kentucky's history and culture, defining what makes the Bluegrass State such a special place. Screenings are offered on the hour 11am-4pm Tuesday-Saturday and 1pm-4pm Sunday.

Thomas Edison House

Before he invented the lightbulb, Thomas Edison was a Western Union telegraph operator in Louisville. The small four-room boarding house where he lived during that period, 1866-1867, is now the **Thomas Edison House** (729 E. Washington St., 502/585-5247, www.edisonhouse.org, 10am-2pm Tues.-Sat., $5 adults, $4 seniors, $3 youth 6-17). On a short tour of the property, visitors see his re-created room and can take a close look at a number of his inventions, including a working telegraph and phonograph.

Riverboat Cruises

The oldest river steamboat in operation, the *Belle of Louisville* (401 W. River Rd., 502/574-2992, www.belleoflouisville.org, May-Oct.) is both a National Landmark and a local icon. Using her big red paddlewheel, the *Belle* carries passengers up and down the Ohio River offering exceptional city views, all to the tune of her distinctive calliope. The Belle's sister boat, the *Spirit of Jefferson,* is a newer and

boarding the *Belle of Louisville* for a cruise

© THERESA DOWELL BLACKINTON

smaller riverboat with modern conveniences. See the *Belle of Louisville* website for schedules for both boats, as well as information on special event cruises. Price depends on the type of cruise chosen, with options for lunch, dinner, sightseeing only, history, and moonlight tours.

Notable Architecture

Louisville's **West Main Street** is second only to New York City's SoHo in the number of cast-iron facade buildings. The eight-block area is also home to Greek Revival, Italianate, Richardsonian Romanesque, international, and postmodern architecture. Pick up a Walking Tour brochure from the **Main Street Association's Visitor and Information Center** (627 W. Main St., 502/589-6008, www.mainstreetassociation.com, 11am-3pm Mon.-Fri.) and explore the history and style that makes this one of Louisville's most architecturally interesting areas. Highlights include Mies van der Rohe's "rusted" **American Life and Accident Building** (3 Riverfront Plaza), Michael Graves's postmodern **Humana Building** (500 W. Main

St.), and the abundance of cast-iron buildings in the 600 and 700 blocks of West Main.

The gothic revival **Cathedral of the Assumption** (433 S. 5th St., 502/582-2971, www.cathedraloftheassumption.org) is the home of the Archdiocese of Louisville and a downtown landmark. Built in 1852, the cathedral was completely renovated in 1994. It boasts one of the oldest American-made stained-glass windows as well as a beautiful starred ceiling complete with restored fresco.

The collections at the **main branch of the Louisville Free Public Library** (301 York St., 502/574-1611, www.lfpl.org, 9am-9pm Mon.-Thurs., 9am-5pm Fri.-Sat., 2pm-5pm Sun.) are not limited to books and magazines, but also include photos and artifacts related to local history. Even if you're not a bibliophile, the library is worth a visit for a look at the South Building. Built in 1906 with funds from Andrew Carnegie, the beaux arts building features Ionic columns, ornamental friezes, marble floors, bronze doors, and large-scale mosaics and paintings.

PORTLAND

Located a bit west of downtown at the Falls of the Ohio, the current neighborhood of Portland was once an independent town and an important stop for riverboat traffic. Though the area has seen some hard times in the past decades, many Louisville old-timers have fond memories of Portland, and notable Louisvillians such as football great Paul Hornung grew up in the neighborhood.

Portland Museum

The **Portland Museum** (2308 Portland Ave., 502/776-7678, www.goportland.org, 10am-4:30pm Tues.-Thurs., $7 adults, $6 seniors, $5 students) explores the history of the land, river, and people who called Portland home and helped turn Louisville from a shipping port into a city. A light-and-sound-enhanced exhibit with detailed dioramas and lifelike human models tells the story of Portland, while additional galleries host rotating exhibits that illuminate life in this vibrant and historic district.

OLD LOUISVILLE

Home to the largest collection of Victorian mansions in the United States and showcasing a variety of impressive architectural styles of the late 19th and early 20th centuries, Old Louisville is a spirited neighborhood rich in history and perfect for on-foot exploration. It's also where you'll find the University of Louisville, which helps keep this old neighborhood young, hip, and richly diverse.

◖ Old Louisville Tours

To get the most out of a visit to Old Louisville, consider a tour. Do-it-yourselfers can choose from five self-guided walking/driving tours outlined in brochures produced by the **Old Louisville Visitors Center** (1217 S. 4th St., 502/637-2922, www.oldlouisville.org, 10am-4pm Tues.-Sat.). Those looking for a real insider's view should sign up for one of the outings with **Louisville Historic Tours** (502/637-2922, www.louisvillehistorictours. com), which employs neighborhood residents as guides. Guided walking tours include the

Old Louisville Grand Walking Tour (11am and 3pm Tues.-Sat., $15), the Old Louisville Ghost Walk (1pm Tues.-Thurs. and Sat., $20), and the Lantern Ghost Walk (7pm daily, $25). Guided bus tours include the Mansions & Milestones Tour (2:30pm Fri.-Sat., $25) and the Ghosts of Old Louisville Tour (7:30pm Fri., $25). Tours depart from the Old Louisville Visitors Center and last 1.5-2 hours. Reservations are recommended. For a chance to peek inside some of the neighborhood beauties, put the Holiday House Tour (www.oldlouisvilleholidayhometour.org, $30), held annually on the first weekend of December, on your calendar. The Hidden Treasure Garden Tour (www.oldlouisvillegardentour.com, $15), held annually in early July, offers a look at what's behind the wrought-iron fences of many neighborhood homes.

Conrad-Caldwell House

Of the many historic homes in Louisville, the **Conrad-Caldwell House** (1402 St. James Ct., 502/636-5023, www.conradcaldwell.org, $10 adults, $6 seniors, $4 students), a grand three-story Victorian mansion from the 1890s, might just be the most interesting to tour (1pm and 3pm Wed.-Sun., additional tour 11am Sat.). Named for Theophilus Conrad, who built and occupied the house for its first 10 years, and the William E. Caldwell family, who lived in the house through the 1920s, the house boasts beautiful parquet floors patterned after quilts; a remarkable attention to detail in the woodworked walls, staircases, and decorative features; and original furniture, books, and belongings from the Caldwell family. If you're lucky, you'll be guided through the house by a direct descendant of William Caldwell, bursting with intimate knowledge of the family and great stories about the house.

Crane House

Since 1987, **Crane House** (1244 S. 3rd St., 502/635-2240, www.cranehouse.org, 9:30am-4:30pm, Mon., Tues., Thurs., and Fri.) has been exposing Louisville residents and visitors to the culture of East Asia through a variety

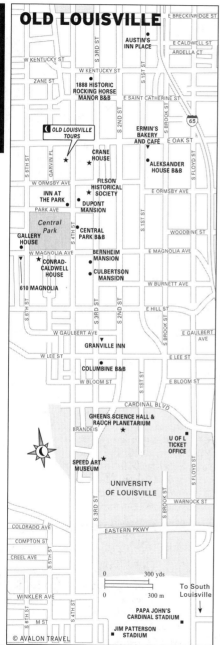

OLD LOUISVILLE

of programming. Visitors are welcome to take a free tour of Crane House, which includes a visit to the Asia Gallery, an exhibit of contemporary and historical Asian artifacts, as well as an introduction to Chinese tea and tea drinking. Crane House also offers Chinese cooking classes, Chinese and Japanese language classes, and Tai Chi classes. A regular lecture series is free and open to the public; check the online calendar.

Filson Historical Society

Home to extensive library collections chronicling local and Southern history, the **Filson Historical Society** (1310 S. 3rd St., 502/635-5083, www.filsonhistorical.org, 9am-4:30pm Mon.-Fri., free) is a gem for researchers. The excellent lecture series is also a boon to the community. Visit the website for a schedule of events. The Ferguson Mansion, home of the society, is worth a visit on its own merit. A self-guided tour describes the luxurious elements that made this beaux arts mansion the most expensive house in the city when it was built in 1905 and also allows visitors to view many of the society's artifacts, including a carving done by Daniel Boone, Civil War uniforms, a moonshine still, antique quilts, and a strong art collection.

University of Louisville

The **University of Louisville,** a public university, bustles with the energy of more than 21,000 students who come from around the state, country, and world to study in more than 170 fields. The urban campus isn't just for students, however; it also offers much to the community. Go ahead and take a stroll on the manicured grounds of Belknap Campus. You'll want to keep an eye out for one of the original casts of Rodin's *The Thinker,* which sits eternally lost in thought in front of the main administrative building, as well as the grave of U.S. Supreme Court Justice Louis Brandeis, which can be found under the portico of the law school that bears his name.

One of the most visited on-campus sites by the public is the **Speed Art Museum** (2035

© THERESA DOWELL BLACKINTON

the Conrad-Caldwell House

SOUTH LOUISVILLE

South Louisville has had a bit of a roller-coaster existence, soaring in the late 19th and first half of the 20th centuries as Churchill Downs and Iroquois Park laid claim to the area and a railcar line made the connection to downtown simple, then falling in the late 1900s as the factories that employed many of the area's middle-class workers left town. Now, this area, once a summer retreat and still the location of some of the city's most historic sites and homes, is again on the way up. A favorite area for new immigrants, South Louisville mixes local tradition with newly introduced customs.

Kentucky Kingdom

It's been a bumpy ride for **Kentucky Kingdom** (Crittenden Dr., Kentucky Exposition Center, www.kentuckykingdom.com, 11am-7pm Sun.-Fri. and 11am-9pm Sat. late May-mid-Aug, 5pm-9pm Mon.-Fri. and 12pm-9pm Sat.-Sun. mid-late Aug., 11am-7pm Mon., Sat., and Sun. Sept., $44.95 general admission, $34.95 children under 48 inches and seniors, $8 parking), the local amusement park, since it was dropped by Six Flags in 2010. However, Kentucky Kingdom finally has new owners, and will reopen on May 24, 2014, with new and long-time favorite rides, a dedicated kids' area, and an expanded Hurricane Bay waterpark. Season passes ($59.95) are a great deal for those planning to visit the park more than once.

◖ Kentucky Derby Museum and Churchill Downs

If you can't make it to the Derby, experiencing the thrill of the most exciting two minutes in sports on the 360-degree high-definition screen at the **Kentucky Derby Museum** (704 Central Ave., 502/637-7097, www.derbymuseum.org, 8am-5pm Mon.-Sat., 11am-5pm Sun., Mar. 15-Nov., 9am-5pm Mon.-Sat., 11am-5pm Sun., Dec.-Mar. 14, $14 adults, $13 seniors, $11 youth 13-18, $6 youth 5-12) is the next best thing. In addition to the film, interactive exhibits and authentic artifacts allow you to get a taste of Derby Day, discover what it takes to create a champion thoroughbred, and learn

S. 3rd St., http://speedmuseum.org), home to Louisville's best art collection, with more than 13,000 works spanning 6,000 years. At the time of research, it was undergoing a three-year renovation and is scheduled to reopen in 2016. Check the website for updated information.

The nearby **Gheens Science Hall & Rauch Planetarium** (108 W. Brandeis Ave., 502/852-6664, www.louisville.edu/planetarium, $8 adults, $6 seniors and youth 12 and under) exposes the public to the wonders of space through a wide range of shows illuminating the night sky, the planets, our solar system, and far beyond. Locals might particularly enjoy the seasonal Skies over Louisville program, which explains exactly what it is you're seeing in the sky right over your own backyard. Also popular are the laser shows, which are set to tunes of the Beatles, Led Zeppelin, Radiohead, and other popular bands. Shows are generally offered at 8pm, 9pm, 10pm, and 11pm Friday; 1pm, 2pm, and 3pm Saturday; and 11am and noon Sunday. Check the website for complete show listings.

about the pursuit of victory from the perspective of jockey, trainer, and owner. The museum was damaged extensively by flooding in early 2009, and while closed for recovery, museum exhibits were overhauled and updated. Your admission ticket also allows you to take a guided walking tour of **Churchill Downs,** the racetrack where the Derby is run every May under the famed twin spires. For a more in-depth look at the historic track, the museum also offers an Inside the Gates Walking Tour ($11), a Barn & Backside Van Tour ($11), a Twilight Tour (3rd Thurs. of the month, $15), and a Horses & Haunts Tour (Oct. only, $15).

THE BIRTH OF THE HAPPY BIRTHDAY SONG

There are some things that seem as if they've simply always existed—the Happy Birthday song being a fine example. Sung to us annually by friends and family to mark the passing of another year, and memorably spiced up by Marilyn Monroe for President Kennedy, "Happy Birthday to You" is so omnipresent in our society that healthcare officials even suggest we sing it as we wash our hands to ensure that we scrub for the proper amount of time needed to kill germs.

But once upon a time, not long before the 19th century turned to the 20th, the Happy Birthday song did not exist. How they celebrated birthdays then, heaven knows, but apparently they did still have parties, because it was at a birthday celebration on what is now the Little Loomhouse property in South Louisville that sisters Patty and Mildred J. Hill introduced the song for the first time. Both kindergarten teachers, the sisters had originally written a song in 1893 called "Good Morning to All," which was well loved by their students. By keeping the melody but changing the simple lyrics, the Hill sisters created history and made birthdays better for all of us.

Little Loomhouse

Preserving the legacy of Lou Tate, a master weaver whose work was admired by the likes of first ladies Eleanor Roosevelt and Lou Hoover, the **Little Loomhouse** (328 Kenwood Hill Rd., 502/367-4792, www.littleloomhouse. org, 10am-3:30pm Tues.-Thurs. and 3rd Sat. of the month, $5) offers tours of her home and workshop. You'll set foot in the cabin where "Happy Birthday" was first sung, see samples of the intricate patterns Lou Tate helped preserve, and learn to weave on a little loom. More in-depth weaving classes are offered in multiweek sessions. The gift shop sells a guidebook to the surrounding neighborhood that will allow you to better explore the area.

Waverly Hills Sanatorium

If your idea of a good time is having the living daylights scared out of you, then add **Waverly Hills Sanatorium** (4400 Paralee Ln., 502/933-2142, www.therealwaverlyhills.com) to your must-see list. This former tuberculosis health care facility and geriatric center is said to be one of the most haunted sites in the United States. For those brave enough, the sanatorium offers half-night (midnight-4am Fri., Mar.-Aug., $50) and full-night (midnight-8am Sat., Mar.-Aug., $100) paranormal investigations that are said to have turned up sightings of ghosts, ectoplasm clouds, and lights where there is no electricity, as well as the sounds of voices, cries, screams, slamming doors, and bouncing balls. A shorter two-hour tour is also available (Fri. and Sat., Mar.-Aug., $22). If just reading this makes you want to hide under a blanket, then opt for the two-hour historical tour (2:30pm Sun., Mar.-Aug., 8pm Wed., Sept.-Oct., $22). All tours must be reserved in advance and are often booked months ahead. Proceeds fund the restoration of the building.

Riverside, The Farnsley-Moremen Landing

Experience life at a 19th-century Ohio River farm on a visit to **Riverside, The Farnsley-Moremen Landing** (7410 Moorman Rd., 502/935-6809, www.riverside-landing.org,

© THERESA DOWELL BLACKINTON

A horse races at Churchill Downs.

10am-4:30pm Tues.-Sat., year-round, 1pm-4:30pm Sun., Mar.-Nov. only, final tour at 3:30, $6 adults, $5 seniors, $3 youth 6-12), a popular stop for boat traffic back when the river was equivalent to today's interstate. A tour will take you into the house, remarkable for its two-story Greek Revival portico. You'll notice that it's decorated in two different styles: the first floor re-creates life in 1840 when Gabriel Farnsley lived in the house as a bachelor; the second draws its style from 1880 when three generations of the Moremen family occupied the house. You'll also visit the detached kitchen, as well as the kitchen garden, where volunteers grow plants that very likely would have been served at mealtime in the 1800s. Be sure to enjoy the view of the river from the grounds; it's photo worthy.

FRANKFORT AVENUE AND EAST LOUISVILLE

Frankfort Avenue, running east from downtown, is a lively neighborhood known more for its restaurants and shopping than its attractions, though it's easy to spend a day exploring the area and enjoying the ambience. Once the gateway between Frankfort (hence the name) and Louisville, Frankfort Avenue is chockablock with historic buildings that have maintained their style despite finding new uses. Continuing east from Frankfort Avenue, you'll find yourself in East Louisville, a popular residential area that also houses interesting sights, primarily historical. With amorphous boundaries—you'll get a lot of different answers if you ask a local just what East Louisville includes—the sights in this section are located as close as 5 minutes and as distant as 30 minutes from downtown.

American Printing House for the Blind

The museum of the **American Printing House for the Blind** (1839 Frankfort Ave., 502/895-2405, www.aph.org, 8:30am-4:30pm Mon.-Fri., 10am-3pm Sat., free), the oldest and largest producer of materials for the visually impaired, features hands-on

FRANKFORT AVENUE AND EAST LOUISVILLE

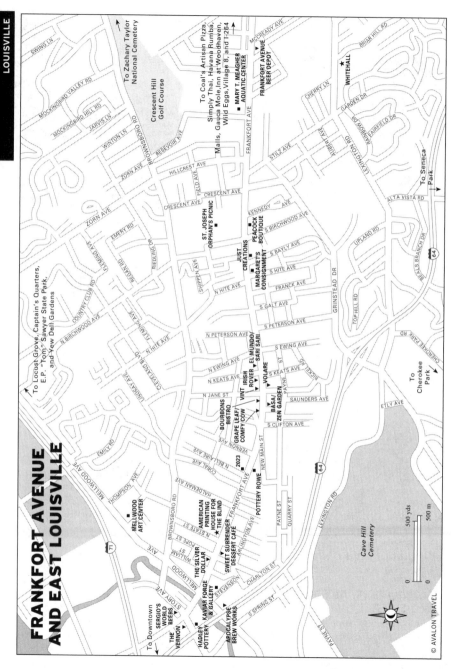

exhibits that document the evolution of tactile reading systems for the blind, and contains items such as a 142-volume Braille translation of an encyclopedia, a Braille bible used by Helen Keller, and a variety of Braille typewriters you can try. For a more in-depth look at the fascinating work done by the APH, take a free tour (10am and 2pm Mon.-Thurs.), where you'll get to see the printing press in action and listen in on the recording of Talking Books.

Whitehall

Although it began its life as a modest red-brick Italianate farmhouse, **Whitehall** (3110 Lexington Rd., 502/897-2944, www.historichomes.org, 10am-2pm Mon.-Fri., $5 adults, $4 seniors, $3 youth 6-18) grew from its humble 1855 origins to become an imposing Southern-style Greek Revival mansion. On a tour of its 15 rooms, you'll learn the history of the home and see the elaborate stylings introduced by the home's two most prominent owners. The Middleton family, who bought

the house in 1909, renovated it into the style we see today, while the Hume family, who occupied the house from 1924 to 1992, made the necessary arrangements for Whitehall to become a historic property. Intricate fireplaces and wood floors, period wallpaper, and beautifully carved furniture imported from around the world give Whitehall its sumptuous feel. Don't forget to check out the gorgeous gardens, which can be visited for free dawn-dusk.

Zachary Taylor National Cemetery

Originally the family burial grounds of the 12th President of the United States, **Zachary Taylor National Cemetery** (4701 Brownsboro Rd., 502/893-3852, www.cem.va.gov, sunrise-sunset daily) was given federal status in 1928, 78 years after Old Rough and Ready was laid to rest. Now joining President Taylor and his family in eternal rest are U.S. military members who served the nation in the years ranging from the Spanish-American War to the

© THERESA DOWELL BLACKINTON

Locust Grove

Persian Gulf War. A life-size statue atop a 50-foot granite monument marks the grave of the Kentuckian president.

Locust Grove

Visited by three presidents as well as the returning Lewis and Clark, and lived in by Louisville founder George Rogers Clark for the last nine years of his life, **Locust Grove** (561 Blankenbaker Ln., 502/897-9845, www.locustgrove.org, 10am-4:30pm Mon.-Sat., 1pm-4:30pm Sun., last tour at 3:15pm, $8 adults, $7 seniors, $4 youth 6-12) has played host to more than its share of history. Now this carefully restored 18th-century Georgian mansion, its grounds, formal gardens, and outbuildings are open to the public. A visit begins with a short film at a quarter past the hour and then moves on to a 45-minute tour of the property, followed by a chance to explore the museum. You'll learn about early Kentucky history, westward expansion, frontier life, and slave life all while enjoying the beautiful setting. Each December, special holiday candlelight tours are offered, giving visitors a taste of an old-fashioned Christmas.

Yew Dell Gardens

Recognized by the Garden Conservancy for its exceptional nature, **Yew Dell Gardens** (6220 Old Lagrange Rd., Crestwood, 502/241-4788, www.yewdellgardens.org, 10am-4pm Tues.-Sat., noon-4pm Sun., Apr.-mid-Dec., 10am-4pm Mon.-Fri., mid-Dec.-Mar., $7 adults, $5 seniors, free youth under 12) is 33 acres of bliss for anyone who loves plants and remarkable landscaping. The once private gardens of renowned horticulturist Theodore Klein, who died in 1998, opened to the public in 2005. Visitors can now marvel at the more than 1,000 specimens of rare trees and shrubs in his arboretum and explore a variety of themed gardens. Favorites include the Secret Garden, the formal Topiary Garden, the English Walled Garden, the summertime Bloom Garden, and the evergreen Serpentine Garden.

BARDSTOWN ROAD AREA

For many residents of Louisville, Bardstown Road, which runs south from downtown toward the suburbs, perfectly sums up the Derby City. As with Frankfort Avenue, Bardstown Road is a happening hub that, despite not having too many tourist attractions per se, is a place where you could easily pass an entire day. It's the place to experience a Louisvillian's Louisville.

Cave Hill Cemetery

Cave Hill Cemetery (701 Baxter Ave., 502/451-5630, www.cavehillcemetery.com, 8am-4:45pm daily) is not just a burial ground; it's also an arboretum, a masterpiece of landscape architecture, and a sculpture park. While strolling the grounds, you can admire the artwork adorning graves, identify more than 500 species of tree and shrub, and feed the waterfowl that live on the lake. Don't forget to pay your respects to Colonel Sanders (section 33, marked with a bust) and other Kentucky notables such as city founder George Rogers Clark (section P). In the spring and fall, historical and geological tours are offered; visit the website for dates and fees.

Farmington Historic Plantation

Farmington (3033 Bardstown Rd., 502/452-9920, www.historichomes.org, 10am-4pm Tues.-Fri., $9 adults, $8 seniors, $4 youth 6-18), the Federal-style home that sits at the heart of a former hemp plantation owned by the venerable Speed family, gives visitors a peek into genteel life in the early 1800s. Known for their philanthropic giving around Louisville, the Speed family was ties to both Thomas Jefferson and Abraham Lincoln, and Farmington gives special attention to the family's relationship with the latter. A permanent exhibition explores what life was like at Farmington when Lincoln spent three weeks there in 1841 and details Lincoln's relationships with Joshua Speed, whom he called his "most intimate friend," and James Speed, who served as Lincoln's attorney general. Another

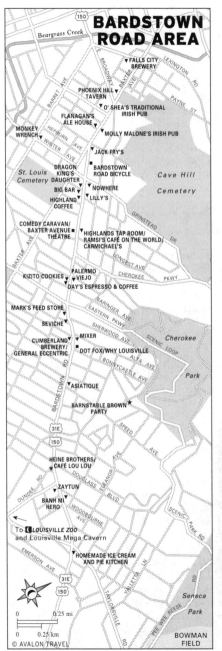

permanent exhibition details the lives of slaves at Farmington. Try to time your visit to coincide with one of their reenactments, which really bring history to life.

◖ Louisville Zoo

With its nationally recognized four-acre Gorilla Forest and its award-winning Glacier Run, which allows for underwater and aboveground viewing of polar bears, the **Louisville Zoo** (1100 Trevilian Way, 502/459-2181, www.louisvillezoo.org, 10am-4pm daily, Sep.-mid-Mar., 10am-5pm daily, mid-Mar.-Aug., $15.95 adults, $11.50 seniors and youth 3-11, $5 parking fee) is one of the best zoos in the country. Follow the simple loop layout to catch all 1,300 residents of the zoo, ranging from the tiny frogs of the Amazonian rainforest to the giant elephants of the African plains. Regularly scheduled training and feeding programs add to the experience, as do the natural settings and informational panels. Going beyond animals, the zoo hosts a few

© THERESA DOWELL BLACKINTON

giraffes at the Louisville Zoo

extremely popular events. August's **Brew at the Zoo** is a celebration of local and regional microbrews and good music that always sells out in advance. For kids, October's **World's Largest Halloween Party,** which features trick-or-treating around the decorated zoo, is a real treat.

Louisville Mega Cavern

Lying underneath the Louisville Zoo and much of the surrounding area, **Louisville Mega Cavern** (1841 Taylor Ave., 877/614-6342, www.louisvillemegacavern.com), which was once a limestone quarry, is now a tourist spot. You can explore it on a one-hour historic tram tour (tours at 10am, noon, 2pm, and 4pm daily, mid-Jan.-mid-Mar., on the hour 10am-4pm daily, mid-Mar.-Memorial Day and Labor Day-Oct., on the hour 9am-5pm Mon.-Fri. and 9am-6pm Sat.-Sun., Memorial Day-Labor Day, $13.50 adults, $12 seniors, $8 youth 3-11) or on a two-hour tour via six underground zip lines (reserve online; $59-79). During the Christmas season, the cavern is decked out in holiday lights, which can be enjoyed on a self-drive tour.

Entertainment and Events

BARS AND CLUBS

Louisville has a happening bar and club scene that centers around three areas: downtown, Frankfort Avenue, and the Bardstown Road/ Baxter Avenue corridor. Vibes range from neighborhood joint to upscale bar, so no matter your taste, you'll find something that's your style. While most cities go dark around 2am, Louisville is unique in that some nightlife locales don't shut down until 4am.

Downtown

Louisville's downtown has been undergoing a nightlife reawakening in the past decade, with the opening of the KFC Yum! Center in 2010 and the revitalization of the area known as NuLu further spurring it on. For those fond of tradition, a few longtime institutions have opened outposts downtown, including Irish pub **Patrick O' Shea's** (123 W. Main St., 502/708-2488, www.osheaslouisville.net, 11am-1am Mon.-Wed., 11am-4am Thurs.-Sat.) and **Bluegrass Brewing Company** (300 W. Main St., 502/562-0007, www.bbcbrew.com, 11am-midnight Mon.-Thurs., 11am-1am Fri.-Sat.), a well-loved microbrewery.

Additionally, multiple new establishments have flung open their doors, turning cool old buildings into hot new spots. From west to east, the following locales are worth checking out.

St. Charles Exchange (113 S. 7th St., 502/618-1917, http://stcharlesexchange.com, 4pm-midnight Mon.-Thurs., 4pm-2am Fri., 5pm-2am Sat., 5pm-10:30pm Sun.) serves top-notch cocktails as well as American wines, craft beers, and bourbons (plus a fine menu of contemporary American fare) from a long handsome bar on a black-and-white checked floor, giving it the feel of old-fashioned elegance. As one might expect, **Down One Bourbon Bar** (321 W. Main St., 502/566-3259, www.downonebourbonbar.com, 11am-11pm Mon.-Thurs., 11am-1am Fri., 4pm-1am Sat.) stocks an impressive array of bourbons, to be sampled by the glass, in flights, or in a cocktail, but they also have a fine beer list as well as wines and non-bourbon cocktails. Another bourbon-based hot spot is **Sidebar** (129 N. 2nd St., 502/384-1600, www.sidebarwhiskeyrow.com, 11am-1am Mon.-Wed., 11am-2am Thurs.-Sat., noon-1am Sun.), which is fittingly located in a loft in Louisville's old Whiskey Row; try one of the aged cocktails or ask the knowledgeable bartenders for their picks. For some live music with your choice of drink (more than 50 whiskeys as well as bottled beers and seven craft beers on tap), try **Haymarket Whiskey Bar** (331 E. Market St., 502/442-0523, http://haymarketwhiskeybar.com, 4:20pm-midnight Tues.-Thurs., 4:20pm-2am Fri.-Sat.).

the NuLu neighborhood

Downtown's **Fourth Street Live!** (400 S. 4th St., www.4thstlive.com) likes to bill itself as the place to be, but to be honest, most locals aren't big fans of it. Besides **Maker's Mark Bourbon House & Lounge** (502/568-9009, www.makerslounge.com, 11am-11:30pm Mon.-Thurs., 11am-3am Fri.-Sat., 11am-midnight Sun.), where you can kick back in a leather chair and sip one of the more than 70 bourbons on offer, few of the bars have any sort of Louisville feel, and you're most likely to find tourists and frat boys hanging out here. If you do want to check it out, the other nightlife establishments here are **Kill Devil Club,** a cocktail bar open Thursday-Saturday nights; **Marquee Bar,** a dance club with table service open only on Friday and Saturday nights; and **PBR Louisville,** a cowboy-themed club open Thursday-Saturday nights.

Frankfort Avenue

In addition to multiple fine restaurant bars, Frankfort Avenue also boasts destinations where drinking is the focus. **The Vernon** (1575 Story Ave., 502/584-8460, www.vernonclub. com, 5pm-midnight Mon.-Tues., 5pm-1am Wed.-Thurs., 3pm-1am Fri., noon-1am Sat., 1pm-1am Sun.)—part club, part bowling alley with bar—has played a part in Louisville history since the late 1800s. The club hosts shows by up-and-coming bands (check the online schedule), and The Vernon's eight lanes are the coolest place in town to doff bowling shoes. For a change from the usual scene, The Vernon is your spot.

Sergio's World Beers (1605 Story Ave., 502/618-2337, www.sergiosworldbeers.com, 2pm-midnight Mon.-Thurs., 2pm-2am Fri.-Sat., 2pm-11pm Sun.) is not the place to go if you think that beer is beer. If, however, you are a discerning beer drinker, then you'll want to locate this discreet (there's no signage) temple to beer to surround yourself with like-minded individuals and get lost in the selection of 1,400 beers, more than 40 of which are on tap.

For bourbon fans, you'll want to head to one of two destinations. **Bourbons Bistro** (2255 Frankfort Ave., 502/894-8838, www.

LOUISVILLE'S CRAFT BEER SCENE

Louisville's contemporary craft beer scene dates back to the early 1990s, long before the country went mad for microbrews, but it's grown substantially in the past decade. Fans of local brews will want to check out the following microbreweries, some of which focus exclusively on beer while others have a restaurant element as well. True aficionados will want to be in Louisville in September for the nine-day **Louisville Craft Beer Week,** which features beer dinners, beer pairings, beer walks, brewery parties, and more at locations all around town.

AGAINST THE GRAIN

Located in the old train station at Louisville Slugger Field, **Against the Grain** (401 E. Main St., 502/515-0174, www.atgbrewery.com, 11pm-midnight Mon.-Wed., 11am-2am Thurs.-Sat., noon-9pm Sun.) brews beers in six broad categories—session, hop, whim, malt, dark, and smoke—with the particular beers on tap constantly rotating. The 15-copper-barrel brewhouse is also a smokehouse restaurant.

APOCALYPSE BREW WORKS

Opened in 2012, **Apocalypse Brew Works** (1612 Mellwood Ave., 502/589-4843, http://apocalypsebrewworks.com, 5pm-11pm Fri.-Sat.) is a homebrew operation that focuses on small-batch beers. Their beers run the gamut from stouts, porters, and IPAs to fruit and specialty beers. On their 10 taps, you might find Creamation, Atomic Amber, Apollo IPA, or Smokin Pyres Porter.

BLUEGRASS BREWING COMPANY

The oldest of Louisville's microbreweries and the largest microbrewery in Kentucky, **Bluegrass Brewing Company** (known locally as BBC) has been keeping Louisville in beer since 1993. They have three restaurant locations (http://bbcbrew.com; 3929 Shelbyville Rd., 502/899-7051, 11am-midnight Mon.-Thurs., 11am-1am Fri.-Sat., noon-10pm Sun.; 660 S. 4th St., 502/568-2224, 11am-midnight Mon.-Thurs., 11am-1am Fri.-Sat.; 300 W. Main St., 502/562-0007, 11am-midnight Mon.-Thurs., 11am-1am

Fri.-Sat., 1pm-10pm Sun.) where you can try their American Pale Ale, Dark Star Porter, German Alt Beer, Nut Brown Ale, or Raspberry Mead, as well as rotating specials. Additionally, their **production brewery** (636 E. Main St., 502/584-2739, http://bluegrassbrew.com, 4pm-10pm Tues.-Fri.), which hosts a taproom and a museum of objects representing brewing history in Louisville, is also open to the public.

CUMBERLAND BREWERY

An integral part of the Bardstown Road scene, **Cumberland Brewery** (1576 Bardstown Rd., 502/458-8727, www.cumberlandbrewery.com, 4pm-2am Mon.-Thurs., noon-2am Fri.-Sat., 1pm-2am Sun.) keeps their regulars happy with their selection of cream ales, pale ales, porters, wheat ales, bocks, meades, and saisons, as well as their tasty menu of bar favorites.

FALLS CITY BREWERY

First opened in 1905, but then closed in 1978, **Falls City Brewery** (545 E. Barrett Ave., www.fallscitybeer.com, 4pm-8pm Thurs.-Fri., 2pm-8pm Sat.) was revived in 2010 as a craft brewery. Their first new beer after coming back onto the scene was an English pale ale. At the brewery and taproom, you can sample the goods or grab a growler to go.

NEW ALBANIAN BREWING COMPANY

Technically not in Louisville, but instead across the bridge in Indiana, **New Albanian Brewing Company** (www.newalbanian.com) has a hearty Louisville fan base. Since opening in 2002, New Albanian has brewed more than 30 beers, including Hoptimus, an imperial IPA; Black & Blue Grass, an ale spiced with lemongrass, black pepper, and agave; and Bob's Old 15B, a brown porter. The brews can be tried at their **pub and pizzeria** (3312 Plaza Dr., New Albany, IN, 812/944-2577, 11am-midnight Mon.-Sat.), from which you have a view of the R&D brewery, or at the **Bank Street Brewhouse** (415 Bank St., New Albany, IN, 812/725-9585, 11am-10pm Tues.-Thurs., 11am-11pm Fri.-Sat., 10am-9pm Sun.), a bistro-style restaurant where the production brewery is located.

bourbonsbistro.com, 5pm-10pm Tues.-Thurs., 5pm-11pm Fri.-Sat., 5pm-9pm Sun.) pours more than 130 bourbons, and also hosts bourbon dinners and other events in addition to serving a regular bourbon-based dinner menu. **The Silver Dollar** (1761 Frankfort Ave., 502/259-9540, www.whiskeybythedrink.com, 5pm-2am daily), which has a bit of a honky-tonk feel and serves Southern-meets-Californian food, has a four-page bourbon list, a three-page beer list, and substantial numbers of whiskeys and tequilas.

Bardstown Road

Louisville's nightlife center for decades, Bardstown Road is still where many locals go to meet and mingle or just grab a stool at the neighborhood watering hole. Many a weekend gets kicked off at Louisville's Irish corner, located just past where Bardstown Road turns into Baxter Avenue. It's the home of **O'Shea's Traditional Irish Pub** (956 Baxter Ave., 502/589-7373, www.osheaslouisville.net, 4pm-2am Mon., 11am-2am Tues., 11am-4am Wed.-Sat.), **Flanagan's Ale House** (934 Baxter Ave., 502/585-3700, http://flanagansalehouse.com, 11am-2am Sun.-Wed., 11am-4am Thurs.-Sat.), and **Molly Malone's Irish Pub** (933 Baxter Ave., 502/473-1222, www.mollymalonesirishpub.com, 11am-2am Sun.-Wed., 11am-4am Thurs.-Sat.). Molly's draws in a large college student contingent, while O'Shea's, with its three bars and two lovely courtyards, and Flanagan's, with more than 100 beers on tap, cater to a more mixed crowd. It's not unusual to find people hopping among all three.

A newer addition to the scene, beer mecca **Holy Grale** (1034 Bardstown Rd., http://holygralelouisville.com, 4pm-1am Mon.-Thurs., 1pm-2am Fri.-Sat.) is a temple to craft beer (and craft beer only) located in a former Unitarian church. They've got 26 taps, lots of bottles, and a good bar menu to boot, with an unbeatable indoor area and a lovely beer garden.

When the weather is nice, make **Monkey Wrench** (1025 Barrett Ave., 502/582-2433,

4pm-2am Tues.-Fri., noon-2am Sat., 10am-2am Sun.) your destination. Located in a former Laundromat, this spacious bar has a fantastic rooftop deck where you can enjoy inexpensive drinks. A small cover may be charged if you opt to drink inside and enjoy the live music, but the deck is always free.

More interested in nightclubs than bars? Then **Phoenix Hill Tavern** (644 Baxter Ave., 502/589-4957, www.phoenixhill.com, 8pm-4am Wed. and Sat., 8pm-3am Thurs., 5pm-4am Fri.) is a good bet. On weekends, live music plays from three stages, and in summer, the dance party moves outdoors to the deck. Phoenix Hill also hosts national acts and special events. Check the online calendar.

Although members of the GLBQT demographic should find themselves comfortable anywhere listed here, a few Bardstown Road establishments are known for being especially gay-friendly. They aren't gay bars, but bars that are welcoming to all and have a higher percentage of GLBQT patrons than some other places. Regardless of your sexual orientation, the following sites are worth checking out for a good time. **NoWhere** (1133 Bardstown Rd., http://nowherelouisville.com, 4pm-4am Mon.-Sat., 2pm-4am Sun.) attracts a fun-loving crowd with its DJ and dance floor as well as pool tables and a chill patio. **Big Bar** (1202 Bardstown Rd., 502/618-2237, 4pm-4am Mon.-Sat., 2pm-4am Sun.), a small place despite its name, has the welcoming feel of a neighborhood bar, and its patio is great for people-watching. **Mixer** (1565 Bardstown Rd., 502/384-1565, http://mixerlouisville.com, 5pm-4am Tues.-Sun.), a piano bar with good cocktails, has a relaxed but classy atmosphere.

LIVE MUSIC
Downtown

Stevie Ray's Blues Bar (230 E. Main St., 502/387-7365, www.stevieraysbluesbar.com, 4pm-midnight Mon.-Tues., 4pm-1am Wed.-Thurs., 4pm-3am Fri., 6pm-3am Sat.) brings in some of the nation's best blues musicians as well as top local talent. Crowds regularly pack the bar, which is equally welcoming to those who like to enjoy their blues with a drink at a table and those who feel the need to get up and dance.

In the basement of the Glassworks building, **Jazzyblu** (815 W. Market St., 502/992-3243, www.jazzyblu.com, 8pm-midnight Wed., 5pm-11pm Thurs., 8pm-2am Fri.-Sat., 6pm-11pm Sun.) appeals to the artsy crowd with its upscale lounge feel and its schedule of jazz, blues, and neo soul shows.

Bardstown Road
Highlands Tap Room (1279 Bardstown Rd., 502/459-2337, www.highlandstaproom.com, 4pm-4am daily) offers live music seven days a week and never charges a cover. The music is diverse, ranging from rock and indie to blues and bluegrass, and bands are both local and regional. The bar also hosts open mic and karaoke nights. On busy nights, getting to the bar to order one of the 13 microbrews they have on tap can be difficult, but the crowd is friendly.

COMEDY CLUBS
Bardstown Road
Comedy Caravan (1250 Bardstown Rd., 502/459-0022, www.comedycaravan.com) has been making Louisville laugh for more than two decades. Nationally known comedians share the stage with up-and-coming performers, all of whom know how to tell a joke or two. Check the website for a schedule of shows. You must be 18 or older to attend. Reservations are recommended.

MOVIE THEATERS
Bardstown Road
Louisville has plenty of theaters showing blockbuster hits and offering stadium seating. But if you're looking to catch a foreign or independent film, you'll want to get a ticket at **Baxter Avenue Theatre** (1250 Bardstown Rd., 502/456-4404, www.baxter8.com). Blockbuster films are also shown. Film freaks won't want to miss Midnight at the Baxter,

a series in which cult classics appear in all their 35-mm glory on the big screen on select Saturdays.

East Louisville
For a cheap night out, screen a flick at **Village 8** (4014 Dutchmans Ln., 502/894-8697, www.village8.com), Louisville's discount theater. Tickets are only $4 in the evening, $3 before 6pm. Every Friday, a new first-run independent, foreign, or art-house film opens at Village 8 as part of the Louisville Exclusive Film series.

PERFORMING ARTS
Kentucky Center for the Performing Arts
The stages of the **Kentucky Center for the Performing Arts** (501 W. Main St., 502/562-0100, www.kentuckycenter.org) are home to the **Louisville Ballet** (www.louisvilleballet.org), **Louisville Orchestra** (www.louisvilleorchestra.org), **Kentucky Opera** (http://kentuckyopera.org), the **Broadway Across America** series (http://louisville.broadway.com), and the **Stage One** (www.stageone.org) children's theater. The center also puts on concerts, shows, and performances from nonresident groups and popular artists in a series called Kentucky Center Presents. With three stages on-site, ranging from the tiny experimental MeX to the kid-friendly Bomhard to the crowd-welcoming Whitney Hall, as well as the grand stage of the nearby Brown Theatre (315 W. Broadway), the Kentucky Center is where you go to see great performing artists from every genre. All shows draw big crowds, but for the Broadway series in particular, be sure to get tickets well in advance, as the best seats for these shows sell out quickly.

Actor's Theatre
For powerful performances of both groundbreaking and classic plays, **Actor's Theatre** (316 W. Main St., 502/584-1205, www.actorstheatre.org) is the hottest act in town. The Tony Award-winning theater is known

for its daring and innovation, introducing more than 300 plays into the greater theater world and premiering three Pulitzer Prize winners. It's also known by locals for its annual production of *A Christmas Carol,* which seems to get better every year. The theater's three stages are reached through a magnificent lobby that was originally built as the imposing Bank of Louisville building in 1837.

Louisville Palace

When big-name comedians, musicians who like to provide their audience with an intimate experience, and other performers of national note come to town, you can often find them at the **Louisville Palace** (625 4th Ave., 502/583-4555, www.louisvillepalace.com). This performing arts space lives up to its high-reaching name thanks to its many visual pleasures. Built in 1928, it cost $2 million—a remarkable amount then—and you'll understand why immediately. The Spanish Baroque design translates into a lobby of bright red, gold, and blue with a vaulted ceiling featuring carvings of such greats as Shakespeare and Beethoven. Entering the theater, you'll feel as though you've stepped into a Spanish courtyard due to the plethora of arcades, balconies, and turrets, and the ceiling painted like the midnight sky. Come for the show or come for the theater; either way you'll have an amazing experience.

ART GALLERIES

Art is thriving in Louisville, with galleries popping up all around town. In fact, the gallery scene has exploded so much that two monthly hops are needed to keep patrons happy, though galleries are, of course, open outside of trolley hop hours.

◖ First Friday Trolley Hop

Since the most recent turn of the century, downtown Louisville's Main and Market Streets have transformed into the place to be for art lovers. Galleries abound, and thanks to the **First Friday Trolley Hop** (www.first-fridaytrolleyhop.com), they're all easy to visit

and welcoming to both the committed art patron and the casual browser. From 5pm-11pm on the first Friday of each month, historic trolleys circulate through the art district, offering free rides between art galleries and the nearby restaurants, bars, and shops. Galleries often hold exhibition openings on First Friday nights, while restaurants offer special menus and deals. A full listing of participating galleries with links to their individual websites can be found on the Trolley Hop website, so you can plan in advance where you want to stop. On First Fridays, most galleries stay open until 9pm. Free parking is available at Slugger Field, the Fourth Street Live! parking garage, and on the street after 6pm.

A few noteworthy galleries are **Glassworks** (815 W. Market St., 502/584-4510, www.louisvilleglassworks.com, 10am-5pm Mon.-Sat.), which has two glass studios, two glass galleries, and a workshop space where you can take classes; **Flame Run** (828 E. Market St., 502/584-5353, www.flamerun.com, 10am-4pm, Mon.-Fri., 10am-5pm Sat.), another excellent glass studio that plays host to an array of exhibitions; **Zephyr Gallery** (610 E. Market St., 502/585-5646, www.zephyrgallery.org, 11am-6pm Tues.-Sat.), a cooperative gallery with 14 members who show their work on a rotating basis; and **Pyro Gallery** (909 E. Market St., 502/587-0106, www.pyrogallery.com, noon-6pm Thurs.-Sat.), another cooperative with artists working in everything from clay to film to found objects.

F.A.T. Friday Hop

Trolley-hop fun isn't limited to the first Friday of the month; it's also scheduled for 6pm-10:30pm on the last Friday of the month, when the beloved TARC trolley makes its way to Frankfort Avenue for the **F.A.T. Friday Hop** (www.fatfridayhop.org), offering free rides to hop participants. Though the Frankfort Avenue area boasts less art galleries than downtown, it's still a bustling area of boutiques, specialty shops, and restaurants. A map of participants can be found on the F.A.T. Friday website.

Most participating galleries stay open until at least 9pm on F.A.T. Fridays.

Whether on the trolley hop or on your own time, here are a few galleries worth seeking out. The **Mellwood Art Center** (1860 Mellwood Ave., 502/895-3650, www.mellwoodartcenter.com), located in a 360,000-square-foot industrial building that once housed the Fischer Meat Packing plant, now houses more than 200 artist studios and galleries, running the entire gamut of arts and crafts. Though the center is open 9am-9pm daily, not all artists are there at all times. For the best chance of finding the artist you're looking for in studio, visit during the trolley hop or during market hours (11am-4pm Wed.-Sat.). At **Pottery Rowe** (2048 Frankfort Ave., 502/896-0877, www.potteryrowe.com, 10am-5pm Mon.-Sat.), Melvin Rowe creates outstanding pieces from clay, ranging from functional dishes to decorative ornaments. At **Kaviar Forge & Gallery** (1718 Frankfort Ave., 502/561-0377, www.craigkaviar.com, noon-6pm Wed.-Fri., noon-4pm Sat.), artist Craig Kaviar turns out award-winning forge work and also presents pieces by other artists in his gallery.

FESTIVALS AND EVENTS
◖ Kentucky Derby Festival

The Kentucky Derby might be known as the most exciting two minutes in sports, but to Louisville, the Derby lasts far longer than two minutes. In fact, thanks to the **Kentucky Derby Festival** (www.kdf.org), Derby excitement lasts for a complete two weeks.

The party kicks off on the Saturday two weeks before the Derby (which is always the first Saturday in May) with **Thunder Over Louisville,** the largest annual fireworks display in the world. For nearly 30 minutes, eight 400-foot barges anchored in the Ohio River around the Second Street Bridge shoot a barrage of pyrotechnics into the night, turning Louisville's downtown sky into an explosion of color. Crowning the show is the mile-long waterfall of fireworks that cascades down from the bridge. The celebration begins long before

A balloon version of Secretariat gallops down the street during the Pegasus Parade.

© THERESA DOWELL BLACKINTON

dark, however, with an air show that lifts off in mid-afternoon and features performances by skydive and aeronautic teams as well as flyovers by military jets. The best viewing spots are at Waterfront Park (129 E. River Rd.). Claim yours early.

Next on the agenda for most Derby Festival attendees is the **Great BalloonFest,** which takes place the weekend after Thunder, stretching from Thursday through Saturday. Events include a Balloon Glimmer at Waterfront Park on Thursday, a Rush-Hour Race departing from Bowman Field (2815 Taylorsville Rd.) at 7am on Friday, a Balloon Glow Friday night at the Kentucky Exposition Center (937 Phillips Ln.), and the Great Balloon Race departing from Bowman Field at 7am on Saturday. All balloon events are weather permitting. Also taking place on the Saturday one week before Derby is the **Derby Festival Marathon and Mini-Marathon,** both of which take runners on a tour of Louisville, including a lap around Churchill Downs.

During Derby week, the Festival really heats up, with the end of the week especially loaded with popular events. On Wednesday evening you'll want to make your way to the Waterfront for the **Great Steamboat Race** (6pm), which pits the hometown *Belle of Louisville* against the *Belle of Cincinnati.* The two boats race a course down the Ohio River and back to port, but the first boat across the finish line isn't necessarily the winner of the coveted gilded antlers. Instead, the winner is the boat that accumulates the most points in a competition involving five predesignated tasks, one being a calliope-playing contest. If you're not content to watch the race from shore, you can purchase a dinner cruise ticket for either boat.

On Thursday afternoon at 5pm, the festival's original event, the **Pegasus Parade,** gets underway. Broadway, from Campbell Street to 9th Street, is taken over by floats, marching bands, equestrian units, celebrities, clowns, and inflatables, and cheering crowds cram the sidewalks. Tickets are available for bleacher seats and chairs, but many people just bring their own blankets and lawn chairs and claim

a street-side spot. If you're a true parade aficionado, get an in-depth look at the floats and performers during the Parade Preview, which takes place on the Tuesday evening before the race at the Kentucky Exposition Center.

As much as Louisville loves fireworks, balloons, and parades, by Friday of Derby week all thoughts have turned to horse racing. Though the big event is still a day away, you'll find Churchill Downs nearly as packed. Locals, who often spend Derby Day itself at parties rather than at the track, flock to Churchill Downs for the running of the **Kentucky Oaks,** a premier race for fillies established alongside the Derby in 1875. As with the Derby, the infield is open for the full day of racing, and attendance routinely tops 100,000. The scene is a bit more laid-back than on Derby Day, making it a favorite for families (Oaks Day is a school holiday in Louisville). General admission tickets, which allow you entrance to the infield and first-floor paddock, are $25 and available at the gate. Reserved seats must be purchased in conjunction with Derby tickets. After the races, one final pre-Derby event takes place: the **Barnstable Brown Party,** a Derby Eve gala attended by celebrities of every stripe. Legions of fans line up outside the home of Patricia Barnstable Brown (1700 Spring Dr.) in the hopes of spotting their favorite stars.

The denouement of all the celebrating and the reason the festival takes place at all is the **Kentucky Derby,** run every year since 1875 at Churchill Downs, making it the longest-running sporting event in the United States. Though the actual Run for the Roses is the 10th race of the day, with the traditional singing of "My Old Kentucky Home" and the call to the post taking place around 6pm, the gates at Churchill Downs open at 8am, and the racing starts at 11am. Join the more than 150,000 people who attend the Derby each year for an experience everyone should have at least once. In the grandstands, women wear extravagant hats, men wear seersucker suits, and everyone enjoys at least one mint julep. When it's time to watch the best three-year-old thoroughbreds in the nation race, all eyes turn to the track.

Overhead in Millionaires Row, Hollywood celebrities air kiss each other and pose for the camera in designer outfits. And in the 40 acres of infield, where most Derby attendees end up, anything goes. Though you can catch a glimpse of the horses passing by if you push your way up to the fence and you can see all the races on the infield's big-screen TVs, most people come to the infield to party rather than watch the horses run. The area near the third turn is particularly notorious for its raucous behavior, which almost always involves alcohol snuck in via ingenious methods and frequently involves mud, nudity, and other behavior that your parents would not approve of. But don't fear; if that's not your scene, just head toward the first turn, where families tend to congregate and even Miss Manners would find little to shake her head at. General admission tickets cost $40 and an unlimited number are available at the gate. Reserved seats are much, much harder to come by. Without a lot of money or luck, obtaining reserved seats for the Derby is nearly impossible. Tickets for the Derby and Oaks are sold together in a package. You can submit a ticket request to Churchill Downs via their website (www.churchilldowns.com), which will enter you into a lottery for tickets. Additionally, a few thousand tickets are released for public sale, again via the website, in December or January. These tickets range in price from $172 for a grandstand bleacher seat to $6,390 for a six-seat box in the third-floor clubhouse.

Aside from the Oaks and Derby, all events mentioned here are free to spectators with a Derby pin. Pins can be purchased at the entrance to all events for $5, as well as at local grocery stores, drugstores, and other retailers for $4. The Kentucky Derby Festival consists of many more events than those outlined here, so check the website for a full calendar of events with descriptions. You'll also want to confirm dates, times, and locations for all events.

Humana Festival of New American Plays

Be the first to know about the next hot thing in theater by attending the annual **Humana Festival of New American Plays** (www.actorstheatre.org). This internationally renowned festival, held for seven consecutive weeks between February and April, unveils the best new works by American playwrights. Many of these plays have gone on to win prestigious prizes. The excitement in the air is palpable. For theater buffs, attending the festival is a must. In addition to single performance tickets, packages are also available.

Forecastle Festival

Billing itself as a music/art/activism festival, the **Forecastle Festival** (http://forecastlefest.com) is a huge three-day outdoor concert. The festival, which is held at Waterfront Park in early July, features more than 100 bands and is considered one of the premier outdoor events in the nation. In 2013, performers included the Black Keys, Tift Merritt, Old Crow Medicine Show, the Avett Brothers, Big Boi, and a slew of other artists from a wide variety of genres. For many attendees, the event is as much about the experience as the music. Single-day and three-day tickets are available.

Abbey Road on the River

Though you might assume the world's largest Beatles music festival would be held in England, you'd be wrong. It's actually held in Louisville over Memorial Day weekend. At **Abbey Road on the River** (www.abbeyroadontheriver.com), more than 60 bands pay tribute to The Beatles during five days of rocking and rolling at the waterfront Belvedere Park. When the official partying ends around 1am, many attendees head to the nearby Galt House for sing-alongs of Beatles favorites. The hotel also hosts film viewings as well as a few indoor stages. If you can't get enough of John, Paul, George, and Ringo, you won't want to miss this festival. Five-day tickets offer the best value, but you can also buy single-day tickets.

Kentucky Shakespeare Festival

Every summer from mid-June to mid-July, the **Kentucky Shakespeare Festival** (www.kyshakes.org) raises the curtain on the stage

© THERESA DOWELL BLACKINTON

Saying hello to Freddy Farm Bureau is a State Fair tradition.

of late August every year, is an end-of-summer rite. From fine-arts competitions to tobacco judging, from livestock shows to beauty pageants, from the thrill of pig races to the suspense of the pipe-smoking contest, the Kentucky State Fair offers something for everyone. A huge midway, as well as a series of free and ticketed concerts, rounds out the offerings. Admire the skill of quilters, judge for yourself which goat deserves a blue ribbon, pick up as many freebies as you can carry, say hello to giant Freddy Farm Bureau, or just people watch. To fit it all in, you'll need a few days, especially if you want to take in events such as the World Championship Horse Show. You'll also want to come hungry as there's a feast of food to be had. For a real taste of the Bluegrass State, forgo the carnival classic corndog and gyro stands and instead visit the Kentucky Proud Tent for your choice of locally produced treats. The pork chop sandwiches are hard to beat. Tickets are available at the gate. Before the fair begins, discounted tickets are available at area Kroger grocery stores.

at the C. Douglas Ramsey Amphitheatre in Old Louisville's Central Park and presents two or three of the Bard's works. No matter what plays they're putting on, expect elaborate costumes, impressive scenery, and accomplished actors. Dating back to 1949, making it the oldest free and independent Shakespeare festival in the United States, Shakespeare in Central Park is a Louisville tradition and draws big crowds. The amphitheater can seat 1,000 people, but you're also welcome to view your "Free Will" from a blanket on the lawn. Bring a picnic to enjoy before the 8pm show and make it an evening.

〖 Kentucky State Fair

The **Kentucky State Fair** (Kentucky Exposition Center, 937 Phillips Ln., www. kystatefair.org), occupying an 11-day stretch

St. James Court Art Show

Fine art and fine homes go well together, which may explain why the **St. James Court Art Show** (Old Louisville, www.stjamescourtartshow.com, 10am-6pm Fri.-Sat., 10am-5pm Sun., free), which takes place in the heart of Old Louisville on the first full weekend in October, is such a well-attended event. Consistently ranked by artists and art organizations as one of the top art shows in the nation, St. James features 750 artists from across the continent. At booths set up amid the mansions on St. James and Belgravia courts as well as on Magnolia, 3rd, and 4th Streets, you'll find works in 16 mediums, ranging from fiber to clay, metal, wood, and photography—and in price ranges to fit any budget. Artists are chosen through a competitive selection process, and all work is juried.

Shopping

SHOPPING DISTRICTS

Like every midsize city in the United States, Louisville has its share of shopping malls and big box stores, but it also has some great local stores. Shopaholics will want to hit NuLu, Frankfort Avenue, and Bardstown Road to find the best Louisville goods.

NuLu

Currently the hottest area in town, NuLu stretches from Main Street on the north to Jefferson Street on the south, and from Hancock Street on the west to Wenzel Street on the east, with most of the action clustered on Market Street in the middle. It's all easily walkable, so take an afternoon to stroll from shop to shop, stopping for drinks and food when the urge hits. Can't-miss stops include **Gifthorse** (805 E. Market St., 502/681-5576, 11am-6pm Tues.-Thurs., 11am-7pm Fri.-Sat.), an awesome

sweets for sale at Muth's Candies

source for fun fashion and gifts, much of them locally made; **Revolver** (707 E. Market St., 502/468-6130, www.revolverlouisville.com, 10am-5pm Tues.-Thurs. and Sat., 10am-6pm Fri., 11am-3pm Sun.), with drool-worthy furnishings and home decor; **Joe Ley Antiques** (615 E. Market St., 502/583-4014, www.joeley. com, 10am-5pm Tues.-Sat.), which overwhelms with two acres of amazing antiques; **Muth's Candies** (630 E. Market St., 502/585-2952, www.muthscandy.com, 8:30am-4pm Tues.-Fri., 10am-4pm Sat.), Louisville's confectionary since 1921; **Taste Fine Wines and Bourbons** (634 E. Market St., 502/409-4646, http://taste-finewinesandbourbons.com, 11am-8pm Tues.-Wed., noon-late Thurs.-Fri., 10:30am-late Sat.), where you can sample and buy a wide variety of the namesake products; and the **Louisville Beer Store** (746 E. Market St., 502/569-2337, www.louisvillebeerstore.com, 3pm-10pm Tues.-Thurs., 1pm-midnight Fri., noon-midnight Sat., 1pm-7pm Sun.), which has hundreds of craft beers by the bottle as well as eight rotating taps and a tasting bar.

Frankfort Avenue

Frankfort Avenue, with a long history as a central area for local business, is another good place to pound the pavement in search of fun finds. If you're after high fashion, pop in at **Peacock Boutique** (2828 Frankfort Ave., 502/897-1158, www.shopthepeacock.com, 10am-7pm Mon.-Sat.), or for a more budget-friendly option, try **Margaret's Consignment** (2700 Frankfort Ave., 502/896-4706, www. margaretsconsignment.com, 10am-5pm Mon.-Sat., noon-4pm Sun.), which specializes in higher-end clothing. If you're looking to outfit your home, browse the 20th-century antiques at **2023** (2023 Frankfort Ave., 502/899-9872, 11am-5pm Tues.-Sat.) or the fair-trade goods from 35 developing nations at **Just Creations** (2722 Frankfort Ave., 502/897-7319, www.just-creations.org, 10am-6pm Mon.-Sat.).

© THERESA DOWELL BLACKINTON

Bardstown Road

The Highlands is a true Louisville original, a neighborhood chock full of well-loved houses and local shops, bars, and restaurants, and Bardstown Road is the epicenter of it all. For shoppers, the one-mile stretch between Eastern Parkway and Baxter Avenue is full of fun and funky options. If you're looking for an original Louisville souvenir, such as a T-shirt that you won't find anywhere else, drop in at **WHY Louisville** (1583 Bardstown Rd., 502/456-5400, www.whylouisville.com, 11am-8pm Mon.-Fri., 10am-8pm Sat., noon-6pm Sun.), where all the goods are made by local and regional designers. You can also find cool T-shirts at nearby **Dot Fox** (1567 Bardstown Rd., 502/452-9191, www.dotfoxclothingculture.com, 11am-8pm Mon.-Thurs., 11am-9pm Fri.-Sat., noon-6pm Sun.), a local take on Urban Outfitters where trendy clothing is sold alongside kitsch. For more fashion fun, head down the street to **General Eccentric** (1600 Bardstown Rd., 502/458-8111, www.geneccentric.com, 11am-8pm Mon.-Thurs., 11am-9pm Fri.-Sat., noon-6pm Sun.), where you can always find the latest trends, though if you like it, you'd better buy it, since they stock limited quantities of each style. You'll also want to be sure to visit **Carmichael's** (1295 Bardstown Rd., 502/456-6950, www.carmichaelsbookstore.com, 8am-10pm Sun.-Thurs., 8am-11pm Fri.-Sat.), Louisville's favorite bookstore, winning over customers with its book-loving sales staff, its handpicked collection, and its neighborhood feel.

ARTS AND CRAFTS

Since 1815, **Louisville Stoneware** (731 Brent St., 502/582-1900, www.louisvillestoneware.com, 10am-6pm Mon.-Fri., 10am-5pm Sat.) has been providing the Derby City with original dinnerware and house decor. The stoneware—designed, fired, and painted at the Brent Street studio—comes in a variety of motifs and colors, both traditional and modern. The mint julep cups, Hot Brown trays, and Kentucky Pie plates make great souvenirs, and the Equine and Fleur de Lis patterns are very popular. If you'd like to see the stoneware being created, visit at 10:30am or 1:30pm, when studio tours are offered for $7. If none of the designs suit your fancy, then you're welcome to paint your own stoneware. The $25 paint-your-own price includes a tour.

Though it has a shorter history than Louisville Stoneware—dating back to 1940—**Hadley Pottery** (1570 Story Ave., 502/584-2171, www.hadleypottery.com, 9am-5pm Mon.-Fri., 9am-3pm Sat.) is also a well-loved local institution. The "Hadley blue" paint appearing on all the pottery is instantly recognizable, and the whimsical designs, originally created by Mary Alice Hadley and now painted by her protégées, have a strong fan base. The holiday plates make for fun collector's items, and kids in particular love the animal designs. Many of the items can be personalized. Hadley Pottery is sold throughout the country, but the factory in Louisville is where it's all created, and you're welcome to take a tour (2pm Mon.-Thurs.) as well as browse the showroom.

MALLS

Louisville's most popular indoor malls are located directly next to each other. **Mall St. Matthews** (5000 Shelbyville Rd., 502/893-0311, www.mallstmatthews.com) is anchored by Dillards and J. C. Penney, while **Oxmoor Center** (7900 Shelbyville Rd., 502/426-3000, www.oxmoorcenter.com) is anchored by Sears, Macy's, and Von Maur. **The Paddock Shops** (4300 Summit Plaza Dr., 502/425-3441), an outdoor shopping center with such popular stores as Banana Republic, J.Crew, and Pier 1, is another favored shopping destination.

Sports and Recreation

PARKS

More than a hundred parks dot Louisville, providing 14,000 acres of green space, so no matter where you are, there's a park nearby. To find the one that most suits your interests, visit the Metro Parks website (http://louisvilleky.gov/metroparks) and use the Park Finder, which allows you to search by name, location, or park amenities.

◖ Olmsted Park System

Although landscape architect Frederick Law Olmsted is probably best known for New York's Central Park, many critics consider the park system he designed for Louisville to be his greatest accomplishment. Locals certainly think so. Consisting of three large flagship parks—Cherokee, Iroquois, and Shawnee—connected by six tree-lined parkways, with 15 smaller parks and playgrounds along the way, Louisville's **Olmsted Park System** (www.olmstedparks.org) is where Louisvillians go for a breath of fresh air.

CHEROKEE PARK

Cherokee Park (Willow Ave. and Cherokee Pkwy.) is the most popular park in the city, drawing nearly 500,000 visitors annually. In the Beargrass Creek Valley, Cherokee's 409 acres boast wide-open spaces perfect for picnics and pick-up games and broad vistas that reward hikers, joggers, and bikers. The always-busy 2.4-mile Scenic Loop is a mixed-use, one-way road, with one lane for cars and another dedicated to person-powered transport. Other favorite areas include the sport-lover's Frisbee Field, the dog run at Cochran Hill, the playground at Hogan's Fountain, and the eternal hangout of Big Rock. The park also sports an archery range, bird sanctuary, nine-hole golf course, and a series of trails shared by hikers and mountain bikers. Thanks to Cherokee Park's many entrances and exits, even locals are known to get confused when driving through,

so it's best to consult the park and trail maps online to plan your outing.

IROQUOIS PARK

The southern anchor of the Olmsted Park System, **Iroquois Park** (Southern Pkwy. and Taylor Blvd.) is known for its rugged terrain and the 10,000-plus-year-old forest that constitutes the heart of the park. From the park summit, home to one of many outlooks that dot Iroquois's 739 acres, visitors can take in a grand panorama of Louisville. Take a bike up to the summit for a challenge, or test your athletic prowess on the basketball courts, disc golf course, or 18-hole golf course. The Iroquois amphitheater, home to warm-weather productions and concerts, is another highlight of the park.

SHAWNEE PARK

Shawnee Park (Southwestern Pkwy. and Broadway), in western Louisville, makes the most of its riverfront setting with a Great Lawn popular for family reunions and other large gatherings. The basketball courts, baseball fields, and tennis courts are often busy, and the 18-hole golf course is the only city park course to offer a complete driving range facility.

Waterfront Park

Encompassing 85 acres of riverfront real estate in downtown Louisville, **Waterfront Park** (www.louisvillewaterfront.com, 6am-11pm daily) is home to most of the city's outdoor celebrations. Huge crowds gather on the Great Lawn and its surrounding green spaces for **Thunder Over Louisville,** the kickoff to the Derby Festival, as well as the **Waterfront Independence Festival,** a celebration of music and fireworks every July 3 and 4. The park also hosts numerous smaller festivals, concerts, and fundraiser walk/runs. In the summer, outdoor yoga classes and **Waterfront Wednesday,** a free after-work concert series scheduled for

taking a walk on the Big 4 Pedestrian & Bicycle Bridge at Waterfront Park

© THERESA DOWELL BLACKINTON

divided into five sections, three of which are completely or partially completed and open to the public, and two of which were still in the planning phases at the time of research. The biggest complete section is the 23-mile stretch of the Ohio River Valley section, running from Waterfront Park to Farnsley-Moremen Landing. Other open sections of the trail include 1.5 miles of the Shale Lowland section in southwest central Jefferson County and two miles of the Floyds Fork section in the far eastern section of the county. Visit the website for updated information and trail access points.

Louisville Extreme Park

The **Louisville Extreme Park** (Clay St. and Franklin St., www.louisvilleextremepark.org, 6am-11pm daily) features a 24-foot pipe, seven bowls ranging 4-11 feet, a 12-foot wooden vertical ramp, and plenty of ledges and rails, which invite skateboarders, in-line skaters, and bikers to show off their best moves. A rating system similar to that used on ski slopes identifies areas suitable for those with beginner, intermediate, and advanced skills. Don't forget your helmet; a local ordinance requires a helmet to be worn by all park users.

E. P. "Tom" Sawyer State Park

The only state park in Louisville, **E. P. "Tom" Sawyer State Park** (3000 Freys Hill Rd., 502/429-3280, http://parks.ky.gov, daylight-dark, free) doesn't lack for anything. Among its more standard offerings are a basketball and badminton gym, 12 tennis courts, a plethora of fields (14 soccer, 5 lacrosse, 3 softball, 1 rugby), fitness and nature trails, and picnic shelters. A number of leagues use these facilities, and information about joining one can be found on the park's website. The park's less common features include a model airplane airfield, an archery range, and a BMX track (Mar.-Oct.). A four-acre dog park welcomes canines and their companions, and an Olympic-size pool (noon-6pm Sun.-Fri., 11am-6pm Sat., Memorial Day weekend-Labor Day, $5 ages 13 and up, $4 ages 3-12) is a park favorite. For a unique treat, take part in one of the monthly Star Parties

the last Wednesday of each month, are popular with downtown workers and visitors. Visit the park's website for a complete listing of the many events held here each year.

It doesn't take a festival, however, for the park to be bustling. It's a prime spot for a picnic, a bike ride, a walk, or a pick-up game of ultimate Frisbee or touch football. For kids, the playground and waterplay areas are the biggest draws. For a place to sit quietly and thick, try the Lincoln Memorial, which celebrates Abe's connections to the state. The most recent addition, the **Big 4 Pedestrian & Bicycle Bridge,** is a big hit. This converted railroad bridge over the Ohio River connects Louisville with Jeffersonville, Indiana, and is a great place to get some exercise with a view. Parking is available on the street and in lots, most of which are free, along River Road.

Passing through Waterfront Park is the **Louisville Loop** (www.louisvilleloop.org), an approximately 100-mile multiuse trail that, when completed, will encircle the city. It is

© THERESA DOWELL BLACKINTON

water-spraying fish at Waterfront Park

forest in the United States. Hikers in particular love this park, as it offers more than 35 miles of trails. The longest and most challenging of these is the 6.2-mile, one-way Siltstone Trail, while the 0.2-mile Tuliptree Trail is the shortest and easiest (it's also wheelchair accessible). In between these two are a multitude of one-way and loop trails offering hikes of varying degrees of difficulty. Whichever you choose, you'll get to enjoy the bountiful plant life—50 types of trees and 17 species of ferns—as well as wildlife not often found in an urban setting—bobcats, coyotes, red foxes, white-tailed deer, great blue herons, and horned owls. For bird-watchers, a bird blind is available by appointment.

GOLF
Louisville Metro Parks

Nine of Louisville's Metro Parks feature public golf courses (http://louisvilleky.gov/metroparks/golf), with six of these offering a full 18 holes. Varying in difficulty, the courses invite golfers of all abilities to play at affordable prices. Of the nine courses, the two most popular are **Seneca Golf Course** (2300 Pee Wee Reese Rd., 502/458-9298) and **Charlie Vettiner Golf Course** (10207 Mary Dell Ln., 502/267-9958). Seneca, with its hilly par-72 course running aside Beargrass Creek, has been ranked the sixth most difficult course in the state, while Charlie Vettiner, with 50 sand traps and three ponds, is ranked right behind Seneca as the seventh most challenging.

Quail Chase

Boasting country club standards without the membership fees, **Quail Chase** (7000 Cooper Chapel Rd., 502/239-2110, www.quailchase.com) is a public golf course with 27 championship regulation holes. Water hazards, bunkers, and tree-lined fairways make every round a challenge.

Valhalla

The premier golf course in Louisville, **Valhalla** (15503 Shelbyville Rd., 502/245-4475, http://valhalla.pgalinks.com) is a private club that has hosted the PGA Championship, the

sponsored by the Louisville Astronomical Society and held at the park (www.louisville-astro.org).

The Parklands of Floyds Fork

One of the city's most exciting outdoor projects since the creation of the Olmsted Park System, the **Parklands of Floyds Fork** (http://theparklands.org) is an in-progress work in Eastern Louisville, which, when finished in 2015, will consist of four parks connected by a park drive, about a hundred miles of hike and bike trails, and 19 miles of canoe trails. At the time of research, Beckley Creek Park was open, Pope Lick Park was set to open, and ground was being broken on Turkey Run Park and Broad Run Park. Visit the website for updated information.

HIKING

Covering a remarkable 6,218 acres, **Jefferson Memorial Forest** (11311 Mitchell Hill Rd., 502/368-5404, www.memorialforest.com, 8am-dusk daily) is the largest municipal urban

Senior PGA Championship, and the Ryder Cup. Valhalla is partially owned by the PGA and considered a difficult course by even the world's best golfers. If you're a top-notch golfer and want to give the course a go yourself, you'll need to be the guest of a member or arrange guest privileges through the club. Check the website for details of upcoming events if you'd like to be a spectator.

SWIMMING

The **Mary T. Meagher Aquatic Center** (201 Reservoir Ave., 502/897-9949, http://louisvilleky.gov/metroparks), named for Louisville's own Olympic champion, features an indoor Olympic-size pool open year-round for both exercise and recreational swimming. The pool is open 5am-9pm Monday-Friday and 9am-6pm on Saturdays, but recreational swim is restricted to noon-3:30pm Monday-Friday with the addition of a 7pm-9pm time slot on Friday, and noon-6pm on Saturday. Swim lessons, exercise classes, and lifeguarding classes are offered at the center. A day pass costs $4.50 for those over age 13, while those 12 and under pay $2.25. For frequent users, a membership is the best option.

BIKING

Bike Louisville is an effort of the city government to encourage biking. To map a route, find roads with bike lanes, connect to local bike organizations, or find a bike shop, visit http://louisvilleky.gov/bikelouisville. Among the most popular places for road biking in the city are Cherokee and Iroquois parks and Jefferson Memorial Forest. Mountain bikers also like Cherokee and Iroquois, while BMX bikers stake claim to E. P. "Tom" Sawyer State Park.

Bike Clubs

The **Louisville Bicycle Club** (www.louisvillebicycleclub.org) organizes rides and events and advocates for cyclists. If you're looking for a group to ride with, check the calendar on their website, as they have rides scheduled nearly every day. The LBC also sponsors the annual **Old Kentucky Home Tour,** a two-day ride with

route options of 50, 72, and 102 miles. The century route takes riders from E. P. "Tom" Sawyer State Park to Bardstown, Kentucky, where they overnight before returning the next day.

Bike Shops and Rentals

For all your biking needs, visit **Bardstown Road Bicycle Co.** (1051 Bardstown Rd., 502/485-9795, www.bardstownroadbicycles.com, 10am-7pm Mon.-Wed., 10am-5pm Thurs.-Sat.), where the knowledgeable staff can help you pick out a new bike, fix up an old bike, or gear up for any type of bike adventure. They also rent bikes.

At **Wheel Fun Rentals** (Waterfront Park at the Big 4 Bridge, 502/589-2453, www.wheelfunrentals.com, 10am-9pm mid-May-mid-Aug., hours are weather-dependent rest of the year), you can rent a bicycle and explore Louisville's downtown and waterfront. Bikes available for rental range from your standard cruiser to tandem bikes to a double surrey that can transport your entire family.

SPECTATOR SPORTS
Horse Racing

Under the iconic spires of **Churchill Downs** (700 Central Ave., 502/636-4400, www.churchilldowns.com, $3 general admission), the world-famous Kentucky Derby is run every year on the first Saturday of May. The racetrack also hosts a spring meet (late April-early July), a Homecoming meet (September), and a fall meet (late October-November), where you can experience a full day of thoroughbred racing on both dirt and turf at the historic track. Pick up a program, wander over to the paddock for an up-close look at the contenders and their jockeys, place a bet, and then hurry down to the rail to cheer your pick on to the finish line. It's a classic way to pass a day in the Derby City. For a twist on traditional horse racing, check out Downs After Dark, a Saturday night racing event that tends to draw a younger crowd.

College Sports

Consistently drawing some of the largest crowds

WIN, PLACE, OR SHOW: PLACING A BET AT CHURCHILL DOWNS

First, get a program. You're going to need to know what horses are racing, and you might want to know what jockey is on board what horse, what the horses' previous race results are, or maybe just what color silks the jockeys will be wearing. There are as many ways of picking a winner as there are people, ranging from complicated mathematical formulas to lucky numbers and colors, so go with whatever feels right to you.

Second, scan the tote board to see the current odds for each horse. They change continually as people place bets. At Churchill Downs, odds are listed as a single number, such as 5. This translates to 5 to 1 odds, which means that you'd get a $5 payout for every $1 bet if said horse wins. Though there are payouts for second and third places, the winnings are impossible to calculate until the race has been run because they vary based on which three horses end up in the money and in what order. It's complicated. Don't worry about it.

Third, once you've picked a horse, decide how much you want to bet (there's a $2 minimum), and whether you want to bet on the horse to win, place (finish second), or show (finish third). Be aware that if you bet a horse to place, you get a payout if it wins or places, and if you bet a horse to show, you get a pay-out if it wins, places, or shows. The payout for a show bet on a winning horse isn't as much as the payout on a win bet, however.

Fourth, once you're certain you've picked the winner, head to the betting window. Approach the teller and place the bet. To make sure the teller gets all the info straight, give him or her your bet in the following manner: "Xth race, X dollars to (win, place, show) on horse number X." (For example: "Fourth race, two dollars to win on number four.") Check your ticket before walking away from the window to make sure all the information is correct.

Finally, return to your seat and scream your lungs out in an effort to get your horse to cross the finish line first. If your horse does win (or place or show, depending on your wager), wait until the results are posted as final and then return to the betting window, where the teller will cash your ticket.

Once you've gotten the hang of the straight bet, you can venture into the world of exactas (pick in correct order the first- and second-place finishers), trifectas (pick in correct order the first-, second-, and third-place finishers), pick threes (pick the winner of three designated races), and other exotic wagers, which someone at the race track will gladly explain to you if you just ask nicely. Good luck!

winning Kentucky Derby ticket

© GREGORY DOWELL

MORE THAN A RIVALRY: THE NATION'S BIGGEST HIGH SCHOOL FOOTBALL GAME

On a Friday evening in late September, more than 35,000 fans pack Papa John's Cardinal Stadium to watch a football game, but not one played by the University of Louisville. Instead, these fans, wearing St. Xavier green-and-gold or Trinity green-and-white sweatshirts, face paint, and hats, have come to watch Louisville's two largest Catholic all-male high schools have it out on the gridiron. It's the nation's best high school football rivalry.

Year in and year out, one, if not both, of these teams end up in the state championship game, but to many players and fans, the annual **St. X-Trinity game** is just as important,

if not more so. Sure, the approximately 1,400 students from each high school attend, but so also do their parents, neighbors, friends, and their friends' friends. Alumni turn out with their families in tow, some coming all the way across the country to what has become an unofficial annual reunion. Tailgating reaches a fever pitch in the parking lot pregame, though officials do ask that you keep it alcohol-free. Going far beyond a high school event, the St. X-Trinity game is a Louisville event, so no matter what your connection is, you'll want to join the crazed fans in seeing high school football like you've never seen it before.

in college athletics, the **University of Louisville Cardinals** (502-852-5732, www.uoflsports. com), who will join the ACC in 2014 after years in the Big East, are Louisville's team. The men's basketball team, NCAA 2013 National Champions, are the crowd favorite, packing in the fans at every one of their home games at the 22,000-seat **KFC Yum! Center** (S. 2nd St. and W. Main St). The basketball rivalry with the cross-state Kentucky Wildcats is rabid, and was made even more so when the University of Louisville landed Rick Pitino as their head coach in 2001. For many Wildcat fans, this made Pitino a bigger traitor than Benedict Arnold himself, as Pitino had led the Cats for eight years in the 1990s, but for Louisville fans it was the coup of the century. No matter whom they're playing, however, expect exciting hoops and fans who live and die Cards basketball.

Behind men's basketball, U of L football is the passion of local fans, who religiously fill the 56,000 seats of **Papa John's Cardinal Stadium** (2800 S. Floyd St.) and go whole-hog in pregame tailgating. A stretch of highly successful seasons was crowned by a victory over Florida at the 2013 Sugar Bowl.

Though overshadowed by men's basketball, the women's basketball program is also

top-notch, playing for the national championship most recently in 2013, which was one of the best years ever for the Cardinals in general. The women share KFC Yum! Center with the men's team.

Additionally, the Louisville baseball team has come into its own in the past decade, making their second appearance in the College World Series in 2013. The team plays at Jim Patterson Stadium (Central Ave. and 3rd St.).

Tickets for men's basketball games are nearly impossible to come by, so your best bet is to check www.stubhub.com to find someone selling theirs. For other sports, tickets may be purchased online at www.ticketmaster.com or at the **U of L Ticket Offices** (Belknap Campus, Student Activities Center, 3rd floor, corner of Floyd St. and Brandeis St., 502-852-5863, or Papa John's Cardinal Stadium Gate 2, 9am-5pm Mon.-Fri. and starting at 9am game days).

Professional Baseball

As the AAA affiliate of the Cincinnati Reds, the **Louisville Bats** (502-212-2287, www.milb. com) offer baseball fans a chance to see tomorrow's big-league stars in an intimate setting. The Bats play home games at **Louisville Slugger Field** (401 E. Main St.), a 13,000-seat stadium with views of downtown and the Ohio River. The stadium, which opened in 2000, preserves a part of historic Louisville in that it incorporates the Brinly-Hardy Warehouse, a train shed built in 1889, into its design. With tickets starting at $7, a Bats game at Slugger Field makes for a fun date, a night out with friends, or a family outing. Come early to get autographs, then enjoy the game, knowing that if the kids get restless, there are two in-stadium playgrounds, a carousel, a speed pitch activity, and the never-ending antics of mascot Buddy Bat.

Accommodations

Most visitors to Louisville will want to reserve a room in one of the downtown hotels or Old Louisville B&Bs. From either of these two areas, you can easily access the city's major sights and restaurants. If you don't mind being a little bit out of the action, East Louisville has two nice options as well. Look for weekend deals downtown when business travelers have gone home, and midweek specials at the B&Bs. Prices soar all over town at Derby time, and you'll also find higher prices in Old Louisville during the St. James Court Art Show.

DOWNTOWN
$100-150

One of Louisville's golden-era hotels, the four-star **Brown Hotel** (335 W. Broadway, 502/583-1234, www.brownhotel.com, $107-499) offers all the luxuries one expects from a hotel built in the high-rolling 1920s: a grand lobby fit for movie star entrances, marble flooring, mahogany furniture, and faultless service. If you can afford it, spring for one of the spacious suites, which honor the formal English Renaissance architecture of the hotel while remaining entirely comfortable. The deluxe rooms can be small, but worth the price if ambience is your interest. Located in the theater district, the Brown is within easy walking distance of all downtown attractions.

$150-200

Although the current **Galt House** (140 N. 4th St., 502/589-5200, www.galthouse.com, $145-350) dates back to only 1971, the establishment's first incarnation played host to the likes of Jefferson Davis and Charles Dickens in the 1800s. Now the Galt House is the largest hotel in Kentucky and the only waterfront hotel in Louisville, its twin towers a distinctive part of the downtown skyline. For a view out onto the Ohio River, choose one of the 591 rooms in the Rivue Tower. Deluxe rooms are spacious but not special, while suites have the luxury of balconies, wet bars, and an extra half-bath. For an upgrade, choose the neighboring Suite Tower, which offers 600 premium rooms decked out with all the amenities. The hotel is often used for large conventions, so you may want to inquire whom you will be sharing the hotel with when you reserve a room.

If you're a *Great Gatsby* fan, then you can't pass on a night at the downtown **Seelbach Hotel** (500 4th St., 502/585-3200, www.seelbachhilton.com, $169-209), the inspiration for the site of Tom and Daisy Buchanan's wedding. Though now part of the Hilton family, the Seelbach still clings to the old-world elegance that has attracted the likes of F. Scott Fitzgerald, Al Capone, and John F. Kennedy. Rooms have a somewhat standard Hilton feel with some era-appropriate touches. Get out of your room to have a bourbon in the Oak Room alcove where Capone played cards, sneak a peek at the Grand Ballroom that inspired Fitzgerald, and admire the medieval style of the Rathskellar, the only surviving Rookwood Pottery room in the world.

Over $200

If you like modern, artsy, hip hotels, then check yourself into **◖ 21C Museum Hotel** (700 W. Main St., 502/217-6300, www.21chotel.com, $229-439), the most innovative hotel in the

FINDING ACCOMMODATIONS FOR THE DERBY

Locating a place to rest your bones during Derby week, especially on Derby weekend, is not easy. It's also not cheap. But with persistence, a willingness to compromise, and a bit of money saved up, you can find something to fit your taste and budget.

If you're committed to doing the Derby in high style, then you'll want to stay at one of downtown Louisville's classic hotels. In order to make this a reality, you must do two things: 1) plan early, and 2) pay the big bucks. It's not uncommon for Derby regulars to book their room for next year when they arrive for the current year's Derby. For a choice of rooms, you'll want to begin planning by January, though you can pick through leftovers into early spring. Most of the downtown hotels only offer rooms as part of package deals and usually have a two- or three-night minimum. Expect to pay thousands of dollars for a weekend stay.

The B&Bs of Old Louisville also offer an excellent Derby experience, particularly if you like intimate spaces and the opportunity to get really personalized advice on how to best enjoy the Derby. They are also very well located, just 2.5 miles from Churchill Downs. Unfortunately, the biggest of Louisville's B&Bs have no more than eight rooms, and some have as few as two. This means that they book up quickly, often with repeat customers. Expect to pay rates much higher than average if you do manage to find a room.

For those less picky about the ambience of their accommodations, but desirous of a location within city limits, Louisville's chain hotels offer the best option. Come Derby Day you'll find that almost all of them are at capacity, but they don't fill as quickly as the local hotels, giving you a little more time to get your plans together. Be aware that you won't find any deals here, however. Prices generally start around $300 for a typical double room. Visit a hotel aggregator website such as www.hotels.com to sort through your options.

If $300 for the Holiday Inn sounds ludicrous to you, then start looking farther afield. Once you get outside of Louisville and the immediate surrounding communities, you'll find prices that more closely resemble regular rates. You'll have to drive further and won't have all the amenities of the city, but if your main goal is to make it to the Derby without breaking the bank, this is the way to go. Begin by checking for hotels in Southern Indiana (New Albany, Jeffersonville, Clarksville), La Grange, and Shepherdsville, where prices will range greatly but be more affordable overall. You can also consider making the Derby just part of a Kentucky vacation, opening up hotel possibilities in Bardstown (30 miles), Frankfort (50 miles), and Lexington (70 miles).

Finally, go local and look for apartments, condos, and homes available for lease during Derby week. More than a few Louisvillians move in with friends and family for the weekend, renting their digs to out-of-towners. For large groups, this can be an especially good deal. Check the vacation rental and sublet sections of www.craigslist.org for available properties, as well as www.vrbo.com.

state and recipient of endless honorifics. Every one of the 90 rooms in this boutique hotel incorporates contemporary art into its design, but in no way is 21C too cool for school. Southern hospitality is the rule here, and the hotel doesn't just cover all the bases—it goes above and beyond with amenities like iPods, flat-screen HDTVs, wireless Internet, and silver mint julep cups in each room. Look for the red penguins adorning the roof of this hotel right in the heart of Museum Row.

OLD LOUISVILLE
$50-100

The three rooms at **Gallery House** (1386 S. 6th St., 502/922-6329, www.thegalleryhouse.com, $85-95) offer the most affordable stay in Old Louisville, though you should be aware that despite the home's High Victorian appearance, it was actually built in 1997 after a fire destroyed the previous property. The spirit of the house remains true to the neighborhood, and you'll enjoy the fact that all rooms have en suite bathrooms and modern systems. Plus it's hard to find owners better suited to the job: Gordon is an artist, meaning you'll find original artwork all over the house, and Leah is a chef, known for making some of the best cakes in town, so you can bet that breakfast will be a treat.

$100-150

Slip back in time at **1888 Historic Rocking Horse Manor Bed and Breakfast** (1022 S. 3rd St., 502/583-0408, www.rockinghorse-bb.com, $105-195), a meticulously restored Richardsonian Romanesque mansion in the heart of Old Louisville. The attention to architectural detail—original stained glass, relaxing claw-foot soaking tubs, and splendidly carved fireplace mantels—is matched only by the attention afforded each guest by the innkeepers, who serve a delicious two-course breakfast each morning and provide snacks and drinks in the evening. Each of the six rooms is tastefully decorated in period style and has its own bathroom. For a splurge, go for the Victorian Suite with its king-size canopy bed and hot tub.

Although the six rooms—all of which are named for the innkeeper's family members—at **Aleksander House Bed and Breakfast** (1213 S. 1st St., 502/637-4985, www.aleksanderhouse.com, $115-209) have distinct feels, the overall vibe of this 1882 Victorian mansion is warm and inviting, like the French Impressionist paintings in the dining room. Among Aleksander House's more unique offerings is a suite that can sleep 4-6 people, making it perfect for a family or girlfriend getaway. Additionally, the gourmet breakfast menu offers equally delicious options for vegans, diabetics, and celiacs.

Austin's Inn Place (915 S. 1st St., 502/585-8855, www.austinsinnplace.com, $135-155) combines two three-story houses to offer guests a choice of eight rooms, each fitted with either a king or queen bed with top-of-the-line bedding. The expansive inn also offers plenty of communal space, including a library, bar, game room, and garden. Exposed red brick features throughout the inn, which was once the home of Kentucky governor Augustus Everett Willson. For those who rise before it's time for the full breakfast, a spread of tea, coffee, juice, cereal, fruit, and pastries will help tide you over.

Thanks to its great columned portico and Greek Revival style, the (**Columbine Bed and Breakfast** (1707 S. 3rd St., 502/635-5000, www.thecolumbine.com, $125-175) stands out in this neighborhood of Victorian homes. Guests also love its sunny porches, welcoming back garden, friendly innkeepers, and breakfasts with a raved-about homemade syrup. Built for a mahogany magnate in 1896, the house is filled with this sumptuous wood. It's also remarkably well decorated, with the six large rooms classic and understated. If you fear frilliness, lace, and floral decor, then this is the B&B for you. The only negative is that bathrooms, though private, are often across the hall, but the plush bathrobes provided make this only a minor inconvenience.

One of the most magnificent homes on what was once known as Millionaires' Row, the 20,000-square-foot (**Culbertson Mansion** (1432 S. 3rd St., 502/634-3100, www.culbertsonmansion.us, $109-179) boasts more than 50 rooms, all decadently decorated, including the seven bedrooms available to guests. Built by Samuel Culbertson, president of Churchill Downs during the 1920s and 1930s and the man behind the garland of roses awarded to the Derby winner, the mansion was home to many formal dinner parties and dances. Now whether you're entering through the marble mosaic door, savoring breakfast at the original dining table, having a complimentary drink with the hosts in the downstairs bar, or relaxing amid the 100 varieties of roses in the formal courtyard, you'll feel like an honored guest. Splurge for the Knights of Kentucky Suite, replete with its own baby grand piano, and you'll feel like royalty.

$150-200

Built for the wealthy industrialist family for which it is named, the (**DuPont Mansion**

(1317 S. 4th St., 502/638-0045, www.dupontmansion.com, $129-239) is a conscientiously restored 1879 Italianate mansion with details that will make your jaw drop. While you eat breakfast under sparkling chandeliers, enjoy the murals covering the wall of the dining room. In the evening, take your snack of homemade goodies and wine in the formal gardens. And at night, luxuriate in the whirlpool tub found in each of the B&B's seven rooms. All of the rooms are elegant and decorated with period furniture and reproductions, but the two suites are particularly magnificent. If the DuPont Mansion is all booked up, check the availability at **Inn at the Park** (1332 S. 4th St., 502/638-0045, www.innatpark.com, $129-209), a sister property just across the street with eight rooms with private baths.

Step through the triple entry of the Richardsonian Romanesque **Bernheim Mansion** (1416 S. 3rd St., 502/638-1387, www.bernheimmansion.com, $119-225), and you'll immediately notice the abundance of exotic woods and intricate woodwork, as well as the curved stairwell lit by stained glass windows. This B&B is heavy on style and true to its roots as the home of distiller and philanthropist Bernhard Bernheim. If you're looking for luxury, choose between the Bernheim Suite and the Carriage House. The Bernheim Suite swells with old-world charm and includes a private library and office. The Carriage House impresses with its soaring 30-foot wood ceiling and exposed beams, combining contemporary architecture with antique decor. Of the remaining three rooms, one has a king bed with antique bath (but no shower), and the other two are queen rooms with a shared bath.

True to its 1884 origins but with the modern amenities travelers love, **Central Park Bed and Breakfast** (1353 S. 4th St., 502/638-1505, www.centralparkbandb.com, $135-195) offers three guest rooms on the second floor, three on the third floor, and a carriage house out back. Each room has a queen or king bed and its own private bathroom. The Rose Garden Room is especially spacious at 700 square feet, with its own sitting room with a bird's-eye view of the area. A large breakfast is served in the dining room, and other common spaces inside and out are open to guests.

EAST LOUISVILLE
$100-150

Once you enter the **Inn at Woodhaven** (401 S. Hubbards Ln., 888/895-1011, www.innatwoodhaven.com, $119-255), a 19th-century Gothic Revival home painted a cheery yellow, you'll forget that the inn is located next to an apartment complex. Beautifully decorated with period furniture, the inn makes sure no detail is forgotten. Choose among four rooms in the main house, three rooms in the carriage house out back, or the octagonal Rose Cottage. The main house's Attic Room is bigger than most apartments; in fact, the bathroom, with its spa tub and steam shower for two, is bigger than most hotel rooms. Enjoy the three-course gourmet breakfast in the dining room or in the comfort of your own room.

While most Louisville B&Bs are from the Victorian era, **Tucker House Bed and Breakfast** (2406 Tucker Station Rd., 502/297-8007, www.tuckerhouse1840.com, $105-125) transports you to the era of antebellum country living, with its four bed chambers, dining areas, and living areas all decorated true to the 1840s. Located a bit outside of town, the brick Federal-style Tucker House is a great place to stay if you're looking for a true getaway, especially if you love peace and quiet and the great outdoors. Bring your hiking shoes to explore the five acres of woods and the spring-fed lake. As much as you'll love the period decor, you'll also enjoy the modern pool, decks, and amenities.

Food

Louisville has a remarkable food scene that is constantly evolving. Many of Louisville's restaurants and chefs have received national recognition, and there is much to be impressed by. These days, downtown, especially the NuLu area, might be the most happening area, but tasty destinations abound throughout the city. The following listings make up only a small fraction of what Louisville has to offer. Ask around for favorites or hop online and visit sites such as www.hotbytes.com or http://louisville.eater.com for the latest news and reviews.

DOWNTOWN
Breakfast
Momma knew what she was talking about when she said breakfast was the most important meal of the day, so start your day right at **Toast on Market** (620 E. Market St., 502/569-4099, www.toastonmarket.com, 7am-2pm Tues.-Fri., 7am-3pm Sat.-Sun., $5.75-9.75). The King French Toast, a tribute to Elvis with its peanut butter and bananas, will get you singing, while Cliffie's Plate, involving eggs, meat, hash brown casserole, and pancakes, makes eating the rest of the day optional.

Coffee Shops
Pick up a pick-me-up in the form of a coffee drink, a baked good, or a vinyl record at **Please & Thank You** (800 E. Market St., www.pleaseandthankyoulouisville.com, 7am-6pm Mon.-Fri., 9am-6pm Sat., 9am-4pm Sun.), a small shop that is part coffee shop, part record store.

Cafés
Though they bill themselves as an "Appalachian tea and hooch café"—probably haven't been to one of those, have you?—**Hillbilly Tea** (120 S. 1st St., 502/587-7350, http://hillbillytea.com, 10am-9pm Tues.-Thurs., 10am-11pm Fri.-Sat., 10am-4pm Sun., $8-18) also serves some mighty fine food, including a very popular

brunch. Try the moonshine pork ribs, French toast with sweet grass syrup, braised lamb on succotash, or buttermilk fried quail with corn pone pudding.

If you're in the mood for a good sandwich—hearty bread, crisp vegetables, savory meats, and tasty dressings with a nice atmosphere on the side—head to **The Café** (712 Brent St., 502/589-9191, http://thecafe.ws, 7am-4pm Mon.-Sat., $5.95-8.95). The very large sandwiches are served with a choice of fresh sides; try the bean salad. For breakfast, choose from baked goods or the heartier biscuits and gravy, twice-baked French toast, or Southern grits scramble.

Casual American
If you get hungry while museum-hopping downtown, make the short walk to **Dish on Market** (434 W. Market St., 502/315-0669, http://dishonmarket.com, 8am-10pm Mon.-Thurs., 8am-midnight Fri.-Sat., 8am-8pm Sun., $6.50-10.75), where everyone in the family should find something to satisfy them. Dish offers a huge selection of salads, burgers, and sandwiches, as well as entrées of fried chicken, fish and chips, and the like. Additionally, breakfast is served daily until 2pm, and they have a bakery where you can grab pastries or sweet treats.

Play a game of table tennis or just relax with a drink at the funky **Garage Bar** (700 E. Market St., 502/749-7100, www.garageonmarket.com, 5pm-10pm Mon.-Wed., 5pm-11pm Thurs., 4pm-midnight Fri., 11am-midnight Sat., 11am-10pm Sun., $11-16), a restaurant in a converted garage that focuses on pizza. Local ingredients, including house-made sausage and pepperoni and herbs grown right out front, top the pies, and should you just want to nibble, Garage Bar also boasts a country ham and oyster bar.

Don't let the basement location discourage you from a meal at **Hammerheads** (921

The sign at Garage Bar makes it clear what they're all about.

Swan St., 502/365-1112, www.louisvilleham-merheads.com, 5pm-10pm Mon.-Sat., $7-14), where you can get unique spins on some comforting favorites. Sink your teeth into a burger (standard beef or elk, venison, or chorizo), a taco (pork, brisket, duck, or soft shell crab), a sandwich (maybe the pork belly BLT), or the signature sweet potato waffle with chicken wings.

Contemporary American

With its clean lines and white-and-black decor, **Relish** (1346 River Rd., 502/587-7007, www.relishlouisville.com, lunch 11am-3pm Mon.-Sat., dinner 5pm-9pm Mon.-Thurs., 5pm-10pm Fri.-Sat., $12-26) has a modern Euro feel, and the food is forward-looking as well. Mindful eating is the mission behind the dishes, which include small plates, such as flatbread with lamb, mint, pomegranate molasses, and feta, and main plates, such as Asian-style salmon. A gourmet-to-go menu makes for excellent picnics. For lunch ($8.50-12), try a salad or sandwich.

The chefs at **Rye** (900 E. Market, 502/749-6200, http://ryeonmarket.com, 5pm-11pm Sun.-Thurs., 5pm-midnight Fri.-Sat., $20-32), who sharpened their knives at Tom Colicchio's Craft, use sustainable and seasonable ingredients to create outstanding dishes, such as a carrot and cantaloupe gazpacho and a Florida red grouper with curry-coconut nage and mango. Enjoy the back porch in season; otherwise watch the action in the kitchen from the elegant interior.

Locals are thankful the chef at ◖ **Decca** (812 E. Market St., 502/749-8128, http://deccarestaurant.com, 5:30pm-10pm Mon.-Thurs., 5:30pm-11pm Fri.-Sat., $14-27) decided to make the move from California to Kentucky, bringing the city an outstanding menu with such treats as diver scallop crudo, ricotta *cavatelli* with braised rabbit, wood grilled broccoli, and made-from-scratch ice cream sandwiches. Cozy up on the plush banquette in the 1870s building or snag a courtyard seat in good weather.

With most of their food coming from within 100 miles and a restaurant decked out with former church pews and large artistic photos of the farmers who grow the food, ◖ **Harvest** (624 E. Market St., 502/384-9090, www.harvestlouisville.com, lunch 11am-2:30pm Tues.-Fri., 10am-2:30pm Sat., dinner 5pm-10pm Tues.-Thurs., 5pm-11pm Fri.-Sat., brunch 11am-2:30pm Sun., $15-24) treats diners to an upscale rustic experience that is constantly changing. Try the Kentucky menu, where you might find beer cheese made with a local brew, pork loin with sweet potato grits, or johnny-cake with smoked vegetable ragout. The lunch menu features sandwiches and pizza ($12-16).

As innovative as the hotel in which it is located, 21C's **Proof on Main** (702 W. Main St., 502/217-6360, www.proofonmain.com, breakfast 7am-10pm Mon.-Fri. and 7am-noon Sat.-Sun., lunch 11am-2pm Mon.-Fri., dinner 5:30pm-10pm Sun.-Thurs., 5:30pm-11pm Fri.-Sat., $22-36) transforms locally sourced food into magical dishes. The entrées are fantastic (try the enormous pork chop), but you could easily make a dinner from the starters, which

© THERESA DOWELL BLACKINTON

Rye, one of many popular restaurants in NuLu

might include cucumber gazpacho, bison carpaccio, and country ham falafel. The bold artwork for which the hotel is known continues in Proof, and the design is modern yet inviting.

The newest restaurant of Edward Lee, whose fame has extended beyond Louisville thanks to *Top Chef,* **Milkwood** (316 W. Main St., 502/584-6455, http://actorstheatre.org/milkwood, 5:30pm-10pm Tues.-Sun., $11-28) is located at Actor's Theatre, but its popularity goes far beyond the theatre crowd. The menu at this elegant restaurant focuses on small plates of comfort bar food with Asian influence as well as larger dinners, all of which changes regularly. Try a sampling of tastes, such as cured wagyu and lamb salami, octopus bacon, and rock shrimp sausage, or order the miso smothered chicken or pork shoulder with coconut rice.

French

La Coop (732 E. Market St., 502/410-2888, www.coopbistro.com, 5:30pm-10:30pm Tues.-Thurs., 5:30-11:30 Fri.-Sat., $12-24) transports you straight to the streets of Paris with its French bistro cuisine of perfectly prepared escargot, *moules,* steak *frites,* coq au vin, and cassoulet. The atmosphere is also spot-on, right down to the sidewalk seating. On Tuesdays, a three-course prix fixe menu is offered for $25.

Latin American

The smoky notes of chiles infuse the authentic Latin American food at **Mayan Café** (813 E. Market St., 502/566-0651, www.themayancafe.com, lunch 11am-2:30pm Mon.-Fri., dinner 5pm-10pm Mon.-Thurs., 5pm-10:30pm Fri.-Sat., $12-25). Start with the *salbutes* (topped corn tortillas), which have garnered acclaim since the chef's days driving a taco truck, then pick from such entrées as wild-caught fish in achiote lime sauce or *cochinita pibil,* a slow-roasted pork. Add the lima beans as a side (trust me). When the weather's nice, sidewalk seating is available.

For a quick but tasty meal, place your order at **Taco Punk** (736 E. Market St., 502/584-8226, www.tacopunk.com, 11am-8pm Mon.-Thurs., 11am-9pm Fri.-Sat., 11am-3pm Sun.,

© THERESA DOWELL BLACKINTON

LOUISVILLE'S CATHOLIC LEGACY

With more than 100 parishes in the Archdiocese of Louisville and more than 20,000 students attending Catholic schools in the archdiocese, the Catholic Church holds strong influence in the city, which is not surprising if you consider that many Louisvillians come from Catholic German, Irish, and French stock. Although certainly not the only faith in town—both the Southern Baptists and Presbyterians have important seminaries in the city with congregations to match, Southeast Christian Church is one of the nation's largest megachurches, and residents of nearly every faith can find a church home in Louisville—the Catholic Church has a way of injecting itself into the city's cultural life. Two of the more popular ways are Friday fish fries and parish picnics.

On Fridays in Lent, nearly every Catholic parish puts on a fish fry, where for a low price anyone is welcome to feast on a plate of fish and Southern sides (think mac 'n' cheese, green beans, and the like). Stop in at the Catholic church nearest you to find out the schedule; if they're not hosting one, they'll know where the nearest one is.

In summer, there's not a single weekend that's without a church picnic. These aren't low-key affairs, but rather big events where the beer and brats flow freely, carnival rides keep the kids happy, and booths offer the chance for you to win a cake, a tin of popcorn, or an enormous stuffed animal. One of the most popular picnics is August's St. Joseph Orphan's Picnic (2823 Frankfort Ave.), which brings volunteers from parishes all over the city together to man more than 60 booths, with all proceeds benefiting the St. Joseph Children's Home. For a schedule of picnics, visit the Archdiocese of Louisville's website (www.archlou.org).

$3.25-4.65 per taco), where you build your gourmet taco by choosing your meat from options such as chorizo and potato, pineapple pork, and Yucatan-style shrimp. Then top it with your pick of shredded cabbage, pickled onion, jalapeños, and cilantro. Housemade tortillas hold it all together.

Dessert

Only the finest natural ingredients go into the sweet treats baked daily at **Cake Flour** (909 E. Market St., 502/719-0172, www.cakeflouronmarket.com, 7am-2pm Mon., 7am-6pm Tues.-Fri., 8am-2pm Sat.-Sun.). White chocolate cheesecake, banana truffle cupcakes, and lemon tarts are just some of the tempting goodies on offer.

Though the savory menu of French-style sandwiches, soups, salads, and crepes at **Ghyslain on Market** (721 E. Market St., 502/690-8645, www.ghyslain.com, 7am-9pm daily) makes for fantastic meals, the chocolates and pastries are what really tempt. Try a chocolate caramel cup, a vanilla cheesecake, or one of the many mousses, or put together a goodie bag of truffles.

OLD LOUISVILLE
Cafés

Artisan homemade breads are still cooked in imported European ovens and the pastries are lovingly made each day at **Ermin's Bakery and Café** (1201 S. 1st St., 502/635-6960, www.erminsbakery.com, 7am-7pm Mon.-Fri., 8am-5pm Sat., 9am-3pm Sun. $3.95-6.95). Try choosing between the cinnamon roll and apple strudel for breakfast or the petit four and sin bar (a rich combination of chocolate and peanut butter) for dessert. Whatever you end up with, your sweet tooth will be satisfied. For lunch, a half sandwich of your choice with the house tomato basil soup makes a satisfying meal.

Casual American

Popular with U of L students, the **Granville Inn** (1601 S. Third St., 502/635-6475, 11am-1am daily, $3.95-7.95) is a constant competitor for the title of best burger. The signature burger is a half-pound of hand-formed beef charbroiled to order and topped with lettuce, tomato, onion, and cheese and served with a heaping side of fries. The bar serves up cheap pints of craft draft beer, and the atmosphere is that of a local joint—a bit dark, with TVs, electronic dartboards, and a pool table.

Contemporary American

If you consider yourself a gourmand, make a reservation at **C 610 Magnolia** (610 W. Magnolia Ave., 502/636-0783, www.610magnolia.com, Thurs.-Sat., dinner only, reservations required) and prepare to be wowed. Widely considered to be one of the best restaurants in the region, the elegant but minimalist 610 Magnolia offers a three- ($45) or four-course ($55) prix-fixe menu that changes every night, but always centers around in-season, local, organic ingredients. What exactly will end up on your plate is a surprise, but Chef Edward Lee, cooking here long before he became a household name thanks to *Top Chef,* consistently turns out sophisticated American food enhanced with global flavors. The atmosphere of this house restaurant is understated, creating an elegant and intimate setting for a special-occasion dinner.

SOUTH LOUISVILLE
Diners

If you like to talk horse racing while you eat, stop in at **Wagner's Pharmacy** (3113 S. 4th St., 502/375-3800, www.wagnerspharmacy.com, 8am-2:30pm Mon.-Fri., 8am-noon Sat. as well as Sun. during racing meets, $3.29-8.99), just across the street from Churchill Downs. Since 1922, Wagner's has been the gathering place for those in the horse industry, and inside the simple white building decorated with images of Derby winners you're likely to share the counter with jockeys, trainers, and owners. The diner-style menu is simple: Lunch is a choice between a long list of sandwiches and the daily special (roast beef on Wednesday, fried fish on Friday), while breakfast options include a selection of omelettes, à la carte pancakes, and

platters with your choice of ham, sausage, or bacon with eggs, biscuits, and potatoes.

Asian

Don't let its strip mall location mislead you. It might not look like much, but **Vietnam Kitchen** (5339 Mitscher Ave., 502/363-5154, www.vietnamkitchen.net, 11am-10pm Sun.-Tues. and Thurs., 11am-11pm Fri.-Sat., $6-13.35) is where Louisville's many Vietnamese immigrants come to be transported back home. From the staple pho (rice-noodle soup traditionally served with beef) to meat, seafood, and vegetarian stir-fry, curry, and clay-pot dishes, the taste will take you to the other side of the world. Vegetarian options abound, and the spice level of each dish can be adjusted, from benign all the way up to "Vietnam spicy."

Indian

In an unassuming strip mall locale, **DakShin** (4742 Bardstown Rd., 502/491-7412, www.my-dakshin.com, 11am-9pm daily, $5.99-10.99) surprises with its authentic taste of India. The extensive menu covers Northern Indian dishes such as *malai kofta,* lamb vindaloo, and chicken korma; Southern Indian dishes such as paneer *dosai, bagara baigan,* and Kerala fish curry; and Indo-Chinese noodle, rice, and stir-fry dishes. It's the best Indian food in town.

FRANKFORT AVENUE
Coffee Shops

A favorite place to work, study, or just relax, **Vint** (2309 Frankfort Ave., 502/894-8060, 6:30am-10pm Mon.-Wed., 6:30am-11pm Thurs.-Fri., 7:30am-11pm Sat., 8am-9pm Sun.) can satisfy your craving for coffee or beer and wine. If you're on the go, hit the drive-through.

Barbecue

The **Frankfort Avenue Beer Depot** (3204 Frankfort Ave., 502/895-3223, www.frankfortavenuebeerdepot.com, 11am-10pm, bar open until 2am daily, $5-14), is a super casual joint, basically a dive, that serves amazing brisket, ribs, chicken, and pulled pork, smoked right in the front parking lot, along with fantastic coleslaw, potato salad, baked beans, macaroni and cheese, and spicy fries. As the name suggests, there's plenty of beer on offer, and many people come by just to have a drink and play the mini-golf course out back or a round of cornhole.

Pizza

Everyone knows the crust is the key to a good pizza, and the pies at **Coal's Artisan Pizza** (3730 Frankfort Ave., 502/742-8200, http://coalsartisanpizza.com, 11:30am-10pm Mon.-Thurs., 11:30am-11pm Fri.-Sat., noon-9pm Sun., $12-15) have the perfect crust—thin, smoky, and just a little sweet. Choose a specialty pizza named for one of Louisville's neighborhoods or deck your own with gourmet ingredients like caramelized onions and piquillo peppers. The weekday lunches are a great deal.

Asian

At ◖ **Basa** (2244 Frankfort Ave., 502/896-1016, www.basarestaurant.com, 5pm-10pm Mon.-Thurs., 5pm-11pm Fri.-Sat., $15-29), a 2008 James Beard Best New Restaurant semifinalist, local ingredients are transformed into tantalizing modern Vietnamese cuisine. The menu is small and focused, with many of the appetizers and entrées featuring seafood—prawns, tuna, oysters, mussels, and the like. One of the most raved-about entrées, however, is the Shaking Beef, cubed filet mignon cooked with garlic, watercress, cherry tomatoes, and red onions in a very hot wok. Expect elegant presentation and fine service at one of Louisville's more exciting restaurants.

A longtime favorite of vegetarians, **Zen Garden** (2240 Frankfort Ave., 502/895-9114, http://zengardenasian.com, 11am-3pm and 5pm-9:30pm Mon.-Thurs., 11am-3pm and 5pm-10pm Fri., noon-10pm Sat., $7.95-10.95) serves up popular dishes such as pad Thai, udon, and various stir-fries, all sans meat. The entire menu is available for carry-out.

Don't overlook tiny but colorful **Sari Sari** (2339 Frankfort Ave., 502/894-0585, 5pm-9pm Tues. and Sat., 11:30am-9pm Wed.-Fri., $4.95-12.95), where you can get a delicious and filling meal of Filipino favorites, a cuisine that combines Asian and Latin flavors in such dishes as chicken coconut curry, pork menudo, and pork adobo.

Irish

A traditional Irish pub, the **Irish Rover** (2319 Frankfort Ave., 502/899-3544, www.theirishroverky.com, 11:30am-11pm Mon.-Thurs., 11:30am-midnight Fri.-Sat., $6.95-14.95) is where the large percentage of Louisvillians who claim Irish heritage come for a taste of the old country. The menu features such hearty standards as fish and chips, bangers and mash, smoked salmon and potato gratin, and cottage pie—a bread bowl filled with steaming Guinness beef stew and topped with mashed potatoes and cheese. You certainly won't go home hungry.

Italian

Sophisticated **Volare** (2300 Frankfort Ave., 502/894-4446, www.volare-restaurant.com, 5pm-10pm Sun.-Thurs., 5pm-11pm Fri.-Sat., $18-39) satisfies with modern Italian food that is locally sourced and house-made. You'll find favorites such as osso buco and chicken marsala as well as exciting specials. For something lighter, try the small plates at the bar, where there's live music Wednesday-Saturday.

Latin American

Neighborhood anchor **El Mundo** (2345 Frankfort Ave., 502/899-9930, www.502elmundo.com, 11:30am-10pm Tues.-Sat., $7.25-14.95) serves up Mexican food with a twist. In addition to considering the burritos, enchiladas, and other favorites, see what's on special. The fish tacos and the grilled fajitas of the day are always good choices, and the margaritas and sangria are top-notch. The two-story restaurant offers counter service downstairs and waiter service upstairs and on the patio. It's a tight space, so expect to get friendly with your neighbors and to wait if you come at peak hours.

Mediterranean

A Frankfort Avenue institution, **Grape Leaf**

(2217 Frankfort Ave., 502/897-1774, www. grapeleafonline.com, 11am-9pm Mon.-Thurs., 9:30am-10pm Fri.-Sat., 9:30am-9pm Sun., $11-18.50) keeps regulars coming back for their tenderloin kabobs, moussaka, and falafel. On a nice day, sit outside and munch from the sampler appetizer, which comes with your choice of three items, including hummus, grape leaves, and spanakopita.

Dessert

What is life without dessert? **Sweet Surrender Dessert Café** (1804 Frankfort Ave., 502/899-2008, www.sweetsurrenderdessertcafe.com, 10am-10pm Tues.-Thurs., 10am-11pm Fri.-Sat.) certainly makes you wonder just that, with its sinful selection of cakes, tortes, pies, cupcakes, cookies, and dessert bars. Selection varies, which means that if your favorite is unavailable, you'll just have to come up with a new favorite. It's not hard to do.

You can stick with the tried-and-true at **The Comfy Cow** (2221 Frankfort Ave., 502/409-4616, http://thecomfycow.com, 11am-10pm Sun.-Thurs., 11am-11pm Fri.-Sat.) and you'll be more than happy, but this impossible-to-miss bright pink ice cream parlor churns out an impressive array of original flavors. Why not try dulce de leche de salte, bourbon ball, or Vermont maple walnut? No pick is a bad pick.

EAST LOUISVILLE
Breakfast

As you'd expect from the name, you can get eggs any way you want them—served Tex-Mex or Benedict style, in omelettes or burritos, in scrambles or skillets—at **Wild Eggs** (3985 Dutchmans Ln., 502/893-8005, www. crackinwildeggs.com, 6:30am-2:30pm Mon.-Fri., 7am-3pm Sat.-Sun., $4.50-11.95). If the thought of eggs isn't making you go wild, then choose from a variety of other breakfast favorites, like stuffed French toast or variations on pancakes, waffles, and crepes.

Casual American

Located at Harrods Creek on the Ohio River, **Captain's Quarters** (5700 Captain's Quarters

The Comfy Cow, a favorite ice cream destination

© THERESA DOWELL BLACKINTON

Rd., 502/228-1651, www.cqriverside.com, 11:30am-10pm Mon.-Thurs., 11:30am-11pm Fri.-Sat., 10:30am-10pm Sun., $7.95-17.95) is Louisville's go-to restaurant for casual riverside dining. Though the dining room is bright and spacious with windows providing water views, it's the multilevel deck overlooking the river that attracts people to Captain's Quarters. As you might expect, the menu is heavy on seafood, offering fried cod, pan-seared salmon, seafood tortellini, and more, in addition to sandwiches, pizzas, and chicken and beef entrées. The fried banana peppers are a favorite of the happy hour crowd. Captain's Quarters offers tie-ups for hungry or thirsty boaters.

Asian

Whether you want pineapple fried rice, *pad kee mow*, or *massaman* curry, **Simply Thai** (323 Wallace Ave., 502/899-9670, www.simplythaiky.com, lunch 11am-2:30pm Mon.-Fri. and noon-3pm Sat., dinner 4:30pm-9:30pm Mon.-Thurs., 4:30pm-10:30pm Sat., 5pm-10:30pm Sat., $9-17) will satisfy. Portions are large and presentation is not overlooked at this small restaurant full of flavorful dishes.

Latin American

Rather than the usual Tex-Mex more common to the area, **❰ Guaca Mole** (9921 Ormsby Station Rd., 502/365-4822, 11am-9:30pm Mon.-Thurs., 11am-10pm Fri., noon-10pm Sat., noon-8:30pm Sun., $8-16), a Mexican cantina-style restaurant, focuses on more authentic dishes, including melt-in-your-mouth carnitas, chicken *tinga sopes,* and short rib *enfrijoladas.* You'll even find proper moles as well as seviche.

Since most of us can't legally travel to Cuba, the best we can do to get a taste of the bright flavors of that forbidden Caribbean island is have a meal at **Havana Rumba** (4115 Oechsli Ave., 502/897-1959, http://havanarumbaonline.com, 5pm-9:30pm Mon.-Wed., 11am-9:30pm Thurs., 11am-10pm Fri., noon-10pm Sat., noon-8:30pm Sun., $7.50-15.99), where the Cuban-born chef-owner dishes up an extensive menu of family recipes in a warm, festive atmosphere. Try the *papas rellenos* (mashed potato balls filled with seasoned ground beef), the Cubano sandwich, or the *lechon asado.*

BARDSTOWN ROAD AREA
Coffee Shops

Day's Espresso & Coffee (1420 Bardstown Rd., 502/456-1170, www.dayscoffee.com, 6:30am-10pm Mon.-Thurs., 6:30am-11pm Fri.-Sat.) claims to have the finest cappuccino in town, and customers declare the iced latte to be unbeatable. Without pretension, Day's is friendly, and service is good.

Heine Brothers (2200 Bardstown Rd., 502/515-0380, www.heinebroscoffee.com, 6:30am-10pm Mon.-Thurs., 6:30am-11pm Fri.-Sat., 7am-10pm Sun., $2-5), Louisville's neighborhood coffee shop, serves the coffee that keeps the Derby City chugging. Having cofounded a first-of-its-kind organic, fair-trade, and green coffee co-op as well as a nonprofit that turns coffee grounds into compost, Heine Bros. isn't just good for a pick-me-up—it's also good for your soul. Multiple outposts are located around town, welcoming you to bring a book, a computer, or a friend and hang out for as long as you like.

Highland Coffee (1140 Bardstown Rd., 502/451-4545, www.highlandcoffeelouisville.com, 6am-10pm Mon.-Wed., 6am-11pm Thurs., 6am-midnight Fri., 6:30am-midnight Sat., 6:30am-10pm Sun.), which draws a young, artsy crowd, claims to be "keeping Louisville wired" with their selection of coffee drinks and baked goods. Breakfast wraps are available in the morning, and panini are made fresh later in the day.

Contemporary American

Exuberant is the best way to describe **Café Lou Lou** (2216 Dundee Rd., 502/459-9566, www.cafeloulou.com, 11am-10pm Sun.-Thurs., 11am-11pm Fri.-Sat., $9-16), a fun and funky favorite with bold decor, spunky servers, and creative food. Though at first glance, the menu seems strongly Italian/Mediterranean thanks to its wide selection of pastas and pizzas, a closer look will reveal the chef's Louisiana and Louisville connections. Pasta jambalaya, muffuletta sandwiches, and Hot Brown pizzas share space with Italian meatball calzones, spinach and tomato crispy lavash, and blue cheese polenta.

Jack Fry's (1007 Bardstown Rd., 502/452-9244, www.jackfrys.com, lunch 11am-2:30pm Mon.-Fri., dinner 5:30pm-11pm Mon.-Thurs., 5:30pm-midnight Fri.-Sat., 5:30pm-10pm Sun., $21-43) is an anchor of the Louisville restaurant scene, pleasing regulars and newcomers alike with its upscale American cuisine, with hints of Southern and French flavors, served in a warm bistro setting. Appetizers range from the signature shrimp and grits to foie gras, while entrées include lamb chops, filet, and herb-brined chicken. Presentation and service are top-notch. Those on a budget should check out the lunch menu ($12-16).

Long before it was the cool thing to do, **Lilly's** (1147 Bardstown Rd., 502/451-0477, www.lillyslapeche.com, 11am-3pm and 5pm-10pm Tues.-Sat., $14-32) established an award-winning menu based almost exclusively on locally sourced food. That means the beet and arugula salad, the housemade lobster agnolotti, and the pulled Moroccan lamb shoulder are bursting with fresh flavor. The menu changes seasonally, but you're guaranteed to find local food transformed into refined dishes influenced by international flavors at this Kentucky bistro.

Barbecue

In the tradition of good barbecue restaurants, **Mark's Feed Store** (1514 Bardstown Rd., 502/458-1570, www.marksfeedstore.com, 11am-10pm Sun.-Thurs., 11am-11pm Fri.-Sat., $7.29-16.59) keeps things simple. Choose among pork, beef, or chicken sandwiches or platters or a rack of fall-off-the-bone ribs. Everything's hickory smoked and, in Kentucky barbecue style, doused with thick and slightly spicy sauce. Sides are what you'd expect: spicy fries, coleslaw, baked apples, baked beans, and the like.

Asian

The cooking as well as the decor is bright and crisp at **Asiatique** (1767 Bardstown Rd., 502/451-2749, www.asiatiquerestaurant.com, 5pm-10pm Mon.-Thurs., 5pm-11pm Fri., noon-3pm and 5pm-11pm Sat., 4pm-10pm Sun. $18-28), an upscale Pacific Rim restaurant with a global view. Malaysian-born Chef Looi, who has been a guest chef at the James Beard Foundation three times, turns out well-executed and mouthwatering cuisine, which changes seasonally, though favorites like the wok-seared salmon usually aren't off the menu for long. Five-course tasting menus are also offered nightly.

Dragon King's Daughter (1126 Bardstown Rd., 602/632-2444, www.dragonkingsdaughter.com, 3pm-11pm Mon.-Wed., noon-midnight Thurs.-Sat., noon-10pm Sun., $8-12) gets creative with sushi, tempura, teriyaki, and other Japanese dishes. For example, you can order a sashimi pizza, made with long strips of red tuna, white tuna, and salmon laid on top of mixed greens and placed on a piece of flatbread dressed with Japanese mayo, or tacos with shrimp tempura, Asian barbecue beef, or chicken katsu. Regular sushi rolls are also available in this casual—and sometimes noisy—storefront restaurant. The happy hour menu (3pm-6pm and 10pm-midnight daily) is a good deal.

Vietnamese sandwiches are the focus at **Banh Mi Hero** (2245 Bardstown Rd., 502/456-2022, http://bahnmihero.com, 11am-9pm Mon.-Thurs., 11am-10pm Fri.-Sat., $4-8), where traditional and unique takes on *banh mi* are made with fresh bread, homemade pâté, house aioli, fresh veggies, and quality meats. Warning: *Banh mi* can be addictive.

International

Ramsi's Café on the World (1293 Bardstown Rd., 502/451-0700, www.ramsiscafe.com, 11am-1am Mon.-Thurs., 11am-2am Fri.-Sat., 10am-11pm Sun., $9-22) isn't kidding about the "world" part. Although Ramsi and his family hail from Lebanon, their restaurant serves up dishes from all over the map (as well as ingredients from their own farm), and they aren't afraid to mix and match the best of what the world has to offer. The East Meets South Fajitas, for instance, take traditional fajita ingredients and wrap them in Indian paratha bread, while the ribs are served with a Caribbean-style mango sauce. Vegetarians, vegans, and those with gluten allergies are generously catered for. Expect enormous portions, an eclectic and friendly staff, and very possibly a wait thanks to all the loyal patrons.

Latin American

Named for the trendy neighborhood in Buenos Aires, **Palermo Viejo** (1359 Bardstown Rd., 502/456-6461, 5pm-11pm Mon.-Sat., $12-17) serves up the tasty steaks (plus *chimichurri*) for which Argentina is known. True meat lovers can indulge in the *parrillada,* a mixed grill of chorizo, short ribs, tenderloin, and sweetbreads. Order a side of the parsley and garlic fries to complete your meal. In a nod to other popular Argentinean cuisine, the menu also offers empanadas and a selection of pasta. In summer, when you can sit outdoors and people watch, the small restaurant gains a few seats.

Garnering national recognition for its Nuevo Latino cuisine, including multiple James Beard nominations, **C Seviche** (1538 Bardstown Rd., 502/473-8560, www.sevicherestaurant.com, 5pm-10pm Mon.-Thurs., 5pm-11pm Fri.-Sat., 5pm-9pm Sun., $19-25) entices diners with its namesake seviches and its tightly curated entrée list. Those who can't choose between the big-eye tuna seviche with coconut and lemongrass and the wild-caught shrimp with chipotle can opt for a seviche tasting of three or five options. Although the way each dish is served changes with the season, entrée options usually include multiple seafood plates as well as chicken and steak. With a creative menu,

warm atmosphere, ample outdoor seating, and excellent service, what's not to like?

Mediterranean

Take it from a girl who spent a year in Greece eating gyros every day—**Zaytun** (2286 Bardstown Rd., 502/365-1788, 11:30am-10pm Mon.-Thurs., 11:30am-11pm Fri.-Sat., noon-9pm Sun., $7.95-11.95) has the best gyros in town. The pita isn't traditional, more of a flatbread instead, but it's delicious, and the meat (choose between chicken or a mix of lamb and beef) is seasoned, cooked, and cut just right.

Dessert

At **Homemade Ice Cream and Pie Kitchen** (2525 Bardstown Rd., 502/459-8184, www. piekitchen.com, 7am-10pm Sun.-Thurs., 7am-11pm Fri.-Sat.), they don't mislead you with their name. The scrumptious homemade ice cream, pie, and other desserts are what have kept Louisvillians coming in for more than a quarter century (when what was a lunch counter became dessert heaven thanks to its oft-requested pies). The caramel-iced Dutch apple pie and the seasonal pumpkin ice cream win raves, but the kitchen probably makes a delicious version of whatever flavor is your favorite. If you've been really good, reward yourself with a combo of the store's two namesake dishes: ice cream pie. Multiple other locations are scattered throughout town.

Legend has it that Elizabeth Kizito of **Kizito Cookies** (1398 Bardstown Rd., 502/456-2891, www.kizito.com, 7am-5pm Tues.-Fri., 8am-5pm Sat.) was born under a banana tree, then learned to bake from her father in Africa before immigrating to the United States at age 17. Whether that's true or not, Kizito cookies are certainly legendary in their own right. Big enough to share and perfectly chewy, the cookies come in 12 different flavors. Stick with traditional chocolate chip or try the pecan-and-chocolate Lucky in Kentucky; it's impossible to go wrong.

Information and Transportation

INFORMATION

The **Louisville Visitors Center** (301 S. 4th St., 502/379-6109, www.gotolouisville.com, 10am-5pm Mon.-Sat., noon-5pm Sun.), located between the Kentucky International Convention Center and Fourth Street Live!, offers advice, maps, reservations, brochures, and everything else you need to arrange your visit.

If you're downtown and looking to mail a postcard home, the 4th Street **post office** (411 S. 4th St., 9am-5pm weekdays) is most central.

The **Courier-Journal** (www.courierjournal. com), Kentucky's largest newspaper, is published daily in Louisville. **LEO Weekly** (www. leoweekly.com) is the city's alternative newspaper and the source for what's happening around town. You can pick it up free at restaurants, bars, shops, and stands around the city.

GETTING THERE
Air

Although UPS is the only carrier flying internationally from the amusingly named **Louisville International Airport** (600 Terminal Dr., 502/368-6524, www.flylouisville.com)—still referred to by many locals as Standiford Field (the former name and the source of airport code SDF)—you can't find many other faults with the airport. It's conveniently located only about five miles south of downtown, and it's notably simple to navigate, with two terminals, each branching off from the main hall and each easily reached on foot. Airlines offer nonstop flights to 20 destinations and a slew of connecting flights to cities around the world. To get to or from the airport, you can take a taxi, rental car, hotel shuttle, or bus.

TARC Route 2 runs between downtown, Old Louisville, and the airport. The bus runs from about 6am to about 10pm daily, with the trip taking about 20 minutes to Old Louisville and 30 minutes to downtown. Buses depart every 40-90 minutes depending on the day and

time. Adult fare is $1.75. Check the schedule at www.ridetarc.org.

Bus

Greyhound services Louisville with a downtown station (720 W. Muhammad Ali Blvd., 502/561-2805, www.greyhound.com).

Car

Lying at the intersections of I-65, I-64, and I-71, Louisville is easily accessed by car from north, south, east, and west. If you're coming from within the state, Louisville is 40 miles (45 minutes) from Bardstown via northbound I-65, 80 miles (1.5 hours) from Lexington via westbound I-64, 100 miles (1.5 hours) from Covington via southbound I-71, 195 miles (3 hours) from Ashland via westbound I-64, 110 miles (2 hours) from Owensboro via northbound U.S. 231 and eastbound I-64, and 220 miles (3.25 hours) from Paducah via U.S. 9001 and northbound I-65.

From out-of-state locations, Louisville is 260 miles (4 hours) east of St. Louis via I-64, 115 miles (1.75 hours) south of Indianapolis via I-65, 100 miles (1.5 hours) southwest of Cincinnati via I-71, and 175 miles (2.5 hours) north of Nashville via I-65.

GETTING AROUND
Car Rental

Your best bet for exploring Louisville, especially if you want to go beyond downtown, is to rent a car. **Advantage** (800/777-5500, www.advantage.com), **Alamo** (800/462-5266, www.alamo.com), **Avis** (800/331-1212, www. avis.com), **Budget** (800/527-0700, www.budget.com), **Dollar** (800/800-3665, www.dollar. com), **Enterprise** (800/261-7331, www.enterprise.com), **Hertz** (800/654-3131, www.hertz. com), **National** (877/222-9058, www.nationalcar.com), and **Thrifty** (888/400-8877, www. thrifty.com) all have desks at the airport. Cars can be reserved online through the companies' national websites.

Metered street parking is available downtown with limits of 1-4 hours. All meters take coins, and the newer meters also take credit cards. Parking is free on the streets after 6pm and on Sundays. The city runs six lots and 14 garages, most of which have an all-day rate of $5 or $10, with hourly rates also available. Look for blue PARC signs to identify these parking areas.

Bus

Public transportation within Louisville is offered by **TARC** (www.ridetarc.org), the Transit Authority of the River City, and is limited to buses and trolleys. Getting across town via bus is not a particularly efficient way of travel, but the Main-Market and Fourth Street trolleys cover nearly all of downtown's tourist sites. Use the "Plan Your Trip" feature on TARC's website to determine your options. Bus fare is $1.75 for adults, $0.80 for students, seniors, and riders with disabilities. Transfers are free. Trolley rides are free. A Day Tripper pass offers unlimited rides on the day of purchase for $3.50 and can be purchased at the Louisville Visitors Center.

Taxi

Although it's not too difficult to flag down a taxi in the city center, it's almost always easier and safer to call and order a cab. All hotels and many restaurants and sights will arrange a taxi for you; just ask at the concierge, hostess, or information desk. Cabs in Louisville are metered with rates set by the city. Taxi options include **Green Cab** (502/635-6400), **Yellow Cab** (502/636-5511), and **AAA Taxi Cab** (502/225-4901).

Pedicabs and Horse Trams

If you're looking for an alternative way of getting from point A to point B, hop in one of the bright red vehicles operated by **Derby City Pedicabs** (502/338-0877, www.derbycitypedicabs.com), most often found near Fourth Street Live!, Slugger Field, Waterfront Park, and along Bardstown Road. Drivers work for tips only, so you decide the fare. Don't be cheap; it's not easy to pedal passengers around town, and the drivers do their best to make the ride fun.

If elegant is more your style, then opt to see downtown Louisville from an old-fashioned carriage crafted by Amish artisans and pulled by majestic draft horses on a ride with **Louisville Horse Trams** (502/581-0100, www.louisvillehorsetrams.com). A standard 30-minute ride for up to three people costs $40, with prices going up from there depending on length of trip and number of people. You can often find the carriages out on the town, especially on summer weekends and near Waterfront Park.

Tours

If you'd rather leave the planning to someone else, contact **Mint Julep Tours** (866/986-8779, www.mintjuleptours.com, from $59) to sign up for their Historic Louisville Tour, which hits city highlights downtown, along the Ohio River, and in Old Louisville. They also offer Bourbon Trail and Horse Country tours and can customize a tour especially for you.

Vicinity of Louisville

For day excursions, you have a number of options. You can head southwest to Fort Knox to get a dose of military history, southeast to Taylorsville to enjoy a day at the lake, or east to Shelbyville to visit standardbred horse farms.

FORT KNOX AND MEADE COUNTY

Located south of Louisville, Fort Knox is a city-size army base with a population of 23,000 soldiers and civilians located in Meade County, which is also home to the wonderful Otter Creek Outdoor Recreation Area. As you approach Fort Knox, don't be surprised to hear the thunder of tanks, as Fort Knox is home to the U.S. Armor Center and School and is the training grounds for the M1 Abrams Main Battle Tank used by both the Army and the Marines. Additionally, as one of five basic combat training facilities in the nation, Fort Knox sees a constant stream of new recruits pass through its gates.

To the general public, Fort Knox is most well known as the home of the U.S. Bullion Depository, or in lay terms, the Gold Vault. Its aura of impenetrability has introduced Fort Knox into the popular vernacular, and it has appeared in many movies such as the James Bond flick *Goldfinger*. Unfortunately, without a presidential order, the vault, which contains more than 5,000 tons of gold, is as inaccessible as claimed, but Fort Knox itself is open to visitors.

Sights

For military buffs, the **General George Patton Museum** (4554 Fayette Ave., 502/624-3812, www.generalpatton.org, 9am-4:30pm Tues.-Fri., 10am-5:30pm Sat., free) is a must-see. Established shortly after the end of World War II, the museum has two main focuses: artifacts related to General George S. Patton Jr. and mechanized cavalry and armory. Unless you're a member of the armed forces, you probably won't get a more up-close look at armored vehicles dating back to 1917. And for fans of Old Blood and Guts, this museum is where you come to pay tribute to the man, the myth, and the legend.

Recreation

Consisting of 2,600 gorgeous acres of wild space, **Otter Creek Outdoor Recreation Area** (KY 1638, Brandenburg, 502/942-9171, http://fw.ky.gov, dawn-dusk Wed.-Sun.) abounds with outdoor opportunities: hiking, mountain biking, horseback riding, fishing, boating, picnicking, and wildlife watching. It also features archery and shooting ranges and a disc golf course. Hunting is allowed in season. For those wishing to stay overnight, a campground ($12-20) offers sites for tents, RVs, and those with horses. There is a $3 entry fee for all visitors 12 and older and an additional $7 permit fee for use of horse trails, mountain bike trails, and the archery and shooting ranges.

Getting There and Around

Fort Knox is located 35 miles (45 minutes) south of Louisville, off of U.S. 31. All vehicles and visitors are subject to search, and weapons are not permitted on base. To reach Otter Creek, take U.S. 31W to KY 1638.

TAYLORSVILLE LAKE

Stretching through three counties and covering 3,050 acres, Taylorsville Lake is the closest destination to Louisville for water recreation. The fishing is good here, whether you're looking to cast for bluegill and sunfish along the shore or are angling to land a bass. Skiing, swimming, and other water sports are also popular. Built in the 1960s by the U.S. Army Corps of Engineers to control flooding, Taylorsville Lake is surrounded by 12,093 acres of protected land used for wildlife management as well as recreation.

Whether you wish to get out on the water or explore land-based activities, you'll want to base yourself at Taylorsville Lake State Park.

Recreation

Located right on the water, **Taylorsville Lake State Park** (2825 Overlook Rd., 502/477-8713, http://parks.ky.gov, free) draws anglers, water skiers, personal watercraft users, and pleasure boaters looking for a day in the sun. The park maintains four boat ramps that are free and accessible to the public. If you don't have your own watercraft, the **Taylorsville Marina** (1240 Settlers Trace Rd., 502/477-8766, www.taylorsvillelakemarina.com) will set you up for the day. You can rent pontoons, deck boats, and jon boats by the day.

Beyond the lake, the park encompasses 1,200 acres of forest and field. The 24-mile trail system is a favorite for horseback riding, though it's officially a mixed-use trail also open to mountain bikers and hikers. During wet periods, the horses can really tear up the trail, so if you're looking to hike, check conditions before you lace up your boots. The trails are particularly nice in autumn when the trees are ablaze with color and the weather is mild.

Accommodations

Edgewater Resort (1238 Settlers Trace Rd., 502/477-9196, www.edgewatertaylorsville-lake.com, $189-299), the only development on Taylorsville Lake, offers fully furnished cottages complete with decks with hot tubs. The majority of the cottages sleep four, though some can accommodate up to eight guests—perfect for a family vacation. From the cottages, a series of paths provide access to the lake, while boaters can launch their craft from a nearby ramp. A beach area has been created for resort guests, and Edgewater also offers trail bikes, canoe rentals, and guided boat excursions.

Geared toward RV campers, the **Taylorsville Lake Campground** (1320 Park Rd., 502/477-8713, http://parks.ky.gov) is open year-round and has 45 large sites with

full hookups ($25). In a nod to the park's popularity with horse lovers, 10 additional sites are designated for horse camping ($27), and there are 15 primitive tent sites ($18). All campers share a central service building that includes laundry facilities.

Food

Aside from a selection of pizza, sandwiches, and burgers sold at the Taylorsville Marina, no food vendors operate in the park. Bring what you need with you or stock up at **Settlers Trace Grocery & Deli** (25 Overlook Rd., 502/477-9676, 5am-8pm Mon.-Sat., 7am-7pm Sun.), which is right up the road from the marina.

Getting There and Around

Taylorsville Lake State Park is located about 20 miles (30 minutes) southeast of the intersection of I-265 and I-64. From Louisville, take eastbound I-64 to Taylorsville Road (Exit 32A) and then follow signs to the lake and park entrances.

SHELBYVILLE

Known as the Saddlebred Capital of the World, Shelbyville is to equestrian events what Lexington is to thoroughbred horse farms. In fact, the eminence of the Shelbyville horse farms helped Kentucky land the 2010 World Equestrian Games, an international competition that had never before taken place outside of Europe.

Beyond its horse farms, Shelbyville is a friendly small town with a center that begs you to get out of your car and explore it on foot. Main and Washington Streets are particularly pedestrian-friendly with a slew of storefronts selling antiques, art, and home decor.

Sights

Though none of Shelbyville's American saddlebred horse farms have regularly scheduled hours for visits from the public, the **Shelbyville Visitors Bureau** (800/680-6388) organizes tours of a working farm. Tours last 60-90 minutes and occur year-round, though you'll need to make reservations two or three days ahead of your visit. If you stay at a local hotel, the tour is free, and your hotel can help with the arrangements. For those not overnighting in Shelbyville, tours cost $6 for adults and $3 for youth 5-12.

For a taste (both literal and figurative) of farm life, locals swear there isn't a better place in the area than **Gallrein Farms** (1029 Vigo Rd., 502/633-4849, www.gallreinfarms. com, 9am-6pm Mon.-Sat., 1pm-5pm Sun.), especially if you have kids. The farm is open spring through fall and contains a produce market as well as a petting zoo and duck pond loved by both the young and the young at heart. Spring and summer offer berry picking, while fall is particularly popular thanks to horse-drawn wagon rides, pumpkin picking, and a corn maze.

Shopping

Antiques hunters seek out Shelbyville's **Wakefield-Scearce Galleries** (525 Washington St., 502/633-4382, www.wakefieldscearce. com, 10am-5pm Mon.-Sat.), which has 32,000 square feet of showrooms dedicated to English antiques. Even if you aren't in the market for any of the amazing pieces on sale here, stop in to browse the impressive collection of antique silver, paintings, furniture, and other home accessories.

Recreation

Favored by bass anglers, the 325-acre **Guist Creek Lake** (11990 Boat Dock Rd., 502/647-5359, www.guistcreek.com, $5 launch fee) also contains catfish, crappie, and bluegill, and it's a rare day when you can't find a quiet spot to cast your line. For those without their own boat, 14-foot jon boats are available for rent at the marina, which also stocks tackle, boat gear, fuel, food, and drinks. From the end of May to the end of September, water skiing is allowed in a specially designated area. For those who like to do some night fishing or who want to make a weekend of it, a campground is open March-November with both tent ($17) and pull-through ($20) sites.

Accommodations

Many people visit Shelbyville on a day trip and spend the night in either Louisville or Frankfort because the options in Shelbyville are limited, though the usual chain hotel suspects do exist.

In nearby Simpsonville, which lies between Louisville and Shelbyville, the **Yellow Carriage House** (4876 Shelbyville Rd., 502/376-9754, www.yellowcarriagehouse.com, $159) is a secluded bed-and-breakfast surrounded by horse fields. Choose between the King and Queen suites in the main house, each with marble shower and private balcony or veranda, or elect for the separate Carriage House, where the candlelight breakfast available to all guests is delivered straight to your room on a silver platter.

Food

Turns out it wasn't just the Colonel who could cook. At **Claudia Sanders Dinner House** (3202 Shelbyville Rd., 502/633-5600, www. claudiasanders.com, 11am-9pm Tues.-Sun., $8.99-18.95), you can choose from a long list of Kentucky specialties straight from the cookbook of Mrs. Colonel Sanders. Though fried chicken and country ham take up a prime portion of the menu, you can also select steaks, chops, fish, and seafood, as well as salads and sandwiches. Dinner is served with family-style sides and a bread bowl that never empties, and of course, all meals are served with a heavy helping of Southern hospitality.

For a pick-me-up, stop in at **Sixth and Main Coffee House** (547 Main St., 502/647-7751, www.6amcoffee.com, 7am-6pm Mon.-Sat., 8am-1pm Sun.), where the brightly colored walls and expertly brewed coffee drinks will get you going again. If you'd rather relax, grab a book from the shelf running the length of the café or just watch out the window as small-town life occurs.

Get friendly with the locals at the monthly **Lake Shelby Fish Fry** (717 Burks Branch Rd., 502/633-5059, www.shelbycountyparks.com), held 5pm-7:30pm on the third Friday of the month May-September. For $8.50, you'll get a heaping plate of fish, coleslaw, hush puppies, and potato wedges, as well as ice cream for dessert and your choice of tea or lemonade. The conversation is free.

Not quite in town but just a few miles away, Simpsonville's **Old Stone Inn** (6905 Shelbyville Rd., 502/722-8200, www.old-stone-inn.com, 4pm-10pm Mon.-Sat., $14-27) is worth the trip. This limestone building from the early 1800s has seen life as a stagecoach stop as well as a tavern and inn, though it's been operating as a restaurant since 1920. Enjoy the warm ambience created by the four original fireplaces while feasting on elegantly plated Southern favorites like country ham, shrimp and grits, and chicken livers. When the weather's nice, take advantage of happy hour on the patio complete with live local music.

Getting There and Around

From Louisville, Shelbyville is an easy 30-mile (40-minute) drive straight east on I-64. You can continue east on I-64 to both Frankfort (25 miles, 35 minutes) and Lexington (50 miles, one hour).

BARDSTOWN, THE BOURBON TRAIL, AND FRANKFORT

The spirit of Kentucky flows out of the central region that includes Bardstown, the Bourbon Trail, and Frankfort. For some, this spirit is religious. Bardstown is Kentucky's holy land, home to the first Catholic diocese in the West. Today, multiple religious orders base themselves here, and landmark religious sites draw the faithful. For many more, however, the spirit they think of when the towns of this region spring to mind is amber-colored and comes in a bottle. Here in central Kentucky, the world's best bourbon—America's only native spirit—is distilled, bottled, and aged.

The locations featured in this chapter are not cities; they're towns. Even Frankfort, the unassuming capital of Kentucky, is no more than a large town. You can explore each and every destination on foot, strolling down revitalized Main Streets lined with historic buildings hosting restaurants, B&Bs, and shops as you make your way from site to site. Expect people to say hello, to ask where you're from, to point out their favorite places. This is small-town America, where festivals are still begun with parades, where neighbors are never strangers, and where the best cooking is home cooking.

Leave each of the towns that dot the route between Bardstown and Frankfort, and you'll find yourself amid farmland. The limestone layer that makes the water so fine for bourbon is good for growing things, too. Weathered barns, tall silos, bright green fields, and large herds of cattle or other livestock enhance the scenery as you travel from distillery to distillery. Many of the distilleries themselves are located essentially on farmland; the warehouses

© THERESA DOWELL BLACKINTON

HIGHLIGHTS

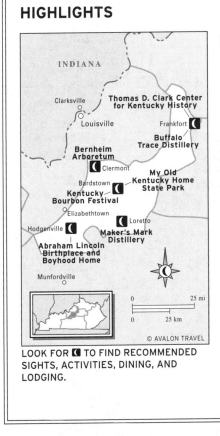

LOOK FOR **◖** TO FIND RECOMMENDED SIGHTS, ACTIVITIES, DINING, AND LODGING.

◖ My Old Kentucky Home State Park: Take a tour of the Federal-style home that inspired Stephen Foster to write what would become Kentucky's state song (page 91).

◖ Kentucky Bourbon Festival: Meet master distillers, sip premium bourbons, and celebrate American's native spirit (page 94).

◖ Abraham Lincoln Birthplace and Boyhood Home: Walk in the footsteps of young Abe Lincoln at the sites where he spent his formative years in what was then the American frontier (page 100).

◖ Bernheim Arboretum: Immerse yourself in natural beauty while hiking, fishing, or admiring a variety of gardens (page 104).

◖ Maker's Mark Distillery: Watch as workers hand-dip bottles of Maker's Mark in the signature red wax on a tour of this idyllic distillery (page 105).

◖ Thomas D. Clark Center for Kentucky History: Trace the history of Kentucky back through thousands of years by way of interactive exhibits and performances (page 115).

◖ Buffalo Trace Distillery: Passionate guides make for an excellent tour that concludes with a tasting of your choice of spirits (page 117).

where barrels of bourbon age are easy to pick out once you know what you're looking for.

One of the most idyllic regions of Kentucky, as well as the area attracting the most new tourists, Bardstown, the Bourbon Trail, and Frankfort are where you go to partake in Kentucky's spirit.

PLANNING YOUR TIME

For a satisfying taste of the region, you need to give yourself, at minimum, a four-day weekend. Spend the first day in Bardstown, visiting the distilleries there and in nearby Clermont. Fill any free time with visits to Bardstown's

historic and religious sites. For the next two days, dedicate yourself to enjoying the small towns along the Bourbon Trail—Loretto, Lebanon, and Lawrenceburg. End your trip in Frankfort, where you can fill up on Kentucky history and then finish your bourbon adventure at Buffalo Trace Distillery. Those without an interest in bourbon could still follow this same path, enjoying the scenery and substituting historical and cultural attractions for distilleries. This route—Clermont, Bardstown, Loretto, Lebanon, Lawrenceburg, Frankfort—makes the most sense if you're starting from Louisville. If you're starting from Lexington,

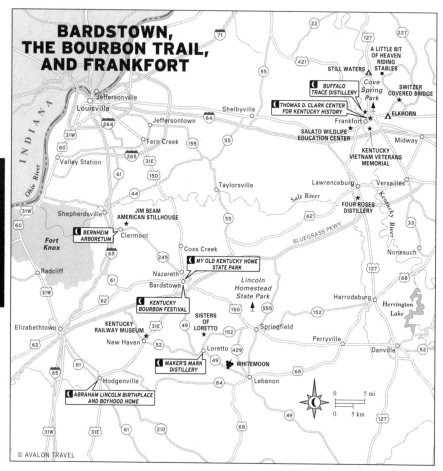

the other popular jumping-off spot for a trip through bourbon country, you can simply flip the route.

To really immerse yourself in this region of Central Kentucky, give yourself a week. You could fit each of the towns in this section into your itinerary with that amount of time, or you could spend a more leisurely time in the towns that interest you the most. Add Hodgenville and Springfield with their many Lincoln attractions to the agenda, and get outdoors either by hiking the Millennium Trail

in Bernheim Arboretum or by paddling with Canoe Kentucky.

If your primary goal is to make it to each of the area's distilleries, you could schedule your trip in two days. You'd have to be meticulous about your itinerary, however, as distilleries offer tours only at set times. You should also note that the distilleries have reduced hours on Sunday, and a few are even closed then. Time of year is also crucial when planning a distillery-based trip. Those with a real interest in the distillation process will want to avoid summer because many of the distilleries go into shutdown during the hottest months. You can still tour the facilities and taste the goods, but you won't see the process in action. Spring and fall are the ideal times to visit this region.

Bardstown

The second oldest town in Kentucky, Bardstown, at first impression, feels a bit like it belongs in the Northeast. Remarkable Federal-style homes line the major thoroughfares, which meet at a traffic circle in which the courthouse sits. Historic markers are chockablock, pointing out the importance of building after building. But take a moment to get to know the town, and you'll realize it's definitively Kentucky. My Old Kentucky Home, the landmark location made into an icon by the state song, is located here, after all. So are major distilleries as well as a craft distillery, the first Catholic cathedral in the West, one of the nation's best Civil War museums, and a slew of restaurants that know how to fry chicken. In Bardstown, you'll find all the components that make this region notable—bourbon sites, religious sites, and historical sites—making it a great starting point for a trip along the Bourbon Trail.

BOURBON SIGHTS
Heaven Hill Distillery
Built of limestone and copper, two elements important to bourbon making, the Bourbon Heritage Center at **Heaven Hill Distillery** (1311 Gilkey Run Rd., 502/337-1000, www.bourbonheritagecenter.com, 10am-5pm Mon.-Sat. year-round, noon-4pm Sun., Mar.-Dec.) is an attractive building loaded with museum-quality exhibits on the history of bourbon that are free to visitors. For those wanting a tour and tasting, you have options: a half-hour Mini-Tour ($4), which includes a guided tour of the Heritage Center and a single tasting; a 1.25-hour Deluxe Tour ($6), which includes a film, a visit to the warehouse, and a tasting of two bourbons; or a 3-hour Behind the Scenes

Tour ($25), which gives you an in-depth look at the entire process behind Heaven Hill's Elijah Craig and Evan Williams bourbons and includes the tasting of two premium bourbons. The tastings, which take place in the barrel-shaped tasting room, are very professionally done, with the guide leading you through a discussion of the taste, smell, and feel of the bourbons. The Behind the Scenes Tour should be booked in advance; other tours can be booked at the center. The last Deluxe Tour departs at 3:40pm Monday-Saturday and at 2:40pm on Sunday.

Barton 1792 Distillery
The **Barton 1792 Distillery** (300 Barton Rd., 502/331-4879, www.1792bourbon.com, 9am-4:30pm Mon.-Fri., 10am-4pm Sat.) is one of a few distilleries that still offer complimentary tours and tastings, so it's a good stop for bourbon fanatics as well as those who aren't sure just how interested they are in distillery touring. The one-hour tours are quite comprehensive, covering everything from the receipt of grains to the fermentation process to bottling and storage, and the guides are both friendly and knowledgeable. When bourbon isn't being distilled, you can still take a tour of the facility and might instead witness the bottling of other liquors. Each tour ends with a tasting of Very Old Barton and 1792 bourbons. Tours are offered on the hour 9am-3pm Monday-Friday and 10am-2pm Saturday.

Willett Distilling Company
On January 18, 2012, the **Willett Distilling Company** (1869 Loretto Rd., 502/348-0899, www.kentuckybourbonwhiskey.com) cooked up its first batch of bourbon using mash bills

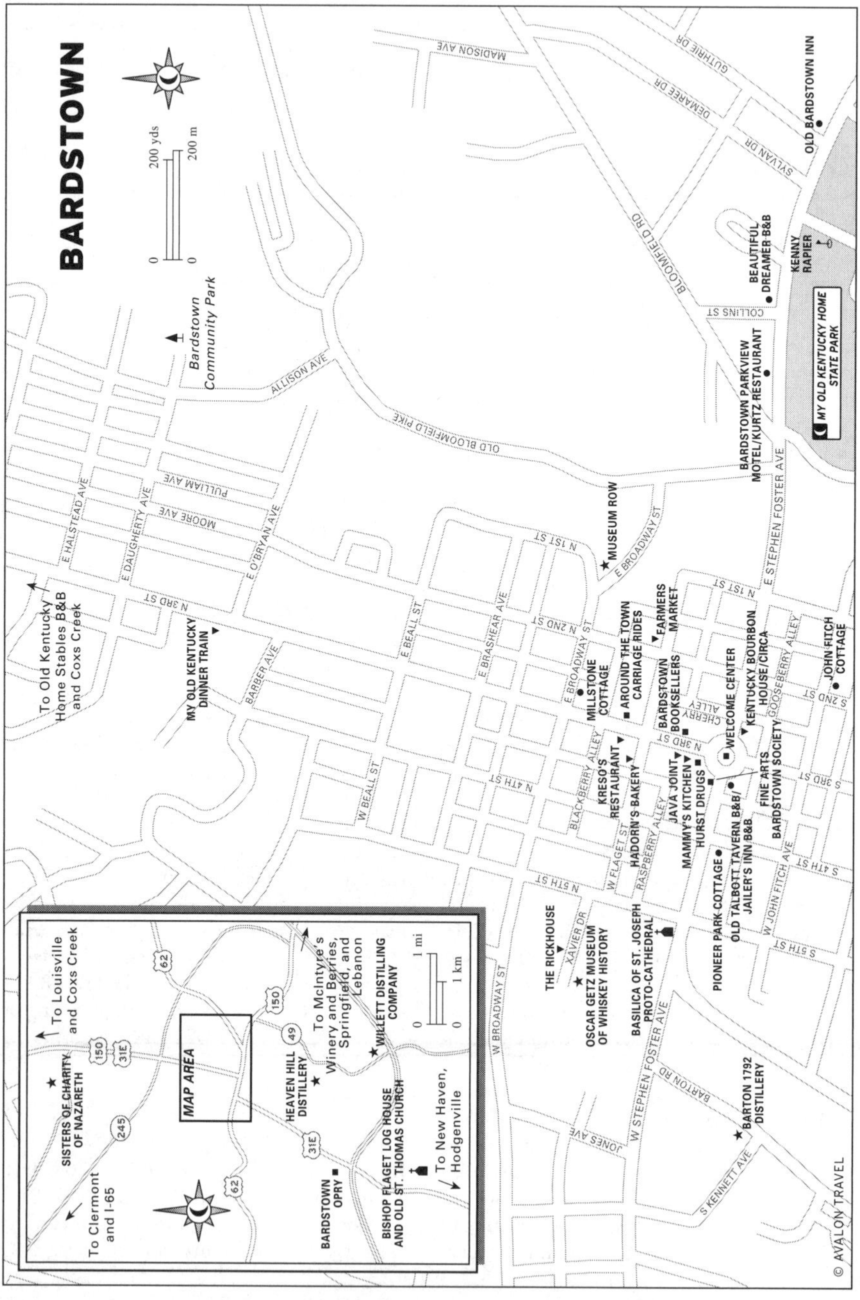
BARDSTOWN
0 200 yds
0 200 m
Bardstown Community Park
MADISON AVE
GUTHRIE DR
DEMAREE DR
SYLVAN DR
OLD BARDSTOWN INN
BLOOMFIELD RD
BEAUTIFUL DREAMER B&B
KENNY RAPIER
COLLINS ST
BARDSTOWN PARKVIEW MOTEL/KURTZ RESTAURANT
MY OLD KENTUCKY HOME STATE PARK
ALLISON AVE
OLD BLOOMFIELD PIKE
PULLIAM AVE
MOORE AVE
E HALSTEAD AVE
E DAUGHERTY AVE
E O'BRYAN AVE
N 1ST ST
MUSEUM ROW
E BROADWAY ST
E STEPHEN FOSTER AVE
To Old Kentucky Home Stables B&B and Coxs Creek
N 3RD ST
MY OLD KENTUCKY DINNER TRAIN
E BEALL ST
E BRASHEAR AVE
N 2ND ST
AROUND THE TOWN CARRIAGE RIDES
FARMERS MARKET
BARBER AVE
E BROADWAY ST
MILLSTONE COTTAGE
BARDSTOWN BOOKSELLERS
CHERRY ALLEY
WELCOME CENTER
KENTUCKY BOURBON HOUSE/CIRCA
GOOSEBERRY ALLEY
JOHN FITCH COTTAGE
S 2ND ST
N 3RD ST
W BEALL ST
N 4TH ST
BLACKBERRY ALLEY
KRESO'S RESTAURANT
HADORN'S BAKERY
JAVA JOINT
MAMMY'S KITCHEN
HURST DRUGS
FINE ARTS BARDSTOWN SOCIETY
S 3RD ST
W FLAGET ST
RASPBERRY ALLEY
OLD TALBOTT TAVERN B&B/ JAILER'S INN B&B
PIONEER PARK COTTAGE
W JOHN FITCH AVE
S 4TH ST
N 5TH ST
THE RICKHOUSE
XAVIER DR
OSCAR GETZ MUSEUM OF WHISKEY HISTORY
BASILICA OF ST. JOSEPH PROTO-CATHEDRAL
S 5TH ST
W BROADWAY ST
W STEPHEN FOSTER AVE
BARTON RD
BARTON 1792 DISTILLERY
JONES AVE
S KENNETT AVE
To Louisville and Coxs Creek
SISTERS OF CHARITY OF NAZARETH
150
31E
62
245
MAP AREA
To McIntyre's Winery and Berries, Springfield, and Lebanon
150
49
WILLETT DISTILLING COMPANY
0 1 mi
0 1 km
HEAVEN HILL DISTILLERY
31E
To Clermont and I-65
BARDSTOWN OPRY
BISHOP FLAGET LOG HOUSE AND OLD ST. THOMAS CHURCH
To New Haven, Hodgenville
62

© AVALON TRAVEL

WHAT MAKES BOURBON BOURBON?

Remember in geometry class when you learned that all squares are rectangles, but not all rectangles are squares? Well, bourbon is just like that. All bourbons are whiskeys, but not all whiskeys are bourbons. For a whiskey to be a bourbon whiskey, it must meet a very specific set of criteria.

- It must be made with at least 51 percent corn.
- It must consist of only grain, yeast, and water. No color or flavor can be added.
- It must be aged in brand-new charred white oak barrels for a minimum of two years.
- It must be distilled to no more than 160 proof and barreled at no more than 125 proof.
- It must be bottled at no less than 80 proof.

Additionally, as America's only native spirit, bourbon must be distilled in the United States. Although technically, it can be distilled anywhere in the country, 95 percent of the world's bourbon comes from Kentucky. Two things in particular make Kentucky an ideal place to produce bourbon. The first is the abundance of limestone springs, which produce water that is rich in nutrients but free of flavor. The second is that Kentucky has four very distinct seasons. When bourbon enters the barrel, it is a clear liquid not all that different from moonshine. When it exits the barrel, it is an amber-colored liquid rich with flavors that range from vanilla to spice to caramel to butterscotch. All of bourbon's color and flavor comes from the charred white oak barrel. The charring brings out the sugars in the wood, which the bourbon then absorbs through a process of expanding into the barrel during hot Kentucky summers and then contracting out of it in cold winters. Different varieties of bourbon are produced through both alterations in the recipe and changes in the amount of time the bourbon ages.

Now about the name bourbon. Many residents of and visitors to Kentucky think that Bourbon County was named for the drink, whereas, in fact, the drink was named for the county (which was named for the French royal family). Once an enormous county, Bourbon County was home to the Ohio River port, from which barrels of Kentucky corn whiskey were shipped out to the rest of the country. As the barrels were loaded onto boats, they were stamped with the word "Bourbon" to indicate their port of origin. As Kentucky whiskey gained a following, people began to refer to the liquor as bourbon thanks to the stamp on the barrel. The name stuck, and the best whiskey in the world has been known as bourbon ever since.

Bourbon becomes bourbon while aging in the warehouse.

© THERESA DOWELL BLACKINTON

© THERESA DOWELL BLACKINTON

BARDSTOWN

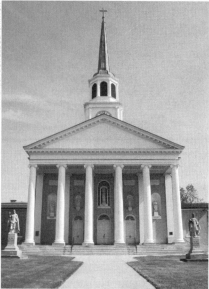

Basilica of St. Joseph Proto-Cathedral

that date back to the original incarnation of this distillery, which produced its first whiskey in 1937. The enormous effort put into restoring the site has paid dividends; this craft distillery, built with wood ceilings and beams and rough-hewn stone walls, is among the most handsome around. Currently, a variety of whiskeys are bottled here, including four boutique bourbons: Kentucky Vintage, Noah's Mill, Pure Kentucky, and Rowan Creek. The very personal and hands-on tours ($7) of the distillery and grounds last between 45 minutes and an hour. Tours are offered 10am-4pm on the hour Monday-Saturday and at 12:30pm, 1:45pm, and 3pm Sunday March-December.

Oscar Getz Museum of Whiskey History

Bourbon and whiskey aficionados can't miss the **Oscar Getz Museum of Whiskey History** (114 N. 5th St., 502/348-2999, www.whiskeymuseum.com, 10am-5pm Mon.-Fri., 10am-4pm Sat., noon-4pm Sun., May-Oct., 10am-4pm Tues.-Sat., noon-4pm Sun., Nov.-Apr., free

admission), which bursts with whiskey-related paraphernalia. You'll find clever advertising art, moonshine stills, Abraham Lincoln's liquor license, antique distilling vessels, and more. The museum, which is a bit tricky to find, is located in Spalding Hall on the St. Joe campus and shares space with the **Bardstown Historical Museum,** a single hall filled with items related to local history.

RELIGIOUS SIGHTS
Basilica of St. Joseph Proto-Cathedral

In 1808, Pope Pius VII created the Diocese of Bardstown, the first Catholic diocese in the West, with jurisdiction over Kentucky, Tennessee, and the entire Northwest Territory. In order to formalize Bardstown's position, Bishop Flaget oversaw the creation of **St. Joseph** (301 W. Stephen Foster Ave., 502/348-3126, www.stjoechurch.com), a majestic cathedral built from bricks baked on the grounds and poplar trees cut from nearby forests and decorated with artwork donated by European royalty. In 1841, when the diocese moved to Louisville, St. Joseph's became a parish church, but as the first cathedral built in the West, it received the name St. Joseph's Proto-Cathedral. In 2001, it was honored with the title of basilica, one of only two in the state. Though you're welcome to explore the basilica on your own, it's best to take advantage of the guided tours, which provide insight into the construction and history of the church as well as the magnificent artwork adorning it. Tours are available on a walk-in basis 9am-5pm Monday-Friday, 9am-3pm Saturday, and 1pm-5pm Sunday, Easter Monday-October. Tours, which may be canceled due to special services, are free, although donations are appreciated.

Bishop Flaget Log House and Old St. Thomas Church

The first permanent residence of the first bishop of the West, the **Bishop Flaget Log House** (870 St. Thomas Ln., 502/348-3717, www.st-thomasparish.org) is considered the oldest structure associated with Catholicism

© THERESA DOWELL BLACKINTON

My Old Kentucky Home

in the Midwest. The restored home is set up to represent the year 1812, when the log building served as a seminary. Old St. Thomas Church, consecrated in 1816 and renovated in 2006, is still the parish home of an active community of Catholics, and visitors are welcome to attend Mass at the church. Tours of the log house are conducted by appointment.

Sisters of Charity of Nazareth

Founded at the Bishop Flaget Log House in 1812 by Mother Catherine Spalding, the **Sisters of Charity of Nazareth** (Nazareth Rd., 502/348-1500, www.scnfamily.org, 9am-4pm Mon.-Sat., 1pm-4pm Sun.) now work in 17 states as well as in Belize, Botswana, India, and Nepal. On a visit to their Nazareth campus, you can watch a short video detailing the good work the sisters do around the world, become acquainted with their heritage in the history room, attend services at St. Vincent, and chat with members of the order. You're also free to explore the manicured grounds, which are graced

with many quiet spots ideal for reflection. Additionally, the sisters offer a full schedule of guided spiritual retreats as well as accommodation for private retreatants.

HISTORIC SIGHTS
◖ My Old Kentucky Home State Park

Federal Hill, the home of the distinguished Rowan Family, has become known to generations as My Old Kentucky Home, thanks to Stephen Foster and the song he penned while visiting the home in 1852. The three-story brick house is the centerpiece of **My Old Kentucky Home State Park** (501 E. Stephen Foster Ave., 502/348-3502, http://parks.ky.gov, 9am-4:45pm daily, Mar.-Dec., Wed.-Sun. only, Jan.-Feb.), and costumed tour guides lead visitors through the house, doling out information and anecdotes about family history and the artifacts in the home. An impressive 75 percent of the items in the house, which is decorated in the style of the mid-1800s, actually belonged to the Rowan family. Tours of the house cost $7 for adults, $5 for seniors, and $3.50 for youth 6-12, but visitors to the park are welcome to stroll the grounds, visit the family cemetery, and picnic on the beautifully landscaped lawn free of charge. A designated picnic area with tables, a covered pavilion, and a playground is located on Loretto Road. The park also includes a golf course and campground.

KENTUCKY'S STATE SONG

Every year on Derby Day, as the contenders in America's most prestigious horse race head to the post, the crowd stands for the singing of "My Old Kentucky Home." And without fail, this simple song by Stephen Foster, America's first great composer, brings tears to the eyes of men, women, boys, girls, and jockeys alike. Don't be the only one who doesn't know the words.

My Old Kentucky Home

The sun shines bright on my old
    Kentucky home
'Tis summer, the children are gay
The corn top's ripe and the mead-
    ow's in the bloom
While the birds make music all the
    day
The young folks roll on the little
    cabin floor
All merry, all happy and bright
By 'n' by hard times come a-knock-
    ing at the door
Then my old Kentucky home good-
    night
Weep no more, my lady
Oh, weep no more today
We will sing one song for the old
    Kentucky home
For the old Kentucky home far away

Stephen Foster

Historic Walking Tour

Ask for a copy of the **Historic Walking Tour** brochure at the Welcome Center (1 Court Sq., 502/348-4877), or download it from the tourism website (www.visitbardstown.com); then set out on a 48-stop tour. All sites are within a three-block radius of Court Square. While the brochure gives cursory information on each site, many sites also have informative signs relaying information about architecture and history.

OTHER SIGHTS
Museum Row

Made up of five distinct museums, each of which can be visited individually or as part of a package, **Museum Row** (310 E. Broadway, 502/349-0291, www.civil-war-museum.org, 10am-5pm daily Mar.-Oct., 10am-5pm Fri.-Sun. Nov.-Dec. 15) focuses primarily on history. Tickets ($10 adults, $5 youth 5-15) provide admission to all five museums for two consecutive days.

CIVIL WAR MUSEUM

The most significant of the five museums is the **Civil War Museum,** which has been named the fourth best museum of its type by *North & South,* the official magazine of the Civil War Society. The museum focuses on the action that took place in the Civil War's Western theater (Kentucky, Tennessee, Mississippi, Georgia, and the Carolinas) and portrays the war from both Union and Confederate perspectives. The outer exhibit tells the chronological history of battles while the inner exhibit focuses on more detailed stories, with authentic artifacts illustrating the information. The artifacts on hand are most impressive and include flags, uniforms, weaponry, personal and medical kits, and more, much of which belonged to generals and other high-ranking officers.

WOMEN'S CIVIL WAR MUSEUM

Complementing the Civil War Museum is the **Women's Civil War Museum,** which documents the many ways in which women contributed to the war effort, from acting as nurses, spies, and even soldiers to stepping up to fill roles at home and in the factories.

THE WAR MEMORIAL OF MID AMERICA MUSEUM

The **War Memorial of Mid America Museum** is the final military-themed attraction on Museum Row. This museum presents artifacts from the Revolutionary War through Desert Storm and tells the story of those who have fought in defense of the United States, with special attention paid to local men and women.

PIONEER VILLAGE

Representing the oldest era of regional history, the **Pioneer Village** strives to authentically re-create a 1790s village. The cabins come from the local area and date back more than 200 years.

WILDLIFE MUSEUM

The final museum in the group, the **Wildlife Museum** focuses on natural history, showcasing professionally stuffed animals of North America in natural-like settings. The preservation is top-notch and the displays are attention-grabbing, especially the one depicting wolves in pursuit of an elk.

McIntyre's Winery and Berries

At **McIntyre's Winery and Berries** (531 McIntyre Ln., 502/507-3264, www.mcintyreswinery.com, 10am-9pm Mon.-Sat., 1pm-9pm Sun.), homegrown blueberries and blackberries are transformed into both sweet and dry fruit wines. Visitors are welcome to stop by for a tour and a tasting.

ENTERTAINMENT AND EVENTS
Nightlife

Freestanding bars are uncommon in Bardstown and definitely not where the action is. Instead, locals and visitors alike seek out restaurant bars for a drink and evening entertainment. The **Bourbon Bar at Old Talbott Tavern** (107 W. Stephen Foster Ave., 502/348-3494, www. talbotts.com, 4pm-9pm Mon.-Wed., 4pm-1am Thurs.-Sat., 1pm-8pm Sun.) is a popular gathering place with (loud) live music, and the bar at **The Rickhouse** (112 Xavier Dr., 502/348-2832, 11am-9pm Tues.-Thurs., 11am-10pm Fri.-Sat.) offers a fine selection of bourbons, beers, and wines.

Performing Arts

The Stephen Foster Story (Drama Dr., 502/348-5971, www.stephenfoster.com) is Bardstown's signature performance, drawing big crowds every summer with its song-and-dance-filled story of America's first great composer. Unless it rains, the evening performances take place at the large outdoor theater on the grounds of My Old Kentucky Home State Park. In addition to putting on the classic *Stephen Foster Story,* the Stephen Foster Productions company rounds out the schedule with other musical performances. For instance, the 2013 schedule featured *Shrek the Musical.* The season runs mid-June-mid-August, and tickets cost $19-24 for adults and $11-13 for youth 6-12.

Live Music

The **Live at the Park Concert Series** (502/348-5971, www.stephenfoster.com) brings popular (but sometimes dated) musicians to town to perform onstage at My Old Kentucky Home State Park. The 2013 concerts featured John Michael Montgomery, Jana Kramer, The Monarchs, The Devonshires, and Beatles and CCR tribute bands. Tickets range $15-25; those interested in multiple shows should consider purchasing season tickets, which are good for the concerts as well as the Stephen Foster Story productions.

Music lovers will also want to avail themselves of the free **Summer Band Concerts,** which are held 7pm-9pm every Friday Memorial Day-Labor Day in the **Bardstown Community Park** (E. Halstead Ave., www. cityofbardstown.org). Bands and genres change every week, so pack a picnic and make it a recurring date.

The Bardstown Opry (426 Sutherland Rd.,

859/336-9839, www.musicmansoundstage. com, $10 adults, $6 youth 6-12) caters to bluegrass fans with shows every Friday night. Doors open at 6pm, with music from 7:30pm to 10pm.

Festivals and Events
◖ KENTUCKY BOURBON FESTIVAL
For six days in mid-September, the Bourbon Capital of the World hosts the **Kentucky Bourbon Festival** (800/638-4877, www.ky-bourbonfestival.com), an absolute must for lovers of America's native spirit. Highlights of the festival include the Great Kentucky Bourbon Tasting and Gala and the Kentucky Bourbon All-Star Sampler. Each of these events allows participants to meet with master distillers and taste the best bourbons being made. Although much of the schedule is filled with events directly related to bourbon (demonstrations, seminars, tastings, and more), you'll also find golf tournaments, fun runs, art festivals, concerts, and other types of entertainment to keep you satisfied between sips.

BARDSTOWN ARTS, CRAFTS & ANTIQUES FAIR
Nearly 200 artists and craftspeople descend on Bardstown on the second weekend of October for the **Bardstown Arts, Crafts & Antiques Fair** (www.visitbardstown.com), held on the streets of downtown. Shop for jewelry, pottery, woodwork, photography, prints, and more while enjoying music and local food.

SHOPPING
North Third Street is lined with shops selling gifts, apparel, and local souvenirs, so window shop as you walk, popping in whenever something catches your eye. At **Bardstown Booksellers** (129 N. 3rd St., 502/348-1256, 9am-6pm Mon.-Thurs., 9am-7pm Fri.-Sat., 11am-4pm Sun.), books about Kentucky fill the most prominent shelves, so it's a great place to shop if you're looking for a cookbook of traditional recipes or a coffee table book of beautiful photos. The store also stocks locally made

crafts, jewelry, and food, including a mouthwatering selection of truffles, as well as popular and antiquarian books.

Old-fashioned **Hurst Drugs** (102 N. 3rd St., 502/348-9261, 8am-6pm Mon.-Sat.) stocks a broad selection of Kentucky souvenirs, including Derby glasses, U of L and UK themed gifts, pottery, and Kentucky Proud food products. You're also welcome to have a seat at one of the red stools at the counter and enjoy a shake, malt, float, or soda.

At the gallery of the **Fine Arts Bardstown Society** (90 Court Sq., 502/348-0044, www.fineartsbardstown.com, 10am-6pm Tues.-Sat., noon-6pm Sun.), you'll find photography, pottery, sculpture, jewelry, and all sorts of other artwork produced by the society's members.

SPORTS AND RECREATION
Golf
The **Kenny Rapier Golf Course** (668 Loretto Rd., 502/349-6542, http://parks.ky.gov, Apr.-Oct.), which is part of My Old Kentucky Home State Park, is an 18-hole, par-71 course. It was awarded four stars by *Golf Digest* in 2009 after a redesign that updated the original 1928 course to a more modern style.

ACCOMMODATIONS
$50-100
Bardstown Parkview Motel (418 E. Stephen Foster Ave., 502/348-5983, www.bardstown-parkview.com, $60-100) doesn't claim to offer all the amenities of new hotels, but instead preserves the style that made motels popular in the first place. Service at this family-owned place is friendly, the grounds are nicely manicured, and a courtyard area with pool is popular with families. Though dated, rooms and suites (which have desks and cooktops) are clean and come with Internet connections. The location directly across the street from My Old Kentucky Home can't be beat. Breakfast isn't worth getting up for.

The 33 units at **Old Bardstown Inn** (510 E. Stephen Foster Ave., 502/349-0776, www.angelfire.com/ky3/oldbardstowninn, $55) offer standard motel amenities with clean rooms, each with two queen beds, wireless Internet access, and refrigerators. A continental breakfast is served in the lobby, and a pool provides a welcome escape on hot summer days. Leave your car in the lot and just cross the street to visit My Old Kentucky Home or play a round of golf.

The five rooms at **Old Talbott Tavern Bed and Breakfast** (107 W. Stephen Foster Ave., 502/348-3494, www.talbotts.com, $69-109) are named for famous Tavern guests: Abraham Lincoln, Generals Clark and Patton, Anton Heinrich, Daniel Boone, and Washington Irving. All rooms are furnished with period antiques, such as claw-foot tubs and canopy beds, but contain modern (but worn) amenities like private baths, refrigerators, and TVs. Beware that the rooms can be very noisy due to both street traffic and the music played in the bar below. Breakfast is disappointing, especially considering the B&B is part of a restaurant.

$100-150

At the **Jailer's Inn Bed and Breakfast** (111 W. Stephen Foster Ave., 502/348-5551, www.jailersinn.com, $110-155), you don't have to break any laws to spend the night in the slammer. While the back jail remains preserved, the front jail has been renovated to contain six guest rooms. Five feel like typical B&B rooms, while one room, decorated in black and white and with the original bunks, maintains the aura of a jail cell. Plenty of ghost stories surround the jail, so a stay here might not be for the faint of heart. A family suite ($235) with one king bed, one queen bed, and a living area is also available.

Book a room at **Old Kentucky Home Stables Bed and Breakfast** (115 Samuels Rd., Cox's Creek, 502/294-0474, $115), located 10 minutes from downtown Bardstown, and you'll be spending the night at America's oldest continuously operating saddlebred horse farm. The pre-Civil War home, with original plank floors and double-sided brick fireplace, offers large rooms with all the modern amenities, including whirlpool tubs and cable TV. Views stretch far and wide over rural countryside, and are only occasionally interrupted by a peacock strutting past, feathers spread. Owner Frankie is a history and horse buff and can ply you with trivia or spin a good story. You can also arrange riding lessons with him, though be aware that the saddlebreds he breeds, trains, and shows are big, powerful animals, not ponies.

$150-200

Named for one of Stephen Foster's songs, ◖ **Beautiful Dreamer Bed and Breakfast** (440 E. Stephen Foster Ave., 502/348-4004, www.bdreamerbb.com, $159-189) sits on property that was once part of My Old Kentucky Home. Now a street divides it from this landmark, but you can still enjoy a view of the park from the second-floor veranda. The four spacious bedrooms have large bathrooms, flat-screen TVs, reclining chairs, and big beds. Decor is crisp and classic, and the walls are painted in shades of rich wine, forest green, and Kentucky blue. Breakfast is served family style, and drinks and snacks, along with games and DVDs, are available on the second-floor landing. If you have questions about the Stephen Foster Story, which you can walk to from the B&B, just ask host Lynell. She's seen the show more than 200 times!

The **Colonel's Cottage Inns** (502/507-8338, www.colonelscottageinns.com) are three meticulously restored 19th-century cottages, each of which is available to be rented by those looking for a private retreat along the Bourbon Trail. **Millstone Cottage** (107 E. Broadway, $169) has two bedrooms, one with a queen bed and the other with two single beds, and a bathroom with whirlpool tub for two and shower. **Pioneer Park Cottage** (114 S. Fourth St., $189) also has two bedrooms, one with a queen bed and the other with two single beds, but it has two bathrooms, one with a whirlpool tub and one with a shower. **John Fitch Cottage** (211 E. John Fitch, $129) has one queen bedroom and a bathroom with both whirlpool tub and shower. All have kitchens, living areas, and outdoor space. The cottages are tidied up daily and breakfast is left in the kitchen, but otherwise guests are left in privacy.

Campgrounds

My Old Kentucky Home State Park hosts a **campground** (Loretto Rd., 502/348-3502, http://parks.ky.gov, Apr.-Oct., $23), which has 39 improved sites for RVs and a separate grassy area for tent campers. Showers and restrooms are located in a central building.

FOOD
My Old Kentucky Dinner Train

Take your dinner in a vintage 1940s dinner car while enjoying a ride through the countryside on **My Old Kentucky Dinner Train** (N. 3rd St., 502/348-7300, www.rjcorman.com, dinner trip $84.95 adult, $54.95 youth 5-12, lunch trip $69.95 adult, $44.95 youth 5-12). During the 2.5-hour trip, a four-course dinner or three-course lunch is served, with travelers choosing from a small selection of options for their salad, entrée, and dessert. The train runs year-round, although there are more departures during summer months. Visit the website to view the schedule and make reservations.

Kentucky Bourbon House

At the 【 **Kentucky Bourbon House** (107 E. Stephen Foster Ave., 502/507-8338, www.chapezehouse.com), Colonel Michael and Margaret Sue Masters bring together the best of bourbon and Southern cooking for a memorable lunch or dinner experience. Lunch is served as part of **Kentucky Bourbon University** ($99), where participants learn about bourbon history, production, and etiquette and how to drink and serve bourbon. The class features 10 premium Kentucky bourbons, two rye whiskies, one Tennessee whiskey, and one white dog, and it ends with a classic lunch of burgoo, country ham, Benedictine, potato salad, and bread pudding. Dinners ($29.95) are intimate events limited to 20 guests. They begin at 6:30 with bourbon and cocktails and then proceed into a dinner of bourbon-marinated pork chops accompanied by a bevy of fresh sides and finished with dessert. Reservations are required for both lunch and dinner, which are unique experiences akin to dining with gracious Southern friends in their historic home.

Farmers Market

Pick up crisp veggies, juicy fruits, and other farm-fresh products at the **Farmers Market** (N. 2nd and E. Flaget Sts., 7:30am-12:30pm Tues., Fri., and Sat., May-Oct.), held three times a week in a permanent building in downtown Bardstown.

Cafés and Bakeries

If you've got a hankering for a pastry or other baked goodie, head to **Hadorn's Bakery** (118 W. Flaget St., 502/348-4407, 7am-1pm Tues.-Sat., $0.95-3.95), where treats are turned out fresh each day.

Java Joint (126 N. 3rd St., 502/350-0883, 7:30am-5:30pm Mon.-Sat., $5.50-6.75) keeps Bardstown fueled with coffee and specialty drinks all day long, and during the lunch stretch offers a selection of soups, salads, and sandwiches. In addition to the common chicken and egg salad, Java Joint also serves muffulettas, Cubans, and a roasted pepper pimento cheese.

Contemporary American

Located right on Bardstown's main circle in a yellow-painted stone house dating to around 1780, 【 **Circa** (103 E. Stephen Foster Ave., 502/348-5409, www.restaurant-circa.com, lunch 11am-2pm Tues.-Fri., dinner 5pm-9pm Tues.-Sat., $21-30) serves a small menu of upscale contemporary Southern food at reclaimed poplar tables spread throughout various rooms of the house. Dinner choices might include lamb pot pie or coq au vin. The lunch menu ($7-10) ranges from fish tacos to chicken crepes to mac and cheese with turkey, bacon, and tomato. Expect excellent service and a special-occasion feel. Reservations are recommended.

Classic American

Hidden away in the basement under the Oscar Getz Museum, **The Rickhouse** (Xavier Dr., 502/348-2832, http://market8media.com/therickhouse, 11am-9pm Tues.-Thurs., 11am-10pm Fri.-Sat., $14-27) serves well-prepared classic American dishes while playing to a bourbon theme. Steaks are a signature item, but other favorites include a barbecue bourbon chicken, a porterhouse pork chop, and a Hot Brown. Try the Brussels sprouts as a side… seriously.

If you want to know what good fried chicken tastes like, get a table at **Kurtz Restaurant** (418 E. Stephen Foster Ave., 502/348-8964, www.bardstownparkview.com, 11am-9pm Tues.-Sat., noon-8pm Sun., $13.95-18.95), where it's served piping hot and without a hint of grease though it's cooked the way grandma used to do it—in a skillet full of lard. You also don't want to miss the fried cornbread, enormous pieces of meringue pie, or the biscuit pudding with bourbon raisin sauce. Kurtz has been serving fried chicken and other Southern favorites since 1937, and when you step into the home-turned-restaurant, you'll be treated like one of the family. The atmosphere is cozy with dining tables spread through the rooms of the house.

Those who like their meals served with a side of history will appreciate the **Old Talbott Tavern** (107 W. Stephen Foster Ave., 502/348-3494, www.talbotts.com, 11am-9pm Mon.-Thurs., 11am-10pm Fri.-Sat., 11am-7pm Sun., $14.95-29.95), which dates back to 1779 and maintains much of its original architecture. George Rogers Clark used the tavern as his base during the Revolutionary War, and other famous figures who have passed through the doors include Andrew Jackson, Abraham Lincoln, John James Audubon, and General George Patton. Though portions of fried chicken, catfish, pork chops, and country ham are large, flavors need to be kicked up a notch. Unlike the atmosphere, the food is rather bland.

Mammy's Kitchen (114 N. Third St., 502/350-1097, 6:30am-8pm Mon.-Tues., 6:30am-9pm Wed.-Fri., 8am-2pm Sun.) is your destination if you're after no-fuss but tasty home cooking along the lines of chicken fried chicken, open-faced roast beef sandwiches, and meatloaf. Breakfast is served until 11am, and there's always pie, with the meringue on the chocolate, coconut, and butterscotch piled high. It's a small place that's nearly always busy, but service is speedy, so your wait shouldn't be too long.

European

Kreso's Restaurant (218 N. 3rd St., 502/348-9594, www.kresosrestaurant.com, lunch 11am-3pm Mon.-Fri., dinner 5pm-11pm Mon.-Fri., 11am-11pm Sat., noon-10pm Sun., $9.95-26) exudes charm thanks to the fact that it's located in an old theater. Run by a Bosnian family, the menu offers old-world favorites like schnitzel and goulash, as well as an excellent selection of steaks and seafood (and not the fried kind most popular in these parts). Start any meal with the Bosnian salad, a mix of leaf lettuce, tomato, cucumber, hard-boiled egg, red onion, and feta cheese. The lunch menu ($6.95-9.95) includes lighter versions of popular dinner entrées as well as salads and sandwiches. Service can be hit-or-miss.

INFORMATION AND SERVICES

Gather all the information you can handle at Bardstown's **Welcome Center** (1 Court Sq., 502/348-4877, www.visitbardstown.com), located in the courthouse building smack in the middle of the main traffic circle. Bardstown's main **post office** (205 W. Stephen Foster Ave.) is located just down the street.

GETTING THERE

Bardstown is about 40 miles (45 minutes) south of Louisville. Take I-65 South to KY 245 South (Exit 112). After 15 miles, turn right on 3rd Street, which leads straight to the center of town. For a more scenic drive, take U.S. 31E (Bardstown Road) all the way from Louisville to Bardstown. From Frankfort (55 miles; one hour) or Lexington (60 miles; one hour), going eastbound on Blue Grass Parkway (KY 9002) will connect you to U.S. 31.

Bardstown lies 165 miles (2.25 hours) northeast of Nashville via northbound I-65 to the Blue Grass Parkway (Exit 93) to U.S. 31. Bardstown is 302 miles (4.5 hours) from St. Louis, 154 miles (2.5 hours) from Indianapolis,

BARDSTOWN

© THERESA DOWELL BLACKINTON

Heaven Hill Distilleries Trolley

and 140 miles (2.25 hours) from Cincinnati. Coming from any of these three cities, you'll first travel to Louisville, and then follow the directions from there.

GETTING AROUND
Trolley Tours
See Bardstown from the windows of the **Heaven Hill Distilleries Trolley** (www.bourbonheritagecenter.com) on a narrated half-hour tour. The handsome vintage trolley leaves from

the distillery and circles past the town's main attractions. The tours run at 10am and 1pm.

Carriage Tours
Take in historic Bardstown at a relaxed pace with **Around the Town Carriage Rides** (223 N. 3rd St., 502/249-0889, 9am-10pm daily). Horse-drawn carriages, buggies, and stagecoaches provide the most stylish rides in town. A 30-minute narrated tour for two people costs $40.

Vicinity of Bardstown

A few small towns surround Bardstown to the south and east and are worth a visit for their religious and historical sites. Railway enthusiasts and those moved by the writings of Thomas Merton will want to add New Haven to their itinerary, while Lincoln fans shouldn't miss Hodgenville, the president's hometown, and Springfield, his ancestral home.

NEW HAVEN
Abbey of Gethsemani
Since 1848, Trappist monks have called the **Abbey of Gethsemani** (3642 Monks Rd., Trappist, 502/549-3117, www.monks.org) home, dedicating the time they spend at this beautiful sanctuary to formal prayers and the manual labor that provides their livelihood.

© THERESA DOWELL BLACKINTON

Abbey of Gethsemani

BARDSTOWN

10am-4pm Tues.-Sat., noon-4pm Sun., $5 adults, $2 youth 2-12) and a ride on one of their trains. The trains cover 22 miles of countryside on a 90-minute ride, with a brief layover at the turnaround point allowing a chance to grab a snack or drink. Those who have dreamed of engineering a train can opt to ride in the locomotive ($50 adults, $25 youth 7-12). Special events are held throughout the year. Among the most popular are the Great Train Robbery weekends, Mystery Theatre nights, and holiday-themed trips. If you have kids, you won't want to miss Thomas the Tank Engine's visit, which occurs each summer and draws huge crowds. Train rides are offered at 2pm on Saturday and Sunday March-May and mid-August-mid-December; and at 11am and 2pm on Saturday, 2pm on Sunday, and 1pm on Tuesday and Friday mid-June-mid-August. Train fares ($17 adults, $12 youth 2-12 on diesel trains; $2 more on steam trains) include admission to the museum, which features rail artifacts, and the model train center, which hosts detailed displays that can be activated by visitors.

Gethsemani is widely known thanks to Thomas Merton, a Trappist monk at the abbey who wrote multiple books, including his famous autobiography *The Seven Storey Mountain,* and attracted admirers with his interest in interfaith understanding. Visitors to the abbey are greeted in the Welcome Center (9am-5pm Mon.-Sat.) with a video that explains the monastic life, and are also invited to join the monks at prayers or Mass. In the longstanding tradition of monks offering hospitality, people interested in prayer and reflection are welcome to reserve a stay at the **abbey** (502/549-4133, by donation). Directed retreats are also available through the **Merton Institute Retreat Center at Bethany Spring** (502/549-8277, www.bethanyspring.org). Visitors to the Abbey of Gethsemani should remember that it is a place of silent prayer.

Kentucky Railway Museum

Chug back in time with a visit to the **Kentucky Railway Museum** (136 S. Main St., New Haven, 502/549-5470, www.kyrail.org,

Getting There and Around

New Haven is located 13.5 miles (18 minutes) south of Bardstown and can be reached via southbound U.S. 31E. To reach the Abbey of Gethsemani, you don't have to travel all the way into New Haven. Instead, after eight miles on U.S. 31E, turn left onto Monks Road.

HODGENVILLE

Though Illinois claims to be the Land of Lincoln, America's 16th president was a Kentuckian by birth and spent the first seven years of his life in the Bluegrass State. More specifically, young Abe grew up in the area that came to be known as Hodgenville, but was a frontier town at the time. The early years of his life, a time of struggle (although his family would have been considered middle class), certainly helped shape the man who would become president. In fact, in an autobiography he wrote for his 1860 campaign, Lincoln noted that his earliest memories revolved around his boyhood home on Knobs Creek. Today's

BARDSTOWN

© THERESA DOWELL BLACKINTON

Memorial Building at Abraham Lincoln Birthplace

Hodgenville celebrates this connection with a number of Lincoln-related sites.

Abraham Lincoln Birthplace and Boyhood Home

Part of the National Park Service, the **Abraham Lincoln Birthplace** (2995 Lincoln Farm Rd., 270/358-3137, www.nps.gov/abli, 8am-4:45pm daily, Sept.-May, 8am-6:45pm daily, June-Aug., free) and **Boyhood Home** (7 miles north on U.S. 31E) preserve a sense of how the Lincoln family lived in Kentucky. Begin your visit at the Birthplace Visitors Center, where you can view a 15-minute film about Lincoln's childhood and check out the Lincoln family bible and other artifacts. The site's main attraction is the Memorial Building, a marble and granite structure that houses a cabin symbolic of that in which Lincoln was born. Fifty-six steps, one for each year of Lincoln's life, lead up to the memorial and past the Sinking Spring, for which the family farm was named. (The Pathway of a President trail provides wheelchair access to the memorial.) A 0.7-mile interpretive

hiking trail is open to those who want to stretch their legs and learn a bit about what the Lincoln homestead would have been like. After visiting the Birthplace, continue on to Lincoln's Boyhood Home, where he lived from 1811 to 1816. Poke your head in the family cabin of Lincoln's friend Austin Gollaher, wander down to the creek where Lincoln almost drowned in a flash flood, and examine a garden planted with crops the Lincolns likely grew.

Lincoln Museum

At the **Lincoln Museum** (66 Lincoln Square, 270/358-3163, www.lincolnmuseum-ky.org, 8:30am-4:30pm Mon.-Sat., 12:30pm-4:30pm Sun., $3 adults, $2.50 seniors, $1.50 youth 5-12), 12 life-size dioramas depict important events in the life of the 16th president—from his cabin years in Kentucky to his assassination at Ford's Theatre. The well-done dioramas make history accessible to children and those with only a cursory interest in the subject, while accompanying photos, newspaper articles, letters, and descriptive panels cater to those seeking more in-depth information. A second floor contains Lincoln artwork as well as Civil War artifacts, including items unearthed from battlefield digs.

Lincoln Square Statues

In the center of Hodgenville, two statues of Abraham Lincoln sit facing each other. Dedicated in 1909, Adolph Weinman's Abraham Lincoln Statue depicts the Kentuckian seated and looking as he did when he was president. Directly across from this classic statue you'll find the more whimsical Boy Lincoln Statue, added to the square in 2008. This statue shows young Abe, accompanied by a dog and a fishing pole, leaning against a tree stump and reading from a Webster's spelling book.

Entertainment

For a toe-tapping good time that apparently even the President would have loved, make plans to attend the **Lincoln Jamboree** (2579 Lincoln Farm Rd., 270/358-3545, www.lincolnjamboree.com, 7:30pm-10:30pm Sat., $8.50), an old-fashioned country music show that's been going strong for more than 50 years. Come early to enjoy free music on the patio (6pm).

Events

To honor the city's, as well as the state's, greatest resident, Hodgenville celebrates **Lincoln Days** (270/358-8710, www.lincolndays.org) annually in late September or early October. The weekend festival includes an oratory contest, Mary Todd and Abraham Lincoln lookalike contests, and pioneer games, as well as art and car shows, a parade, a fun run, and live music.

Food

Laha's Red Castle (21 Lincoln Square, 270/358-9201, 9am-4pm Mon.-Tues. and Thurs.-Sat., 9am-1:30pm Wed., $1.95-4.95) has been keeping Hodgenville in hamburgers for more than 65 years. Follow the smell of fried onions to the tiny corner diner, where you'll most likely have to wait for a stool at the counter to open up before you can place your order for a fresh-made hamburger and an ice-cold bottled Coke.

Follow up your lunch with a treat from **The Sweet Shoppe** (100 S. Lincoln Blvd., 270/358-0424, www.sweetshoppefudge.com, 11am-6pm Mon.-Sat.), which offers 35 flavors of fudge, along with ice cream and other desserts. A half-pound of fudge sells for $4.99.

Information and Services

The **LaRue County Visitors Center** (60 Lincoln Sq., 270/358-3411, www.laruecountychamber.org, 9am-4pm Mon.-Fri.) can set you up with all the information you need on Hodgenville's attractions as well as other regional sites of interest.

Getting There

Hodgenville is located 25 miles (30 minutes) southwest of Bardstown via southbound U.S. 31E. Hodgenville can also be reached by exiting I-65 at southbound KY 61 (Exit 91), which will lead you right to the center of town.

SPRINGFIELD

Complementing Hodgenville is the town of Springfield, which is where President Lincoln's pioneer grandparents settled and where both of his parents were born and raised.

Lincoln Homestead State Park

Abraham Lincoln's ancestors entered Kentucky in the late 1700s via the Wilderness Road, establishing a homestead in the area that is now Springfield. **Lincoln Homestead State Park** (5079 Lincoln Park Rd., 859/336-7461, http://parks.ky.gov) is home to three structures that preserve the history of the Lincoln family. The Lincoln Cabin is a replica of the log house in which Abraham Lincoln's grandmother lived and raised five children, including President Lincoln's father, Thomas. A second log house at the park, which is a bit fancier with a second floor and glass windows, was the home of President Lincoln's mother, Nancy Hanks. This original cabin was moved to the park from

© THERESA DOWELL BLACKINTON

BARDSTOWN

President Lincoln's mother's house at Lincoln Homestead State Park

about a mile away. A third building, a stately white home that belonged to President Lincoln's favorite uncle, Mordecai Lincoln, is also in the park, having been moved from across the street. Tours of the cabins along with a blacksmith's shop cost $2 for adults and $1.50 for youth, and are offered 10:30am-5:30pm daily, May-September, and on weekends in October. The grounds, which are complete with signage relaying the history of the buildings and area, are free and open year-round.

Opposite the road from the homes is an 18-hole golf course, allowing you to play a round on the rolling hills where the Lincolns once lived.

Mt. Zion Covered Bridge

At 246 feet long, the **Mt. Zion Covered Bridge** (KY 458), which crosses the Beech Fork River, is one of the longest remaining multispan bridges in Kentucky. Built in 1871, Mt. Zion Covered Bridge is the only one of Washington County's seven covered bridges to remain standing, although it is no longer in use.

Accommodations

◖ **Maple Hill Manor** (2941 Perryville Rd., 859/336-3075, www.maplehillmanor.com, $139-199) deserves the many raves and honors it has received, and it's worth going a bit out of your way to stay here. Set on a 15-acre working alpaca and llama farm and surrounded by horse, tobacco, and cattle farms, this wonderfully preserved antebellum home has seven lovely guest rooms, each with private bath. The large, light-filled rooms are luxurious with plush bedding, towels, and robes, along with high-end bath products, fireplaces, TVs, and Internet access. Homemade desserts and beverages are offered each evening in the parlor, and a candlelight breakfast is served on fine china in the formal dining room each morning. Guests are invited to tour the grounds, which are complete with flower gardens, fish ponds, and an orchard from which you can pick fresh fruit in season. Although convenient to Springfield attractions and the Bourbon Trail, Maple Hill Manor is also the perfect place to go and do nothing but relax. Football fans take note: Maple Hill Manor was the childhood home of Super Bowl MVP and Giants quarterback Phil Simms.

Food

Signature dishes at **Mordecai's on Main** (105 W. Main St., 859/336-3500, www.mordecaisonmain.com, 11am-midnight Tues.-Sat., 10am-2pm Sun., $6.99-18.49) include honey bourbon salmon, chicken in a mushroom bourbon cream sauce, New York strip marinated in bourbon, and bourbon-marinated pork chops, making it a perfect place for Bourbon Trail visitors to dine. If you've already had enough bourbon, the menu also offers burgers, sandwiches, and entrées prepared in other tasty ways. Located in a downtown building, Mordecai's is decorated with historic photos and offers a variety of seating options, including patio seating in the summer. Good food and good service make this Springfield's best dining option. The Friday and Saturday buffet is extremely popular, offering a selection of entrées as well as soup and salad.

THE BOURBON CHASE

Although most people choose to cover the Bourbon Trail in an automobile, some believe the best way to take in the landscape of this part of Kentucky is on foot—hence, the reason the annual **Bourbon Chase** (www.bourbonchase.com), a 200-mile relay race along the Bourbon Trail, sells out every year months before its October start date.

Teams of 6 or 12 members begin the race at Jim Beam Distillery in Clermont, with teams taking off every 15 minutes during the first day. Each runner covers 3-9 miles before being replaced by a teammate. The course moves from Clermont to Bardstown, then passes through Loretto, Lebanon, Springfield, Perryville, Stanford, Danville, Harrodsburg, Lawrenceburg, Versailles, Frankfort, and Midway before ending in Lexington, where a huge party awaits participants. The race can take up to 35 hours, with runners pounding the pavement both day and night. Towns along the way are set up to support and celebrate the teams regardless of what hour the runners and their teammates pass through.

Autumn is a beautiful time of year to visit the Bourbon Trail region of Kentucky, so whether you're interested in participating in the race or just cheering on the runners, put the Bourbon Chase on your calendar.

Information and Services

The **Springfield Tourism Commission** (127 W. Main St., 859/336-5440, www.seespringfieldky.com, 9am-5pm Mon.-Fri.) has an office in the restored Opera House. After you gather any information you need, take a few minutes for an informal tour of the building, which was built around 1900 and renovated in 2004.

Getting There and Around

Springfield is 17 miles (25 minutes) east of Bardstown on U.S. 150. Located right past the intersection of U.S. 150 and KY 55, Springfield is on the route between Bardstown and Lebanon and thus easy to add to any Bourbon Trail itinerary.

The Bourbon Trail and Nearby Towns

In 1999, the Kentucky Distillers Association decided to turn one of the state's most distinct industries into what is now one of its biggest tourist attractions, creating an official Bourbon Trail. This official trail, which highlights seven distilleries, serves as a great starting point for those seeking to get a taste of Kentucky, both literally and figuratively. However, bourbon fanatics will want to go beyond the trail to visit additional major distilleries as well as the craft distilleries that have opened in recent years, feeding off the bourbon craze. Not all of Kentucky's bourbon sites are located in this region, but the area is definitely the heart of bourbon country. It's also home to small towns and rolling countryside, where the Kentucky spirit is distilled day in and day out.

CLERMONT

For those starting the trail from Louisville, Clermont will be your first stop. Not actually a city or even a town, Clermont is just a small stretch of road that happens to be home to the world's largest bourbon distillery. Most bourbon tourists group Clermont in with Bardstown, which is just a bit further down the road.

Jim Beam American Stillhouse

In an idyllic setting, **Jim Beam American**

Stillhouse (526 Happy Hollow Rd., 502/543-9877, www.americanstillhouse.com, 9am-5:30pm Mon.-Sat., noon-4:30pm Sun. Mar.-Dec.) is definitely worth a visit since the distillery's upgrade and expansion in 2012. Guided tours ($10) begin at the natural limestone water well and don't end until you've seen every part of the process, from mashing to distilling, barreling, storing, and bottling. Tours end with your choice of two tastings from a selection of 15 options. The 1.25-hour tours, which are very hands-on and allow you to participate in the distilling process, are offered on the half-hour 9:30am-3:30pm Monday-Saturday and 12:30pm-3pm Sunday. Twice a month, a six-hour bourbon experience ($199) that includes a meeting with the master distiller, a meal, and a commemorative bottle of bourbon are offered, giving the true connoisseur an insider's experience. Reservations are highly recommended.

Four Roses Warehouses

Although their distillery is located in Lawrenceburg, **Four Roses** maintains their bottling facilities and warehouse off-site (624 Lotus Rd., Cox's Creek, 502/543-2664, http://fourrosesbourbon.com). Unique among bourbon distilleries, Four Roses uses single-story warehouses to age their bourbon, believing this helps minimize temperature fluctuations and creates a more consistent taste. True bourbon aficionados may want to arrange a tour of the facilities, available by reservation only.

◖ Bernheim Arboretum

Grateful for his success in the whiskey business, Isaac W. Bernheim chose to give back to the state of Kentucky by purchasing 14,000 acres for use as an arboretum. Designed by the Olmsted landscape firm, **Bernheim Arboretum and Research Center** (2499 Old State Hwy. 245, 502/955-8512, www.bernheim.org, 7am-sunset daily, free weekdays, $5 per car weekends and holidays) opened to the public in 1950 and has since become an oasis for people all around the region. Begin your visit at the LEED Platinum Certified Visitors Center, a magnificent "green" building where you can pick up maps, learn about the arboretum, browse the gift shop, or enjoy a snack or light lunch at the café. The arboretum offers plenty of activities. Those seeking more passive recreation opportunities can picnic, view wildlife, and wander around the arboretum's many gardens and collections, including an open prairie habitat and the largest holly collection in North America. If you're after something more active, take advantage of the arboretum's 35 miles of hiking trails, 3.7-mile bike trail, roadside bike lanes, and the fishing areas at Lake Nevin. Be sure to check out the Canopy Tree Walk, a boardwalk that puts you 75 feet over the forest floor and offers splendid views year-round, though autumn is especially breathtaking. Hikers will find the 13.75-mile Millennium Trail through the knobs of Kentucky to be one of the region's best trails. Bernheim offers a robust schedule of events that includes moonlight hikes, ECO Kids activities, art classes, and seasonal festivities. Check their website for a full listing.

Accommodations and Food

Just north of Bernheim and Jim Beam, you'll find a strip of fast-food restaurants as well as a chain hotel or two. There's no real reason to stay overnight in the area, and with Clermont located between Bardstown and Louisville, you have plenty of options in either direction. Your best bet for lunch is to bring a picnic and enjoy it on the grounds of Bernheim or check out the tasty sandwiches at their café.

Getting There

Clermont is about 15 miles (20 minutes) northwest of Bardstown. From the center of Bardstown, take Third Street to northbound KY 245, where you'll turn left and then travel about 13.5 miles to reach Clermont's attractions.

Clermont is about 27 miles (30 minutes) south of downtown Louisville. To get to Clermont, simply follow southbound I-65 to the KY 245 exit (Exit 112). Turn left onto KY

245, and you'll find Bernheim on your right and Jim Beam just past it on your left.

LORETTO

After you check out the distilleries in Clermont and Bardstown, the next stop on your west-to-east tour of Kentucky's bourbon distilleries is Loretto. Best described as a hamlet, Loretto, with a population of about 600, probably wouldn't make the map if it weren't for the iconic Maker's Mark distillery being located here.

◖ Maker's Mark Distillery

Set on a village-like campus, **Maker's Mark Distillery** (3350 Burks Spring Rd., 270/865-2099, www.makersmark.com) wins the award for most picturesque distillery. The buildings are uniformly dark brown, tan, and red—the trademark colors of Maker's Mark—with cut-out bourbon bottles on every window shutter. The tour starts in a home museum decorated to the 1950 period when the Samuels family began Maker's Mark. It then takes in the spotless distillery, where bourbon is still brewed in

© THERESA DOWELL BLACKINTON

Maker's Mark Distillery

wooden vats; the bottling line, where the bottles are dipped in their famous red wax; and the warehouse, where barrels are still rotated during their six-year aging process. The finale is a well-conducted tasting of bourbon at four different stages, complemented with a bourbon ball. Tours ($9) are offered once an hour on the half-hour 9:30am-3:30pm Monday-Saturday year-round and 11:30am-3:30pm Sunday, March-December.

Sisters of Loretto

Founded on the Kentucky frontier in 1812, the **Sisters of Loretto** (515 Nerinx Rd., 270/865-7096, www.lorettocommunity.org) moved to their current campus in 1824. Visitors are welcome on the campus, a place of mesmerizing beauty that, in addition to preserving vast wild spaces, also supports a working farm and many historical buildings. Don't miss the Rhodes Hall Art Gallery, where the amazing sculptures of Sister Jeanne Dueber are displayed. You'll also want to stroll the walking paths and visit the cemetery and AIDS garden. A Heritage Center (10am-noon and 1pm-3:30pm Tues.-Fri., 1pm-3:30pm Sat.-Sun.) documents the history of the order and this community through museum displays. The Sisters of Loretto welcome retreatants. Those seeking solitude and reflection should inquire about staying in one of the seven Cedars of Peace cabins on campus.

Accommodations and Food

Although **Hill House Bed and Breakfast** (110 Holy Cross Rd., 877/280-2300, www.thehillhouseky.com, $105-135) dates to the 1800s, the house has been completely gutted and renovated. Save for the original floors and staircase, Hill House is basically a brand-new house and thus sports completely modern rooms and amenities, though antique furniture and classic stylings make the four queen guest rooms as well as the common areas feel warm and inviting. Guests are not only treated to a delicious breakfast, but are also offered wine and cheese in the afternoon.

Loretto is a very small community. For additional accommodation options, as well as a selection of restaurants, head to Lebanon, which is just a few miles southeast.

Getting There

From Bardstown, the easiest way to get to Maker's Mark, which is about 30 minutes away, is to travel south on KY 49 for 9.6 miles. At this point, KY 49 will turn off to the left, but you'll want to stay straight onto KY 527 and drive 3.7 miles to where it intersects with KY 52. Turn left onto KY 52 and drive 4.4 miles to Burkes Spring Road, which leads back to the distillery. You'll pass through "downtown" Loretto on your way. To reach the Sisters of Loretto, stay on KY 49 when it turns left and follow it for five miles to a T-intersection with Nerinx Road, onto which you'll turn left.

From Frankfort (61 miles; 1.5 hours) or Lawrenceburg (48 miles; 1 hour), take southbound U.S. 127 to westbound Blue Grass Parkway and drive 16.9 miles to KY 555 (Exit 42). Proceed 14.7 miles on KY 555 to KY 152. Turn right onto KY 152, and drive 2.8 miles to KY 429. Turn left onto KY 429 and drive 4.2 miles to Burkes Spring Road, onto which you'll turn right to reach the distillery. From Lexington (65 miles; 1.5 hours), take westbound U.S. 60 to the Blue Grass Parkway and then follow the directions from Frankfort. From Louisville (60 miles; 1 hour 20 minutes), head to Bardstown first and then follow the directions from there.

A nine-mile stretch of KY 49 connects Loretto with Lebanon (15 minutes).

LEBANON

Lebanon likes to call itself the heart of Kentucky, as it's located at the state's geographic center. It's also about the midway point on the Bourbon Trail. Besides being the gateway to Maker's Mark, Lebanon, named for the biblical Promised Land location, is home to the cooperage where many of Kentucky's bourbon barrels originate, as well as a young craft distillery.

Kentucky Cooperage

One visit to a distillery and you'll know how important the barrels are to bourbon making. It wouldn't be bourbon without them. Therefore, to get a full understanding of bourbon, you need to head to **Kentucky Cooperage** (712 E. Main St., 270/692-4674, www.independent-stavecompany.com, tours at 9:30am and 1pm Mon.-Fri., free), where most of Kentucky's bourbon barrels are made. The tour has three stops—one in the stave, where barrels are constructed; one in the finishing room, where the all-important charring is done; and one at the cooper's, where barrels that don't pass inspection are repaired by hand. Informative videos are shown at each stop, filling you in on any processes that you might not see firsthand. Because this is a factory tour, closed-toe shoes are required and cameras are not permitted.

Limestone Branch Distillery

Descended from a long line of distillers, brothers Steve and Paul Beam are carrying on the family tradition at their **Limestone Branch Distillery** (1280 Veterans Memorial Hwy., 270/699-9004, www.limestonebranch.com, 10am-5pm Mon.-Sat., 1pm-5pm Sun.), which opened in 2012. While their first batches of bourbon age, the micro-distillery is focusing on single-barrel batches of fruit-flavored moonshine (also called sugarshine). The free half-hour tours, which depart on the hour, take you into the one room where the whole operation is currently centered, allowing you to see the 150-gallon hand-hammered copper still, the fermentation barrels, and the bottling area. Tours end with a tasting. Limestone Branch is a fun diversion from the larger bourbon distilleries, allowing you to experience a much smaller operation and taste something a bit different.

WhiteMoon Winery

Lebanon might be a small town, but they've got all your drinking needs covered—bourbon, moonshine, and now, thanks to **WhiteMoon Winery** (25 Arthur Mattingly Rd., 270/865-4564, 10am-6pm Mon.-Sat.,

1pm-5pm Sun.), wine as well. In the hilly countryside between Maker's Mark and Limestone Branch, WhiteMoon Winery is producing red, white, and rosé wines, ranging from dry to sweet. Stop in to sip some wines while enjoying the scenic views.

Marion County Heritage Center

Through artifacts and rotating exhibits, the **Marion County Heritage Center** (120 W. Main St., 270/699-9455, 10am-4pm Mon.-Fri., 10am-1pm Sat., free) documents the history of the region all the way up to the present day, which means it includes an entire section dedicated to Turtleman (aka Ernie Lee Brown, Jr.), the Lebanon native now known to Animal Planet viewers everywhere.

Lebanon National Cemetery

Designated a national cemetery in 1867, the land that became **Lebanon National Cemetery** (20 KY 208, sunrise-sunset daily) was first used to bury 865 Union dead from the 1862 Battle of Perryville. Since then, service members from all of the United States's wars have been, and continue to be, interred here. Take a stroll on the somber grounds to remember the sacrifices made by soldiers standing in defense of the United States. Services take place on Memorial and Veterans Day, and the cemetery participates in the Wreaths Across America program in December.

Agritourism

Lebanon is surrounded by agricultural land, with farmers growing crops and raising livestock on acres of rich soil. Many of these farms welcome visits by the public, although because they are all working farms, they do ask that visitors make arrangements in advance.

Alpacas have become a popular farm animal in recent years, and at **Serenity Farm** (1380 Frogg Lane, Raywick, 270/692-8743 www.alpacasatserenityfarm.com), owner Tim Auch will gladly show you around and introduce you to his animals. More common to Kentucky are horses, which you can find at **Meadow Creek Farm** (KY 49 & KY 84, 270/692-0021).

Although Kentucky is best known for its thoroughbred horses, the area around Lebanon is standardbred territory, and Meadow Creek produces the best standardbreds around, including world champion Sportswriter.

One of many such displays in the state, the **Marion County Quilt Trail** takes visitors on a tour of the countryside in search of 45 quilt patches decorating barns and other structures. Pick up a brochure at the Lebanon visitors center for more information on each of the designs as well as suggestions for other sites to look for along the way. You'll even learn how to identify different breeds of cow.

Tours

Because Lebanon was home to a train depot and Union Commissary, it felt the wrath of Confederate General John Hunt Morgan on all three of his Civil War raids into Kentucky. A self-guided walking or driving tour points out sites of interest located along the **John Hunt Morgan Trail.** After completing this tour, head to nearby Bradfordsville to explore the **William Clark Quantrill Trail,** a route that commemorates sites related to the notorious outlaw's guerilla attacks.

Architecture buffs may prefer the **Historic Homes & Landmarks Tour,** which offers separate walking and driving tours and points out buildings of note, many of which date to before the Civil War. Brochures with maps for all tours are available at the visitors center.

Nightlife

Once a famous party town thanks to the former Club 68, which hosted the likes of Tina Turner, CCR, and Little Richard, Lebanon is no longer as wild as it once was, but the town still knows how to have a good time. To get in on the fun, set your sights on **Chasers** (110 N. Proctor Knott Ave., 270/699-2221, 4:30pm-1am Mon.-Sat.) or **McB's Bar and Grill** (212 W. Main St., 270/692-3970, http://mcbsbargrill.webs.com, 9pm-1am Tues. and Thurs.-Sat.).

Festivals and Events

Lebanon complements their nightlife with a

packed schedule of festivals, oftentimes putting on two or three events at once. Check the tourism website for a full listing of festivals.

The year's biggest event is **Marion County Country Ham Days** (www.visitlebanonky. com), held on the last weekend of September. In addition to offering all the country ham a person could possibly consume, the festival features the PIGasus parade, a hog calling contest, a car show, carnival, 5K race, and live entertainment.

Fans of radio-controlled planes won't want to miss the weeklong **Jets Over Kentucky** (www.visitlebanonky.com), which takes place at the Lebanon-Springfield Airport in early July. As many as 200 pilots put their jets to the test in dogfights, aerobatic competitions, and other contests. Spectators are welcome to enjoy the show and chat with pilots.

Beat the winter doldrums by attending the **Kentucky Bluegrass Music Kickoff** (www.visitlebanonky.com), which features jam sessions, workshops, and a Saturday night concert headlined by big names in bluegrass. The kickoff is held on a Friday and Saturday in January.

Recreation

Two fishing spots are located just outside downtown Lebanon. Both **Fagan Branch Reservoir** (370 Fagan Branch Rd.) and **Marion County Sportsman's Lake** (716 Sportsman Lake Rd.) are stocked with largemouth bass, smallmouth bass, bluegill, and other popular species. At Fagan Branch Reservoir, you'll also find the Cecil L. Gorley Naturalist Trail, a 3.2-mile loop around the lake that has a notable 43 bridges. The grounds at Sportsman's Lake are open for deer, squirrel, and waterfowl hunting, and also contain archery and skeet ranges.

Take in a 100-mile view that encompasses three counties at **Scott's Ridge Lookout** (KY 84). From a maintained perch, you can look out over a wide swath of farmland, the panorama seemingly endless. The view takes on remarkably different characteristics with each season.

Accommodations

Apparently even John Hunt Morgan and his Raiders found the classic home that is now **Myrtledene Bed and Breakfast** (370 N. Spalding Ave., Lebanon, 270/692-2223, www. myrtledene.com, $95) to be beautiful, as they spared it during their raids through the state. In fact, instead of setting it on fire, they turned it into their headquarters while in Lebanon. Reserve either the queen room or the room with two twin beds, and enjoy the sense of history preserved in the B&B, which is furnished in antiques. On a nice day, take advantage of the grounds, which are complete with fish ponds, hammocks, and swings. Should the weather not cooperate, the rooms are fully equipped with television and wireless Internet, and the house has a library and piano.

Those looking for a standard hotel should book a room at the **Hampton Inn** (1125 Loretto Rd., 270/699-4000, www.hamptoninn.com, $99), which is fresh and clean and provides all the modern amenities. A free all-you-can-eat hot breakfast is offered each morning.

The **Rosewood Cabins** (520 Fairway Dr., 270/692-0506, www.rosewoodgolfcourse.com) are an excellent choice for families or groups of friends, as each cabin has two bedrooms with two double beds in each, as well as a living room and a kitchenette. Golfers will particularly enjoy these cabins because they are located on a course, and cabin rental allows for unlimited golf. A one-night stay is $100, with nightly rates decreasing the longer you stay.

Food

For breakfast or lunch, check out **Joe's Deli on Main** (101 S. Spalding Ave., 270/321-4033, www.joesdelionmain.com, 7am-4pm Mon.-Fri., 8am-2pm Sun., $1.50-7.99). Lighter eaters can choose a breakfast biscuit sandwich, while those who like to start their day with a hearty meal will want to consider the biscuits and gravy, pancakes, or traditional breakfast of eggs, bacon or sausage, potatoes, and biscuit or toast. For lunch, choose from deli sandwiches and wraps, hot sandwiches, burgers, chicken tenders, and salads.

The people behind **Ragetti's Fine Italian Dining** (213 W. Main St., 270/692-1322,

11am-9pm Mon.-Thurs., 11am-10pm Fri.-Sat., noon-9pm Sun., $5.95-10.95) have transformed a former Hardee's into a cozy restaurant decorated with old photos of Lebanon. You'll find hearty pastas, filling pizzas, and a broad selection of subs and strombolis on the menu. Half-portions are available at lunch, and unless you skipped breakfast, it's more than enough food to take you to dinner.

If you're looking for a little flavor in your life, consider **La Fuente** (784 W. Main St., 270/692-3800, 11am-10pm Sun.-Thurs., 11am-10:30pm Fri.-Sat., $5.25-11.99). Though you might wonder how good a Mexican restaurant in the heart of Kentucky can be, you'd be wrong not to give it a chance. Thanks to the area's agricultural nature, a significant population of Hispanics call Lebanon home, and the food at La Fuente is made to please. Lunch specials, which include tacos, tamales, enchiladas, chalupas, and tostadas, start at $3.75.

Information and Services

Tucked away on the second floor of the former junior high school, in what is now called Centre Square, the friendly folks at the **Lebanon Tourist & Convention Commission** (239 N. Spalding Ave., Ste. 200, 270/692-0021, www.visitlebanonky.com, 8am-5pm Mon.-Fri.) will gladly help you plan your visit to Lebanon.

Getting There and Around

From Bardstown (35 minutes), take eastbound U.S. 150 about 15 miles to southbound KY 55, which will, after an additional 9 miles, land you on Lebanon's Main Street. If you're coming from Frankfort or Lexington (both 1.25 hours), take westbound Blue Grass Parkway to southbound KY 555 (Exit 42). After about 15 miles, KY 555 becomes KY 55; continue straight for another 9 miles to reach Lebanon.

Lebanon is located along U.S. 68, which is designated a scenic highway in Kentucky. It begins in Western Kentucky near Illinois, and then travels east and northeast, passing through Land Between the Lakes, Bowling Green, Lexington, and many smaller towns in between before exiting into Ohio at Maysville. If you're

looking for a scenic driving route, U.S. 68 is a good one. Locally, you can take it to reach Perryville and Harrodsburg in the Lexington and Horse Country region of the state.

When driving around the area, be particularly watchful for deer as they are abundant in the area and dangerous to motorists. If you see one cross the road, proceed with extreme caution because others are usually nearby.

LAWRENCEBURG

Lawrenceburg specializes in the fine things in life, which here in Kentucky are bourbon, wine, and cigars made with Kentucky tobacco. Visitors are invited to tour sites related to all three, and no one's going to stop you from taking as many souvenirs of each with you as you'd like. Within easy reach of Frankfort, Lawrenceburg is a small town with a quaint downtown surrounded by farmland.

Four Roses Distillery

Well-known in the United States in the first half of the 20th century, Four Roses then dropped off of most people's radar for the rest of that century as it became an export-only product, sold in Europe and Japan but not in its home country. However, that all changed in 2003, when it came back on the domestic market, and since then, Four Roses' 10 bourbons have caught on big-time. Learn more about the bourbons on a tour of the **Four Roses Distillery** (1224 Bonds Mill Rd., 502/839-3436, http://fourrosesbourbon.com), which is notable for its Spanish Mission-style architecture. Complimentary tours depart on the hour 9am-3pm Monday-Saturday and noon-3pm Sunday. Because the aging warehouses and bottling facilities are located off-site in Clermont, the tour is shorter than those offered at other distilleries, but it does end with a tasting of three different bourbons.

Wild Turkey Distillery

The tour ($5) at **Wild Turkey Distillery** (1525 Tyrone Rd., 502/839-2182, www.wildturkeybourbon.com) provides one of the most in-depth looks at the process by which raw grains

BARDSTOWN

© THERESA DOWELL BLACKINTON

Four Roses is known for its unusual Spanish Mission-style architecture.

are turned into smooth bourbon, though the facilities are a bit more industrial than some of the others. After watching a short film featuring master distiller Jimmy Russell, who has been at Wild Turkey for more than 55 years, visitors witness production step-by-step. Watch a grain truck empty its load, see the yeast starter and grain mash being pumped into the fermenter, poke your head into vats in various stages of fermentation, compare the bourbon-to-be after the first and the second condensation and distillation, and observe the filling of barrels. A new visitors center and upgraded facilities were being added in 2013. Tours are offered on the hour 9am-3pm Monday-Saturday year-round and noon-3pm Sunday, March-November.

Lovers Leap Vineyards & Winery

With 30 acres of vines set on a total of 66 acres, **Lovers Leap Vineyards & Winery** (1180 Lanes Mill Rd., 502/839-1299, www.loversleapwine.com, 11am-6pm Wed.-Sat., 1pm-5pm Sun.) is scenically set on the hills above the Kentucky River. The Leet Family, who bought the vineyard in 2008 and do every step from growing the grapes to bottling the final product on-site, produce white, blush, red, and dessert wines that have medaled at competitions in California, New York, Texas, and Kentucky. Stop in for a tour and tasting.

Rising Sons Winery

With 10 acres of grapes located on their 45-acre family-run winery, **Rising Sons Winery** (643 N. Main St., 502/600-0224, www.risingsonswinery.com, 11am-7pm Sat., 1pm-5pm Sun.) offers visitors the chance to indulge in wine while relaxing on the farm. Rising Sons produces four dry reds, one semisweet red, one semisweet white, one sweet white, and a blackberry dessert wine.

Kentucky Gentlemen Cigars

At **Kentucky Gentlemen Cigars** (1056 Ninevah Rd., 502/839-9226, www.kentuckygentlemencigars.com, 10am-5pm Mon.-Sat.), two of Kentucky's most heralded products—bourbon and tobacco—are combined to make cigars that have gotten the attention of cigar fans around the nation and world. To make the hand-rolled cigars, tobacco is aged for six months in used bourbon barrels. Though the bourbon cigars are most popular, Kentucky Gentlemen Cigars also produces moonshine, mint julep, wine, and other flavored cigars. Stop by to see the production process and learn about this Kentucky Proud business.

Events

Exalting burgoo, a spicy barbecue-style stew popular in Kentucky, the **Anderson County Burgoo Festival** (www.kentuckyburgoo.com) is held annually in Lawrenceburg on the last weekend of September. The main point of the festival is to sample as much burgoo as you can handle, but for a little balance, live music, art and history exhibitions, pageants, and tractor pulls are also on the schedule.

Accommodations

Lawrenceburg Bed & Breakfast (643 N. Main St., 502/930-8242, http://lawrenceburgbb. com, $125) accommodates guests in two spacious suites, each with king bed and private bathroom. For larger groups, an extra room is available, but it shares the bathroom with a suite. Guests are treated to a four-course gourmet breakfast as well as wine and cheese in the afternoon and home-baked desserts in the evening, which can be enjoyed on the large and inviting front porch.

Food

C **Heavens to Betsy** (124 Main St., 502/859-9291, 11am-6pm Tues.-Fri., 11am-4pm Sat., $6.75-8.50) is the place to stop for lunch along the Bourbon Trail. The menu is deceptively simple—nine cold sandwiches, five hot sandwiches, two soups, and an assortment of side salads—but the sandwiches are enormous and made with the finest ingredients. It's not uncommon to hear someone say "best sandwich ever" after they finish their reuben or the H2B pretzel panini, which features deli ham, beer cheese, and mild banana peppers on a pretzel bun. You might feel too full for dessert, but you'll still want to get a piece of cake—take it to go if you must.

Information and Services

The **Anderson County Tourism Commission** (502/517-6362, www.visitlawrenceburgky. com) can provide you with information on Lawrenceburg. While in town, stop into City Hall (100 N. Main St., 9am-5pm Mon.-Fri.), where tourist information is available in the foyer of the historic building.

Getting There and Around

Lawrenceburg lies at the intersection of U.S. 62 and U.S. 127. It's about 15 miles (25 minutes) south of Frankfort on U.S. 127, and about 25 miles (40 minutes) west of Lexington if you take U.S. 60 to Versailles and then switch to U.S. 62. From Bardstown (45 minutes), travel 34 miles on eastbound Blue Grass Parkway to northbound U.S. 127, which after 5 miles will lead to Lawrenceburg. If you're coming from nearby Danville (30 miles; 40 minutes) or Harrodsburg (20 miles; 25 minutes), just follow northbound U.S. 127.

BARDSTOWN

KENTUCKY DISTILLERIES, BIG AND SMALL

Created by the Kentucky Distillers Association, the Bourbon Trail is an official route that was put together as a means of drawing tourists to member distilleries. It does not, however, include all of the distilleries in the state, many of which are located in the area covered by this chapter, the heart of the bourbon distilling area, but some of which are located elsewhere. For those wishing to be comprehensive in their distillery touring, the list below covers all of Kentucky's major bourbon distilleries and their locations, moving from west to east.

- Evan Williams Bourbon Experience (www.evanwilliams.com), Louisville

- Jim Beam Distillery (www.americanstillhouse.com), Clermont

- Heaven Hill Distillery (www.heavenhill.com), Bardstown

- Barton 1792 Distillery (www.1792bourbon.com), Bardstown

- Maker's Mark Distillery (www.makersmark.com), Loretto

- Four Roses Distillery (www.fourrosesbourbon.com), Lawrenceburg

- Wild Turkey Distillery (http://wildturkeybourbon.com), Lawrenceburg

- Buffalo Trace (www.buffalotrace.com), Frankfort

- Woodford Reserve Distillery (www.woodfordreserve.com), Versailles

- Town Branch Distillery (www.kentuckyale.com), Lexington

In addition to the major distilleries, Kentucky is also home to multiple craft distilleries, not all of which make bourbon. Some focus specifically on other spirits (moonshine being particularly popular); some produce bourbon in addition to other spirits. These craft distilleries and their locations, again from west to east, are as follows.

- Silver Trail Distillery (http://lblmoonshine.com), Hardin

- MB Roland Distillery (www.mbrdistillery.com), Pembroke

- Corsair Artisan Distillery (www.corsairartisan.com), Bowling Green

- Willett Distillery (www.kentuckybourbonwhiskey.com), Bardstown

- Limestone Branch Distillery (http://limestonebranch.com), Lebanon

- Barrel House Distillery (http://barrelhousedistillery.com), Lexington

New distilleries continue to pop up throughout the state. At the time of research, the following distilleries had plans to open to the public for tours and tastings.

- Angel's Envy Distillery (www.angelsenvy.com), Louisville

- Michter's Distillery (www.michters.com), Louisville

- Nth Degree Distillery (www.nthdegreedistilling.com), Bellevue

All distilleries that were open at the time of research, big and small, receive full write-ups in the relevant chapters of this guidebook.

© THERESA DOWELL BLACKINTON

Willett Distillery

Frankfort

A favorite Kentucky joke asks "How do you pronounce the capital of Kentucky: Loo-IS-ville or Loo-EE-ville?" And while neither of those is the correct way to pronounce Louisville, the joke is that no matter how you pronounce it, Louisville is not the capital of Kentucky. Small, unassuming Frankfort is actually the capital of the Bluegrass State. Unlike many state capitals, Frankfort is neither big nor bustling. Sure, when government is in session, there's a bit more traffic on the roads and in the restaurants, but life still goes on at a measured pace and remains overwhelmingly hassle-free. Though politics can be ugly, Frankfort is charming. Attractive historic buildings line downtown streets, through which trains still pass daily; a "singing" bridge helps traffic move across the Kentucky River, which flows right through the city; and a plethora of parks preserve tracts of lush land perfect for picnicking, hiking, biking, and wildlife watching.

GOVERNMENT SIGHTS
Kentucky State Capitol
The **Kentucky State Capitol** (700 Capital Ave., 502/564-3449, http://capitol.ky.gov, 8am-4:30pm Mon.-Fri., 10am-2pm Sat., free), a beaux arts building with classical French influences throughout, celebrated its centennial in 2010. Visitors to the capitol will first notice the statues in the first-floor rotunda, which represent important figures in Kentucky history: President Abraham Lincoln, Statesman Henry Clay, Dr. Ephraim McDowell, Vice President Alben Barkley, and President of the Confederacy Jefferson Davis. Each level of the government occupies a floor of the capitol: The executive branch is located on the first floor, the judicial branch on the second, and

© THERESA DOWELL BLACKINTON

inside the Kentucky State Capitol

BARDSTOWN

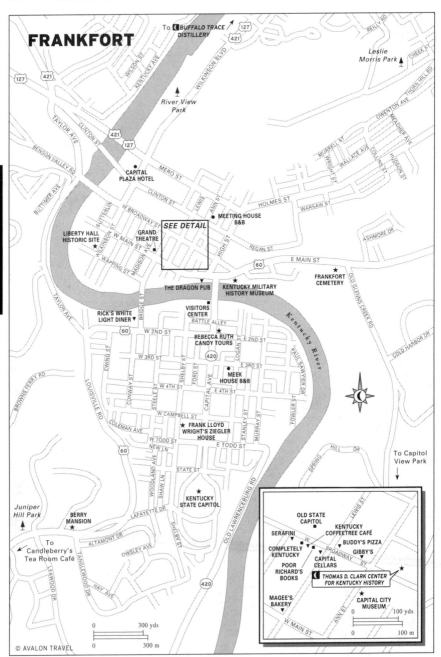

FRANKFORT

To **(** BUFFALO TRACE DISTILLERY

Leslie Morris Park

River View Park

CAPITAL PLAZA HOTEL

MEETING HOUSE B&B

SEE DETAIL

LIBERTY HALL HISTORIC SITE

GRAND THEATRE

THE DRAGON PUB

KENTUCKY MILITARY HISTORY MUSEUM

FRANKFORT CEMETERY

RICK'S WHITE LIGHT DINER

VISITORS CENTER

BATTLE ALLEY

REBECCA RUTH CANDY TOURS

MEEK HOUSE B&B

FRANK LLOYD WRIGHT'S ZIEGLER HOUSE

KENTUCKY STATE CAPITOL

Juniper Hill Park

BERRY MANSION

To Candleberry's Tea Room Café

To Capitol View Park

Kentucky River

0   300 yds
0   300 m

© AVALON TRAVEL

Detail inset:

OLD STATE CAPITOL

SERAFINI

KENTUCKY COFFEETREE CAFÉ

BUDDY'S PIZZA

COMPLETELY KENTUCKY

GIBBY'S

CAPITAL CELLARS

POOR RICHARD'S BOOKS

(THOMAS D. CLARK CENTER FOR KENTUCKY HISTORY

MAGEE'S BAKERY

CAPITAL CITY MUSEUM

W MAIN ST

0   100 yds
0   100 m

the legislative branch on the third. In addition to visiting the House and Senate chambers and the Supreme Court, don't miss the State Reception Room on the second floor, which puts one in mind of the Palace of Versailles thanks to its mirrors and chandeliers as well as its intricate decor. Visitors can ask for a map at the tour desk or download it from the website and explore the capitol on their own, or inquire about guided tours being offered that day. An ID is required for admission.

The grounds of the capitol are notable in their own right, designed by the Olmsted brothers, sons of legendary landscape architect Frederick Law Olmsted. The **Capitol Grounds Walking Tour** brochure, available at the desk inside the capitol or on the capitol website, outlines a route with stops at 37 sites. One of these stops is at the **Floral Clock,** which measures 34 feet across and is filled seasonally with more than 10,000 plants.

The Executive Mansion (www.governorsmansion.ky.gov), home to the governor and his family, is also located in the capitol complex. The mansion, built in the same beaux arts style as the capitol and specifically fashioned after one of Marie Antoinette's villas, is one of only a handful of executive residences in the nation that are open to the public. Free tours are offered 9am-11am on Tuesday and Thursday, but require an appointment (502/564-3449) and may be canceled if an event is being held at the mansion.

MUSEUMS AND HISTORICAL SIGHTS
◖ Thomas D. Clark Center for Kentucky History

As the one and only museum dedicated to Kentucky history—12,000 years of it—the **Thomas D. Clark Center for Kentucky History** (100 W. Broadway, 502/564-1792, http://history.ky.gov, 10am-4pm Wed., 10am-8pm Thurs., 10am-5pm Fri.-Sat., $4 adults, $2 youth 6-18) is home to a rich collection of artifacts, a portion of which are displayed in the center's permanent exhibit, with others appearing in temporary exhibits. The permanent exhibit, A

Kentucky Journey, tells the story of the state era by era with the help of authentic items as well as hands-on activities and animatronic characters. Don't miss Museum Theater, an impressive performance series in which on-staff actors write and present short plays about various aspects of Kentucky history. Performances take place on Saturday afternoons at 1pm and 3pm as well as at varying times during the week. Check the online calendar for the current schedule. Admission to the center also includes admission to the Old State Capitol and the Kentucky Military History Museum.

Genealogists will want to visit the center's **Martin F. Schmidt Library,** which is the premier center for Kentucky genealogy research. Family history workshops held 6:30pm-7:30pm every Thursday help those interested in tracing their roots establish a plan and identify resources.

Old State Capitol

Because the plans for the current state capitol required more space than was available at the site of the third capitol (the first two burned down), the **Old State Capitol** (Broadway and St. Clair St., 502/564-1792, http://history.ky.gov, 10am-4pm Wed., 10am-8pm Thurs., 10am-5pm Fri.-Sat., $4 adults, $2 youth 6-18) was not demolished when the new capitol was opened in 1910, and to this day still stands as a monument to history. Designed by Gideon Shyrock and meant to resemble a Greek temple, the Old State Capitol was built out of Kentucky marble (aka limestone) and was considered architecturally advanced when completed in 1830. The circular staircase, held in place by a single keystone, is indeed remarkable and a must-see for architecture buffs. Tours take you into the House and Senate chambers, furnished mainly in reproduction furniture but with original paintings; the library; the court chambers; and the first-floor office rooms, which house an exhibit on the capitol lawn—host to everything from cattle to concerts. Admission to the Old State Capitol also includes admission to the Thomas D. Clark Center for Kentucky History and the Kentucky Military History Museum.

© THERESA DOWELL BLACKINTON

Old State Capitol

Kentucky Military History Museum

After a five-year renovation, the Old State Arsenal has opened as the **Kentucky Military History Museum** (125 E. Main St., 502/564-1792, http://history.ky.gov, 10am-4pm Wed., 10am-8pm Thurs., 10am-5pm Fri.-Sat., $4 adults, $2 youth 6-18), with exhibitions that detail Kentucky's involvement in conflicts from the War of 1812 to the recent engagements in Iraq and Afghanistan. Artifacts and oral histories from veterans help visitors get a sense of military history. Admission to the Kentucky Military History Museum also includes admission to the Thomas D. Clark Center for Kentucky History and the Old State Capitol.

Capital City Museum

Housed in the former Capital Hotel, which dates to the 1850s, the **Capital City Museum** (325 Ann St., 502/696-0607, www.capitalcitymuseum.com, 10am-4pm Mon.-Sat., free) presents the story of Frankfort, from the founding of the town on the Kentucky River to its successful bid to become the state capital to its current state. Photos, artifacts, and life-size dioramas make the history accessible and interesting in this small museum.

Liberty Hall Historic Site

Built at the end of the 18th century for U.S. Senator John Brown, **Liberty Hall** (202 Wilkinson St., 502/227-2560, www.liberty-hall.org, tours at noon, 1:30pm, 3pm Tues.-Sat., spring-fall, $6 adults, $5 seniors, $2 youth 5-18) was one of the first brick buildings in Frankfort and remains an important landmark. The neighboring Orlando Brown House, though built in the Greek revival style, also belonged to Senator Brown, who had it built in 1835 so that each of his sons would inherit a house. Today, hour-long tours take visitors through both properties, with guides helping to interpret history, architecture, and decor through the story of the Brown family. The tour doesn't include the grounds, but you should pad your schedule so that you have time

BARDSTOWN

© THERESA DOWELL BLACKINTON

bourbon tasting at Buffalo Trace

to wander the lawn and gardens, which lead down to the Kentucky River.

Berry Mansion

Once owned by a wealthy family involved in the whiskey industry, the 22-room **Berry Mansion** (700 Louisville Rd., 502/564-3449, www.historicproperties.ky.gov, 8:30am-4pm Mon.-Fri., free), built from stone quarried on the property, now houses government offices and hosts special events, including weddings. Tours, which include highlights of the foyer, dining room, library, drawing room, music room, service wing, and grounds, can be scheduled through the capitol tour desk at the listed phone number. Go ahead and gawk at the large pipe organ in the ornate music room; that room alone, which was added in 1912, cost nearly as much as the entire Executive Mansion.

Frankfort Cemetery

Though governors, artists, military heroes, and the developer of Bibb lettuce all rest eternally at **Frankfort Cemetery** (215 E. Main St.,

502/227-2403, dawn-dusk), the burial ground's most famous residents are the Boones: Daniel and his wife, Rebecca. Though both Boones died and were buried in Missouri, they were brought back to Kentucky and interred in Frankfort in 1845. A tall rectangular monument, which stands on a bluff overlooking the Kentucky River and the capitol, marks their shared grave. Pick up a map and brochure at the information center or just follow the signs to Daniel Boone's grave.

BOURBON SIGHTS
◖ Buffalo Trace Distillery

Thanks to the fact that it was allowed to remain open during Prohibition as one of four distilleries authorized to produce "medicinal" liquor, **Buffalo Trace Distillery** (1001 Wilkinson Blvd., 502/696-5926, www.buffalotrace.com) owns the title of the oldest continually operating distillery in America. A complimentary tour of Buffalo Trace starts with a short video that relays the history of the region and the distillery; continues with a peek at Warehouse D, where the 13 different bourbons made at the distillery are aged; segues into a visit to the line where premium bourbons are hand-bottled; and ends with a tasting, where you can choose two tastes from a selection that will include a couple of bourbons as well as other spirits made at the distillery. Tours, which depart on the hour, are offered 9am-4pm Monday-Saturday year-round and noon-3pm Sunday April-October.

In addition to the standard tour, Buffalo Trace also offers a Hard Hat Tour (10:30am and 1:30pm Mon.-Fri. and 10:30am Sat.), which shows the step-by-step process by which bourbon is made—from grain delivery through fermentation and distillation. Architecture and history aficionados will want to sign up for the National Historic Landmark Tour (11:30am Mon.-Fri.), which focuses on the growth that took place at Buffalo Trace from 1930 to 1950 as Americans were once again allowed to legally consume alcohol. Believers in the supernatural will want to check out the Ghost Tour (7pm Thurs.-Sat.), on which you'll hear stories of the ghosts said to haunt the distillery and see some of its spookier sites. All three of the specialty tours are complimentary, but they do require reservations.

Rebecca Ruth Candy Tours

Thanks to the creation of the now-famous bourbon ball, products from **Rebecca Ruth Candy** (112 E. 2nd St., 502/223-7475, www. rebeccaruth.com, 10am-noon and 1pm-5:30pm Mon.-Sat., Apr.-Nov.) are enjoyed around the country and even internationally. The business didn't start out with such global aspirations, however. Instead, it was founded by two substitute schoolteachers, Ruth Hanly and Rebecca Gooch, who decided they had more of a knack for making candy than for teaching. Your sweet tooth will agree. Take a 20-minute tour ($3) of the small facility (which somehow manages to produce more than three million pieces of candy each year) to learn about the history of the business and the women, see the century-old stove where candy is made, and hear the story of how an offhanded comment led to the development of their signature candy. Samples are included on the tour.

OTHER SIGHTS

Salato Wildlife Education Center

Run by the Department of Fish and Wildlife, the **Salato Wildlife Education Center** (1 Sportsman Ln., 502/564-7863, http://fw.ky. gov, 9am-5pm Tues.-Fri., 10am-5pm Sat., $4 adults, $2 youth 5-18) seeks to teach visitors about Kentucky ecosystems and the creation and protection of wildlife habitats. Start your visit in the exhibition hall, where you can check out live snakes, frogs, and fish and dioramas of larger stuffed animals. Then hit the paved path for a circuit that will take you through a diversity of habitats and past large, natural enclosures housing eagles, black bears, elk, bison, bobcats, and deer. Those looking for a little more adventure will want to lace up their hiking books and explore the 0.5-mile red-blazed HabiTrek Trail, which connects with the 0.2-mile yellow-blazed Prairie Trail, or try out the three-mile white-blazed Pea Ridge Loop Trail.

The complex also offers two fishing lakes and picnic areas, so pack your lunch and make it a day. There is no fee to access the hiking trails, lakes, and picnic areas.

Kentucky State University

Created in 1886 to provide higher education to Kentucky's African Americans, **Kentucky State University** (400 E. Main St., 502/597-6000, www.kysu.edu) remains proud of its heritage while now serving a diverse student body. Visitors to the campus will want to stop in the Jackson Hall gallery and lobby, as well as the Visitor and Information Center in the Carroll Academic Services building to see rotating exhibitions culled from the collections of the Center of Excellence for the Study of Kentucky African Americans. A Kentucky Civil Rights Hall of Fame, which honors 52 inductees, can be viewed in the Carl Hill Student Center Ballroom. Campus maps are available at the Visitor and Information Center.

Kentucky Vietnam Veterans Memorial

The **Kentucky Vietnam Veterans Memorial** (300 Coffee Tree Rd., www.kyvietnammemorial.net) honors the 125,000 Kentuckians who served in the conflict, including the 1,103 who were killed. The design, by architect and veteran Helm Roberts, is unusual: The memorial is a very large sundial. The base, which is granite, is inscribed with the names of those who lost their lives and is patterned in such a way that on the anniversary of their death, the shadow of the sundial pointer falls on their name. Verses from Ecclesiastes are also inscribed in the base.

Frank Lloyd Wright's Ziegler House

Architecture fans will want to drive by the **Ziegler House** (509 Shelby St.), which was designed by architect Frank Lloyd Wright in his famous prairie house style. Though the clean-lined white house is distinctive, it fits in seamlessly on the street, on which a number of impressive houses of varying styles are located.

KENTUCKY'S DRY COUNTIES

As the number one producer of America's only native spirit, Kentucky appears on the surface to be a state that likes its liquor. Dive deeper, and you'll see that alcohol sales are a contentious issue in the Bluegrass State. After all, Carrie Nation, the radical hatchet-wielding leader of the temperance movement, was a Kentuckian.

Although most Americans consider it their right in post-Prohibition America to buy alcohol anywhere so long as they are of legal age, that's not the case in Kentucky. Only 32 of Kentucky's 120 counties are wet, meaning that alcoholic beverages can be sold by businesses for on-site or off-site consumption. A surprising 39 counties are completely dry, meaning alcohol sales are prohibited throughout the entire county. The remaining 49 counties are "moist," which means they are primarily dry, but they may have a city that is completely wet (such as Bowling Green in Warren County), have cities that allow sales by the drink in certain restaurants, or have golf courses or wineries that are allowed to serve alcohol.

Dry areas can be found in every region in the state, although they are most concentrated in southern, eastern, and far western Kentucky, which are Bible Belt areas, and the ban on alcohol has everything to do with religious beliefs. In these areas especially, you'll have to go a long way before you find alcohol—at least legal alcohol, that is. Moonshine is alive and well in Kentucky, despite what officials may try to tell you. It should be noted that it is not illegal to possess alcohol for private consumption in dry counties; it is simply illegal to sell it. The majority of the wet counties are in the vicinity of Louisville, Lexington, Northern Kentucky, and Owensboro. Not only are these the state's most populated and urban areas, but they also have strong Catholic communities. Interpret that how you will.

A map showing the distribution of wet and dry counties is available through the website of the Kentucky Department of Alcoholic Beverage Control (http://abc.ky.gov).

A historical marker indicates the house, which is private and may only be viewed from the street. The Ziegler House is the only Wright-designed house in Kentucky.

Switzer Covered Bridge

One of only a handful of covered bridges remaining in Kentucky, the **Switzer Covered Bridge** (KY 1262 and KY 1689) is a 120-foot-long Howe truss bridge built in 1855 to span the Elkhorn River. In 1954, the bridge was closed to traffic, a concrete structure taking its place. Restored multiple times since its construction, the bridge can now be crossed by foot, and though the external structure is in good condition, graffiti scars the interior.

ENTERTAINMENT AND EVENTS
Nightlife

Frankfort is not really known for its nightlife.

Many government workers head back to their hometowns on weekends, while locals often opt to see what's going on in nearby Lexington. Standalone bars are few and far between, but many restaurants buzz in the evenings with locals seeking out a drink and entertainment. The bar at Serafini, for instance, is always crowded.

The hottest place in town for a drink is **Capital Cellars** (227 W. Broadway, 502/352-2600, http://capitalcellars.net, 10am-9pm Mon.-Thurs., 10am-10pm Fri.-Sat.). It's where people come together, especially those interested in arts, culture, and meeting new friends. With an enormous selection of wines at reasonable prices ($4-6 per glass; a bottle can be enjoyed in-store for $2 over retail), as well as a short menu of sandwiches, salads, and snacks such as cheese plates, olive trays, and smoked salmon, it's a great place to grab a light dinner, then hang out, as art exhibitions open, musicians start impromptu jam sessions, and people meet and mingle. For those not inclined toward wine, Capital Cellars also offers 35 Kentucky bourbons as well as a wide choice of other drinks.

Though the **Kentucky Coffeetree Café** (235 W. Broadway, 502/875-3009, www.kentuckycoffeetree.com, 7am-9pm Mon.-Wed., 7am-10pm Thurs.-Fri., 8am-10pm Sat., 8am-7pm Sun.) serves up coffees, smoothies, sandwiches, and pastries during the day, on weekend evenings it's the place to go for live music. The intimate setting makes it feel as if the musicians are playing just for you. Some performances are ticketed; others require a cover. Check the website for details.

For a more traditional bar experience, grab at table at **The Dragon Pub** (103 W. Main St., 502/875-9300, www.dragonpub.com, 11am-2am Mon.-Fri., 10am-1am Sat.), where Tuesday night is trivia night and Fridays and Saturdays feature live music. Expect a young professional crowd, ready to relax after work.

Performing Arts

Built in 1911 as a small vaudeville theater, the **Grand Theatre** (308 St. Clair St., 502/352-7469, www.grandtheatrefrankfort.org) was converted into a large movie theater in the 1940s before closing in 1966. Now, thanks to a group of activist citizens, the Grand is back as a community arts center. In addition to again showing films, the theater also hosts art exhibitions, concerts, and other performances. Check the online schedule for upcoming events and ticket information.

Festivals and Events

Head to the lawn of the Old State Capitol for the **Summer Concert Series** (www.downtownfrankfort.com) every other Friday in the summer at 7pm. Bring a blanket, bring a friend, bring a picnic; entertainment is provided.

On the first weekend of June, Frankfort shows off its goods at the **Capitol Expo Festival** (www.capitalexpofestival.com). The three-day event includes a cornhole tournament, a lip sync contest, a fireworks show over the Kentucky River, an arts and crafts show, and lots of live music.

SHOPPING
Bookstores

Bookstore lovers will delight in **Poor Richard's Books** (233 W. Broadway, 502/223-8018, http://poorrichards.indiebound.com, 10am-6pm Mon.-Fri., 10am-5pm Sat., 12:30pm-5pm Sun.), where the front shelves are dedicated to Kentucky authors while the rest of the store contains popular offerings in every genre. It's nearly impossible to leave without a new read in hand.

Kentucky Products

From horse brooches to carved wooden benches, **Completely Kentucky** (237 W. Broadway, 502/223-5240, www.completelykentucky.com, 9:30am-6pm Mon.-Fri., 9:30am-5pm Sat., 12:30pm-5pm Sun.) covers the entire spread of Kentucky-made arts, crafts, and souvenirs. Items range from the decorative (glass pieces and prints) to the useful (ceramic dishes) to the mouthwatering (gift baskets of Kentucky food) to the absurd (junkyard animals). There's something for everyone.

For other unique local products, be sure to check out the gift shops at the Center for Kentucky History and Buffalo Trace Distillery.

SPORTS AND RECREATION
Parks

Stop at **River View Park** (Wilkinson Blvd., across from Capital Plaza) for a walk along a one-mile path that runs parallel to the Kentucky River. Sixteen sites of historical interest are marked along the trail. The park also offers a fishing pier, boat dock, and picnic area, and hosts the farmers market May-October.

Juniper Hill Park (800 Louisville Rd., 502/696-0607, www.frankfortparksandrec.com, 7am-11pm, Apr.-Oct., 7am-dusk, Nov.-Mar.) offers some of the best recreational facilities in the city with an Olympic-size pool, sand volleyball courts, tennis courts, and an 18-hole golf course. You'll also find extensive picnic facilities and a playground at Juniper Hill.

shops of downtown Frankfort

© THERESA DOWELL BLACKINTON

Pull over at the **scenic overlook** on U.S. 60 as you head out of downtown Frankfort and go toward Louisville for an excellent view of the capitol, which sits directly in front of and below the overlook.

Hiking

Start your visit to **Cove Spring Park** (100 Cove Spring Rd., 502/696-0607, www.frankfortparksandrec.com, 8am-11pm Apr.-Oct., 8am-dusk Nov.-Mar.) with a stop at the waterfall located right next to the parking lot, then create a hiking route from the park's four trails and multiple connectors. No matter what path you choose to use to explore the park's 100 acres, you'll pass through riverine forest that is home to deer, wild turkeys, great blue herons, and other wildlife.

From Fort Hill, Frankfort militia protected the city from an attempted Confederate invasion in 1864. Today, **Leslie Morris Park** (400 Clifton Ave., 502/696-0607, www.frankfortparksandrec.com, dawn-dusk daily) preserves the remains of the forts built on this hill and

allows visitors to experience them on a series of trails that loop through acres of forest, where deer and other wildlife are known to live. A brochure available from a box in the parking lot outlines a 0.6-mile route that takes you past many of the sites and provides a wonderful panorama of the entirety of Frankfort. Those looking for a good workout can actually ascend the hill from the city via the Old Military Road Walking Trail, which begins behind the Capital Plaza tower.

Biking

Capital City Cycles (475 Versailles Rd., 502/352-2480, http://capitalcitycyclesky.com, 10am-6pm Mon.-Sat., noon-5pm Sun.) is Frankfort's go-to place for all biking needs. The shop services and sells bikes and also rents road, mountain, and hybrid bikes by the day and week. Staff members are avid cyclists and can answer any question you have about where to bike in Frankfort, and the store also organizes group rides. Call or stop in for more information.

In addition to soccer and softball fields, **Capitol View Park** (Glenns Creek Rd., 502/696-0607, www.frankfortparksandrec.com, 8am-11pm, Apr.-Oct., 8am-dark, Nov.-Mar.) features 10 miles of mountain bike trails. The trails run along the river and through the woods and connect to make one large loop.

Water Sports

The Kentucky River and Elkhorn Creek offer excellent canoeing and kayaking waters, and there's no outfitter better suited to help get you out on those waters than **Canoe Kentucky** (7323 Peaks Mill Rd., 888/226-6359, www.canoeky.com). They offer instruction for those new to the activity, sales for those who can't get enough, and both guided and self-guided boat trips for paddlers of all levels. Options range in length and distance, from short evening paddles in the moonlight to all-day trips. Children are welcome, but if they weigh less than 35 pounds, you'll have to provide your own life jacket for them. All activities should be booked in advance.

Horseback Riding

A Little Bit of Heaven Riding Stables (3226 Sullivan Ln., 502/223-8925, www.kystable.com) offers horseback riding lessons on their Appaloosa horses. No experience is necessary, but you do need to call ahead to arrange a lesson. Because of the size of the horses, a weight limit of 185 pounds is strictly enforced. Those too timid to climb onboard are welcome to take a tour of the paddock and meet the nearly 50 horses boarded there.

ACCOMMODATIONS
$50-100

The **Capital Plaza Hotel** (405 Wilkinson Blvd., 502/227-5100, www.capitalplazaky.com, $89-99) offers 189 guest rooms outfitted with standard hotel amenities, including cable television and wireless Internet, and decorated in standard, but now somewhat dated, hotel style. Located next to the convention center, the hotel is popular with business travelers, but is also within walking distance of Frankfort's main sights.

$100-150

Built prior to the Civil War, ◖ **The Meeting House Bed and Breakfast** (519 Ann St., 502/226-3226, www.themeetinghousebandb.com, $115-125) retains many of the features of the original building, including the poplar floors, the walnut banister on the three-floor staircase, the high ceilings, and the many fireplaces. Period pieces throughout the house, which is located within easy walking distance of most attractions, add to the historic feel. The house has been updated, however, so that each of the four guest rooms has its own private bath with walk-in shower. Rooms are large with desks and comfortable chairs and feature cable TV and wireless Internet. Three rooms have full beds and one has a queen. Homemade cookies are served each afternoon, and breakfast is served in courses. Scottish eggs are the house specialty. Don't let the Boston accent of hosts Gary and Rose throw you; they know more about Frankfort than many of its life-long residents.

The bathroom attached to the Red Room at **Meek House Bed and Breakfast** (119 E. 3rd St., 502/227-2566, www.bbonline.com, $115) was, in its last incarnation, most likely a bedroom. It's that big. It features a claw-foot tub and walk-in shower and even has its own door to the patio overlooking the tranquil garden. The bedroom is itself quite large, with plenty of open space left despite the room having a king-size bed and loveseat. The B&B's other room, the Green Room, is perfect for traveling partners who prefer separate beds as it contains two twins as well as a pull-out couch. Both rooms have stocked refrigerators and TVs. At the multicourse breakfast, you might be treated to a Mexican quiche, herbed eggs with cheese on an English muffin, or cinnamon chip French toast, as well as a starter course of yogurt and homemade granola.

A number of chain hotels are located in Frankfort, including a **Hampton Inn** (1310 U.S. 127 S., 502/223-7600, www.hamptoninn.com,

$109) and a **Best Western** (80 Chenault Dr., 502/695-6111, www.bestwesternkentucky.com, $104), both of which offer nice rooms with all the amenities one would expect. Although each is convenient to I-64, neither is located in the heart of the city.

Campgrounds
RVers will be happy with the services at **Elkhorn Campground** (165 N. Scruggs Ln., 502/695-9154, www.elkhorncampground.com), which offers 125 sites, 61 of which have full hookups. For entertainment, choose from the campground's pool, mini-golf facility, horseshoe pit, basketball and volleyball courts, and playground. Located on the banks of the Elkhorn, the location is peaceful as well as convenient to Frankfort sites.

Those more interested in outdoor offerings than historic sites will want to check out **Still Waters Campground** (249 Strohmeier Rd., 502/223-8896, www.stillwaterscampground.com), which is located on the Kentucky River and features boat ramps and offers canoe and kayak rentals. In addition to full-service sites, the campground has two primitive camping areas.

FOOD
Farmers Market
Fresh fruits, vegetables, and assorted other agricultural products are available for purchase at the **Frankfort Farmers Market** (River View Park, 7am-noon Tues., Thurs., and Sat.) three times each week.

Cafés and Bakeries
Candleberry's Tea Room & Café (1502 Louisville Rd., 502/875-0485, www.candleberrytearoom.com, 11am-2pm Tues.-Fri., $5.95-7.95) offers light lunches served in a cozy atmosphere. Take your pick from a list of sandwiches or daily quiche and soup specials. If you can't decide, they'll let you mix and match. Finish your meal with a perfectly sweet piece of chess pie, said to be made from a vintage recipe. Of course, you'll want to have tea with your meal—the only trouble is you have to pick from

a long, tempting list. For the true tea connoisseur, book a reservation 48 hours in advance for afternoon tea on Saturday ($18.95), where you'll be treated to scones, soup, and a selection of sweet and savory goodies to go along with your tea. It's perfect for an outing with the girls or a mother-daughter date, though men are plenty welcome.

For a breakfast treat or an afternoon sweet, visit **Magee's Bakery** (225 W. Main, 502/223-7621, http://frankfortmagees.com, 7am-2pm Tues.-Fri., 8am-2pm Sat.) and choose from a tasty selection of fresh-baked doughnuts, cookies, cupcakes, breads, tarts, pies, and other pastries. Magee's also offers a small menu of sandwiches, wraps, and soups at lunch.

Casual American
Although **Gibby's** (204 W. Broadway, 502/223-4429, www.eatatgibbys.com, 10:30am-9pm Mon.-Sat., $3.49-14.99) offers pasta, meat, and seafood entrées, it's primarily known for filling sandwiches and stuffed spuds. Located in the revitalized downtown, Gibby's does a bustling lunch business, popular with locals looking for a quick, tasty lunch before heading back to work.

Fans of the old-fashioned diner, where the chef/owner has a colorful history and the gift of gab, won't want to miss **Rick's White Light Diner** (114 Bridge St., 502/696-9104, www.whitelightdiner.com, 11am-5pm Tues.-Fri., 8am-3pm Sat., $7.75-19.50). The menu leans toward Cajun, with crawfish pie, a variety of po' boys, and a New Orleans muffuletta all finding a spot on the menu. Though the space and style is traditional decor, the food is high-quality, with local meats, eggs, and produce used whenever possible. Food Network fans might recognize the place from *Diners, Drive-Ins, and Dives*.

Italian
Hole-in-the-wall **Buddy's Pizza** (212 W. Broadway, 502/352-2920, 11am-9pm Mon.-Thurs., 11am-10pm Fri., noon-9pm Sat., $8-17.50) offers the best pies in town. Choose from a specialty pizza or create your own combo to

be baked to perfection in Buddy's brick oven. Salads and Italian sandwiches ($4-7) round out the menu. At lunch on weekdays, pizza is available by the slice ($2.50).

◖ **Serafini** (243 W. Broadway, 502/875-5599, www.serafinifrankfort.com, 11am-3pm Mon.-Fri. and 4:30pm-10pm Mon.-Sat., $15-36) is Frankfort's nicest restaurant, serving up an excellent selection of pastas and meat and fish dishes. The menu changes seasonally, but might feature Shanghai scallops, grilled filet mignon, or a pork chop marinated in sweet tea. The risotto of the day is always a good choice. Desserts are decadent, so consider sharing. Tall booths provide privacy, though you can also opt for an open table or even open-air seating when the weather is nice. At lunch ($8-13), the menu runs primarily to pastas, sandwiches, and pizzas.

INFORMATION AND SERVICES

Located in a beautiful Queen Anne-style house, the **Visitors Center** (100 Capital Ave., 502/875-8687, www.visitfrankfort.com, 8am-5pm Mon.-Fri., 9:30am-2:30pm Sat. May-Sept.) stocks brochures and maps, and the friendly staff can provide you with information on dining and hotel options in Frankfort and Franklin County. The center also offers free wireless Internet.

A **post office** is located at 1210 Wilkinson Boulevard, near Buffalo Trace Distillery.

GETTING THERE

Frankfort is located just north of I-64. From Louisville (one hour), take eastbound I-64 for nearly 50 miles to northbound U.S. 127 (Exit 53B), which will lead into downtown Frankfort after about 5 miles. From Lexington (45 minutes), you can take westbound I-64 for 21 miles to westbound U.S. 60 (Exit 58). After 2.5 miles, U.S. 60 will hit Main Street. If you prefer to avoid the interstate or are on the western side of Lexington, drive 20 miles on northbound U.S. 421, at which point you'll hit Main Street. From Bardstown (one hour), travel on eastbound Blue Grass Parkway for 34 miles

to northbound U.S. 127 (Exit 59B). Then drive an additional 16 miles, passing through Lawrenceburg, to reach Frankfort.

Frankfort is 315 miles (4.75 hours) from St. Louis (4.75 hours) via eastbound I-64; 165 miles (2.5 hours) from Indianapolis via southbound I-65 to Louisville and then eastbound I-64; 80 miles (1.5 hours) from Cincinnati via southbound I-71 and southbound U.S. 127; and 210 miles (3.25 hours) from Nashville via northbound I-65 and eastbound Blue Grass Parkway.

Frankfort's Capital City Airport is not served by commercial airlines. The nearest airports are Blue Grass Airport in Lexington and Louisville International Airport.

GETTING AROUND
Public Transportation

Listen for the friendly ring of Frankfort's free **downtown trolley** (www.visitfrankfort.com, 10am-3pm Tues.-Fri.), then hop onboard to enjoy old-fashioned transport among the city's most popular sites. Among the many stops are the Capitol, Rebecca Ruth Candy, Frankfort Cemetery, The Center for Kentucky History, Liberty Hall, River View Park, and Buffalo Trace Distillery. Departures are scheduled at 40-minute intervals, making the trolley a fun and convenient way to see Frankfort.

Tours

Multiple walking tours of Frankfort are offered throughout the year. **Russ Hatter's Downtown Tour,** which costs $5 for adults and is free for those under 12, provides an in-depth look at Frankfort history. Call 502/696-9127 for reservations. Those who delight in the fact that trains still run right through Frankfort will be interested in **Chuck Bogart's Railroad Walking Tour,** an hour-long trip through railroad history. Reservations for the free tour can be made by calling 502/227-2436. Naturalists will want to sign up for **Russ Kennedy's Kentucky River Walk,** a free tour focusing on the history of the river and its impact on Frankfort. Call 502/803-0242 for reservations. If you're visiting Frankfort during the witching month, get in the mood for Halloween with a **Murder and Mayhem Tour,** held every Thursday night in October at 7:30pm. Guides, costumed like early 20th-century policemen, tell tales of 30 grisly Frankfort murders while leading a tour through the nighttime streets of Frankfort. The tour, which costs $10 and departs from the Capital City Museum, is restricted to those 18 and older. Reserve a spot on the tour by calling 502/696-0607.

For those who prefer to tour at their own pace, walking and driving tour brochures are available at the visitors center. To uncover the stories behind the many historic buildings that form the heart of downtown Frankfort, request a copy of the **walking tour brochure.** Brief histories of 40 different sites, all within a 10-block radius, are provided in the brochure. Civil War buffs will want to pick up a copy of the **Civil War Driving Tour** brochure and follow the route to 15 sites with connections to the war. All sites are within the city, so driving distances are short, but the tour is long on interesting facts.

LEXINGTON AND HORSE COUNTRY

Lexington and Horse Country is, for many, quintessential Kentucky. It's what you see in your mind if you've never been to the Bluegrass State and your whole knowledge of it is based on passing images. This is where you'll find endless rolling hills of bluegrass, immense fields marked by wooden fences, and foals dancing in the morning sunlight. This is where champion thoroughbreds, legends like Secretariat, Man O' War, and Seattle Slew, were born and where they stood stud, siring a new generation of racehorses after their own championship days were through. The soil in this area, underlain by shelves of limestone, is some of the richest in the world. Beyond thoroughbreds, this region also produces burley tobacco, bourbon, and wine.

Lexington itself is Kentucky's second most populated city, a Southern-style metropolis where modern office buildings and historic storefronts mix. Surrounding the city are the horse farms that make Lexington the center of the equine universe, and you'll also find plenty of lovely old Southern homes, complete with the requisite front porch. But Lexington is not all seersucker and sweet tea; it's also home to the University of Kentucky, the state's largest university, and thus has a good-time college atmosphere as well. Somehow the forces of Southern respectability and youthful exuberance come together here as smooth as a bourbon cocktail. Lexington is just as much symbolized by opening day at Keeneland as it is by the first home basketball game at Rupp Arena.

Lexington is the heart of this region, its pulse carrying out into the many towns that

© THERESA DOWELL BLACKINTON

HIGHLIGHTS

◖ **Keeneland:** With unrivaled atmosphere and great beauty, this track is one of the best places in the world to watch thoroughbred horse racing (page 131).

◖ **Kentucky Horse Park:** Immerse yourself in everything equine at this enormous park, which covers all aspects of the horse world (page 132).

◖ **Mary Todd Lincoln House:** This in-depth home tour gives you a look at the life of one of this nation's most talked-about and misunderstood first ladies (page 133).

◖ **Woodford Reserve Distillery:** Learn what makes Woodford Reserve one of the world's most acclaimed bourbons on an in-depth tour of the production process (page 156).

◖ **Old Friends Equine Center:** At this retirement farm for some of racing's biggest names, you get to meet each horse, learn their story, and even pet and feed some of the gentler residents (page 161).

◖ **Claiborne Farm:** If you only have time for one working horse farm, consider Claiborne, one of the most storied farms and the final resting place of Secretariat (page 164).

◖ **Fort Boonesborough State Park:** Meet Daniel Boone and learn about life at Kentucky's second settlement through visits with re-enactors who occupy the reconstructed fort (page 172).

◖ **Shaker Village:** Explore what it meant to belong to the Shaker movement on a tour through the buildings and lands of this living history museum (page 178).

LOOK FOR ◖ TO FIND RECOMMENDED SIGHTS, ACTIVITIES, DINING, AND LODGING.

surround it. Much smaller than Lexington, these towns are charming, distilling the region's finest qualities into easy sips. Versailles, Midway, and Paris play huge roles in the thoroughbred industry. In fact, many of the farms that people group under Lexington are actually located in these three nearby towns. Georgetown and Nicholasville also have their share of horse farms, but they're further defined by the small colleges located in them and their other resources, such as the Toyota plant in Georgetown. Winchester, Richmond, Harrodsburg, and Danville share the bond of history with Lexington. The state's earliest settlements were built here, Kentucky declared its statehood here, and important Civil War battles took place here.

To enjoy Lexington and Horse Country, you don't have to care about horses, history,

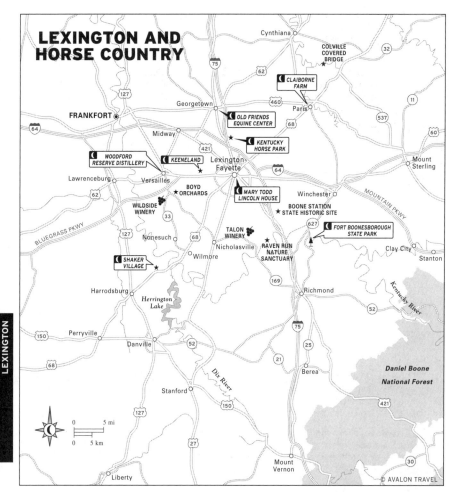

LEXINGTON AND HORSE COUNTRY

or basketball (though it does, of course, help). You could simply come here to enjoy the outstanding restaurants and first-class bed-and-breakfast accommodations. The scenery is nothing short of spectacular. Shoot, even a drive down the interstate here is an attractive option, although country roads are obviously a more enticing choice. The area is a lovely place to visit, and what many people take for hospitality is, well, simply just the way things are done around here.

PLANNING YOUR TIME

Lexington is a great weekend destination. You can choose to be selective about what you see and move at a leisurely pace, or you can get up and go each morning and have two very packed days. If you've never been to the races at Keeneland before, try to plan your trip to Lexington for April or October, when the meets are held. Opening weekends are especially packed, though all weekends are busy. If possible, plan in advance to get reserved seats, which provide for a much nicer experience. Attending the races at Keeneland will fill an entire day, leaving you one additional day for sightseeing. For the Kentucky Horse Park you need at least a half-day. Most shows at the park are held twice, once in the morning and once in the afternoon, so aim to arrive right when the park opens or immediately after lunch.

For a really enjoyable visit to this area, aim for an extended weekend of three or four days. With the additional days, you can visit some of the sites in the surrounding towns. Versailles, Midway, Georgetown, Paris, Winchester, and Nicholasville are all less than a 30-minute drive from Lexington, making any of their attractions easy add-ons to a Lexington itinerary. Richmond is only a few minutes farther. One good way to schedule your time is to spend two days seeing Lexington, one day seeing sites in the towns to the east, and one day seeing sites in towns to the west.

Danville and Harrodsburg are a bit farther from Lexington, taking about 45 minutes to reach by car. The extra time it takes to reach them is worth it, however, and for history buffs especially, it may be worth replacing visits to the towns immediately surrounding Lexington with visits to these two towns. With the fantastic Beaumont Inn in Harrodsburg, you'd be smart to consider staying overnight there if you're interested in the area's attractions.

Of course, if Lexington and Horse Country really interest you, you can easily fill a week immersing yourself. This is especially true if you want to visit a lot of the horse farms, because with limited tour offerings at each, it can be hard to fit more than one, or at most two, into a day. Of course, those with a less specific interest in certain farms and horses can opt for a guided tour that will give you your fill of horse farms in one day.

Many people opt to base themselves in Lexington because of the way the area is laid out, with Lexington at the center and the other towns circling it. Lexington also has the most food and hotel options. However, the entire region is actually quite rich when it comes to food and dining. The options in Versailles and Midway are among my favorites, though nearly every town in this area has an amazing bed and breakfast and restaurant. You're actually spoiled for choice, and with the region so compact, you can pretty much stay in whichever place you fancy most and easily make your way to any other for sightseeing. Be aware that hotel rooms can be harder to find during Keeneland meets and sales.

The entire area is a year-round destination. Spring and fall are best for those interested in horses, while fall and winter draw sports fans interested in UK football and basketball. Although summer is peak season in most of the state and hot summer days see plenty of action in this area as well, it's actually a bit quieter in Lexington in the summer thanks to the fact that school is out. If the college scene doesn't interest you, this might be a good time to visit Lexington, though be prepared for heat and humidity.

Lexington

Named after the Massachusetts town successfully defended by colonists in the first battle of the Revolutionary War, Lexington is Kentucky's second-biggest city. Many local residents, however, consider it Kentucky's first city, the one that best epitomizes just what Kentucky is.

Lexington prides itself on being a cultured city. Back in the early 1800s, Lexington was nicknamed the Athens of the West and visited by many people of national importance. Today, as the home of the University of Kentucky, the state's largest university, and a diverse population that is the most well educated in the state, Lexington remains a thriving city.

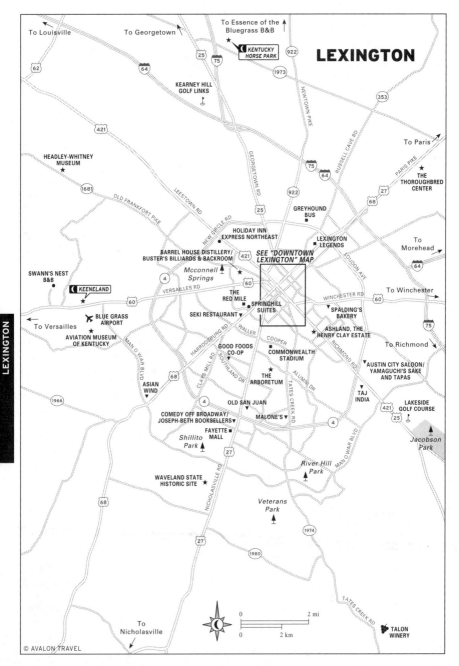

LEXINGTON

© THERESA DOWELL BLACKINTON

racehorse on the Keeneland track

LEXINGTON

Though forward-looking and liberal-leaning when it comes to politics, Lexington is also very traditional, rich with historic homes, horse farms that have been passed down through many generations, and a racetrack that is still firmly rooted in the community. The epitome of a Southern city, Lexington is all manners and hospitality...at least when it's not basketball season. Then, anything goes, especially when the University of Kentucky is playing the University of Louisville. Rivalry is alive and well between Kentucky's two largest cities, especially when it comes to sports. UK basketball is, after all, a religion to most of the state, and the entire city of Lexington bleeds blue.

With interesting history, beautiful landscape, great restaurants, and a strong sense of identity, Lexington is a fun place to visit. Home to both horse-industry millionaires and nearly 30,000 college students, it manages to be a proper Southern city and a good-time college town all at once.

HORSE SIGHTS
Keeneland

Churchill Downs might be host to the Kentucky Derby, but **Keeneland** (4201 Versailles Rd., 859/254-3412, www.keeneland. com) is Kentucky's most popular racetrack. It's also the state's (and maybe the world's) most beautiful, with lush, meticulously landscaped grounds and stone buildings. It is unabashedly Southern and genteel, a place where ladies can still carry white parasols and men look dapper in seersucker. The live racing season is short, restricted to April and October, making every race day, especially those on weekends, feel like an event. General admission is $5 and allows access to the paddock area and first-come, first-served bench seating right along the racetrack. For an additional $3 you can upgrade to grandstand seating, which gives you a guaranteed seat. On Saturdays, grandstand seating is usually sold out in advance, but on other days you can get such a seat upon arrival if you come early. Gates open at 11am on race days, and

LEXINGTON

first post is at 1:15pm. The quality of races is high during the short season, with the most popular events being spring's Bluegrass Stakes, a Derby prep race, and Fall Star weekend, when nine stakes races are run over three days in the lead-up to the Breeders Cup.

Keeneland, although definitely a wonderful place for horse racing, is about so much more than race day. If you find yourself in Lexington outside of April or October, Keeneland should still be on your itinerary, preferably for first thing in the morning. Rise and shine early and head straight to Keeneland for breakfast at the **Track Kitchen** (6am-11am daily), where the public is welcome to share sausage biscuits, breakfast burritos, and other oh-so-good but probably not-so-good-for-you dishes with owners, trainers, and jockeys talking shop. After breakfast, you'll want to make your way to the track, where you can watch morning workouts. It's an intimate look at horse racing, and the park-like grounds look stunning in the early morning light. Most workouts end by 10am, so you really do want to arrive early. Another site of interest is the **library** (8:30am-4:30pm Mon.-Fri.), home to one of the world's biggest collections of information on thoroughbreds and the repository for the entire history of Daily Racing Forms. If you're not looking to do research, just flip through the scrapbooks documenting the history of Keeneland in five-year increments and check out the racing-related artifacts on display. Before you leave Keeneland, pop into the **gift shop** (9am-5pm daily), where you can find a wide array of horse-related gifts as well as the perfect Derby hat.

For those in the horse industry, Keeneland is as much about horse sales as it is about racing. Four times a year (January, April, September, and November), thoroughbreds are sold at Keeneland. It's a fascinating process, and it's open to the public. Check it out if you get the chance.

◀ Kentucky Horse Park
A combined working horse farm, equine competition facility, and horse-based theme park of sorts, the **Kentucky Horse Park** (4089

Iron Works Pkwy., 859/259-4257, www.ky-horsepark.com, 9am-5pm daily mid-Mar.-Oct., 9am-5pm Wed.-Sun. Nov.-mid-Mar.) is the best place—not just in Lexington, but probably the entire world—to get up close and personal with horses. A visit to the park is easily an all-day affair, thanks to the many things to see and do. A good way to start a trip is on a horse-drawn trolley tour, which will allow you to get a sense of the park. You'll then want to work out your schedule so that you catch both the Hall of Champions presentation, which introduces such renowned horses as Kentucky Derby winner Funny Cide and Horse of the Decade Cigar to visitors, and the Horses of the World show, in which costumed handlers present horses of various breeds in a show ring. With more than 40 breeds of horses represented at the park, you might see anything from a miniature horse to a draft house. During June and July, you'll also want to stick around for the mare and foal show, where you can see the darling baby horses with their mommas. At the heart of the park is the International Museum of the Horse, which has exhibits tracing the ancestry and evolution of horses, detailing the domestication of horses and the many roles horses have served throughout history, capturing the golden age of the horse, and citing the many different known breeds of horses. A wing that opened in 2010 is dedicated to the Arabian horse, from which the thoroughbred descended, and is the most hands-on of the exhibit halls. A second museum, the American Saddlebred Museum, is also part of the park complex and offers a detailed look at Kentucky's only native breed of horse. If you find that you have time left to spare, take a walk around the grounds, saying hello to the big beauties at the Draft Horse Barn, witnessing the horseshoeing process at the Farrier Shop, and visiting the gravesites of Man O' War and War Admiral. For an additional fee, you may also go on a 35-minute guided trail ride ($25). Pony rides ($5) are offered for youngsters. Admission is $16 for adults and $8 for youth 7-12 mid-March-October, and $10 for adults and $5 for youth 7-12 November-mid-March. Parking costs an additional $3. With your admission sticker, you may come and go as you please both the day of purchase and the next day. If you plan to visit more than once, a season pass is a worthwhile investment.

The Thoroughbred Center

Whereas most casual racing fans are satisfied with viewing a morning workout session at Keeneland, those with a stronger interest in how thoroughbreds are trained to race should schedule a tour of **The Thoroughbred Center** (3380 Paris Pike, 859/293-1853, www.thethoroughbredcenter.com, guided tours 9am Mon.-Sat., Apr.-Oct., Mon.-Fri., Nov.-Mar., $15 adults, $8 youth 12 and under). On the tour, which lasts 1-1.5 hours, visitors watch as horses are put through their morning workouts, see horses in the barn and paddocks, and witness trainers caring for the horses.

HISTORIC SIGHTS
Ashland, The Henry Clay Estate

More than a beautiful home, **Ashland** (120 Sycamore Rd., 859/266-8581, www.henryclay.org, 10am-4pm Tues.-Sat., 1pm-4pm Sun., Mar.-Dec., $10 adults, $5 youth 6-18) is a shrine to Henry Clay, Kentucky's most renowned statesman and the man known as the Great Compromiser for his role in preserving the union as the nation expanded westward during the difficult decades prior to the Civil War. The estate, which once consisted of nearly 700 acres, is that of Clay, but the house is not the exact one he lived in. Following his death in 1852, his son James had the original house, which had become architecturally unsound, demolished, rebuilding the house on the exact same spot with the exact same floor plan. He did change some of the stylings, adding Italianate touches to the Federalist home, and later descendants, who would occupy the house until 1950, added some of their own personality. The grand 18-room mansion is furnished and decorated almost entirely with items from the family, including a huge wealth of Clay's personal belongings. Among the most interesting are a walking stick he owned with George Washington's head atop it, a book he personally inscribed to Abraham Lincoln, and a handwritten copy of his license to practice law. Tours are guided, depart on the hour, and last about an hour. You'll learn all kinds of interesting tidbits about Henry Clay, including the fact that he was an active horse breeder who owned two mares to which 11 Kentucky Derby winners can trace their lineage. Though a national figure, Clay was a true Kentuckian if there ever was one. If you arrive while a tour is in progress, you can view a 12-minute film on Henry Clay and Ashland and take in the permanent exhibits, which capture the many aspects of Clay—farmer, citizen, statesman, and presidential candidate.

◖ Mary Todd Lincoln House

Although Mary Todd met and wed Abraham Lincoln in Springfield, Illinois, she, like Abraham, was a native Kentuckian. Unlike Abraham, however, Mary Todd was not born in a cabin on the frontier, but was instead born into a prominent family, well known in Lexington high society. Visitors to the **Mary Todd Lincoln House** (578 W. Main St., 859/233-9999, www.mtlhouse.org, 10am-3pm Mon.-Sat., Mar. 15-Nov. 30, $10 adults, $5 youth 6-12), a 14-room home in which she lived from 1832 to 1839, will gain better insight into this most intriguing first lady. The guided tour, which begins on the hour and lasts about one hour, is very in-depth, with the knowledgeable guides sharing insight on her upbringing, her impressive amount of education, her political views, her marriage to Abraham, her experience as first lady, and her family life. Many Todd family belongings remain in the house, along with a few items that came from the Lincoln family, and although most of the house is strictly hands-off, you can run your hand down the original banister, which Abraham himself used on a visit to the house in 1847.

Hunt-Morgan House

Built in 1814 by John Hunt, a merchant who became the first millionaire west of the Alleghenies, the **Hunt-Morgan House** (201 N.

TOURING KENTUCKY'S HORSE FARMS

A visit to a horse farm is high on the list of many visitors to Kentucky. Most, however, aren't sure how to go about making this happen or don't know what to expect. First, any prospective visitor should be aware that Kentucky's horse farms are working operations, not tourist attractions. Although many farms do enjoy welcoming visitors, business always comes first, and that business is breeding (not training, as many people wrongly assume). Tours are restricted to set times and dates, and reservations are always required. Additionally, thoroughbreds, especially the stallions, are high-strung animals not generally suited to up-close encounters with unfamiliar people. Working horse farms aren't petting zoos, and you shouldn't expect to get to touch a horse or pose for a photo with one. On occasion, you may be able to, but in that case, you should consider yourself lucky.

Now, with business taken care of, let's get down to the details of how to plan a visit. Basically you have three options: Sign up for a regularly scheduled guided tour, organize a custom tour with a professional guide, or arrange visits on your own with individual farms.

For most casual visitors—those with an interest in seeing a horse farm or two, but no burning desire to visit a specific farm or see a particular horse—a regular guided tour is the preferred option. These tours typically average three hours and visit one or two horse farms along with additional horse-related sites of interest such as Keeneland Race Track. Each tour is slightly different, so you should compare options before booking. Reputable tour operators include:

- **Blue Grass Tours** (www.bluegrasstours. com)
- **Horse Farm Tours Inc.** (859/268-2906, www.horsefarmtours.com)
- **Thoroughbred Heritage Horse Farm Tours** (800/979-3370, www.seethechampions.com)

- **Unique Horse Farm Tours** (800/259-4225, www.kyhorsepark.com)

If you have a deep interest in thoroughbred horses or specific ideas on exactly what you wish to see, you should consider organizing a custom tour. By doing this, you will have control of your itinerary and the pace of your trip. You'll also have direct access to a knowledgeable guide with insider contacts who can help you gain access to farms that you may not be able to should you opt to go alone. Although many assume the cost of a private tour will be out of their budget, if you have a couple of people in your group, it may come out cheaper than a regular organized tour. Many of the organized tour operators will arrange custom tours on request, although there are also guides who specialize in private tours. The best way to find the right guide is to call a few, discuss your wishes with them, and then see what they can do for you. You may wish to start with the following:

- **Karen Edelstein** (859/266-5465, www.kyhorsefarmtours.com)
- **Martha Martin and Nancy Hapgood** (859/333-8940, www.unbridledhorsetours.com)
- **John Midbo** (859/278-9488, www.lexingtonprivatetours.com)

Independent travelers who like to make all their arrangements on their own can opt to contact horse farms directly to try to arrange visits. Although some farms can accommodate you with only a day's notice, it's best to contact the farms you wish to tour as far in advance as possible. Throughout this chapter, horse farms that welcome independent visitors are given full listings. A few of the more popular farms are:

- **Ashford Stud** (5095 Frankfort Rd., Versailles, 859/873-7088, www.coolmore.com)
- **Claiborne Farm** (703 Winchester Rd., Paris, 859/233-4252, www.claibornefarm.com)

- **Lane's End Farm** (1500 Midway Rd., Versailles, 859/873-7300, www.lanesend.com)

- **Taylor Made Farm** (2765 Union Mill Rd., Nicholasville, 859/885-3345, www.taylormadeadvantage.com)

- **Three Chimneys Farm** (1981 Old Frankfort Pike, Versailles, 859/873-7053, www.threechimneys.com)

- **WinStar Farm** (3301 Pisgah Pike, Versailles, 859/873-1717, www.winstarfarm.com)

No matter how you choose to visit Kentucky's beautiful and iconic horse farms, there are a few things you should keep in mind. First, know that you'll be expected to tip the groom that shows you around the farm. A tip of $5-10 is standard depending on the quality of the tour. If you're on an organized tour, inquire in advance as to whether the price includes tips. Second, wear appropriate clothing. You're walking around a working farm, so closed-toe shoes with good soles are the best choice. Third, think carefully before bringing your children to a horse farm. Although the farms themselves have no restrictions against children, keep in mind that kids without an express interest in horses may find the tours boring (no petting, no running, no loud talking) or they may be exposed to information that may not be age-appropriate (the details of horse breeding). Finally, remember that tours may be limited during certain events or times of year, such as breeding season, horse sales, Derby week, or Keeneland meets. The best way to avoid disappointment is to plan as far in advance as possible.

© THERESA DOWELL BLACKINTON

LEXINGTON

Mill St., 859/253-0362, www.bluegrasstrust. org, 1pm-4pm Wed.-Fri. and Sun., 10am-3pm Sat., $7 adults, $6 seniors, $4 students), known to its former residents as Hopemont, was saved from the wrecking ball in 1955 by the Bluegrass Trust for Historic Preservation. The trust now leads guided tours of the restored house, telling the story of one of Kentucky's most interesting families. Descendants of John Hunt include the legendary Confederate raider John Hunt Morgan, whose mother inherited the house directly from her father, John Hunt, and Dr. Thomas Hunt Morgan, who won the Nobel Prize in 1933 for his work in genetics. Tours of the house take visitors to the home's many rooms, pointing out both family and period furniture of note as well as unique architectural features. A one-room Civil War museum with authentic artifacts from the war is located on the second floor. Tours last about 45 minutes and begin on the hour.

Waveland State Historic Site

Waveland State Historic Site (225 Waveland Museum Ln., 859/272-3611, http://parks. ky.gov, 10am-4pm Wed.-Sat., 1pm-4pm Sun., Apr.-Dec.) preserves the plantation home of the Joseph Bryan family, direct descendants of Daniel Boone, providing insight into life in Kentucky in the 1840-1860 period. The tours ($7 adults, $6 seniors, $4 students) are excellent, given by enthusiastic tour guides, who dress in period costume and take on the persona of the family. Their monologues are both informative and at times amusing and allow plenty of opportunity for questions. Although slave quarters have disappeared from most historic homes, they remain at Waveland, and tours include a stop in both the downstairs working quarters and the upstairs living quarters, allowing for an interesting conversation on slavery in Kentucky. If you're a believer in paranormal activity, ask to hear a few of the house's ghost stories. Special events are held regularly and include spirit walks around Halloween and candlelight tours around Christmas. Tours depart on the hour and last about an hour.

The park grounds, which are open

© THERESA DOWELL BLACKINTON

plantation home at Waveland State Historic Site

year-round from dawn to dusk, are free to the public. Amenities include picnic tables, a playground, a 0.25-mile nature trail, and a flower garden.

Lexington Cemetery

The **Lexington Cemetery** (833 W. Main St., 859/255-5522, www.lexcem.org, 8am-5pm daily) is the final resting place of many notables, including Henry Clay, John Hunt Morgan, and Adolph Rupp. The cemetery also has a large Civil War section with memorials to both Union and Confederate soldiers. The enormous old trees, attractive landscaping, and impressive statuary make the cemetery not just a place to pay your respects, but also a place for contemplative reflection.

MUSEUMS
Explorium

If you have kids with energy to burn, take them to the **Explorium** (440 W. Short St., 859/258-3253, www.explorium.com, 10am-5pm Tues.-Sat., 1pm-5pm Sun., open Mondays as well Memorial Day-Labor Day, $8) for a solid few hours of hands-on discovery. The only dedicated children's museum in Kentucky, the Explorium strives to create eureka moments for kids while they're engaged in play. Exhibits run the gamut from healthy bodies to space to dinosaurs to caves to music. In a nod to local life, kids can dress up like a jockey and mount a life-size stuffed horse, care for a stuffed horse by brushing its mane, and learn about the horse industry. Other kid favorites are a bubble room, where you can step inside a bubble, and a 70-foot water table that re-creates a section of the Kentucky River. Admission to the museum also allows kids to enter the art studio and take part in the day's activity or create a masterpiece of their choosing. The museum will validate parking tickets for the Victorian Square garage for up to three hours.

Headley-Whitney Museum

In an unlikely location surrounded by horse farms, you'll find a unique art museum, the **Headley-Whitney Museum** (4435 Old Frankfort Pike, 859/255-6654, www.headley-whitney.org, 10am-5pm Wed.-Fri., noon-5pm Sat.-Sun., adults $10, seniors $7, students $7). Opened in 1968 on the family farm (hence the location) by George W. Headley, a jewelry designer to the stars, to show off his works and his eccentric collection of art and oddities, the museum now exists as a nonprofit with the same goals. Those who find their way to the museum start in the main building, which houses the dollhouse collection of Headley's wife, Marylou Whitney, along with a collection of Oriental ceramics and rotating exhibits. After touring this building, guests join a guide for a look at the Shell Grotto, a building whimsically decorated entirely in shells, and a visit to the Jewel Room, which houses a fine collection of dazzling and unusual jewelry and bibelots (a French work for knickknacks) created by Headley, and the Library, where you'll find a broad array of art books along with Headley's collection of items no longer considered collectible (thank goodness)—elephant tusks, rhino horns, whale vertebrae, and the like. The pretty grounds are certainly worth a stroll as well.

Aviation Museum of Kentucky

Fans of flying will enjoy the **Aviation Museum of Kentucky** (Blue Grass Airport, 4029 Airport Rd., 859/231-1219, www.aviationky.org, 10am-5pm Tues.-Sat., 1pm-5pm Sun., $7 adults, $5 seniors, $4 youth 6-16). On display are restored airplanes, both military and civilian, including barnstormers and a variety of warbirds. The museum also contains a hall of fame honoring Kentuckians who have contributed to the field of aviation. The staff is made up of plane enthusiasts who are eager to share their knowledge with visitors.

Living Arts & Science Center

Although more known for their educational programs and their events that spotlight both art and science, the **Living Arts & Science Center** (362 N. Martin Luther King Blvd., 859/252-5222, www.lasclex.org, 8am-5pm Mon.-Fri. and 10am-2pm Sat. Sept.-May, 8am-5:30pm Mon.-Fri. June-Aug., free) also

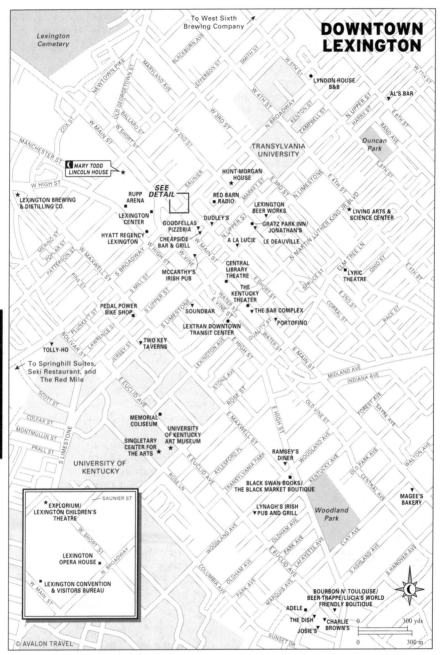

LEXINGTON

DOWNTOWN LEXINGTON

To West Sixth Brewing Company

Lexington Cemetery

LYNDON HOUSE B&B

AL'S BAR

TRANSYLVANIA UNIVERSITY

Duncan Park

MARY TODD LINCOLN HOUSE

HUNT-MORGAN HOUSE

SEE DETAIL

LEXINGTON BREWING & DISTILLING CO.

RUPP ARENA

RED BARN RADIO

LEXINGTON BEER WORKS

LIVING ARTS & SCIENCE CENTER

LEXINGTON CENTER

GOODFELLAS PIZZERIA

DUDLEY'S

GRATZ PARK INN/ JONATHAN'S

HYATT REGENCY LEXINGTON

CHEAPSIDE BAR & GRILL

A LA LUCIE

LE DEAUVILLE

LYRIC THEATRE

MCCARTHY'S IRISH PUB

CENTRAL LIBRARY THEATRE

THE KENTUCKY THEATER

PEDAL POWER BIKE SHOP

SOUNDBAR

THE BAR COMPLEX

PORTOFINO

LEXTRAN DOWNTOWN TRANSIT CENTER

TWO KEY TAVERNS

TOLLY-HO

To Springhill Suites, Seki Restaurant, and The Red Mile

MEMORIAL COLISEUM

UNIVERSITY OF KENTUCKY ART MUSEUM

SINGLETARY CENTER FOR THE ARTS

RAMSEY'S DINER

UNIVERSITY OF KENTUCKY

BLACK SWAN BOOKS/ THE BLACK MARKET BOUTIQUE

MAGEE'S BAKERY

LYNAGH'S IRISH PUB AND GRILL

Woodland Park

EXPLORIUM/ LEXINGTON CHILDREN'S THEATRE

SAUNIER ST

LEXINGTON OPERA HOUSE

BOURBON N' TOULOUSE/ BEER TRAPPE/LUCIA'S WORLD FRIENDLY BOUTIQUE

LEXINGTON CONVENTION & VISITORS BUREAU

ADELE

THE DISH

CHARLIE BROWN'S

JOSIE'S

0   300 yds

0   300 m

© AVALON TRAVEL

hosts rotating exhibits related to both topics. It's worth popping in to see what's on display as the exhibits are very well done and usually hands-on. Check the website for programming details.

BREWING, DISTILLING, AND WINEMAKING SIGHTS
Lexington Brewing and Distilling Co.
Lexington Brewing and Distilling Co. (401 Cross St., 859/255-2337, www.kentuckyale.com, 10am-5pm Mon.-Sat., noon-5pm Sun.), the newest addition to the Bourbon Trail, is unique in that it is a joint beer and bourbon operation. The brewing business got underway first, and currently five beers are produced on-site, including the popular Kentucky Bourbon Barrel Ale and Kentucky Bourbon Barrel Stout, each of which get their finish from a multi-week stay in a used bourbon barrel. The distillery, which became the first new distillery in Lexington in more than 100 years, produces Town Branch Bourbon. Forty-five-minute tours ($7), which include both the brewhouse and the distillery, depart on the hour.

Barrel House Distillery
In the old barrel house of a long-gone distillery, **Barrel House Distillery** (1200 Manchester St., 859/259-0159, http://barrelhousedistillery.com, noon-5pm Wed.-Fri., 11am-3pm Sat.-Sun., free) is making a fresh go of it, distilling craft rum, vodka, moonshine, and bourbon. Although the bourbon has been distilled and barreled, it has not yet been declared ready, though rumor has it that 2014 might be the year the first of the bourbon gets bottled. Tours of this boutique distillery depart at 15 minutes past the hour and include a tasting.

Talon Winery
Located on farmland dotted with barns and ponds, **Talon Winery** (7086 Tates Creek Rd., 859/971-3214, www.talonwine.com, 10am-7pm Mon.-Thurs., 10am-8pm Fri.-Sat., noon-6pm Sun., Apr.-Oct., 10am-6pm Mon.-Thurs., 10am-7pm Fri.-Sat., noon-6pm Sun., Nov.-Mar.) is a pretty spot to enjoy a glass or two of wine. Start your visit with a walk through the five-acre vineyards, stopping to peek in at the production facilities if you wish. Then enter the 18th-century farmhouse that serves as the tasting room at Talon Winery to imbibe some of their award-winning wines, including Coyote Red, a highly regarded semi-sweet red wine. Six tastings cost $5. During the summer, the winery hosts multiple music events, including jazz on the porch and Friday night concerts.

UNIVERSITY SIGHTS
University of Kentucky
The **University of Kentucky** (500 S. Limestone St., 859/257-9000, www.uky.edu) is the state's largest public university and the reason that people throughout the state claim to bleed blue. Always bustling, even in the summer, the University of Kentucky has a profound impact on Lexington, and a number of campus sites are of interest to students and non-students alike.

The **University of Kentucky Art Museum** (405 Rose St., 859/257-5716, www.uky.edu/artmuseum, noon-5pm Tues.-Sun., until 8pm Fri., free) boasts a collection of more than 4,500 objects. Genres represented include painting, drawing, photography, printmaking, and sculpture, and works come from Europe, Africa, Asia, and the Americas. Names that you might recognize as you browse the exhibitions include Childe Hassam, Louis Tiffany, Roy Lichtenstein, and Alexander Calder. The museum also has a strong collection of work done by regional artists. Special exhibitions are hosted at the museum regularly and may have an admission fee.

The **Arboretum** (500 Alumni Dr., 859/257-6955, www.ca.uky.edu/arboretum, dawn-dusk daily, free) is a popular destination for Lexingtonians of all ages. A two-mile paved path attracts joggers and dog walkers, while the lovely gardens appeal to those looking to relax and rejuvenate. Even at the peak of the hottest summer or the coldest winter, something is in bloom.

LEXINGTON

© THERESA DOWELL BLACKINTON

University of Kentucky Arboretum

Quilters and art enthusiasts will want to take the elevator to the fifth floor of the William T. Young Library (401 Hilltop Ave., 859/257-0500, www.uky.edu, 8am-8pm daily) to view the **Wade Hall Quilt Collection.** Consisting of more than 100 quilts, 64 of which are on display, the collection encompasses quilts from throughout the Ohio Valley, focusing on quilts created not with the intention of being displayed, but with the purpose of being used. The oldest quilt in the collection dates to 1860.

Transylvania University
The oldest college west of the Alleghenies, **Transylvania University** (300 N. Broadway, 859/233-8300, www.transy.edu) was established in 1780, predating the state of Kentucky by 12 years. Old Morrison, a Greek Revival building completed in 1843 by well-known architect Gideon Shyrock, sits at the heart of the campus and is listed as a National Historical Landmark. Old Morrison is open to the public year-round, and guests are also welcome to stroll the grounds of Transy, as the university

is known locally. If you're visiting with your sweetheart, be sure to locate the Kissing Tree, a white ash located near the library where young lovers would steal a kiss back in the days when public displays of affection were not only frowned upon, but actually forbidden. Today, a bench circles the tree, making it a fine place to sit and read if you don't have someone to smooch.

ENTERTAINMENT AND EVENTS
As you'd expect from the city that is home to the state's biggest university, Lexington hosts a large amount of nightlife. Though plenty of places cater to the college student, there are also more upscale bars for those wanting a spot with a bit more class and a bit less noise.

Bars and Clubs
The ever-popular **Cheapside Bar & Grill** (131 Cheapside, 859/254-0046, www.cheapsidebarandgrill.com, 11:30am-2:30am daily) is located downtown. Cheapside's huge deck with

its own bar makes it a great destination when the weather's nice. A Victorian-style pub can meet your drinking needs when the weather's not so fair. For the standard Irish pub experience, **McCarthy's Irish Pub** (117 S. Upper St., 859/258-2181, www.mccarthysirishbar.com, 11am-2:30am daily) delivers. The pub doesn't offer food, but you're welcome to order from local restaurants. Offering more of an upscale lounge scene is **Soundbar** (208 S. Limestone, 859/523-6338, www.soundbarlex.com, 4:30pm-2:30am daily), which serves classic cocktails in an updated art deco building on the southern edge of downtown. Soundbar is especially popular Thursday-Saturday, when a DJ spins live beginning at 10pm and crowds take to the dance floor. Recognized by *Out Magazine,* **The Bar Complex** (224 E. Main St., 859/255-1551, www.thebarcomplex.com, 4pm-midnight Mon.-Wed., 4pm-2:30am Thurs.-Sat.) caters to Lexington's gay and lesbian crowd, although people of all sexual orientations are welcome. The Bar hosts often-outrageous drag shows and has three bars and a dance floor to keep the customers happy.

As you would expect, the area near the University of Kentucky campus is also a hot spot for nightlife, particularly for the younger crowd. **Two Keys Taverns** (333 S. Limestone, 859/254-5000, 11am-2:30am daily) is, for many UK undergrads, the place to go for a good time. Wildcat central, Two Keys is packed for all the games with raucous fans. **Lynagh's Irish Pub and Grill** (384 Woodland Ave., 859/255-1292, www.lynaghsirishpub.com, 11am-2:30am Mon.-Sat., noon-11pm Sun.) does live music on the weekends and hosts trivia nights on Thursday. The pub is also a popular place to watch UK games if you can't get a ticket. **Charlie Brown's** (816 E. Euclid Ave., 859/269-5701, 11am-1am Mon.-Thurs., 11am-2am Fri.-Sat., noon-midnight Sun.) has a bit more of a laid-back atmosphere with worn but comfy couches, fireplaces, and walls lined with bookshelves. It is, however, about as dark as a pub can get. Escape to the lively patio if the dark starts to get to you.

If you're into home brews, craft brews, and the local beer scene, Lexington has some solid options for you. For a taste of Lexington beer, check out **Country Boy Brewing** (436 Chair Ave., 859/554-6200, http://countryboybrewing.com, 4pm-10pm Mon.-Tues., noon-midnight Wed.-Sat., 1pm-10pm Sun.), where you can enjoy a beer produced on-site or choose from a selection of other craft beers, and **West Sixth Brewing Company** (501 W. Sixth St., 859/951-6006, www.westsixth.com, 3pm-10pm Mon.-Wed., 3pm-11pm Thurs., noon-midnight Fri.-Sat., noon-10pm Sun.), where an ever-changing variety of house-produced craft brews are on tap. Both are laid-back, get-together-with-friends kind of places, particularly perfect on a hot summer's evening. Food trucks can usually be found nearby both to provide accompaniment to the beer. Home brewers can load up with supplies at **Lexington Beer Works** (213 N. Limestone St., 859/359-6747, http://lexingtonbeerworks.com, 3pm-11pm Mon.-Wed., 1pm-midnight Thurs., 1pm-1am Fri., noon-1am Sat., noon-11pm Sun.), which also has 12 taps rotating through craft beers from around the world as well as more than 100 bottled beers. Also worth adding to the list is the **Beer Trappe** (811 Euclid Ave., 859/309-0911, www.thebeertrappe.com, 4pm-10pm Mon., 11am-midnight Tues.-Sat., 1pm-10pm Sun.), which, with its eight rotating taps of rare craft beers and more than 500 bottled beers, is a beer-lover's paradise.

Live Music

Al's Bar (601 N. Limestone, 859/309-2901, www.alsbarlexington.com, 4pm-midnight Mon.-Thurs., 4pm-2am Fri.-Sat., 4pm-midnight Sun.) has established itself as the best place for bluegrass music in Lexington. Live shows are held Wednesday-Saturday. Though the bar has a bit of a dive feeling, it serves good burgers and has a quite credible bourbon list.

Country music fans will find a haven at **Austin City Saloon** (2350 Woodhill Dr., 859/266-6891, www.austincitysaloon.com, 7pm-2:30am Wed.-Sat.). Hosting live, local country acts every night, Austin City Saloon is the hometown bar of country star John Michael Montgomery.

Jazz fans should check out **Live at the Library** (www.jazzartsfoundation.org), a free monthly show sponsored by the Jazz Arts Foundation and the Lexington Public Library. The shows are held on the second Thursday of the month 7pm-8:30pm at the Central Library Theatre (140 E. Main St.).

The best venue in town for medium-size rock, punk, metal, and indie shows is **Buster's Billiards & Backroom** (899 Manchester St., 859/368-8871, www.bustersbb.com, 7pm-2:30am Wed.-Sat.), which is located in an old distillery, with the shows taking place in the large back room. A list of shows, most of which are ages 18+, is on the website.

Two live radio shows are taped in Lexington and welcome crowds to enjoy the music in person. **Woodsongs Old Time Radio Hour** (300 E. Third St., 859/252-8888, www.woodsongs.com, $10) tapes its show, which features folk and acoustic music, every Monday at the Lyric Theatre. The show begins taping at 7pm, and audience members must be in their seats by 6:45pm. It's best to reserve tickets in advance, although unfilled seats are available on a standby basis. A schedule of artists is available on the website. **Red Barn Radio** (161 N. Mill St., www.redbarnradio.com, 7pm Wed., $8) is dedicated to old-time Kentucky and bluegrass music. Their one-hour show, which features music as well as conversation with the artists, is taped on Wednesdays at 7pm. Tickets can be purchased at the door.

Comedy

If you're looking for a good laugh, try **Comedy Off Broadway** (161 Lexington Green Cir., 859/271-5653, http://comedyoffbroadway.com), which hosts famous national acts as well as more regional comedians.

Movie Theaters

The **Kentucky Theatre** (214 E. Main St., 859/231-7924, www.kentuckytheatre.com) transports moviegoers back to Hollywood's glory days. The magnificently restored 1920s theater has stained glass, murals on its walls, and a grand lobby. Films usually lean to the more artistic and independent, although blockbusters such as the *Twilight* series have also been shown at the Kentucky Theatre. During the summer, the theater hosts a classic film series, and midnight showings of *The Rocky Horror Picture Show* draw legions of dedicated fans who dress up and act out scenes from the cult classic. General admission tickets are $7.50, although shows before 6pm are only $5.50.

Art Galleries

Lexington hosts a downtown **art gallery hop** (www.galleryhoplex.com) five times a year, on the third Friday of February, April, June, September, and November. The LexTran trolley provides free transportation among the nearly 30 studios and galleries that participate in the hop. Many participating venues schedule openings and events to coincide with the hop, which is held 5pm-8pm. Artwork on display covers a wide range of genres, including folk art, jewelry, pottery, painting, printmaking, and sculpture.

Performing Arts

The **Singletary Center for the Arts** (405 Rose St., 859/257-4929, www.uky.edu), located on the UK campus, is a top-notch center for performing arts in Lexington. The Singletary Signature Series presents a full schedule of dance, jazz, classical, and world music. The center also hosts performances by UK Theatre, UK Opera Theatre, the **Lexington Philharmonic Orchestra** (www.lexphil.org), and such special events as music festivals and the Miss Kentucky pageant. Tickets for all events can be purchased online, over the phone, or in person at the box office (10am-5pm Mon.-Fri.).

The historic **Lexington Opera House** (401 W. Short St., 859/233-3535, www.lexingtonoperahouse.com) is not just a venue for opera. In fact, opera actually makes up just a small portion of the schedule, with other dates filled with ballet, comedy, Broadway series, and children's presentations. Companies that perform at the Lexington Opera House include the

Lexington Opera Society (www.lexingtonopera.com), the **Lexington Ballet** (859/233-3925, www.lexingtonballet.org), and the **Kentucky Ballet** (859/252-5245, www.kyballet.com).

A special treat put on by Lexington's ballet companies is **Ballet Under the Stars,** which is held for four nights in August at Woodland Park (601 E. High St.). For $5, attendees enjoy ballet in the beautiful park setting and are invited to bring a picnic to nibble on during the show.

Exposing children to the wonders of live theater since 1938, the **Lexington Children's Theatre** (418 W. Short St., 859/254-4546, www.lctonstage.org) offers a full season of fun favorites every year. Recent performances have included *Shrek the Musical, The Legend of Sleepy Hollow, Jack and the Wonder Beans,* and *The Best Christmas Pageant Ever.*

Festivals and Events

For many Lexingtonians, the year's biggest events are sporting events—opening weekend at Keeneland and the first game of UK's basketball season. For Kentucky Wildcat fans, life revolves around basketball, making Midnight Madness, also known in these parts as **Big Blue Madness** (www.ukathletics.com), a red letter day. Midnight Madness takes place on the first day that the NCAA allows formal basketball practice to be held (mid-October), marking the beginning of what UK fans consider to be the best time of the year. The University of Kentucky holds the record for most attendees at a Midnight Madness event, with fans camping out days in advance to try to get tickets.

Another much anticipated annual event is early June's **Festival of the Bluegrass** (www.festivalofthebluegrass.com). This four-day festival draws bluegrass music fans from the world over to the Kentucky Horse Park for some serious jamming. Many attendees bring their RVs, and after the day's official events end, the party goes on within the community of fans.

Theatre fans won't want to miss **Summerfest** (www.mykct.org), a three-week festival put on by the Kentucky Theatre Conservatory, in which two plays—which change every year and range from Shakespeare to modern classics to musicals—are performed in the open air of the UK Arboretum.

SHOPPING
Downtown Shopping Centers

The **Lexington Center** (430 W. Vine St., 859/233-4567, www.lexingtoncenter.com, 10am-6pm Mon.-Sat.) is home to Rupp Arena and the convention center as well as two levels of shops, including **Kentucky Korner,** which sells all things UK; the **Kentucky Proud Market,** where you can stock up on food items produced by farmers throughout the state; **Old Kentucky Chocolates,** where you can create a grab bag of bourbon chocolates, Kentucky Derby mints, and chocolate thoroughbreds (known elsewhere as turtles); and **Artique,** which is chock-full of arts and crafts from more than 1,000 American artisans.

Boutiques

Lexington is a city with style and, as such, has a lovely array of boutiques carrying everything from the latest fashions to home furnishings to fun gifts. Locals all have their favorites, so don't be afraid to ask for recommendations, but here are a few centrally located places to get you started. **Adelé** (445 S. Ashland Ave., 859/266-9930, www.adelelexington.com, 10am-6pm Mon.-Fri., 10am-4pm Sun.) carries home decor, gift items, baby items, and jewelry that will make you look good, whether you keep it for yourself or give it to a friend. **The Black Market Boutique** (516 E. High St., 859/281-1421, www.theblackmarketboutiqueky.com, 11am-6pm Mon.-Sat.) specializes in both new and vintage fashion and jewelry, and also sells artwork and handcrafted goods. **Lucia's World Friendly Boutique** (523 E. High St., 859/389-9337, www.luciasboutique.com, 11am-6pm Mon.-Sat., 1pm-5pm Sun.) stocks fair-trade and eco-friendly clothes, jewelry, accessories, and gifts from artisans around the world.

Bookstores

Joseph-Beth Booksellers (161 Lexington Green Cir., 859/273-2911, www.josephbeth.

com, 10am-10pm Mon.-Thurs., 10am-11pm Fri.-Sat., 11am-9pm Sun.) is Lexington's go-to bookstore. The two-story bookstore carries a huge selection of books, has a dedicated children's area, and hosts an endless array of authors and public figures. Joseph-Beth plays a very active role in Lexington life. **Black Swan Books** (505 E. Maxwell St., 859/252-7255, www.blackswanbooks.net, 11am-5:30pm Mon.-Sat.) is a dedicated champion of Kentucky authors, hosting readings and signings, and carrying books from names and publishers big and small. One of the dwindling number of locally owned, independent bookstores, Black Swan is a bibliophile's paradise with knowledgeable staff and a rich collection of hard-to-find books.

Malls

Mall rats will be right at home at **Fayette Mall** (3401 Nicholasville Rd., 859/272-3495, www.shopfayette-mall.com, 10am-9pm Mon.-Sat., noon-6pm Sun.), which has more than 120 stores. Macy's, JC Penney's, Dillard's, and Sears anchor the mall.

SPORTS AND RECREATION
Parks

An important site in the founding of Lexington, **McConnell Springs** (416 Rebmann Ln., 859/225-4073, www.mcconnellsprings.org, dawn-dusk daily) was used as a resting station by 18th-century pioneers as they explored the Kentucky wilderness. Today, the spring, which is referred to as the blue hole thanks to its vibrant color, is protected as a park. Wetlands, an old quarry, and century-old trees are also contained within this park, which provides a way for city dwellers to quickly get back to nature. An education center is open 9am-5pm Monday-Saturday and 1pm-5pm Sunday.

When Boonesborough became too crowded for Daniel Boone's tastes, he founded a smaller settlement named Boone Station. Today, nothing remains of the structures that composed the settlement, but **Boone Station State Historic Site** (240 Gentry Rd., 859/527-3131, http://parks.ky.gov, free) commemorates the location.

The verdant green landscape welcomes picnickers as well as those looking for open space to play a game of Frisbee or football. The park also has a one-mile trail.

Convenient to downtown, **Woodland Park** (601 E. High St.) is one of Lexington's most popular parks. In addition to basketball and tennis courts, horseshoe pits, and a baseball field, Woodland Park also has a skate park with 12,000 square feet of bowls, ramps, pipes, and platforms and an aquatic center (11am-8pm Mon.-Sat., 1pm-8pm Sun., $5 adults, $4 youth under 16) with slides, high dive, children's water play area, sand and grass play areas, and lap lanes.

On a water company reservoir, **Jacobson Park** (4001 Athens-Boonesboro Rd.) provides water sports facilities in addition to the typical playground, picnic, and green space offerings. During fair weather, a marina rents pedal boats and also allows you to launch your own non-motorized watercraft for a small fee. Fishing is also allowed from the bank or handicap-accessible docks. If you have a dog, bring it along and let it run free in the dog park.

Hiking

Raven Run Nature Sanctuary (5888 Jack's Creek Pike, 859/272-6105, www.lexingtonky.gov, 9am-5pm daily), a 734-acre preserve located south of the city, invites hikers to use its 10 miles of trails. The trails cross meadows, meander along creeks, and lead through woodlands characteristic of the Kentucky Palisades. On your hike, you may see the remains of structures built by early settlers and can try to identify as many of the sanctuary's 600 plant species and 200 bird species as possible. A nature center is located at the head of the trail system, and visitors are asked to sign in before hiking.

Biking

The Lexington Convention & Visitors Bureau and the Blue Grass Trust for Historic Preservation have teamed up to encourage visitors to see Lexington on two wheels by publishing a bicycle tour of the city's historic sites. The

BLEEDING BLUE: UNIVERSITY OF KENTUCKY BASKETBALL

There is no reasonable explanation for the passion Kentucky residents feel for the UK Wildcats men's basketball team, but that in no way makes it any less real. Just find a way inside Rupp Arena on game day to see the fervor for yourself.

UK basketball has a long and proud tradition (aside from two periods of NCAA probation, one in the 1950s, and one in the late 1980s/ early 1990s). The program, which was begun in 1903, did not immediately have great success or prominence, but by 1912, the UK men's basketball team was regularly putting up winning seasons. The worst season in early UK basketball history came in 1927, when the Wildcats posted a losing season record. This would be the last time this happened until 1989, and it has not happened again since.

Wildcat basketball rose to prominence under the coaching of Adolph Rupp, who led the team for an impressive 42 years, from 1930 to 1972, when he was forced out by a policy that required state employees to retire at age 70. The winningest coach in college basketball history at the time of his retirement (with a total of 876 wins), Rupp led his teams to national championships in 1948, 1949, 1951, and 1958. His teams also won 27 Southeastern Conference regular season championships and 13 SEC tournaments. The most famous of Rupp's teams was his 1966 team, affectionately nicknamed Rupp's Runts, because no player on the team was taller than 6'5." This all-white team faced Texas Western's all-black starting team in that year's championship, losing 72-65. Rupp, who recruited teams that were 80 percent in-state players, did not sign his first black player until 1969.

In the years since Rupp retired, Kentucky has had six coaches and won four more national championships: the 1978 championship under Joe B. Hall, the 1996 championship under Rick

Pitino, the 1998 championship under Tubby Smith, and the 2012 championship under John Calipari. Remarkable teams in the recent history of Kentucky basketball include 1992's The Unforgettables; 1996's The Untouchables, who went undefeated through the conference regular season before winning the national championship; and 1998's Comeback Cats, who rebounded from huge deficits in the last three games of the tournament to win the national championship. The 1992 team, which was led by four seniors (Richie Farmer, Deron Feldhaus, John Pelphrey, and Sean Woods), three of whom were from eastern Kentucky, brought Kentucky back to prominence after two years of NCAA probation. This team, however, is probably best known for their loss to Duke in the Elite Eight, when Christian Laettner hit a game-winning shot just as the clock expired. Regarded as one of the most memorable games in college basketball, it remains a nightmare for UK fans. Don't even consider mentioning Laettner's name or Duke University, which in addition to Louisville, remains one of the Wildcat's biggest non-conference rivals.

In the first three years under John Calipari, who came to Kentucky in 2009, Kentucky went from advancing to the Elite Eight of the NCAA tournament to the Final Four to winning it all. However, in 2012-2013, the defending champion Wildcats failed to make the NCAA tournament and lost in the first round of the NIT. That's the same year that the University of Louisville went on to capture the NCAA title, making the already difficult season for UK fans even worse.

In total, as of 2013, Kentucky has won eight national titles, second behind only UCLA; made 52 NCAA tournament appearances, more than any other team; and is the winningest program in college basketball history. Perhaps that's why fans are so crazy about their Big Blue.

11-mile route takes cyclists through historic districts and to such sites as the Hunt-Morgan House, the Opera House, and Memorial Coliseum. The brochure with map and details is available online (www.visitlex.com) or at the visitors bureau.

Cycling past horse farms as you roll through the gentle hills of the Bluegrass on back roads is nothing short of spectacular. Most roads in and around Lexington are bike-friendly, so feel free to explore as you wish. Those unfamiliar with the area would do well to contact the **Bluegrass Cycling Club** (www.bgcycling.org) for suggested routes. The club also organizes near-daily rides for those looking to ride in a group. Check the website for more information.

A number of annual bike events are held in Lexington. One of the most well attended is the **Horsey Hundred,** held annually on Memorial Day weekend. This event has route options of 26, 35, 53, 75, and 100 miles, so that anyone who likes to cycle can participate. The ride is not a race but a chance to see horse country from your bike in the company of others. The Horsey Hundred is sponsored by the Bluegrass Cycling Club, and more information about this and other events is available on their website.

If your bike needs servicing or you'd like to pick up some new gear, try **Pedal Power Bike Shop** (401 S. Upper St., 859/255-6408, www.pedalpowerbikeshop.com, 9am-6pm Mon.-Fri., 9am-5pm Sat.). The staff is knowledgeable and can also offer suggestions on their favorite rides in the region.

Golf

Kearney Hill Golf Links (Kearney Rd., 859/253-1981, www.lexingtonky.gov) is a favorite of area golfers and has hosted numerous national professional and amateur events. The Scottish links-style course has deep bunkers, three manmade lakes acting as water hazards, and wide open terrain that makes wind a major factor in your play.

Host of a Senior PGA golf qualifier and many state events, **Lakeside Golf Course** (Coy Dr., 859/263-5315, www.lexingtonky.gov) has the longest par-5 hole in the state. The course

is gently rolling and situated on the shores of Jacobson Lake, making it a scenic place for a round of golf.

Disc Golf

Disc golf is a popular pastime in Lexington, and three parks contain courses. **River Hill Park** (3800 Crosby Dr.), which opened in 2009, is the newest of the courses, and the 2,100-foot course provides a good introduction to the sport. The course at **Shillito Park** (300 W. Reynolds Rd.) is a challenging course that is very wooded and has lots of elevation change. **Veterans Park** (650 Southpoint Dr.) has a course similar to that at Shillito, with most of the action in wooded areas.

Spectator Sports

Horse racing and basketball are at the center of the sporting world in Lexington. In all seriousness, opening day at Keeneland and March Madness are bigger than Christmas here, so if you really want to see what Lexington is about, you need to get in on the action at Keeneland, which has meets in April and October, and Rupp Arena, home to the University of Kentucky Wildcats.

Rupp Arena (430 W. Vine St., 859/233-4567, www.rupparena.com) is the largest basketball arena in the United States, and on game days, it's absolutely packed with Wildcats fans. **UK basketball** is a passion that sweeps the entire state, with Louisville the possible exception, although there are plenty of Cats fans there, too. With a total of 2,111 wins as of the 2012-2013 season, including eight national championships, Kentucky is the winningest college basketball program in the nation. To experience the madness, try to get a ticket for a home game, though be warned—your chances aren't very good. Season ticket holders make up the bulk of nonstudent attendees at the game, with single-game tickets available only if student demand is low, and I'm not sure that's ever happened. If hell freezes over and it does happen, tickets will be available online through www.ticketmaster.com on dates listed on the UK athletics website (www.ukathletics.

© THERESA DOWELL BLACKINTON

Even the water tower is for the Wildcats in Lexington.

com). Your best bet is to find a season ticket holder who is unable to use his or her tickets. Check www.stubhub.com to see if anything is available. Be aware that scalping is illegal in Kentucky.

Believe it or not, the University of Kentucky does participate in a slew of other sports at the Division I level. Women's basketball has had its own success, and you'll have much better luck getting a ticket to one of the women's games at **Memorial Coliseum** (Euclid Ave. at Lexington Ave.). Tickets may be purchased by calling the UK Ticket Office (859/257-1818) or ordering online. Behind basketball, football is the most popular sport at UK. Although the football program hasn't had the success the basketball program has, **Commonwealth Stadium** (1540 University Dr., 859/257-8000), which can seat more than 67,000, still draws good crowds for UK football games. Tickets for UK football games may be purchased through www.ticketmaster.com.

In addition to Keeneland, which has meets

in April and October, Lexington is home to **The Red Mile** (1200 Red Mile Rd., 859/255-0752, www.theredmile.com, $2), a one-mile, red clay harness racing track. Live racing takes place August-October. A pretty track with an unusual round barn, Red Mile offers the chance to see standardbred horses instead of thoroughbreds.

The **Lexington Legends** (www.lexington-legends.com) offer an alternative to horse racing and UK athletics. The Class A affiliate of the Kansas City Royals, the Lexington Legends take on their opponents in the South Atlantic League's Northern Division at **Whitaker Bank Ballpark** (207 Legends Ln., 859/422-7867). As with most minor league baseball teams, the Lexington Legends do a ton of promotions, and attending a game is a fun way to spend a summer afternoon or evening. Lawn seats are $4, bleacher tickets are $5, and box seats start at $9.

ACCOMMODATIONS

As you would expect, Lexington has a healthy selection of hotels, although the majority of them are chain hotels. These chains run the gamut from family-friendly budget hotels to upscale hotels. The city does have a few unique inns and bed-and-breakfasts, which are detailed here. If you can't find a place to stay in Lexington, consider the surrounding communities included in this chapter.

$100-150

Convenient to the University of Kentucky, **SpringHill Suites** (863 S. Broadway, 895/225-1500, www.marriott.com, $139) pleases guests with clean, comfortable rooms that come with mini-kitchens and sitting areas. The pool, workout room, continental breakfast, and free wireless Internet also have their fans. Some rooms face the Red Mile racetrack, which some people like and others don't. If you're choosy, specify a preference at booking.

Connected to Rupp Arena and the convention center, the **Hyatt Regency Lexington** (401 W. High St., 859/253-1234, http://lexington.hyatt.com, $139) attracts both basketball fans and businesspeople. Rooms are spacious and well appointed with comfy beds, a chair with ottoman, flat-screen TVs, iPod docking stations, and wireless Internet access. The hotel is within walking distance of most downtown Lexington restaurants and attractions.

If you don't mind not being centrally located, the **Holiday Inn Express Northeast** (1780 Sharkey Way, 859/231-0657, www.hiexpress.com, $145.99) is a good choice. New in 2008, the hotel maintains a fresh, contemporary feel, and the rooms are clean and comfortable. The staff is friendly, and the standard Holiday Inn Express continental breakfast is included. The hotel is located just inside New Circle Road, with downtown a quick 2.5-mile drive south on U.S. 421.

$150-200

Located among the horse farms north of the city, **◖ Essence of the Bluegrass Bed and Breakfast** (4343 Mt. Horeb Pike, 859/255-0067, www.essenceofthebluegrass.com, $149-249) gives guests the choice of four large rooms, each with either a king or queen bed and private bathroom. The entire residence is spotless and all your needs are catered to, with snacks and drinks available around the clock, hosts who are friendly and full of helpful suggestions for the area, and a delicious breakfast to start your day. The grounds are ideal for relaxing if you just want to get away, but the B&B is still within easy access to Lexington if you've got a packed schedule.

Location is the big draw for **Swann's Nest Bed and Breakfast** (3463 Rosalie Ln., 859/226-0095, www.swannsnest.com, $149-235), a stately home located on Cygnet Farm and as close to Keeneland as you can get. From your balcony, you can look out over lovely gardens to see racehorses in open fields. You have a choice of a standard room or a suite, all of which have their own bathrooms. The suites are very large, while standard rooms are cozy but big enough to accommodate king-size beds. Rooms have a bit of a shabby chic feel, and some people notice a hint of smoke throughout the house, so if you're sensitive to that, you might want to look elsewhere. The B&B name

is a bit of a stretch because the breakfast is only packaged pastries rather than a full, hot meal.

The **Gratz Park Inn** (120 W. 2nd St., 859/231-1777, www.gratzparkinn.com, $179-259) is a historic property very well located in the downtown area with easy access to Lexington attractions. Though the property bills itself as a luxury boutique inn, the rooms feel a little tired and could certainly use better lighting. The rooms are individually decorated and vary in size and style. The mahogany beds are comfortable, and amenities include wireless Internet. Breakfast is not included.

Over $200

◖ Lyndon House Bed and Breakfast (507 N. Broadway, 859/420-2683, www.lyndonhouse.com, $169-249) is a gracious 19th-century home located in downtown Lexington. The seven rooms and all common areas are decorated in an elegant Southern style that invites comfort and relaxation. Rooms are very spacious with nice furniture, artwork, and luxurious beds. Gathering places are located both upstairs and downstairs, and guests are invited to relax in the sunroom or in the garden as well. The owner has worked hard to preserve historical details like stained-glass windows, carved moldings, and a Jacobean staircase while also offering modern amenities like wireless Internet and even elevator access. A full breakfast is offered daily in the dining room.

Campgrounds

A very large, high-quality campground is located on the grounds of the **Kentucky Horse Park** (4089 Iron Works Pkwy., 800/370-6416, www.kyhorsepark.com). This campground has 260 back-in sites with electric and water hookups ($32), along with an area designated for tent camping ($20-26). Facilities at the campground include bathhouses, grocery store, tennis, basketball, and volleyball courts, and a large swimming pool. The campground is open year-round, although water hookups are not available November-March. RV sites are by reservation, while tent sites are on a first-come, first-served basis.

FOOD

Lexington has an abundance of great dining options that span the spectrum in style, price, and type of food. There's great Southern food to be had, as well as amazing ethnic food. The listings here are just a sample, so be sure to ask locals about their favorite places to dine. And for a tasty look at what's cooking in Lexington, consider signing up for a food tour with **Bleu Plate Tours** (www.bleuplatetours.com).

Farmers Market

The **Lexington Farmers Market** in Cheapside Park on Saturdays (251 W. Main St., www.lexingtonfarmersmarket.com, 7am-3pm) is about more than just fresh food from local farmers. It's a community gathering place, with musicians and chef demonstrations keeping you there long after you've loaded up on tomatoes and sweet corn.

Cafés and Bakeries

The café at **Good Foods Co-Op** (455 Southland Dr., 859/278-1813, www.goodfoods.coop, 8am-10pm daily, $4.99-7.99), a local grocery store focusing on healthy and organic foods and supporting local producers whenever possible, is a great place for tasty yet good-for-you food. Vegetarians will find that there are just as many options for them as there are for meat eaters on the panini and deli-sandwich menu. The hot buffet (11am-8pm Mon.-Fri., 9am-8pm Sat.-Sun.), salad bar (9am-10pm daily), and weekend brunch (9am-2pm) are extremely popular and can be eaten in or taken to go. Smoothies, milkshakes, and espresso and juice bar drinks make for good midday pick-me-ups.

For breakfast pastries, you've got two bakeries to choose from, both with diehard fans known to line up before the doors open in anticipation of the goodies awaiting them. **Spalding's Bakery** (760 Winchester Rd., 859/252-3737, www.spaldingsbakery.com, 6:30am-noon Wed.-Sat., 7am-noon Sun., $0.75-1.50) has been Lexington's go-to place for doughnuts since 1929. The doughnuts are always hot and fresh and worth lining up for. For those who prefer a more diverse selection of pastries, **Magee's Bakery** (726 E. Main St., 859/255-9481, www.mageesbakery.com, 6:30am-2pm Mon. and Sat., 6:30am-4pm Tues.-Fri., 8am-2pm Sun.) caters to many whims. In addition to doughnuts, Danish, cinnamon rolls, scones, and muffins, Magee's offers breakfast casseroles and biscuit sandwiches ($0.75-$2.50). They also go beyond breakfast to serve a short selection of deli sandwiches ($5.95-9.75) and are well known for their cakes and desserts.

Cheap Eats

Although it recently changed locations, **Tolly-Ho** (606 S. Broadway St., 895/253-2007, www.tollyho.com, open 24 hours daily) remains a UK tradition, a place where students gather, especially when they get hungry at the wee hours of the morning. The Tolly-Ho, a quarter-pound hamburger, comes in at $2.89, and most things on the menu are under $5. Breakfast is available around the clock.

There's nothing fancy about 〔 **Bourbon n' Toulouse** (829 Euclid Ave., 859/335-0300, www.bntlex.com, 11am-9pm Mon.-Sat.), where your meal is served on a Styrofoam plate, but the Cajun cooking is bayou perfect. The on-the-mark menu offers half orders ($4.50) and full orders ($6.50) of chicken étouffée, jambalaya, chicken Creole, red beans with smoked sausage, gumbo, and a few other New Orleans favorites. Multiple gluten-free options are available.

Often packed at 2:30am after final call at the bars, **Goodfellas Pizzeria** (110 N. Mill St., 859/281-1101, www.goodfellaspizzeria.com, 11am-9pm Mon.-Wed., 11am-3:30am Thurs.-Fri., 5am-3:30am Sat.) serves New York-style pizza by the slice or by the pie. The large is an enormous 22 inches, which makes it a favorite of the college crowd. Calzones and oven-baked subs are also available.

Classic American

Although **Josie's** (821 Chevy Chase Pl., 859/538-8328, www.josieslex.com, 8am-9pm Mon.-Sat., 8am-2pm Sun., $6.50-13.50) serves generous and tasty lunches and dinners of classic American favorites, the real reason to go is breakfast, which is available all day. Try the pork chop and eggs or order a waffle with Georgia pecans. Options are pretty traditional, but it's all cooked perfectly.

Contemporary American

A Lexington institution since 1981, **❰ Dudley's** (259 W. Short St., 859/252-1010, www.dudleysrestaurant.com, 11am-2:30pm daily, 5:30pm-10pm Sun.-Thurs., 5:30pm-11pm Fri.-Sat.) is a beautiful restaurant with a wall of windows fronting the sidewalk, rich red and muted green painted walls, molded plaster, and hardwood floors. Vested waiters serve diners seated at freestanding tables or tables lined up against a leather booth lining the wall. Popular for business lunches, Dudley's is just as ably a date spot or special occasion destination. The menu also covers all bases. At lunch ($11-13), choose from a Greek-style lamb burger, a Downtown Debbie Brown version of a Hot Brown, or the Pasta Dudley, which bursts with fresh veggies and big pieces of chicken. At dinner ($22-30), such scrumptious dishes as seared salmon with watermelon gazpacho and braised short ribs with hominy pudding might make the menu.

You'll have a tough time choosing among the options at **The Dish** (438 S. Ashland Ave., 859/317-8438, http://thedishlex.com, 5pm-9pm Mon.-Tues., 5pm-10pm Wed.-Thurs., 5pm-10:30pm Fri.-Sat., $16-26), where you might be tempted with pork shanks braised in West 6th Amber Ale, grouper in guava sauce, or simply the house-made burger. The atmosphere is between that of upscale casual and fine dining, so whether you're on a date or out with friends, it makes a fine destination.

Fresh flavors are the star at **Jean Farris Winery & Bistro** (6825 Old Richmond Rd., 859/263-9463, www.jeanfarris.com, 5:30pm-9pm Tues.-Sat., noon-9pm Sun.), a contemporary, elegant eatery with strong ties to the land. The menu is built around seasonal availability, including herbs, heirloom tomatoes, and a variety of fruit and vegetables grown on-site, as well as local meats whenever possible. Charcuterie

and cheese plates are great for sharing. Pair any meal with a glass of wine made from grapes grown in the vineyard just outside. If the weather's nice, opt for a meal on the patio.

Southern

The redefined Kentucky cuisine at **❰ Jonathan's** (120 W. 2nd St., 859/252-4949, www.japg.info, 11am-2pm and 5:30pm-10pm daily, $24-38) has become so well regarded that chef Jonathan Lundy has given away some of his most popular recipes in a cookbook titled *Jonathan's Bluegrass Table*. What Lundy strives to do is put a contemporary spin on traditional Kentucky dishes made with local products, and with dishes like short ribs braised with bourbon, lamb chops topped with mint julep jelly, and filet wrapped in house-cured bacon, he has succeeded. Food is expertly prepared and presented, and portion sizes are good. The atmosphere is refined but casual, with a large main dining room with cozy booths and open tables as well as a wood-paneled room with a bar that has the feel of a club where good ol' boys can gather and talk politics and UK basketball over supper, which is what they call the evening meal here.

A La Lucie (159 N. Limestone St., 859/252-5277, www.alalucie.com, 11am-2pm Tues.-Fri., 5pm-10pm Mon.-Thurs., 5pm-11pm Fri.-Sat., $18.95-29.95) serves a fantastic menu of upscale food, but there's nothing stuffy about the atmosphere. It's a fun place with brightly painted walls, pink napkins, leopard-print booths, and eclectic artwork. It feels a bit like someplace you might find in New Orleans, where the strangest things come together in a way that feels hip, not crazy. The menu is just as unusual as the decor, with entrées ranging from Kentucky rabbit and bourbon Tabasco pork chops to paella and bouillabaisse. At lunchtime, smaller portions of entrées are offered along with sandwiches that range from a fried green BLT to a grilled portabella. On paper, it seems like a strange place, but somehow A La Lucie works.

❰ Ramsey's Diner (496 E. High St., 859/259-2708, www.ramseysdiners.com,

11am-11pm Mon.-Fri., 9am-11pm Sat.-Sun., $8.95-11.95) is your classic meat-and-three restaurant. For your meat, choose from meatloaf, chicken livers, fried catfish, pot roast, pork chops, and the like. For your "veggies," you have to make your way through a list of 20 options, which, of course, include such classics as fried okra, mac 'n' cheese, pinto beans, and greens. Real butter and lots of gravy are the standard here, so dieters beware, though there are some sandwiches if you want a slightly (and only slightly) lighter option. And oh yeah, you need to save room for pie. The atmosphere is friendly, with the diner attracting a legion of loyal regulars. The High Street location is the original, but Ramsey's has been so successful that there are now three additional locations around town.

Steakhouses

Lexington so loves a good cut of meat that **Malone's** (3347 Tates Creek Rd., 859/335-6500, www.bluegrasshospitality.com, 11:15am-10:30pm daily, $13.99-44.95), a local venture designed to bring prime cuts to the city, has three locations that all do a bustling business. Steaks are obviously at the heart of the menu, with diners choosing from prime filets, sirloins, rib eyes, prime ribs, and porterhouses. Fresh fish and pastas dishes are also well prepared. As you'd expect from a fine steakhouse, wood dominates the decor and a large bar covers all your drink needs.

Asian

A nondescript place, **Seki Restaurant** (1093 S. Broadway Rd., 859/254-5289, lunch 11am-2:30pm Mon.-Fri., dinner 5:30pm-9:30pm Mon.-Sat., $3.95-9.95) serves what many Lexingtonians consider to be the area's best sushi. Run for years by an older couple whom restaurant regulars referred to, à la *Seinfeld,* as the Sushi Nazis for the strict yet unspoken rules they had for dining at their restaurant, Seki was sold in 2010 to Korean owners after the passing of Mrs. Seki. The menu, however, remains nearly the same, with fresh traditional-style sushi and sashimi the stars of the menu.

Prices are among the best you'll see for sushi, especially of this quality. Reservations are a must because of the restaurant's small size and its popularity.

◖ **Yamaguchi's Sake and Tapas** (1205 Codell Dr., www.sakeandtapas.com, 8pm-midnight Mon.-Thurs., 8pm-2am Fri.-Sat., $6-18) is a unique find that also happens to be well off most people's radar. This small place (they can only accommodate parties of six or less) focuses on small plates of Japanese cuisine and a well curated list of sakes. Diners receive an intimate experience in a cozy, unrushed environment, and the food is excellent and entirely unlike that offered at most Japanese places (no sushi, Bento boxes, or teriyaki). They don't take incoming calls, and all seats are first-come, first-served.

Rooted in Hunan- and Szechuan-style Chinese cooking, **Asian Wind** (3735 Palomar Centre Dr., 859/223-0060, www.asianwindrestaurant.com, 11:30am-9:30pm Sun.-Thurs., 11:30am-10:30pm Fri.-Sat., $7.95-14.95) also serves popular dishes from other Asian nations. The menu is thus quite extensive, even more so if you consider that they offer vegan and vegetarian options of every dish. The food is fresh, and service is efficient. If you're craving Asian food, you won't go wrong at Asian Wind.

French

Connoisseurs of French food should reserve a table at **Le Deauville** (199 N. Limestone, 859/246-0999, www.ledeauvillebistro.com, 5:30pm-11pm Mon.-Sat., $24-34). Starters at this bistro-style restaurant include escargot, pâté *maison,* and mussels prepared in five different ways, while entrées include duck confit, coq au vin, and bouillabaisse. Specials include all-you-can-eat crepes on Mondays and all-you-can-eat mussels and *frites* on Tuesdays. Le Deauville is small, with a curving bar taking up one wall and cozy tables dressed in white tablecloths lining the other and filling the interior. Mirrors and a high pressed tin ceiling keep it from feeling crowded, and a few outdoor tables expand seating options during warm weather.

LEXINGTON

Indian

Taj India (154 Patchen Dr., 859/268-0055, www.tajindiaindianrestaurants.com, lunch 11:30am-3pm daily, dinner 5pm-10pm Sun.-Thurs., 5pm-10:30pm Fri.-Sat., $8.99-13.99) can satisfy your craving for butter chicken, garlic naan, lamb vindaloo, *malai kofta,* or *channa masala.* The lunch buffet is a fantastic deal and lets you sample an array of dishes. With fresh food, pleasant decor, and friendly service, Taj India is the best Indian in Lexington. Its location between New Circle Drive and Man O' War Boulevard makes it a bit of a drive if you're in downtown, but it's worth it if you're after authentic Indian food.

Italian

Portofino (249 E. Main St., 859/253-9300, www.portofinolexington.com, lunch 11am-2:30pm Mon.-Fri., dinner 5pm-10pm Sun.-Thurs., 5pm-11pm Fri.-Sat., $16-38) is Lexington's top Italian restaurant, specializing in upscale Northern Italian food and boasting an extensive wine list. The restaurant is located in a restored downtown building and strives for casual elegance. The dinner menu features pasta selections such as veal marsala meatballs and gnocchi *di casa* along with meat and seafood dishes such as bison short ribs and Atlantic salmon. The lunch menu ($8-12), which offers pastas, sandwiches, and pizzas, is popular with the business crowd. Choose from seating in the bustling bar area, the more intimate dining room, or the patio.

Latin American

Half grocery, half restaurant, ◖**Old San Juan** (247 Surfside Dr., 859/278-2682, 11am-8pm Tues.-Wed., 11am-9pm Thurs.-Sat., $5-12) is a hole in the wall that does delicious authentic Cuban food. Try the *ropa vieja,* the Cubano sandwich, the shrimp in Cuban sauce, or the roasted pork and sweet plantains, and you'll feel that you've been transported to the Caribbean. Old San Juan also has a wide variety of flavored soft drinks and malts that are hard to find elsewhere. Simple but friendly, this mom-and-pop joint is a secret that needs to be shared.

INFORMATION AND SERVICES

The **Lexington Convention & Visitors Bureau** (401 W. Main St., 859/233-7299, www.visitlex.com, 8:30am-5pm Mon.-Fri., 10am-5pm Sat. year-round, noon-5pm Sun. summer only) is happy to help you plan your visit to Lexington. You can request an information packet in advance or stop in and see them once you arrive. Their website is excellent, with all the information you expect along with a long list of suggested itineraries based around a multitude of interests.

The *Lexington Herald* (www.kentucky.com) is Lexington's daily newspaper.

The most centrally located **post office** (210 E. High St.) is open 9am-5pm Monday-Friday. If you need to mail something on Saturday, a post office just north of New Circle Road (1088 Nandino Blvd.) is open 9am-5pm.

GETTING THERE
Air

Five major commercial carriers (Allegiant Air, American Eagle, Delta, United, and US Airways) serve **Blue Grass Airport (LEX)** (4000 Terminal Dr., 859/425-3114, www.bluegrassairport.com), which, thanks to its central location, is a good place to start a visit to not only Lexington, but also most of the state. Nonstop flights are available to 13 destinations, primarily in the eastern United States. From these cities, which include large hubs like Chicago, Atlanta, and Houston, you can connect to flights around the globe. The airport has only 13 gates and is very easy to navigate. Located directly across from Keeneland, Blue Grass Airport is about six miles west of downtown Lexington off of U.S. 60.

Transportation options to/from the airport include rental car, taxi, hotel shuttle, and LexTran bus (www.lextran.com). LexTran Route 21 connects the downtown transit center (200 E. Vine St.) with Keeneland and Blue Grass Airport. The bus is convenient if you happen to catch it, but its hours are very limited: Monday-Friday only from about 6:30am to about 6:30pm.

Car

Lexington is centrally located in Kentucky at the intersection of I-64 and I-75, making it easily accessible from all directions. Louisville, to the west of Lexington, is about 75 miles (1 hour 20 minutes) away via I-64, and Covington, to the north of Lexington, is about 85 miles (1 hour 20 minutes) away via I-75. To get to and from Frankfort, which is 25 miles (40 minutes) east of Lexington, U.S. 421 provides the most direct route.

With the easy interstate access, getting to Lexington from out of state is also simple. From St. Louis, it's 335 miles (five hours) directly east on I-64. From Indianapolis, which is 190 miles (three hours) northwest, the easiest route is to take I-65 south to Louisville and then I-64 east to Lexington. From Cincinnati, the route is exactly the same as from Covington, just a few miles further. From Nashville, which is 215 miles (3.25 hours) southwest of Lexington, the most direct route is to take I-65 north to Exit 93 and then follow the Bluegrass Parkway east to Lexington.

Bus

Greyhound (477 W. New Circle Rd., 859/299-0428, www.greyhound.com) has a station in Lexington.

GETTING AROUND

The roadways in Lexington are set up in a wheel-and-spoke system. New Circle Road (KY 4) circles the city, with downtown and the inner suburbs inside the circle. Major thoroughfares then run from downtown out to New Circle Road. U.S. 68 runs in a northeast/southwest direction, U.S. 25 runs in a northwest/southeast direction, U.S. 27 runs in an almost north/south direction, and U.S. 60 runs in an east/west direction. Though fairly easy to get around, traffic on city roads

can be fairly heavy, especially during morning and evening rush hours. Give yourself a little more time than you think you'll need to get where you're going.

Car Rentals

Four car rental agencies have offices at the airport. The rental counters are located in the baggage claim area, and there is one central facility directly next to the terminal for drop-off and pick-up. The agencies at the airport are **Avis** (800/230-4898, www.avis.com), **Enterprise** (800/261-7331, www.enterprise.com), **Hertz** (800/654-3131, www.hertz.com), and **National** (800/227-7368, www.national-car.com). **Budget** (800/527-0700, www.budget.com) also rents cars from an off-airport location.

Taxis

Three companies provide cab service to and from the airport and around Lexington. They are **Bluegrass Cab** (859/223-8888), **Wildcat Taxi** (859/231-8294), and **Yellow Cab** (859/231-8294).

Public Transportation

LexTran (859/253-4636, www.lextran.com) provides bus service around Lexington. More useful than the bus to most visitors is the free trolley (www.colttrolley.com), which runs two routes. The blue route (11:30am-2pm Mon.-Fri., 6pm-1am Thurs.-Sat.) makes an east-to-west loop along Main and Short Streets, while the green route (9pm-3am Thurs.-Sat.) makes a north-to-south loop between UK and Transylvania University along Upper and Limestone Streets. During horse racing season, an additional trolley ($1) runs to Keeneland from downtown. A full list of routes and schedules for the buses and trolley is available on the LexTran website.

Versailles and Midway

Woodford County, home to the towns of Versailles and Midway, produces some of the finest products to come out of Kentucky—Woodford Reserve bourbon and thoroughbred racehorses. Both the towns are small but wealthy and offer food and accommodation of a quality that far exceeds their size. Versailles—which is pronounced Vur-SALES because this is Kentucky and not France—is the bigger of the two cities, named in honor of General Lafayette, a friend of the city's founder. Midway, which isn't much more than a main street and a whole lot of surrounding farmland, was Kentucky's first railroad town. It is strategically situated midway (hence its name) between Frankfort and Lexington. Both towns are exceedingly charming, and the drive between the two is on a scenic byway lined with gorgeous horse farms. Very close to Lexington, either city makes a good base for exploring the entire region.

HORSE FARMS

Woodford County is home to more than 100 horse farms. At times, while driving around the area, it can seem as if there is nothing else. Everywhere your gaze falls, you'll find stone and wood fences enclosing rolling bluegrass hills dotted with horses. The majority of the farms are closed to the public, though those listed here welcome visitors with advance reservations.

Ashford Stud

Derby winners Fusaichi Pegasus and Thunder Gulch are two of the stallions that stand in the distinctive blue-trimmed barns at **Ashford Stud** (5095 Frankfort Rd., Versailles, 859/873-7088, www.coolmore.com). Free tours of the breeding complex at this beautiful facility are offered by reservation. The horses may travel south during the latter half of the year, so aim to visit Ashford Stud between February and June if possible.

Lane's End

Outside of the breeding season, **Lane's End** (1500 Midway Rd., Versailles, 859/873-7300, www.lanesend.com) offers free tours of their stallion complex at 10am on Thursdays July-January. Meet the horses, learn about the industry, and admire Lane's End's park-like setting. Among the more well-known horses on-site is Curlin, a two-time Horse of the Year. The facility hosts a couple of open houses each year, which are open to both breeders and the public. Check the website to find out if an open house is on the schedule.

Three Chimneys Farm

Three Chimneys Farm (1981 Old Frankfort Pike, Versailles, 859/873-7053, www.threechimneys.com, 1pm Tues.-Sat., $10) has been home to a long list of thoroughbreds that any horse racing fan will know, including Seattle Slew, Silver Charm, Genuine Risk, and Big Brown. Kentucky Derby 2008 winner Big Brown is currently standing stud at Three Chimneys Farm and is often brought out and walked for visitors. If a breeding session is scheduled during your visit, you may be allowed to watch. With notable stone architecture and lush green fields, Three Chimneys Farm is not just a premier stud farm, but also a pretty place to tour.

WinStar Farm

For an insider's look at how champion thoroughbred horses are bred, visit **WinStar Farm** (3301 Pisgah Pike, Versailles, 859/297-1328, www.winstarfarm.com), owner of 2010 Kentucky Derby winner Super Saver. Tours begin with a video that features 2000 Horse of the Year Tiznow. Visitors then move into the stallion complex, where they are introduced to the farm's stallions, including attention-loving Tiznow, and are informed about the process of breeding. Guides can answer any and all questions you might have about thoroughbreds,

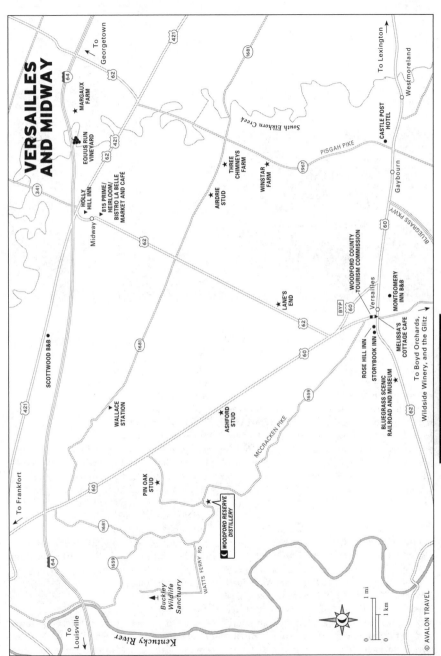

VERSAILLES AND MIDWAY

LEXINGTON

© AVALON TRAVEL

LEXINGTON

© THERESA DOWELL BLACKINTON

thoroughbreds on the horizon at a horse farm

racing, breeding, sales, and training, so don't be shy. Free tours are offered at 1pm Monday, Wednesday, and Friday.

Additional Farms

Other horse farms that provide free tours of their facilities include **Airdrie Stud** (2641 Old Frankfort Pike, Midway, 859/873-7270, www. airdriestud.com), **Margaux Farm** (596 Moore's Mill Rd., Versailles, 859/846-4433, www.margauxfarm.com), and **Pin Oak Stud** (830 Grassy Springs Rd., Versailles, 859/873-1420, www. pinoakstud.com).

BOURBON DISTILLERIES AND WINERIES

Woodford Reserve Distillery

Though Woodford Reserve bourbon has been produced only since 1996, the **Woodford Reserve Distillery** (7855 McCracken Pike, Versailles, 859/879-1812, www.woodfordreserve.com), the National Historic Landmark where it is made, is one of the oldest distilleries in the state. Join a one-hour tour for an in-depth look at the process by which this premium bourbon, the official bourbon of the Kentucky Derby, is made. You'll see the only stone aging warehouses in America, learn that Woodford Reserve is the only bourbon to be distilled three times before being barreled, and visit the only bourbon fermenting facility to use wood tanks exclusively. Tours end with a tasting, and visitors are allowed to take their shot glass home with them. Tours ($7) are offered on the hour 10am-3pm Monday-Saturday year-round, with additional tours at 1pm, 2pm, and 3pm on Sundays April-December. Two specialty tours ($25)—a National Landmark Tour, which focuses on the distillery's architecture, and a Corn to Cork Tour, which is a more in-depth look at the bourbon-making process—are also offered, but they require advance reservations.

Equus Run Vineyards

Nestled between horse farms and South Elkhorn Creek, **Equus Run Vineyards** (1280 Moores Mill Rd., Midway, 859/846-9463, www.equusrunvineyards.com, 11am-7pm Mon.-Sat., 1pm-5pm Sun. Apr.-Oct., 11am-5pm Mon.-Sat., 1pm-5pm Sun. Nov.-Mar.) has been producing award-winning wines since 1998. A complimentary guided tour is offered at 1:30pm Monday-Thursday and at 1:30pm and 4pm Friday and Saturday. Guests who arrive outside those hours are welcome to take a self-guided tour of the grounds. Regardless of whether you take a tour, tastings ($5), which include six wines and a souvenir glass, are offered until 15 minutes before closing. The vineyard produces 15 red, white, and rosé wines, and as the official wine of the Derby, also creates special-edition wines each year. A number of events are held at the vineyard, including a very popular summer concert series. Check the website for a schedule of upcoming events.

Wildside Winery

Wildside Winery (5500 Troy Pike, Versailles, 859/879-3982, www.wildsidevines.com, 1pm-7pm Tues.-Sat., 1pm-5pm Sun.) makes a long list of wines, focusing especially on dry red and sweet fruit wines. In addition to the usual strawberry and blackberry, Wildside also does peach mead, cranberry, and pomegranate wines, plus a few other less common selections. Among the reds, you'll find a syrah, a cabernet sauvignon, and a cynthiana, along with a bourbon barrel red, which is a cabernet that is aged in a bourbon barrel. A couple of whites are also available. Tastings are free, and the winery occasionally hosts outdoor concerts.

OTHER SIGHTS
Bluegrass Scenic Railroad and Museum

Get a taste of rail travel on a one-hour train ride with **Bluegrass Scenic Railroad and Museum** (175 Beasley Rd., Versailles, 859/873-2476, www.bluegrassrailroad.com, 1pm-4pm weekends). The rides, which are offered at 2pm on weekends mid-May-October, take passengers through the bluegrass countryside. You'll pass through Trackside Farm, where thoroughbreds

are raised, and see cattle, tobacco fields, and other rural Kentucky sites. Special train rides are held throughout the year and include Civil War train robbery rides, mystery theater rides, haunted Halloween rides, and a Christmas ride with Santa. Come early or hang around after the ride to explore the one-room museum, which has exhibits on the work the railroad did for the United States, the jobs of those who worked for the railroad, and the trains that used to pass through the area. Tickets ($11.50 adults, $10.50 seniors, $9.50 youth 2-12) can be purchased online or in person. Plan to arrive 30 minutes before departure, because trains here run on a Swiss timetable, departing right on schedule.

Boyd Orchards

As fifth-generation fruit growers, the Boyd family knows a little something about fruit, and a visit to **Boyd Orchards** (1396 Pinckard Pike, Versailles, 859/873-3097, www.boydorchards.com, 9am-6pm Tues.-Sat., noon-6pm Sun.) is a treat for your taste buds. The only problem is that after tasting their strawberries, peaches, apples, blackberries, raspberries, grapes, and pears, you might be too spoiled to ever again settle for grocery store produce. Beyond producing mouthwatering fruit that you can purchase already picked or head to the fields to pick yourself, Boyd Orchards also has an enormous playground and animal area ($5) that kids love and a great gift shop full of unique products. During the seven weeks leading up to Halloween, Boyd Orchards hosts an extremely popular fall festival with a petting zoo, live music, corn maze, face painting, pony rides, mini-train rides, hayrides, and of course, plenty of pumpkins, mums, and gourds. Their **Apple Blossom Café** has a full kitchen that turns out tasty lunches that often feature fruit fresh from the farm. Try the fruit slushes and the sandwiches and salads built around the produce of the moment (maybe a strawberry goat cheese salad or a Cuban sandwich with asparagus). For dessert, good luck choosing between apple cider doughnuts and fried apple or peach pies.

LEXINGTON

© THERESA DOWELL BLACKINTON

Boyd Orchards

RECREATION
Hiking
The **Buckley Wildlife Sanctuary** (1305 Germany Rd., 859/873-5711, www.audubon. org, 9am-5pm Wed.-Fri., 9am-6pm Sat.-Sun., $4 adults, $3 youth) has four trails, ranging in length from 0.3 to 1.5 miles and easily connectable, which lead into field, pond, and forest habitats. A bulletin board in the parking lot has a box filled with binders that provide information on the trails and point out sights you'll encounter along the way. Bird lovers will enjoy the bird blind, which is perched on the edge of a pond that many avian species like to visit. Field guides are provided for identification of species, but bring your own binoculars. The Nature Center is open 1pm-6pm weekends April-December.

ACCOMMODATIONS
Versailles and Midway offer a surprising number of accommodation options, none of which are chains. With their close proximity to Lexington and especially Keeneland, the B&Bs in Versailles and Midway are a good option for those looking to spend time all around the region.

$150-200
Dating back to 1795, the house that is now **Scottwood Bed and Breakfast** (2004 E. Leestown Pike, Midway, 859/846-5037, www. scottwoodbedandbreakfast.com, $175-195) journeyed from its original location in Scott County to its present location in 1971. An addition was built at that point, but the house maintains the beautiful period woodwork and floors. Two guest rooms are located in the house, one on the main floor, the other occupying the entirety of the second floor. The upstairs suite, which can accommodate a family or group thanks to the twin beds in the room that adjoins the main bedroom, is decorated in Shaker style, while the down bedroom is done in the style of Williamsburg. Both rooms have private baths. A carriage house is located behind the main house and offers a private retreat with working fireplace and a lovely deck

overlooking South Elkhorn Creek. Breakfast is provided each morning, and the rooms are equipped with satellite television and wireless Internet.

No one stays at **(Rose Hill Inn** (233 Rose Hill Ave., Versailles, 859/873-5957, www.rose-hillinn.com, $139-184) and doesn't love it. The seven tastefully decorated rooms in this historic 1823 home have private baths, comfy beds, and TVs, and come with special touches like robes, homemade cookies, and candles. All rooms are spacious, and the various configurations—kings, queens, twins—can accommodate couples, families, or groups of friends. Some rooms feature whirlpool tubs and kitchen areas, and three of the rooms are even able to accommodate pets. The owners are excellent hosts who serve up a delicious breakfast daily and will do everything in their power to make sure you have a wonderful stay.

The **Montgomery Inn Bed and Breakfast** (270 Montgomery Ave., Versailles, 859/251-4103, www.montgomeryinnbnb.com, $139-179) has 10 guest suites, each with a private bathroom with whirlpool tub, queen or king bed, TV with DVD player, and Internet access. Some have private entryways, and all have access to complimentary snacks and drinks. Rates include a full breakfast. The decor can be a little bit busy, with patterned wallpapers, bed covers, and upholstery overwhelming those with simpler tastes. Those with allergies should be aware that multiple cats call the inn home.

Over $200

(Storybook Inn (277 Rose Hill Ave., Versailles, 859/879-9993, www.storybook-inn.com, $259-325) is an upscale bed-and-breakfast where not a single detail is overlooked. An antebellum-style mansion dating to 1843, Storybook Inn was renovated in 2009-2010. In the inn's four suites, you'll find such niceties as rain showerheads, soaking tubs, towel warmers, and fireplaces, not to mention luxurious linens, mattresses, and furniture. A guesthouse with 3 bedrooms, 3.5 bathrooms, an office that can be used as an

additional bedroom, a kitchen, and a private deck is perfect for those seeking privacy or traveling in a group. Common areas include a beautiful garden and a library stocked with books and movies. Homemade treats and refreshments are available all day, and the delicious breakfasts can be tailored to accommodate any restrictions. Innkeeper Elise is a delight and will dedicate her full attention to helping you plan your visit.

It's impossible to drive down Pisgah Pike and not see the **Castle Post Hotel** (230 Pisgah Pike, Versailles, 859/879-1000, www.thecastlepost.com, $195-420). It is, after all, a castle with turrets, 12-foot wooden doors, and stone walls, smack in the middle of horse country. Though there are a lot of people who want to tour it, the only way you can gain admission to the castle is by booking an overnight room. It's not cheap, but how many people can say they've slept in a castle in Kentucky? Rooms are luxuriously decorated (for better or worse, they don't feel at all medieval) and come with all the amenities.

FOOD

You will not go hungry while visiting Versailles and Midway. Locally owned restaurants rule, and they're doing exciting things with food here.

Cafés

For a fantastic sandwich in downtown Midway, pop in at **Bistro La Belle Market + Café** (121 E. Main St., Midway, 859/846-4233, 11am-2pm Tues.-Sat., $6.50), where roasted chicken salad, white cheddar pecan spread, Kentucky country ham, and other sandwich fixings are served on a selection of freshly baked bread.

Casual American

The Big Brown burger at **(Wallace Station** (3854 Old Frankfort Pike, Versailles, 859/846-5161, www.wallacestation.com, 8am-8pm Mon.-Thurs., 8am-9pm Fri.-Sat., 8am-6pm Sun., $5.95-8.95) was named a top five burger by Guy Fieri of Food Network's *Diners, Drive-Ins, and Dives,* who visited this deli and bakery in 2010. If you're not into burgers, you can choose from a very long list of sandwiches, all of which are excellent, or opt for soup or salad. A special fried chicken dinner is offered on Mondays, and Fridays feature fried catfish. For breakfast, try one of the country Benedict sandwiches or grab a treat from the bakery. Wallace Station is completely low-key with a few mismatched tables and chairs inside and a number of picnic tables on a deck. Live bluegrass music adds to the ambience on Saturday evenings. A special gluten-free menu is available.

Classic American

Depending on your mood, choose to sit at either the casual and cozy downstairs pub or the more refined upstairs dining room at **815 Prime** (131 E. Main St., Midway, 859/846-4688, www.815prime.com, 5pm-10pm Tues.-Sat., $10-22), both of which serve the same menu of American favorites, which range from a burger, fish and chips, and a prime rib sandwich to a bone-in pork chop, wild-caught walleye, and a New York strip. Though the menu isn't as creative as some in the area, the food is solid, the atmosphere is nice, and the service is good.

Contemporary American

Details matter at **❰ Heirloom** (125 E. Main St., Midway, 859/846-5565, www.heirloom-midway.com, 11:30am-2pm and 5:30pm-9pm Tues.-Sat., $12-33). The dining room is elegant but comfortable, decorated in shades of brown, tan, and white and furnished with extra-tall booths and granite tables. Presentation is an art, with each dish expertly plated on unique dishes, and the tastes are spectacular. The menu is short, featuring about seven entrées, but each is carefully thought out and executed. The menu changes regularly, but might include duck breast with pumpkin ricotta ravioli or capellini with Alaskan king crab. The lunch menu ($9-13) tempts diners with favorites such as buttermilk-brined fried chicken and fish and chips.

Although open only limited hours, **❰ Holly Hill Inn** (426 N. Winter St., Midway,

859/846-4732, www.hollyhillinn.com, 11am-2pm Fri.-Sun., 5:30pm-10pm Thurs.-Sat.) is worth working into the schedule. James Beard-nominated chef Ouita Michel impresses guests with elevated Southern cuisine prepared with local ingredients and served in the charming surroundings of an 1845 country inn. Lunch and Sunday brunch are three-course affairs ($18), in which you choose from such options as local chicken crepes and eggplant *involtini*. The three-course dinner ($35) is built around such entrées as spicy lamb sausage harissa and roulade of beef tenderloin. A six-course tasting menu ($65) is also offered. Reservations are highly recommended at this deservedly popular restaurant.

For a rather unusual dining experience, head out of town to a tiny place called Nonesuch, Kentucky, where you'll find an enormous antiques gallery called Irish Acres. Proceed to the lower level to a restaurant named **The Glitz** (4205 Ford's Mill Rd., Nonesuch, 859/873-6956, www.irishacresgallery.com, 10am-5pm Tues.-Sat.), which makes complete sense when you see the place. The Glitz serves a three-course luncheon menu, with multiple selections for each of the courses. For dessert, you'll want to try the signature dish, the Nonesuch Kiss, which involves a meringue shell, ice cream, chocolate sauce, whipped cream, almonds, and a cherry. The food is carefully prepared, and the atmosphere incomparable. Beverages are included with the meal, which costs $21.50. Reservations are required.

Southern

Fans of comfort food will find refuge at **Melissa's Cottage Café** (167 S. Main St., Versailles, 859/879-6204, 11am-9pm Mon.-Sat., $6.95-11.95), where meatloaf, chicken pot pie, and hamburger steak are some of the most popular entrées. Portions are generous and come with good Southern-style sides. The menu does change often and is presented to you on a chalkboard. Unlike many comfort food spots, Melissa's is a charming (albeit tiny) place with tasteful decor.

INFORMATION AND SERVICES

Stop into the visitor information center run by the **Woodford County Tourism Commission** (190 N. Main St., Versailles, 859/873-5122, www.woodfordcountyinfo.com, 10am-4pm Mon.-Fri.) for information on the area.

GETTING THERE AND AROUND

Versailles is located directly west of Lexington on U.S. 60, which connects the two cities. From the center of Lexington, Versailles is about 13 miles (25 minutes) away, although Versailles is only about 6 miles (10 minutes) from Keeneland, making it equally as convenient as Lexington if you're in the area for horse racing. Midway is north of Versailles, located just south of I-64. To travel between Versailles and Midway, drive 7.5 miles (15 minutes) on westbound U.S. 62. From Lexington, the most direct route to Midway is via northbound U.S. 421. Lexington and Midway are separated by 15 miles (25 minutes). From Louisville and points westward, take I-64 to Exit 58 to reach Versailles (64 miles; one hour) and Exit 65 to reach Midway (60 miles; one hour). From Covington (90 miles; 1.5 hours) and points north or west, travel to Lexington and proceed from there.

Georgetown

Georgetown is one of the bigger cities in the area surrounding Lexington, thanks in particular to the Toyota plant that opened in the late 1980s. The plant brought many jobs to the area as well as an influx of foreign visitors. Hotels sprung up, many located at Exit 126 along I-75, which is convenient to the plant. But Georgetown existed long before Camrys began rolling off the assembly line. Founded in the 1780s, Georgetown is home to a liberal arts college, is said to be the place where bourbon was first made, has a still-active historic downtown, and is, of course, the location of a fair share of horse farms.

SIGHTS

◖ Old Friends Equine Center

Established as a retirement farm for at-risk racehorses, **Old Friends Equine Center** (1841 Paynes Depot Rd., 502/863-1775, www.old-friendsequine.org) has rescued more than 100 horses, including stallions, that have reached the end of their careers, providing them with a beautiful space to live out their days while receiving excellent care. The center welcomes visitors to take a one-hour walking tour of the farm, which involves visiting with the horses and learning each of their stories. Visitors are even welcome to feed and pet some of the more people-friendly residents. After spending time with these gorgeous creatures, it's hard to believe that people could abuse these horses or consider sending them to a slaughterhouse. Tours, which take place at 10am, 1pm, and 3pm daily, March through October, and at 11am only, November-February, are free, but donations are always gladly accepted and go toward the care of the horses. Reservations are required. For an up-close look at thoroughbreds, many with champion pedigrees and race histories, there's not a better place in the area.

Toyota Motor Manufacturing Plant Tour

Some of the most popular cars in the United States—the Camry, Avalon, and Venza—are manufactured at Georgetown's **Toyota Motor Manufacturing Plant** (1001 Cherry Blossom Way, 502/868-3027, www.toyotageorgetown.com, free). The plant offers tours, allowing you to see auto assembly from start to finish. The tour, which is given via tram, is limited to 30 people and lasts one hour. Tours, which are scheduled for 10am, noon, and 2pm on

LEXINGTON

weekdays, regularly book up in advance, so make reservations as soon as possible. A visitors center (9am-4pm Mon.-Fri.) has exhibits on the production process and Toyota's commitment to the environment and the community.

Historic Walking Tour

Georgetown has a well-preserved historic downtown with grand 19th-century buildings hosting restaurants and businesses. To get the most of a stroll through downtown, opt to take a two-mile self-guided tour of the area. Begin by picking up a free brochure with map and details on each stop at the Welcome Center, which is located inside the old **Scott County Jail** (117 N. Water St., 502/570-8366), the tour's first stop. Additional stops on the tour include the Courthouse, built in 1877 in Second Empire style; the old post office, which is now home to the **Georgetown-Scott County Museum** (229 E. Main St., 502/863-6201, 9am-4pm Mon.-Sat., free); and **Georgetown College** (400 E. College St., 502/863-8000, www.georgetown-college.edu), a liberal arts college with Baptist ties that dates to the early 1800s.

SPORTS AND RECREATION
Parks

Yuko-En on the Elkhorn (700 Cincinnati Pike, www.yuko-en.com, dawn-dusk daily, free) is a Japanese friendship garden planted with native Kentucky plants. The garden does, however, adhere to Japanese principles and careful thought was given to the selection of plants. Native cane stands tall like Japanese bamboo, and redbuds provide spring color instead of Japanese cherry trees. Other features include Japanese-style gates, a snow lantern, a koi pond, a bright red arched bridge, a teahouse, and sculptures. A walking path leads through the six-acre garden, inviting visitors to relax and enjoy their surroundings. A free self-guided tour brochure available at the garden entrance explains many of the park's features.

The people of Georgetown claim that Reverend Elijah Craig, who helped found the city, distilled the world's first bourbon at a site now preserved as **Royal Spring Park** (Water St.

and W. Main St.). Right at the edge of downtown, Royal Spring Park protects a spring that is still used as the main source of water for Georgetown. The park features a grassy area good for picnicking and a restored log cabin.

Fishing

Elkhorn Creek runs right through Georgetown, and its waters are great for fishing. Many people choose to cast a line from shore, but the Richard O. Winder boat ramp, located on Cincinnati Pike directly across from Yuko-En, allows you to put in a canoe, kayak, or small motorboat.

Horseback Riding

Saddle up and take a trail ride through the woods on one of the horses at **Whispering Woods Riding Stable** (265 Wright Ln., 502/570-9663, www.whisperingwoodstrails.com, Mar.-Nov.). One-hour rides are $25 with each additional hour costing $20, and payment is by cash or check only. Riders must be at least eight years old. You should call in advance to schedule a ride.

FESTIVALS AND EVENTS
Festival of the Horse

Each year in late September or early October, Georgetown pays tribute to the horse and its significance to the local community with the **Festival of the Horse** (www.festivalofthe-horse.org). The event kicks off on Thursday evening with a fireman's chili cook-off and continues through Sunday afternoon. The schedule includes a horse-themed kids parade, pony rides, riding competitions, a parade of horses, a blessing of animals, and a horse show. Between events, you can enjoy live music, dancing, and a carnival.

Georgetown International Kite & Cultural Festival

The **Georgetown International Kite & Cultural Festival** (www.kitefest.com) invites you to go fly a kite. Seriously. Held every year in mid-April, the weekend festival centers around kite making and kite flying. Bands provide entertainment, and food booths offer international cuisine. The festival was created to honor Georgetown's sister city in Japan, Tahara, which is known for its kite festivals, and each year, Tahara residents come to Georgetown for the festival. The free weekend event is held on the grounds of the Cardome Center (800 Cincinnati Pike).

ACCOMMODATIONS
$50-100
The bright yellow **Pineapple Inn Bed and Breakfast** (645 S. Broadway, 502/868-5453, www.pineappleinnbedandbreakfast.com, $80-100) near Georgetown College has four rooms, each with private bath. The Derby Room has a queen bed and spa tub, while the other three rooms have double beds. The Americana Room, which has two beds, is set up for families. Decor is a little bit fussy, which can make fairly big rooms feel crowded.

$100-150
Located on a 20-acre working horse farm, **Jordan Farm Bed and Breakfast** (4091 Newtown Pike, 859/321-5707, www.jordanfarmbandb.com, $100-125) gives guests the choice of two carriage house suites, each with queen bed, Jacuzzi tub, and a sitting area, or a two-bedroom cottage that's great for families. The rooms are quite comfy and the breakfast, while somewhat simple, is tasty, but it's the setting that's the real star. Guests are invited to jump in the pool, sit by the lake, or stroll the grounds, meeting the horses and learning about life on a horse farm.

$150-200
The 10,000-square-foot, Georgian-style **Blackridge Hall Bed and Breakfast** (4055 Paris Pike, 502/863-2069, www.blackridgehall.com, $109-229) is not a historic mansion, but rather a new building constructed with an eye for historic detail. The six guest rooms are decorated in an upscale country style, with lots of flower patterns and silk flower arrangements. Rooms are spacious and all have their own private bath, though some are not connected to

the room. The mansion sits on five acres from which you can view horses grazing on nearby farms. The host is very gracious and can help arrange visits to horse farms or other attractions. Breakfast is served on fine china in the dining room each morning.

FOOD
Cafés
The **Upbeat Café and Music Venue** (117 N. Broadway, 502/863-5445, www.upbeatcafe.com, 8am-3pm Mon.-Fri., $4.75-6.99) is a good lunch spot with a strong offering of sandwiches and salads. The café uses artisan bread and makes homemade croutons and salad dressings. The café also acts as a coffeehouse, serving a variety of espresso drinks, smoothies, and Italian sodas. On Thursday, Friday, and Saturday nights, the café is open 6pm-10pm for live music.

Diners
Opened in 1910 as a confectionery, **Fava's Restaurant** (159 E. Main St., 502/863-4383, 6:30am-9pm Mon.-Sat., $2.99-8.95) has evolved through the years to become a diner-style restaurant. The menu is long on breakfast specials as well as burgers and sandwiches. Dinner options include pork tenderloin, country ham, and catfish during the week, while rib eyes, oysters, and jumbo shrimp are added to the menu on Friday and Saturday. The cream pies are delicious and worth stopping in for on their own.

Classic American
For a nice dinner, **Rodney's on Broadway** (222 N. Broadway, 502/868-7637, www.rodneysonbroadway.com, 5pm-10pm Tues.-Sat., $18-30) should be your destination. In this historic 1840s home, chef Rodney Jones turns out a menu of excellently prepared classic dishes, including a rib eye topped with wild mushrooms, shrimp, and scallops in a Woodford Reserve cream sauce, and roasted duck in a port wine reduction. With only a couple of tables per room, the restaurant has an intimate feel, and the service is warm and knowledgeable.

LEXINGTON

INFORMATION AND SERVICES

The **Georgetown/Scott County Tourism Commission** (502/863-8600, www.georgetownky.com) maintains a website with information on attractions, hotels, dining options, and other facets of Georgetown. The best place to pick up information once you're already there is the Welcome Center located in the old jail (117 N. Water St.).

GETTING THERE AND AROUND

North of Lexington, Georgetown is located at the intersection of U.S. 25 and U.S. 460, just to the east of I-75 and north of I-64. To reach Georgetown from Lexington, travel 14 miles (30 minutes) on northbound U.S. 25.

From Louisville, which is 70 miles (1 hour 10 minutes) west, take I-64 to Exit 69. Proceed 3.3 miles on eastbound U.S. 62, then turn right on U.S. 460. Drive 1.7 miles, and then turn left on U.S. 25, which will lead you directly into town in 1.8 miles. From Versailles (18 miles; 30 minutes) and Midway (10 miles; 20 minutes), take eastbound U.S. 62 to U.S. 460 and follow the same directions as from Louisville. If you are coming from Covington (70 miles; 1 hour 5 minutes), take southbound I-75 to Exit 126. Drive 0.6 miles on westbound U.S. 62, then turn right onto U.S. 460, which will put you in downtown in one mile. Georgetown is also very convenient to Frankfort. To get from Georgetown to Frankfort, drive 19 miles (30 minutes) on eastbound U.S. 460.

Paris

The town of Paris, which adopted the name in 1790 in tribute to the French for their assistance during the Revolutionary War, is located in Bourbon County, which was named after the French royal family. The naming, however, is about the only connection the area has to France. It is, instead, very much a Kentucky city, a small place whose growth is completely constrained by the horse farms that surround it. More than 50 of these horse farms, including the famous Claiborne Horse Farm, claim portions of the county's rolling acreage. Before the horse farms, the rich land attracted settlers and was roamed by buffalo. In fact, Main Street—which has brick sidewalks, antique lampposts, and a hearty handful of restaurants and shops in revitalized historic buildings—was constructed along a buffalo trace. Take time to walk around downtown, stopping in to see the courthouse, which dates to 1905 and is supposedly the most beautiful in the state. While there, be sure to check out the cartouche that depicts Bourbon County as the home of "fast horses, beautiful women, and good whiskey." What more could you want?

SIGHTS
◖ Claiborne Farm

Claiborne Farm (703 Winchester Rd., 859/987-2330, www.claibornefarm.com) has bred thousands of horses in its 100-year history, many of which have had stellar careers, but it's one horse in particular that makes Claiborne an immediately recognizable name to any horse aficionado: Secretariat. Triple Crown Champion and the fastest horse to ever run the Kentucky Derby, Secretariat was conceived at Claiborne and then retired to the farm to stand stud after his racing career. When he died at age 19, he was embalmed and then buried at Claiborne. Today, breeding champion horses remains the number one goal and the main business at Claiborne Farm. The farm does, however, also offer free tours. The approximately 45-minute walking tours are led by a knowledgeable groom, who shows visitors the breeding shed, the stables and paddocks where the stallions are kept, and the equine cemetery where Secretariat and other horses are buried. Somewhat uniquely, the tour also directly introduces participants to one or two of the

© THERESA DOWELL BLACKINTON

An impressive list of horses have stood stud at Clairborne Farm.

stallions, allowing for photographs with and petting of the horse. Tours are held daily at 10am and 11am, but it's imperative that you make advance reservations. During sales and other busy times of year, the farm may cancel all tours.

Cane Ridge Meeting House

In 1791, Scots-Irish Presbyterians who had settled nearby on the rich, fertile land covered in cane built what is now the largest one-room log building on the continent to serve as their meeting house. A decade later, the **Cane Ridge Meeting House** (1655 Cane Ridge Rd., 859/987-5350, www.caneridge.org, 9am-5pm Mon.-Sat., 1pm-5pm Sun., Apr.-Oct., free) was the site of the Great Revival, a religious revival that attracted upwards of 20,000 people at a time when the Second Great Awakening was sweeping across the country. Only a few years later, in 1804, the family of churches that includes the Disciples of Christ and the Church of Christ was born at Cane Ridge Meeting

House during a gathering of Presbyterian ministers. Today, the meeting house, which was used by the Cane Ridge Christian Church until 1921, remains, protected by a stone superstructure that was erected in the 1950s. Guided tours of the meeting house are available, and visitors are also welcome to tour the graveyard and a museum that accommodates memorabilia related to the religious movements that occurred here, as well as a small room filled with 19th-century tools.

Duncan Tavern

Dating to 1788, **Duncan Tavern** (323 High St., 859/987-1788, www.duncantavern.com, 10am-noon and 1pm-4pm Wed.-Sat., Apr.-mid-Dec.) is packed with history, both literally and figuratively. In the three-story stone building where Daniel Boone, Simon Kenton, and other pioneers gathered, the Kentucky Society of the Daughters of the American Revolution now have their state headquarters. Guided tours of the building ($8 adults, $6 seniors, $2 youth 6-12), which was a marvel in a time when every other nearby building was made of logs, are offered at 1:30pm and by appointment. Neighboring the tavern in the Anne Duncan House is a genealogical library also open to the public.

Hopewell Museum

If you're interested in learning more about Paris, visit the **Hopewell Museum** (800 Pleasant St., 859/987-7274, www.hopewellmuseum.org, noon-5pm Wed.-Sat., 2pm-4pm Sun., $3), located in the beaux arts building that once housed a post office. The museum contains exhibits relaying local history and also hosts a rotating schedule of art exhibits.

Colville Covered Bridge

One of 13 remaining covered bridges in Kentucky, Colville Covered Bridge is still in use, transporting vehicle traffic over Hinkston Creek on KY 3118. The bridge, which is painted green and white on each end, is worth a pass through, but unfortunately there is no real pull-off available for those who would like to take a closer look at the bridge.

LEXINGTON

SECRETARIAT'S LEGACY

Considered by many to be the best racehorse to ever run, Secretariat has become an icon, a name recognized even by people who know nothing about thoroughbred racing. Owned by Penny Chenery, one of only a few women owners in the 1970s, Secretariat first gained attention as a two-year-old, winning the title of American Horse of the Year and the Eclipse Award. As a three-year-old, he catapulted to fame. He began his pursuit of the Triple Crown by first winning the Kentucky Derby by 2.5 lengths, running the 1.25-mile race in 1:59 ^{2}/s, a record time that still stands today. In the second leg of the championship series, Secretariat won the Preakness Stakes by 2.5 lengths. After this victory, he appeared on the cover of *Time*, *Newsweek*, and *Sports Illustrated*. In the Belmont Stakes, the third and final leg of the series, Secretariat faced only four other horses and entered the race as the 1-10 favorite. He raced at a blazing speed, finishing the 1.5-mile race in a world record 2:24 and winning by an astounding 31 lengths. With this win, Secretariat became the ninth horse in history to win the Triple Crown. He was, of course, again named Horse of the Year.

Secretariat retired from racing after his three-year-old season with a total record of 16 wins out of 21 races. He then stood stud at Claiborne Farm in Paris, Kentucky, until his death in 1989 at the age of 19. Secretariat was buried at Claiborne Farm, where visitors can now visit his gravesite.

In 2010, Disney released a movie titled *Secretariat*, with Diane Lane starring as Penny Chenery.

Secretariat is buried at Claiborne Farm.

© THERESA DOWELL BLACKINTON

ACCOMMODATIONS
$50-100

Relax in the gorgeous countryside that surrounds Paris at **Country Charm Historic Farmhouse Bed and Breakfast** (505 Hutchison Rd., 859/988-1006, www.countrycharm.net, $90), which is located in easy proximity to both Paris and Lexington. The country house, which is both the married and the childhood home of owner David Snell, has been lovingly decorated and furnished, with antique pieces and hardwood floors mingling nicely with bright, fresh bedding and first-rate artwork. Guests can choose from a king room or queen room in the main house. Each room is spacious with private bath, wireless Internet, and TV. A stocked refrigerator is located on the landing between the rooms. The queen room can be converted to a suite ($150) with a second room with full bed that can be accessed through the bathroom, which would then be shared. A three-bedroom cottage with two bathrooms and kitchenette is also available for rent and is a great option for families. A fantastic breakfast is served each morning in the dining room by owners David and LaVonna, who make warm, wonderful hosts.

If you're the type of person who wants to hook up with a local who can show you all the places the average visitor would never see, set your sights on Pat Conley, the owner of **The Treehouse at Stoner Creek** (131 Taylor Ave., 859/987-6251, www.treehouseatstonercreek.com, $85-100). He'll gladly take you for a cruise down the creek in his pontoon boat; show you where to enjoy a burger underneath a disco ball; set you up for an afternoon float in an inner tube, kayak, or canoe; lead you on a personal walking tour of the town; or assist you in doing whatever else it is you wish. And then you get to stay at his waterfront B&B, a raised wooden home with a dreamy wraparound deck. The B&B has two rooms, a queen room with its own personal elevator and private deck, and a smaller room with two twin beds that is ideal for mother-daughter getaways and the like. The two rooms share 1.5 bathrooms as well as a lounge area with TV (though each room also has its own) and computer. A full breakfast is served each morning.

$100-150

If you've ever wanted to pretend you lived on a horse farm, sipping a bourbon on a porch while the sun sets on a field of thoroughbreds, **The Guesthouse at Rosecrest Farm** (1276 Winchester Rd., 859/987-7500, www.rosecrestfarm.net, $125-165) is your spot. Fulfill your fantasy in one of the two queen rooms on the first floor or in the upstairs king suite. All rooms have private bath, Wi-Fi access, and views of the farm, and a delicious breakfast is served every morning.

FOOD
Farmers Market

If you're looking to make your own picnic, make the farmers market (720 High St., 859/987-6614, 9am-5pm Mon.-Fri., 9am-2pm Sat.) your first stop. Open year-round, the market offers fresh fruits and veggies during the growing season and fresh local eggs and meats every month.

Cafés

Step back in time with lunch at **The Fountain at Ardery's** (627 Main St., 859/987-8180, 7am-3pm Mon.-Sat., $3.95-7.95), an authentic restored soda fountain located inside an antiques store. The Fountain offers hot specials, sandwiches, ice cream, and homemade desserts.

Casual American

The Grey Goose (509 Main St., 859/897-4700, www.greygooserestaurants.com, 11am-10pm Sun.-Thurs., 11am-11pm Fri.-Sat., $8.95-18.95), which is located in a lovingly restored old pharmacy building featuring exposed brick and the original hardwood floors, is a solid choice for lunch or dinner. The menu emphasizes brick-oven pizza, which ranges from a traditional Italian option to more original choices such as the Hot Brown. Burgers, steaks, and fish and chips make up the rest of the menu.

Asian

For your favorite Asian dishes as well as some fusion-type cuisine, give **Paradise Café** (731 Main St., 859/987-8383, 11am-9:30pm Mon.-Sat., 11:30am-9pm Sun., $6.50-12.99) a try. Located in the tallest three-story building in the world and decorated extravagantly, Paradise Café can satisfy a craving for lo mein, sesame chicken, or beef with broccoli.

INFORMATION AND SERVICES

The **Paris Tourism Office** (720 High St., 859/987-8744, http://parisbourbonky.com, 9am-5pm Mon.-Fri.) is located right next to the farmers market. Brochures and maps are available for you to grab and go, or you may chat with staff about the area.

GETTING THERE AND AROUND

Paris is located to the northeast of Lexington along U.S. 68. To get from Lexington to Paris, it's a 19-mile straight shot down U.S. 68 (33 minutes). Georgetown, which is 17 miles (26 minutes) west of Paris, is directly accessible via U.S. 460. Winchester lies 17 miles (25 minutes) to the south of Paris, with KY 627 connecting the two cities.

Winchester

Winchester sits on the eastern edge of the Bluegrass region, connected both to the horse farms of Lexington and the mountains of the east. As you approach Winchester from Paris to the north, you drive past horse farm after horse farm. As you proceed out of town in the other direction, you're more likely to encounter historic markers, stone fences, and the remains of early settlers. The Winchester area has a long history, with many of today's residents tracing their heritage back to the men and women who entered Kentucky with Daniel Boone. That history is seen in the city's museum, in its Civil War heritage, and in the historic buildings of downtown that host everything from old-fashioned hardware stores to contemporary diners where you have to order an Ale-8-One, the local soft drink, with whatever it is you eat.

SIGHTS

Bluegrass Heritage Museum

Through a collection of quality artifacts professionally displayed and interpreted, the **Bluegrass Heritage Museum** (217 S. Main St., 859/745-1358, www.bgheritage.com, noon-4pm Mon.-Sat., $3) preserves the history of Winchester and Clark County.

Exhibits focus on such subjects as agriculture, transportation, military history, music, and domestic life, and you'll see such items as a dulcimer made by Homer Ledford, a collection of quilts dating back to the 1800s, and memorabilia from the hemp and turkey farms that once made Clark County the largest grower of both. The building in which the museum is housed is an exhibit in itself. Built in 1895, the Romanesque revival house served as the Guerrant Mountain Mission Hospital and Clinic from 1927 through 1989, catering to the needs of local residents as well as those who lived in the mountains to the east. The third floor honors this history in three rooms that use authentic articles to re-create the operating room, scrub room, and patient room. Though locally focused, the museum is of broad interest.

Ale-8-One Factory Tour

Created in the 1920s by local businessman G. L. Wainscott, Ale-8-One is Kentucky's soft drink. A ginger ale type of soda, Ale-8-One is sold throughout Kentucky and surrounding states, but it's particularly prevalent in this region of the state. Though Ale-8-One is still sold primarily in glass bottles, you'll also find it in cans and plastic bottles, as well as from soda fountains and even slushie machines around Winchester. A tour of the **Ale-8-One Factory** (25 Carol Rd., 859/744-3484, www.ale8one. com, free) allows Ale-8-One aficionados and factory tour fans to file through the bottling plant and peek in at the quality control room and the warehouse. Before or after the tour, you can visit the gift shop and purchase Ale-8-One salsa and barbecue sauce as well as T-shirts and other paraphernalia. Tours are offered by reservation and last 30-45 minutes.

Downtown Cell Phone Tours

Those who like to peel back the layers and learn about the history and architecture of a place will enjoy the free downtown cell phone tour. The tour encompasses 25 buildings in downtown Winchester, including churches, banks, municipal buildings, theaters, and other locations significant to the city. Taking the tour is a great way to get to know Winchester. Pick up a brochure at the tourism office or download it from their website (www.tourwinchester. com). Then call 859/592-9166 and enter the stop number (found on the brochure or on audio stop signs around town) to learn more about each site.

The Civil War Fort at Boonesboro

On a palisade bluff overlooking the Kentucky River, Union soldiers established an earthwork **Civil War Fort** (1250 Ford Rd., www.civilwarfortatboonesboro.com) to protect a ford and ferry. Two walls of the fort, which will be obvious to Civil War buffs, remain, while those less familiar with such structures will be able to identify the site thanks to a cannon situated in the middle of it. To reach the fort, you must hike up a fairly steep 0.5-mile trail. Interpretive signage lines the trail, covering topics ranging from history related to the fort to the geology of the palisades to the biology of the many flowers growing trailside. The signs also provide regular rest stops for those who find the hike difficult. Be sure to check out the mural on the retaining wall in the parking lot, which depicts scenes of life on the river through history.

FESTIVALS AND EVENTS
Beer Cheese Festival

On the must-taste list for any visitor to Kentucky is beer cheese, and there's no better place to dip into your first batch than at the **Beer Cheese Festival** (www.beercheesefestival.com), held on the second Saturday of June in Winchester. Beer cheese—which, naturally, is made with beer and cheese, along with garlic and an assortment of other spices—was created in Winchester in the 1940s by the Allman family, who ran a restaurant on the river. The spread is usually served with carrots, celery, and saltines and comes in mild, medium, and hot varieties. At the Beer Cheese Festival, you can get a sample of the very many interpretations of beer cheese out there, and you can even enter your own version into the amateur division competition. The festival also features live music, craft vendors, and food vendors.

Daniel Boone Pioneer Festival

The **Daniel Boone Pioneer Festival** (www. danielboonepioneerfestival.com) celebrates Winchester's long history and its connection to some of the state's earliest settlers. The Labor Day weekend festival kicks off with a street dance on Friday night and continues through the weekend with an arts and crafts festival, fun run, antiques appraisals, live music, and concessions. The festival wraps up on Sunday evening with a concert featuring country music and fireworks.

SPORTS AND RECREATION
Hiking

Many Kentucky hikers consider **Lower Howard's Creek Nature & Heritage Preserve** (1945 Athens-Boonesboro Rd., 859/744-4888, www.lowerhowardscreek.org, sunrise-sunset) to be one of the most beautiful sites in the state. Wildflowers are abundant in spring, when the creek and waterfall are also at their best and the trills of birds fill the air inside the gorge. Fall is another popular time to explore the site, which showcases both nature as well as the remains of a mill that was one of Kentucky's earliest industrial sites. The John Holder Trail is open to the

LEXINGTON

public daily, while the rest of the preserve can be visited by appointment only.

MAKE YOUR OWN BEER CHEESE

Beer cheese is a Kentucky staple, and any good Bluegrass hostess has a recipe for this tasty dip in her collection. It's perfect for Kentucky Derby parties, as a snack while watching football games, or at backyard barbecues.

A search for beer cheese recipes will reveal that there are many different ways of making this dish. Feel free to increase or decrease spice amounts and experiment with different styles.

INGREDIENTS

12 ounces of beer, preferably your favorite Kentucky brew
16 ounces sharp cheddar cheese, grated
½ teaspoon garlic powder (or 2 cloves, minced)
½ teaspoon minced onion
¼ teaspoon hot sauce
¼ teaspoon Worcestershire sauce
¼ teaspoon coarse ground black pepper
⅛ teaspoon salt
pinch cayenne
1 teaspoon dry mustard

DIRECTIONS

Pour a 12-ounce bottle of beer into a glass and let it sit for one hour or until flat. Combine cheese and remaining ingredients in a food processer and pulse until slightly blended. Then, while the food processor is on, pour beer slowly through the food processor chute. Once blended, remove mixture from food processer, place in an airtight container, and store in the refrigerator. If possible, make the recipe a day or two in advance, so the flavors have time to mingle. Regardless, the beer cheese will need to be refrigerated before serving so that it hardens to the proper consistency. Serve with saltines, pretzels, celery, and carrots.

Water Sports

There's no better way to enjoy the magnificent beauty of the Kentucky Palisades than from the river. To get out on the water, contact **Three Trees Canoe & Kayak Rental** (300 Athens-Boonesboro Rd., 859/749-3227, www.threetreeskayak.com), located right on the banks of the Kentucky River. The outfitter offers two-hour, half-day, and full-day rental options in which you paddle out from their dock and then paddle back in, as well as six-mile shuttle trips.

ACCOMMODATIONS
$100-150

The former nurses' home of Winchester's mission hospital has been converted by the current generation of Guerrants, the family that began the hospital, into a warm and welcoming bed-and-breakfast. Guests to the **Guerrant Mountain Mission Bed and Breakfast** (21 Valentine Ct., 859/745-1284, www.bbonline.com, $125-150) can choose among three rooms, two of which are on the second floor, and the third of which is on the first floor and can be rented with an additional attached room. Each suite has a large bedroom with queen or king bed plus a sitting room and a full private bathroom. Amenities include stocked refrigerators, robes, TVs, and access to wireless Internet. Furniture and decor is in tune with the historic nature of the house, but is at the same time completely comfortable. Historic photos hang in the hallways, shedding light on the unique history of the home, and owner Wally Guerrant loves to share stories about the house, his family, and the hospital. You can take breakfast at the cozy dining table already set in your suite or join the Guerrants at the same dining table used by the nurses. Guests are also invited to gather in the downstairs common areas or on the large deck.

Three guest rooms have been tastefully appointed at **House on Belmont** (331 Belmont Ave., 859/745-0177, www.houseonbelmont.com, $130-150) to cater to the needs and whimsy of a range of guests. Sharlotte's Room is rich with bursts of fiery red, and a queen four-poster bed, fireplace, and private bath with both shower and whirlpool tub make it a great couple's retreat. Couples who prefer a softer touch can opt for Rebecca's Room, which is decorated in blues and greens and features a queen-size bed, fireplace, and bathroom with double-headed shower. Friends or family members traveling together will find comfort in Francesa's Room, which has two twin beds and its own private bathroom. House on Belmont also welcomes pets.

FOOD
Casual American
Make **Stinky & Coco's Diner** (1 N. Main St., 859/744-8100, www.stinkyandcocos. com, 6am-2pm Mon.-Sat., $1.75-7.95) your choice for breakfast or lunch. Though a traditional diner in the sense that you can sit at the counter and watch as they prepare your food, Stinky & Coco's is no greasy spoon. The restaurant is fresh and contemporary with a touch of nostalgia, and the food is prepared with attention to detail and a splash of creativity. The shrimp and grits is a favorite for both breakfast and lunch, and the burgers are hand-formed and come with hand-cut fries. A few daily specials complement the small menu. The atmosphere is small-town friendly with regulars filling the seats. As for the name, don't fear—it has nothing to do with the food or the building, but is instead the name of the owner's cats.

Hall's on the River (1225 Athens-Boonesboro Rd., 859/527-6620, www.hallsontheriver.com, 11:30am-10pm Mon.-Sat., 11:30am-9pm Sun., $9.95-23.95) is a regional institution. Its location on the banks of the Kentucky River has always been favored as a dining site, Holder's Tavern occupying the location as far back as 1783. Today, Hall's keeps that history alive with a bar they refer to as Holder's Tavern. A casual place with fireplaces to keep you warm in the winter and a deck for summer dining, Hall's is known for its beer cheese as well as its fried banana peppers. Popular entrées include catfish, a Hot Brown, and Southern favorites like chicken livers and country ham.

INFORMATION AND SERVICES
If you need assistance with your travels around the region, contact or visit the **Winchester-Clark County Tourism Commission** (2 S. Maple St., 859/744-0556, www.tourwinchester.com, 9am-5pm Mon.-Fri.). You'll definitely want to pick up copies of their free driving tour brochures.

GETTING THERE AND AROUND
Winchester is almost directly east of Lexington, just a bit south of I-64. To travel from Lexington to Winchester, the most direct route is to drive 19 miles (35 minutes) on U.S. 60, which provides door-to-door access. Winchester is connected to Paris, which is 17 miles (25 minutes) north, by KY 627. From Winchester, KY 627 continues south, and if you follow it for 21 miles (30 minutes), you'll reach Richmond. If you're traveling on I-64, take Exit 96A, and proceed two miles south on KY 627. From I-75, take Exit 95 and follow northbound KY 627 for nearly 14 miles.

While driving around Winchester and Clark County, be sure to note the many stone fences lining the roads. Here you'll find the most extensive collection of dry masonry quarried stone fences in the United States. The majority of these fences were built in the early 1800s after a law was passed requiring property owners to keep their livestock from roaming onto other people's property. Though often referred to as "slave fences," Irish and Scottish immigrants actually brought the trade to the region. Slaves were often required to help with the construction, and after emancipation, many used the skill to make a living. The fences come in a variety of styles, with the majority of the fences in Clark County in the turnpike, plantation, or edge style. A brochure available at the tourism office has a map highlighting the roads where you will find stone fences.

LEXINGTON

Richmond

Although Richmond is home to Eastern Kentucky University and is located in the same county as Berea, which is firmly entrenched in Appalachia, Richmond more closely identifies with Lexington. It's actually the sixth-biggest city in Kentucky, but it's often overlooked, more of a stopover than a stopping place. The city itself isn't particularly notable, but there are a slew of interesting attractions in its vicinity, particularly for those with an interest in history.

SIGHTS
◖ Fort Boonesborough State Park

Commemorating Kentucky's second settlement, established by Daniel Boone and company in 1775, **Fort Boonesborough** (4375 Boonesboro Rd., 859/527-3131, http://parks. ky.gov, 9am-5pm Wed.-Sun., mid-Apr.-Oct.,

10am-4pm Fri.-Sun., Nov.-mid-Apr. $8 adults, $5 youth 6-12) is one of Kentucky's most popular parks, and for good reason. The reconstructed fort has working cabins, with interpreters and artisans dressed in accurate period garb re-creating life in the fort. Start the visit with a viewing of the 15-minute orientation film, then proceed from cabin to cabin, learning from weavers, tool makers, distillers, spinners, woodworkers, gunsmiths, candle makers, soap makers, and other fort residents. Interpreters welcome visitors to ask questions, touch artifacts, and interact on many levels. Be sure to visit Daniel Boone, who will gladly help you purchase a piece of property at Boonesborough, and stop in the Transylvania Store, which sells period items, including many of the products made by the on-site artisans. In late September, the fort hosts a fascinating re-enactment of the siege of 1778, in which Native

Re-enactors bring Fort Boonesborough to life.

© THERESA DOWELL BLACKINTON

LEXINGTON

Americans attacked the fort. On weekends Memorial Day-Labor Day, admission to the fort includes admission to the Kentucky River Museum (10am-4pm), which contains exhibits about life on the river during the 1900s.

Outside the fort, the state park also offers recreational facilities, including picnic areas, a mini-golf course, a playground, a very popular pool with a big twisting slide, and access to the Kentucky River, as well as a campground.

White Hall State Historic Site

White Hall State Historic Site (500 Whitehall Shrine Rd., 859/623-9178, http://parks.ky.gov, 9am-5pm Mon.-Sat., noon-4pm Sun., Apr.-Oct.) preserves the home and interprets the life of Cassius Clay (the outspoken emancipationist, not the boxer better known as Muhammad Ali). Tours (Wed.-Sat. only, $7 adults, $7 seniors, $4 youth 6-12) of the 44-room Italianate mansion are led by costumed guides who share stories about the home, which is restored to its 1860s state, and the Clay family. Tour participants will also visit the slave quarters and outbuildings, learning what influenced Clay, who came from a wealthy, slave-owning family to become a noted emancipationist.

Battle of Richmond Visitors Center and Driving Tour

The Battle of Richmond, which took place in late summer 1862, was a major Confederate victory that was, unfortunately for the South, negated by the lack of a plan for how to proceed post-battle. Those interested in learning about this battle should begin with a stop at the **Battle of Richmond Visitors Center** (101 Battlefield Memorial Hwy., 859/624-0013, 10am-4pm daily, free), located in a historic home that witnessed fighting on all sides. After exploring the visitors center, you can then take a 13-stop self-guided tour of the battle. The tour starts in the southern part of the county near Berea, making its way north toward Richmond along U.S. 25. A brochure detailing the route and providing information on each stop is available at the Richmond Tourism office and through their website. Civil

War enthusiasts can also purchase a CD at the tourism office, with much more detailed information on the battle.

Downtown Walking Tour of Historic Homes

Encompassing 60 buildings in three distinct National Register Historic Districts, the downtown walking tour is a must for history and architecture buffs. A free 77-page booklet provides detailed information on the features of each building along with a photo of each. Buildings on the tour cover a wide variety of architectural styles—federal, Queen Anne, Italianate, classic revival, T-plan, gothic—and uses, from private homes to courthouses to churches. The tour begins and ends at the **Irvinton House** (345 Lancaster Ave.), which is where the tourism office is located and the booklet can be picked up.

Acres of Land Winery

Located on 400 acres used for more than 50 years to grow burley tobacco, **Acres of Land Winery** (2285 Barnes Mill Rd., 859/328-3000, www.acresoflandwinery.com, 10am-5pm Mon.-Sat., 12:30pm-5pm Sun.) is a family-run enterprise with on-site vineyards as well as production facilities. The winery welcomes guests to visit for a walk through the vineyards followed by a tasting. The lovely grounds make a great picnic location, and there's no need to worry if you didn't bring your own; the on-site restaurant is happy to fix one up for you using produce and herbs grown on the grounds. The best days to visit are Friday-Sunday, when the winery offers free guided tours of the winery buildings and wagon tours of the grounds on the hour between 1pm and 4pm, which allow you to see the production process and ask all the questions you can come up with.

ENTERTAINMENT

Thanks to its large patio, cheap beer, and raved-about wings, **Madison Garden** (152 N. Madison Ave., 859/623-9720, www.madisongarden.net, 11am-1am Tues.-Sat., noon-9pm Sun.) has been a happening gathering place since 1982. Weekly events include beer pong on Tuesday, karaoke on Wednesday, a DJ on Thursday, and live music on Friday and Saturday. Expect to find a lot of Eastern Kentucky University students having a good time here.

Another popular good-time kind of place is **Paddy Wagon Irish Pub** (150 E. Main St., 859/625-1054, 3pm-1am Mon.-Fri., noon-1am Sat.). This typical pub with exposed brick and a wraparound bar serves more than 80 beers from around the world and has billiards tables and live music.

SPORTS AND RECREATION
Parks
Lake Reba Recreational Complex (Gibson Bay Dr., 859/623-8753) is where Madison County residents go to enjoy the great outdoors. The 75-acre lake accommodates boats (with trolling motors only) and bank fishing, while the grounds surrounding it offer nature trails, baseball and soccer fields, basketball and volleyball courts, batting cages, a horseshoe pit, playgrounds, picnic areas, and two dog parks. The complex also hosts an 18-hole golf course and driving range along with an 18-hole mini-golf course. In summer, the most favored feature is the **Paradise Cove Water Park** (274 Lake Reba Dr., 859/626-7665, 11am-7pm Mon.-Sat., 1pm-6pm Sun. Memorial Day-Labor Day, $7 adults, $4 seniors, $5 youth 14-17, $4 youth 4-13), which has a lap pool with one-meter diving boards and a play pool with four slides. Rates are reduced by $2 at 4pm.

Horseback Riding
Deer Run Stable (2001 River Circle Dr., 615/268-9960, www.deerrunstable.com) leads guided trail rides along six miles of trail, which cut through forest and over creek, passing old cabins and a cemetery predating the Civil War. Call in advance to make a reservation.

Spectator Sports
Richmond Raceway (328 Greens Crossing, 859/626-4189, www.richmond-raceway.net) is a 0.3-mile oval dirt track that hosts stock car races every Saturday night April-September.

ACCOMMODATIONS
$100-150
The Bennett House (419 W. Main St., 859/623-7876, www.bennetthousebb.com, $125-200) is an elegant property with architecture worthy of a house museum. The late 19th-century home built in Queen Anne style with Romanesque details has a stone archway entrance, turret, stained-glass windows, hand-carved mantles, and a magnificent cherry wraparound staircase. Two guest rooms are located on the second level, and one is located on the ground floor. Each room is large with a king or queen bed as well as a comfy sitting area with TV and wireless Internet access. A large private bathroom with 1950s tiling is attached to each room. Family pieces and antiques decorate the rooms in a traditional style. A cottage located behind the house was added in the 2000s and offers two suites. One suite has a king bed and a full kitchen while the other has two full beds and a kitchenette. Both have private bath with whirlpool tubs, TV, wireless Internet access, and private deck. A multi-course breakfast is served in the dining room each morning.

Campgrounds
The campground at **Fort Boonesborough State Park** (4375 Boonesboro Rd., 859/527-3131, http://parks.ky.gov, $30-35) is large, with 167 sites with full hookups situated along the Kentucky River. Back-in and pull-through sites are available. Amenities include restrooms, a shower house, laundry facilities, and a small grocery. Though large, the campground does often fill completely in the summer. It's open year-round.

FOOD
Casual American
Jackson's (203 S. 3rd St., 859/623-2090, 7am-7pm Mon.-Thurs. and Sat., 7am-8pm Fri., 8am-4pm Sun., $6-10) will fill you up right

with home-cooking favorites, such as fried pork chops, catfish, meatloaf, and mac and cheese. Take a stroll down the cafeteria-style food line, opting for a meat with one, two, three, or four sides, or order a hamburger, sandwich, or omelet from the menu. Whatever you choose, save room for the big slices of pie for dessert.

Indian

Masala Fine Indian Cuisine (1000 Center Dr., 859/623-8589, www.masalafinecuisine.com, lunch 11am-2:30pm Mon.-Fri. and 11:30am-3pm Sat.-Sun., dinner 5pm-10pm Sun.-Thurs., 5pm-10:30pm Fri.-Sat., $9.95-14.95) does a fine job with food from the subcontinent. Their lunch buffet is especially popular. Those ordering off the menu can choose from tandooris; lamb, chicken, or seafood specialties; rice dishes; and vegetarian options. Flavors are authentic, although not as spicy as you'd find in India. Beautiful murals depicting traditional Indian scenes adorn the walls.

Mediterranean

The gyros at **Babylon** (213 W. Main St., 859/625-1212, 10am-10pm Mon.-Sat., $5.99-12.99) could trick you into thinking that you're somewhere a bit more Mediterranean than central Kentucky. Plates, which include shawarma, kabobs, and falafel, are hearty. The atmosphere isn't much to speak of, but the owner is a real character, so take a minute to chat with him.

INFORMATION AND SERVICES

The **Richmond Tourism & Visitors Center** (345 Lancaster Ave., 800/866-3705, www.rich-mondkytourism.com, 8am-4:30pm Mon.-Fri.) is located in the heart of the city, convenient for those seeing downtown's sights but a bit far from the interstate. Brochures and maps are available, and staff can provide suggestions on Richmond area sights, accommodation, and food. While there, be sure to check out the Irvinton House Museum (free) with which it shares a space. The museum houses artifacts related to local history, as well as one of only seven remaining Revolutionary War uniforms.

GETTING THERE AND AROUND

Richmond is located 25 miles (35 minutes) south of Lexington on I-75. From I-75, take Exit 90A, and then follow southbound U.S. 25 for three miles into the city. To travel to Nicholasville (30 miles; 40 minutes), take KY 169, which will take you to the Kentucky River, which you can cross via the **Valley View Ferry** (KY 169, 859/258-3611, 6am-8pm Mon.-Fri., 8am-6pm Sat., 9am-6pm Sun., free), the oldest continuously operated business in Kentucky. Chartered in 1785 when Kentucky was still part of Virginia, the three-car cable-guided ferry still flies both Kentucky and Virginia flags. Once over the river, continue along KY 169, which leads to Nicholasville.

Nicholasville and Jessamine County

Nicholasville is a rapidly growing city with strong ties to Lexington. People who work in Lexington but seek a smaller place with a lower cost of living to call home often choose Nicholasville. Nearby Asbury College and Seminary also draws people to the region. Currently the 11th largest city in Kentucky, Nicholasville is working hard to draw new residents and to establish fresh new businesses in the historic buildings of downtown. Despite the development, Nicholasville has also managed to protect its natural beauty, which is rich thanks to its location in the Kentucky Palisades.

SIGHTS
Camp Nelson Heritage Park

On 4,000 acres of land naturally protected by

LEXINGTON

© THERESA DOWELL BLACKINTON

Oliver Perry House at Camp Nelson Heritage Park

the Kentucky Palisades, the Union Army established **Camp Nelson** (6614 Danville Rd., 859/881-5716, www.campnelson.org, dawn-dusk daily, free), which had more than 300 buildings and fortifications. This camp was used as a commissary depot, staging ground, hospital, and defensive site. It was also used to recruit, muster, and train troops, perhaps most significantly eight regiments of African American troops. Visitors to the site of this camp are invited to explore the 525 acres that are preserved as a heritage park. A trail with interpretive signage provides context. The **Oliver Perry House,** now commonly referred to as the White House, is the only structure that remains from that era. Built in 1846, the house was confiscated by General Burnside for use as officers' quarters during the war. Free tours of the house are given 10am-4pm Tuesday-Saturday. In September, a reenactment event called Camp Nelson Civil War Days is held at the park.

Taylor Made Farm

Taylor Made Farm (2765 Union Mill Rd., 859/885-3345, www.taylormadefarm.com) is a 1,600-acre horse farm and a top agent for horse sales. Among the stallions stabled at Taylor Made are Florida Derby winner Unbridled's Song and Arkansas Derby winner Old Fashioned. The farm welcomes visitors to call and arrange a free tour. Tours may be limited during the spring breeding season.

Chrisman Mill Vineyards & Winery

Ten different types of wine are produced at **Chrisman Mill Vineyards & Winery** (2385 Chrisman Mill Rd., 859/881-5007, www.chrismanmill.com, 11am-5pm Wed.-Sat.) using both estate-grown grapes and grapes from more than 14 Kentucky farmers. At the vineyard, owners Chris and Denise Nelson, who got their start by making wine for their own wedding, give tours and offer tastings ($5). A tapas and dessert menu is available if you want to nibble while enjoying the view.

SPORTS AND RECREATION
Parks

High Bridge Park traces its history back to 1877 when High Bridge, the first cantilevered bridge in North America, was constructed over the Kentucky River. At that time, the park was used for religious meetings, dances, and picnics. With the passing of time, and as passenger trains quit using High Bridge, the park fell out of favor and into disrepair. In recent years, however, the park has been revitalized, and again boasts a pavilion, as well as a playground and a viewing platform that extends out over the river. Located on KY 29 south of Wilmore, where the road dead-ends at the river, High Bridge Park is a great place to have a picnic and admire the Kentucky Palisades. It's also a good bird-watching spot, with herons commonly seen along the river.

ACCOMMODATIONS
$50-100

Located on the grounds of Asbury Theological Seminary, the **Asbury Inn** (1 June Ryan Circle, Wilmore, 859/858-3581, www.asburyseminary. edu, $89.95) offers 27 rooms with either king bed and sleeper sofa, two queen beds, or two double beds. The rooms, which were updated in 2010, are simple but fresh and are well maintained. Complimentary Internet access and breakfast come with the room. The inn is open to everyone, not just those with a connection to the seminary.

The **Corner House Bed and Breakfast** (228 Richmond Ave., Nicholasville, 877/571-5777, www.cornerhousebedandbreakfast.com, $75-85) is a welcoming place with three guest rooms, each with a queen bed, private bath, TV, and Internet access. The 1911 house is decorated in Victorian style and retains its original floors and mantles. A video library is available to guests as is a game room with billiard table and dartboard. The curved porch furnished with rocking chairs is a great place to relax after enjoying the very good breakfast. Corner House also rents out a two-bedroom cottage, which is located just across the street, and three townhouses located closer to Lexington.

FOOD
Contemporary American

Euro Winebar (102 S. Main St., 859/885-3139, http://eurowinebar.com, 5pm-midnight Wed.-Thurs., 5pm-1am Fri.-Sat., $6-13) is a unique addition to the area, serving tapas-style portions of American favorites, including mini Hot Browns, pan-fried ravioli, a meatloaf slider, baked brie, and other tasty bites. Furnished with a mix of couches and tables, it's part restaurant, part bar, with a fine wine and cocktail list.

Hawaiian

A somewhat unlikely find, **◖ Ogata's Hawaiian Grill** (1001 Elizabeth St., 859/881-0703, 11am-7pm Mon.-Thurs. and Sun., 11am-8pm Fri.-Sat., $6.25-8) serves plate lunch specials just like you'd find in Hawaii. This little joint has all the expected menu items—Hawaiian beef, Kalua pork, *mochi,* and even Spam sushi—and the food is truly *ono* (that's "delicious" in Hawaiian). The Hawaiian mixed plate, which includes the beef and pork plus Hawaiian-style chicken, rice, and macaroni salad, is a steal at $8. If you're lucky, they might even have *malasadas* (Portuguese doughnuts).

INFORMATION AND SERVICES

Information about Nicholasville and Jessamine County can be obtained through the website of the **Nicholasville Tourism Commission** (508 N. Main St., 859/887-4351, www.nicholasvilletourism.com).

GETTING THERE AND AROUND

Nicholasville is located 12 miles (20 minutes) south of Lexington on U.S. 27. From most everywhere, the easiest way to get to Nicholasville is to first go to Lexington. From Richmond (30 miles; 40 minutes), however, you can take KY 169. The Kentucky River cuts across KY 169, and the only way across it at this point is via the **Valley View Ferry** (KY 169, 859/258-3611, 6am-8pm Mon.-Fri., 8am-6pm Sat., 9am-6pm Sun., free).

Chartered in 1785, the Valley View Ferry is the oldest continuously operated business in Kentucky. While riding or waiting for the ferry, which is guided by cable and can only carry three cars at a time, look for the ferry's flags. Because it began operation when Kentucky was still part of Virginia, the ferry flies both Kentucky and Virginia flags.

Harrodsburg

Kentucky's oldest town, Harrodsburg still deals on its pioneering past, throwing in a strong dose of Southern charm for balance. The town itself is small, although worthy of a stroll. Its attractions, however, can easily fill a day. Great hotels and food make it an excellent place to overnight while seeing both Harrodsburg and surrounding towns.

SIGHTS
Old Fort Harrod State Park
Settled in June 1774, Harrodsburg was the first permanent European settlement west of the Allegheny Mountains. Today, **Old Fort Harrod State Park** (100 S. College St., 859/734-3314, http://parks.ky.gov) commemorates the settlement, with a replica of the original fort taking center stage. During the high season, costumed interpreters occupy the fort's buildings and portray life on the frontier. Watch as interpreters make dolls, soap, and candles; spin wool; work wood; smith metal; and perform other tasks while discussing daily life at Harrodsburg. Admission to the fort ($5 adults, $4 seniors, $3 youth 6-12) also includes entrance to a museum that houses an eclectic collection of artifacts dating from pioneer days through much of the 19th century. The Lincoln Marriage Temple, a church built around the cabin where President Lincoln's parents were wed, is also located on the park grounds, as is the Pioneer Cemetery and a playground and picnic area. The grounds are open 8am-dusk daily and are free to access. The fort and Lincoln Marriage Temple are open 9am-5pm Wednesday-Saturday and noon-5pm Sunday, March-November, and 8am-4:30pm Monday-Friday, December-February. The museum is open only Friday-Sunday, mid-April-October.

Shaker Village
Home to a thriving Shaker religious community from 1805 to 1910, **Shaker Village** (3501 Lexington Rd., 800/734-5611, www.shakervillageky.org, 10am-5pm daily Apr.-Oct., 10am-4pm daily Nov.-Mar., $15 adults, $5 youth 6-12 Apr.-Oct., $7 adults, $3 youth 6-12 Nov.-Mar.) was restored in the 1960s and transformed into a living history museum. Visitors are now welcome to enter 14 of the 34 restored buildings, many of which are staffed by costumed interpreters. Take a 45-minute tour of the enormous Centre family dwelling, enjoy a musical performance in the Meeting House, learn about Shaker inventions and agricultural practices in the historic farm area, and watch artisans craft the furniture and textiles for which the group is known in the Brethren's and Sisters' Shops. Wagon rides ($6) and Dixie Belle Riverboat rides ($10 adults, $5 youth) are offered in high season. Allow three hours for a cursory visit, a full day if you wish to participate in tours and demonstrations.

The 3,000 acres on which Shaker Village sits are protected as a nature preserve, which can be explored via a 40-mile trail system. From three trailheads, hikers, bikers, and horseback riders can access 13 different trails, ranging in distance from 1-6 miles and covering meadow, palisade, river, and forest terrain. The trails, open from sunrise to sunset, are free to hikers and bikers. Equestrian trail users must pay a $10 fee. All users must check in and sign a waiver at Shaker Village, at which time they will be issued a map and trail information.

To really immerse yourself in Shaker Village, consider overnighting at the **Inn at Shaker Village** ($100-200). The simple rooms

© THERESA DOWELL BLACKINTON

sheep at Shaker Village

LEXINGTON

are adorned with beautiful Shaker furniture, including a choice of beds (twin, double, or queen), a dresser, and rocking chairs, as well as modern bathrooms and televisions. (Though many people wrongly associate Shakers with the Amish, Shakers were, in fact, early adopters of technology and avid inventors.) Overnight guests as well as day visitors are welcome to enjoy a meal at the candlelit **Trustees' Office Dining Room** (breakfast 7:30am-10am, lunch 11:30am-3pm, dinner 5pm-8:30pm daily). The menu changes seasonally, but always features fresh, local food, some of which is grown right on the property. Dinner ($15.95-22.95) offerings might include rack of lamb or prawn risotto, while the lunch ($10.95-12.95) menu might feature a pork sandwich or johnnycakes. During the winter months (Jan.-mid-Feb.), lunch and dinner are served in the Winter Kitchen. Reservations are strongly recommended for all meals, though walk-ins are welcome to inquiry about availability.

Shaker Village hosts a multitude of annual events. Some of the most popular events are the Chamber Music Festival of the Bluegrass (Memorial Day Weekend), Antique Show (mid-June), Shaker Music Day (mid-July), and Shaker Village Craft Fair (early August).

ENTERTAINMENT
Live Music
The Kentucky Strangers, a local country music group, entertains the crowds every week at **The Barn** (345 Buster Pk., Burgin, 859/748-9689, 7pm-10pm Fri., $10). Special guest performers are regularly on the schedule.

Movie Theaters
Although drive-ins have gone the way of the dodo in most of the United States, at Harrodsburg's **Twin Hills Drive-In Theatre** (1785 Louisville Rd., 859/734-3474, 6:30pm Fri.-Sat. spring-fall, $5 adults, $2.50 youth 3-11), you can still enjoy a movie while parked in your car. Make sure your car radio works, because you'll need to tune in to 106.1 FM to receive the movie soundtrack.

WHO WERE THE SHAKERS?

During the 1800s, Kentucky had two Shaker communities, one in Harrodsburg and one west of Bowling Green in South Union. The Shakers were a unique religious sect that originated in England and then migrated to the United States, with the first communities located in New York. Shaker beliefs were centered around communalism, in which members of each village lived in family groups, although members were not actually related by blood. In fact, true Shakers practiced celibacy, and buildings were divided so that men and women each had their own side. Because Shakers did not procreate, the religion expanded through conversion and the adoption of orphans. Socially, the Shakers were actually quite progressive, with men and women given equal responsibility and rights.

Religiously, Shakers believed in Jesus as the embodiment of the masculine side of God, and Mother Ann, the religion's founder, as the embodiment of the feminine side of God. Their faith was centered around four values: virgin purity, Christian communism, confession of sin, and separation from the world.

Shakers made a number of contributions to today's world. They are known for their style of furniture, which is simple and functional but of the highest craftsmanship. Authentic Shaker pieces go for very high prices today, with reproductions also flooding the market. Shaker music, which was a vital part of worship services, also made it to the outside world. "Simple Gifts" is the most widely known of their songs. Prolific inventors, Shakers introduced circular saws, clothespins, flat brooms, wheel-driven washing machines, and other home and farm implements to the world.

By the early 1900s most Shaker communities had died out. Shaker Village at Pleasant Hill was abandoned in 1910, while the village in South Union closed in 1922. Today the only active Shaker community is located in Sabbathday Lake, Maine.

old-fashioned plowing at Shaker Village

© THERESA DOWELL BLACKINTON

SPORTS AND RECREATION
Horseback Riding
Ride your way across 1,000 acres of blue-grass on a mount from **Big Red Stables** (1605 Jackson Pike, 859/734-3118, www.bigredstablesky.com). Horseback riding is available by appointment. Riders must be at least 12 years old and cannot weigh more than 220 pounds.

Water Sports
The deepest lake in the state, **Herrington Lake** is a popular fishing and water recreation spot. Among the species anglers cast a line for are bluegill, catfish, crappie, and bass. Multiple marinas are located on the lake, offering services from bait purchase to boat rentals. The lake can be reached by traveling east on U.S. 152 from Harrodsburg for nine miles.

ACCOMMODATIONS
$100-150
Each of the three rooms at **Southern Charm Bed and Breakfast** (363 N. East St. 859/734-9340, www.southerncharmbb.com, $125) has a distinct personality. Choose the first-floor Magnolia Room if you want a spacious understated room with queen bed; opt for the Flower Garden Room if you like antique decor and claw-foot tubs; or reserve the Gold Room with whirlpool tub and fireplace if romance is what you're after. The Greek Revival-style house is smartly decorated and wireless Internet enabled, and the yard boasts a built-in pool. Guests should be aware that only a continental breakfast is served.

$150-200
The oldest family-operated inn in Kentucky, **Beaumont Inn** (638 Beaumont Inn Dr., 859/734-3381, www.beaumontinn.com, $143-230) is also one of the most beautiful. The inn consists of three distinct buildings: the original Beaumont Inn, a Greek Revival mansion that served as a girls' school from the mid-1800s to the early 1900s; Goddard Hall, a white frame building directly across the drive; and Greystone, a Colonial Revival limestone building constructed in 1931.

Antique wood furniture, chandeliers, and decor are found in all guest rooms, which are uniformly lovely. For true luxury, book a suite in the Greystone House and relax on the king-size bed, in front of the electric fireplace, or in the two-person whirlpool bath. Wireless Internet is not available in Greystone, but guests are welcome to hop online while enjoying the many common areas in the main inn. The complimentary breakfast is served buffet style, but you have to ask for an order of the renowned cornmeal battercakes. Sunday rates are significantly lower—practically a steal—and the inn offers discounts for stays of three days or more.

FOOD
Casual American
You don't normally expect soda fountains to be handsome, but **Dedman Drugstore** (225 S. Main St., 859/733-0088, www.kentuckyfudgecompany.com, 9am-8pm Tues.-Thurs., 9am-9pm Fri.-Sat., $5.95-8.95) is. Stained-glass windows, cherrywood paneling and cabinetry, and a high decorative ceiling make Dedman's more than a great place to savor a shake at the counter or try the more than 20 types of homemade fudge. You can also take a table and order from a selection of sandwiches, quiches, soups, salads, and daily specials.

With an enormous stage, **Eddie Montgomery's Steakhouse** (180 Lucky Man Way, 859/734-3400, www.eddiemontgomerysteakhouse.com, 4pm-9pm Tues.-Wed., 4pm-11pm Thurs., 11am-1:30am Fri.-Sat., 11am-8pm Sun., $10-25) is as much about entertainment as food. This won't come as a surprise to anyone who recognizes the name, since Eddie Montgomery is half of the country music duo Montgomery Gentry. Performances occur most weekends, and Mr. Montgomery himself makes regular appearances. Steak and classic American dishes are menu mainstays. Expect long waits.

Southern
You don't have to stay at **Beaumont Inn** (638

LEXINGTON

Beaumont Inn Dr., 859/734-3381, www. beaumontinn.com) to partake in a meal at one of their three restaurants. The claim to fame at the white-tabled **Beaumont Inn Dining Room** (lunch 11:30am-1:30pm Wed.-Fri., dinner 6pm-7:30pm Wed.-Fri. and 6pm-8pm Sat., brunch 11am-1:30pm Sun., $19.95-24.95) is yellow-legged fried chicken served with Kentucky country ham. It's the best of country cooking served in an elegant atmosphere. If you're looking for good food but a more casual atmosphere, grab a table at the **Old Owl Tavern** (4pm-9pm Mon.-Thurs., 4pm-10pm Fri., 11:30am-10pm Sat., $12-18), a cozy bar and restaurant with brick columns and exposed wood beams on the inn's lower level that serves Southern favorites such as shrimp and grits and slow-braised beef brisket. **Owl's Nest Lounge** (5pm-10pm Wed.-Sat., $12-18), opened in 2009, is the inn's newest establishment and, though it maintains the inn's classic character, it also feels a bit hip. You can order from the same menu as is served at the Old Owl Tavern, or just sit and sip one of 50 available bourbons.

INFORMATION AND SERVICES

Diamond Point Welcome Center (488 Price Ave., 859/734-2364, www.harrodsburgky. com, 9am-5pm Mon.-Fri., additional Sat. hours June-Oct.) offers the usual collection of brochures and maps. Ask for the free Harrodsburg & Mercer County Walking and Driving Tour brochure, which directs you to 85 points of interest in the area, many of which are on the National Register of Historic Places.

GETTING THERE AND AROUND

From Lexington, follow westbound U.S. 68 for 32 miles (50 minutes) to Harrodsburg. Harrodsburg is also easily accessible from Frankfort; just travel 33 miles (45 minutes) south on U.S. 127. From nearby Danville, travel 10 miles (17 minutes) north on U.S. 127.

Danville and Perryville

Danville is small-town America epitomized. In fact, *Time* magazine named Danville one of the 10 most successful small towns in America. It's home to an award-winning Main Street, a liberal arts college that keeps the old town young, festivals that capture the spirit of Americana, and residents who love their hometown and aren't afraid to show it. Located along the Wilderness Trail, Danville's history is a long one, but the town, while celebrating its past, doesn't get stuck in it. Nearby Perryville is the site of one of the most important Civil War battles to take place in Kentucky, and the perfectly preserved battlegrounds deserve a place on any area itinerary.

SIGHTS
Historic Downtown Danville
Recipient of a 2001 Great American Main Street Award from the National Trust for Historic Preservation, Danville's downtown has been carefully preserved, with new shops maintaining the elegant facades of yesteryear. Get to know the town on a walking tour that visits 50 sites of interest, including the iconic courthouse, a number of churches that date to the early 1800s, the first college building west of the Alleghenies, the first state-supported school for the deaf, and other buildings of note. A free brochure with map and details of each site can be picked up at the visitors bureau or downloaded from their website.

McDowell House Museum
Marvel at the bravery of both Dr. Ephraim McDowell and patient Jane Todd Crawford on a visit to the **McDowell House Museum** (125 S. 2nd St., Danville, 859/236-2804, www. mcdowellhouse.com, 10am-noon and 1pm-4pm Mon.-Sat., 2pm-4pm Sun., closed Mon.

© THERESA DOWELL BLACKINTON

Constitution Square

LEXINGTON

Nov.-Feb., $7 adults, $5 seniors, $3 students 13-20, $2 youth 5-12), site of the world's first successful abdominal surgery, performed in 1809 sans anesthesia and with a prayer in the doctor's pocket. Tours of the restored house encompass private dwelling areas, the apothecary shop, and gardens and are offered on a walk-in basis. In addition to learning specifically about Dr. McDowell, you'll also learn about life in that time period and might even discover where the phrase "sleep tight" comes from.

Great American Dollhouse Museum

Although the **Great American Dollhouse Museum** (344 Swope Dr., Danville, 859/236-1883, www.thedollhousemuseum.com, 11am-5pm Tues.-Sat., $7.50 adults, $6.60 seniors, $5 youth 4-12) does indeed feature dollhouses—more than 200 of them, in fact—it's much more than a collection of dolls and miniatures. It's also a history museum. The first exhibit provides a timeline of American social history via dollhouse displays, while the second exhibit portrays a century-old fictional village. The attention to detail is phenomenal, with commissioned dolls and intricate scenes. The thousands of miniatures could easily overwhelm the non-enthusiast, but short, and sometimes humorous, quotes create a story for each house and focus your attention.

Constitution Square State Historic Site

On the grounds of what is now known as **Constitution Square** (134 S. 2nd St., Danville, 859/239-7089, http://parks.ky.gov, 9am-5pm daily, free), Kentucky was officially born, its first constitution signed here on June 1, 1792, after a series of conventions. The original buildings built by pioneers who entered Kentucky via the Wilderness Road no longer remain, but replicas stand in place of the meetinghouse, courthouse, jail, and first post office in the West. Visitors are welcome to take a self-guided tour of the buildings and imagine what Danville was like when it stood at the crossroads of settlement.

Chateau du Vieux Corbeau Winery

At **Chateau du Vieux Corbeau** (471 Stanford Ave., Danville, 859/236-1808, www.oldcrowinn.com, 11am-6pm Mon.-Sat.), Kentucky's youngest vintner creates blends that result in award-winning wine. The winery produces four whites, four reds, one blush, and five fruit wines. Tastings are free, and cellar tours are available with advance notice. While sipping a glass of wine, enjoy a stroll around the property, where you'll find the oldest stone structure west of the Alleghenies, dating to the 1780s, and may encounter the wildlife—including a flock of 100 wild turkeys—that roams the 27 acres.

Perryville Battlefield State Historic Site

Thanks to limited development in the area, **Perryville Battlefield** (1825 Battlefield Rd., Perryville, 859/332-8631, http://parks.ky.gov) is considered one of the most pristine Civil War battlefields in the country, meaning that visitors to the site are treated to an accurate view of the terrain where the battle for Kentucky took place. The battle, which occurred on October 8, 1862, was the biggest to take place in the state. Although the Confederates won the tactical battle, they were outnumbered and forced to retreat from what would be their high water mark in the western sphere. Visitors are welcome to walk all or parts of the 9.8 miles of interpretive trails on the battlefield (dawn-dusk, free). A 30-minute video about the battle can be viewed at the museum (9am-5pm daily, Apr.-Oct., Wed.-Sun., Nov.-Dec. and Mar., closed Jan.-Feb., $3.50 adults, $2.50 youth), which also houses Civil War artifacts. The Battle of Perryville is reenacted each year on the first weekend of October.

ENTERTAINMENT AND EVENTS
Performing Arts

A small town in the middle of Kentucky might not be the most obvious place to find big-time shows, but Centre College's **Norton Center for the Arts** (600 W. Walnut St., Danville, 859/236-4692, www.nortoncenter.com) deals in world-class performances. Artists such as Willie Nelson, Yo-Yo Ma, and Tony Bennett, and shows such as *Riverdance, Stomp,* and *Rent,* have graced the stage of the Norton Center. Additionally, Newlin Hall, the Center's main stage, hosted the 2000 vice-presidential debate between Dick Cheney and Joe Lieberman and the 2012 debate between Joe Biden and Paul Ryan. Tickets for all performances can be purchased online or at the box office (10am-4pm Mon.-Fri.).

Theater under the stars has become popular throughout the state, but Danville's **Pioneer Playhouse** (840 Stanford Rd., Danville, 859/236-2747, www.pioneerplayhouse.com, $16 adults, $9 youth 12 and under) can boast of being the oldest outdoor theater in Kentucky. The playhouse's repertory company presents six productions each year, with performances taking place at 8:30pm Tuesday-Saturday, early-June-mid-August. Although an integral part of the community, Pioneer Playhouse is not a community theater. In fact, stars such as John Travolta and Lee Majors have spent time onstage at Pioneer Playhouse. Tickets can be reserved by phone and picked up at the box office. The playhouse offers a buffet dinner before the show (7:30pm). A campground is also located on site.

Art Galleries

Jones Visual Arts Center (600 W. Walnut St., Danville, 859/238-5727), located on the Centre College campus, hosts exhibitions and houses the studios of Centre faculty artists. Internationally recognized glass artist Stephen Rolfe Powell maintains his primary studio here, and a viewing area allows visitors to observe as Powell creates masterpieces from hot glass.

The **Community Arts Center** (401 W. Main St., Danville, 859/236-4054, www.communityartscenter.net, 10am-6pm Wed.-Thurs., 10am-7pm Fri., 10am-4pm Sat.) hosts rotating exhibits, featuring work in various genres created by regional artists. The center goes beyond visual arts to also offer dance and music programming in their elegant beaux arts building. Starry Night Studio, an event that lets you paint your own version of a famous artwork while sipping wine, is held multiple times each month and is so popular that it often books up in advance.

Nightlife

Since Danville elected to go wet in 2010, a handful of spots have opened where you can enjoy a beer or sip a glass of bourbon or wine. At **V The Market** (130 S. Fourth St., 859/236-9774, http://vthemarket.com, 4pm-9pm Tues.-Thurs., 4pm-10pm Fri., 11am-9pm Sat.), you can purchase a well-curated selection of bourbons, craft beers, wines, chocolate, and cheese to take with you or enjoy the best of each in their attached **Wayne and Jane's Wine and Whiskey Bar.** Though **BeerEngine** (107 Larrimore Ln., 859/209-4211, www.kybeerengine.com, 4pm-11pm Mon.-Thurs., 4pm-midnight Fri.-Sat., 4pm-10pm Sun.) is Kentucky's smallest brewery, they still boast a substantial selection of beers, with three of their own brews on tap in addition to nine other craft beers.

Festivals and Events

For four days in mid-June, the best brass bands in the nation, accompanied by a band or two from outside the United States, converge on Danville for the **Great American Brass Band Festival** (www.gabbf.com). Free concerts, most of which take place on stages set up on the Centre College campus, are the highlight of the festival, but festival goers will find many other activities to keep them entertained between sets. The entire town gets in on the celebration, making it a wonderful time to visit Danville.

About 30 minutes west of Danville, the town of Forkland is a quiet place proud of its history and tradition. Those who appreciate small-town celebrations will want to put October's **Forkland Heritage Festival** (KY 37, www.forklandcomctr.org, $2 adults, $1 youth) on their calendars. Held on the second Friday and Saturday of October, this event includes live country music provided by local musicians, horse-drawn wagon rides, exhibits of old-time skills, arts and crafts demonstrations, a fox and hound race, a pancake breakfast, and a bean supper followed by a drama presentation.

SHOPPING

Many cute shops can be found in the historic buildings lining Danville's Main Street. Pop in at **Maple Tree Gallery** (225 W. Main St., Danville, 859/236-0909, 10am-5:30pm Mon.-Fri., 10am-4:30pm Sat.), where jockey silk aprons are just one of many unique items available. If you're in need of new reading material, head across the street to **Centre Bookstore** (110 S. 3rd St., Danville, 859/238-1516, 9am-6:30pm Mon.-Fri., 10am-4pm Sat.), where you can find popular titles mixed in with textbooks and Centre College paraphernalia.

Much of Perryville was devastated by the Civil War battle that took place here, with hardly a house left untouched. However, **Merchant's Row** (S. Buell St., Perryville, 859/332-1862), a strip of original buildings from the 1840s, survived and has been restored to house gift shops, cafés, and other stores.

ACCOMMODATIONS
$50-100

The two guest rooms at **The Golden Lion Bed and Breakfast** (243 N. Third St., 859/583-1895, www.thegoldenlionbb.com, $95-99) are decorated to fit the style of the men for which they are named: one a Revolutionary War soldier, the other an 18th-century tobacco grower. Both rooms feature queen beds, fireplaces, and private baths. A gourmet breakfast is served in the dining room, which looks out on the tranquil garden. The 1840 Greek Revival home will be of special interest to those with the surname Jones, as it hosts a genealogical museum tracing the origin of the name. A collection of 200 military items is also available for guests to browse.

Over $150

For a taste of country living that doesn't lack

for comfort, book a bed at **The Farm** (450 Waterworks Rd., 859/583-0244, www.thefarmllc.com, $175-240), a 200-year-old home on a working farm. Choose from seven rooms, a private cottage, or even set up camp on the grounds. The rooms are tastefully decorated and comfortably outfitted, so if you just want to get away and relax in a lovely setting, you'll be pleased, but The Farm is especially great for active vacationers or those with kids, as guests are invited to fully take part in farm living—from milking the goats to feeding the calves to collecting the chicken's eggs. Breakfast is bountiful and includes homemade jams and dishes made using goods straight from the farm.

FOOD
Bakeries
Burke's Bakery (121 W. Main St., 859/236-5661, 7am-6pm Mon.-Fri., 7am-5pm Sat., noon-4pm Sun., $0.50-4.50) is a Danville institution. Their rich breakfast pastries, lush cream pies, crowd-pleasing cookies, and old-fashioned salt-rising breads draw a steady stream of customers. Regulars know to bring cash, because greenbacks are the only currency accepted.

Cupcake lovers will think they've found heaven at **The Twisted Sifter** (128 Church St., 859/238-9393, www.thetwistedsifter.com, 10am-7pm Tues.-Sat., $1.25), where "sugar architect" Pam Birt and staff whip up cupcakes in 89(!) different flavors. Vanilla and chocolate are available every day along with five or six special flavors. Check out the webpage to keep up with the day's offerings, especially if you're after a specific taste like chocolate bourbon, Vietnamese coffee, or orange creamsicle. Creamy icing atop fluffy cake makes these cupcakes truly decadent. If a cupcake isn't enough, order one of their specialty cakes, available for weddings, birthdays, anniversaries, or just because it's Wednesday.

Cafés
In addition to serving breakfast, lunch, and drinks, **The Hub Coffee House and Café** (236 W. Main St., 859/936-0001, www.thehubcoffeehousencafe.com, 6:30am-8pm Mon.-Thurs., 6:30am-9pm Fri., 7am-9pm Sat., 8am-8pm Sun.) also serves up the latest news on what's going on in Danville. The breakfast menu runs from muffins to burritos ($1.60-4.95), while soups, salads, sandwiches, and wraps make up the lunch and dinner menu ($3.50-7.25). Keep things simple with a BLT or chicken salad, or engage your taste buds with the hummus platter, gyro wrap, or Thai peanut salad. Vegetarians will find many options on the menu here. The Hub offers free wireless Internet to customers, so surf the Web at this busy corner spot while enjoying one of the many coffees, teas, hot chocolates, or specialty drinks.

Delis
Join Danville locals on their lunch break at **Melton's Great American Deli** (247 E. Main St., 859/236-9874, www.meltonsgreatamericandeli.com, 9:30am-4pm Mon.-Fri., $2.89-6.49), a family-run place where regulars trade good-natured ribbing with the friendly staff. Choose from a handful of sandwiches made to order, then complete your meal with a bag of chips, a bottle of Ale-8-One, and a soft, chewy cookie.

Casual American
Opened in 2010 after Danville voted to become a wet town, **Bluegrass Pizza and Pub** (235 W. Main St., 859/236-7737, www.bluegrasspizzaandpub.com, 11am-9pm Tues., 11am-10pm Wed.-Sat., $6.25-12.99) became an instant hit. The food menu focuses on brick-oven pizza, which comes generously topped with your choice of ingredients or as one of seven specialty pies. Stromboli, Philly, and other classic sandwiches are also available. Beer connoisseurs will be pleased with the selection of drinks, which includes microbrews from around the country.

Lulu's Tavern (219 S. 4th St., 859/238-2040, www.lulustavern.com, 11am-11pm Mon.-Thurs., 11am-midnight Fri.-Sat, $8-17) emphasizes local food in its entrées, which include pasta made with farmers market ingredients and Kentucky-fresh fried chicken and rib eye. Comfort-food seekers will want to try the meatloaf, while those looking for something a bit lighter might opt for the you-pick-two combo of sandwiches, salad, and soup. The tavern rocks to live music on the weekends.

INFORMATION AND SERVICES

The **Danville-Boyle County Convention & Visitors Bureau** (105 E. Walnut St., 859/236-7794, www.danvillekentucky.com, 9am-4:30pm Mon.-Fri., 10am-4pm Sat.) does an excellent job of informing visitors about all there is to see and do in Danville. Stop in to load up on tips, brochures, and maps, as well as to download their latest smartphone apps, which make it easy for the tech-savvy visitor to get info on the go.

GETTING THERE AND AROUND

Danville is about smack in the middle of the state and thus easily accessible from all directions. From Lexington (50 minutes), Danville can be reached by traveling south on U.S. 27 for about 29 miles, then taking westbound KY 34 for the remaining 7 miles. From Frankfort, drive south on U.S. 127 for 26 miles (45 minutes) to reach Danville, passing through Lawrenceburg and Harrodsburg on the way.

Perryville lies 10 miles (15 minutes) west of Danville on U.S. 150. Perryville can also be reached by traveling 11 miles (20 minutes) west on U.S. 68 from Harrodsburg or by traveling 19 miles (25 minutes) east on U.S. 68 from Lebanon.

LEXINGTON

NORTHERN KENTUCKY AND COVERED BRIDGE COUNTRY

The Ohio River, which forms the northern border of Kentucky and directly influences the life of the city and towns that grew up along its shores, is the common thread tying this region together. It is, to put it simply, the reason many of these places exist. The river brought people west. Some people stopped in Kentucky, found it to their liking, and stayed; others kept on moving, but needed a place to overnight, a stop where they could provision. Entrepreneurs looked at the river traffic and saw a means of selling their ideas and goods and built businesses long before there were interstates or even railways. The river gave life to this area, and sometimes, when it overflowed its bank, took it as well. Today, although life is less dependent on the river, it still influences, acting as a constant presence in the lives of area residents and as an attraction to visitors.

Although tied by the river, this area is actually made up of two very distinct subregions: Northern Kentucky and Covered Bridge Country. Northern Kentucky—which traditionally consists of the state's three northernmost counties but can be expanded, as it is here, to include a few counties to the south—is primarily urban. Situated directly across the river from Cincinnati, Northern Kentucky, which includes the cities of Covington, Newport, and Florence, is intimately connected with the Queen City. Cincinnati's airport, after all, is located in Northern Kentucky, and Northern Kentucky residents consider the Reds to be their hometown baseball team, even though the stadium is on

© THERESA DOWELL BLACKINTON

HIGHLIGHTS

(Oktoberfest: The beer flows freely at one of the biggest Oktoberfests in the nation, inviting you to celebrate your German heritage, real or imagined (page 196).

(Newport Aquarium: Rare shark rays, glowing orange jellyfish, poisonous lionfish, and all sorts of other species fill one million gallons of saltwater and freshwater tanks (page 202).

(Newport Gangster Tour: Learn why Newport used to be called the Sin City of the South on an engaging tour that transports you back to the days of Prohibition (page 204).

(Kentucky Gateway Museum Center: One of the nation's best miniature collections will have you gaping in awe at the intricacy of the pieces, which include working musical instruments, beer taps, and more (page 225).

(Old Pogue Distillery: This craft bourbon distillery, in a somewhat unlikely location, is worth seeking out for its historic nature, lovely setting, and for the intimate tours and tastings on offer (page 226).

(Historic Old Washington: Costumed guides lead tours around a pioneer settlement that is also an active modern-day community (page 226).

(Blue Licks Battlefield State Resort Park: Enjoy canoe trips and battlefield tours all in one place, the site of the last battle of the Revolutionary War (page 232).

(Fleming County's Covered Bridges: Fleming County, the Covered Bridge Capital of Kentucky, invites you to visit three covered bridges, one of which is still in use (page 233).

LOOK FOR **(** TO FIND RECOMMENDED SIGHTS, ACTIVITIES, DINING, AND LODGING.

the Ohio side of the river. In fact, Northern Kentucky markets itself as the "Southern Side of Cincinnati," claiming all the assets of Cincinnati and then complementing them with Southern hospitality and a slower pace of life. The true Northern Kentucky area is densely populated, with Newport running into Covington running into Erlanger running into Florence. Move east and south, and

you'll find more agricultural communities, but as the region continues to grow, development spreads.

As for actual attractions in this area, a few of the state's big hitters are here. The Newport Aquarium is a major regional draw, and the Creation Museum has drawn shockingly big numbers from around the nation since it opened in 2007. Horse racing and auto racing have

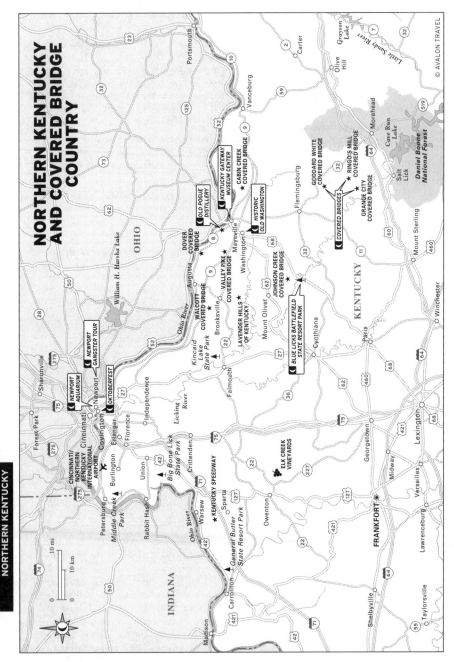

found homes in this part of the state, which has a long, interesting history—just check out the mammoth bones at Big Bone Lick State Park for a glimpse of it. And of course, there's Cincinnati just a stone's throw away.

The second subregion, Covered Bridge Country, is overwhelmingly rural. Farming remains a viable way of life here, and in this area tobacco lives on post-buyout as a major cash crop. Adding to the idyllic scenery of fields and barns are covered bridges. Eight of the state's 13 covered bridges are located in this region, transporting those who stop and take notice back to a different era. The majority of these bridges have long since been closed to traffic, but a few let you cross either by car or foot, and all pose prettily for photos. Another attraction that plays on the region's rural nature are the barn quilts, blocks painted with quilt patterns and hung on barns. Lewis County's Barn Quilt Trail makes for a fine Sunday (or any day of the week) drive. Complementing the countryside are a handful of small towns, the best of which are Augusta and Maysville. Here historic buildings are lovingly preserved, chewing the fat is a legitimate afternoon activity, and kids can still ride their bikes to the river to fish or take an unsupervised stroll to the library. In Augusta, the *Jenny Ann,* one of the oldest ferries on the Ohio River, continues to take foot and car traffic across to Ohio and then back again. Life is different here, slower, maybe sweeter, certainly intended to be savored.

PLANNING YOUR TIME

Give yourself a weekend to explore Northern Kentucky. Covington and Newport are separated only by the small Licking River, so close to each other that those unfamiliar with the area often aren't sure what city they're in. Add in Florence, which is just a very short cruise down the interstate, and the attractions in its vicinity, and you're looking at a full itinerary. The Newport Aquarium can easily fill half a day, and those interested in touring the Creation Museum need to block off a good portion of a day for it. Fill in the blanks with a riverboat cruise or Gangster Tour, an excursion to Big Bone Lick State Park, and dinner and evening entertainment at the Newport Levee or Covington's MainStrasse, and you've got yourself a plan.

Most visitors to this region combine Northern Kentucky with Cincinnati, squeezing highlights of both into an action-packed weekend. Regardless of which side of the river you expect to spend more time in, the Kentucky side makes a great base. Hotels are a bit more affordable on the southern side of the river, and the many bridges—both vehicle and pedestrian—make it extremely easy to cross back and forth. The Kentucky side also has the benefit of the airport for those flying rather than driving.

To venture into Covered Bridge Country, you're going to need to budget at least a weekend, simply due to the distance between sites and the fact that getting to some of these covered bridges or barn quilts means you've got to hit the back roads. Additionally, hotels and restaurants are limited in the area, so rather than moving from town to town, you're going to need to pick a base and explore on day trips from there. Augusta and Maysville are the best candidates for bases, since both have good accommodation options as well as unique local restaurants.

As with most of the state, spring through fall is the best time to visit, with summer the peak season for travelers, particularly those with children. In the metropolitan areas of Northern Kentucky, however, winter travel shouldn't be written off. The aquarium and museums are just as nice in winter as they are in summer and much less busy. In the rural areas, snow and ice can make for treacherous roads, so winter travel is less advisable. Planning ahead (or staying away, depending on your tolerance for crowds) is a good idea around certain events, including races at Kentucky Speedway, Cincinnati Bengals games, and Oktoberfest.

NORTHERN KENTUCKY

Covington

By the time it was incorporated in 1815, Covington was already linked to Cincinnati, thanks to the city's founding fathers laying out the streets in such a way that they lined up with those on the opposite bank. Perhaps this made sense for the ferries, which at the time provided the only transportation across the river. Destined to never grow in the same way as Cincinnati because of the shallower riverbed on the Kentucky side, Covington nonetheless attracted many European immigrants in the 1800s, particularly those of German heritage. That influence is still felt, especially during Oktoberfest and along MainStrasse.

In 1867, Covington was finally connected to the north via the John A. Roebling Suspension Bridge. Take a glance at the bridge, which is still used by vehicle and pedestrian traffic today, and you might think it looks familiar. That's because this bridge served as the prototype for the much more famous Brooklyn Bridge. While investigating the bridge, another piece of architecture might catch your eye. The curving, sail-like glass building at the base of the bridge was constructed by starchitect Daniel Libeskind and houses condos. Its formal title is The Ascent at Roebling Bridge. Bridges and buildings helped Covington grow through the early 1900s. The city peaked in 1930, then declined with the Great Depression and the era of urban flight. Now, Covington sits comfortably as the fifth largest city in Kentucky with a population of around 41,000. Redevelopment in the 1990s and early 2000s has heightened the profile of the town and led to flowering tourism, with its historic churches and neighborhoods, German spirit, and proximity to Cincinnati its biggest draws.

SIGHTS
Behringer-Crawford Museum
The four levels of the **Behringer-Crawford Museum** (1600 Montague Rd., Devou Park,

859/491-4003, www.bcmuseum.org, 10am-5pm, Tues.-Sat., 1pm-5pm Sun., $7 adults, $6 seniors, $4 youth 3-17) relay Northern Kentucky history through the vehicle of transportation. The first floor—which, like the second and fourth, is not a full floor—focuses on rail transportation, displaying the last streetcar to run in the area and an amazingly intricate model railroad. The theme of the second floor is roads, with the exhibits telling the story of migration from downtown to the suburbs. The third floor explores river transportation, touching on the Civil War, the Underground Railroad, and early inhabitants of the area. The very small fourth floor continues with the river exhibit while also briefly mentioning air transport. Adults will enjoy the detailed panels relaying historical information, while kids will be entertained by the many hands-on features. You can crawl into the center of the model railroad, listen to passengers on the streetcar tell their stories, sit in a 1959 Electra parked at a mock drive-in, play 1950s hits on a working jukebox, and dress up in period costumes on an interactive packet boat.

Carroll Chimes Bell Tower
Make your way to the 100-foot, German-style clock tower that sits on the edge of MainStrasse Village near the top of the hour to see the clock come to life. Every hour on the hour, the 43-bell carillon chimes as mechanical figures depicting the Pied Piper of Hamlin move onto the balcony. Introduced in 1978, the **Carroll Chimes Bell Tower** (W. 6th St. at Philadelphia St.) fell into disrepair with time, but was restored back to life in 2004 to the delight of adults and children alike.

St. Mary's Cathedral Basilica of the Assumption
One of only two Catholic basilicas in Kentucky and 35 in the United States, **St. Mary's Cathedral Basilica of the Assumption** (1140

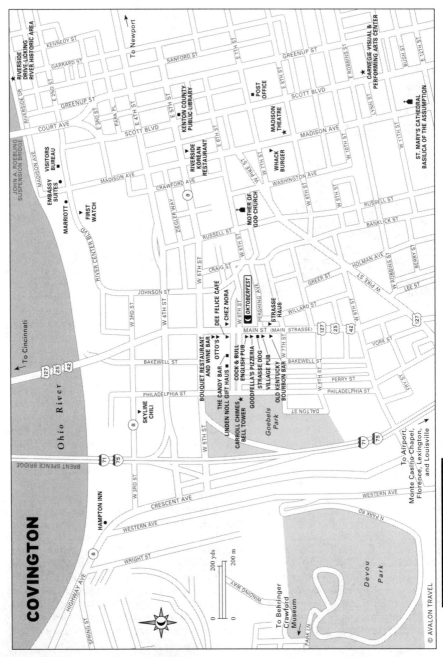

NORTHERN KENTUCKY

© AVALON TRAVEL

© THERESA DOWELL BLACKINTON

Carroll Chimes Bell Tower

Madison Ave., 859/431-2060, www.covcathedral.com) is a tremendous gothic-style church modeled after two landmark French churches. The interior, which is shaped like a cross and was begun in 1895, is based on the design of Abbey Church of St. Denis, while the facade, which was added in 1910, is reminiscent of Notre Dame. Outstanding features of the basilica include the porcelain and mother-of-pearl mosaic stations of the cross, 26 Italian-carved gargoyles, and 82 German-made stained-glass windows, including two rose windows and an immense window depicting the Council of Ephesus. A free brochure provides information on the architecture and artwork, allowing for self-guided tours of the basilica.

Mother of God Church

Constructed in 1870-1871, the Italian Renaissance **Mother of God Church** (119 W. 6th St., 859/291-2288, www.mother-of-god. org) has long been home to the area's German-American population, with Mass celebrated in German until recently. Stop in the imposing church to enjoy some impressive artwork, including a beautifully detailed wood-carved altar and pulpit, large stained-glass windows, and five murals by artist Johann Schmitt, whose art also appears in the Vatican.

Monte Casino Chapel

Collectors of roadside oddities will want to visit the **Monte Casino Chapel** (333 Thomas More Pkwy., Crestview Hills, 859/341-5800), which Ripley's named the Smallest Church in the World in 1922. The six-by-nine-foot stone church was built by Benedictine monks in 1878 and was moved in 1965 to the campus of Thomas More College, where it was restored and is now located.

Riverside Drive-Licking River Historic Area

Bounded by the Ohio River on the north, 8th Street on the south, the Licking River on the east, and Scott Street on the west, the Riverside Drive-Licking River Historic Area encompasses 13 blocks of magnificent homes, many of which date back to the first half of the 19th century. One of the first areas of Northern Kentucky to be settled thanks to its riverfront location, the neighborhood, which is listed on the National Register of Historic Places, is the perfect destination for an early morning or late evening stroll. Admire the wonderfully restored and maintained homes, then follow the Riverwalk to check out seven life-size bronze statues depicting local people of historical significance.

Walking Tours

Experience Covington has created six self-guided tours that help locals and visitors alike become better acquainted with the city. Choose from the Faith Tour, Arts Tour, Historic Tour, Architecture Tour, Neighborhood Tour, and Unexpected Covington Tour. For each tour, a map and audio guide can be picked up at the Kenton County Public Library (502 Scott Blvd., 859/962-4060) or downloaded from the website (www.experiencecovington.com).

NORTHERN KENTUCKY

© THERESA DOWELL BLACKINTON

home in the Riverside Drive-Licking River Historic Area

ENTERTAINMENT AND EVENTS
Bars and Clubs

MainStrasse is the hub of Covington's social scene and offers a number of nightlife options. The **Village Pub** (619 Main St., 859/431-5552, www.mainstrassevillagepub.com, 3pm-2:30am daily) caters to beer connoisseurs with more than 200 different imports and microbrews on offer at any time. If you don't know which to choose, ask the knowledgeable bartenders or go for the daily special. The pub is a popular place to watch Reds and Bengals games, for which they open early on Sundays during football season (11am). Entertainment options include pool tables, dartboards, and video games, and every Monday night, there's live music from 10pm to 2am.

The major draw at **Strasse Haus** (630 Main St., 859/261-1199, www.strassehauspub.com, 11am-2am daily) is the large patio area and outdoor bar. Popular with the college crowd, Strasse Haus is not for those looking for a quiet night or lots of personal space. It's a meet-and-mingle kind of place. The bar offers live music daily along with plenty of drink specials.

Those with a taste for Kentucky's native spirit will appreciate **Old Kentucky Bourbon Bar** (629 Main St., 859/581-1777, 4pm-midnight Tues.-Sun.), where the expert bartenders can help you choose the right bourbon for your tastes or deftly mix you a bourbon cocktail. Check out the chalkboard centered among the shelves of bourbon for the bourbon of the day, drink of the day, and flight of the day.

Two popular restaurants are equally loved for their nightlife options. The **Cock & Bull** (601 Main St., 859/581-4253, www.theenglishpub.com, 11am-2am daily) is a traditional English pub that offers nearly 50 different beers on draught, including the required Boddington's, Smithwick's, and Guinness, as well as an impressive selection of microbrews. For a more upscale evening, consider the rooftop jazz club at **Chez Nora** (530 Main St., 859/491-8027, www.cheznora.com, 11am-1am daily), which

NORTHERN KENTUCKY

© THERESA DOWELL BLACKINTON

Chez Nora, one of many popular restaurants on Main Street

offers live music as well as incredible panoramic views.

Live Music

The renovated art deco-style **Madison Theater** (730 Madison Ave., 859/491-2444, www.madisontheateronline.com) offers a packed schedule of live music, drawing smaller national acts and also hosting some bigger local bands. You might find indie punk one night, bluegrass the next. An online calendar lists upcoming shows. The theater has three full-service bars and can be set up in three different styles (club, cabaret, or theater) depending on the show.

Art Galleries

The **Carnegie Visual & Performing Arts Center** (1028 Scott Blvd., 859/491-2030, www.thecarnegie.com, 10am-5pm Mon.-Fri., noon-3pm Sat., free), originally constructed in 1904 as a Carnegie Library, is home to five small galleries, each of which displays different rotating exhibits. Expect all types of visual arts

from prints and photography to sculpture and folk art.

Performing Arts

In addition to hosting visual art exhibits, the **Carnegie Visual & Performing Arts Center** (1028 Scott Blvd., 859/491-2030, www.thecarnegie.com) has a theater, which is used for plays, concerts, and dance performances. Current performance schedules are posted on the website. Tickets can be purchased online or in person at the on-site box office.

Festivals and Events
◖ OKTOBERFEST
Held on the second weekend of September, **Oktoberfest** (www.mainstrasse.org) celebrates Covington's German heritage with a grand party centered around MainStrasse. Drawing nearly 350,000 people annually, Covington's Oktoberfest is one of the biggest in the nation. A keg tapping starts the festivities each day, and beer, sauerkraut, and wursts flow freely after that. German music and dancing fill the streets. Kids will love the midway, and adults will want to check out the arts and crafts fair between beers.

MAIFEST
Because it's too much to ask that locals wait an entire year to celebrate German culture, Covington also hosts **Maifest** (www.mainstrasse.org), a mid-May festival intended to welcome spring. You'll find many of the same things at Maifest as at Oktoberfest—plenty of German food, arts and craft vendors, live entertainment, and a midway. The main difference is that instead of beer, Maifest is a toast to spring wines.

SHOPPING

Interspersed among MainStrasse's restaurants and bars are a number of locally owned shops that make for interesting browsing and buying. If you've enjoyed the German culture of the area and want to take a souvenir back with you, visit **Linden Noll Gift Haus** (506 W. 6th St., 859/581-7633, 11am-5pm Tues.-Sat.), where beer steins are sold alongside European collectibles. For the beloved canine in your life, pop into **Strasse Dog** (605 Main St., 859/431-7387, 4pm-8pm Mon., Wed., Thurs., noon-9pm Fri., noon-8pm Sat., noon-7pm Sun.) and pick up a unique treat. Kids and the kid inside all of us will delight at **The Candy Bar** (422 W. 6th St., 859/261-3367, www.thecandybar-ky.com, noon-8pm Tues.-Thurs., noon-9pm Fri.-Sat.), an old-fashioned neighborhood candy store that sells more than 200 different candies.

SPORTS AND RECREATION
Parks
Those looking for an escape from city life without actually having to lose sight of the city will love **Devou Park** (790 Park Ln.), which boasts 550 acres of green space. Most of this space is open, without any specific purpose. Throw down a blanket and have a picnic. Gather friends for an impromptu game of football or Frisbee. Let the kids run wild. For those seeking structured play, Devou Park has an 18-hole golf course, playgrounds, tennis courts, a 1.25-mile nature trail, a fishing pond, and some very hilly jogging/walking/biking paths. An amphitheater hosts summer concerts put on by the Northern Kentucky University symphony. No visit to the park is complete without a trip to Drees Pavilion, which boasts an outstanding view of the skyline on both sides of the Ohio River.

ACCOMMODATIONS
Chain hotels outfitted for the business traveler but also catering to the casual visitor are the main game in Covington. For bed and breakfast options, head to nearby Newport.

$100-150
The **Hampton Inn** (200 Crescent Ave., 859/581-7800, www.hamptoninn.com, $129-149), which was renovated in 2010, offers rooms with refrigerator, microwave, flat-screen TV, and wireless Internet at a competitive rate for the area. Its location near the river just west of I-75 means the hotel is convenient to all area attractions.

$150-200
The **Embassy Suites** (10 E. RiverCenter Blvd., 859/261-4800, www.embassysuites.com, $169-325) at RiverCenter is a popular option for families. One- and two-bedroom suites are available, both featuring a sleeper sofa in the living area, meaning entire families can room together. Remodeled in 2008, the facilities at Embassy Suites are fresh and contemporary, and amenities include flat-screen HD televisions and wireless Internet access. A daily hot breakfast is included with all reservations, as is an evening reception with snacks and drinks. The riverfront location is prime, with easy access to Covington, Newport, and Florence sights as well as the attractions across the river in Cincinnati.

The **Marriott** (10 W. RiverCenter Blvd., 859/261-2900, www.marriott.com, $169-199) impresses with its soaring atrium and glass elevators, but unfortunately the design also leads to one of the hotels biggest negatives—noise. Because the bar is located in the open atrium, noise carries throughout the hotel and can be an issue for those who want to go to bed before last call. If noise isn't a problem for you, the rooms offer standard amenities and clean, comfortable surroundings, and rooms on the north side have nice views. As with many business hotels, Internet access, on-site parking, and breakfast are available for a fee.

FOOD
Breakfast
If the hotel breakfast isn't cutting it, start your morning at **First Watch** (50 E. RiverCenter Blvd., 859/491-0869, www.firstwatch.com, 7am-2:30pm daily, $3.49-8.79). Choose from 11 types of pancakes; a traditional breakfast of eggs, choice of meat, English muffin, and potatoes; or something more unusual, like the Chickichanga, a breakfast chimichanga. Each table gets its own carafe of fresh coffee, so you won't need to wait for refills. Sandwiches, soups, and salads are available for lunch.

Cheap Eats
Skyline Chili (617 W. 3rd St., 859/261-8474,

ACROSS THE RIVER IN CINCINNATI

Almost all visitors to Northern Kentucky venture over one of the many bridges at least once to see what's happening on the Ohio side of the Ohio River. Cincinnati, which is directly across from Covington and Newport, is a bustling metropolis with a nice skyline and plenty of things to do. It's worth checking out, even if it is Ohio, which we all know isn't as nice as Kentucky. But hey, not every place can be. Here are a few itinerary-worthy sights. For a more detailed list of attractions, as well as hotel and restaurant information and money-saving combos and coupons, visit www.cincinnatiusa.com.

THE CINCINNATI REDS

For most Kentuckians, the Cincinnati Reds are the closest Major League Baseball team and are thus the main cheering interest of many Bluegrass baseball fans. The Reds play in the **Great American Ball Park** (100 Joe Nuxhall Way, 581/381-REDS, http://cincinnati.reds.mlb.com), which sits right on the Ohio River. Opened in 2003, the state-of-the-art stadium has good views from all seats, with tickets starting as low as $5.

CINCINNATI MUSEUM CENTER

Museum buffs and those caught in the area on a rainy day will enjoy the **Cincinnati Museum Center** (1301 Western Ave., 513/287-7000, www.cincymuseum.org), located in historic Union Terminal. Museums located here include the Cincinnati History Museum, the Duke Energy Children's Museum, the Museum of Natural History & Science, and an OMNIMAX theater.

Tickets for all three museums are $14.50 for adults, $13.50 for seniors, $10.50 for youth 3-12, and $5.50 for toddlers 1-2. OMNIMAX tickets can be added for $3.50 for adults and seniors, $2.50 for youth, and free for toddlers.

CINCINNATI ZOO AND BOTANICAL GARDENS

More than 500 animals and 3,000 plant species make their home at the **Cincinnati Zoo and Botanical Gardens** (3400 Vine St., 513/281-4700, www.cincinnatizoo.org, 9am-5pm daily, Labor Day-Memorial Day, 9am-6pm daily, Memorial Day-Labor Day, $15 adults, $11 seniors and youth 2-12, $8 parking). Zoo favorites include the western lowland gorillas, Sumatran orangutans, black and Sumatran rhinoceros, African penguins, and manatees. The very well-rated zoo has excellent exhibits that allow you to see animals in natural settings.

NATIONAL UNDERGROUND RAILROAD FREEDOM CENTER

With Ohio a free state and Kentucky a slave state, Cincinnati was a very critical stop on the Underground Railroad. The **National Underground Railroad Freedom Center** (50 E. Freedom Way, 513/333-7500, www.freedomcenter.org, 11am-5pm Tues.-Sun., $12 adults, $10 seniors, $8 youth 3-12) commemorates the Underground Railroad and presents exhibits related to slavery and freedom throughout history and the world. The three contemporary buildings, symbolizing courage,

www.skylinechili.com, $4.99-7.99) has become synonymous with Cincinnati-style chili, so you might as well pop in and see what the fuss is all about. Although your food will come fast, Skyline is a sit-down kind of place, so grab a table and give your order to a waitress. The 3-Way (chili, spaghetti, and cheese) is their rather tasty signature dish, though Coneys (dressed hot dogs) are also quite popular. This is filling food,

so only order the large if you haven't eaten in a day or so.

Available by the slice (starting at $3) or the pie (starting at $7.95), the NY-style pizza at **Goodfella's Pizzeria** (603 Main St., 859/916-5209, www.goodfellaspizzeria.com, 11am-11pm Sun.-Wed., 11am-2:30am Thurs.-Sat.) would hold its own in a contest with pizza straight from the streets of the Big Apple. Go for a simple slice of cheese or try cooperation, and perseverance, host both permanent and temporary exhibits.

KINGS ISLAND

Kings Island (6300 Kings Island Dr., Mason, 513/754-5700, www.visitkingsisland. com, $56.99 everyone 48 inches and taller and under age 62, $33.99 everyone under 48 inches tall or over 62, free under 3, $15 parking) is one of the region's most popu-

lar amusement parks. The park has seven themed areas (two specifically for kids) with 40 rides, including many roller coasters and thrill rides, an Australian-themed water park, a huge outdoor amphitheater, and numerous smaller stages offering live entertainment. The park is open daily late May-August with weekend hours in April, May, September, and October. Discounted tickets can be purchased online.

© RUDI1976/DREAMSTIME.COM

Cincinnati skyline

NORTHERN KENTUCKY

the Fuhgetaboutit, which comes loaded with every available topping. Calzones, salads, and subs round out the menu at this casual joint, with outdoor deck seating and an upstairs bar.

Whack Burger (715 Madison Ave., 859/360-3361, http://whackburger.com, 11am-3pm and 5pm-9pm Tues.-Wed., 11am-3pm and 5pm-10pm Thurs.-Sat., $7.95-9.95) focuses solely on burgers, but still offers plenty of variety. Begin by choosing your burger (beef, turkey, or black

bean) and your bun (brioche, whole wheat, or none), then pick from one of 14 styles of toppings, and finally pick from one of six sides. With bright walls and comic book decor (from which the name Whack comes), this burger place keeps things fun while you wait for your burger to be freshly prepared.

Contemporary American

With its bright multicolored chairs and large

artworks, **€ Otto's** (521 Main St., 859/491-6678, www.ottosonmain.com, lunch 11:30am-2:30pm Mon.-Sat., dinner 5pm-10pm Tues.-Sat., 5pm-9pm Sun., brunch 10am-2pm Sun.) exudes a fun, hip vibe that hasn't escaped the young working crowd looking for a good lunch or a place to gather with friends for dinner. Lunch ($9-14) favorites include a tomato pie; a Hot Brown; and a bacon, lettuce, egg, and fried-green tomato sandwich. Sandwiches are overstuffed and come with a choice of salad, soup, or sweet potato fries. The dinner menu ($21-31) is short, made up of no more than 10 entrées, but tasty, built around contemporary Southern favorites like shrimp and grits, braised short ribs, and lemon tilapia. Run by a young and enthusiastic husband-and-wife team, Otto's is a gathering place that also happens to serve great food.

Bouquet Restaurant and Wine Bar (519 Main St., 859/491-7777, www.bouquetrestaurant.com, 5pm-10pm Tues.-Thurs., 5pm-1am Fri.-Sat.) offers an upscale dinner experience in an intimate and warm environment. With an emphasis on farm-to-table cuisine, the small restaurant offers a large selection of small plates ($4-15), which might include ramp ricotta ravioli or Kentucky pork sausage, accompanied by a short selection of entrées ($17-29), such as Kentucky lamb and chicken Provence. Great attention is paid to presentation, and there's a wine for every taste. Upon request, dishes can be made vegetarian, vegan, or gluten-free. Reservations are helpful.

Crab cakes are the specialty at **Chez Nora** (530 Main St., 859/491-8027, www.cheznora.com, 11am-1am daily, $13-25), but the menu covers a wide range of options. Filet mignon, baby back ribs, and a number of Cajun specialties are mainstays on the dinner menu, while a handful of daily specialties add variety. Sandwiches and quesadillas make up the lunch menu ($7-9), and a Sunday brunch (10am-2pm) features breakfast pizza and *croque madame*. A 100-year-old mahogany bar dominates the casual main dining room, and it's almost always packed. If the weather is nice, outside seating is available. A late-night menu of small bites

and pub food is available if you get a case of the munchies while enjoying the rooftop jazz bar.

Asian

€ Riverside Korean Restaurant (512 Madison Ave., 859/291-1484, www.riversidekoreanrestaurant.com, lunch 11:30am-2pm Tues.-Fri., dinner 5pm-9pm Tues.-Thurs. and Sun., 5pm-10pm Fri.-Sat., $15.95-21.95) serves highly praised authentic Korean food in an atmosphere to match. Low tables with floor cushions line one wall, while grilling booths line the other wall of this historic downtown building. The menu is divided into nine dinner categories—rice, fish and seafood, seafood soup, deep fried, stir fried, grilled, stew and soup, noodle, and adventure. More common choices include grilled beef short ribs, spicy stir-fried shrimp, and pan-fried salted yellowfish, while the adventure dinners feature marinated spicy beef intestine stew and raw flank beef. A plethora of sides, including kimchi, come with each dinner. The lunch menu ($8.95-9.95) is decidedly smaller, but the lunch box selections, which come in pork, chicken, beef, seafood, and tofu options, make for tasty midday meals.

Cajun

Enjoy jazz with your dinner at **Dee Felice Café** (529 Main St., 859/261-2365, www.deefelicecafe.com, 5pm-10pm daily, $16.95-36.95), a Main Street staple since long before Main Street was revitalized. Decorated in a casual New Orleans style, Dee Felice serves Cajun and Creole specialties like jambalaya, shrimp Creole, crawfish étouffée (a portobello option is available for vegetarians), and blackened halibut. Though not exactly what you'd get if you were in the Big Easy, the food is good, and half portions are available for lighter eaters. Dee's Filet, which comes with a shrimp cream sauce, garners rave reviews. As you'd expect, the restaurant has a well-stocked bar that offers a long list of beers, wines, and cocktails. Tables are pretty close together, and the atmosphere is that of a jazz club (a bit dark and loud) in this historic building with tiled floor and tin ceiling. Service, from black-tie-clad waiters, is excellent. Reservations are recommended. In the summer you can opt for a sidewalk table.

European

If you're craving fish and chips, then **Cock & Bull English Pub** (601 Main St., 859/581-4253, www.theenglishpub.com, 11am-9pm Sun.-Thurs, 11am-10pm Fri.-Sat., $7.99-16.49) is your place. The deep-fried Icelandic cod, which is accompanied by seasoned fries or pub chips, has received regional recognition. Burgers, wraps, sandwiches, and salads complete the menu at this traditional British pub. Outdoor seating overlooks the Goose Girl statue and is a hot option on nice days.

INFORMATION AND SERVICES

The **Northern Kentucky Convention and Visitors Bureau** (50 E. RiverCenter Blvd., Suite 200, 877/659-8474, www.nkycvb.com) has teamed up with Cincinnati to promote the entire region, which means that, oddly enough, www.cincinnatiusa.com is the best place to get information on the area. That website has an online trip planner, maps, as well as special offers on hotels, admission tickets, and packages. Unfortunately, there are no walk-in information centers in Covington.

The **post office** at 700 Scott Street is open 8:30am-5pm Monday-Friday and 8:30am-2pm Saturday.

GETTING THERE
Air

Although everyone refers to it as the Cincinnati Airport, the official title of this region's airport is the **Cincinnati/Northern Kentucky International Airport (CVG)** (2939 Terminal Dr., Hebron, 859/767-3151, www.cvgairport. com), thank you very much, and it's located entirely in Kentucky. The airport, by whatever name you call it, offers direct flights to 70 different cities, including Cancun, Punta Cana, and Paris, thus earning the international part

of its name. Airlines that fly out of CVG are Air Canada, American, Delta, Frontier, United, and U.S. Airways. The airport, which has two passenger terminals, is easy to navigate.

Rental cars and taxis are both available at the airport. Conveniently located just off of I-275, the airport is 9 miles from Florence (11 minutes), 10 miles from Covington (15 minutes), and 12 miles from Newport (20 minutes). The least expensive option for getting into town is to take the TANK (Transit Authority of Northern Kentucky) bus, which picks up outside of Terminal 3 and transports you to downtown Covington for $2. The trip takes about 30 minutes, and buses depart every 75 minutes. A schedule is available at www.tankbus.org.

Car

Covington is located in northernmost Kentucky on the bank of the Ohio River immediately across from Cincinnati. I-71/I-75 runs directly through the city before crossing into Ohio via the double-decker Brent Spence Bridge and provides the most direct route between Covington and Cincinnati as well as points north and south.

From Louisville, northbound I-71 provides a direct route to Covington, which is nearly 100 miles (1.5 hours) to Louisville's northeast. From Lexington, the drive is as easy; simply take I-75 north for 80 miles (1.5 hours). The AA Highway (KY 9) runs from Covington all the way across the northern stretches of the state, providing access to Augusta (40 miles; 1 hour), Maysville (65 miles; 1 hour 20 minutes), and other locations in Covered Bridge Country.

I-74 provides a direct connection to Indianapolis, which is about 110 miles northwest (1 hour 45 minutes). From Nashville, it's 270 miles (4 hours) on I-65 and I-71, and from St. Louis, it's 350 miles (5.5 hours) via I-64 and I-71.

Bus

Greyhound does not directly service Northern Kentucky, but it does have a terminal in Cincinnati (1005 Gilbert Ave., 513/352-6012, www.greyhound.com).

GETTING AROUND

Covington is fairly compact and easy to get around. To move between Covington and Newport, which would touch if it weren't for the Licking River, use 4th Street. To get to Cincinnati sans car, use the pedestrian lanes on the Roebling Suspension Bridge, which ends on the Ohio side just a few short blocks from the Great American Ball Park, where the Reds play, and Paul Brown Stadium, where the Bengals play, as well as the rest of downtown Cincinnati. Free parking is available on the street throughout Covington, but it can take a little patience to find a spot near MainStrasse, especially on weekend evenings.

Car Rental

Eight car rental companies are located at the airport, allowing you to hunt for the best deal. If you haven't reserved a car in advance, courtesy phones located in the airport baggage claim area will connect you with the rental companies, which include **Avis** (800/331-1212, www.avis.com), **Enterprise** (800/261-7331, www.enterprise.com), **Hertz** (800/654-3131, www.hertz.com), and **National** (877/222-9058, www.nationalcar.com), among others.

Public Transportation

In addition to providing transportation to and from the airport, **TANK** (www.tank-bus.org, $1.50 per ride) buses run throughout the entire region, with routes that cover MainStrasse, Newport on the Levee, the Florence Mall, and downtown Cincinnati. The Southbank Shuttle ($1) runs one of the busiest routes, triangulating between Covington, Newport, and Cincinnati. If you want to see the Reds or Bengals play, the shuttle is the best way to get to the game, with the shuttle picking up at 10 stops in Covington, including one at the Covington Convention Center, and dropping fans off directly in front of the stadiums. On game days, it runs from 2 hours before game time until 30 minutes after the game ends. Visit the website for a route map and schedule.

Newport

Directly east of Covington, bordered by the Ohio River on the north and the Licking River on the west, Newport is Covington's older but smaller sibling. It's also the fun sibling. While Covington is Northern Kentucky's business hub, Newport is its entertainment capital. Some think this is a historically recent development, related to the opening of the Newport Aquarium in 1999 followed by Newport on the Levee, but that's not the case. Newport has been an entertainment destination for much of its history; it just wasn't always as family-friendly as it is now.

Before Vegas, there was Newport. The cute little storefronts of downtown Newport haven't always supported antiques shops and restaurants. During the first half of the 1900s, these buildings housed casinos, adult clubs, and prostitution rings. Gangsters essentially ran Newport through the late 1950s, until exposés by major national magazines and newspapers forced a crackdown on Kentucky's Sin City. Now a fun place to take the kids, Newport has worked hard to evolve into a very different place, where card sharks have been replaced with sand tiger sharks and the only real danger is in ordering a second stein of beer at the Hofbräuhaus.

Immediately to the east of Newport is the enclave of **Bellevue,** which offers a few noteworthy accommodation and restaurant options and is included herein.

SIGHTS

◖ Newport Aquarium

From sharks to seahorses, the 15 galleries at the **Newport Aquarium** (1 Aquarium Way, 859/261-7444, www.newportaquarium.com,

NORTHERN KENTUCKY

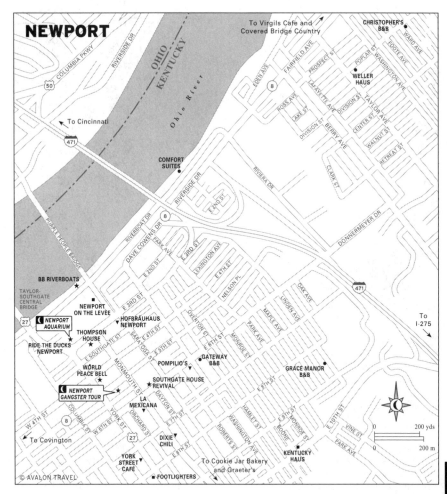

NORTHERN KENTUCKY

9am-7pm daily, Memorial Day-Labor Day, 10am-6pm daily, Labor Day-Memorial Day, $23 adults, $15 youth 2-12) allow visitors to get up close and personal with a wide range of aquatic creatures. In fact, you can do more than observe at two touch stations, one of which features tide-pool creatures such as hermit and horseshoe crabs and a second extremely popular station where you can pet sharks. See-through floors and walk-through tunnels that allow you to observe sharks, rays, eels, turtles, and many species of fish swimming above, below, and next to you are another highlight. Additional standout exhibits include the Jellyfish Gallery, the Bizarre & Beautiful collection, and the Kingdom of Penguins. To really view the many tanks and supporting exhibits, plan to spend at minimum a half day in the aquarium. Coupons are widely available. Check with the visitors bureau, your hotel, and local Kroger stores. A season pass is a worthwhile investment if you live in the region.

sharks at the Newport Aquarium

© THERESA DOWELL BLACKINTON

World Peace Bell

Weighing in at more than 70,000 pounds, the **World Peace Bell** (425 York St., 859/581-2971) rings daily at noon, its chime a call for harmony around the globe. Unfortunately, the accompanying visitors center is open by appointment only.

◖ Newport Gangster Tour

Newport may be a family-friendly destination these days, but it hasn't always been that way. Take the **Newport Gangster Tour** (859/951-8560, www.newportgangsters.com, $20) to learn why this city used to be called the Sin City of the South and how it actually inspired the development of Las Vegas. The tour begins with a picture-packed presentation on the history of Newport from the 1920s through the 1960s and the characters who ruled the area. Participants then set out on an eight-block walking tour, with costumed tour guides pointing out locations of interest and telling stories about what happened at each. Tours depart from Gangsters Dueling Piano Bar (18 E. 5th

St.) at 5pm on Saturdays May-October and last two hours. Tickets should be purchased online in advance.

Ride the Ducks Newport

Hop onboard an amphibious vehicle for a tour of the area with **Ride the Ducks Newport** (1 Aquarium Way, 859/815-1439, www.newportducks.com, $17 adults, $12 youth 2-12). The 45-minute tour takes riders from Newport on the Levee, through downtown Newport, along the Cincinnati riverfront, and out onto the Ohio River. Kids in particular love the corny jokes, the sing-alongs, and the quackers—a special whistle that participants are encouraged to blow loudly and proudly. Adults are more likely to appreciate the bits of history and trivia doled out by the tour guide.

BB Riverboats

For a classier trip down the muddy waters of the Ohio River, opt for a cruise with **BB Riverboats** (101 Riverboat Row, 859/261-8500, www.bbriverboats.com). Choose from brunch (noon-2pm Sun., $40 adults, $23 youth 4-12), lunch (noon-2pm Tues.-Sat., $38 adults, $35 seniors, $23 youth 4-12), or a variety of dinner (Tues.-Sun., $48-55 adults, $33-38 youth 4-12) cruises aboard the flagship *Belle of Cincinnati* or the *River Queen*. Both boats feature dining areas, bars, dance floors, and open-air top decks and are decorated in the sumptuous style of the riverboat era. Meals are served buffet style, and the food is better than you'd expect. Take time on your cruise to poke your head in and say hi to Captain Al, and if he looks like he has a free minute, ask him to tell the story of how the *Belle of Cincinnati* came to fly the pirate flag. A 1.5-hour sightseeing cruise ($20 adults, $14 youth 4-12) is also offered, and it's possible to purchase a sightseeing-only ticket for the lunch and dinner cruises. Reservations are recommended, but tickets for unreserved spots can be purchased the day of the trip.

ENTERTAINMENT
Bars and Clubs
Newport on the Levee (1 Levee Way, www.newportonthelevee.com) is the entertainment center of Newport, with venues that span the spectrum. **Star Lanes on the Levee** (859/652-7250, www.starlaneslevee.com, 11am-midnight Sun.-Wed., 11am-2am Thurs.-Sat.) is where bowling alley meets nightclub. The 12 public lanes, over which hang enormous TV screens playing movies or the big game, are almost always full, with bowlers sipping cocktails in between turns. The atmosphere is sleek and sophisticated, with a large bar and a few plush booths accommodating those without a lane. Star Lanes shares a restaurant (which serves awesome fried mac and cheese) with **Toro** (859/652-7260, www.torolevee.com, 9pm-2am Fri.-Sat.), a bar with DJ, lounge seating, and a mechanical bull. Both facilities enforce a dress code (casual but classy is fine).

Bar Louie (859/491-2222, www.barlouieamerica.com, 11am-2am daily), a chain based out of Chicago, has set up shop at the Levee. Have a seat at the bar or snag one of the elevated booths along the wall, and then order a martini, the house specialty. The intimate setting and low lighting makes this a great place to kick off or end a date or just get together with friends for conversation. If martinis aren't your style, Bar Louie also offers a wide selection of beer and wine. Weekday happy hours are held 5pm-7pm and 10pm-midnight. The full-service restaurant, which serves lunch and dinner, dishes out $1 burgers on Wednesday after 5pm with purchase of a drink.

In July 2013, **The Still** (859/581-6700, http://thestillnewport.com, 4pm-2:30am Mon.-Fri., 11am-2:30am Sat.-Sun) became one of the newest additions to the Levee, tapping into the bourbon obsession sweeping the state and beyond. This upscale bar offers 50 bourbons, 12 craft beers, and live music, as well as a bourbon-inspired menu.

A night out at **Funny Bone Comedy Club** (859/957-2000, www.funnyboneonthelevee.com) is certain to add some laughter to your life. The club hosts nationally known comedians, with tickets going on sale about a month prior to the event. The club is open to adults age 21 and older only. Shows are at 8pm Thursday, 8pm and 10:30pm Friday, 7:30pm and 10pm Saturday, and 7:30pm Sunday.

Live Music
Music knows no boundaries at **The Southgate House Revival** (111 E. 6th St., 859/431-2201, www.southgatehouse.com, 3pm-2:30am Mon.-Sat.), the reincarnation of the Southgate House, which closed at the end of 2011. The Southgate House Revival hosts national and regional artists and bands that play everything from reggae to rock to folk and country to indie pop in an old church that still retains its stained-glass windows and pipe organ. Shows, some of which are restricted to patrons 18 and older or 21 and older, take place in one of three spaces—the Lounge, the Sanctuary, and the Revival Room. A calendar of shows can be found on the website, and tickets can be purchased online or at the door.

In the 1814 mansion where the former Southgate House was located, you'll now find **Thompson House** (24 E. 3rd St., 859/261-7469,

NORTHERN KENTUCKY

http://thompsonhousenewport.com, 11am-2:30am Mon.-Sat., 1pm-2:30am Sun.), which takes advantage of its spacious location with three stages and four bars. In addition to a far-reaching schedule of live music, the Thompson House also hosts open mic and karaoke nights. Admission into the general areas is free, but some shows require tickets. See the website for a full listing of events.

Performing Arts

The **Kentucky Symphony Orchestra** (859/431-6216, www.kyso.org), which is composed of a 90-piece orchestra as well as several quartets, quintets, and small bands, brings classic and contemporary musical performances to the Northern Kentucky area, with performances at varying venues. Tickets can be purchased online or over the phone. A summer concert series takes place at the Devou Park Amphitheatre in Covington. Summer performances are free (although donations are appreciated), and patrons are encouraged to bring blankets and picnics and make it an evening. It's a great way to introduce youngsters to the orchestra as the summer selections are fun and the atmosphere is relaxed.

Presenting four musicals each year in a season that runs fall-spring, **Footlighters** celebrated its 50th anniversary in 2013. The community theater has received national recognition and been invited to perform internationally. Even if you can't make it to a show, try to check out their Stained Glass Theatre (802 York St., 859/291-7464, www.footlighters.org), which is located inside the former Salem United Methodist Church, hence the name. Tickets cost $20 and may be purchased online, by phone, or at the door.

Events

Foodies will want to put the **Goettafest** (www.goettafest.com) on their schedule. This annual three-day festival held on the first weekend of August at Newport on the Levee is all about goetta, a breakfast sausage-like food made from pork, beef, and steel-cut oats. Though goetta has German origins, it's now practically unknown there, and has instead become a trademark food of this region. At the festival, you can taste goetta in more ways than you can imagine—goetta nachos, goetta Hot Browns, goetta coneys, goetta fried rice, goetta sushi, goetta brownies, and even ice cream with goetta topping. Live music, games, and other entertainment complement the goetta.

Every Thursday night from Memorial Day through Labor Day, make the most of summer evenings at the free **Live at the Levee Summer Concert Series** (www.newportonthelevee.com). From 7pm to 10pm on the plaza outside the aquarium, regional bands perform, giving you a chance to get your weekend started early.

SHOPPING

Amid the many chain shops located in the mall at Newport on the Levee, you'll find **Art on the Levee** (1 Levee Way, 859/261-5770, www.artonthelevee.com, 10am-9pm Mon.-Sat., noon-6pm Sun.), a gallery showcasing the work of local artists. The stunning rocking chairs made by Wayne Burnett and the earthy ceramic creations of Wade Summers would make lovely additions to any home. Photography, paintings, jewelry, sculpture, and more are on display and available for purchase.

Kentucky Haus (411 E. 10th St., 859/261-4287, www.kentuckyhaus.com, noon-5pm Sat., 1pm-5pm Sun.) centers itself around craft items made in the Bluegrass State. You'll find Hadley and Bybee pottery, the work of Berea artisans, and Kentucky-made food products. If you're searching for a unique gift, Kentucky Haus is a good place to start.

ACCOMMODATIONS
$100-150

For some, a stay at **Christopher's Bed and Breakfast** (604 Poplar St., Bellevue, 859/491-9354, www.christophersbb.com, $125-189) is akin to a religious experience, not least because the bed-and-breakfast was a Christian church in its former life, and the original stained-glass windows and hardwood floors remain. The classic building has been converted to contain three guest rooms—two junior suites with queen beds and whirlpool tubs, and one suite with king bed, living room, and his-and-her baths. All rooms have a romantic feel, with intricate wallpaper, antique furnishings, and stained-glass windows. During the week, a deluxe continental breakfast of fruit, muffins, and granola is served, while weekend breakfasts are plumped up with a main dish.

Owners Ken and Sandy Clift, upon purchasing **(** **Gateway Bed and Breakfast** (326 E. 6th St., Newport, 859/581-6447, www.gatewaybb.com, $129-169) in 1989, set about restoring the 1878 Italianate home to its Victorian glory. The success of their mission is in the details—the reproduction lighting, refinished pine floors, antique mantels, irregular glass windows, period wallpaper, and plaster moldings. While the furnishings in each of the three guest rooms as well as the parlor and dining room adhere to this period, the amenities are all modern. Rooms have wireless Internet access and bathrooms have such luxuries as heated floors, air jet tubs, and rain showerheads. A full country breakfast is served each morning in the dining room, and guests are invited to relax in a lovely patio garden.

Grace Manor Bed and Breakfast (828 Linden Ave., Newport, 859/491-4213, www.gracemanorbb.com, $115) offers two rooms, each with a queen bed, small television, and Wi-Fi. Each room has a private bathroom, although it's located off the main hallway and not directly connected with the room. The 1906 home is decorated to keep with the period, albeit with a little added quirkiness, like a mannequin beside the staircase. The breakfast is both extremely generous and delicious.

For families with younger children, **Comfort Suites** (420 Riverboat Row, 859/291-6700, www.choicehotels.com, $135-190) offers double and king rooms with sofa beds, allowing up to five people to share one room. All rooms have refrigerator, microwave, and wireless Internet access and come with complimentary continental breakfast. Located along the riverfront, the hotel offers easy access to Newport and Cincinnati attractions.

$150-200

Period antiques and contemporary furnishings mingle in the two side-by-side 1880s Victorian Gothic homes that comprise **Weller Haus** (319 Poplar St., Bellevue, 859/391-8315, www.wellerhaus.com, $149-219). In each of the five guest rooms, you'll find such 21st-century amenities as iPod docking stations, heated mattress pads, flat-screen TVs, and wireless Internet access. In all but the Garden Room, you'll also find fireplaces and whirlpool tubs. Depending on your room, breakfast, which comes with a choice of entrées, can be served in your room or in the dining room. A flower-filled garden offers a quiet spot to start or end your day. For a romantic getaway, choose from the Church Steeple Suite, Margaret's Porch Suite, or Dream Suite, all of which have two-person tubs.

FOOD
Bakeries

In business for more than 85 years, **(** **Cookie Jar Bakery** (919 Monmouth St., 859/261-3345, 3am-3pm Sat. and Mon., 1am-5pm Tues.-Fri.) lovingly bakes mouthwatering treats in the wee hours of the night. Come early for the best selection of doughnuts, cookies, eclairs, coconut rolls, coffee cakes, cinnamon rolls, bread, and all sorts of other goodies.

Cheap Eats

On a trip to Northern Kentucky, you must plan to eat Cincinnati-style chili for at least one meal. Family-owned **(** **Dixie Chili** (733 Monmouth St., 859/291-5337, www.dixiechili.com, 9am-1am Mon.-Thurs., 9am-3am Fri.-Sat., 10am-1am Sun., $1.50-$5.79), the first restaurant of its type to open on the southern side of the Ohio River, has been dishing up secret-recipe chili since 1929 at this Newport location. The menu is simple, centered around chili that you can get plain, with beans, with spaghetti, or as a three- (chili, spaghetti, cheese), four- (plus beans or onions), five- (plus both beans and onions), or even six-way (everything plus garlic). Coneys (dressed hot dogs) are a popular alternative to straight-up chili, and deli sandwiches are also available, but really, if you're not going for the chili, why go?

Contemporary American

Located in a Queen Anne that was home to a pharmacy and the Fraternal Order of Eagles in its past lives, **York Street Café** (738 York St., 859/261-9675, www.yorkstonline.com, 11am-10pm Tues.-Thurs., 11am-11pm Fri.-Sat.) is an eclectic place that will appeal to those who like their meals served with a side of character. A beautiful old pharmacy cabinet now filled with an array of collectibles lines one wall, and a hip mannequin hangs out in the window. At lunch, choose from a tasty selection of salads, wraps, and sandwiches ($7.95-8.95), or go for one of the conversation platters, like the Swiss fondue or the Mediterranean board, which are also available in the evening. Dinner entrées ($18-23) might include free-range Amish chicken, vegan cauliflower steak, or the day's fresh catch. A second-floor lounge is located above the dining room, and an art gallery is one floor higher.

Virgil's Café (710 Fairfield Ave., Bellevue, 859/491-3287, www.virgilscafe.com, lunch 11am-10pm Mon. and Wed.-Sat. 11am-2pm Sun., $8-24) keeps things local with a menu built around what nearby farmers and producers have on offer. Virgil's also keeps things simple, letting the food shine on its own and catering to local tastes. The day's menu might give you a choice between a burger and the much-loved house-made pastrami, between steak poutine and shrimp Creole, or between fresh pasta and frog legs. Located in a historic brick storefront on Bellevue's main thoroughfare, Virgil's was featured in a 2011 episode of *Diners, Drive Ins, and Dives.*

Pizza

Dewey's Pizza (1 Levee Way, 859/431-9700, www.deweyspizza.com, 11am-10pm Mon.-Thurs., 11am-11pm Fri.-Sat., noon-9pm Sun., $11.95-15.45) is a crowd pleaser, regardless of the makeup of the crowd. Kids and adults alike love the pizzas at Dewey's. Order one of the specialty pizzas or create your own

gourmet creations with toppings that range from your standard meats and veggies to capers, black bean corn salsa, pine nuts, goat cheese, and Amish chicken. They'll gladly do half-and-half pizzas if the table can't agree. The atmosphere is cool, casual, and kid-friendly, with the on-tap microbrews making it adult-friendly as well.

Italian

A mainstay since the 1930s, **Pompilios** (600 Washington Ave., 859/581-3065, www.pompilios.com, 11am-10pm Sun.-Thurs., 11am-midnight Fri.-Sat., $9.99-24.99) is pretty much the unofficial official Italian restaurant of Newport. It's also a place with a lot of history, home to a handsome hand-carved bar that was the first in Kentucky to acquire a post-Prohibition liquor license. If it looks familiar but you know you've never been here, thank *Rainman.* Scenes from that movie were filmed here, and in many ways the restaurant still looks the same, though it's been brightened up in the years since. The restaurant has the warm, welcoming feel you expect from a family Italian restaurant, and the menu centers around hearty red-sauce foods like lasagna, ravioli, and veal parmigiana. The food is merely average, but the prices are fair for the portion size, the atmosphere is fun, kids are more than welcome, and the bocce court is a hit. Plus, next time you watch *Rainman,* you can say, "I've been there" during the toothpick scene.

German

The first authentic Hofbräuhaus outside of Germany, **◗ Hofbräuhaus Newport** (200 E. 3rd St., 859/491-7200, www.hofbrauhausnewport.com, 11am-11pm Sun.-Thurs., 11am-2am Fri.-Sat., $7.49-31.99) transports you directly to Munich. From the beer garden to the indoor hall decked with long tables and benches, from the beer brewed on-site to German specifications to the enormous steins, from the hostesses in dirndls to the musicians with accordions, Hofbräuhaus Newport is the real deal. The food is excellent as well. To keep things authentic, go with the pretzels, wurst, or schnitzel. Portions, as you would expect, are hearty.

Latin American

La Mexicana (642 Monmouth St., 859/261-6112, 10am-9pm daily) is the closest you'll get to an authentic taqueria in Northern Kentucky, and it's pretty darn close. The only complaint you could make is that perhaps it's a bit too nice for a hole-in-the-wall, with its plush booths and small but bright dining area. The tacos are served in a double corn tortilla with onions, cilantro, and lime, and the burritos are so enormous that they are a meal unto themselves. Meat choices run the gamut from carne asada and chicken to goat and tripe. Immediately upon arrival, you're greeted with a bowl of chips served with a green salsa. Ask for the salsa *fuerte* if you want a hot red salsa. Service is snappy, and the price is right, with tacos starting at $2.49 each, specials coming in around $6, and nothing on the menu going over $11.99. Order a Mexican Coke for the complete experience.

Dessert

Dessert is an easy decision in Northern Kentucky. **Graeter's** (1409 North Grand Ave., 859/781-7770, www.graeters.com, 7am-11pm Mon.-Sat., 9am-11pm Sun.), which was founded just across the river in 1870, has built up a dedicated fan base thanks to its rich French pot ice cream. Still made in small two-gallon batches, Graeter's ice cream comes in multiple original and signature flavors as well as seasonal offerings. Try the coconut chip for a real treat.

INFORMATION AND SERVICES

The **Northern Kentucky Convention and Visitors Bureau** (50 E. RiverCenter Blvd., Suite 200, Covington, 877/659-84748, www.nkycvb.com) has teamed up with Cincinnati to promote the whole region, and therefore www.cincinnatiusa.com is the best place to get information on the area. The website has an online

trip planner, maps, as well as special offers on hotels, admission tickets, and packages.

GETTING THERE
Air

Despite the fact that the local airport is casually referred to as the Cincinnati Airport, the **Cincinnati/Northern Kentucky International Airport (CVG)** (2939 Terminal Dr., Hebron, 859/767-3151, www.cvgairport.com) is located in Kentucky. Direct national and international flights are offered on Air Canada, American, Delta, Frontier, United, and U.S. Airways. The airport has two easy-to-navigate passenger terminals.

Rental cars and taxis are both available at the airport. Conveniently located just off of I-275, the airport is 9 miles from Florence (11 minutes), 10 miles from Covington (15 minutes), and 12 miles from Newport (20 minutes). The least expensive option for getting into town is to take the TANK (Transit Authority of Northern Kentucky) bus, which picks up outside of Terminal 3 and transports you to downtown Covington for $2. The trip takes about 30 minutes, and buses depart every 75 minutes. From Covington, you can transfer to the Southbank Shuttle to get to Newport or hop a cab for a short, inexpensive ride. A schedule is available at www.tankbus.org.

Car

Newport is just east of Covington, with 4th Street providing the most direction connection between the neighboring cities. For those heading across the river to Cincinnati, U.S. 27 provides the most direct vehicle access via the Taylor-Southgate Bridge.

From Louisville and Lexington and points further afield, follow directions to Covington, and then travel westbound on 4th Street to reach Newport. The AA Highway (KY 9) is the most direct route between Newport and the attractions in Covered Bridge Country.

GETTING AROUND

Newport's attractions are all within easy walking distance of each other. A parking garage at

Newport on the Levee offers convenient access to most attractions. To save a few bucks, try the open-air lot at the corner of Monmouth and 4th Streets. To cross from the Levee to Cincinnati, use the Purple People Bridge. This bridge, which dates to 1872 and was used by the L&N railroad, is now a pedestrian-only bridge that is painted purple, hence the name.

Car Rental
Eight car rental companies are located at the airport, allowing you to hunt for the best deal. If you haven't reserved a car in advance, courtesy phones located in the airport baggage claim area will connect you with the rental companies, which include **Avis** (800/331-1212, www.avis.com), **Enterprise** (800/261-7331, www.enterprise.com), **Hertz** (800/654-3131, www.hertz.com), and **National** (877/222-9058, www.nationalcar.com), among others.

Public Transportation
In addition to providing transportation to and from the airport, **TANK buses** (www.tank-bus.org, $1.50) run throughout the entire region, providing transportation from Newport to Covington, Florence, and Cincinnati. If you're trying to get to a Reds or Bengals game in Cincinnati, consider taking the Southbank Shuttle ($1), which picks up at Newport on the Levee and takes you right to the stadium.

Florence and Boone County

You know for certain that you've made it to Northern Kentucky when, coming from the south, you pass the water tower painted with the words "Florence Ya'll." The sign once read Florence Mall, an advertisement for a soon-to-open shopping center, but because the sign violated local laws, it had to be changed. The least expensive option was to change the "M" to a "Y," and though a bit corny, the change was a hit and the water tower became a landmark. The largest city in Boone County, Florence is more of a commercial destination than a tourist destination, but the county (which includes Union, a rural area southwest of Florence; Burlington, a quaint town northwest of Florence; and Petersburg, a community near the Ohio River border with Indiana) is home to a number of attractions. By far the biggest is the Creation Museum, which opened in Petersburg in 2007 amid a lot of hullabaloo. Despite the fact that it denies all scientific findings about the creation of the earth—or perhaps because of it—the museum draws in hundreds of thousands of people each year, topping the one million visitor mark in only three years. Those who favor science might find it interesting to note that the Creation Museum is only a short drive from Union's Big Bone Lick State Park, home to fossils from prehistoric megafauna that roamed the earth long before the Creation Museum says the world even existed. Regardless of which side you're on, it's likely we can all at least agree that the nature preserves in Boone County are just plain pretty.

SIGHTS
Creation Museum
Operated by an evangelical Christian ministry, the **Creation Museum** (2800 Bullittsburg Church Rd., Petersburg, 888/582-4253, www.creationmuseum.org, 10am-6pm Mon.-Fri., 9am-6pm Sat., noon-6pm Sun., $29.95 adults, $23.95 seniors, $15.95 youth 5-12) dedicates itself to espousing the creationist view of history through an extremely modern and high-tech museum facility, complete with animatronic people and dinosaurs (shown, at one point, living happily together), a special effects theater, and a planetarium ($7.95). Many visitors begin their tour in the special effects theater for a showing of a video titled *Men in White,* which challenges commonly accepted scientific principles and practices as well as the teaching

NORTHERN KENTUCKY

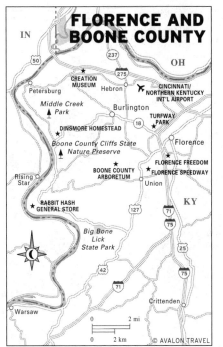

FLORENCE AND BOONE COUNTY

© AVALON TRAVEL

Big Bone Lick State Park

Big Bone Lick State Park (3380 Beaver Rd., Union, 859/384-3522, http://parks.ky.gov, dawn-dusk daily, free) is both an educational and a recreational park. Located at the site of an ancient salt lick that attracted Pleistocene-era animals like mastodons and glacial buffalos, Big Bone Lick proclaims itself the birthplace of American paleontology, thanks to a dig that took place here in 1807 and was supervised by explorer William Clark. A museum (8am-4:30pm Mon.-Thurs., 9am-5pm Fri.-Sun., Apr.-Dec. only, free) contains fossilized bones from the megafauna that visited the site, and an outdoor diorama depicts these animals at a marsh bog. A small bison herd that grows with the birth of a few babies each spring is also kept at the park. Recreational facilities include a 7.5-acre fishing lake, 4.5 miles of hiking trails, a mini-golf course, tennis and basketball courts, two playgrounds, and a campground.

Dinsmore Homestead

Get a taste of what rural life was like in the 19th and early 20th centuries on a visit to the **Dinsmore Homestead** (5656 Burlington Pike, Burlington, 859/586-6117, www.dinsmorefarm.org, 1pm-5pm Wed., Sat., and Sun., Apr.-mid-Dec., $5 adults, $3 seniors, $2 youth 5-17). Tours are offered of the home, which is furnished and decorated with items belonging to five generations of the well-connected and well-to-do Dinsmore family. Guests are also welcome to explore the grounds and hike trails leading through the homestead's 30 acres. A harvest festival with costumed interpreters, bluegrass musicians, and country ham sandwiches is held each September at Dinsmore Homestead and makes for a fun family outing.

SPORTS AND RECREATION
Parks

Boone County remains largely rural and, as such, has numerous parks that beckon residents and visitors alike to get outdoors. **England-Idlewild Park** (5550 Idlewild Rd., Burlington, www.boonecountyky.org) caters to a diversity of outdoor interests. Located on its 290 acres are

of evolution. A walking journey through exhibits portraying the Book of Genesis is at the heart of the museum. Displays present the six days of creation, the fall of man, and the story of Noah's ark, with text panels seeking to provide "scientific" evidence for the biblical version of creation and disprove other interpretations. A whole host of lectures and special events are held at the museum daily, making it possible to spend an entire day or longer here (tickets are good for two days) immersed in either belief or disbelief, depending on your religious views. Try to make time to visit the gardens, which are stunning. A one-mile nature trail leads around a lake and to a petting zoo, and three on-site cafés cater to your earthly needs. The museum also plays host to a zip-line course, which doesn't tie directly into the museum's mission in any obvious way, beyond bringing in money for the cause ($29 for two "flights," $89 for the entire course).

NORTHERN KENTUCKY

diorama of mammoths at Big Bone Lick State Park

© THERESA DOWELL BLACKINTON

NORTHERN KENTUCKY

three fishing ponds, a 24-hole disc golf course, baseball and soccer fields, basketball courts, a 1.8-mile fitness walking path, and 12 miles of mountain biking trails divided into four routes that range from a 0.5-mile beginners loop to a 6-mile advanced trail. Picnic and playground areas are spread throughout the park, and a dog park is adjacent to the main park.

The **Boone County Arboretum** (9190 Camp Ernst Rd., Union, 859/384-4999, www.bcarboretum.org, dawn-dusk daily, free), which has more than 3,000 trees and shrubs, is located within **Central Park,** a popular recreation spot with soccer, tennis, and baseball facilities. Among the most loved arboretum areas are a children's garden and a native Kentucky grassland where wildlife likes to feed. The arboretum also has two paved walking trails, the 1.1-mile Dogwood Trail and the 1.3-mile Loop Trail.

Aquatic Park

The **Florence Aquatic Park** (8200 Ewing Blvd., Florence, 859/647-4619, www.florence-ky.gov/florence-family-aquatic-center,

11am-7pm daily, Memorial Day-mid-August, $10 adults, $7 seniors and youth 3-15, discounted rates are available for residents, annual memberships available) is not your typical public pool. Instead, it goes beyond that to also offer a lazy river, two spray grounds, slides, and a zero-depth area for small children. For beating the summer heat, it's the place to be.

Hiking

Explore cliffs created by glacial outwashes some 700,000 years ago on a hike through the 75-acre **Boone County Cliffs State Nature Preserve** (http://naturepreserve.ky.org). A moderate 2.4-mile looping trail takes you up and down ridges and along Middle Creek through rich forests. Many of the plants have been labeled, and the area is home to a variety of birds, so bring your binoculars. The preserve is located on Middle Creek Road in Burlington, 1.5 miles from the intersection with Burlington Pike. Look for a small gravel parking lot on the left.

Just 0.5 mile west of the turnoff to Boone

County Cliffs State Nature Preserve and adjacent to the Dinsmore Homestead, you'll find **Dinsmore Woods State Nature Preserve** (http://naturepreserve.ky.org). This 107-acre preserve protects a mature maple-ash forest that has never been commercially logged. A moderate 1.7-mile trail leads up to a ridge and through wildflower-rich woods. Another great birding spot, Dinsmore Woods can easily be combined with Boone County Cliffs for a great outing.

Also nearby to the nature preserves is **Middle Creek Park** (5501 Middlecreek Rd., www.boonecountyky.org), a 230-acre wooded habitat home to both wildflowers and wildlife. More than 5.5 miles of trails meander through the park, allowing hikers and equestrians to enjoy this unspoiled terrain. During deer hunting season, the park is closed.

Spectator Sports

Turfway Park (7500 Turfway Rd., Florence, 859/371-0200, www.turfway.com, free) is the small town of Kentucky's racetracks, a friendly place welcoming to both track regulars as well as newbies to the sport of champions. The first track in North America to use a synthetic track, Turfway hosts two meets a year: a holiday meet that runs the month of December, and a winter/spring meet that runs January-March. The grandstand, which dates to the 1950s and can feel like it at times, is completely enclosed, making even the coldest winter day a great day for racing. Weekday races (Thurs.-Sun. holiday and winter) are evening affairs, with first post at 5:30pm during the holiday and winter meets, while weekend races begin at 1:10pm during all meets.

The **Florence Freedom** (7950 Freedom Way, Florence, 859/594-4487, www.florencefreedom.com, $10-14) is a professional baseball team that plays in the independent Frontier League. The league is not affiliated with Major League Baseball, and most players were either undrafted or released from MLB teams. The level of play is roughly equivalent to Single-A minor league baseball. Although it's unlikely that you'll ever see any of these guys in the Big Leagues, you'll still get to enjoy a quality baseball game in a fun, family-friendly environment.

The half-mile, high-banked, clay oval track at **Florence Speedway** (12234 U.S. 42, Walton, 859/485-7591, www.florencespeedway.com) hosts late-model, modified, and pure stock car races on Saturdays March-October. The track's more prestigious races include March's Spring 50, June's Ralph Latham Memorial, and August's North/South 100, all of which are dirt late-model events. Pit gates usually open around 4pm, with racing starting around 7:30pm, but check the online schedule for exact details. General admission prices range $12-35 depending on the event, but youth 6-11 never pay more than $3, except for the North/South 100, when youth admission is $7. Fans are allowed to bring in coolers and alcohol (but no glass), so expect a rowdy (but generally family-friendly) good time.

ACCOMMODATIONS
Airport Area

Two Marriott properties, the **Courtyard** (3990 Olympic Blvd., Erlanger, 859/647-9900, www.marriott.com, $99-139) and the **Residence Inn** (2811 Circleport Dr., Erlanger, 859/282-7400, www.marriott.com, $109-159), provide excellent accommodation in close proximity to the airport. The Courtyard offers large, clean, comfortable rooms, while the Residence Inn offers nice suites with full kitchens, living rooms, and separate bedrooms. Both offer free wireless Internet and free airport shuttles. The Residence Inn also offers a complimentary hot breakfast daily and an evening reception on weekdays.

Burlington

Burlington's **Willis Graves Bed and Breakfast Inn** (5825 N. Jefferson St., Burlington, 859/689-5096, www.burligrave.com, $135-235) consists of a meticulously restored 1830s Federal brick home listed on the National Register of Historic Places and an 1850s two-story log cabin that was rescued from planned airport expansion and

LOST IN TIME: RABBIT HASH

On the banks of the Ohio River, just across the river from Rising Star, Indiana, sits a community unlike any other in Kentucky: Rabbit Hash. A tiny place, whose exact population is unknown but thought to be less than 40, Rabbit Hash transports visitors back in time. Though unarguably sleepy-looking at first glance, this unique community has its fair share of unique offerings, especially for those who love off-the-beaten-path sights and places with proud and well-preserved heritages. Motorcyclists flock to Rabbit Hash and the country roads that lead to it, and it's a place anyone who makes their way to Boone County (home to Florence, Big Bone Lick State Park, and the Creation Museum) should add to their itinerary. After all, have you ever been anywhere else with a dog for a mayor?

Established in 1813, this rural community sprung up around the steamboat. The **Rabbit Hash General Store** (10021 Lower River Rd., 859/586-7744, www.rabbithash.com, 10am-7pm daily), which remains the heart and soul of the community, was built in 1831 to store goods waiting for steamboat transport. Although floods have continually wreaked havoc on the town, destroying homes and businesses, the General Store has stood strong, a system of rods and hooks anchoring the building so that it won't float away. That doesn't mean it hasn't flooded—mud from the 1937 flood is still in the attic—but it's always bounced back. Today the General Store carries food, beverages, and staples needed by the local community, as well as Rabbit Hash souvenirs and a range of Kentucky arts and crafts. Antiques collections spill out

into two buildings across the street. Make the General Store your first stop to find out what's going on in Rabbit Hash. You'll always find at least a few locals hanging out on the porch or in the store.

If you can, try to time your visit to coincide with the monthly barn dance (second Friday of the month, 7:30pm-11pm). It's a great way to meet locals and enjoy some old-fashioned entertainment. To really immerse yourself in life in Rabbit Hash, see if the apartment room at the **Old Hashienda** (10021 Lower River Rd., 859/586-7744, www.rabbithash.com, $155) is available. The 1,200-square-foot rustic property has a bedroom with queen bed, sitting room with queen futon, kitchen, bathroom, living and dining rooms, and a front porch with a swing from which you can observe the comings and goings of Rabbit Hash. If you feel like going for a stroll, be sure to pop into the local craft shops and the Rabbit Hash Museum.

Surely you're wondering how a community came to be called Rabbit Hash. Unfortunately, no one knows the exact answer, but there certainly are a lot of stories to go around. It was originally called Carleton, until the post office asked the community to change its name when residents' mail kept ending up down the river in the city of Carrollton. Legend has it that locals had already been calling the town Rabbit Hash and so decided to make it official with the post office. Rabbit hash, a type of stew, was reportedly a popular dish around here, thanks to the abundance of area bunnies, but why residents would name their town after their supper remains a mystery.

moved to the property. An elegant yet understated classic style pervades the inn, and luxury is the name of the game in the guest rooms. Expect fine quality linens, plush robes and towels, top-of-the-line mattresses, and cookies on the pillow. All rooms have private bathrooms with whirlpool tubs, televisions, wireless Internet access, and espresso machines, and some come with fireplaces or steam showers. Three rooms are located in

the main house, with two additional rooms in the cabin. A delicious full gourmet breakfast is served daily, although you can opt for a continental version if you're in a hurry.

Petersburg

If you're looking for a real country retreat, check out **First Farm Inn** (2510 Stevens Rd., Petersburg, 859/586-0199, www.first-farminn.com, $135-144), which offers two

As for the mayor, Lucy Lou, a red and white border collie, took office in 2008. She faced stiff competition for the position, competing again nine other dogs, one cat, one opossum, one jackass, and one human being. After a rip-roaring campaign and election, Lucy Lou became the third canine mayor of Rabbit Hash. She's known for the warm greetings she bestows on visitors.

To get to Rabbit Hash—you know you want to go—take I-75 to Exit 178 and proceed west on Mt. Zion Road. Continue straight on Mt. Zion Road as it becomes Hathaway Road and Rabbit Hash Road. When Rabbit Hash Road (KY 536) intersects with East Bend Road and Rabbit Hash Hill Road, take Rabbit Hash Hill Road down to the river, where it intersects with Lower River Road. Take the left fork to reach the General Store and the heart of Rabbit Hash, which is about 16 miles from the interstate.

© THERESA DOWELL BLACKINTON

Rabbit Hash General Store

guest rooms in their 1870s farmhouse. Both rooms have queen beds and private bathrooms and offer lovely countryside views. Although the rooms are comfortably outfitted, you won't want to stay inside when you can enjoy the outdoor hot tub, take a walk to the farm ponds, get acquainted with the inn's cats and dogs, or take one of the inn's horses out for a two-hour ride ($55). A hearty breakfast is served daily, consisting of a hot entrée accompanied by fruit and homemade breads.

Campgrounds

Big Bone Lick State Park (3380 Beaver Rd., Union, 859/384-4267, http://parks.ky.gov, Apr.-Oct., $23) has a 62-site campground with full utility hookups at each site and a pool for campers. The campground also features restrooms, showers, laundry facilities, and a grocery store.

FOOD
Florence

Chicago-style deep-dish pizza fans can order up an authentic pie at **Bourbon House Pizza** (7500 Oakbrook Rd., Florence, 859/282-7999, www.bourbonhousepizza.com, 11am-9pm Mon.-Thurs., 11am-10pm Fri.-Sat., noon-9pm Sun., $5.99-13.95). Choose a specialty pizza, such as the Chicago's Favorite (sausage, mushrooms, and onions), or build your own pizza. Many types of hoagies are also available, and non-deep-dish pizza is an option as well.

Mai Thai (7710 U.S. 42, Florence, 859/282-1888, lunch 11am-3pm Mon.-Fri., noon-4pm Sat., dinner 5pm-10pm Mon.-Thurs., 5pm-10:30pm Fri., 4pm-10:30pm Sat., $9.95-14.95) hits the spot if you're craving Thai, with an extensive menu of well-prepared favorites, including pad Thai, pineapple fried rice, Panang curry, and cashew chicken. The lunch menu is a bargain, with entrées coming in at $6.95. Mai Thai also offers maki rolls and sushi.

Burlington

Whether you order a filet mignon or the Tuesday night special of family-style fried chicken, your meal at **Tousey House Tavern** (5963 N. Jefferson St., Burlington, 859/586-9900, www.tousey-house.com, 11am-9pm Tues.-Sat., 10am-8pm Sun., $7.95-29.95) will be expertly prepared and elegantly served. In addition to steak, fish, pork, and chicken entrées, the tavern offers sandwiches, including a shrimp BLT and a Hot Brown, as well as specialties such as Creole mac and cheese. The restaurant runs on Southern hospitality and the atmosphere is that of a gentrified Southerner's home, with tables arranged throughout the restored rooms of an 1822 Federal-style house. Two covered porches with ceiling fans are open when the weather is agreeable and are the ideal place to sip some bourbon and share an appetizer of Kentucky beer cheese or fried green tomatoes.

INFORMATION AND SERVICES

As part of Northern Kentucky and the Greater Cincinnati area, the best place to get information on Boone County is www.cincin-natiusa.com.

GETTING THERE
Air

The **Cincinnati/Northern Kentucky International Airport** (2939 Terminal Dr., Hebron, 859/767-3151, www.cvgairport.com) is located in Boone County. Direct national and international flights are offered on Air Canada, American, Delta, Frontier, United, and U.S. Airways. The airport has two easy-to-navigate passenger terminals.

Rental cars and taxis are available at the airport, and shuttles are provided by many of the nearby airport hotels, including those mentioned here.

GETTING AROUND

Florence is situated along I-71/I-75, about 10 miles (20 minutes) southwest of Covington via the interstate. The interstate also provides direct connections with Louisville, which is 90 miles (1 hour 20 minutes) southwest of

Welcome to Florence.

© THERESA DOWELL BLACKINTON

NORTHERN KENTUCKY

Florence via I-71, and Lexington, which is 80 miles (1 hour 20 minutes) south of Florence via I-75.

Burlington is just 6 miles (12 minutes) east of Florence via Burlington Pike (KY 18), while Petersburg is 20 miles (30 minutes) east of Florence in the far northeast corner, just south of I-275, which provides the most direct route to the Creation Museum. Union, home to Big Bone Lick State Park, is in the southern part of the county, to the east of I-71. From Florence (13 miles; 22 minutes), it's best to take southbound U.S. 127 to eastbound KY 338, from which you enter the park. If you're coming from the south, exit I-71 at U.S. 127 (Exit 62) and follow it northbound to eastbound KY 338.

Car Rental

Eight car rental companies are located at the airport, including **Avis** (800/331-1212, www. avis.com), **Enterprise** (800/261-7331, www. enterprise.com), **Hertz** (800/654-3131, www. hertz.com), and **National** (877/222-9058, www.nationalcar.com).

Carroll, Owen, and Gallatin Counties

The area to the south of true Northern Kentucky is primarily rural. Carrollton, with a population of about 4,000, is a big town for the area. Most other map dots have fewer than 2,000 residents; many have only a couple hundred. If it weren't for I-71, which passes through this region as it connects Louisville and Covington, most people would never make it here. Auto racing fans, however, would see to it that they found a way here, thanks to the Kentucky Speedway, which hosts major NASCAR races. Beyond the speedway, attractions are limited, although General Butler State Resort Park makes for a relaxing getaway, and both oenophiles and hunters will find something they like at Elk Creek. Because the three counties are close together and share the same characteristics, all sights in this area are listed together.

SIGHTS
Kentucky Speedway

The 1.5-mile track at **Kentucky Speedway** (1 Speedway Dr., Sparta, 859/578-2300, www. kentuckyspeedway.com) features two big weekends of racing that include NASCAR Nationwide Series, NASCAR Sprint Cup Series, NASCAR Camping World Truck Series, and ARCA Racing Series races, with the Quaker State 400 the biggest race on the ticket. Camping and tailgating are essential parts of the race experience and are encouraged by Kentucky Speedway on race weekends. Outside of race weekends, you can sign up for a tour of the speedway ($5), which includes a ride around the track, a trip to the garage area and victory lane, a stop in the grandstands, and a peek at a luxury suite. Wannabe race car drivers will want to save their pennies for one of the driving schools offered at the Speedway. These schools allow participants to actually get behind the wheel of a race car and take it for a spin on the track. A schedule of classes is posted online along with requirements and fees.

General Butler State Resort Park

General Butler State Resort Park (1608 KY 227, Carrollton, 502/732-4384, http://parks. ky.gov, dawn-dusk daily, free) was built around the home of the last commander-in-chief of the military during the Mexican War, General William Orlando Butler. This 1859 country home is now a living house museum that can be explored on guided tours ($5 adults, $3 youth). On a 45-minute tour of the Butler-Turpin House, you'll learn about the family's storied military background as well as the lifestyle of both the family and their slaves. A self-guided tour of the cemetery and grounds can be taken after the guided tour is complete. Tours are

NORTHERN KENTUCKY

© THERESA DOWELL BLACKINTON

jumping into the pool at General Butler State Resort Park

offered at 1pm, 2pm, and 3pm Thursday-Saturday June-October.

Visitors to General Butler State Resort Park can, in addition to history lessons, get a strong dose of the outdoors. A nine-hole golf course open year-round beckons serious players, while those who still need to work on their putting can play a round at the mini-golf course (daily Memorial Day-Labor Day, weekends Apr.-May and Sept.-Oct.). Lake Butler, which was built by the Civilian Conservation Corps in the 1930s, can be explored via pedal boats, rowboats, and canoes that can be rented at the dock. Hiking trails include the 1.5-mile Woodland Trail, the 0.25-mile Boy Scout Trail, and the 1.2-mile Butler Lake Trail. The 4.5-mile looping Fossil Trail is open to both hikers and mountain bikers. Basketball and tennis courts and multiple playgrounds provide additional recreational opportunities. Picnic tables are scattered throughout the park, and you must be sure to take in the wide view of the Kentucky and Ohio Rivers and their surrounding valleys from the stone overlook.

As a resort park, General Butler also offers a lodge, cottage, and campground accommodations, and a restaurant.

Wineries

There must be something just right with the soil in the southern reaches of Northern Kentucky, because a growing number of vineyards have staked their claim to the area. **Elk Creek Vineyards** (150 KY 330, Owenton, 502/484-0005, www.elkcreekvineyards.com) is part of an enterprise that also offers lodging, food, and, perhaps most uniquely, a hunt club. The vineyard, which produces red, white, and fruit wines, offers a variety of tasting and tour options. The basic tasting allows you to sip five light and sweet ($5) or dry and full-bodied wines ($8), while the classic tour and tasting (minimum of 8 people, $12) includes a tour of the winery, four tastings, a cheese and cracker platter, and a glass of the wine of your choice. Other attractions at the vineyard include an art gallery and an outdoor stage that hosts local bands every Friday and Saturday evening

NORTHERN KENTUCKY

May-August. The hunt club offers top-notch sporting clays facilities, along with deer, turkey, and other bird hunting packages in season. The vineyard is open 10am-7pm Monday-Thursday and 10am-10pm Friday-Saturday, June-mid-September, 10am-6pm Monday-Thursday and 10am-9pm Friday-Saturday, mid-September-December, 11am-6pm Monday-Thursday and 10am-9pm Friday-Saturday, January-March, and 11am-7pm Monday-Thursday and 10am-9pm Friday-Saturday, April-May.

Operating on a much more intimate scale is **River Valley Winery** (1279 Mound Hill, Carrollton, 502/750-0594, www.rivervalley-winery.com, noon-5pm Tues.-Fri., also Sat. in winter, free), which welcomes visitors to taste their award-winning white, blush, and red wines in their tasting room or on an attractive arbor-covered patio. Beyond rows and rows of grapes, the winery is also home to llamas, sheep, dogs, and ducks. A concert series is held on the grounds during the summer, with the option to enjoy dinner at the vineyard before the show.

FESTIVALS AND EVENTS

Fans of honest-to-god small-town festivals will enjoy the **Carroll County Tobacco Festival** (www.carrolltontobaccofestival.com), held annually in early October in Carrollton to celebrate the region's agricultural heritage. In addition to a carnival, live entertainment from local bands and Elvis impersonators, and a parade right through the heart of town, the festival also includes pageants, a 5K race, an outhouse race, and a cornhole tournament. Getting to the heart of the festival, the tobacco judging takes place on Saturday morning. If you've always wondered what makes for good tobacco, here's your chance to find out.

ACCOMMODATIONS
Speedway Area
Racing fans will want to get a room at the **Ramada** (525 Dale Dr., Sparta, 859/567-7223, www.ramada.com, $85-95), the only hotel located in the immediate vicinity of Kentucky Speedway. It's literally at the speedway entrance, so if you want to crash near the track and didn't bring your RV, book a room (well in advance) here. The rooms are well maintained and spacious, and have wireless Internet access. The only real negative is the somewhat thin walls that let in the sound of your neighbor's television or snoring. A complimentary breakfast of pastries, cereals, and waffles is served each morning. Rates are much higher on race weekends than on non-event days.

From May through September, **Magnolia Inn** (1519 Sparta Pike, Sparta, 859/743-0058, http://magnoliainn.org) offers guests a choice of six rooms, each named for a Civil War general. The rooms are decorated in a classic Southern style, and each has a private bathroom. The entire main floor is a common area, and guests are also welcome to enjoy the porches, a hot tub, more than 80 acres of land for hiking and biking, and two fishing ponds.

Stately **C Riverside Inn** (85 U.S. 42 E., Warsaw, 859/567-1239, www.riversideinnbb.com, $249), an 1869 riverfront mansion, underwent an enormous renovation in 2011 and then opened as a high-end bed and breakfast. The five king suites and two queen rooms are luxuriously appointed and richly decorated. In addition to a full breakfast buffet, guests will also enjoy the afternoon wine and cheese reception and 24-hour access to snacks and refreshments. Soak in the sunset over the river from the gazebo, kick back in the library, music room, or billiards room, or schedule a massage for true relaxation. More active guests may wish to borrow a bicycle or play a game of croquet on the lawn. You certainly won't want to leave.

Carrollton
General Butler Lodge (1608 Hwy. 227, Carrollton, 502/732-4384, http://parks.ky.gov, $109.95), which boasts a beautiful cathedral-like common room, has 53 guest rooms, each with private balcony or patio. Choose from two double beds or one king bed. The rooms have a rustic feel that some people adore and others find dated. The park also offers cottages with one-, two-, and three-bedroom configurations

NORTHERN KENTUCKY

($159.95-259.95). They're perfect for families and groups, offering privacy as well as easy access to park activities. The cottages are bigger than they look from the outside, and exposed beams and skylights give them an airy feeling. A pool is open to lodge and cottage guests. Additionally, the park has a 111-site campground ($23) with utility hookups available year-round. Two service buildings provide showers and restrooms for campers.

A pack of chain hotels is located right off of I-71 at the Carrollton exit. The **Holiday Inn Express** (147 Hospitality Way, Carrollton, 502/732-6770, www.hiexpress.com, $100-155) ranks highest among the options, with friendly staff, clean rooms, and a good continental breakfast. The **Hampton Inn** (7 Slumber Ln., Carrollton, 502/732-0700, www.hamptoninn.com, $119) is another solid option for those looking for a standard hotel room and amenities.

Owen County

For a relaxing getaway, try **Ragtime Bed, Barn, and Breakfast** (2310 Breck Rd., Owenton, 517/980-0380, www.ragtimebb.com, $65-110), which offers far-reaching views of the Kentucky countryside from its porch rockers as well as from each of the three guest rooms. Floor-to-ceiling windows, a stone fireplace, and a private bath give the master suite a sense of luxury. The other two rooms, one with a double bed and one with two twin beds, share a bathroom, but are spacious and comfortable.

FOOD
Speedway Area

C Jewell's on Main (100 E. Main St., Warsaw, 859/567-1793, 11am-9pm Tues.-Thurs., 11am-10pm Fri., noon-10pm Sat., $7-17) is a little bit of a contradiction: You order at the counter, but then they seat you and deliver your meal, which is not anything like the type of food you get at most places with a counter. Instead, you'll get chef-prepared, delicious renditions of such favorites as shrimp and grits, meatloaf, pan-fried catfish, and hand-cut rib eye at prices that are more than reasonable. Located in a

100-plus-year-old storefront with the original floors still intact, Jewell's is always busy, and for good reason—it's a great place to eat, and not just for the area.

Carrollton

Two Rivers Restaurant (1608 Hwy. 227, Carrollton, 502/732-4384, http://parks. ky.gov, 7am-9pm daily, $5.99-11.99) at General Butler State Resort Park pays homage to the nearby convergence of the Ohio and Kentucky Rivers with fish camp decor. The restaurant serves breakfast, lunch, and dinner daily, focusing on family favorites. The lunch buffet and a Sunday brunch are particularly popular.

Serving breakfast all day, **Welch's Riverside Restaurant** (505 Main St., Carrollton, 502/732-9118, 5am-8pm Mon.-Sat., 6am-3pm Sun., $3.99-8.99) is your basic hometown diner with a counter and booths, a daily newspaper waiting to be read, and a view of the Ohio River. If you're not the breakfast-for-dinner type, you can opt for a burger or sandwich, try the seafood platter or country ham dinner, or go for the daily special of a meat and two (vegetables, that is). Friday's special is fish, of course.

INFORMATION AND SERVICES

The **Carroll County Tourism Office** (511 Highland Ave., Carrollton, 502/732-7036, 9am-5pm Mon.-Fri.) is your best source for information about the area. For online information, visit www.carrolltontourism.com, where you'll find information on a country drive route.

GETTING THERE AND AROUND

Carrollton sits nearly exactly halfway between Louisville and Covington, 50 miles (55 minutes) northeast of Louisville and 50 miles southwest (55 minutes) of Covington at Exit 44 on I-71. General Butler State Resort Park is right in Carrollton; you'll pass it as you take KY 227 from the interstate to the center of Carrollton. Sparta and the Kentucky Speedway are about 15 miles (20 minutes) northwest of Carrollton at Exit 57 on I-71. Owenton is located very near to the center of the triangle formed by I-71, I-75, and I-64. The most direct route is to exit I-71 at U.S. 127 (Exit 62) and then follow U.S. 127 south to Owenton.

Covered Bridge Country

There's no doubt that the towns scattered throughout Covered Bridge Country, which sits east of I-75, north of I-64, and south of the Ohio River, are in tune with the 21st century. Yet somehow, they still manage to maintain an aura of yesteryear. It's not that they cling to the past, but that they've managed to create a present where the best of the past has been preserved. Neighbors look out for each other. People make the time to stop and chat, valuing personal connections. And even those who move away don't forget where they came from. George Clooney, after all, brought the premiere of *Leatherheads* to Maysville, which neighbors his hometown of Augusta, where his parents still reside.

Augusta is one of the most popular destinations in the region, along with Maysville, which is the largest town with around 9,000 residents. Because of the fine hotel and restaurant options in these towns, most visitors to this area base themselves in one of the two. The rest of the area is primarily rural. Tobacco farming is still a common way of life here, although farmers are branching out to other crops, including such unexpected ones as lavender. Barns, many of which are decorated with quilt patches, dot the landscape, but it's the bridges that attract most people. With 8 of the state's remaining 13 covered bridges in this region, this area is a magnet for those looking for a relaxing getaway in a place with a tangible link to the days before interstates and iPhones.

© THERESA DOWELL BLACKINTON

brightly painted storefronts in downtown Augusta

NORTHERN KENTUCKY

COVERED BRIDGES DRIVING TOUR

If covered bridges are your passion, northern Kentucky is a great destination. The best way to see the bridges is on a multiday trip, where you can also visit the surrounding towns and small communities. If, however, you're just passing through or are simply out for a long Sunday drive, here's how to visit all eight of the region's bridges in a looping day's drive.

Begin your adventure in Covington, where you'll take Exit 75 off of I-275 to the AA Highway (KY 9). Drive east for 31 miles on the AA Highway to reach stop number one: **Walcott Covered Bridge.** This bridge, located at the intersection with KY 1159, is visible from the highway, although you can turn off for a closer look.

From Walcott Covered Bridge, continue east on the AA Highway for 4.7 miles, then turn left on KY 19. Drive 3.2 miles, and then turn right on KY 8. Drive 6.9 miles on eastbound KY 8 to Lee's Creek Road. Turn right on Lee's Creek Road, and you'll reach **Dover Covered Bridge** in 0.1 mile.

Get a double dose of Dover Bridge by driving through it, then U-turning and driving back through it to return to KY 8. Turn right onto KY 8 and continue east for 1.6 miles. Turn right onto Tuckahoe Road, drive 3.9 miles, and then turn right on Minerva Tuckahoe Road. Drive 0.9 mile, and then turn left onto Valley Pike. The short **Valley Pike Covered Bridge** (23 feet) is privately owned, but you may view it at a turn-off.

From the Valley Pike Bridge, you'll now head to the easternmost bridge before looping south and then back west. Begin by traveling 1.5 miles on Valley Pike to Germantown Road. Turn right and drive 0.8 mile to the AA Highway. Turn left, drive 2.9 miles, and then turn left onto KY 10. Continue on KY 10 for 3.2 miles through Maysville and onto combined KY 10/KY 8. Drive 6.4 miles on KY 10/KY 8, and then turn left on Springdale Road. After 1.8 miles, turn right on Cabin Creek Road and drive 1.7 miles to **Cabin Creek Covered Bridge.** This bridge is closed to traffic, so get out to admire it and then return to your car.

You're now off to see Fleming County's three covered bridges. Begin by retracing your path on Cabin Creek Road for 1.2 miles, turning left onto Owl Hollow Road. Proceed for 2.1 miles, and then turn left onto KY 8. Drive 0.6 mile, and then stay right onto KY 1237. After 3.7 miles, turn right onto KY 57 and drive 11 miles into Flemingsburg. Go straight through the roundabout, and then turn left onto eastbound KY 32. Drive 8.2 miles on KY 32 to the **Goddard White Covered Bridge,** which is located just off of KY 32 on Parkersburg Road. It is open to traffic, so go ahead and pass through. You'll then want to pull off for some photos, which are more attractive if you shoot from KY 32.

After you're done taking photos of the Goddard White Bridge, continue east on KY 32. Drive 6.5 miles to Rawlings Road, where you'll

AUGUSTA AND BRACKEN COUNTY

Located on the banks of the Ohio River, where boys on bikes still come to fish and a ferry chugs back and forth to Ohio in a tradition that dates back more than 200 years, Augusta feels like it could step in for Mayberry at any moment. Riverside Drive and Main Street compose the heart of the town, their sidewalks lined with grand homes, historic storefronts, and log buildings. Augusta is a perfect place to come for a day's escape. Stroll the streets, browse the shops, tour the museum, or take a ride on the ferry, and then have lunch at your choice of tasty restaurants. While there, you might want to have a sip of the local water, which must have something special in it. Although the town has only about 2,000 residents, it's the hometown of both George Clooney and Miss America 2000.

Rosemary Clooney House Museum

Actress and singer Rosemary Clooney, perhaps best known to younger generations as the aunt of George Clooney, although certainly a star in turn right. Proceed 2.8 miles to the intersection with KY 158. **Ringo's Mill Covered Bridge,** which is no longer used, is right next to the road at this intersection.

From Ringo's Mill Bridge, it's just a short drive to the second-to-last bridge on your tour. Turn right on KY 158, and drive 3.5 miles, turning left at the dead end, to reach KY 111. Turn left on KY 111, and drive 2.9 miles to **Grange City Covered Bridge,** which is on the side of the road to your right.

To reach the tour's final bridge, retrace your path on KY 111, driving a total of 10.4 miles to westbound KY 32. After 0.9 mile, continue onto KY 32 bypass. Drive 3.3 miles on the bypass before turning left back onto KY 32. Continue 4.7 miles on KY 32 to KY 165, where you'll turn right. Drive 6.2 miles on KY 165 to where it dead-ends at U.S. 68. Turn left onto U.S. 68, drive 1.8 miles, and then turn right on Mt. Pleasant Road. Continue 1.9 miles to Old Blue Lick Road, where you will take a sharp right, and proceed 1.5 miles to **Johnson Creek Covered Bridge,** the eighth and final covered bridge in this region.

If you'd like to complete the loop and return to Covington, follow Old Blue Lick Road and Mt. Pleasant Road back to U.S. 68. Turn right onto U.S. 68, drive two miles, and then turn right onto KY 165. Remain on KY 165 for 20.6 miles until you reach KY 19. Stay right on KY 19, and drive 0.9 mile to KY 10. Drive 10.5 miles on KY 10, and then turn right on Lenoxburg Foster Road, which will connect to the AA Highway in 2.7 miles. At the AA Highway, turn left and drive 26.8 miles back to I-275.

This entire loop totals 217 miles, and it will take 5-5.5 hours to drive the whole circuit, not counting time spent at each bridge. It's certainly a full day's trip, but it's a very scenic route and a lovely way to explore the rural areas of this region.

For those using a GPS, coordinates for each of the bridges are as follows:

- Walcott Covered Bridge: N 38° 43.992 W 084° 05.868

- Dover Covered Bridge: N 38° 45.018 W 083° 52.719

- Valley Pike Covered Bridge: N 38° 40.470 W 083° 52.320

- Cabin Creek Covered Bridge: N 38° 36.574 W 083° 37.277

- Goddard White Covered Bridge: N 38° 21.738 W 083° 36.930

- Ringo's Mill Covered Bridge: N 38° 16.110 W 083° 36.624

- Grange City Covered Bridge: N 38° 15.294 W 083° 39.192

- Johnson Creek Covered Bridge: N 38° 28.950 W 083° 58.722

her own right, was born and raised in nearby Maysville, purchasing a riverfront house here in Augusta in 1980. This house, which served as her retreat from the world of show business for more than two decades, has been turned into the **Rosemary Clooney House Museum** (106 E. Riverside Dr., Augusta, 606/756-2603, www.rosemaryclooney.org, noon-3pm Thurs.-Fri., 11am-4pm Sat., 1pm-4pm Sun., $5) thanks to the efforts of former Lt. Governor Steve Henry and his wife, Miss America 2000, Heather French Henry. Participants on a tour of the house will visit Clooney's living room, dining room, bedroom, and library, all of which are filled with her furnishings and mementos from her movies and shows. Additional displays exhibit the Miss America memorabilia of Mrs. Henry and some articles from George Clooney's television and movie performances.

Augusta Historic Tour

Founded in 1797 and occupied by Native Americans long before that, Augusta is a town teeming with history and culture. Although just strolling the streets to see the magnificent homes and buildings is enjoyable in itself, a tour of the town is made more engaging with the aid of the **Augusta Historic Tour** brochure. The brochure identifies 57 sites of interest, including the homes of important people, buildings with distinct architectural features, and locations of historic importance, such as a home on the Underground Railroad and businesses that were attacked during one of Morgan's Raids. History buffs can also take a self-guided tour of the 1811 Augusta Jail, with its log dungeon, debtor's prison, and jailer's living quarters. Free brochures for all tours can be picked up at the **Welcome Center** (corner of Main St. and Riverside Dr.).

Walcott Covered Bridge

As you approach Augusta from Northern Kentucky, you'll pass the **Walcott Covered Bridge** (AA Highway at KY 1159) on your left. Though hundreds of covered bridges once provided passage all across the state, the Walcott Covered Bridge is thought to have been the only one built in Bracken County. Dating to the 1880s, the 74-foot king-and-queen-post truss bridge once helped traffic across Locust Creek. It is now closed to motorized transport, but pedestrians are welcome to cross. The creek running below the bridge reflects it perfectly in early morning and late evening hours, making for a great photo.

Agritourism

An abundance of agritourism destinations are located in the rich farmland of Bracken County. **Baker-Bird Winery** (4655 Augusta/Chatham Rd., Augusta, 859/620-4965, http://bakerbirdwinery.com, 1pm-5pm Sat.-Sun.) continues a long tradition of wine producing, sitting on land used as a winery as far back as the mid-1800s. New vines were planted in 2006, and visitors can now taste one of seven wines produced there as well as tour the historic site.

Between May and July, the lavender peaks at **Lavender Hills of Kentucky** (229 Conrad Ridge Rd., Brooksville, 606/735-3355, www.lavenderhillsofkentucky.com, noon-6pm Sat.-Sun. June-Oct.), with the more than 600 lavender plants in 19 different varieties giving the entire area a wonderful aroma. A gift shop carries an enormous variety of products made from the lavender, including sachets, eye masks, sugar scrubs, bath teas and salts, candles, cleaning products, and decorative items.

For fresh-from-the-farm produce, head to **Brackenridge Berry Farm** (1090 Belmont Rd., Brooksville, 606/735-2490, www.brackenridgeberryfarm.com), where you can pick blueberries in season, or to **Hillside Orchard and Country Store** (4979 AA Hwy., Foster, 606/747-5635, www.hillsideorchardandcountrystore.com, 10am-6pm Fri.-Sat., 1pm-6pm Sun.), where seasonal bounty includes apples, pumpkins, honey, and various fruits.

Entertainment and Events

The **Augusta Riverfest Regatta** (www.augustaky.com) brings riverboats and their admirers to town for a fun weekend celebration. In addition to being able to tour the many boats that dock at Augusta for the regatta, festival attendees can enjoy live music, wander through car and antique tractor shows, sign up for a beauty contest or Huck Finn/Becky Thatcher lookalike contest, participate in a wine tasting, observe the rubber duck regatta, and relax in the beer garden. The festival, which is held annually in late July, draws from across the region with its family-friendly, small-town fair atmosphere.

Accommodations

Choose from 10 themed bed-and-breakfast-style rooms at **The Parkview Country Inn** (103 W. 2nd St., Augusta, 606/756-2603, www.parkviewcountryinn.com, $95-145), a historic property built in the early 1800s in the heart of town. Room arrangements vary with double, queen, and king bed options, although all have their own private bath. Each room is decorated with stylish antique furniture related to its unique theme, with popular rooms including the fun Train Room, the romantic Victorian Room, and the handsome Riverboat Room. A complimentary full country breakfast is served each morning in the inn's restaurant, which also does lunch and dinner.

A popular spot for weddings, **Asbury Meadow** (3737 Asbury Rd., Augusta, 606/756-2100, www.asburymeadow.com, $90-125) is a gorgeous former plantation home in the Augusta countryside. Two guest rooms are located in the main house: one with a queen bed, twin Murphy bed, and private attached bath; the other with a king bed, twin Murphy bed, twin day bed, and private bath across the hall. A unique offering is the cottage that was once the slave quarters. With murals on the walls, a vaulted ceiling, and a soaking tub, the cottage is now a cozy hideaway, certainly much different than it was in the 1800s. A full breakfast is included with all stays.

Food

If you're in the mood for a hamburger or simple sandwich, pop into the old-fashioned **Augusta General Store** (109 Main St., Augusta, 606/756-2525, $4.99-7.99), where you can browse the shop for gifts or pick up a handful of penny candy while you wait for your food. A few simple wooden tables are located at the front of the shop. One peek at the dessert counter and you'll be having a piece of cream pie or cobbler regardless of whether you're already full.

Chandler's at the Beehive Tavern (101 W. Riverside Dr., Augusta, 606/756-2202, 4pm-9pm Thurs., 11am-9pm Fri., 11am-10pm Sat., 11am-6pm Sun. $8.95-29.95) is a local landmark. Built in the 1790s to serve as a riverside tavern, the historic building has been restored to its original character, making you feel like you've stepped back in time. The menu sticks to tried-and-true classics like catfish, chicken pot pie, and rib eye steak, but weekly specials mix things up. Service is consistently good, and it remains the local favorite.

Information and Services

The **Augusta Welcome Center** is located in an old red caboose at the intersection of Main and Riverside. Pick up a walking tour brochure and let the staff on duty inform you about what's going on in Augusta. Plan your visit in advance with the help of www.augustaky.com.

Getting There and Around

To reach Augusta from Covington (40 miles; 1 hour), travel south on the AA Highway (KY 9) for about 23 miles to the junction with KY 154, which will, after just over a mile, link you with KY 8. Travel an additional 15 miles on eastbound KY 8, which parallels the river, to make your way to Augusta. From Lexington, it's 66 miles (1 hour 40 minutes) north on U.S. 62 and KY 19. From Louisville, Cincinnati, or Indianapolis, you'll first go to Covington and then proceed from there on the AA Highway.

Continuing east on KY 8 for another 20 miles (30 minutes) will put you in Maysville. Be careful while traveling the AA Highway, which sees more than its share of accidents. The road is in good condition; speed is the main problem.

If you need to get to or from Higginsport, Ohio, or just want to go for a ride, the *Jenny Ann* ferry runs 8am-8pm daily. Foot passengers are free, but it costs $5 to take a vehicle across. Catch the ferry on Riverside Drive, just west of Main Street.

MAYSVILLE AND MASON COUNTY

Maysville is Covered Bridge Country's big city, offering visitors to this region the most selection with regard to accommodation and food. It's also centrally located, with all area attractions within an easy and scenic drive. More than a place to sleep and eat, however, Maysville has attractions of its own that deserve a bit of your attention. You'll want to set aside some time to take a stroll past churches and the courthouse, preserved row houses and renovated storefronts, as well as visit the Old Pogue Distillery, a historic site brought back to life as a craft distillery by the original founder's descendants.

◖ Kentucky Gateway Museum Center

The **Kentucky Gateway Museum Center** (215 Sutton St., Maysville, 606/564-5865, www.

© THERESA DOWELL BLACKINTON

downtown Maysville

re-creations of real places such as Princess Diana's ancestral home and the Maysville Bethel Baptist Church.

Floodwall Murals

Ten scenes relevant to the history of Maysville are illustrated on the **floodwall murals** (E. McDonald Pkwy., Maysville, www.cityof-maysville.com) along the Ohio River. The story begins with the use of the area as a hunting ground by Native Americans in the 1600s; continues with important events of the 1800s, such as the visit of the Marquis de Lafayette, the growth of the town thanks to steamboat traffic, and the role of the town in the Underground Railroad; pays tribute to the area as a prime tobacco-growing region; and salutes hometown golden girl Rosemary Clooney.

◖ Old Pogue Distillery

Nearly a century and a half after H. E. Pogue founded a distillery in Maysville and nearly eight decades after it last operated, the **Old Pogue Distillery** (716 W. 2nd St., Maysville, www.oldpogue.com) is back in the business of producing craft liquor. Using family recipes, the fifth- and sixth-generation descendants of H. E. Pogue are distilling two small-batch rye whiskeys and one small-batch 91-proof bourbon. On a one-hour tour (10am and 2pm Wed.-Sat., 2pm Sun., book online) of the distillery, you'll learn about the distilling process, visit the grain-holding and barrel-storage areas, and imbibe in the tasting room. This is a boutique distillery with minimal staff, so be sure to book ahead online so they know you're coming and so you can secure one of the 15 spots available for each tour time.

◖ Historic Old Washington

Now a historic district, **Old Washington** served as the gateway to the West to pioneers in the late 1700s, establishing itself as one of Kentucky's largest settlements during frontier days. Many significant sites and buildings have been preserved and visitors are welcome to explore them. Although a self-guided tour brochure provides brief

kygmc.org, 10am-4pm Tues.-Fri., 10am-3pm Sat., $10 adults, $2 students) is much more than your typical small-town museum. Although a significant portion of the 1881 building and its modern additions are given over to a regional history museum, the displays and artifacts are not haphazard, but are instead professionally displayed and curated to illustrate the story of Maysville and the surrounding counties from prehistoric days to the current era. On the second floor, you'll find a genealogical and historical research library that is ranked the third best in the state and houses an extraordinarily complete set of records that can help you trace your family history. The gem of the museum, however, is the Kathleen Savage Browning Miniatures Collection, which is on display in a state-of-the-art facility on the first floor. Considered one of the top miniature collections in the world, the exhibits here will take your breath away with their intricacy. You'll find tiny tables set with real bone china and Waterford crystal, a working beer tap and working musical instruments, and amazing information on 33 sites, the best way to experience Old Washington is on a guided tour with an interpreter. Tours, which are offered 11am-3pm Monday-Saturday and noon-3pm Sunday, last approximately two hours and cost $10 for adults and $4 youth 6-12. You can call in advance to reserve a spot or just show up at the **Visitors Center in Paxton Inn** (2030 Old Main St., Washington, 606/759-7411, www.washingtonky.com, 10am-4:30pm Monday-Saturday and noon-4:30pm Sunday) and hop on the next tour. Among the many sites visited on the tour are the Simon Kenton Shrine, which is located in an authentic 1790s cabin and set up like a general store the pioneer leader owned; the Harriet Beecher Stowe Slavery to Freedom Museum, which details the story of the slave auction Stowe witnessed here and later used in *Uncle Tom's Cabin;* and the Washington Post Office, which is the only working log cabin post office in the United States. A number of antique shops are also located in Old Washington.

Dover Covered Bridge

Constructed in the 1830s, **Dover Covered Bridge** has the distinction of being the oldest covered bridge in Kentucky still open to vehicle traffic and one of the oldest, accessible or not, in the state. The 61-foot-long queen-post truss bridge, which has been reinforced with iron beams, spans Lees Creek, and can be traveled by turning south off of KY 8 onto Lees Creek Road, which is just 0.4-mile east of the small town of Dover, and driving a short 0.1 mile. Dover is located between Augusta and Maysville, 7.5 miles east of Augusta and 11.5 miles west of Maysville.

Performing Arts

The fifth oldest theater in the nation still in operation, dating back to 1898, the **Washington Opera House** (116 W. 2nd St., Maysville, 606/564-3666) is the home of the **Maysville Players** (www.maysvilleplayers.com), a community theater group that packs the house with audiences from a large surrounding radius. During the nearly year-round season, the players put on five performances, ranging from kid-friendly acts like *Peter Pan* to family holiday shows to old-time favorites such as *Always, Patsy Cline.* If you can't catch a show, at least try to pop in to see the elegantly renovated historic theater. Hollywood fans will be interested to know that *Leatherheads,* the 2006 movie starring George Clooney and Renée Zellweger, premiered right here at the Washington Opera House in little ol' Maysville.

George, however, was not the first Clooney to premiere a movie in Maysville. Rosemary premiered her first motion picture, *The Stars Are Singing,* at the nearby **Russell Theatre** (9 E. 3rd St., Maysville, www.russelltheatre.org) in 1953. Opened in 1930, the theater, which was marketed as a movie palace, stood out thanks to its Spanish Colonial Revival architecture, complete with statues, gargoyles, and other over-the-top elements. Unfortunately, the theater closed as a movie house in 1983, operating in the following years as a variety of stores before being allowed to fall into disrepair. Thankfully, the community has rallied to save the theater, which is undergoing renovation. For now, you can admire the outside, but hopefully in the not-too-distant future, feature films will again be playing on the Russell Theatre's big screen.

Festivals and Events

Old Washington hosts a number of annual events, the most popular of which are the **Simon Kenton Festival,** held on the third weekend in September, and the **Frontier Christmas Festival,** held the first weekend of December. At the Simon Kenton Festival, reenactors demonstrate pioneer life, while you'll find strolling carolers and hands-on period craft activities at the Frontier Christmas Festival. Information on both events can be found at www.washingtonky.com.

Recreation

Although there's fresh air just about everywhere you turn in this part of the state, if you still need an outdoors escape, pay a visit to **Maysville-Mason County Recreation Park**

(2340 Old Main St., Maysville, 606/759-5604, www.cityofmaysville.com), a 57-acre park offering most every type of recreational activity. The park has an Olympic-size pool, golf and mini-golf courses, tennis courts, softball fields, sand volleyball court, shuffleboard and croquet areas, a walking trail, playground and picnic areas, and a fishing lake.

If you have a mind to catch one of the enormous catfish rumored to live in the Ohio River, cast a line from the fishing pier at Limestone Landing, located where McDonald Parkway and Limestone Street meet in downtown Maysville. A boat dock allows for an easy transition from on-the-water fun to downtown's shops and restaurants.

For some high-flying adventure, visit **The Big Zipper** (8157 Stonelick Rd., Maysville, 606/564-8283, www.bigzippermaysville.com), where you can soar over the area on three zip lines. Call or go online to reserve a time.

Accommodations

French Quarter Inn (25 E. McDonald Pkwy., Maysville, 606/564-8000, www.frenchquarterinn.com, $89-175) is the premier place to stay in Maysville and probably the entire river region. Each of the rooms in this four-floor hotel is richly decorated in its own individual style, but amenities such as wireless Internet, whirlpool tubs, and microwaves and refrigerators are standard throughout. Rooms facing the river have outstanding views, especially when the lit bridge is reflected in the water at night, but as a trade-off you must deal with the sometimes bed-shaking noise of the trains that pass literally right outside the window. The floodwall murals are in the parking lot of the hotel and all other sites are within easy walking distance of this downtown hotel.

Two rooms welcome guests at the **Moon River Bed and Breakfast** (320 Market St., Maysville, 606/563-8812, www.moonriverbedandbreakfast.com, $80), an 1888 row house located in the center of downtown activity. Both the Maysville Room and the Civil War Room have private bathrooms, TVs, and Internet access. A continental breakfast is served on weekdays, with a full breakfast offered on weekends.

Food

Chandlers (212 Market St., Maysville, 606/564-6385, 11am-2pm Mon.-Wed., 11am-9pm Thurs., 11am-10pm Fri.-Sat.) is one of the top dining options in Maysville, and reservations can be a good idea. Dinner entrées ($10-20) range from comfort foods like fried country ham and chicken livers to much-loved porterhouse pork chops to lobster ravioli. At lunch ($5.50-8.50), you can choose from a long list of sandwiches, accompanied by boardwalk-style fries, and salads. The atmosphere is casual, although the historic building in which Chandlers is located lends it character.

DeSha's (1168 U.S. 68, Maysville, 606/564-9275, http://deshas.com, 11am-10pm Mon.-Thurs., 11am-11pm Fri.-Sat., 11am-9pm Sun.) menu is loaded with classic American favorites, such as Southern fried chicken salad, fish and chips, a steak sandwich, and chicken fettuccini. The broad menu means almost everyone can find something they'll be happy with, and the friendly service and comfortable atmosphere make it a family favorite.

Repeat winner of the best hamburger in town award, **Delites** (222 Market St., Maysville, 606/564-7047, 7:30am-5pm Mon.-Sat.) is a diner-style restaurant that also serves gyros and Greek salads along with breakfast platters and an array of sandwiches. Rosemary Clooney is said to have loved Delites' coneys. Very little on the menu comes in at over $5, making it a great place for an inexpensive meal. Be aware that it's cash only.

In business in the same location for more than 160 years, **Hutchison's Grocery** (1201 E. 2nd St., Maysville, 606/564-3797, 9am-4pm Mon.-Fri., 9am-3pm Sat., $3.99-5.99) might look more like a place to provision your kitchen than grab a bite to eat, and really it is, but you haven't tasted country ham until you've tasted theirs. Every holiday season they send hundreds of their hams out across the nation. Luckily, you don't have to wait for Christmas to have a taste. The grocery serves up country ham and other sandwiches to go. Grab one to enjoy on a bench in town as you observe small-town life.

Information and Services

Contact the **Maysville-Mason County Convention & Visitors Bureau** (201 E. 3rd St., Maysville, 606/564-9419) with any questions you might have about visiting the area. A small section of the city's website, www.cityof-maysville.com, is dedicated to tourism.

Getting There and Around

Maysville is located about 60 miles (1 hour 20 minutes) from Covington, which you'll pass through if coming from Cincinnati or Indianapolis. From Covington, travel east on the AA Highway (KY 9) for 55 miles, then turn north on KY 10, which leads to downtown. Maysville is just over 60 miles (1.5 hours) from Lexington, the two cities directly connected by U.S. 68. To reach Maysville from Louisville (140 miles; 2.5 hours), the quickest route is through Lexington.

To travel to Augusta, which is 19 miles (30 minutes) to the east, use KY 8. To get to Vanceburg, which is 28 miles (40 minutes) to the west, use the AA Highway. Flemingsburg, which is 17 miles (25 minutes) to the south, is directly linked via KY 11.

Train aficionados should note that the **Amtrak Cardinal,** which connects Chicago and Washington DC, runs through Maysville, offering a unique way of traveling to this Kentucky town. The train serves Maysville three times a week. A schedule can be found at www.amtrak.com.

LEWIS COUNTY

Lewis County makes up the eastern boundary of this region, surrounded on both the south and the east by the Appalachian area of Kentucky, but tied to the Northern Kentucky area by the river and its covered bridge. Like the neighboring counties, Lewis County is primarily agricultural. The barns here, however, do more than hang tobacco and store other crops; they come together to form a particularly nice barn quilt trail, as well as a specialized

Patriot Trail. Vanceburg, the county seat, is a sleepy place, with a pretty riverfront park, the nation's only Union monument south of the Mason-Dixon Line that was erected by public subscription, and a quaint downtown historic district. At the foothills of the Appalachians, the landscape is rolling, the hills and valleys dotted with farms and forests, making Lewis County a lovely place to go for a drive.

Cabin Creek Covered Bridge

Like many of the other covered bridges in the area, **Cabin Creek Covered Bridge** is closed to all traffic. Built in 1867, this 114-foot-long bridge has a laminated arch design. Funding for restoration of this bridge, which has been damaged by weather and time, has been acquired, with the hopes of restoring the bridge to a condition that would allow special-event traffic to use it. The Cabin Creek Covered Bridge is located at the intersection of KY 984 and Cabin Creek Road, between Maysville and Vanceburg, the seat of Lewis County.

Lewis County Barn Quilt Trail

Barn quilts are popular throughout Kentucky. For those unfamiliar with the art form, barn quilts are painted versions of quilt squares affixed on barns. If you've driven in any rural area of the state, you've probably seen them. The **Lewis County Barn Quilt Trail** stands out, however, due to the overwhelming agricultural nature of the entire county and the ease of tracking down the quilt squares thanks to a detailed brochure that provides a map as well as information on each location. There's really no one route that will lead you past all the barn quilts unless you're willing to weave your way around the county, but there are a few roads where you'll find a concentration of the quilts. For example, six quilts, with designs ranging from a red hat girl and farmer boy to a trip-around-the-world pattern, are located along the AA Highway (KY 9) between the Mason County line and Vanceburg. A unique addition to the regular Barn Quilt Trail is the **Patriot Trail,** a collection of 11 barn quilts all located along Quicks Run Road, with patriotic

KENTUCKY'S BARN QUILTS

Quilting has a long legacy in Kentucky. From the days of the early pioneers, when women would patch together scraps of cloth to make coverings that would keep their families warm, to the present day, when art quilts decorated with such luxuries as Swarovski crystals hang in the National Quilt Museum in Paducah, quilts have found a way into the lives of Kentuckians. Decorative and functional, quilts are passed down from generation to generation, their patterns and materials telling stories. In rural areas, particularly, quilting is a way of life.

Founded in Adam County, Ohio, by Donna Sue Groves as a way of honoring her mother, a quilter, the Quilt Trail project quickly spread to surrounding communities and took off like wildfire in Kentucky, where people were eager to pay homage to the traditions and qualities that quilts symbolize. To participate in the project, people painted quilt squares with traditional quilt patterns or personalized images onto their barns. Those without barns painted them on floodwalls, other buildings, or even on freestanding pieces of wood. As you travel throughout Kentucky, the bright colors and interesting patterns of barn quilts catch your eye and lift your spirit. From east to west, you can spot the barn quilts from major highways as well as winding country roads.

More than 60 counties in Kentucky have established quilt barn trails. The size of the trails varies greatly. Some projects have dozens of participants, whereas others have only a few. Some trails are located in a concentrated area of the county, while others weave their way throughout the entire county. Some are well publicized with brochures and maps, whereas others are left for you to discover by chance. On a trip through Kentucky, you're bound to spot a number of the barns, but quilt and community arts fans may wish to plan their routes around the trails. In addition to seeing some great artwork, you'll also get to observe and enjoy rural life in Kentucky. Overview information on the Kentucky Quilt Trail project as well as an interactive map with links to individual quilt trails can be found at http://artscouncil.ky.gov.

designs and a quilt for each branch of the military. Download a brochure from www.visitlewiscountyky.com to plan your route. Be aware that the quilts are located on private property, and you should not approach them unless invited to do so. Also be careful on the winding country roads and try to find a safe place to pull over and take photos or admire the quilts rather than stopping in the middle of the road.

Information and Services

The **Vanceburg Visitors Center** (3rd and Main Sts., Vanceburg, 606/796-0238, www.visitlewiscountyky.com) is located in the George Morgan Thomas House, a bright green historic home that is worth a peek whether you need any information or not. The kind staff can suggest a place to stay or load you up with maps for the Barn Quilt Trail and a historic walking tour of Vanceburg. The visitors center is open 9am-5pm weekdays except Wednesday.

Getting There and Around

Vanceburg is about 30 miles (40 minutes) east of Maysville on the Ohio River, and can be reached by following KY 8, KY 9, or KY 10, which all come together near Vanceburg before again separating. When they do separate, stay with KY 8 to reach downtown Vanceburg.

PENDLETON COUNTY

The westernmost of the counties in Covered Bridge Country does not have a covered bridge, but it does have some of the best outdoor recreation opportunities in the area. The Licking River weaves its way through the county, offering excellent fishing holes as well as paddling opportunities.

NORTHERN KENTUCKY

© THERESA DOWELL BLACKINTON

one of many barn quilts in the region

Kincaid Lake State Park

The 183-acre lake at **Kincaid Lake State Park** (565 Kincaid Park Rd., Falmouth, 859/654-3531, http://parks.ky.gov, dawn-dusk daily, free) attract anglers thanks to its abundance of largemouth bass, channel catfish, crappie, bluegill, and sunfish. Those without a boat can rent pontoons and fishing boats as well as rowboats and pedal boats at the marina. A lakeside pool is open to the public Memorial Day-mid-August ($4 adults and youth 13 and older, $3 seniors and youth 3-12). Kincaid Lake State Park also has a nine-hole golf course and two connected hiking trails that make a 2.25-mile loop. A popular 84-site campground ($17-24) with hookups is open April-October.

Canoeing and Kayaking

The gentle Class I Middle Fork of the Licking River makes for great paddling for first-time canoers or kayakers or for those just looking for a relaxing way to spend time in the great outdoors. **Thaxton's Licking River Canoe Rental** (Cartons Camp Rd., Butler, 859/472-2000, www.paddlersinn.com, 9am-4pm Mon.-Fri., 8am-5pm Sat.-Sun.) can set you up with a canoe or kayak and shuttle you to a starting point, from which you can leisurely make your way down the river. Wildlife, including many species of birds and mammals, is often seen near the river.

Paddlers looking for an extended retreat should inquire about **Paddler's Inn** (Cartons Camp Rd., Butler, 859/472-2000, www.paddlersinn.com, $59.95-99.95), which is run by the same people as Thaxton's. The five riverside cabins are supplied with linens and towels, and have cable television, microwave and refrigerator, a deck with gas grill, and access to an outdoor hot tub. Guests are welcome to fish and are given complimentary access to canoes and kayaks.

Information and Services

Pendleton County does not have a tourism

NORTHERN KENTUCKY

bureau, but the Northern Kentucky River Region website (www.nkytourism.com) provides information on Pendleton County's attractions.

Getting There and Around

The location of Thaxton's Canoe and Paddler's Inn is very close to Northern Kentucky, just a 40-minute drive from Covington. The easiest way to get there is to take the AA Highway (KY 9) to southbound U.S. 27. The facilities are located at the U.S. 27 bridge over the Licking River. To reach the state park, you'll turn off of U.S. 27 at the Licking River onto southbound KY 177, which will end at KY 159. Turn right onto KY 159 and travel five miles to the park entrance.

If you go over the Licking River on U.S. 27 and continue south, you'll reach Falmouth, the seat of Pendleton County. There's not a lot to Falmouth, but you should be able to find something to eat there.

From Falmouth or the state park, northbound KY 159 leads to the AA Highway, from which you can access Augusta and Maysville.

ROBERTSON COUNTY

By population, Robertson County is the smallest county in Kentucky, with only around 2,000 people calling it home. Visitors shouldn't be surprised, then, that there isn't much in the way of tourist amenities. The county is, however, home to one of the region's covered bridges as well as a great state park that is both a fine place for recreation and an interesting historic site.

Johnson Creek Covered Bridge

Restored in 2007, the **Johnson Creek Covered Bridge** stretches 110 feet over the creek for which it is named. It was used from 1874 to 1966 to conduct traffic along KY 1029, but is now closed to both vehicle and pedestrian traffic. To reach this Smith-truss bridge, travel west on KY 165 for 1.9 miles from U.S. 68, then proceed north on KY 1029.

◖ Blue Licks Battlefield State Resort Park

Although most people believe the Revolutionary War ended at Yorktown, the last battle actually took place on the grounds of what is now **Blue Licks Battlefield State Resort Park** (10299 Maysville Rd., Carlisle, 859/289-5507, http://parks.ky.gov, dawn-dusk daily, free). Here, on August 19, 1782, a group of settlers led by Daniel Boone suffered a brutal defeat at the hands of loyalists and their Native American allies after chasing the enemies down following a two-day siege of their fort. The **Pioneer Museum** (9am-5pm Wed.-Sun., mid-Apr.-mid-Dec., $4 adults, $3 seniors and youth 5-12) does an excellent job of relaying the story of this oft-forgotten battle with artifacts, three-dimensional maps, and text panels. The museum then proceeds back in time through settlement and the Native American presence back to the era when mastodons and other prehistoric creatures fed at the riverside licks. A video about Daniel Boone and the Western expansion is shown downstairs, where you'll also find rotating exhibits and a diorama of what the park looked like during the age of buffalo. The museum also hosts an interesting series of activities related to the pioneer age on Friday afternoons June-September. The activities are free with admission to the museum and include making lye soap, arrows, and salt; woodworking; and cooking. A battle reenactment weekend is held annually on the August weekend closest to the actual battle date.

Although the park is making a push to highlight its historical background, it's also a popular recreational park. Blue Licks is home to a 15-acre nature preserve that protects the last known stand of Short's goldenrod in the world. Visitors are welcome to venture into the preserve via a 0.15-mile hiking trail that follows an old buffalo trace, but are asked not to venture off-trail. Five additional trails, ranging in length from 0.5 mile to 2.5 miles, are open to those looking to do more hiking. During the summer, free one-hour guided battlefield walks are also offered. With the Licking River surrounding Blue Licks on three sides, water is another big focus of activity. A boat ramp is available for those with their own boat. The calm Licking River makes for excellent canoeing, and in the summer months a 2.5-hour guided morning canoe trip ($15, register at Pioneer Museum) is run by the park staff on Tuesday, Thursday, and Saturday mornings, weather permitting. A pool, mini-golf course, ball field, and playground are also available for public use.

Accommodations and Food

A variety of accommodation options are available at **Blue Licks Battlefield State Resort Park** (Hwy. 68, Mt. Olivet, 859/289-5507, http://parks.ky.gov). The 32-room lodge ($109.95) offers standard motel-style rooms with two double beds or one king bed. Each room has a private balcony or patio. Two two-bedroom cottages ($179.95) with views of the Licking River are also available. A 51-site campground ($17-23) with full hookups and restroom and shower facilities is open April-October. The campground is often full in the summer.

Southern favorites like country ham and fried catfish are served at the casual **Hidden Waters Restaurant** (8am-8pm Sun.-Thurs., 8am-9pm Fri.-Sat., $5.99-11.99), which is located in the lodge. A seafood buffet ($17.99) is offered on the first Friday of every month.

Getting There and Around

Robertson County is located south of Mason County. U.S. 68 is the county's main thoroughfare, directly connecting the state park with Maysville, 25 miles (30 minutes) to the northwest, and Lexington, 42 miles (1 hour) to the southeast.

FLEMING COUNTY

For covered bridge lovers, Fleming County is at the center of Kentucky's covered bridge universe. Here you'll find 3 of the state's 13 and this region's 8 covered bridges, thus gaining Fleming County the title of Covered Bridge Capital of Kentucky. Beyond the bridges, there's not a whole lot to attract attention in the area, at least outside of Labor Day weekend, when it plays host to a fantastic bluegrass festival. It's pleasant Sunday driving country, however, as you'll get to enjoy the covered bridges, acres of farm land, and barn quilts.

◖ Covered Bridges

The **Goddard White Covered Bridge** is the most northern of Fleming County's three bridges and the most photographed. Open to both vehicle and pedestrian traffic, this attractive bridge over Sand Lick Creek has been reconstructed to make it traffic-worthy. Bridge aficionados will be interested to know that the Goddard White Bridge, which dates back to the 1820s, is the only remaining Ithiel Town lattice design in the state. For those not up on bridge architecture, this means that a lattice is made using small planks placed close together on a diagonal. Interestingly, wooden pegs instead of nails join the timbers. Located on KY 32, nine miles southeast of Flemingsburg and just north of Goddard, this bridge is particularly photogenic thanks to a white country church that fits into the frame with the bridge.

Fleming County's two other covered bridges are no longer in use, but stand as reminders of a time long gone. **Ringo's Mill Covered Bridge** is an 86-foot bridge crossing the Fox Creek. This Burr truss bridge was built in the late 1860s. Ringo's Mill Covered Bridge is located at the intersection of KY 158 and Rawlings Road. Just a bit east, **Grange City Covered Bridge** is the same length as Ringo's Mill and crosses the same creek. It was also constructed in the same style, just after Ringo's Mill was completed. Grange City Covered Bridge is located on KY 111, a tad north of Grange City.

Fleming County Covered Bridge Museum

A bit misnamed, the **Fleming County Covered Bridge Museum** (119 E. Water St., Flemingsburg, 606/845-6224, 10am-4pm Wed., noon-4pm Sat., Mar.-Dec., free) is

© THERESA DOWELL BLACKINTON

The Goddard White Covered Bridge remains in use.

dedicated not to covered bridges (though they're not ignored), but to the history of the region, displaying artifacts related to the growth and development of Fleming County. A visit to the museum is a bit like rifling through your grandmother's attic, as you'll find all sorts of mementos donated by local residents.

Mandolin Farm Bluegrass Festival

For three days each year, the Thursday through Sunday of Labor Day weekend, the high lonesome sound of bluegrass draws fans to Fleming County for the **Mandolin Farm Bluegrass Festival** (387 Owens Lane, Flemingsburg, 606/845-3693). An impressive lineup of bluegrass bands keeps the music going for about 12 hours each day, and jam sessions extend long into the night. Daily passes cost $15 for Thursday and $30 for Friday and Saturday. A three-day pass is $65 if purchased before August

1, $75 if purchased after. For an additional $75, you can bring your RV and set up camp at the farm for the entire week of the festival.

Information and Services

The **Fleming County Chamber of Commerce** (116 S. Main Cross St., Flemingsburg, 606/845-1223, www.flemingkychamber.com) handles visitor inquiries and dedicates a section of their website to tourism.

Getting There and Around

Flemingsburg is the seat of Fleming County and a good starting point for any forays into the countryside. Flemingsburg is 21 miles (35 minutes) north of I-64, where it passes through Morehead. Exit 137 will put you on KY 32, which you can follow westbound to Flemingsburg. From Maysville, Flemingsburg is 17 miles (25 minutes) south on KY 11.

NORTHERN KENTUCKY

APPALACHIA

Go ahead and throw out everything you think you know about Appalachia (which, by the way, is pronounced App-a-LATCH-uh). Clear your mind of *Dateline* specials, movies, and stereotypes. Approach Appalachia with an open mind, and let this land of both immense beauty and terrible hardship reveal itself to you in its own way. Appalachia, after all, is known for doing things its own way.

The Appalachian region of Kentucky is large and it is not homogeneous, but there are certain characteristics that define it north to south, east to west. What ties it together is a pioneering spirit, a respect for tradition, hardiness in the face of hardship, and a creative culture. This is the land of Daniel Boone, the place where European settlers first entered the state and opened the West. This is coal country, where generations of men have spent their lives toiling in mines and now stand ready to defend this way of life against any threat. This is where you'll find some of the oldest mountains in the world, mountains that are so pretty that they can make you cry and so unforgiving—so impossible to farm, so vulnerable to floods—that they can bring you to your knees. This is a place of music and art, where country music stars are born.

To visit Appalachia, you need to be prepared to go slowly. People here like to talk, and to sit and chat is as much of an experience as touring a coal mine or seeing Loretta Lynn's birthplace. Many residents of Appalachia come from families who have lived in this area since before Kentucky was a state. Many have never left. Others left but have since come back.

© THERESA DOWELL BLACKINTON

APPALACHIA

HIGHLIGHTS

◖ **Butcher Hollow:** The lyrics of Loretta Lynn's "Coal Miner's Daughter" jump to life on a visit to the small cabin where she was born. Her brother Herman leads tours, pointing out family photos and personal belongings (page 245).

◖ **Jenny Wiley State Resort Park:** See a professional theater performance under the stars and surrounded by mountains, then rise early in the morning to take part in an elk tour (page 249).

◖ **Portal 31 Underground Mine:** Ride a coal train into a mine to discover what working in the coal mines in the company town of Lynch was like. Follow up the trip with a visit to the Kentucky Coal Miner's Museum (page 259).

◖ **Cumberland Gap National Historical Park:** Hike along the same path used by Daniel Boone as he led settlers into Kentucky and visit the Hensley Settlement, where the homesteading lifestyle was carried into the 20th century (page 264).

◖ **Cumberland Falls State Resort Park:** Find out what a moonbow is at Cumberland Falls, known as the Niagara of the South (page 271).

◖ **Barthell Coal Mining Camp:** This exact re-creation of a coal camp lets you step into the mine where residents worked, as well as into their homes, school, general store, barber's shop, and doctor's office (page 273).

◖ **Studio Artists of Berea:** Watch renowned artists work in mediums ranging from glass to fiber in a progressive town designated the Folk Art Capital of Kentucky (page 277).

◖ **Renfro Valley Entertainment Center:** You can't help but tap your toes to the old-

fashioned entertainment of a barn jamboree, complete with country, gospel, and bluegrass music and a bit of comedy thrown in for good measure (page 283).

◖ **Red River Gorge Geological Area:** Site of the largest collection of natural arches east of the Rocky Mountains, Red River Gorge is a playground for hikers, rock climbers, paddlers, and photographers (page 292).

LOOK FOR ◖ TO FIND RECOMMENDED SIGHTS, ACTIVITIES, DINING, AND LODGING.

They have stories to tell. If you hurry, you'll miss them. If you hurry, you might also miss hearing musicians pickin' on the porch without a bit of formal training, but with more talent than many of today's stars. If you hurry, you won't be able to detour off of U.S. 23, a

modern four-lane road, onto a country road cutting through a holler. To see elk grazing in the morning mist or to watch an artisan turn a pot, you'll need patience.

What you see in Appalachia will linger with you. Not all of it is pretty—stripped mountains, derelict trailers, and illegal dumping, for instance—but this ugliness is the exception and not the rule. More often than not, what you'll find is beauty—in places, in songs, in works of art, and especially in people. People here, like people everywhere, are striving for a better future, and here in Appalachia they're moving forward with a faith that can literally move mountains.

PLANNING YOUR TIME

Kentucky's Appalachian region is big, encompassing everything east of I-75 and south of I-64. With no interstates running through the region, your fastest roads are U.S. highways, although more often than not you'll be on state highways or country roads. You will, at least once, end up behind a coal truck on a road that doesn't have a place to pass. In short, traveling through Eastern Kentucky is not something that can be done quickly. It's also not something that should be done quickly. To cover the entire region, you need a minimum of three weeks. Since traveling for that amount of time isn't an option for most people, the best thing to do is to break Appalachia up into smaller sections.

The Country Music Highway region, which encompasses the sights down the far eastern part of the state along U.S. 23, is a good introduction to the area. To see it from one end to the other, give yourself at least four days. Even then you'll have to be choosy about your time, and you won't be able to venture too far into the hollers. If at all possible, try to time your trip so that you can catch a show at the Paramount Arts Center or Mountain Arts Center, enjoy pickin' on the porch at the U.S. 23 Country Music Highway Museum, and watch a play at Jenny Wiley Theatre. Although you have hotel options in all the towns along the route, you could also plan your overnights so that you're in a different park each night—Greenbo Lake State Resort Park, Jenny Wiley State Resort Park, and Breaks Interstate Park.

Southern Appalachia and the Big South Fork region fit together nicely for a week's adventure. Sites here are unique, with opportunities to walk in Daniel Boone's footsteps, descend into a coal mine, overnight at a coal camp, watch for black bears, and witness a moonbow.

Berea is a great weekend destination, and it's easy enough to slip away one night to enjoy a show at Renfro Valley. Red River Gorge is another fabulous weekend spot, although if you're big into the outdoors, you'll definitely want to give yourself longer. Many cabins can be rented by the week, which makes for a relaxing vacation.

Spring and fall are wonderful times to visit this region. The fall display of leaves draws big crowds, but spring is actually just as beautiful. The mountains are full of redbuds and dogwoods, which impart the landscape with color. The mountains don't really provide much relief in the summer, and it's nearly as hot and humid in Appalachia as it is anywhere else. This, however, is when you'll find most activities happening, and it's probably the busiest time of year. Winter is usually mild in Appalachia, but just a little snow on mountain roads can be difficult for unfamiliar drivers, so be careful if you decide to travel to this area then. Keep alert of weather conditions year-round, especially if you're near creeks or rivers, as flooding is not uncommon in Appalachia.

Accommodation options are present but not abundant in much of Appalachia, so you should try to book in advance if possible. The parks are especially likely to be full in the summer and on weekends, and during festivals, concerts, and events, other hotels may book up as well.

For trip planning purposes, www.tourseky. com is a valuable resource. This organization promotes the entire region and is a good place to get an overview of area offerings.

APPALACHIA

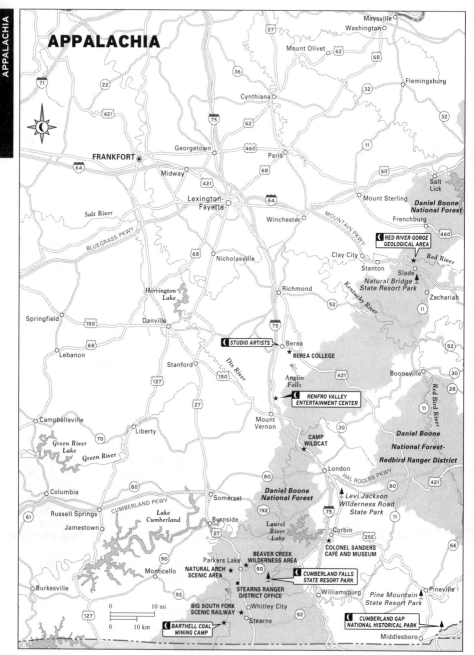

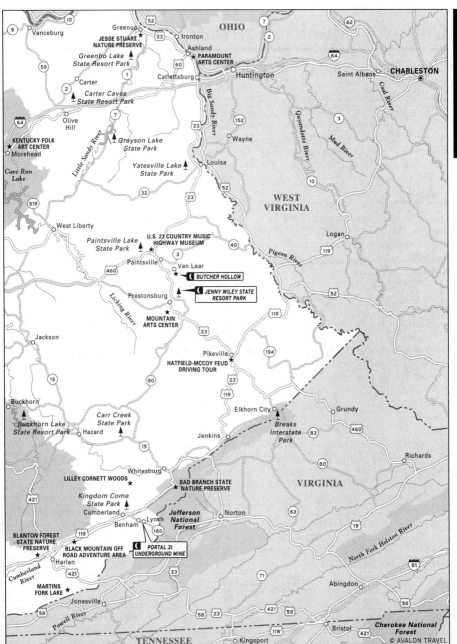

© AVALON TRAVEL

Country Music Highway

The Country Music Highway, labeled as U.S. 23 on your map, traces a path through eight counties in far Eastern Kentucky from which a number of big names in country music have emerged. Making the list are Billy Ray Cyrus, Naomi and Wynonna Judd, Keith Whitley, Ricky Skaggs, Tom T. Hall, Loretta Lynn, Crystal Gayle, Hylo Brown, Rebecca Lynn Howard, Dwight Yoakum, Charlie Gearheart, Patty Loveless, and Gary Stewart. Roadside signs announce the musicians that each county and town can claim as you pass through. Attractions based around this music history—including Loretta Lynn's birthplace, a museum, and a number of performing arts centers—are located down the highway, but those who think the Country Music Highway is all about music will be disappointed. A trip along the highway, which has been designated a national scenic byway, is less about the specific musicians and music than it is about the Appalachian way of life that has influenced all of them. You'll have a chance to visit mountain homesteads, see old coal mining towns as well as mines still in operation, and soak in the beauty of the mountains. Although many people expect that this trip will be entirely rural in nature, the towns along the Country Music Highway are well developed, and U.S. 23 itself is a major thoroughfare that is four lanes wide in many places. Hollers and cricks (that's hollows and creeks to you city folk) are never far away, however, and part of the pleasure of traveling the Country Music Highway is getting off of it every once in a while.

GREENUP COUNTY

The northern terminus of the Country Music Highway is located in Greenup County, which snuggles up against the Ohio River. Here there are more foothills than mountains, and the land is more suited for agriculture, so you might find a produce stand in the summer or spot a field of bright green burley tobacco. Recreation is the number one reason for visiting Greenup County, which is the birthplace of Billy Ray Cyrus, owner of one achy breaky heart, which could possibly be attributed to the recent antics of his daughter Miley.

Greenbo Lake State Resort Park

Fishing and hiking make up the heart of the action at **Greenbo Lake State Resort Park** (965 Lodge Rd., Greenup, 606/473-7324, http://parks.ky.gov, daylight-dark daily, free). Stocked with a wide variety of fish, Greenbo Lake holds two state records for largemouth bass. A launch is available for those with their own boat, while the marina rents pontoons, motorboats, canoes, and pedal boats. A fishing pier is open to those who prefer to cast from shore. Although swimming is not allowed in the lake, a 10-acre scuba area ($12) opened in July 2013, allowing certified divers to explore the lake 10am-6pm April-October.

In the area surrounding the lake, 25 miles of trails draw hikers, bikers, and horseback riders. The shortest trail, the one-mile Fern Valley Loop, is an interpretive trail with 16 information stations located along the path. During wildflower season, the seven-mile Michael Tygart Loop Trail is a good choice, as the plant life is especially rich along it.

History buffs will be interested in visiting the 1850s iron furnace, the one-room schoolhouse that was in use 1926-1955, and the cemetery located on the grounds of the park. A pool with slide and water features for kids is open to the public and can get busy on hot summer days.

Covered Bridges

Greenup County can claim 2 of Kentucky's 13 covered bridges. **Bennett's Mill Covered Bridge** (103 Bennett's Mill, South Shore) dates to 1855, but was restored in 2003, at which time it was raised two feet due to increasing flood levels. Crossing Tygart Creek, Bennett's Mill Covered Bridge is thought to be the oldest and longest (195 feet) single-span covered bridge open to traffic in the world. Crossing the Little Sandy River, the **Oldtown Covered Bridge** (KY 1 near Frazer Branch Rd.) was built in 1880 and restored in 1993, but it no longer accommodates vehicle traffic. You don't have to be a bridge geek to notice the differences between Greenup County's two bridges. Oldtown Covered Bridge is not a single-span bridge, but instead has a center stone support. The facades are also noticeably different.

Recreation
The **Jesse Stuart Nature Preserve** (W. Hollow Rd., Greenup, 502/573-2886, www. naturepreserves.ky.gov) protects 714 acres of the hills and hollows where author Jesse Stuart (1906-1984) lived and found the inspiration for his poems, novels, and short stories. Three miles of trails are open to hikers, birders, and wildlife-watchers. Hikers will be treated to views of the Ohio and Little Sandy Rivers as well as surrounding farmland. The trails also pass a few old buildings that remain on the property.

Accommodations and Food
Most overnight visitors to Greenup County take their meals and bed down at Greenbo Lake State Resort Park or head to nearby Ashland. At the state park, the **Jesse Stuart Lodge** (965 Lodge Rd., Greenup, 606/473-7324, http://parks.ky.gov, $109.95) is a pretty fieldstone building that has 36 rooms on three levels. Some have partial lake views, and all have private patios or balconies. Rooms, which are sufficient but dated, have two double beds and amenities that include wireless Internet. The lodge, which is named for Poet Laureate and Greenup County native Jesse Stuart, has a library stocked with his works and related memorabilia.

The state park's **campground** (965 Lodge Rd., Greenup, 606/473-7324, http://parks. ky.gov, mid-Mar.-mid-Nov., $15-36) has 58 sites that are RV-ready and 35 primitive sites. Two comfort stations with restrooms and showers and a grocery are open to campers.

Anglers Cove Restaurant (965 Lodge Rd., Greenup, 606/473-7324, http://parks.ky.gov, breakfast 7am-10am daily, lunch 11:30am-3pm daily, dinner 5pm-8pm daily, $5.95-13.95) is located in the state park's lodge and serves standard park restaurant fare.

Information and Services
If you need assistance in planning a trip to this area, contact the **Greenup County Tourism Commission** (100 McConnell House Dr., Wurtland, 606/834-0007, www.tourgreenup-county.com).

Getting There and Around
Greenup County is located in the northeastern corner of the state along the Ohio River, 120 miles from Lexington and 190 miles from Louisville. The towns of Greenup and Wurtland both lie on U.S. 23, with Greenup 13 miles (20 minutes) north of Ashland, and Wurtland 10 miles (15 minutes) north of Ashland. To reach Greenbo Lake from I-64, take Exit 172, and then follow northbound KY 1 for 15 miles.

ASHLAND
On the bank of the Ohio River, Ashland is part of a tristate region that includes Ironton, Ohio, and Huntington, West Virginia. The river has always been central to life here, with the coal industry and other companies that rely on riverboat transportation making it one of the biggest inland ports in the nation. Much more industrial than other towns on the Country Music Highway, with refining plants and steel production plants, Ashland is the economic engine of the area. It is still, however, an attractive town, with beautiful Central Park, an active historic center, and strong cultural offerings. Ashland's contribution to the region's country music heritage is mother-daughter duo Naomi and Wynonna Judd, who, along with Ashley Judd, maintain strong ties to the area.

APPALACHIA

© THERESA DOWELL BLACKINTON

Paramount Arts Center

Paramount Arts Center

Built in the 1930s by Paramount Studios to exclusively show their talking pictures, the **Paramount Arts Center** (1300 Winchester Ave., 696/324-3175, www.paramountartscenter.com) is a glorious tribute to the past. Originally, Paramount planned to build one such theater in every state, but the Depression caused only a portion of the theaters to be built, and today an even smaller number remain. Designed in the art deco style of the day, the restored Paramount features brass chandeliers, a ceiling painted with Aztec and Indian designs, an Egyptian design over the stage, murals on the walls, and other unique design elements that have long since been eliminated from most buildings. Today, the Paramount does show a classic film series, but the center is primarily dedicated to the performing arts. On the schedule, you'll find Broadway shows, headliner acts from all genres, and symphony and ballet performances. During business hours (9am-4pm Mon.-Fri.), you can ask at the box office to be let in for a peek at the theater.

Highlands Museum & Discovery Center

The **Highlands Museum & Discovery Center** (1620 Winchester Ave., 606/329-8888, www.highlandsmuseum.com, 10am-4pm Wed.-Fri., 10am-6pm Sat., $6.50 adults, $5 seniors and youth 2-18) has three distinct sections, with exhibits that will appeal to all ages. The History and Heritage section focuses on history with a local angle. Exhibits touch on archaeology and Native American use of the area, war, and education and medicine in past centuries. A second area is dedicated to the musical history of the region, introducing some of the most well-known stars from along the Country Music Highway, with a special focus on the Judd and Cyrus families. Visitors are invited to show off their own musical talents in the karaoke corner. The third part of the museum, the Discovery Center, is tailored to the younger crowd, with hands-on activities that allow them to fly a plane at a simulation station, navigate a towboat, climb around a tree house, crawl into a cave, and play with games, puzzles, and puppets.

Jesse Stuart Foundation

The **Jesse Stuart Foundation** (1645 Winchester Ave., 606/326-2667, www.jsfbooks.com, 9am-5pm Mon.-Fri.) strives to protect and promote the legacy of local author and Poet Laureate Jesse Stuart (1906-1984), who is most noted for the way in which he chronicled rural Appalachian life in his writings. The foundation prints and publishes his work and the work of other regional writers, and sells both used copies of Stuart's work and collector's items such as first editions and signed copies. A small gallery hosts exhibits related to Stuart and the themes on which he focused.

Historical Tour

Settled as early as 1786, Ashland has a long and interesting history thanks to its location on the Ohio River. A two-mile walking or driving tour allows visitors to get a peek at that history through stops at homes, businesses, and churches around town. A free brochure available from the visitors center provides details on the buildings, which all have, in some way, contributed to the history and culture of Ashland. The tour begins at Ashland's lovely **Central Park,** a 47-acre oasis in the heart of town, and ends at the Paramount Theatre. From there, you'd be well served by walking on down to the river to view the **floodwall murals** that depict scenes from Ashland's history.

Art Galleries

Ashland hosts a **First Friday Gallery Walk** each month during which downtown galleries stay open late (5pm-9pm) to introduce patrons to their art. At the center of the walk is the **Pendleton Art Center** (1537 Winchester Ave., 606/920-9863, www.pendletonartcenter.com), which houses the studios of about 20 different local artists who work in genres from watercolor to woodworking, printmaking to pottery. Hours for each studio vary. Check online for information about each artist. Additional downtown events, such as live music or classic car drive-ins, often occur simultaneously with the gallery walk.

Festivals and Events

Two annual events, one in mid-summer and one in mid-winter, anchor Ashland's calendar of events. July's **Summer Motion** (http://beta.summermotion.com) takes place over Independence Day weekend, with four days of concerts by country and rock performers, including some of national note. Other festival highlights include a 10K race, beauty pageant, car show, and arts and crafts festival. The event ends with fireworks over the river. For the winter holidays, Ashland glows, thanks to the **Winter Wonderland of Lights Festival** (www.winterwonderlandoflights.com). During this festival, which begins the week before Thanksgiving and extends through New Year's Day, Central Park is lit up with more than 60 light displays, and homes and businesses add to the festivities by taking part in a decorating contest. On weekends, a toy train takes boys and girls to visit with Santa, and a parade is held during the opening week.

Accommodations

Multiple chain hotels are located in Ashland. Among the best are the **Holiday Inn Express** (13131 Slone Ct., 606/929-1720, www.hiexpress.com, $79-89) and the **Hampton Inn** (1321 Cannonsburg Rd., 606/928-2888, www.hamptoninn.com, $105). Both have good-quality rooms, free wireless Internet access, and complimentary hot breakfast.

Food

Enjoy lunch while surrounded by interesting artwork at **Café Zeal** (1436 Winchester Ave., 606/324-8565, www.discoverzeal.com, 11am-3pm Tues.-Fri., $6.50-7.50), which is located in the Frame Up Gallery. The café offers fresh, tasty sandwiches, like turkey with honey-drizzled apples or a vegetable sandwich with hummus. Homemade desserts include cheesecake, Italian crème cake, and brownies. The café also serves a full list of coffee drinks.

For a breakfast, lunch, or dinner of comfort-food favorites, give **The Lamp Post Café** (1450 Greenup Ave., 606/325-5283, 7am-9pm daily, $4-20) a try. Stuffed French toast and biscuits and gravy are popular breakfast picks. For dinner, try the smoked meatloaf. The enormous desserts are also worth ordering.

If it's a burger you're after, then **Fat Patty's** (1442 Winchester Ave., 606/325-7287, www.fatpattysonline.com, 11am-1am Mon.-Sat., noon-1am Sun., $2.99-12.19) is your place. Although enormous hamburgers are definitely the house special, other bar-type food, including wings, sandwiches, and salads, are on the menu.

Information and Services

The friendly folks at the **Ashland Area Convention & Visitors Bureau** (1509 Winchester Ave., 606/329-1007, www.visitashlandky.com, 9am-5pm Mon.-Fri.) are happy to help in whatever way they can. Maps and brochures are, of course, available in the office.

Getting There and Around

Ashland sits about as far east as you can go in Kentucky, directly on the Ohio River border. Located just north of I-64 on U.S. 23, Ashland is the first place you encounter if you enter Kentucky from the east. It is 120 miles (2 hours) from Lexington, 190 miles (3 hours) from Louisville, 130 miles (2.75 hours) from Covington, and 375 miles (5.75 hours) from Paducah and Kentucky's western border. From eastbound I-64, take Exit 181 to follow eastbound U.S. 60 into Ashland. From westbound I-64, take Exit 191 to enter Ashland via northbound U.S. 23. To continue along the Country Music Highway, it's as easy as heading north on U.S. 23 to Greenup County or south toward Paintsville (60 miles; 1 hour 10 minutes), Prestonsburg (70 miles; 1 hour 20 minutes), and Pikeville (95 miles; 2 hours).

Although most people arrive in Ashland by car, you could also take the train. The **Amtrak Cardinal** stops in Ashland as it travels between Chicago and New York on Wednesday, Friday, and Sunday. The train station (99 15th St.) does not have a ticket counter, so you need to arrange your fare in advance (800/872-7245, www.amtrak.com). **Greyhound** (www.greyhound.com) also services Ashland, leaving from the same transportation terminal as Amtrak.

LAWRENCE COUNTY

A quiet place on the eastern Kentucky border, Lawrence County attracts naturalists with its lake and its hunting opportunities. Beyond that, there's not a whole lot for outsiders to do, although geography buffs may want to drive into the town of Louisa to see where the Tug and Levisa Rivers converge to form the Big Sandy River. Cross over the rivers, and you'll find yourself in West Virginia.

Yatesville Lake State Park

Yatesville Lake State Park (KY 1185, Louisa, 606/673-1492, http://parks.ky.gov, daylight-dark daily, free) offers recreation activities both on the water and on the surrounding shores. The long, narrow lake, which ranges from 1,700 to 2,250 acres at winter and summer pool, respectively, is good for fishing as well as pleasure boating. The marina, which has 140 boat slips, rents pontoons and jon boats and

sells all the supplies you need for a day on the lake. Shoreline fishing is also possible, with an ADA-accessible jetty opening the sport to everyone. An 18-hole golf course challenges players with its rolling terrain. A mini-golf course is also on-site. The **campground** (mid-Mar.-mid-Nov., $14-23) is especially nice. Twenty-seven sites are designated for RVs, with some of the sites situated so as to allow side-by-side RV camping. An additional 20 sites are designated for tent campers; 16 sites are meant to be accessed by boat and 4 by foot. These primitive sites are located in wooded areas with nice views and a secluded feel. Multiple nature trails begin in the campground and weave their way toward and around the lake.

Information and Services

If you'd like more information on Lawrence County, visit the website of the **Lawrence County Tourism Commission** (606/638-4102, www.lawrencecokytourism.com).

Getting There and Around

Yatesville Lake and the town of Louisa are both situated just off of U.S. 23, Yatesville Lake to the west and Louisa to the east. Both are about 30 miles (40 minutes) south of Ashland and 30 miles (40 minutes) north of Paintsville on U.S. 23.

PAINTSVILLE AND JOHNSON COUNTY

Johnson County is home to one of the most frequented sites on the Country Music Highway: Loretta Lynn's home in Butcher Hollow. The opportunity to tour the cabin where she was born is a good reason to come to the area, but there's plenty to keep you here once you arrive. The selection of attractions in Paintsville is the most diverse and interesting on the Country Music Highway and provides the best look at various aspects of Appalachian life. In addition to visiting the county's attractions, you should also schedule some time to poke around downtown Paintsville. Although Walmart and Lowe's drove business out of downtown in the 1990s, a Main Street program is bringing life back to the district's historic buildings. Be sure to check out the **Mayo Mansion and Church,** built in the early 1900s by entrepreneur John C. C. Mayo, one of the first people to recognize the potential for mining in the area.

Mountain HomePlace

For a sense of Appalachian life in the 19th century, visit **Mountain HomePlace** (KY 2275, Staffordsville, 606/297-1850, www.visitpaints-villeky.com/homeplace, 9am-5pm Mon.-Sat., noon-5pm Sun. Apr.-Oct., $6 adults, $5 seniors, $4 youth), a working 1850s farm. Tours begin with a 15-minute movie narrated by local Richard Thomas, better known as John-Boy from *The Waltons* television show, which presents a picture of mountain life. Costumed tour guides then lead visitors through the home-place, which is composed of authentic buildings that were originally located throughout the region. Visitors will get to examine a double-crib barn, saying hello to the donkeys, miniature horses, goats, and sheep that live nearby; sit in the pews, at least one of which dates to 1851, at Fishtrap Church; review the lessons written up on the original blackboard at the one-room McKenzie School, which was built with logs brought by the students; poke around a saddlebag-style cabin furnished with period pieces; and take a peek inside a blacksmith's shop. The length of the tour depends on the interest of the audience. In the fall, Mountain HomePlace sponsors Heritage Days, when you can witness interpreters perform such tasks as making sorghum or crushing wheat.

U.S. 23 Country Music Highway Museum

The **U.S. 23 Country Music Highway Museum** (100 Staves Branch, Paintsville, 606/297-1469, www.us23countrymusichwymuseum.com, 9am-5pm Mon.-Sat., $3 adults, $2 youth) honors the musicians who call the hills and hollows of Eastern Kentucky home. Twelve musicians—Billy Ray Cyrus, Patty Loveless, Dwight Yoakum, Hylo Brown, the Judds, Ricky Skaggs, Gary Stewart, Crystal Gayle, Tom T. Hall, Loretta Lynn, Keith Whitley,

and Rebecca Lynn Howard—are specifically addressed, each receiving their own exhibition case with memorabilia from their lives and careers. A short film shows an interview with Loretta Lynn about the film *Coal Miner's Daughter* and her life. If you're in town on Thursday evening, be sure to pop inside for Pickin' on the Porch, which actually takes place in the reception hall. The event, which draws a couple of hundred people each week, is open mic, with those wishing to perform asked to sign up as they arrive. Maybe you'll see the next star to come from the Country Music Highway.

Paintsville Lake State Park

Paintsville Lake is the premier lake destination in Eastern Kentucky. At 1,139 acres, Paintsville Lake, which is noticeably wider than the other mountain lakes, offers plenty of space for fishing as well as skiing, tubing, swimming, and even houseboating. **Paintsville Lake State Park** (1551 KY 2275, Staffordsville, 606/297-8486, http://parks.ky.gov, daylight-dark daily, free) is a good place to begin your lake visit. From the marina, you can launch your own boat or rent a whole range of watercraft—pedal boats, fishing boats, pontoon boats, and house-boats. Among the fish stocked in the lake by the Kentucky Department of Fish and Wildlife are largemouth and smallmouth bass, crappie, channel catfish, sunfish, trout, and walleye.

◖ Butcher Hollow

Lots of coal miners have had daughters, but there's only one Coal Miner's Daughter— Loretta Lynn—and there's only one place that can claim her as their own: Butcher Hollow. This hollow, named for the family's ancestors, is no more than a sliver of land surrounded by mountains, accessed only by dirt path at the time when Lynn lived there. Today, a rough road leads back to the four-room cabin where Loretta, her younger sister Crystal Gayle, and six other siblings were born and raised. This coal mining family faced plenty of hard times, but they also found joy, particularly in music. Fans of Loretta Lynn and Crystal Gayle or those simply curious about

Butcher Hollow, birthplace of Loretta Lynn

© THERESA DOWELL BLACKINTON

life in one of Eastern Kentucky's hollows are invited to tour the home, which is furnished with family pieces and decorated with family photos. The tours are led by Herman Webb, Loretta's younger brother, who loves to share stories about his life and family. To arrange a tour ($5), stop in at **Webb's General Store** (1917 Millers Creek, Van Lear, 606/789-3397, 10am-5pm Mon.-Sat., noon-5pm Sun.), which is owned by Herman and run by his daughter Madonna. The General Store, which dates back to 1909 and was the company store of the coal operation that employed the people of Butcher's Hollow and surrounding areas, is worth a peek itself. You'll find both practical grocery and home items as well as Loretta Lynn memorabilia in the store. It's best to call ahead to make sure Herman is available. They'll give you directions to the house at the store.

Coal Miners Museum

The Van Lear Historical Society has converted the former headquarters of the Consolidated Coal Company into the **Coal Miners Museum**

(78 Miller's Creek Rd., Van Lear, 606/789-8540, noon-5pm Mon.-Sat., $5 adults, $4 seniors, $2.50 youth 6-10). As one would expect, the museum contains many artifacts directly related to coal mining, but it also has plenty of exhibits that go beyond life in the mines to the daily life of the miners and their families. One room is still set up as the office of the company doctor, while another represents a classroom and is complete with old cheerleading uniforms and coal company baseball team uniforms. The museum, which preserves a unique moment in history unimaginable to many people today, is entirely volunteer-run, and visitors are led through the museum by a volunteer guide with expert knowledge of the area's history.

Festivals and Events

The lack of orchards in Eastern Kentucky has not stopped Paintsville from hosting the **Kentucky Apple Festival** (www.kyapplefest. org) on the first Saturday of October each year since 1962. Events actually unfold all week, and include pageants, an arts and crafts fair,

© THERESA DOWELL BLACKINTON

Coal Miners Museum in Van Lear

a spelling bee, karaoke, live music, clogging and square dancing, and a parade. The Apple Festival is a homecoming of sorts, with people from all over the country returning home, although visitors without the first connection to Paintsville or Johnson County are just as welcome.

Recreation

You might not expect golf to be popular, or even possible, in such a mountainous region, but Eastern Kentuckians love the game as much as anyone else, and Paintsville, which is flatter than many of the towns to the south, is as good a place as any to play a round. The 18-hole **Paintsville Golf Course** (2960 Country Club Rd., 606/789-4234, www.paintsvillegolf-course.com) features a hilly front nine and a flatter back nine with water hazards on nearly every hole. On two holes, you must actually drive your ball over the Big Sandy River, and then get yourself across via a swinging bridge. Be sure to stop into the clubhouse, which was built of cut stone by the WPA in 1939.

In June 2013, the first 18 miles of the **Dawkins Line Rail Trail** (http://parks.ky.gov) opened, with a remaining 18 mile-stretch still under work. Following an old railroad bed, the trail is open to hikers, bikers, and horseback riders and covers 24 trestles and the 662-foot-long Gun Creek Tunnel. One end is located at Hager Hill in Johnson County; the other end is at Royalton in Magoffin County, which is to the west.

Accommodations

The **Ramada Inn** (624 James S. Trimble Blvd., Paintsville, 606/789-4242, www.ramadapa-intsville.com, $84), a locally owned and operated hotel, is not your typical Ramada. Although the hotel offers the well-maintained rooms you expect with comfy beds and all the amenities (including free wireless Internet), its styling is atypical. Rooms overlook an indoor courtyard area with fountains, plantings, a gazebo, and spaces large enough to host a prom. Guests really enjoy the pool, which is large and has both indoor and outdoor sections and a spa.

A full-service restaurant is open year-round, while a snack bar offers additional options during the high season.

Paintsville Lake State Park (KY 2275, Staffordsville, 606/297-8486, http://parks. ky.gov) operates a very popular **campground** ($21-31) right on the shores of the lake. RVs can choose from 32 sites, some of which are pull-through, and all of which have full hookups and large pads. Tent campers will like the 10 primitive campsites set off in a wooded area but still convenient to the showers and restrooms.

Food

Floaters Restaurant (1581 KY 2275, Staffordsville, 606/297-5253, 9am-7pm Tues.-Fri., 9am-9pm Sat.-Sun., $5.95-8.95) has a can't-be-beat location at Paintsville Lake Marina, with outdoor tables literally on the water's edge at this casual-as-can-be eatery. Order a flaky and light fish sandwich or an oversized grilled chicken salad, and enjoy the breeze off the lake and the sight of lunch-hour anglers fishing from the shore.

Wilma's (212 Court St., Paintsville, 606/789-5911, 7am-7pm Mon.-Fri., 7am-4pm Sat.-Sun., $4.95-8.95) caters to fans of down-home country cooking. The decor isn't much to speak of, but people come for the food and not the ambience. Specialties include meatloaf, soup beans and cornbread, and roast beef. At breakfast, biscuits and gravy is a go-to dish, and the homemade cream pies are good no matter what time the clock reads.

Giovanni's Pizza (261 Court St., Paintsville, 606/789-8535, 10:30am-10pm daily, $8.99) is a regional chain with locations spread throughout Central and Eastern Kentucky. Fans of Giovanni's crave the thin-crusted, cheesy pizza; it can be a bit greasy, but some say that's what makes it so good.

Information and Services

The visitors center run by the **Paintsville Tourism Commission** (U.S. 23, 800/542-5790, www.visitpaintsvilleky.com) is located just off of U.S. 23 and shares a parking lot with the Country Music Highway Museum. Brochures about Paintsville and Johnson County attractions as well as sites along U.S. 23 and farther afield are available, and staff is ready and willing to provide personalized information and directions.

Getting There and Around

By the time you reach Paintsville on U.S. 23, you've moved west away from the state's eastern border. You're in the mountains now, but not as much as you will be a bit farther south. There's still a fair bit of flat land, with mountains rarely on both sides, at least outside of the hollows. If you're traveling south on U.S. 23, Paintsville is 30 miles (40 minutes) south of Louisa and nearly 60 miles (1.25 hours) south of Ashland. Prestonsburg, which is the next stop on the Country Music Highway, is only 13 miles (20 minutes) farther south.

PRESTONSBURG AND FLOYD COUNTY

Prestonsburg really stands out for its performing arts, so it's wise to schedule your visit around concerts and plays. Regularly scheduled events that are worth your while include performances by the Kentucky Opry and the Front Porch Pickin' series at the Mountain Arts Center, as well as the professional plays staged by the repertory company at Jenny Wiley Theatre. Recreation is another big draw in Prestonsburg thanks to Jenny Wiley State Resort Park, which runs very cool elk-viewing tours. Arriving in Prestonsburg, from the north especially, you'll really feel that you're in the mountains, with hills rising up on both sides of you almost everywhere you go. Coal mining remains an important industry here, as it does throughout the region, and those curious about the effects of strip mining should be sure to travel up to Stone Crest Golf Course to see what has been done with a reclaimed mine site and to better understand why people here stand firm in their support of mining. You may not agree, but at least you'll have a more rounded view of the many issues at play in this debate.

Mountain Arts Center

The **Mountain Arts Center** (50 Hal Rogers Dr., Prestonsburg, 606/889-9125, http://macarts.com) is the prime performing arts venue in Eastern Kentucky. Opened in 1998, the center hosts more than 140 events each year in its magnificent theater that seats 1,050. The theater, which still feels brand-new, has state-of-the-art sound and stage systems, and there's not a bad seat in the house. The Mountain Arts Center is home to the **Kentucky Opry,** a resident group that puts on a variety show of country, bluegrass, gospel, and a bit of humor on Saturday evenings in July, plus additional dates in August and September (8pm, $15 adults, $13 seniors, $11 students). The Front Porch Pickin' series is also hosted each summer. This open-mic series invites performers to get up on stage and perform, with members of the audience joining in as they see fit (7pm Fri., free). Plays, concerts, dance shows, and other events fill out the schedule. Dedicated to all forms of art, the lobby hosts rotating displays of works by local artists as well as historical photographs and a display of mining artifacts.

Battle of Middle Creek Historic Site

The **Battle of Middle Creek** (KY 114 & KY 404, www.middlecreek.org, free), fought in January 1862, was the most significant Civil War battle fought in Eastern Kentucky, pitting 1,100 Union troops against 2,000 Confederate troops. This battle is a perfect example of the statement that the war forced brother to fight brother, as the forces that lined up against each other here were composed primarily of Kentuckians. A short walking trail with interpretive signage leads around the battlefield. The best time to visit the battlefield is during the annual reenactment, which is held in September.

East Kentucky Science Center

Through an exhibit hall that hosts constantly rotating shows, the **East Kentucky Science Center** (Big Sandy Community and Technical College, 1 Bert T. Combs Dr., Prestonsburg, 606/889-8260, 1pm-4pm Tues.-Fri., noon-4pm Sat., $6 adults, $4 students and seniors) introduces various scientific principles to the local community and visitors. Exhibits are heavily hands-on. The center also has a planetarium that presents both star shows and laser shows. The admission price allows access to the exhibit hall as well as both shows. Planetarium shows, which tend to change weekly, are shown at 2pm on weekdays and at 12:30pm and 2pm on weekends. The laser shows, which change almost daily, are held at 3:15pm.

◖ Jenny Wiley State Resort Park

Named for a legendary pioneer woman who escaped after being held in captivity by Native Americans for 11 months, **Jenny Wiley State Resort Park** (75 Theatre Ct., Prestonsburg, 606/889-1790, http://parks.ky.gov, daylight-dark daily, free) embraces the spirit and heritage of the mountains in which it is located. As expected at a state park, multiple recreational activities are offered. A marina is located on

Elk are abundant in Appalachia.

© THERESA DOWELL BLACKINTON

1,100-acre Dewey Lake, renting pontoon boats to those wishing to motor around the lake. Hikers can choose from more than 10 miles of trail worth exploring. Families will enjoy the 0.75-mile Sassafras Trail, which is interpreted with signs that provide information on the many types of plants you'll see. Serious hikers should opt for the 4.5-mile one-way Jenny Wiley Trail, which provides access to the serene and sometimes strenuous mountain environment of the area. A separate set of trails is open to mountain bikers, with three trails totaling three miles. The park also features a nine-hole golf course.

The naturalist programs at Jenny Wiley are particularly strong, with a wide variety of offerings ranging from primitive fire making to overnight canoe trips. Pick up a copy of the weekly activities schedule at the lodge to see if any of the events interest you. One particularly neat offering is the elk tour. These tours, which take place in the wee hours of the morning on weekends, take wildlife lovers out to known elk habitats to allow viewing of this wonderful species, which was reintroduced to Kentucky in 1997. The tours can last 4-6 hours, depending on how easy it is to find the elk. On a good day, you can see upwards of 100 elk, including both bachelor herds and herds of cows with their young. Tours ($30 adults, $15 youth 12 and under), which are led by very knowledgeable naturalists, are limited to 20 people and should be reserved in advance, although you might check for any available openings if you failed to do so. The tour is worth getting up early for.

Unique to this park is the **Jenny Wiley Theatre** (www.jwtheatre.com), an outdoor theater with a professional repertory company that puts on four shows each summer season (June-Aug.). Performances overlap throughout the season, making it possible to see one show one night and a different show the next night. Performances run the gamut from Broadway shows to children's favorites. Each year one show is held at the accompanying indoor theater, with both matinee and evening options. Performances are top-notch and a lot of fun,

with not only fantastic actors, but also amazing scenery and costumes. The season schedule is usually released by late fall of the preceding year, and tickets can be purchased in advance over the phone (606/896-9274), although last-minute seating is usually available at the box office on the day of the performance.

With so much to do in the park (and at such late and early hours), an overnight stay is a good idea. An on-site lodge and campground cater to visitors.

Festivals and Events

The **Kentucky Highland Folk Festival** (http://macarts.com) celebrates Eastern Kentucky mountain heritage with live music, storytelling, and demonstrations of such mountain skills as blacksmithing, basket making, wood carving, and playing the banjo, dulcimer, fiddle, and guitar. Held annually on the second weekend in September at the Middle Creek National

THE LEGEND OF JENNY WILEY

Jenny Wiley was an American pioneer who moved with her family to the wilderness of what is now the Kentucky-Virginia border region. In this area, she met and married Thomas Wiley in 1778, and together they built a home and had children. In October 1789, when Thomas was away at a trading post, their cabin was attacked by Native Americans. The Native Americans killed Jenny's younger brother and three of her four children, taking Jenny and her baby captive. This baby was later killed, as was the baby that Jenny gave birth to while she was captive. After 11 months of captivity, Jenny was able to escape and make her way back to her husband. They started a new family, having five more children, and around 1800 moved across the Big Sandy River to what is now Johnson County, Kentucky. Jenny lived out the rest of her life in this area and was buried in River, Kentucky, when she died in 1831.

© THERESA DOWELL BLACKINTON

Stone Crest Golf Course in Prestonsburg

Battlefield, this free event also features Civil War reenactors, a pig roast, an arts and crafts festival, and plenty of family-friendly fun.

Recreation

It would be hard to find a golf course in Kentucky with a better view than **Stone Crest Golf Course** (918 Clubhouse Dr., 606/886-1006, http://stonecrestgolfcourse.com). Located on the site of a former surface mine, Stone Crest is high up above Prestonsburg with amazing vistas of the surrounding mountains. The course is challenging—drive too long and your ball may not stop until it reaches the bottom of the mountain—with 18 championship-level holes. Multiple other recreational facilities are located on this former mine site—a testament, locals say, to the ways in which mining has benefited the community—including baseball, softball, and soccer fields, and a 200-stable equestrian complex that hosts multi-day events.

Accommodations

At **Jenny Wiley State Resort Park** (75 Theatre Ct., Prestonsburg, 606/889-1790, http://parks.ky.gov), **May Lodge** ($109.95) has a rustic feel that fits in well with the surrounding mountains and lake. Furnishings and decor are a bit dated, but the rooms are well maintained and comfortable. Each of the 49 rooms has a private balcony or patio, some with views of the lake. One- and two-bedroom **cottages** ($139.95-179.95) are also available for bigger parties or those seeking privacy. A 121-site **campground** (mid-Mar.-mid-Nov., $18-24) often fills in the summer, particularly on weekends. Of the sites, 28 sites are meant for tents only, whereas the other 91 have electric hookups for RVs. The campground has two comfort stations and an on-site convenience store.

In addition to the lodge at the state park, which tops the list of choices, Prestonsburg has four hotels, none of which are particularly memorable. If the park lodge is full, consider staying at the **Comfort Suites** (51 Hal Rogers Dr., 606/886-2555, www.comfortsuites.com, $99), which is located directly next door to the Mountain Arts Center. All rooms have refrigerator and microwave, and a deluxe continental breakfast is included in the room rate.

Food

🎵 **Billy Ray's** (101 N. Front St., 606/886-1744, 6am-8pm Mon.-Fri., 6am-10pm Sat., 8am-4pm Sun., $5.99-9.99) is Prestonsburg's most popular dining option, with the simple chairs and booths almost always filled at mealtimes. Good old-fashioned country cooking is the focus here, with specials such as chicken and dumplings accompanied by two sides (pinto beans, green beans, mac and cheese, and the like) and a choice of biscuit or cornbread. The poolroom hamburger garners raves, and a huge selection of desserts lines the counter, tempting you to indulge even though meals are so hearty that you hardly have room.

El Azul Grande (132 Collins Cir., 606/886-8300, 11:30am-10pm daily, $6.99-12.99) will exceed your expectations for a Mexican restaurant in Eastern Kentucky, satisfying crowds of diners with huge portions of quality food. The menu is long, with choices ranging from tacos *al carbon* to carnitas to *camarones* a la *diabla* (spicy shrimp). Service is attentive, and the casual restaurant decorated in typical Latin style is spotless. A second location is in Pikeville.

If you've got a hankering for barbecue, head to **Pig in a Poke** (341 University Dr., 606/889-9119, 11am-10pm Tues.-Thurs., 11am-11pm Fri.-Sat., 11am-4pm Sun., $6-15). Try the pulled barbecue sliders (brisket, chicken, and pork), barbecue pork nachos, or a more traditional plate of ribs. Meals come with two sides and Texas toast. Service can be a little slow, but the atmosphere is nice.

Lizzie B's Café Bakery (2010 KY 321, 606/886-2844, 10:30am-9:30pm Mon.-Thurs., 10:30am-10:30pm Fri.-Sat., $5.99-8.99) offers a nice selection of sandwiches on homemade bread, pizzas on naan bread, and multiple soups made fresh daily. The sandwiches and pizza options are creative, and vegetarians will have choices here. Lizzie B's also has a full coffee bar and a good beer and wine selection.

Information and Services

The **Prestonsburg Convention & Visitors Bureau** (113 S. Central Ave., 606/886-1341, www.prestonsburgky.org, 9am-5pm Mon.-Fri.) can help you sort out your plans for touring Prestonsburg as well as other stops along the Country Music Highway. While at the office, be sure to check out the **Ranier Racing Museum,** a collection of auto racing memorabilia donated by the Raniers, a local family who ran a very successful racing operation, with drivers such as Buddy Baker and Bobby Allison racing for them. A large gift shop is also located at the tourism office, featuring products made by locals.

Getting There and Around

Prestonsburg is located just 13 miles (20 minutes) south of Paintsville on U.S. 23, and is 26 miles (35 minutes) northwest of Pikeville, the next stop for most people traveling the Country Music Highway. Prestonsburg is also located on the Mountain Parkway, which runs west from Prestonsburg through the Red River Gorge area before connecting to I-64 near Winchester. Primarily a four-lane highway, the Mountain Parkway is the most direct way to get from Prestonsburg to Lexington (120 miles, 2 hours) and points westward.

PIKEVILLE AND PIKE COUNTY

Pike County is Kentucky's easternmost county and also its largest geographically. Most of the county is decidedly rural, with small communities existing in hollows between heavily forested mountains. This amazing terrain is both a blessing, creating great paddling opportunities and enchanting parks like Breaks Interstate, and a curse, leading to flooding of national disaster proportions. Pikeville, thanks to the fact that they literally moved a mountain and changed the course of a river, is largely protected from the flooding, although it is still tucked tightly into a valley with mountains looming on each side. The region's big city, Pikeville is home to four-year Pikeville College, whose 99 steps you should climb for a view of town; a highly regarded hospital; and the Eastern Kentucky Exposition Center, which has hosted big names like Carrie Underwood.

Hatfield-McCoy Feud Driving Tour

One of America's most famous feuds took place in the Appalachian Mountains of Eastern Kentucky and West Virginia. The feud between the Hatfields of West Virginia, led by patriarch Devil Anse, and the McCoys of Kentucky, led by patriarch Randolph, began during the Civil War and continued until the 1890s. Support for differing sides in the Civil War, claims of stolen pigs, and illicit love affairs all contributed to the feud. A self-guided driving tour leads visitors on a tour of sites related to the feud. Sites on the tour are in both Kentucky and West Virginia, and are marked with signs that detail such events as the hog trail, the burning of the McCoy cabin, and the shooting of three McCoy boys in retaliation for the killing of Ellison Hatfield. The tour also visits **Dils Cemetery,** which is thought to be the first integrated cemetery in Eastern Kentucky

and is where Randolph McCoy, wife Sarah, and their daughter Roseanna are buried. A free brochure is available at the **visitors center** (781 Hambley Blvd., Pikeville, 606/432-5063, www. tourpikecounty.com), but to get the most out of the tour, you'll want to purchase the accompanying audio CD and listen to it as you drive. You'll need about three hours to complete the entire circuit.

Big Sandy Heritage Museum

The **Big Sandy Heritage Museum** (773 Hambley Blvd., Pikeville, 606/218-6050, www.bigsandyheritage.org, 10am-5pm Mon.-Fri., $3 adults, $2 seniors and youth) contains more than 2,000 artifacts that illustrate the history of the region. The museum is located in the former C&O passenger station, which can hardly accommodate all the items on display. Exhibits cover mining, the railroad, homestead life, the Civil War, the Hatfields and McCoys, moonshine, the military, and just about every other facet of life in Eastern Kentucky through the ages.

Breaks Interstate Park

Pike County is rich with recreation opportunities that take advantage of the area's natural beauty and resources. One of the richest areas is in the far southern part of the county near Elkhorn City. There you'll find **Breaks Interstate Park** (KY 80, 276/865-4413, www.breakspark.com, 24-hours daily, free), a 4,600-acre playground that spreads the border of Kentucky and Virginia and contains a five-mile-long, 1,650-foot-deep gorge known as the Grand Canyon of the South. For some, a drive through the park, with stops at overlooks showcasing tumbling rivers and outstanding rock formations, is enough, but most visitors hanker to actually get out and surround themselves with the beauty. Hiking is one way to do that. More than 25 miles of trail provide access to the park's natural features, including springs, rock towers, creeks, and meadows. Most trails are short, coming in at a mile or less, but it's easy to connect multiple trails for a longer outing. Additional trails are available for those who

© THERESA DOWELL BLACKINTON

picnic site at Breaks Interstate Park

like to explore on two wheels. Stacked loop trails provide up to 12 miles of moderate to difficult terrain for mountain bikers.

Breaks is best known for water sports, however, particularly whitewater rafting and kayaking. Each year, on the first four full weekends in October, water is released from the dam, turning Russell Fork River into a raging waterway with world-class rapids. Top whitewater paddlers from around the nation and even the world descend on the area in October to test themselves on rapids with such names as Twenty Stitches and Broken Nose. Rapids are rated at up to Class V+ and are known as some of the best in the eastern United States. Outfitters that can get you out on the river, on sections both wild and calm, include **Kentucky Whitewater** (www.kentuckywhitewater. com), **Russell Fork Whitewater Adventures** (276/530-7044), and **Sheltowee Trace Outfitters** (www.ky-rafting.com, 800/541-7238). While October is the premier month, Russell Fork River attracts paddlers year-round, with both rapids for adventure paddlers and breathtaking scenery for recreational paddlers. Serious paddlers should check www.russellfork. info for information on water levels, events, put-in spots, and routes.

Those looking for a more relaxing way to enjoy the water can opt to fish in Russell Fork River, Laurel Lake, or Beaver Pond. Laurel Lake offers pedal boat and canoe rentals. The park also has an Olympic-size pool with diving board and slide.

Nightlife
Bank 253 (253 Second St., 606/432-6566, www.bank253.net, 11am-11pm Mon.-Wed., 11am-1am Thurs.-Fri., 11am-2:30am Sat.) is a sports bar-style restaurant where the younger crowd likes to gather to drink with friends. They have some craft and seasonal beers on tap, bottles of mainstay beers, a cocktail lists, and wines by the glass.

The **Landmark Inn** (190 S. Mayo Trail, 606/432-2545, www.the-landmark-inn. com) is another destination for locals. It offers two hangout spots, the **Top of the Inn**

Lounge (11am-midnight daily) and the **Mark II Lounge** (4pm-1am daily). You'll find karaoke on Thursdays and live music on Wednesdays, Fridays, and Saturdays.

On the first and third Saturday of the month June-October, **Main Street Live** brings people downtown for live music from the mountains from 5pm to 11pm.

Performing Arts
The **Artists Collaborative Theatre** (207 N. Patty Loveless Dr., Elkhorn City, 606/754-4228, www.act4.org) is a delightful community theater that puts on a full season of eight shows every year. Actors are not professionally trained, but are enthusiastic and often quite good, and the productions are popular shows like *Little Women, The Wizard of Oz,* and *Steel Magnolias.* Run entirely on volunteer hours and donations, the theater does a remarkable job with costuming and scenery. Tickets are a bargain $8 for all shows (7:30pm Thurs., Fri., Sat. and 3pm Sun.).

Festivals and Events
Benefitting the Shriner's Children's Hospital in Lexington, **Hillbilly Days** (www.hillbillydays. com) is a great excuse for letting your inner hick out. The three-day festival, which takes place in mid-April on the streets of downtown Pikeville, is packed with activities. There's a carnival, arts and crafts fair, lots of live music, and a Saturday afternoon parade that is the highlight of the event. Although a handful of people feel the festival fuels unfair stereotypes, the festival draws an annual 100,000 people who see it for the fun time that it is.

Recreation
Pine Mountain is one of Kentucky's most beautiful mountains, lush with rhododendrons and mountain laurel and offering incredible vistas. Hikers can really get to know this area on the **Pine Mountain Trail** (www.pinemountain-trail.org). This trail, which will one day run 110 miles and connect Breaks Interstate Park, Kingdom Come State Park, Pine Mountain State Resort Park, and Cumberland Gap

National Historical Park, is only partially complete. Presently, the first 42 miles, from Breaks to U.S. 119, is complete and welcomes hikers to take a multi-day trip and get a taste of the wilderness atop Pine Mountain. It's about as wild of a stretch of forest as you'll find in the United States these days, and those who take the challenge of hiking it will have a taste of what Kentucky was like in the days of Daniel Boone. It's pretty amazing.

Those with their own boat can take advantage of the recreational opportunities at **Fishtrap Lake State Park** (2204 Fishtrap Rd., Shelbiana, 606/437-7496, http://parks.ky.gov, daylight-dark daily, free). Built in the 1960s to help control flooding in Pike County, the 1,100-acre Fishtrap Lake offers prime angling and is a popular pleasure boating site as well.

Accommodations

The (**Historic Mansion Bed and Breakfast** (179 College St., Pikeville, 606/509-0296, www.pikevillehistoricmansion.com, $119-130) is a remarkably restored home dating to the early 1900s. Each of its seven gorgeous rooms is named for a person important to the history of the town and the house, and all are spacious and decorated in a style that is clean and crisp with an understated elegance. The beds are so comfortable that getting out of them is hard, and the bathrooms are nicely equipped. The York Suite has a sitting room that can be shared with the Johnson Room, creating a suite perfect for families or couples traveling together. All rooms have TV and wireless Internet access, and all guests are invited to help themselves to snacks and drinks from a communal refrigerator. Breakfast is served daily at 8am, although guests who would like to take their morning meal earlier or later may opt to dine at the **Hampton Inn** (831 Hambley Blvd., Pikeville, 606/432-8181, http://hamptoninn.hilton.com, $134), which is owned by the same person. This Hampton Inn is an upscale version of your typical Hampton, with everything sparkling and new. Rooms are large with all the amenities, and the hotel has a nice pool, free parking in a garage next

door, and complimentary hot breakfast. The nicest Hampton Inn I've ever seen, Pikeville's Hampton has an over 90 percent occupancy rate, so you'll want to book ahead.

Multiple accommodation options are offered by **Breaks Interstate Park** (KY 80, 276/865-4413, www.breakspark.com). Choose from a wooded spot at the 138-site **campground** ($15-24); a room at the motel-style **lodge** ($99.95); a rustic two-bedroom **cottage** ($150); or a gorgeous two- or three-bedroom hand-hewn luxury log **cabin** ($240-290) right on the lake that comes complete with rocking chairs on the porch.

Food

(**Blue Raven Restaurant and Pub** (211 Main St., 606/509-2583, http://theblueraven.net, lunch 11am-2pm Tues.-Sat., dinner 5pm-10pm Tues.-Thurs. and 5pm-11pm Fri.-Sat., $18-25) brings excellent contemporary American dining to Pikeville. For dinner, try the scallops stir-fried with vegetables in Ale-8; penne with zucchini, carrots, and walnuts cooked in moonshine; or a dry aged steak. The lunch menu ($6.50-9) consists of sandwiches, including a crab cake sandwich and a meatloaf sandwich, as well as soup and salad.

Located in the historic McCoy house, which has been transformed into a cozy, casual place with warm yellow walls and a choice of booths and tables, **Chirico's** (235 Main St., 606/432-7070, www.chiricosristorante.com, 10am-9pm Tues.-Thurs., 10am-10pm Fri., 3pm-10pm Sat., $5.99-17.99) serves hearty portions of traditional Italian favorites. All dishes come with a side salad and tasty garlic bread. If you like only a light coating of sauce on your pasta, make that clear, because most dishes come with healthy helpings of sauce. In addition to homemade pastas and classic dishes such as manicotti and shrimp scampi, the menu also offers sandwiches, pizzas, and calzones. Lunch portions are available.

Two regional favorites have locations in Pikeville. **El Azul Grande** (238 S. Mayo Trail, 606/437-7200, 11:30am-10pm daily, $6.99-12.99) draws consistent crowds with its many

Mexican dishes, while **Dairy Cheer** (344 S. Mayo Trail, 606/432-5222, 7am-10pm Mon.-Thurs., 7am-11pm Fri.-Sat., $2.99-4.99) is known for their smashburgers, hot dogs topped with coleslaw, and about every type of shake you can dream up.

Information and Services

You can't miss the office of the **Pikeville-Pike County Tourism Commission** (781 Hambley Blvd., 606/432-5063, www.tourpikecounty.com, 9am-4:30pm Mon.-Fri.), seeing as it's located in two train cars on Pikeville's main thoroughfare. Get your audio CD for the Hatfield-McCoy driving tour here, as well as all the brochures, maps, and suggestions you need.

Getting There and Around

Pikeville is located 26 miles (35 minutes) southeast of Prestonsburg on U.S. 23. Pike County extends all the way south to the border with Virginia, which is where you'll find Elkhorn City (25 miles; 35 minutes) and Breaks Interstate Park (30 miles; 45 minutes). To reach this area, follow KY 80 from Pikeville. If you'd like to complete the entire length of the Country Music Highway, continue following U.S. 23 southwest for 30 miles (35 minutes) to the town of Jenkins in Letcher County.

The Pikeville Cut-Through, which you'll drive through on U.S. 23, has been labeled the eighth wonder of the world and is one of the largest land removal projects in the western hemisphere. More than 18 million cubic yards of earth were cut from a mountain to open a pass through which four lanes of U.S. 23 as well as a railroad line could pass. In the process, the Big Sandy River was also rerouted, taking it out of downtown Pikeville to ease flooding. The project began in 1973 and took 14 years to complete, costing a total of $80 million.

WHITESBURG AND LETCHER COUNTY

Whitesburg, the seat of Letcher County, is situated in the shadow of Pine Mountain, Kentucky's second-tallest mountain and a destination for outdoor recreation. If you're looking for hiking opportunities, Letcher County has some strong options that will take you into old-growth forest or to a rejuvenating waterfall. You should also make time to walk around downtown Whitesburg, a pretty place with stone buildings constructed by Italian masons during the coal mining heydays of the 1920s. Arts, crafts, and mountain traditions are alive and well here, so pack your dancing shoes along with your hiking boots.

Hiking

Bad Branch State Nature Preserve (www.naturepreserves.ky.gov, free) protects 2,639 acres of biologically diverse habitat on the side of Pine Mountain. The best way to enjoy the lush forest, which is dense with rhododendrons and heavily shaded by old-growth hemlocks, is to hike it. A one-mile trail leads to a picturesque 60-foot waterfall that tumbles down onto large boulders. It's absolutely breathtaking on snowy days and at its peak in the spring, though it does run at some level year-round. The trail to the falls is moderate to begin with, but the last stretch to the falls is tough, requiring sure-footedness as you scramble up rocky inclines. Strong hikers can venture farther into the preserve to High Rock, a sandstone outcropping on the upper level of the mountain from which you can view the Cumberland Plateau and Black Mountain. The hike to High Rock is one-way with a loop at the peak. If you do it all, your total mileage will be nearly seven miles, much of which is strenuous. The preserve is located on KY 932, 1.7 miles from U.S. 119, marked only with a small sign indicating the trailhead parking lot on the left side of the road.

The **Lilley Cornett Woods** (KY 1103, Skyline, 606/633-5828, www.naturalareas.eku.edu, free) is a 554-acre nature preserve that boasts 252 acres of old-growth forest, a true rarity in Kentucky. The woods, which contain more than 500 species of flowering plant and many types of birds, are used as a research station by Eastern Kentucky University, but are also open to the public. You must, however, make an appointment to visit, with access limited to guided walks on designated trails.

Whitesburg is another good access point for the **Pine Mountain Trail** (www.pinemountaintrail.com), particularly the 16-mile Highland Section of the trail, which runs between U.S. 23 and U.S 119. Two shelters are located along this section, and to truly appreciate the natural beauty and the wildlife, you should take advantage and make this a multi-day hike. Detailed topographical maps can be downloaded from the website.

Performing Arts

Appalshop (91 Madison Ave., Whitesburg, 606/633-0108, www.appalshop.org) has been preserving Appalachian traditions and culture, fighting stereotypes, and giving a voice to Appalachian people since 1969. Appalshop projects include Roadside Theatre, which produces and puts on original plays that relate to Appalachia; WMMT radio station, which broadcasts the music and stories of the region; Front Porch, which profiles traditional musicians from Kentucky; and a variety of other theater, film, radio, and music programs. Visit their website to check for upcoming events. You're always welcome to stop in and browse the gallery, which has rotating exhibits of local art.

One of the oldest **community square dances** in the United States is held on the second Saturday of the month April-December 7pm-9pm at the community center in the tiny town of Carcassonne (Square Dance Rd., 606/633-7958), in the northwest corner of Letcher County. Nationally recognized banjo master Lee Sexton regularly provides music. Dancers from Carcassonne have performed at the Smithsonian Folk Life Festival in Washington DC, and are darn good, but even those with a tin ear and two left feet are warmly invited to participate. Contact the Letcher County Tourism office for more information.

Festivals and Events

The **Seedtime on the Cumberland Festival** (http://seedtimefestival.org) is an annual celebration of mountain arts and culture sponsored by Appalshop. The festival, which takes place on the second weekend in June, is expansive, incorporating storytelling, music, dancing, film, and visual arts. In recent years, the event has been timed to coincide with Whitesburg's quarterly Artwalk, which introduces participants to local galleries, and has included such events as a Harley bike ride with pit stops at art sites of interest, an early morning bird-watching hike, and seed spittin' and hollerin' contests. For a real taste of the spirit and creativity of Appalachia, the Seedtime Festival is a must.

Food

When you've had your fill of soup beans and cornbread or entrées covered in brown gravy, grab a table at **The Courthouse Café** (104 N. Webb Ave., Whitesburg, 606/633-5859, $6.95-11.95). A chalkboard lists daily specials, but reliable favorites include chicken Dijon, blackened fish (salmon or trout), grilled pork loin, and rib eye steak. Meals are lighter than the typical fare in these parts, and there's an emphasis on fresh ingredients. You have to make room for the Tanglewood pie, an over-the-top creation that involves bananas, cream cheese, whipped cream, and blueberries.

Another refreshingly different option is **Summit City Lounge** (214 Main St., Whitesburg, 606/633-2715, www.summitcitylounge.com, $5.95-8.95), which is part café, part gallery, part nightclub. Sandwiches range from a healthy hummus sandwich to a meat-stuffed Italian sandwich. High-quality salads built around fresh mixed greens and a large selection of bar snacks and appetizers round out the menu. For those looking for a drink, Summit City offers a good choice of wines along with coffee drinks, teas, and sodas. Works by local artists decorate the walls, and live bands perform regularly. Check the online calendar.

Information and Services

The **Letcher County Convention & Tourism Commission** (156 Main St., Whitesburg, 606/633-2129, www.letchercounty.ky.gov) maintains an office in downtown Whitesburg. In addition to providing your usual information, the staff there should be able to help you arrange shuttles if you plan to do any long-distance hiking.

Getting There and Around

You reach the end of the Country Music Highway in the tiny town of Jenkins, which is located in Letcher County. At that point, U.S. 23 and U.S. 119, which had been one, split, with U.S. 23 heading south into Virginia. To continue on to Whitesburg, you'll want to follow U.S. 119 for about 12 miles (20 minutes). As you approach Whitesburg, you'll again reach a split. U.S. 119 turns south, leading you over Pine Mountain, and then west toward Cumberland. This is a very scenic route, running through the Jefferson National Forest, and is the best way to continue on to the sights

in Southern Appalachia. To actually enter the town of Whitesburg, however, you'll want to veer right at the split onto KY 15. KY 15 runs diagonally across Appalachia from Whitesburg, passing through the city of Hazard and connecting to the Mountain Parkway. It's the route you'll take if you're headed to Lexington (150 miles; 2.75 hours) or Louisville (220 miles; 3.75 hours) after completing your trip down the Country Music Highway.

If you're traveling west to Cumberland and want to take the road less traveled, opt to forgo U.S. 119 for the Little Shepherd Trail (KY 1679). This one-lane (but two-direction) paved road runs across the crest of Pine Mountain for 38 miles to Kingdom Come State Park. It's a twisty, turning route, but you'll have magnificent views.

Southern Appalachia

From the time Europeans arrived in America until the mid-1700s, all the land that lay west of the Appalachian mountains remained unknown. The mountains were too high, the forests too thick, the journey too treacherous for man to venture West, although certainly they did try. A man named Dr. Thomas Walker would, however, change the course of the not-yet-nation when he mapped a way from Virginia into the west via a break in the mountains he named the Cumberland Gap. Later, Daniel Boone would make this path into a viable route called the Wilderness Road, through which hearty pioneers would pass, setting up homes in what would become Kentucky and in regions even farther west. Today, that passageway is protected as a national park, where you can follow in the footsteps of pioneers.

In the early 1900s, long after better routes had been made to the West, another set of men flocked to the mountains of Appalachia. This time, they were after coal and lumber. Companies built entire towns from scratch—homes, banks, schools, churches, stores,

post offices, and police stations—and then brought in workers and their families to populate them. These company towns, as they were known, were the heart and soul of much of this region until the middle of the 20th century, when the companies sold them. Today, although the homes are privately owned, the civil service buildings owned by the government, and the biggest mines closed, the towns still have strong connections to mining, and for those curious about the industry and the way of life it created, there's no better place to experience it firsthand.

TRI-CITY AREA

Planted at the base of Black Mountain, the state's highest peak at 4,145 feet, the tri-city area of Southern Appalachia consists of Cumberland, Benham, and Lynch, each of which would more properly be classified as a town than a city. Cumberland, named for the river that runs through it, is the oldest of the towns as well as the largest. It's also the only one of the three that is not a coal company town, established instead as a trade center.

Benham, founded in 1911 by Wisconsin Steel (which became International Harvester), and Lynch, founded in 1917 by U.S. Steel, began as company towns, and try as you might, it's unlikely that you'll find anyone in the area without a direct link to the mines, which remain the area's largest employer, despite operating on a reduced scale.

All three towns are tiny, surrounded entirely by black bear-inhabited mountains, but the insight the towns provide into the coal culture make them extremely interesting to the curious traveler. Visitor services are limited (but available), and the towns are working hard to fill empty storefronts, turn abandoned mining buildings into sites of interest, and draw tourists. I recommend a visit.

Kentucky Coal Mining Museum

Located in the former International Harvester company store, where mine employees could buy everything from clothes to washing machines, groceries to ice cream sodas, the **Kentucky Coal Mining Museum** (229 Main St., Benham, 606/848-1530, http://kycoalmuseum-portal31.southeast.kctcs.edu, 10am-5pm Tues.-Sat., $8 adults, $6 seniors, $5 high school and college students, $4 youth 3-12) preserves the history of coal mining and the communities that developed around the mines. Display cases are filled with artifacts donated by miners that demonstrate the evolution of the items area miners carry and the equipment they use as they work in underground mines. The museum also has life-size re-creations of the insides of company homes and shops, artifacts such as company scrip and scatter tags, a kid-size mock mine open to exploration, and a floor dedicated to Loretta Lynn and filled with her personal items and mementos. Although you're welcome to explore the museum on your own, it's worth calling ahead to arrange a guide, who can add much color to your experience. Most visitors combine a visit to the mine with a trip into Portal 31. Combination tickets are available ($20 adults, $16 seniors, $12 high school and college students, $9 youth 3-12).

◖ Portal 31 Underground Mine

Between 1917 and 1963, more than 120 million tons of bituminous coal were mined from Portal 31, an underground drift mine owned by U.S. Steel. In October 2009, **Portal 31** (KY 160, Lynch, 606/848-1530, http://kycoalmuseum-portal31.southeast.kctcs.edu, 9:30am-3pm Tues.-Sat., $15 adults, $12 seniors, $9 high school and college students, $6 youth 3-12) reopened for tours, offering visitors a fascinating look at life inside a coal mine. Participants on the 35-minute tour board a mine car for a jostling ride into the mine and through its history. Through animatronic displays featuring miners at work, the history of Portal 31 is told. You'll hear about the people who came to Lynch to work in the mines (33 different nationalities!), the process of mining and the safety measures taken, the unionization of the mine, the importance of the mines during World War I and II, and the evolution of the technology used in mining. The mine is rather dark and may be a bit scary for young children, but it's a must for all others. A combo ticket ($20 adults, $16 seniors, $12 high school and college students, $9 youth 3-12) allows for admission to both the mine and the Kentucky Coal Mining Museum. Because the mine cars can carry only 10 adults at a time, it's best to reserve a tour time in advance.

Godbey Appalachian Center

If you're curious about what the towns of Benham and Lynch looked like during their coal camp heydays, then you'll want to visit the **Godbey Appalachian Center** (700 College Dr., Cumberland, 606/589-2145, 9am-5pm Mon.-Fri., free) on the campus of Southeast Community College. The center is home to a remarkable collection of photographs that document the construction and development of the two towns. Photographers hired by U.S. Steel and International Harvester captured seemingly every facet of the towns—the removal of the mountain cabins that were there when the land was purchased, the building of new homes, men working in the mines, families

© THERESA DOWELL BLACKINTON

preparing to enter Portal 31 Underground Mine

shopping at the commissary, Independence Day celebrations, and more. The center also has a small art gallery with rotating shows, a folk art collection, and a particularly beautiful mosaic mural, but the photography collection is far and away the highlight.

Kingdom Come State Park

One of a number of parks and nature preserves in the Pine Mountain range, **Kingdom Come State Park** (502 Park Rd., Cumberland, 606/589-2479, http://parks.ky.gov, daylight-dark, free) is Kentucky's highest state park at an elevation of 2,700 feet. The mountainside terrain is dense with rhododendron thickets and mountain laurel, which paint the park pretty in late spring and early summer. In fall, the overviews, of which there are many, draw photographers and leaf-peepers thanks to the seemingly endless views. Unusual rock formations are also of interest. They include Raven Rock, a soaring monolith sitting at a 45-degree angle in the center of the park; Log Rock, a natural stone bridge that looks like a fallen log; and

Cave Amphitheater, an outcrop that makes a natural amphitheater.

Hiking is one of the premier activities at Kingdom Come. More than five miles of hiking trails are arranged in a spoke-like manner, connecting the road with Raven Rock. The trails are short, but of varying difficulty, and can easily be combined for those looking for more of a challenge. While hiking, be alert for black bears, as the park is home to a large population that makes Cumberland the black bear capital of Kentucky. The bears tend to avoid humans, but you should read the many park signs about the bears so you know what to do if you should encounter one.

Kingdom Come also has a small 3.5-acre lake stocked with bass, catfish, and trout. Fishing is allowed only from the banks, but those wishing to go out onto the lake can take a spin in a rental pedal boat. Other park facilities include a mini-golf course, multiple playgrounds, basketball courts, horseshoe pit, and volleyball court. Four tent-only campsites (free) are located near the picnic pavilions. There are no shower facilities, but there are restrooms with running water.

Accommodations

Return to your school days with a stay at the **Benham School House Inn** (100 Central Ave., Benham, 800/231-0627, http://kycoalmuseumportal31.southeast.kctcs.edu, $85.95-99.95). The inn's 30 rooms are located in former classrooms of the company school, which operated as a K-12 institution from 1926 to 1961, continuing on as a K-8 school until 1992. Green lockers still line the halls, and you half expect to hear the school bell ring or find kids running up the worn-smooth stairs. Instead you'll find large, nicely furnished rooms with comfy beds, cable TV, standard bathrooms, and desks (adult, not schoolhouse, style). The wireless Internet does not reach most rooms, but can be accessed on the first floor. A unique reappropriation of an out-of-use building, the Benham School House Inn makes for a fun overnight stop on a tour through the region.

Food

El Charritto (35 Black Bear Ave., Cumberland, 606/589-2007, 11am-9:30pm daily, $6.50-9.99) offers a long menu of Mexican dishes, including tacos, burritos, fajitas, flautas, enchiladas, and quesadillas. Red booths and tabletops fill the large, neatly kept restaurant, which is brightly decorated with piñatas, Mexican paintings, sombreros, and colorful dresses and scarves. Service is speedy and portions enormous. Combo meals are a good deal, and lunch specials are available daily.

Skip the Pizza Hut and grab a slice of local pie at **Black Mountain Pizza Company** (217 W. Main St., Cumberland, 606/589-2399, 11am-10pm Mon.-Thurs., 11am-midnight Fri.-Sat., $5.99-9.99). In addition to New York-style pizzas, the restaurant also serves calzones, sandwiches, and salads.

Information and Services

For information on the area and help planning a trip, contact the **Cumberland Tourist Commission** (506 W. Main St., Cumberland, 606/589-5812).

Cumberland Bank (E. Main St., Cumberland) has an ATM where you can get cash. A couple of gas stations are also located in Cumberland, along with a food mart, where you can put together a picnic.

Getting There and Around

The tri-cities are located on Kentucky's southern border with Virginia. The towns of Benham and Lynch lie along KY 160, which branches off from U.S. 119 at Cumberland. From Cumberland, U.S. 119 runs east to the town of Whitesburg (25 miles; 35 minutes), and then merges with U.S. 23 to continue on to Pikeville (60 miles; 1 hour 15 minutes), making it easy to connect from Southern Appalachia to the County Music Highway. To the west, U.S. 119 continues on to Pineville (50 miles; 1 hour), where you can connect to U.S. 25E and go south to access Cumberland Gap (65 miles; 1.25 hours) or head northwest to Corbin (85 miles; 1.5 hours). Be aware that U.S. 119 may be referred to as the Kingdom Come Scenic Parkway, or just as "the parkway" by people in this area.

From most cities in Kentucky, the best way to reach the tri-cities is to take I-75 to Corbin, and then follow southbound U.S. 25E and eastbound U.S. 119 as noted. It's a pretty long haul from most everywhere, but it's worth the trouble.

HARLAN AND VICINITY

Thanks to the FX show *Justified,* Harlan has become a household name to many. Harlan lies in the same county as the tri-cities, but is located about 25 miles west. In this section of the county, recreation is the primary attraction, with opportunities for hiking, fishing, paddling, hunting, and off-road driving. For a long time, many of the recreation areas were completely undeveloped and unadvertised, known only to locals and accessible only to those with their own gear. That's still partially true today, but the city is working hard to provide better information and access and turn Harlan into the adventure tourism destination that it is ready to be.

Hiking

Nature lovers will want to make time to visit **Blanton Forest State Nature Preserve** (KY 840, Harlan, 502/573-2886, www.naturepreserves.ky.gov, free), which protects Kentucky's largest old-growth forest and one of only 13 old-growth forests in the Eastern United States. Trees, some of which date to the 1600s, can reach 100 feet tall and 4 feet in diameter. Although the preserve encompasses 3,124 acres, only a small portion of it is open to the public via about 4.5 miles of hiking trails. The looping Knobby Rock Trail is of moderate difficulty, taking hikers to a sandstone outcropping that you can clamber on for an awesome panoramic view. From the parking lot, the entire hike is 3.2 miles. Those wanting a real adventure can add the 1.3-mile loop Sand Cave Trail to their hike. This strenuous trail climbs through dense forest and past neat rock formations on the slopes of Pine Mountain.

Water Sports

Martins Fork Lake (5965 KY 987, Smith) is a scenic spot most popular with anglers. Many species of fish can be caught here, including bass, crappie, catfish, walleye, and bluegill, as well as rainbow trout below the dam. Many anglers fish from shore, although you are allowed to launch boats with motors of 10 horsepower or less. The Smith Recreation Area has a beach perfect for hot summer days.

Martins Fork of the Cumberland, which runs through the **Martins Fork Wildlife Management Area & State Natural Area,** offers some impressive whitewater runs, including a 15-foot waterfall. The water is crystal clear, the scenery awesome, and the rapids wild (up to Class V+). Unfortunately, access is difficult, and no outfitter is currently providing trips. The Harlan County Tourism Commission is hard at work on improving accessibility, however, and if you're a serious paddler with the skills to handle the run on your own, they can connect you with some people knowledgeable about Martins Fork. Information about paddling this run is also available at http://americanwhitewater.org.

Off-Road Vehicles

Off-road driving is huge in Eastern Kentucky, and Harlan County contains one of the best parks for the sport. **Black Mountain Off-Road Adventure Area** (606/837-3205) offers more than 200 miles of trail on 7,000 acres of mountain terrain prime for exploring by ATV, Jeep, or other off-road vehicles. Routes are designated for beginner, intermediate, and extreme users, and the area has received national attention for its fun and challenging rides. The park can be accessed by two trailheads, one off of KY 38 in Evarts and the other off of U.S. 119 in Putney. A general access permit is required for each vehicle. A 31-day pass costs $20, while an annual pass is $35.

Zip-Lining

Soar through the forests of Harlan County with **Black Mountain Thunder Zipline** (Kelly St., Evarts, 606/837-3205, http://blackmountainthunder.com, $79 adults, $40 youth 12 and under), which offers a tour that lasts about two hours and includes 11 zip lines. Reservations are required.

Accommodations

Built in 1938 to serve as a boarding house for miners, the **Little Inn of Harlan** (508 S. Main St., Harlan, 606/573-7011, www.thelittleinnofharlan.com, $50-80) now welcomes visitors to Harlan to stay in one of their four guest rooms, each of which is complete with private bathroom, TV, and wireless Internet. Rooms are decorated with tasteful Victorian-style furnishings that aren't overly fussy. The Green Room is a bit tight, while the other three rooms are rather spacious. Common areas include a large deck and patio, living room, dining room, and kitchen. The kitchen is fully equipped and guests are welcome to prepare meals there or on the outside grill.

Mount Aire Motel (355 Skidmore Dr., Harlan, 606/573-4660, $59.95-69.95) is a

ELK VIEWING IN EASTERN KENTUCKY

During the days of Daniel Boone, elk were a common sight in Kentucky. By 1847, however, they were gone, and for more than 150 years, Kentucky autumns were no longer heralded by the bugling of the elk. That all changed in 1997, when more than 1,500 elk were reintroduced to 16 counties in Kentucky. This massive project, which involved nonstop cross-country transport with drivers trading off every eight hours, required the cooperation of the Kentucky Department of Fish and Wildlife, the University of Kentucky College of Agriculture, the Rocky Mountain Elk Foundation, and Fish and Wildlife units in Arizona, Kansas, North Dakota, New Mexico, Oregon, and Utah.

The elk, which live in herds and like to graze on open land during the day and sleep in the protection of the forest at night, were introduced onto grasslands created through surface mine reclamation projects. The elk are entirely wild, not bounded by fences, and free to move throughout the region as they wish. Although no one knew exactly how the elk would fare in Kentucky, they have thrived remarkably. Thanks to an absence of predators and an abundance of food, the elk population has grown to an estimated size of 10,000, making it the largest population east of the Rocky Mountains. In fact, in order to manage the population, the state now runs a tightly controlled elk-hunting program, with permits given out by lottery.

Because the elk are free-roaming, you could conceivably see them anywhere in Eastern Kentucky. There are, however, areas that are prime elk-viewing spots. Elk can be viewed year-round, although spring and fall are the best seasons and dawn and dusk are the best times. To do your own self-guided elk-viewing tour, set your sights on the following areas:

· **South Fork Elk View:** The largest elk herd in Kentucky resides in Breathitt County, and a viewing area has been established for visitors. From Jackson, which is located on KY 15 between Hazard and the Mountain Parkway, drive south on KY 15 for 3 miles, and then turn left on KY 1098. Drive 16 miles, and then turn right on a paved road identified as South Fork Elk View.

· **Jewel Ridge Viewing Area:** Located in southern Perry County, the Jewel Ridge Viewing Area is easily accessible from Hazard. Travel south on KY 15 to KY 7. Drive 11 miles on KY 7, and then turn right onto KY 699. After 7.6 miles, turn left onto KY 463. In five miles, you'll reach the viewing station on the left.

· **Elk View Drive:** A very popular elk-viewing spot, Elk View Drive is located in Knott County, north of Hindman. The viewing area is off of KY 1028, a few miles north of where KY 1028 intersects with KY 80.

· **Begley Wildlife Management Area:** A seasonal hunting area located near Harlan, Begley has meadows and forests that attract elk. To reach Begley from Harlan, take northbound U.S. 421 to westbound KY 221, and then turn right on Big Run Road after 8.9 miles to enter the wildlife management area.

A really great way to see the elk is to go on a tour organized through the state parks (http://parks.ky.gov). On these tours, you have the benefit of being accompanied by a knowledgeable naturalist, who can provide you with all kinds of information on the elk, as well as any other wildlife you might spot. Tours are offered from the following parks:

· **Jenny Wiley State Resort Park** (75 Theatre Ct., Prestonsburg, 606/889-1790)

· **Buckhorn Lake State Resort Park** (4441 KY 1833, Buckhorn, 606/398-7510)

For a truly unique way of viewing elk, contact **Saddle Up Elk Tours** (250 Hale Cemetery Rd., Mallie, 606/642-3656), which offers horseback guided tours of elk areas.

single-story motel built in log-cabin style. Rooms have double or king beds and some come with a kitchenette. Wireless Internet is available at the motel, but not all rooms have good connections. Picnic tables are located outside each room, and most people enjoy the local ambience. If you prefer a chain hotel, the **Comfort Inn** (2608 KY 421, Harlan, 606/573-3385, www.choicehotels.com, $89) delivers the clean, comfortable room that you expect, as well as free breakfast and a heated indoor pool.

Off-road drivers flock to the **Harlan County Campground & RV Park** (8331 U.S. 119, Putney, 606/573-9009, www.harlancountycampground.com), which is located right next to one of Black Mountain Off-Road Adventure Area's trailheads. The campground offers 138 acres where you can pitch a tent ($15) along with an open gravel area with hookups for RVs ($27). Bathrooms and shower houses are available to all campers. Cabins ($70-220), ranging from basic one-bedroom units to multistory cabins that can sleep up to 13, are also offered.

Food

Harlan doesn't have many outstanding food options. Your choices are basically limited to fast-food restaurants or low-end steakhouse chains. One good place to grab lunch, however, is **Jac's Coffee Shop** (119 Eversole St., Harlan, 606/573-1271, 10:30am-3pm Mon.-Thurs., $3.99-5.99), which serves tasty sandwiches and draws a large crowd of locals.

Information and Services

The **Harlan County Tourist Commission** (201 S. Main St., Harlan, 606/573-4156, www.harlancountytrails.com, 9am-5pm Mon.-Fri.) is located in a fancy new building in downtown Harlan. The website is well done, compiling good information on the many recreation options in the area as well as food and lodging options. The photos, which were taken by a staff member, are especially nice, providing a good idea of what the various recreation spots offer.

Getting There and Around

The city of Harlan sits just about one mile south of U.S. 119 on U.S. 421. It is 25 miles (30 minutes) west of Cumberland and 32 miles (40 minutes) east of Pineville on U.S. 119.

CUMBERLAND GAP AREA

First traveled by bison, then Native Americans, and then finally European settlers, the Cumberland Gap was the key to America's westward expansion. Located at the convergence of present-day Kentucky, Tennessee, and Virginia, the passageway was first documented in 1750 by Dr. Thomas Walker, who named it Cumberland Gap in honor of a British duke. In 1775, Daniel Boone blazed a path now known as the Wilderness Trail through Cumberland Gap, opening up Kentucky, which he deemed a second paradise, and vast areas beyond to settlers. By 1810—the year in which improved transportation westward made the gap a secondary means of migration—more than 300,000 of these settlers had passed through the gap, some staying in Kentucky while others pressed on. Today the Cumberland Gap and the forested mountains that surround it are preserved as a national park, with multiple historical and recreational opportunities. Just a bit north, Pine Mountain State Resort Park offers additional trails that provide a peek at what Kentucky might have looked like in pioneer days.

The city of Middlesboro serves as the gateway to these parks. The only town in the world known to have been built in a meteorite crater, Middlesboro wasn't founded until 1880, long after the pioneers had passed through. It's one of the area's bigger towns, with a shopping mall, most every fast-food chain you can think of, and a Holiday Inn Express. How you spell the city's name is a matter of choice. Originally spelled Middlesborough, the post office decided to shorten it to Middlesboro, and now no one can decide which is actually correct.

◖ Cumberland Gap National Historical Park

Cumberland Gap National Historical Park preserves the route that pioneers took as they left behind America as they knew it and helped

APPALACHIA

© THERESA DOWELL BLACKINTON

Cumberland Gap National Historical Park

to establish the America that we know today. Any visit to this most important of frontier locations should begin at the **visitors center** (U.S. 25E, Middlesboro, 606/248-2817, www.nps.gov/cuga, 8am-5pm daily), where in addition to speaking with rangers about the park's recreation options and getting maps and brochures, you can watch two excellent videos. A short 10-minute video traces the history of this region from its geological formation through frontier days and the Civil War, while a 25-minute video tells the story of Daniel Boone and the pioneers who migrated west with him. The visitors center also has an exhibition wing that unveils the human history of the park through the tales of individuals, including a Native American trader, Dr. Thomas Walker, Daniel Boone, a Baptist minister, a miner, and a park ranger.

Fittingly for a park that exists because of the foot route that runs through it, Cumberland Gap National Historical Park bills itself as a hiking park. More than 85 miles of trails run throughout the park, offering hiking opportunities for all levels of hikers. Long-distance hikers will want to try the 21-mile Ridge Trail, which runs the length of the park. Backcountry camping permits allow you to break the trip into multiple days. Families and casual hikers should set their sights on the 0.6-mile connector trail, which runs from the Thomas Walker parking area to the Wilderness Road Trail, allowing you to set foot on the actual trail Boone blazed through the gap. Enthusiastic hikers can also make the 2.8-mile hike up to Pinnacle Overlook, which provides a panoramic view of the tri-state area. In summer, haze can limit the view to a few peaks, but on clear days, the view stretches to North Carolina. The autumn landscape is indescribable. Pinnacle Overlook can also be reached by car.

Park visitors with a real interest in the pioneer lifestyle should sign up (preferably in advance) for a Hensley Settlement Tour. These four-hour tours, which depart from the visitors center at 9:30am daily mid-May-October ($10 adults, $5 seniors and youth under 12), take participants to the site of an early 20th-century settlement, where 12 entirely self-sufficient families lived for over 40 years, separated from the rest of the world. It's a long, rough drive to the settlement, but it's an amazingly interesting place. A one-mile walk through the fence-lined settlement allows you to visit the one-room schoolhouse, a springhouse, and other buildings and settled areas.

If you prefer natural history to human history, sign up for a tour of Gap Cave ($8 adults, $4 seniors and youth 5-12). This beautiful cave is rich in stalactites, stalagmites, and flowstone. The two-hour tour requires participants to walk 1.5 miles and negotiate 183 steps. Tours are offered at 10am and 2pm daily, June-August, 10am weekdays and 10am and 2pm weekends, April-May and September-November, and 10am and 2pm weekends only, December-March.

Pine Mountain State Resort Park

Pine Mountain State Resort Park (1050 State Park Rd., Pineville, 606/337-3066, http://parks.ky.gov, daylight-dark daily, free) uses its assets to its advantage, making hiking the focus with 12 miles of trails meandering through the beautiful forests of Pine Mountain. The Hemlock Trail is a must for any visitor to the park, taking hikers on a 0.5-mile loop through a seemingly enchanted forest of 300-year-old hemlocks. The way light filters through the trees onto the rhododendrons and cascades below is simply magical. Another particularly lush trail is the Fern Garden Trail, which is 1.2 miles in length and is rich in ferns that may grow up to 3-4 feet tall. In spring, one of the loveliest hikes in the park is to Honeymoon Falls, which can be accessed via a 1.35-mile loop. Not only is the 25-foot waterfall at its strongest in spring, but the many rhododendrons lining the trail are also in bloom. For a short hike with a view, make your way 0.35 mile along the Chained Rock Trail. As the story goes, this large boulder was chained to the mountain in 1933 to ease the minds of Pineville residents who were afraid it was going to fall on them. From the rock, you have a great view of the peaks in Kentucky Ridge State Forest as well as of the town below.

In the valley at the base of the mountain on which Pine Mountain State Resort Park is located, you'll find the park's Wasioto Winds Golf Course. This 18-hole course is a links-style course that has been applauded by *Golf Digest*.

Festivals and Events

Every May, Pine Mountain bursts into color as the mountain laurel blooms, and the city of Pineville has been recognizing this gorgeous display since 1931 with the **Kentucky Mountain Laurel Festival** (www.kmlf.org). Festival events include a quilt show, a craft fair, a golf tournament, and a headliner concert. The main action takes place on Saturday of Memorial Day weekend, with a morning parade and the afternoon coronation of the Mountain Laurel Queen. That evening, a grand ball open to the public is held to honor the queen and her court.

Accommodations

Pine Mountain State Resort Park (1050 State Park Rd., Pineville, 606/337-3066, http://parks.ky.gov) has a number of fine lodging options. The **Herndon J. Evans Lodge** ($129.95) has 30 rooms, with either two queens or one king bed. Rooms are spacious and each has a private patio or balcony from which you can soak in the beauty of the forest. Eleven **cottages** ($179.95) with two bedrooms with two double beds each, two bathrooms, a living room, and a very nicely updated kitchen are also available for rent. For a really neat stay, opt for one of the nine log **cabins** ($159.95-169.96) set high up on the mountain. Each cabin has one bedroom with queen bed, one bathroom, a living room with sofa bed, and a fully equipped kitchen. The stone fireplaces in the living room give a true rustic feel to the cabins, which are authentic log structures.

Although **Cumberland Gap National Historical Park** (U.S. 25E, Middlesboro, 606/248-2817, www.nps.gov/cuga) does not have a lodge, it does have a year-round campground ($14-20) with 160 sites. All sites can accommodate tents, trailers, or RVs, but only 41 have hookups. Comfort stations provide hot showers and flush toilets. The campsites are first-come, first-served. If you're looking for a unique overnight option that will take you back in time to the days of Daniel Boone, inquire about the Martins Fork Cabin ($10), a primitive cabin with fireplace, three wooden bunk beds (bring your own mattress), and a picnic table that can only be accessed by a minimum five-mile hike. The cabin has no electricity, and a stream provides the water. The cabin can be reserved up to three months in advance. **Backcountry camping** in designated spots is also allowed in the park, but a free permit must be obtained from the visitors center.

Perched on a downtown hillside with views on all sides of the mountains, **Cumberland Manor Bed and Breakfast** (208 Arthur Heights, Middlesboro, 606/248-4299, www.cumberlandmanorbedandbreakfast.com, $109-159) provides a relaxing base after a day spent exploring Cumberland Gap or Pine Mountain. The 21-room Victorian is decorated in a style befitting its history as home to the wealthy Europeans who built the town. Six guest rooms named for U.S. presidents offer a variety of options from full and queen beds to a room with two twins. All have private baths and comfortable furnishings, and host Jill provides extra touches like turndown service and chocolates on the pillow. Evenings are well spent taking in the view from a front porch rocker, while mornings get off to a good start with a delicious full breakfast.

If you're looking for a chain hotel room, try the **Sleep Inn and Suites** (1260 N. 12th St., Middlesboro, 606/576-7829, www.sleepinn.com, $92), which opened in 2011 and still retains a new-hotel feel and provides an excellent breakfast, or the neighboring **Holiday Inn Express** (1252 N. 12th St., Middlesboro, 606/248-6860, www.hiexpress.com, $92).

Food
At Pine Mountain State Park, **Mountain View Restaurant** (1050 State Park Rd., Pineville,

606/337-3066, http://parks.ky.gov, 7am-8pm Sun.-Thurs., 7am-9pm Fri.-Sat., $5.99-13.99) is frequented by both park guests and local residents. Views from the floor-to-ceiling windows are particularly nice at sunset or on a misty morning. The menu is standard for the state parks, featuring catfish fillets, grilled chicken, club sandwiches, and the like. A buffet is also offered.

Although Middlesboro has about every fast-food chain restaurant you can think of, local dining choices are limited. Luckily, your main option is a good one. **Shades of Brown** (2119 Cumberland Ave., 606/248-4315, www.shadescoffeeshop.com, 3pm-9pm Mon.-Tues., 11am-9pm Wed.-Thurs., 3pm-10pm Fri.-Sat., $6-8) offers a scrumptious selection of sandwiches, salads, and soups, as well as grilled pizzas on naan bread, in a cheery coffeehouse atmosphere. If the tables in the front room are full, don't despair; two cozy "study rooms" are located in the area behind the counter, and a cute side patio is an excellent option when it's not too hot or too cold. On Friday and Saturday nights, the coffeehouse becomes a steakhouse ($10-22), serving a selection of steaks, grilled chicken, pork chops, ribs, shrimp, and salmon.

Information and Services
The **Bell County Tourism Commission and Visitors Center** (2215 Cumberland Ave., Middlesboro, 606/248-2482, www.mountaingateway.com, 9:30am-3:30pm Mon.-Fri.) is located in the historic Arthur House, built by town founder Alexander A. Arthur in 1890 to house the headquarters of his company. After gathering all the information you need for a visit to the area, take a walk around the museum section, which contains items that belonged to Mr. Arthur and that detail the establishment of Middlesboro.

Getting There and Around
From Harlan (40 miles; 50 minutes) and the tri-cities (60 miles; 1.25 hours), the Cumberland Gap area is accessible via U.S. 119, which ends right at Pine Mountain State Resort Park at the intersection with U.S. 25E. If you turn right

to proceed north on U.S. 25E, you'll immediately reach Pineville and can continue on another 32 miles to Corbin (40 miles) and I-75. If you turn left to proceed south on U.S. 25E, you'll reach Middlesboro after 12 miles (15 minutes) and can continue a short distance to enter Cumberland Gap National Historical Park. In the park, U.S. 25E passes under the mountains via a tunnel, which spits you out into Tennessee.

If you want to continue on to the Big South Fork area from the Cumberland Gap area, you'll want to take westbound KY 92, which you can access by turning left off of U.S. 25E just three miles north of Pineville. KY 92 is a winding country road that is often traversed by coal trucks, so drive carefully. KY 92 intersects with U.S. 27 after about 52 miles, and if you turn right onto it and follow it north, you will be on your way to Stearns (75 miles; 1 hour 40 minutes), which is just off of U.S. 27.

The Appalachian Interior

In the area west of the Country Music Highway, east of the I-75 corridor, and north of Southern Appalachia lies the Appalachian Interior. This area, which is rarely visited by outsiders, is home to small communities of independent-minded people. Coal mining is big business here, and one of the few economic engines in the area, although the dispersion of the wealth created by coal is terribly uneven. This is one of the poorest areas of Kentucky. It is, however, rich in natural beauty; two state parks and an outcropping of the Daniel Boone National Forest protect this beauty and provide recreational opportunities for those interested in exploring an off-the-beaten-path part of Kentucky.

DANIEL BOONE NATIONAL FOREST REDBIRD RANGER DISTRICT

Separate from the rest of the Daniel Boone National Forest, which runs in one continuous swath from north of I-64 to the Tennessee border, the **Redbird Ranger District** (91 Peabody Rd., Big Creek, 606/598-2192, www.fs.fed. us, 24 hours daily, free) encompasses 145,840 acres of land once owned by the Fordson Coal Company. The primary recreation destination in this part of the forest is the looping 65-mile Redbird Crest Trail. Tracing the ridge tops of the region's mountains, this trail is open to hikers, bikers, and horses, but is most used by ATVs. A permit ($7 one-day, $15 three-day, $40 annual pass) is required to use the trail. Recreation Opportunity Guides with maps can be downloaded from the ranger district website. Hikers looking for more peaceful trails should inquire at the ranger district office about the 25 miles of hiking trails located in the Redbird Wildlife Management Area.

BUCKHORN LAKE STATE RESORT PARK

At 1,230 acres, Buckhorn Lake is a great destination for outdoor recreation. For swimming, boating, and hiking options, you'll want to base yourself at **Buckhorn Lake State Resort Park** (4441 KY 1833, Buckhorn, 606/398-7510, http://parks.ky.gov, daylight-dark daily, free). The park is home to two boat ramps and a marina that rents pontoon and fishing boats. It also has a public beach with a bathhouse, ideal for cooling off on hot summer days. A 1.5-mile hiking trail meanders alongside the lake, offering an easy but scenic walk. Additionally, the park offers a mini-golf course, tennis and sand volleyball courts, a horseshoe pit, picnic and playground areas, a lodge, and a restaurant.

CARR CREEK STATE PARK

As early as the 1770s, pioneers were establishing homes in the area of current-day Carr Creek Lake. A marshy area atypical of Appalachia, the Carr Creek region is rich with wildlife.

GET CRAFTY IN APPALACHIA

The Appalachian region is known for its cultural heritage, with arts and crafts playing a huge role. Beyond Berea, which is the place to head if you want to fully immerse yourself in arts and crafts, there are many places in Kentucky's Appalachians where you can find unique works by local artists. While traveling about the area, check out the following shops, arranged by region.

COUNTRY MUSIC HIGHWAY

- **David Appalachian Crafts** (6369 KY 404, David, 606/886-2377, www.davidappalachiancrafts.com): Run by the St. Vincent Mission, David Appalachian Crafts was founded in the 1970s to assist the wives of laid-off mine workers to provide for their families through the making of clothes and later crafts that could be sold. The program continues to do this, selling Appalachian crafts at a store in the coal town of David and at shows around the eastern United States. Crafts, which include pottery, quilts, woodworked items, jewelry, and more, are made both locally and in Appalachian towns throughout the region.

- **Pike County Artisan Center** (211 Main St., Pikeville, 606/433-0193, www.pikeartisancenter.org): The center hosts artists' studios, leads classes, and sells the work of artisans from all over Pike County.

SOUTHERN APPALACHIA

- **Poor Fork Arts and Crafts Guild Store** (218 W. Main St., Cumberland, 606/589-2545, http://poorforkartsandcrafts.org): Guild members sell a variety of works, including cornhusk dolls, pottery, dulcimers, paintings, furniture, quilts, birdfeeders, and more, at this downtown shop.

- **Cumberland Crafts** (U.S. 25E, Middlesboro, 606/242-3699, www.southernhighlandguild.org): Located in the visitors center of Cumberland Gap National Historical Park, this retail outlet of the Southern Highlands Craft Guild sells works from artists all over the southern Appalachians.

APPALACHIAN INTERIOR

- **Kentucky Appalachian Artisan Center** (16 W. Main St., Hindman, 606/785-9855): Located in the town of Hindman, which is off of KY 80 between Prestonsburg and Hazard, this center is worth seeking out. More than 200 juried members from 49 Eastern Kentucky counties display and sell their goods here. The quality of work is high, with the center helping artists make a living from their work.

- **Marie Stewart Museum and Crafts Shop** (71 Center St., Hindman, 606/785-5475, www.hindmansettlement.org): Part of the very neat Hindman Settlement School, which was established in 1902 and continues to this day to "provide education and service opportunities for people of the mountains, while keeping them mindful of their heritage," this shop also offers juried crafts from Eastern Kentucky.

- **Red Bird Mission Crafts** (70 Queendale Center, Beverly, 606/598-2709, www.rbmission.org): This nonprofit evangelical Christian mission, which provides health care and education to the region's residents, runs a craft store featuring works from artisans within a 60-mile radius.

BIG SOUTH FORK AREA

- **Mountain Craft Center** (6930 Hwy. 90, Parkers Lake, 606/376-3463): Located inside a log cabin dating to 1842 that is just five miles west of Cumberland Falls, the center sells quilts, candles, birdhouses, walking sticks, photographs, and a beautiful collection of wood furniture.

- **Junkyard Pottery** (66 P. P. Walker Ln., Parkers Lake, 606/376-8959, www.junkyardpottery.com): This shop specializes in stoneware pottery that is hand thrown and glazed on-site. Browse dishes, vases, candleholders, planters, and other decorative and utilitarian pieces.

Although small at only 710 acres, Carr Creek is a very pretty lake, surrounded by redbuds and hillsides. **Carr Creek State Park** (2086 Smithboro Rd., Sassafras, 606/642-4050, http://parks.ky.gov, daylight-dark, free) has a long, sandy beach that provides swimming access to the lake. Picnic areas are also located around the lake. A nearby marina offers boat ramps and pontoon and fishing boat rentals.

ACCOMMODATIONS AND FOOD

Overnight visitors at **Buckhorn Lake State Resort Park** (4441 KY 1833, Buckhorn, 606/398-7510, http://parks.ky.gov) can reserve one of the 36 rooms at **Buckhorn Lodge** ($109.95). Rooms have queen beds and patios or balconies with views of the lake. You can also try your luck at snagging one of the park's few **cottages** ($209.95-229.95). Buckhorn has two two-bedroom cottages and one three-bedroom cottage. The cottages have nice front decks where you can relax or grill dinner. A pool is available for overnight guests of the lodge and the cottages.

At **Bowlingtown Country Kitchen** (4441 KY 1833, Buckhorn, 606/398-7510, http://parks.ky.gov, 7am-8pm Sun.-Thurs., 7am-9pm Fri.-Sat., $5.99-13.99), also at Buckhorn Lake State Resort Park, you can choose from a Kentucky ham plate, a country vegetable plate, or a variety of sandwiches, or opt for the soup and salad bar.

At **Carr Creek State Park** (2086 Smithboro Rd., Sassafras, 606/642-4050, http://parks.ky.gov), a 39-site **campground** (mid-Mar.-mid-Nov., $20) with full hookups offers pretty surroundings and easy access to the lake.

GETTING THERE AND AROUND

Both Buckhorn Lake State Resort Park and Carr Creek State Park are in the vicinity of the city of Hazard, which is north of Whitesburg and Cumberland on KY 15. Buckhorn Lake State Resort Park is located northwest of Hazard on KY 1833. From Hazard (22 miles; 35 minutes), drive 8.8 miles on northbound KY 15 to westbound KY 28. Turn left onto KY 28, drive 10.3 miles to where KY 28 meets KY 1883, and stay straight onto KY 1883, which will lead you to the park in about 4 miles. Carr Creek State Park is located between Whitesburg and Hazard on KY 15. It is about 15 miles (25 minutes) north of Whitesburg and about 15 miles (20 minutes) east of Hazard.

The Redbird Ranger District is south of the Hal Rogers Parkway between London and Hazard. From Hal Rogers Parkway, take Exit 24, and then drive south on KY 66 for about three miles to the Redbird Ranger Station.

Big South Fork Area

The Big South Fork Area consists almost entirely of public land, although there are towns and cities with homes and businesses located on this land. Specifically the area consists of the Big South Fork National River and Recreational Area, which encompasses the very southern section of this region and then stretches across the border deep into Tennessee; the Stearns Ranger District of the Daniel Boone National Forest, which in total contains 707,000 acres that stretch from Morehead in the north all the way to the Tennessee border; and Cumberland Falls State Resort Park, which offers one of the most unique sights in the state park system. Nearly all of the land in this region is rugged, covered in forests and containing unique sandstone formations. It is also home to a variety of wildlife, including black bears. Recreation opportunities are varied, but this area offers some of the best paddling opportunities in the state, along with good fishing and hiking. Before this land was proclaimed to be public, much of it was owned by coal

Cumberland Falls

and lumber companies, and the region's heritage is strongly related to these industries. Beyond recreation, tourism in the Big South Fork Area revolves around sites that have preserved this way of life that has been so important to Appalachia.

◖ CUMBERLAND FALLS STATE RESORT PARK

Ever seen a moonbow? If not, then you need to get yourself to **Cumberland Falls State Resort Park** (7351 KY 90, Corbin, 606/528-4121, http://parks.ky.gov, 24-hours daily, free) during a full moon. On clear full-moon nights and the two nights before and after, the light from the moon creates a rainbow over Cumberland Falls, a 125-foot waterfall that drops 60 feet. This phenomenon takes place nowhere else in the Western hemisphere, which might explain why rooms at the lodge book years in advance and thousands of people show up during the nicest months. If you can't make it for the moonbow, don't write off Cumberland Falls. The waterfall is beautiful

year-round, arched over by rainbows in the mist on sunny days, framed by colorful trees in the fall, and magical in the snow and ice of winter.

Hiking at the park is particularly excellent, with more than 17 miles of trails tracing through the surrounding forests and down to the falls. Short trails under a mile are ideal for families, while the 10.8-mile Moonbow Trail draws serious hikers. Backcountry camping is allowed, making multi-day hiking trips or nights spent right alongside the river a possibility. An on-site stable offers 45-minute rides ($18) through the forest for those looking to see it from a different vantage point. Those who prefer a wet and wild time also have options. If low-key is your style, kick back at the community pool. If you want big thrills, see what **Sheltowee Trace Outfitters** (www.ky-rafting.com) is offering in the way of kayaking, canoeing, and rafting from their kiosk near the falls overlooks. A popular run from the park is the 30-minute trip through the mist to the bottom of the falls.

© THERESA DOWELL BLACKINTON

Accommodations

Visitors to **Cumberland Falls State Resort Park** (7351 KY 90, Corbin, 606/528-2141, http://parks.ky.gov) can bunk down at **Dupont Lodge** ($129.95), which has a true lodge feel thanks to hemlock beam ceiling supports, knotty pine walls in common areas, and massive stone fireplaces. The 51 rooms were remodeled in 2006 and are furnished in standard hotel style. Rooms have TVs and wireless Internet, although your time is better spent out on the patio overlooking the Cumberland River and the surrounding hills. One- and two-bedroom **cottages** ($149.99-259.99), including a handful built by the Civilian Conservation Corps, are also available. The cottages have nice decks with forest views, and the interiors have all the expected modern comforts. The park's **campground** (mid-Mar.-mid-Nov., $22-24) offers 50 sites with hookups along with some nice tent sites that offer a bit of seclusion.

Experience rural Eastern Kentucky life on a stay at **Farm House Inn Bed and Breakfast** (735 Taylor Branch Rd., Parkers Lake, 606/376-7383, www.farmhouseinnbb.com, $125). Three guest rooms are located in a 1920s log cabin that sits on a cattle, timber, and hay farm north of Cumberland Falls and is accessible from KY 90. The Loft Room has a king bed and a double bed and shares a bathroom with the Sewing Room, which has a full and twin bed. The downstairs bedroom has a full bed and a bathroom across the hall. This inn is ideal for those looking to retreat from the modern world and relax by fishing in the farm ponds, exploring the trails that crisscross the property, and watching for wildlife. A two-night minimum is in effect April-October.

Accommodations can be difficult to find during moonbow periods. If you can't secure a room at the park lodge or at the Farm House Inn, consider staying in Corbin, where you'll find multiple chain hotels.

Food

Cumberland Falls State Resort Park's **Riverview Restaurant** (7351 KY 90, Corbin, 606/528-2141, http://parks.ky.gov, 7am-8pm Sun.-Thurs., 7am-9pm Fri.-Sat., $5.99-13.99) serves such park standards as fried catfish, Hot Browns, and grilled chicken wraps.

Information and Services

A visitors center is located in the falls overlook area. Guests can also ask at the lodge for maps and other park information.

Getting There and Around

Corbin (19 miles; 30 minutes), which is located on I-75, provides the most direct access to Cumberland Falls for most visitors. From the interstate, take Exit 25 and then proceed eight miles on southbound U.S. 25W. At that point, the road splits, and you'll want to stay right onto KY 90, which will lead to the park in about eight miles. From Western Kentucky, the best way to reach Cumberland Falls is by following the Cumberland Parkway to Somerset (35 miles; 50 minutes), where you'll transfer to southbound U.S. 27. Drive 24 miles on U.S. 27, and then turn left onto KY 1045. After eight miles, KY 1045 will hit KY 90, at which point you'll turn right to reach the park. From Stearns (20 miles, 30 minutes) and recreational areas south, you'll take U.S. 27 northbound to KY 1045, where you'll turn right and continue on to KY 90.

STEARNS

The town of Stearns was founded in 1902 by a Michigan man named Justus C. Stearns, who was interested in logging the surrounding forests. During construction of a railroad to haul the logs out, coal was discovered, and soon the Stearns Coal & Lumber Company was busy emptying the area of its natural resources. The town of Stearns stood at the heart of the company, with 18 coal camps scattered throughout the 30,000-acre territory. By the 1950s, mines began to close as their resources were depleted, and the camps were torn down when the Stearns Company left town in 1976, selling its interests to Blue Diamond Coal Company, which mined its last piece of coal in 1987. Today, the town of Stearns has been restored, and the company sign lights up over the warehouse and former company stores, which now host craft shops, restaurants, and a manufacturing company. For a look at life in a coal town or camp, the attractions in Stearns are hard to beat.

◖ Barthell Coal Mining Camp

From 1902 to 1948, the **Barthell Coal Mining Camp** (552 Barthell Rd., 606/376-8749, www.barthellcoalcamp.com, Apr.-Nov.) was home to 350 people with direct ties to the first of what would be an eventual 18 coal mines owned by Stearns Coal and Lumber Company. Although the camp was disassembled when the mine closed, those curious about coal camp life can get as close of a taste as possible thanks to the Koger family. Wishing to honor miners (of which there were many in their family) and the coal mining culture, the Kogers meticulously reconstructed the camp, using a survey conducted by the University of Kentucky, old photographs, and oral histories to rebuild the camp with buildings in their exact former locations. Tours of the camp are guided, with visitors able to choose from a camp tour ($12), a mine tour ($10), or a combined tour. Buildings that can be visited include a doctor's office, barbershop, bathhouse, machine house, commissary, combined church and school, and a miner's house. Each is stocked with artifacts and mementos that make it seem as if a miner might walk in at any minute. Tours of the mine allow you to enter 300 feet into a shaft that lies 300 feet below the top of the mountain. The seam of coal is still visible, and you can get a good idea of what it was like to work inside this mine. Tours are offered at 9am, 11am, 1pm, and 3pm Wednesday-Sunday; the tour length varies depending on your level of interest. If you can, try to visit during June's annual homecoming, when you'll have the opportunity to meet miners from this camp and their families and hear firsthand accounts of life at Barthell.

To really get the full experience, you can book an overnight stay in the camp at one of the miner's cabins. The Kogers, who are kind as can be, will see that you're well taken care of whether you're visiting for the day or staying overnight.

Big South Fork Scenic Railway

Hop aboard the open-sided cars of the former Kentucky & Tennessee Railway for a scenic journey through Daniel Boone National Forest and Big South Fork National River and Recreation Area. Passengers on the **Big South Fork Scenic Railway** (100 Henderson St., 800/462-5664, www.bsfsry.com, $18 adults, $16.50 seniors, $9 youth 3-12), as the railway is now known, travel a total of 16 miles through thick forest, past streams and rivers, over trestle bridges, through tunnels, and past dramatic rock formations.

After an hour-long ride, the train, which was originally built to haul coal and lumber from the 200-square-mile Stearns Company empire, stops at **Blue Heron Coal Mining Camp.** The last of the Stearns coal camps, Blue Heron is now run by the National Park Service, which interprets the site through "ghost" structures representing the church, school, company store, and residences. The best feature of each site is the accompanying audio recording providing insight into daily life at Blue Heron through the voices of former residents. The stop lasts 1.5 hours, plenty of time to take in the sights as well as have a picnic lunch or grab a hot dog from the on-site concessioner. Before you re-board the train, be sure to stroll out onto the tipple bridge for a view of the Big South Fork of the Cumberland River. The return trip is shorter, making for a total trip time of 3-3.5 hours.

The train runs at 11am Thursday-Friday and 11am and 2:30pm Saturday, April; 11am Wednesday-Friday, 11am and 2:30pm Saturday, and 12:30pm Sunday, May-September; and 11am Tuesday-Friday, 11am and 2:30pm Saturday, and 12:30pm Sunday, October. Special train events take place in November and December; check the website for more information.

McCreary County Museum

Your railway ticket provides for free admission

© THERESA DOWELL BLACKINTON

Big South Fork Scenic Railway

to the **McCreary County Museum** (606/376-5730, www.mccrearymuseum.com, 9am-4pm Thurs.-Sat. Apr., 9am-4pm Tues-Sat. and 11am-4pm Sun. May-Oct., 11am-4pm Thurs.-Sat. Nov.), which is located in the Stearns Company office building just above the depot. The museum contains artifacts that tell the story of the county from its pioneer days through its logging and mining days. If you didn't take the railway, you can purchase a ticket ($5 adults, $4 seniors, $3 youth) and poke around.

Accommodations

Accommodation options are limited in the area. The 12 Company Houses at **Barthell Mining Camp** (552 Barthell Rd., 606/376-8749, www.barthellcoalcamp.com, $100-125) offer the area's most unique experience. Although the one- and two-bedroom cabins look straight out of the camp era on the outside, the interiors are fully modern with carpeting, queen beds, full bathrooms, a kitchen with microwave and refrigerator, and a dining area. In the evening,

enjoy the call of whippoorwills from the front porch swing.

For an in-town option, the **Big South Fork Motor Lodge** (136 Bruce St., Stearns, 606/376-3156, $64) belongs solidly to the old-fashioned mom-and-pop hotel category, and although its decor is dated, the rooms are clean, there's a well-maintained pool and outdoor cooking area, and the staff is friendly and helpful.

Food

At Barthell Mining Camp, the **Coal Miner's Diner** (552 Barthell Rd., 606/376-8749, www.barthellcoalcamp.com, $2.95-7.95) serves breakfast, lunch, and dinner, all three meals best finished with a fried apple pie.

There aren't many other options in Stearns. Nearby Whitley City has slightly more choices, including a couple of pizza places, a Chinese restaurant, a Mexican restaurant, a burger joint, and a few fast-food places.

Information and Services

If you're planning a trip to the area, visit the

website of the **McCreary County Tourist Commission** (606/376-3008, www.mccreary-tourism.com). They don't have a visitors center, but can help over the phone or through their website. Brochures and maps are available inside the depot of the Big South Fork Scenic Railway.

Getting There and Around

Stearns is located one mile west of U.S. 27 on KY 1651, a small road that runs between Whitley City and KY 2279.

BIG SOUTH FORK NATIONAL RIVER AND RECREATION AREA AND DANIEL BOONE NATIONAL FOREST

The Big South Fork National River and Recreation Area and the Stearns District of the Daniel Boone National Forest fit together like puzzle pieces, with recreational opportunities crossing back and forth between the two. For all visitor intents and purposes, there is no need to distinguish between them. All you need to know is that these are wilderness areas, rich with crazy rock formations, wild rivers, and stately forests. Whatever your outdoor interest, you'll likely find a way to pursue it in this area.

Hiking

Hundreds of miles of trails are open to hikers in this area. The majority of the trails are short, with distances ranging from under one mile to more than six miles, although many can be connected for longer outings. Additionally, a nearly 55-mile section of the 269-mile Sheltowee Trace National Recreation Trail runs through this section of the Daniel Boone National Forest. During the spring, a popular hike is the one-mile loop that takes hikers to **Yahoo Falls** (KY 700), which at 113 feet is the tallest waterfall in Kentucky, and then on to Yahoo Arch. The waterfall often dries up in summer, making this a less appealing hike during the hottest months. The **Natural Arch Scenic Area** (KY 927) is another popular hiking destination. A short one-mile trail leads through wooded landscape to the base

of a 50-foot-by-90-foot natural rock arch and then back to the parking area. Those looking for a longer hike can take the five-mile Buffalo Canyon Trail, which also visits the arch before traveling farther into the forest. An overlook is located just a short walk down a paved path from the parking area.

Experienced hikers can test themselves in the 4,791-acre **Beaver Creek Wilderness Area,** a completely undeveloped area of wild forests, sandstone cliffs, and rock shelters. Trails are primitive and un-signed, so you should not venture into this area unless you have strong outdoors knowledge. Those who do, however, will be rewarded with solitude and pristine wilderness.

A list of hikes with mileage as well as downloadable maps can be found on the Stearns Ranger District page at www.fs.fed.us and at www.nps.gov/biso.

Horseback Riding

Horseback riding is one of the most popular activities in the area, with many miles of trails open for equestrian use. Two horse camps, Barren Fork and Bell Farm, are located in the Stearns district of the Daniel Boone National Forest, for those with their own horses. Unfortunately, no camps offer guided rides.

Water Sports

The many forks of the Cumberland River, a state-designated wild river, offer excellent paddling opportunities for all abilities. The main outfitter for these rivers is **Sheltowee Trace Outfitters** (2001 KY 90, Corbin, 800/541-7238, www.ky-rafting.com). Rafting trips are especially popular, with options including a 2.5-hour family fun run, half-day trips, and full-day trips on stretches of the river that offer rapids up to Class IV. Canoe trips on calmer waters are also offered, ranging from a half-day, 5-mile trip to a two-day, 28-mile trip. Trips vary with season and water level and should be reserved in advance. When the water is very low (usually August only), Sheltowee Trace Outfitters also organizes tubing on the Cumberland River.

Those with their own watercraft are welcome to run the rivers without a guide, but all paddlers should be seasoned before hitting the water. Popular stretches include the 17 miles on the Upper Cumberland from KY 204 to KY 90 (Class I and II) and the 11.6 miles on the Lower Cumberland from Cumberland Falls to the Mouth of Laurel Lake (Class III). Sheltowee Trace Outfitters offers shuttle service.

Fishing

The Big South Fork of the Cumberland River is a popular fishing spot, with anglers casting lines for bass, sunfish, and other freshwater species. The area's real treasure, however, is Rock Creek, a blue ribbon trout fishery. Nearly 15 miles of scenic creek are accessible to the public. Once heavily polluted by the mines, this creek has been nurtured back to life and is a favorite of anglers who can cast for brown and rainbow trout.

Camping

Four park service campgrounds are scattered throughout this region. **Barren Fork Horse Camp** (FS Rd. 684, 606/376-5323, www.fs.fed. gov, Apr.-mid-Nov., $9) has 41 sites that can accommodate horse trailers (although non-equestrian campers are also welcome). The camp has fire grates, potable water, a watering pond for horses, and vault toilets. **Bell Farm Horse Camp** (FS Rd. 6303, 606/376-5323, www.fs.fed.gov, Apr.-mid-Nov., free) caters to groups, with five large spots that can accommodate 60 people. The campground has vault toilets, and the only source of water is Rock Creek. Located along Rock Creek, **Great Meadow Campground** (FS Rd. 137, 606/376-5323, www.fs.fed.gov, free) is a small site

available on a first-come, first-served basis. The campground has vault toilets and running water mid-April-November and is ideal for those fishing for trout. The **Blue Heron Campground** (KY 742, 877/444-6777, www. nps.gov/biso, Apr.-Oct., $17) has 41 sites with full hookups, available by reservation, although unreserved spots are offered on a first-come, first-served basis. The campground has showers and flush toilets.

Information and Services

The **Big South Fork National River and Recreation Area** (100 Henderson St., Stearns, 423/286-7275, www.nps.gov/biso) maintains a seasonal office (Apr.-Nov.) in the depot of the Big South Fork Scenic Railway. The ranger office for the **Stearns District of the Daniel Boone National Forest** is located in Whitley City (3320 U.S. 27 N., Whitley City, 606/376-5323, www.fs.fed.gov). Both offices can provide maps (both driving and hiking), information on outfitters and activities, and help you tailor a trip to your ability and interests. Some trail maps are also available online.

Getting There and Around

Recreational opportunities are spread throughout a large swath of forested land, and there's no one specific jumping-off place. To really make the most of your time, plan your activities in advance, and map directions to where you need to go. If you arrive without a plan, try to speak with a ranger, who can help you determine a route. Forest roads are generally in good shape, but can be narrow and winding, so drive carefully and keep a close eye out for wildlife, especially at dawn and dusk.

The Western Foothills

Situated along I-75, where the Appalachian Mountains begin to stretch out, turning into foothills that give way to flatter land in the west, you'll find towns working hard to preserve the Appalachian culture. Arts and crafts, traditional music, and fried chicken are at the heart of the western foothills. This region is more traveled than much of Appalachia thanks to the easy access provided by I-75, but the towns remain small and all have easy access to the trails and waterways of the middle portion of the Daniel Boone National Forest.

BEREA

Berea is an arts and crafts paradise, with seemingly every person in this college town gifted with a talent for woodworking, ceramics, painting, weaving, glassworking, or music. The town has a collaborative spirit with a belief that art is for everyone, so in addition to being able to purchase all kinds of work, you can also witness as it's being made or take classes to learn to create such beautiful items yourself. Progressive in a way that most people don't expect from Appalachia, Berea believes strongly in protecting the earth, promoting equality for all people, and preserving tradition while embracing the future. It is literally a breath of fresh air, and is really a must for any Kentucky itinerary.

Berea College

Since its establishment in 1885, **Berea College** (101 Chestnut St., 895/985-3000, www.berea. edu) has stood out for its progressive stance on education and its commitment to the Appalachian community. All 1,500 students at Berea today receive a full scholarship and earn income for additional expenses through a required work-study program, which has students perform college jobs ranging from working at Boone Tavern Hotel and Restaurant to producing crafts. A beacon in the community and the greater world, Berea was the first college in the South to admit African Americans and women,

and in the present era is noted for its work on sustainable living. Every building on campus is green, and students even have the opportunity to live in an off-the-grid Eco-Village. A remarkable college unlike any other in the state, Berea is worth exploring. Student-led historical tours are offered at 9am, 10am, 1pm, and 3pm weekdays and 9am and 2pm Saturday. A craft tour, which allows visitors an insider's look at the college's renowned program dedicated to preserving the tradition of Appalachian crafts, is offered at 10am and 2pm weekdays. The free tours last about one hour and depart from the Berea College Visitors Center.

(Studio Artists of Berea

Lots of towns have art galleries. What makes Berea unique is the fact that a huge portion of the artwork being sold in Berea is made right here in Berea. The backbone of Berea's status as the Folk Arts and Crafts Capital of Kentucky is the studio artist program, in which working artists operate combined studio galleries, not only selling their work to the public, but also sharing with them their creative process. Square purple signs bearing a four-hand design designate studio artists' galleries, where you can watch artists blow glass, weave, woodwork, throw pots, and more. The majority of studio artists are located in Old Town (Broadway), but a few are in College Square. Because Berea is so easy to walk, you can just wander the two districts, keeping an eye out for the studio artist signs. You can also pick up the Berea Working Artists Studio Map or the Map to Art in Berea brochure from the Old Town Welcome Center.

Although it feels unfair to single out artists, as they all are truly exceptional, I'll go ahead and point out my musts. In College Square, visit **Warren May** (110 Center St., 859/986-9293, www.warrenamay.com), a woodworker who creates beautiful pieces of furniture, but is most known for his Appalachian dulcimers. Jimmy Lou Jackson at **Hot Flash Beads**

© THERESA DOWELL BLACKINTON

hand-crafted dulcimers in a shop in Berea

(2 Artist Circle, 859/986-2411), which shares a building with **Honeysuckle Vine** gallery near the Welcome Center, creates gorgeous lamp-worked beads that she turns into must-have earrings, pendants, and more. Naturally gregarious, Jimmy Lou loves to demonstrate her process and can easily talk you through everything she's doing without missing a beat. To learn about the process of weaving on a variety of looms, visit Neil Colmer at **Weaver's Bottom** (140 N. Broadway, 859/986-8661) in Old Town, where the Berea College graduate turns out bed covers, blankets, rugs, shawls, and more in all kinds of colors and patterns. If I were so lucky to have a beach house to decorate, the first person I'd see would be Michelle Weston at **Weston Studio Glass** (217 Adams St., 859/985-0150), where she turns out blown glass pieces that remind me of the sea. For one-of-a-kind home furnishings, see what brothers Doug and Wally can craft for you at **Haley-Daniels** (119 N. Broadway, 859/986-7243, www.haleydaniels.com). The pieces made from Ambrosia maple, a local maple wood

that takes its remarkable patterning from the Ambrosia beetles that inhabit it, are my favorites. Multiple other studio artists live and work in Berea, and you should try to visit as many as possible. After all, art is personal, so your favorite and mine might not be the same. Most studios are open 10am-5pm Monday-Saturday, but schedules can vary.

Art Galleries

Beyond the studio galleries of working artists, Berea also boasts multiple art galleries that, instead of focusing on the works of one artisan, offer works by many regional artists. In College Square, visit **The Log House Craft Gallery** (200 Estill St., 859/985-3225), the first of Berea's art galleries, which, in addition to selling crafts from Appalachian artists, also features the work of Berea student artists, including such remarkable items as hand-turned beds; **The Promenade Gallery** (204 Center St., 859/986-1609, 10am-5pm Mon.-Sat.), which stocks pottery, textiles, prints, and yard art; **Gallery 103** (103 Jackson St., 859/986-0668,

Hot Flash Beads and Honeysuckle Vine gallery in Berea

© THERESA DOWELL BLACKINTON

10am-5pm Mon.-Sat.), which sells pottery, stained glass, and silversmithed jewelry; and **Appalachian Fireside Gallery** (127 Main St., 859/986-9013, 10am-5pm Mon.-Sat.), which offers a strong mix of the many arts and crafts native to this area. In Old Town, don't miss **Top Drawer Gallery** (202 N. Broadway, 859/985-2907, www.topdrawergallery.com, 10am-5pm Mon.-Sat.), which has lovely furniture and other higher-end pieces.

Art Workshops

To the people of Berea, art is a way of life, and they love to encourage others to share in their passion. A number of local artisans offer classes to help you discover your inner artist. Lindy Evans at **Images of Santa** (139 N. Broadway, 859/582-2065, www.lindyevans.com) hosts workshops that allow you to create your own 18-inch Santa doll. **Ken Gastineau** (859/986-9158, www.gastineaustudio.com) teaches copper and brass jewelry making, while **Tim Weckman** (859/582-1234, bereabonsai.com) introduces people to the art of bonsai. For those

interested in woodworking, the **Kelly Mehler's School of Woodworking** (859/986-5540, www.kellymehler.com) offers a broad schedule of classes. New classes are added each year to keep up with the skills and interests of workshop participants. Dancers looking to learn new steps should sign up for the **Christmas Country Dance School** (859/985-3431), held annually in the week between Christmas and New Year's. The classes focus on traditional dance styles such as clogging, square dancing, Morris dancing, and more.

If you're looking to try your hand at a wide range of arts and crafts, learning from some of the best out there, you'll want to put the annual **Festival of Learnships** on your calendar. This two-week event held in July brings professional instructors from around the nation to Berea to teach more than 100 workshops covering visual arts, performing arts, literary arts, culinary arts, and the art of sustainable living.

Kentucky Artisan Center

Introduce yourself to Berea at the **Kentucky**

Artisan Center (200 Artisan Way, 859/985-5448, www.kentuckyartisancenter.ky.gov, 9am-6pm daily), which is located just off of I-75 and is essentially the best rest stop you'll ever experience. The 25,000-square-foot limestone building, which is a work of art itself, contains a gallery with changing art exhibits and retail space dedicated to work by Kentucky artisans. Demonstrations occur regularly on weekends. The arts and crafts on display are top-notch and will entice you to head into Berea for more.

Entertainment and Events

Art has broad meaning in Berea, as it should, and music and dance are nearly as popular as visual arts. Every Thursday, a local father-daughter team hosts **Jammin' on the Porch** at the Old Town Welcome Center (7pm-9:30pm). Playing music on the porch is a tradition as old as the hills themselves, so get into the spirit of Appalachia by attending. You're welcome to tap your toes, get up and dance, or bring your instrument and jam along.

Another local tradition is the **monthly dance** held at the Russel Acton Folk Center (212 Jefferson St.) and sponsored by the Contraire Dance Association (www.bereacontradance. org). This is no small community get-together, but a serious good time with a professional caller leading approximately 250 people across the dance floor. Don't worry if you don't know how to do-si-do. Each event begins with a 30-minute introductory session that allows newcomers to learn the steps and those with two left feet to get a refresher. The dance is held on the fourth Saturday of the month. The introductory lesson begins at 7:30pm, and the actual dance runs 8pm-11pm. Admission is $7 for adults and $4 for students. A contra dance is also held every third Friday 9pm-midnight. Musicians are invited to bring their instrument and play in the open band.

The largest annual event is the **Berea Craft Festival** (Indian Fort Theatre, 859/986-1585, www.bereacraftfestival.com, 10am-6pm, $6 adults, $5 seniors, free youth under 12), which is held on the second weekend of July. More than 100 artists from across the nation display their goods at the festival. Craft demonstrations, which might include blacksmithing, pottery, or dyeing with plants, take place throughout the weekend, and live traditional music fills the air.

Fabric artists should put the **Quilt Extravaganza** (859/985-9317, www. bereaartscouncil.org, $3 adults, free for youth), held on the first weekend in August, on their calendar. The two-day event features quilt exhibits, workshops, demonstrations, and more.

The **Spoonbread Festival** (www.spoonbreadfestival.com), a mid-September weekend event, involves all kinds of old-fashioned family fun: a parade, a carnival, a car show, live music, and all the spoonbread you could possible consume.

Hiking

Near Berea are multiple hiking options. One much-loved hike follows a 0.7-mile trail to **Anglin Falls,** a 75-foot waterfall that sprays down a rock shelf. Strongest in the spring, the falls can shrink to a trickle during the summer months. The wildflowers are also lovely in the spring. Anglin Falls is located in the John B. Stephenson Memorial Forest State Nature Preserve (www.naturepreserves. ky.gov), named for a former president of Berea College who advocated for conservation of the area. The preserve, which is located off of Himanns Fork Road, is a bit tricky to find. Copy the directions from the website or ask in Berea, where someone at the visitors center or the college can easily give you turn-by-turn directions.

The **Berea College Forest,** which encompasses nearly 8,000 acres, is another good hiking destination. Hikers can choose from 19 miles of trails. Popular routes include the 4.5-mile round-trip to Buzzard Roost and Eagle Nest overlooks, the 6.4-mile round-trip to Robe Mountain, and the 3.5-mile round-trip to East Pinnacle. Many people claim the best views in the state are from the outlooks in Berea College Forest, and during fall especially, it's hard to argue. Access to the forest is through

Indian Fort Theatre, which is three miles east of Berea College on KY 21.

Biking

The **TransAmerica Trail** (www.adventurecycling.org), which leads cyclists across the country, passes through Berea. The town warmly welcomes these cross-country cyclists, as well as anyone else who cares to go for a bike ride through Berea. The tourism office is happy to provide information on various nearby routes, with one suited for most any ability. Drivers in Berea are bike friendly, and a designated bike path even leads from town to the Kentucky Artisan Center.

Accommodations

Built more than a century ago to host the many guests of Berea College, **Boone Tavern Hotel** (100 Main St., 859/985-3700, www.boonetavernhotel.com, $99-155) has evolved to become Kentucky's first LEED-certified hotel, its gold status recognizing the hotel's efforts to be sustainable and environmentally friendly. Although Boone Tavern Hotel works hard to conserve energy and water, guests don't feel as if they're being asked to skimp. The hotel speaks of Southern elegance, grace and comfort mingling easily. Rooms are bright, fresh, and spacious, with crown moldings, high ceilings, and gorgeous woodworked furniture, tiled mirrors, and bedding made by Berea students. Soaking tubs, plush robes and slippers, flat-screen TVs, and wireless Internet access are standard. A large common room off the lobby and a veranda decked out in rocking chairs invite gatherings. Old-fashioned Southern hospitality meets progressive ideas at Boone Tavern Hotel, which shows that the two can get along famously if given the chance. You should give it a try.

The Doctor's Inn Bed and Breakfast (617 Chestnut St., 859/986-3042, www.doctorsinnofbereaky.com, $135-150), a Greek Revival home, offers gorgeous views of the Appalachian foothills while sitting only four blocks from the heart of Berea. The three guest rooms have private bathrooms and are decorated with authentic furnishings from Berea College and stained-glass windows. Guests are treated to a full country breakfast each morning.

A cute home on a quiet street within walking distance of College Square, **The Greathouse Inn Bed and Breakfast** (317 Jackson St., 859/986-7351, www.bbgreathouse.com, $110) has two rooms available for guests, one on the first floor and one on the second. Rooms are spacious and decorated with antiques. The breakfast features Southern favorites like biscuits and gravy and country ham.

If you're looking for your own private retreat, you'll find two interesting options in Berea. **Weaver's Rest Cottage** (106 Churchill Ct., 859/582-3475, www.weaversrestcottage.com, $85) is a one-bedroom cottage with living area, full kitchen, and bathroom with claw-foot tub and shower. Home until 2006 of Churchill Weavers, one of the most renowned Appalachian craft groups, Weaver's Rest Cottage lets you immerse yourself in the history and culture of Berea. Bright, cheerful, and cute as a button, the cottage is within walking distance of sites, or you can just sit on the porch and relax. Another option is the **John G. Fee Cottage** (107 Parkway Ave., 859/625-4111, www.feeguestcottage.com, $85), built by and now named for the founder of Berea College. This cottage has one king bed, one queen bed, and one trundle bed, a full kitchen, two bathrooms, and a sunroom. Both cottages have free wireless Internet.

Food

Boone Tavern Restaurant (100 Main St., 859/985-3700, www.boonetavernhotel.com, 7am-10am, 11am-2pm, and 5pm-8pm daily, $18-28) offers the finest dining option in Berea. Decorated in multiple shades of blue and furnished with handsome carved chairs and large chandeliers, the restaurant has an understated elegance, with a warmth that makes conversation between neighboring tables of once-strangers not uncommon. The restaurant serves all three meals, the menu combining contemporary offerings with traditional favorites like pork chops and creamed chicken in a nest made of shredded potatoes. The restaurant serves as much local food as possible, including many items that come from the Berea College Farm. Spoonbread, for which the restaurant is famous, comes with all meals, as does a salad of greens from the garden. Be sure to choose the orange marmalade dressing, another specialty, which is quite delicious. Students act as servers, and most do a great job, although service can occasionally be slow.

Grab a muffin or bagel for breakfast at **Berea Coffee & Tea Co.** (124 Main St., 859/986-7656, 7:30am-9pm Mon.-Fri., 8am-9pm Sat., 10am-6pm Sun.) or stop in for panini at lunchtime. In tune with the artistic environment of the town, Berea Coffee & Tea is open and inviting, with a chalkboard menu and a smattering of tables as well as couches. A patio provides outdoor seating on sunny days. Vegetarians will find options here.

Main Street Café (106 Main St., 859/986-7656, www.msc-berea.com, 10am-3pm Sun. and Tues., 10am-7pm Mon. and Wed., 10am-8pm Thurs.-Sat., $3.99-14.99) does a popular lunch and dinner service. The lunch menu is long on sandwiches and wraps that cater to every diet, from vegetarian to vegan to gluten-free. Dinner entrées also span the spectrum, ranging from chicken tenders to grilled yellowfin tuna to portobello mushrooms to Danish meatballs. The café's most famous dish is their goat cheese salad. Produce is fresh from local gardens, and Kentucky Proud products are used whenever possible. The atmosphere is cozy, with art on the walls and an old piano at the front door, and live music accompanies dinner on Saturday.

If you're in the mood for pizza, grab a table at **PapaLeno's Italian** (108 Center St., 859/986-4497, www.papalenos.com, 11am-10pm Mon.-Thurs., 11am-11pm Fri.-Sat., noon-10pm Sun., $8.99). This casual restaurant with wooden booths and tables, each equipped with a tall can of Parmesan cheese, is known for their homemade crust, which they toss in plain view. The hot sandwiches are also popular. Pasta dishes complete the menu, but the sandwich bread and pizza crusts are the real highlights here.

Dinner Bell Restaurant (127 Plaza Dr., 859/986-2777, 7am-8pm daily, $4.99-9.99) focuses on country cooking, a good choice for those looking for a local version of Cracker Barrel. Pinto beans and cornbread, an Eastern Kentucky traditional meal, is a favorite. Vegetarians should be aware that choices are few here, since practically everything, vegetables included, is cooked with meat. Breakfast is especially popular at Dinner Bell, the plates large enough to carry you through to dinner or at least a late lunch.

For a sweet treat, head to **Old Town Candy Kitchen and Fudge Factory** (128 N. Broadway, 859/985-0541, 9:30pm-5pm Mon.-Sat.), where you'll have to choose among fudge, bourbon balls, caramels, ice cream, shakes, and malts.

Information and Services

Located in the old L&N Depot, the **Berea Welcome Center** (201 N. Broadway, 800/598-5263, www.berea.com, 9am-5pm daily Apr.-Dec., closed Sun. Jan.-Mar.) is a good place to start any visit to Berea. You can pick up maps and brochures and get advice on how to structure your visit.

Berea College runs its own visitors center (Short St., College Square, 859/985-3145, www.berea.edu, 9am-6pm Mon.-Fri., 9am-5pm Sat.), which is the starting point for historic and craft tours of the college.

The **Kentucky Artisan Center** (975 Walnut Meadow Rd., 859/985-5448, www.kentucky-artisancenter.ky.gov, 8am-8pm daily) is a third place to get information on Berea. A visitors center in the front of the building offers state tourism information as well as specialized resources on Berea. The center also contains a restaurant with good, inexpensive offerings. Bypass the regular roadside fast-food options and enjoy the day's special, consisting of a meat and two sides (or a vegetarian entrée) for only $6.95, or a made-to-order burger or sandwich for about $3. And just so you know, the bathrooms were voted the best on I-75.

Getting There and Around

Berea is located directly off of I-75 at Exits

76 and 77. It is 38 miles (45 minutes) south of Lexington, 38 miles (35 minutes) north of London, and 50 miles (50 minutes) north of Corbin. There are two main sections to Berea, the College Square area, which includes Berea College and the shops along Main and Center Streets, and the Old Town Artisan Village, which is centered around North Broadway and where you'll find many of the working artisans as well as the welcome center. Chestnut Street, which has its own share of galleries and antique shops, connects the two. You could walk everywhere in Berea if you don't mind a little bit of exercise. Most people, however, drive (or bike!) between the two main areas and then explore each on foot.

RENFRO VALLEY

Designated the Country Music Capital of Kentucky, Renfro Valley offers family-friendly performances that feature all forms of traditional music. If you remember *Hee Haw* fondly, then you'll love Renfro Valley. If *Hee Haw* doesn't ring a bell for you, imagine a variety show that is built around country, gospel, and bluegrass music and is interjected with a touch of humor, often self-deprecating. Although in today's world this type of show might be considered hokey, it really is a good time, and the musicians and singers are truly talented. If you can't make it to Renfro Valley, you can catch the Renfro Valley Gatherin' program on radio stations throughout the United States and Canada.

(Renfro Valley Entertainment Center

Music has always been an integral part of Appalachian life, and no place has better preserved the tradition of country, bluegrass, and gospel music that has been passed down from generation to generation than **Renfro Valley Entertainment Center** (U.S. 25, Renfro Valley, 800/765-7464, www.renfrovalley.com). While Nashville has gone glam, at Renfro Valley the jamming still takes place in a barn, and performers address the audience as if it's made up of old friends. A variety of shows

© THERESA DOWELL BLACKINTON

Renfro Valley Entertainment Center

are offered Wednesday-Sunday, ranging from Friday's Front Porch Pickin' Show to Saturday afternoon's Gospel Jubilee to Sunday morning's Renfro Valley Gatherin', which is broadcast across the nation and is followed by a nondenominational religious service. The backbone of Renfro Valley, however, is Saturday night's Renfro Valley Barn Dance (7pm), a lively show combining traditional country, bluegrass, gospel, and a bit of humor that's been held in the Old Barn since 1939. Many people choose to come for the Barn Dance and then stay for the Jamboree (9pm), which is built around contemporary country music and big laughs. Tickets for the various shows range $15-25. Crowds tend toward the senior citizen demographic, although younger folks should not be intimidated by the tour buses. The shows are fun for all ages, the picking and playing are phenomenal, and the voices are strong.

Kentucky Music Hall of Fame and Museum

The **Kentucky Music Hall of Fame and Museum** (2590 Richmond Rd., 606/256-1000, www.kentuckymusicmuseum.com, 10am-6pm Mon.-Sat., 9am-3pm Sun., $7.50 adults, $7 senior, $4.50 youth 6-12) celebrates the state's rich tradition of music. Although country and bluegrass are the heavyweights of Kentucky music, the museum does recognize other genres. The one-story museum is organized so that visitors follow one winding route through exhibits that feature instruments and outfits from legends such as the Everly Brothers, explore the many influences that have contributed to music in the Bluegrass State, and allow for hands-on experimentation with music. Musicians often perform live on the small stage in the museum's front room.

BitterSweet Cabin Village

Learn about both the bitter and the sweet experiences of frontier life in Appalachia on a self-guided tour through the cabins of **BitterSweet Cabin Village** (U.S. 25, 606/256-0715, 10am-5pm Mon.-Tues., 10am-7pm Wed.-Sat., 9am-3pm Sun., by donation). The nine cabins, which demonstrate all four types of log cabin found in Kentucky, are furnished with artifacts that represent different aspects of pioneer life. You'll find a farrier's shop, barn toolshed, family cabin, general store, cobbler's shop, woodwright's shop, broom shop, heirloom room, and loom house. Begin your tour in the theater building, where you can view a nostalgic film about Appalachia and the people who have called it home.

Accommodations

If you're attending one of the evening shows and you don't want to have to go far afterward, the **National Heritage Inn and Suites** (2090 Richmond St., Mt. Vernon, 606/256-8600, www.nationalheritageinn.com, $89) is a good place to lay your head. Within walking distance of the entertainment center, the inn is well cared for, with clean rooms available with one king or two doubles. The continental breakfast goes beyond the basics with eggs, sausages, biscuits, and other hot items.

Food

The **Lodge Restaurant** (U.S. 25, 606/256-2638, www.renfrovalley.com, 11am-7pm Wed.-Fri., 7am-7pm Sat., 7am-3pm Sun., $6.99-10.99), located on the grounds of Renfro Valley Entertainment Center, is where most visitors to town take at least one of their meals. The restaurant serves down-home cooking in a homey atmosphere. Meatloaf, fried chicken, country ham, and the like are at the heart of the menu. Service is quick and friendly. They know how to get crowds in and out in time for the shows.

Information and Services

The **Mt. Vernon-Rockcastle County Tourism Commission** (2325 Richmond St., Mt. Vernon, 606/256-9814, www.rockcastletourism.com) covers Renfro Valley. You can request a visitor's packet online.

Getting There and Around

Renfro Valley is located on U.S. 25, just off of I-75. All the town's attractions are lined up one

© THERESA DOWELL BLACKINTON

Levi Jackson Wilderness Road State Park

after another on U.S. 25, which is known as Richmond Street in town. From Berea, travel south on U.S. 25 for 14 miles (15 minutes). From other locations, take I-75 to Exit 62, and then follow northbound U.S. 25 into town.

LONDON, CORBIN, AND LAUREL COUNTY

KFC, with locations in 120 countries, serves more than 12 million people a day, but once upon a time, in the 1930s, Kentucky Fried Chicken was just a mom-and-pop restaurant in the town of Corbin known as Colonel Sanders Café. For many travelers, that restaurant is the reason to stop at Corbin, more for the bragging rights of having eaten at the original than for the good chicken, which, honestly, is no different than what you'd get at any KFC. There's more to Laurel County, which contains the towns of London and Corbin, than the Colonel, however, especially if you're a nature or history lover. A state park and a portion of the Daniel Boone National Forest are located nearby, offering plenty of outdoor

activities. True KFC fans need to time their visit with the Annual World Chicken Festival, which surely will give you plenty to talk about with friends back home.

Levi Jackson Wilderness Road State Park

Levi Jackson Wilderness Road State Park (998 Levi Jackson Mill Rd., London, 606/330-2130, http://parks.ky.gov, daylight-dark daily, free) exists to both honor the pioneers who settled Kentucky and also to provide recreational opportunities. Those interested in understanding a bit more about the homesteading experience will want to visit the **Mountain Life Museum** (8:30am-4:30pm Wed.-Sun., Apr.-Oct., $3), which consists of seven original log buildings relocated here and filled with authentic artifacts. Among the buildings are a two-room school building, a Methodist church, a smokehouse, a blacksmith's shop, a barn, and family cabins. Tours of the buildings are self-guided with the aid of an information sheet explaining the buildings and the objects they contain. Another historic building on the park grounds is **McHargue's Mill.** This water-powered grist mill was reconstructed in the 1930s with original parts dating to 1805 and a millstone that may date all the way back to 1750. The mill is in working order with demonstrations offered Wednesday-Sunday, Memorial Day-Labor Day.

If it's outdoor recreation that you're after, the park has 8.5 miles of hiking trails, portions of which were traveled by Kentucky's earliest settlers. The park also has a mini-golf course, community pool with waterslides, volleyball and basketball courts, horseshoe pits, and picnic and playground areas, as well as a campground.

Harland Sanders Café and Museum

In the kitchen of a café he operated in Corbin, Colonel Harland Sanders came up with the blend of 11 spices that made his chicken famous and his franchise the most popular in the world. The current building, which was built in

1939 as a café and motel, was run by Sanders until I-75 stole much of his business and he began to sell franchise restaurants built around his secret-recipe fried chicken. Visitors to the **Harland Sanders Café and Museum** (688 U.S. 25 W., Corbin, 606/528-2163, 10am-10pm daily) are now essentially visiting one of those franchises. Although the exterior maintains its 1930s style, and wooden country-style tables stand in place of plastic booths, the counter and menu are the same as you'd find at any KFC. So go ahead and order a meal of fried chicken and mashed potatoes—if ever there were a time to eat Kentucky Fried Chicken, this is it—and when you're finished, browse the exhibits scattered throughout the building. You'll find a model of the Colonel's kitchen and one of his motel rooms and cases filled with his personal belongings as well as dishes and other items from the original restaurant.

Daniel Boone National Forest London Ranger District
HIKING
With 190 miles of trail snaking through the London Ranger District, there's a hike for everyone. Ten sections totaling 113 miles of the Sheltowee Trace National Recreation Trail, which stretches the entire length of the Daniel Boone National Forest, fall within this district. Here the trail is open to both hikers and bikers, and you're welcome to do as much or as little of the trail as you like. Other trails in this district are primarily short, although a handful of trails average around five miles, making for a good morning or afternoon adventure. Recreation Opportunity guides, with descriptions of the trails and maps, are available online on the Forest Service website (www.fs.fed. us). You may also visit the **ranger office** (761 S. Laurel Rd., London, 606/864-4163) to get personalized advice on where to hike.

WATER SPORTS
The wild rivers of the southern section of the Daniel Boone National Forest extend north into this portion, making paddle sports a popular pursuit. Those wishing to get out on the

water with the assistance of an outfitter should contact **Sheltowee Trace Outfitters** (2001 Hwy. 90, Corbin, 800/541-7238, www.ky-rafting.com) to explore the various possibilities. If you have your own canoe or kayak, you have multiple options. For a leisurely class I+ paddle, the six miles on the Upper Rockcastle from Wilderness Road Ford in Livingston to the I-75 bridge and the 10.6 miles on the Upper Rockcastle from the I-75 bridge to the KY 1956 bridge make for a nice outing. For a challenging run, consider the 16.9-mile stretch on the Lower Rockcastle from KY 1956 to KY 192, which has Class III and IV rapids.

For a relaxing float down the river, consider renting a tube from **A Country Pedaler** (9006 KY 25, Livingston, 606/256-0703, $8). You'll drift down a gentle section of the Rockcastle River, with forest on both sides.

Fans of still water will want to make their way to **Laurel River Lake,** which offers 5,600 acres of pretty blue water surrounded by forested shores and cliffs. There are eight boat launch ramps scattered around the lake and two marinas with rental options. Both **Grove Marina** (Forest Service Rd. 558, Corbin, 606/523-2323, www.grovemarina.com) and **Holly Bay Marina** (KY 1193, London, 606/864-6542, www.hollybaymarina.com) rent houseboats, pontoons, and fishing boats.

HISTORIC SITES
On rugged terrain near Rockcastle River, troops engaged in the first Civil War battle to take place in Kentucky on October 21, 1861. Here novice Union troops, upon hearing of a northern advance by the Confederates, established **Camp Wildcat** (www.wildcatbattlefield. org) in late September. The battle, which involved 12 Union army units and 8 Confederate army units, ended with a Confederate retreat. Today, although the site is still remote and rugged, little evidence of the battle remains beyond the outlines of trenches. For all but the most serious Civil War buff, visiting the site may require more effort than it's worth, except for reenactment weekend (www.wildcatreenactment.org), which takes place in mid-October.

Then the battlefield really comes to life, and those without in-depth knowledge of the war can get their minds around what happened here. To reach Camp Wildcat, take Exit 49 off I-75, and turn east on KY 909. Drive 0.6 mile to southbound U.S. 25, and continue another 0.6 mile to Hazel Patch Road on the left. You will turn left once again at a sign indicating the battlefield.

Festivals and Events

Laurel County is proud of its status as the birthplace of Kentucky Fried Chicken, and to show its appreciation for all things chicken, it hosts the **Annual World Chicken Festival** (www.chickenfestival.com) every year in late September. Sure, the festival has typical events such as live entertainment, a carnival, a car show, and a parade, but it also has a very strong chicken component. Festival attendees can participate in a variety of contests, including a clucking contest, a cooking contest, a hot-wings eating contest, an egg drop contest, and a Colonel Sanders lookalike contest. Before you leave, be sure to get yourself a chicken dinner from the world's largest skillet.

Accommodations

Thanks to their location along I-75, both London and Corbin have a host of hotel options. If you have a preferred chain, you'll probably find it at one of the exits for these towns. London's best choice is the **Hampton Inn London-North** (200 Alamo Dr., London, 606/864-0011, www.hamptoninn.com, $109). This well-managed property has friendly staff and fresh rooms with comfortable beds. The complimentary breakfast comes with many selections, and guests are also invited to an evening manager's reception. In Corbin, consider the **Fairfield Inn** (25 KY 770, Corbin, 606/528-7020, www.marriott.com, $94), which should meet expectations for a standard hotel room, although compared with some continental breakfasts, their offerings are a bit weak.

At **Levi Jackson Wilderness Road State Park** (998 Levi Jackson Mill Rd., London,

606/330-2130, http://parks.ky.gov), the large 136-site **campground** ($19-32) is primarily set up for RVs, although tents are also welcome. Although a scattering of trees provides shade, the campground is very open with little seclusion between spaces.

Ten **campgrounds** are located within the **Daniel Boone National Forest London Ranger District,** five of them on Laurel River Lake. The most popular lake campgrounds are **Grove** (Forest Service Rd. 558, $16) and **Holly Bay** (KY 1193, $16-28), which are located next to the marinas of the same name. These two drive-in campgrounds (mid-Apr.-mid-Oct.) have electricity hookups, flush toilets, and shower houses. Reservations should be made in advance for both of these campgrounds by phone (877/444-6777) or online (www.recreation.gov). A boat-in campground with vault toilets and drinking water is also located at Grove ($14) and is open year-round on a first-come, first-served basis. Off the lake, one of the most beautifully situated campgrounds is Bee Rock ($9). Campsites are located on both sides of Rockcastle River and offer good views of the unique rock formations along the river. Bee Rock is located on KY 192, 18 miles west of I-75. A full listing of campgrounds is available on the Forest Service website (www.fs.fed.us).

Food

As with hotels, chains rule in the London and Corbin area. Considering this is the birthplace of KFC, that somehow feels appropriate. For one meal, of course, you must eat at **Colonel Sanders Café** (688 U.S. 25 W., Corbin, 606/528-2163, 10am-10pm daily).

The **Abbey** (132 N. Main St., London, 606/864-0044, 11am-3pm Mon.-Wed., 11am-9pm Thurs.-Sat., $6.99-15.99) satisfies diners with a broad menu of American favorites—burgers, steaks, pastas, soup and salad combos. The menu isn't creative, but the food is well prepared, service is efficient and friendly, and prices are good. In an area without many options, this 2012 addition to the area is a solid choice.

Information and Services

The **London-Laurel County Tourism Information Center** (140 Faith Assembly Church Rd., London, 606/878-6900, www.laurelkytourism.com) should be able to help you with inquiries about the area.

Getting There and Around

London and Corbin are both located directly off of I-75 on U.S. 25. To travel between the two cities, which are 13 miles (25 minutes) apart, with London north of Corbin, use U.S. 25. If you're coming via I-75, take Exit 41 to access London and Exit 29 to access Corbin. London is 75 miles (1.25 hours) south of Lexington, and Corbin is 86 miles (1.5 hours) south of Lexington. From the Cumberland Gap area, Corbin can be reached via northbound U.S. 25E (50 miles; 1 hour).

Northern Appalachia

The section referred to here as Northern Appalachia encompasses the area along I-64 from the boundaries of the Lexington region to the Country Music Highway and south down to the Mountain Parkway. It's a vast area, but you'll find no big cities, and even the towns are spread far and wide. Morehead, home to Morehead State University, is the hub of the region, although the fact that its population is less than 7,000 should give you an idea about the rural nature of the area. What makes this region attractive, aside from the Folk Art Center in Morehead, is its parks and recreation areas. You'll find a couple of good lakes for fishing and water sports; a state park protecting a very neat cave system; and the Red River Gorge Geological Area, a premier destination for hiking and climbing in the eastern United States. The natural beauty wows, especially the rock formations that you just don't expect to find in this part of the country, but which are present in big numbers.

MOREHEAD AND ROWAN COUNTY

In Morehead and Rowan County, you can see the transition from the bluegrass region to the west to the mountains of the east. Farming is still good here, with tobacco and corn grown on many farms, although as you move east, the land becomes hillier and then mountainous. The connection to the east is stronger than it is to the west, both economically and culturally.

Coal and lumber have always been big business here, and Morehead is a destination for folk art and bluegrass music. Additionally, a large percentage of the student body at Morehead State comes from the cities and towns of Eastern Kentucky. Tourism destinations are limited in Morehead proper, but the town benefits from its close proximity to Cave Run Lake and other parts of Daniel Boone National Forest.

Kentucky Folk Art Center

Folk art has a long, rich tradition in Kentucky, particularly in the Appalachian Mountain region, and the **Kentucky Folk Art Center** (102 W. 1st St., 606/783-2204, www.moreheadstate.edu/kfac, 9am-5pm Mon.-Sat., free) seeks to preserve, celebrate, and educate audiences about that tradition. More than 1,300 pieces belong to the center's permanent collection, with many of them on display in the main-level gallery. Visitors to the center will be exposed to Calvin Cooper's woodcarvings, Charles Kinney's paintings, Minnie Adkins's whittling, Robert Morgan's found-materials sculptures, Marvin Finn's wood-carved toys, and many other works by a wide range of artists. The second floor hosts five rotating exhibits each year, which may be displays of folk art or collections related to the many influences of folk art. During your visit, be sure to take some time to watch the video profiling four of Kentucky's most influential folk artists.

CCC Trail Vineyard & Winery

Well off the beaten track, on a 1,200-foot ridge surrounded by tobacco farms, **CCC Trail Vineyard & Winery** (3939 CCC Trail, 606/780-7195, www.rosstica.com, noon-6pm Fri.-Sat.) offers a picturesque setting for sipping wine. The 5.5-acre vineyard is planted with 37 varieties of grapes along with a patch of blackberries, all of which are used to make red, white, and fruit wines. Visitors to the vineyard are welcome to sit for a tasting of five wines served in a souvenir glass ($7.50).

Festivals and Events

In the fall, the **Poppy Mountain Bluegrass Festival** (606/784-2277, www.poppymountainbluegrass.com) brings musicians and fans to Morehead. The festival, which is dedicated solely to bluegrass music, stretches five days in the middle of September, although the campground opens and begins to fill at the beginning of the month with die-hard fans looking to do some pickin' and jammin' with friends new and old. During the actual event, recognizable names from bluegrass occupy the main stage, while a showcase stage premieres musicians looking for their big break. Tickets for the entire festival cost $120, while individual day passes cost $20 for Tuesday and Wednesday, $30 for Thursday, $40 for Friday, and $50 for Saturday.

Accommodations

Chain hotels are pretty much your only option if you want to stay in the city of Morehead. As is the case across much of Kentucky, the nicest chain in town is the **Hampton Inn** (500 Hampton Way, 606/780-0601, www.hamptoninn.com, $109). This Hampton Inn was built in 2008 and retains a new feeling, with rooms and common areas fresh and modern.

If, while you're in the area, you plan to visit Cave Run Lake or other areas within the Daniel Boone National Forest, consider some of the cabin and hotel options listed in that section.

Food

If you're a bookstore fan like me, you'll love Coffee Tree Books and their **Fuzzy Duck Coffee Shop** (159 E. Main St., 606/784-9877, www.fuzzyduckcoffeeshop.com, 7am-8pm Mon.-Sat.). You can grab a hot or cold drink from the coffee bar, or enjoy a healthy meal. Options include wraps, sandwiches, panini, pitas, quesadillas, salads, and soups ($2.59-3.59). Items are made to order and are filled with fresh and tasty meats and veggies. Vegetarians have a number of choices here.

Melini Cucina Italian Ristorante (608 E. Main St., 606/780-8865, 11am-10pm daily, $7.99-14.99) is a local chain with a handful of restaurants in the Kentucky, Ohio, and West Virginia tri-state area. The menu is extensive, covering most everything Italian from pasta to chicken and seafood specialties to pizzas and calzones. The food is consistently good, and service is quick and friendly. Although it's located in what appears to be an old fast-food restaurant, Melini's is a sit-down restaurant with quality food, so don't let the external appearance fool you.

If you're headed out to the CCC Trail Vineyard, consider having lunch at their **Celebration Cafe** (3939 CCC Trail, 606/780-7195, www.rosstica.com, noon-6pm Fri.-Sat., $5-11). Choose from 10 gourmet burgers, firebrick pizza, soup, or salad. On Saturday evenings, they serve a seven-course dinner ($55), with each course paired with one of their wines. Reservations are required for dinner.

Information and Services

The **Morehead Tourism Commission** (111 E. 1st St., 606/780-9694, www.moreheadtourism.com) provides information on sights throughout the county, with a strong emphasis on recreational pursuits, especially at nearby Cave Run Lake.

Getting There and Around

Morehead is situated just south of I-64 on U.S. 60 and is completely surrounded by the Daniel Boone National Forest. To access Morehead from I-64, take Exit 137 and then proceed on eastbound KY 32. Morehead is 65 miles (1 hour 10 minutes) east of Lexington and 65 miles (1 hour 10 minutes) west of Ashland.

DANIEL BOONE NATIONAL FOREST CUMBERLAND RANGER DISTRICT

The Cumberland District of the Daniel Boone National Forest is the northernmost section of the forest and can be broken down into two main areas. The Cave Run Lake area is the northern section, beginning just south of Morehead and centered around the lake. This area primarily draws water-sport enthusiasts, although there are also hiking and biking trails. The second area, the Red River Gorge Geological Area, encompasses some of Kentucky's most magnificent scenery. Here you will find the greatest concentration of natural arches east of the Rocky Mountains. More than 100 natural sandstone arches are scattered among 29,000 acres that also feature lush forests and tumbling waterfalls. Climbers flock to the area's rock formations, which have routes for both new and expert climbers. Red River Gorge is also a hiker's paradise, with miles of interesting trails. The beauty is incredible, of national park stature, throughout all four seasons, and although a drive-through is good if that's all you have time for, this is a park you really want to explore via foot. In this area, you will also find Natural Bridge State Resort Park, which is technically separate from the Daniel Boone National Forest, but only because it is run by Kentucky State Parks and not the Forest Service. Like Red River Gorge, it is known for its rock formations and hiking opportunities, although climbing is not allowed in the park.

Cave Run Lake
RECREATION

At 8,270 acres, Cave Run Lake offers plenty of space for water recreation of all types. The fishing is quite good here, especially for the somewhat unusual muskie, an enormous fish that can be rather tricky to catch. Bass, catfish, and crappie fishing is also good at Cave Run Lake. **Cave Run Marinas** (www.caverunmarinas. com) runs two outlets catering to those who want to get out on the water with a variety of rentals. For day outings, the marinas offer pontoons and fishing boats as well as pedal boats, while those wishing to take an extended trip can rent a houseboat. The Scott Creek Marina is located on KY 801, 1.5 miles south of the dam, and the Long Bow Marina is located on KY 1274 on Beaver Creek in Frenchburg.

Plenty of trails are located in the forests surrounding Cave Run Lake, the majority of which are multi-use, open to hikers, bikers, and horseback riders. ATV trails are also located near the lake. Some information is available online through the **Forest Service** website (www. fs.fed.us), but to get the most current information and maps, stop in at the **ranger office** (2375 KY 801, Morehead, 606/784-6428, 8am-4:30pm Mon.-Fri.).

If you're looking to rent a bike, canoe, kayak, or stand-up paddleboard, visit **Cave Run Bicycle & Outdoor Center** (995 KY 801, Morehead, 606/207-9864, www.caverunbikeshop.com, 10am-6pm Tues.-Sat.). Kayak, canoe, and stand-up paddleboard rentals are by the day ($40-45) or half day ($25-35). Tandem, single, and touring kayaks are all available, and the shop will set you up with life jackets and the materials needed to haul the boat on top of your car. Mountain bike rentals are by the day ($25). Whether you rent or have your own boat or bike, the center can provide suggestions on places to go, and they even have some maps of suggested routes on their website.

SIGHTS

If you've ever stopped to wonder how lakes are stocked, you might be interested in a visit to the **Minor E. Clark Fish Hatchery** (120 Fish Hatchery Rd., 606/784-6872, grounds open sunrise-sunset year-round). This hatchery specializes in cool- and warm-water fish and is the largest muskie hatchery in the world. Tours of the facility are offered 7am-3pm daily during the summer.

EVENTS

The **Cave Run Storytelling Festival** (606/780-4342, www.caverunstoryfest.org)

honors the art of spinning a good thread by bringing some of the nation's best storytellers to Cave Run Lake every September. The festival is held at the Twin Knobs Recreational Area (5195 KY 801), with storytellers creating magic in two tents all day Friday and Saturday. Tickets may be purchased for the entire weekend ($45 adults, $15 youth 6-18), per day ($25 adults, $10 youth 6-18) or for the evening only ($8 adults, $5 youth 6-18). Family rates and advance purchase discounts are also available.

ACCOMMODATIONS

In the area surrounding Cave Run Lake, you will find a large variety of accommodation options. **Cave Run Lodging** (1190 KY 801 S., Morehead, 606/783-1234 www.caverunlodge.com, $99-269), which is among the closest to the lake itself, offers one-, two-, and four-bedroom cabins. An in-ground pool is shared by all the cabins, which can be rented by the day or the week. The cabins are simple but bright and clean, and are fully equipped with linens and kitchen supplies. One cabin is wheelchair-accessible.

Cave Run Cabins and Brownwood Bed and Breakfast (46 Carey Cemetery Rd., Morehead, 606/784-8799, www.caveruncabins.com, $89-140) also offers cabin rentals. Their three deluxe wood cabins accommodate up to four people with a queen bed and a sleeper sofa. The setup is studio style with a kitchenette with microwave and mini-refrigerator instead of a full kitchen. For a couple's getaway, the premium cabin sleeps two and is less rustic in style. Other options include a very large suite in the main house with queen bedroom, living room, eat-in kitchen, sitting room, and bathroom, and a cottage that can sleep six people and is located a short distance from the main property. A continental breakfast is offered daily.

Journey's End Lodge (999 Carrington Dr., Salt Lick, 606/768-2103, $69) is a 16-room inn surrounded by pretty scenery. Each room has an outside entrance, two double beds, refrigerator, and Internet access. A bit farther from the lake than some other properties, Journey's End is in a good location for those interested in visiting both Cave Run Lake and Red River Gorge.

Lakeview Motel (4300 KY 801, Morehead, 606/784-1600, www.caverunlodging.com, $45-65) is, as the name suggests, located right on the lake. Deluxe rooms, which come with two double beds, have views onto the lake, while standard rooms with one double bed do not. Rooms are simple, but do come with refrigerators, microwaves, and Internet access.

Five campgrounds are located in the Cave Run region. The two most popular are the Twin Knobs and the Zilpo Campgrounds (mid-Apr.-mid-Oct.), both of which are located right on the lake. The **Twin Knobs Campground** ($24) has 216 sites, and the **Zilpo Campground** ($22) has 172. Both campgrounds have bathhouses, recreational facilities, beaches, and boat ramps. Reservations are required at these two campgrounds and can be made over the phone (877/444-6777) or online (www.recreation.gov). The Twin Knobs Campground is located on KY 801, nine miles south of I-64 at Exit 133. The Zilpo Campground is located on Forest Road 918, which is most easily accessed from Salt Lick. Other campgrounds include **White Sulphur Horse Camp** (Forest Service Rd. 105, $12), primitive **Clear Creek Campground** (Forest Service Rd. 129, $12), and **Clay Lick Boat-In Campground** ($12). Additional information on the campgrounds can be found on the Forest Service website (www.fs.fed.us).

FOOD

Many visitors to the lake self-cater, bringing picnics with them or arriving with food to cook in their cabins. Others head north to Morehead when mealtime comes around.

INFORMATION AND SERVICES

The **Cumberland Ranger District Office** (2375 KY 801, Morehead, 606/784-6428, www.fs.fed.us, 8am-4:30pm Mon.-Fri.) has a visitors center that focuses on the Cave Run Lake area. A short video highlights regional attractions, and interactive displays tell the history of the area. Maps and brochures are available for free, while a bookstore sells more detailed trail guides and nature guides.

GETTING THERE AND AROUND
Cave Run Lake is big, with many different access points. The visitors center as well as multiple recreational areas are located along KY 801, which is a good place to start. From U.S. 60 in Morehead, travel south on KY 519 for 7.6 miles, then turn right onto KY 801.

◖ Red River Gorge Geological Area
HIKING
Hiking opportunities are abundant in Red River Gorge, and trails vary widely in distance and difficulty. For those with limited time or interest in hiking, there are plenty of short trails that allow you access to some neat bridges and rock formations without much exertion. For instance, the looping trail to Sky Bridge, one of the park's most popular sites and a distinct freestanding rock bridge, is only 0.8 mile long. Even shorter are the 0.2-mile one-way trail to Whistling Arch, the 0.3-mile one-way trail to Angel Windows, the 0.3-mile one-way trail to Chimney Top Rock, and the 0.2-mile one-way trail to Princess Arch. More serious hikers will enjoy the six-mile loop made by hiking Double Arch Trail, Auxier Branch Trail, and Auxier Ridge Trail. This fairly strenuous hike takes you to both Double Arch and Courthouse Rock as well as through some lovely forest. A favorite hike of many Red River Gorge visitors is the 1.4-mile Rock Bridge Trail, which takes you to both Creation Falls and Rock Bridge, a unique sandstone formation that crosses over a river.

If you're looking for an overnight backpacking trip, try the 17 miles of the Sheltowee Trace National Recreation Trail that cut right through the heart of Red River Gorge. Many consider this to be the most scenic part of the 278-mile trail. Very experienced hikers can also opt to hike in the **Clifty Wilderness,** a 12,646-acre area on the southern edge of Red River Gorge that is kept extremely wild. The plant and animal life in this area is incredible, but you really do need to be a skilled outdoorsman to attempt hiking here. The 7.8-mile Swift Camp Creek Trail, the 1.3-mile Wildcat Trail, the 7.0-mile Osborne Bend Loop Trail, and the 1.7-mile Lost Branch Trail are maintained, but there are many more unmaintained trails in Clifty Wilderness. Know how to use a compass and purchase and study a quality map of the area before hiking here.

If you're really interested in hiking in Red River Gorge, consider purchasing *Hiking the Red: A Complete Trail Guide to Kentucky's Red River Gorge*. Casual hikers can make do with the maps and suggestions provided at the visitors center.

ROCK CLIMBING
Red River Gorge draws climbers from all over the country—and the world—thanks to its spectacular sandstone rock formations that practically beg you to find a way to scale them. Bolted routes ranging in difficulty from 5.7 to 5.14 are located throughout the gorge, offering some of the best climbing in the eastern United States. In addition to the routes on federal land in the gorge, the Red River Gorge Climber's Coalition (http://rrgcc.org), an advocate and excellent resource for climbers, has purchased the 700-acre Pendergrass-Murray Recreational Preserve and opened routes there to the public. Survey local climbers on their favorite routes and you'll get a plethora of answers based on ability and interest. Some of the most popular routes, however, are located on Military Wall, Motherlode, and Roadside Crag. The website www.redriverclimbing.com contains some of the best information on rock climbing in the area, with nearly every route covered in their online guidebook. The best way to orient yourself to the area and gather firsthand information is to start your climbing trip at **Miguel's** (1890 Natural Bridge Rd., Slade, 606/663-1975, www.miguelspizza.com), the hangout for climbers.

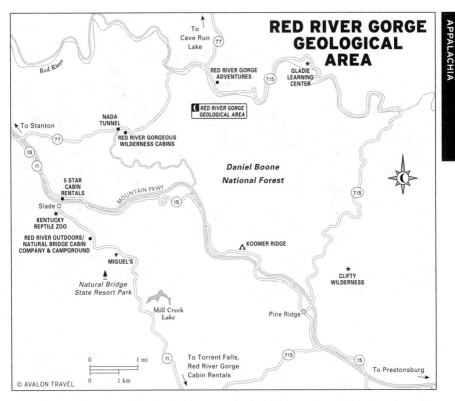

RED RIVER GORGE
GEOLOGICAL
AREA

Daniel Boone
National Forest

© AVALON TRAVEL

Newbies to the sport of rock climbing or those looking to move up to the next level can employ the help of a guide. **Torrent Falls** (1617 N. KY 11, Campton, 606/668-6613, www.torrentfalls.com, 9am-5pm daily Mar.-Nov.) offers half-day and full-day guided climbing and rappelling packages. For a unique experience (no climbing experience necessary), try the Torrent Falls Climbing Adventure, which is the first via ferrata course in the United States. The Climbing Adventure has participants scaling rock faces using iron hand and foot rungs while attached to a cable system. Difficulty levels vary along the course, but multiple exit points make the course accessible to all levels. **Red River Outdoors** (415 Natural Bridge Rd., Slade, 859/230-3567, www.redriveroutdoors.com) also has highly trained guides who have

climbed all over the world and are happy to introduce people to the sport or assist climbers in reaching new goals.

WATER SPORTS

The Red River, a Class I waterway, provides leisurely paddling opportunities for those looking to see the gorge from a different viewpoint. **Red River Gorge Adventures** (606/663-1012, www.redriveradventure.net) can arrange a canoe or kayak rental ($35-50). All rentals are for the entire day, and no matter what part of the river you choose to paddle, you'll have opportunities to swim, fish, picnic, and enjoy the stunning scenery. The outfitter will also help you plan an overnight trip ($70), in which you paddle to a backcountry camping spot along the river and then return the next day. If you

© THERESA DOWELL BLACKINTON

small waterfall in Red River Gorge

have your own boat but need shuttle service, Red River Gorge Adventures can provide that as well. Red River Gorge Adventures is open March-November, although the river can often be too low for paddling in late summer and fall. Red River Gorge Adventures is located on KY 715, just 0.5 mile from the intersection with KY 77 inside the gorge.

The upper portion of the Red River runs through Clifty Wilderness, and during the peak season of January-May, you can find Class II and III rapids here. If you have your own kayak, you can put in at the KY 746 bridge and paddle nine miles to a take-out at the KY 715 bridge.

NEARBY ATTRACTIONS
If you need a break from hiking, climbing, and paddling, you can take a trip to the **Kentucky Reptile Zoo** (200 L&E Railroad Rd., Slade, 606/663-9160, www.kyreptilezoo.org, 11am-6pm daily Memorial Day-Labor Day, Fri.-Sun. only Mar.-May and Sept.-Oct., $7 adult, $5

youth 3-15), where you can view rattlesnakes, pythons, vipers, cobras, tortoises, and alligators. A live venom extraction takes place at 1pm, and reptile programs that cover an array of topics are offered at 3pm and 5pm.

For evening entertainment, load up your car with as many friends as can fit (or just your sweetie if it's romance you're after), and find a spot at the **Mountain View Drive-In Theatre** (1327 E. College Ave., Stanton, 606/663-9988, www.mt-view-drivein.com). This drive-in has two screens, each of which shows a double feature of current releases. Movies begin at dusk Friday-Sunday, April-August. Admission is $7 for adults, and $2 for youth 6-9. You can't beat that for an evening out.

ACCOMMODATIONS
Cabins are an ideal lodging choice in Red River Gorge, and if that's your cup of tea, you have a number of options to choose from. **Red River Gorgeous Wilderness Cabins** (3546 Nada Tunnel Rd., Stanton, 606/663-9824,

www.rrgcabin.com, $59-160) has 12 cabins for rent, which range from one-room, off-the-grid cabins that can only be accessed via hike to cabins stocked with modern amenities and able to sleep up to eight people. Guests need to provide their own linens. Many climbers like to stay at one of the cabins owned by **Red River Outdoors** (415 Natural Bridge Rd., Slade, 859/230-3567, www.redriveroutdoors. com, $135-200). They offer A-frames for 4 adults, as well as a variety of other cabins that can accommodate 6-8 adults. Honeymoon Haven is perfect for a couple seeking a romantic getaway. The cabins are cute and comfortable and are supplied with everything you need. They are located in different areas of Red River Gorge, but all are surrounded by fantastic scenery.

A number of companies, including **Red River Gorge Cabin Rentals** (400 Cliffview Dr., Campton, 606/668-3272, www.redriv-ergorgecabinrentals.com), **Natural Bridge Cabin Company & Campground** (1231 Natural Bridge Rd., Slade, 606/663-3700, www.nbcab-ins.com), and **5 Star Cabin Rentals** (12075 Campton Rd., Slade, 606/663-8858, www. naturalbridgecabinrental.com), manage a wide range of vacation properties that can sleep 2-14 people and vary in style from rustic to luxurious.

Camping is, of course, wildly popular in the area. The **Koomer Ridge Campground** (KY 15, 606/663-7939, $18) is run by the Forest Service and offers 54 wooded sites that are mainly suited toward tent camping. Nineteen sites, however, can accommodate trailers. The campground has flush toilets and showers, although they are not available in the winter. Climbers, especially the young and those on a tight budget, flock to **Miguel's** (1890 Natural Bridge Rd., Slade, 606/663-1975, www.miguelspizza.com), where you're welcome to join the crowd of tents behind the restaurant for only $2 a night. As you might expect, Miguel's can get pretty loud, but most people enjoy the party atmosphere. Pay showers are available.

Backcountry camping is allowed almost everywhere in the park. Pick up a permit ($3 one-day, $5 three-day, $30 annual) at local stores or Forest Service offices. Remember this is black bear country, so be sure you know proper food storage techniques before pitching your tent.

FOOD

Miguel's (1890 Natural Bridge Rd., Slade, 606/663-1975, www.miguelspizza.com, $4-13) is a Red River Gorge institution for climbers especially, although everyone is invited in for a bite. In a bright yellow building across from Natural Bridge State Resort Park, Miguel's is about as casual as it gets. Grab a piece of paper that outlines the many, many toppings you can have on your pizza, and check everything that appeals to you. Then note whether you want a lot or a little sauce and cheese, scratch your name at the top of the sheet, and hand it over to the person behind the counter. Your pizza will shortly be delivered to you at one of the makeshift booths made with old bus seats. Pizzas come in small (two slices), medium (four slices), and large (eight slices) and are very fairly priced based on the number of toppings. Slices are large, heartily topped, and just plain tasty. Salads and pasta are also available, but pizza is the mainstay at Miguel's.

INFORMATION AND SERVICES

The **Gladie Learning Center** (3451 KY 715, Frenchburg, 606/663-8100, 9am-5:30pm daily, mid-Mar.-Nov.) is the National Forest Service's information center for the Red River Gorge Geological Area. The center has a nice set of exhibits on the history, geology, flora, fauna, and culture of the area. You can also pick up park maps and purchase detailed trail maps and backcountry camping permits here. The staff is really knowledgeable and happy to help you plan your visit. Let them know how much time you have and what your interests and abilities are, and they'll be able to offer you really spot-on suggestions for making the most of your time.

GETTING THERE AND AROUND

The heart of Red River Gorge is contained within the area bounded by KY 715, the Mountain Parkway/KY 15, and KY 77. The interior areas are accessed almost exclusively by trails, which have trailheads on one of these roads, although there are also a couple of gravel roads that enter the interior. To tour the area, begin in the gateway town of Slade, which is located at Exit 33 on the Mountain Parkway. From Slade, take KY 15 north to KY 77, where you will turn right, and begin your trip on what has been deemed the Red River Gorge Scenic Byway. As you drive along KY 77, you will approach the Nada Tunnel, which is not your average road tunnel. Unlit and one-way (approach carefully with your lights on and wait for any cars already in the tunnel), the Nada Tunnel is not smooth but remains jagged with rocks jutting out. Driving through it is like driving through a cave. It's very cool. After a total of about 5 miles, you'll reach a fork with KY 715. Stay right onto KY 715, which runs along the Red River before turning south on the western border of Clifty Wilderness. You'll travel about 13 miles on KY 715 before you reach the Mountain Parkway and KY 15. If you're in a hurry, take the Mountain Parkway; otherwise opt for KY 15, which parallels the parkway. In about 10 miles, you'll be back in Slade. For additional scenic byway driving, you can then go south on KY 11, passing Natural Bridge State Park and continuing to the town of Zachariah, or you can go north on KY 11 to the town of Stanton, which is west of Red River Gorge.

The Mountain Parkway is accessible from I-64 at Exit 98.

Natural Bridge State Resort Park
RECREATION

More than 20 miles of trails wind through the forested acres of **Natural Bridge State Resort Park** (2135 Natural Bridge Rd., Slade, 606/663-2214, http://parks.ky.gov, daylight-dark daily, free). The 0.75-mile Original Trail leads from the lodge to Natural Bridge, a 65-foot-high natural sandstone arch that spans 78 feet. The Original Trail climbs over 500 feet through hemlock, pine, poplar, and rhododendron and past rock walls to the arch. When you reach the top, you'll be under the arch. Squeeze up the narrow passage to walk across the top of the bridge and enjoy the vista. If you continue another 0.5 mile, you'll arrive at another viewpoint that allows for a good view of the bridge in its entirety. The arch can also be reached by a **sky lift** (10am-6:30pm daily, Apr.-Oct., $9 adults, $8 seniors, $7 youth 4-12, $6 one-way). Many people take the sky lift up to the arch and then hike back down.

Multiple other trails, many of them short and family-friendly, lead to other natural formations, such as Balanced Rock, Battleship Rock, Henson's Arch, and Whittleton Arch. As you hike, you may also encounter a number of structures, including shelters and staircases, built by the Civilian Conservation Corps. A trail guide can be picked up at the lodge.

Another way to get some exercise is by

© THERESA DOWELL BLACKINTON

sky lift at Natural Bridge State Resort Park

renting a pedal boat or hydrobike and powering yourself around Hoedown Island Lake. Hoedown Island, located in the lake, just below the lodge, is the host of Friday evening square dances. Many talented dancers attend the weekly event (late Apr.-early Oct.), but everyone is invited to do-si-do.

The park's naturalist staff leads a full schedule of events during the park's high season. Activities include guided hikes, wildlife viewing, reptile and amphibian displays, and more. The park also has a pool that is open to the public and accessible to people with disabilities.

ACCOMMODATIONS

Natural Bridge State Resort Park's **Hemlock Lodge** (2135 Natural Bridge Rd., Slade, 606/663-2214, http://parks.ky.gov, $149.95) is located partially up the mountainside, Natural Bridge above it (although out of sight) and the lake and pool below it. The lodge has only 35 rooms, so it is regularly booked up, especially on summer and fall weekends. Rooms, which are a bit dated but well cared for, come with two queen beds and a private balcony where you'll want to spend all of your time drinking in the view. If you'd like more space than a lodge room offers, see if one of the park's **cottages** ($169.95-219.95) is available. Seven one-bedroom and four two-bedroom cottages are nestled in the mountains with wonderful views out of every window. Two **campgrounds** (Apr.-Oct., $17-28) combine to provide 86 sites. Both back-in and pull-through sites are available. The campgrounds also offer primitive sites for tent campers. Comfort stations with restrooms and showers are located in both campgrounds.

FOOD

Sandstone Arches Restaurant (2135 Natural Bridge Rd., Slade, 606/663-2214, http://parks.ky.gov, 7am-9pm daily, $6.49-12.49) builds its menu around Kentucky and Southern favorites like catfish and Hot Browns. Many diners opt for the buffet, which on occasion is a seafood buffet. The restaurant has a relaxed atmosphere

with big windows offering views down on the lake and Hoedown Island.

INFORMATION AND SERVICES

For park maps and a schedule of activities, stop at the front desk of Hemlock Lodge.

GETTING THERE AND AROUND

Natural Bridge State Resort Park is located adjacent to the Red River Gorge Geological Area. To get there, take the Mountain Parkway to Slade (Exit 33), and then proceed south on KY 11 for about 2.5 miles.

CARTER COUNTY

Between Morehead and Ashland, Carter County is drive-through country for many Kentucky travelers, but those who don't get off the interstate are missing out. Carter County doesn't have a lot in the way of city attractions, but it does have two great state parks that offer distinctly different activities.

Carter Caves State Resort Park

Although the Mammoth Cave area can claim the most miles of cave, Carter County boasts the highest concentration of caves in the state. **Carter Caves State Resort Park** (344 Caveland Dr., Olive Hill, 606/286-4411, http://parks.ky.gov, daylight-dark daily, free) protects multiple caves as well as 2,000 acres of forests and streams. Unfortunately, White Nose Syndrome, which is threatening bats across the nation, has caused the park to close some of the caves to the public for the time being. Three caves, however, remain open for tours. Cascade Cave ($9 adults, $5 youth 3-12), named for the 30-foot waterfall within it, can be visited on a 75-minute tour that covers approximately 0.75 mile, including 225 steps. It is the largest cave in the park and has many notable formations. X Cave ($7 adults, $4 youth 3-12), named for its crisscrossing passageways, can be explored on a 0.25-mile, 45-minute tour. X Cave also contains many unique formations, such as the Great Chandelier, which is an enormous collection of stalactites. Although X Cave has only

75 steps, the passageways are narrow and require some stooping. Saltpeter Cave ($7 adults, $4 youth 3-12) has an interesting history, having been used to make gunpowder during the War of 1812. It can be toured on a 0.5-mile tour with 30 steps that lasts one hour. Tours of Cascade Cave and X-Cave are offered year-round, but numbers are reduced in the low season. Tours of Saltpeter Cave are offered only Memorial Day-Labor Day. In summer, tours run every 1-1.5 hours. Flashlight and lantern tours are offered at select times.

Beyond caves, Carter Caves State Resort Park offers a wealth of recreation options. Hiking, especially to the park's many natural arches, bridges, and tunnels, is very popular. Try the 3.5-mile Three Bridges Trail, which loops past Fern Bridge, Raven Bridge, and Smoky Bridge and also offers views of the lake. Those looking for a challenge should try the 8.3-mile, one-way Carter Caves Cross Country Trail, which ventures into the park's backcountry, where you're allowed to camp with a permit. The park's longest trail is the nine-mile looping Kiser Hollow Trail, which is open to horseback riders and bikers as well as hikers. For those looking to explore via horseback, guided 45-minute trail rides are available for $18.

Another center of activity is Smokey Valley Lake, which is stocked with bass, bluegill, and crappie. The park does not rent boats, but those with their own boat can launch from the park (trolling motors only). During the summer season, the park staff leads canoe trips ($10) on the lake. It's a great introduction to canoeing for those new to the sport. To find out about additional staff-led activities taking place at the park, pick up a copy of the weekly program schedule from the welcome center. A nine-hole golf course, mini-golf course, tennis courts, basketball courts, playground, and public pool are also located within the park.

Overnight accommodation is available at the **Lewis Caveland Lodge** ($109.95). This small lodge, with only 28 rooms, has fieldstone and wood construction. Rooms are motel style with outside entrances and private patios or decks. Eleven two-bedroom **cottages** ($219.95), arranged along a cul-de-sac, are also available for rent. Most have two bathrooms and fireplaces, but configurations differ slightly. Covered decks are standard, along with full kitchens. The **campground** (mid-Mar.-mid-Nov., $18-25) has two distinct areas, one with 90 spots with hookups for RVs, and one with 31 tent-only sites. It's a nice setup, especially for tent campers who don't like to be sandwiched between RVs. Equestrian camping ($33) is also offered.

Tierney's Cavern Restaurant (7am-8pm daily, $5.99-13.99) is located inside the lodge. As with other state park restaurants, Tierney's Cavern serves Kentucky Proud products whenever possible. The menu is designed to satisfy a wide range of tastes, so expect standard sandwich and entrée options, such as a traditional club sandwich or a catfish fillet dinner.

Grayson Lake State Park

Located on the shores of 1,510-acre Grayson Lake, an Army Corps of Engineers project, **Grayson Lake State Park** (314 Grayson Lake Park Rd., Olive Hill, 606/474-9727, http://parks.ky.gov, daylight-dark daily) focuses on the water. A boat ramp provides access to anglers seeking bass, crappie, and catfish, while a nearby marina offers pontoon and fishing boat rentals to recreational boaters. The lake is really lovely, long and narrow and surrounded by cliffs that reach up to 200 feet above the lake's surface. Off-the-water activities include golf and hiking. The 18-hole golf course belongs to the park's signature series, with large bunkers and long back tees challenging all levels of players. The short Beech-Hemlock Forest Trail offers 0.8 mile of discovery of plant and animal species and geological formations. In winter and spring, the three-mile Lick Falls Overlook Trail is worth the effort. The rest of the year, the hike, which follows a lakeside cliff-line, is still nice, but the waterfall is likely to be dry. A 71-site **campground** (Apr.-Oct., $23) with hookups allows for overnight visits to the park.

The Army Corps of Engineers runs a recreational area separate from the park and located at the dam. Here you'll find picnic areas, playgrounds, a boat ramp, a marina, and a historic log house.

Information and Services

Carter County doesn't have a tourism office, although staff at both of the parks should be able to help you with any inquiries you might have about the region.

Getting There and Around

Carter County's two state parks lie on different sides of I-64. Carter Caves is to the north, and Grayson Lake is to the south. To reach Carter Caves, take Exit 161 off of I-64, and drive two miles on eastbound U.S. 60. Then turn left on northbound KY 182 and continue three miles to the park entrance. To reach Grayson Lake, take Exit 172 off of I-64 and follow southbound KY 7 for 11 miles to the park entrance.

BOWLING GREEN, CAVE COUNTRY, AND SOUTH-CENTRAL LAKES

The thrill of flying across the glasslike surface of a lake, the excitement of creeping through underground passageways, the warmth of small towns still set around squares, and the buzz of activity indigenous to one of Kentucky's major cities are what draws people to the south-central section of the state. Kentucky families plan vacations here. Ohioans come in such numbers to this region's lakes that they've been nicknamed the Ohio Navy. Travelers making their way to and from Florida and the Gulf Coast on I-65 plan for stops in Cave Country and Bowling Green. A tourism hot spot, this region of Kentucky attracts both active travelers and those who love old-fashioned, family-friendly roadside attractions.

Bowling Green, located on I-65 between Louisville and Nashville, is the hub of the region. It's home to Western Kentucky University, which pumps constant energy into the area, as well as the Corvette, which creates an energy of its own. Excellent museums and attractions and standout restaurants give Bowling Green city cred, but a square where people like to sit and have a drink while watching the world go by is still the heart of downtown.

Leave the city and you'll quickly find yourself in farmland. If you get lucky, you might come across a small animal swap meet while driving down a country road. If you do, stop, order one of the hamburgers that someone is bound to be grilling, and have lunch with the locals. Drive carefully in these rural areas, because you're just as likely to come across a horse and buggy as another automobile. Low land

© THERESA DOWELL BLACKINTON

HIGHLIGHTS

◖ National Corvette Museum: Fall in love with America's sports car on a visit to this Corvette-centric museum. Car geek or not, you'll leave dreaming of getting behind the wheel of one of these beauties (page 304).

◖ Lost River Cave & Valley: Although a boat tour through the cave is the highlight here, the beautiful grounds filled with hiking trails, wildlife-rich wetlands, and butterfly gardens are also worth your time (page 308).

◖ Kentucky Down Under: Pet a kangaroo, watch a sheep roundup, and tour a cave at this Australian outpost smack in the middle of Kentucky cave country (page 322).

◖ Mammoth Cave National Park: Choose from a variety of tours that allow you to explore

a tiny fraction of the world's longest cave system. Above ground, hiking trails and paddle-friendly rivers beckon (page 327).

◖ Diamond Caverns: Beating out the region's many other caves for the title of Most Attractive, Diamond Caverns impresses with its many outstanding formations (page 332).

◖ Dale Hollow Lake: Clear turquoise waters make this one of the prettiest lakes in this part of the country. Anglers and recreational boaters mingle easily at this island-dotted lake (page 342).

◖ Lake Cumberland: Gather your friends, rent a houseboat, and get your party on at one of the South's most happening lakes (page 345).

BOWLING GREEN

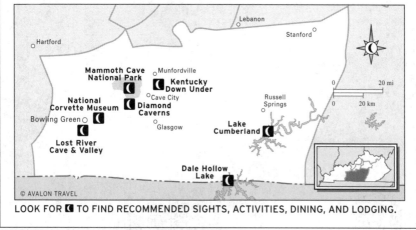

LOOK FOR ◖ TO FIND RECOMMENDED SIGHTS, ACTIVITIES, DINING, AND LODGING.

prices, rich soil, and community acceptance have brought numerous Amish and Mennonite families to this area. Many run small businesses that welcome visitors, these old-order communities easily mingling with their modern neighbors.

North of Bowling Green, along I-65, is Cave Country. Here, there is not much in the way of solid ground. Hundreds of miles of passageways

exist just below the surface, creating the largest known cave system in the world—Mammoth Cave—and a slew of other smaller caves. The caves vary wildly in size and structure. Some still have water running through them; others are entirely dry. Some have wide passages and open rooms; others demand that you creep, crouch, and crawl. Some have few formations; others are thick with stalactites and stalagmites.

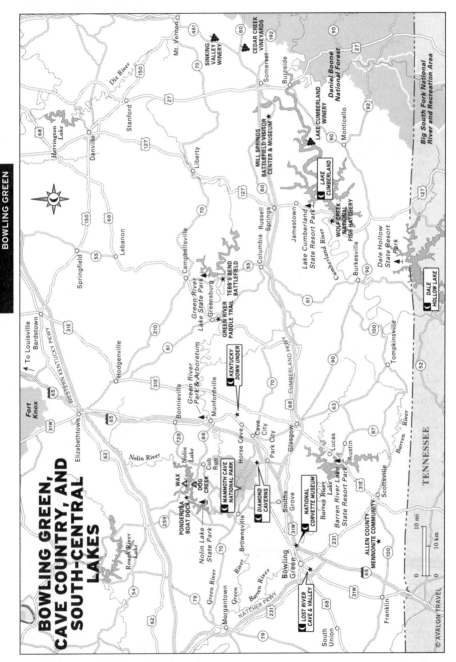

Above ground, in addition to farms, you'll find charming small towns like Munfordville that take pride in their historic buildings and storied past, as well as towns like Cave City that seem to run entirely on tourism. Non-cave attractions in this area range from the entertaining and the educational to the decidedly hokey, but all are 100 percent family friendly.

Move east from Bowling Green and Cave Country and you'll find yourself surrounded by lakes considered to be among the best in the southeastern United States. Anglers, driven by dreams of landing the big one, cast lines into Green River Lake and Barren River Lake. Recreational boaters love the turquoise waters of Dale Hollow, which practically begs you to dive in for a swim. And those who equate "lake" with "party" come en masse to Lake Cumberland, where houseboats rule. In the lake's hard-partying coves, almost anything goes, despite the fact that Lake Cumberland is located in the heart of Kentucky's Bible Belt, where the sale of alcohol is illegal and billboards are just as likely to be religious as commercial.

So what are you waiting for? The water's nice. Go ahead, dive in. South-central Kentucky is waiting to offer you a taste of both what's hot—a summer day at the lake, the classic Corvette—and what's cool—caves, caves, and more caves.

PLANNING YOUR TIME

Geographically, the Bowling Green, Cave Country, and South-Central Lakes region is large with a wide diversity of attractions, so trying to take it all in on one trip would be a mistake. Instead, decide what you're interested in—do you want to crawl through caves, relax at the lake, or explore Corvette culture?—and delegate your time accordingly.

Bowling Green is a destination in itself, perfect for a weekend getaway. It's also the only major city in the region. With an abundance of hotels and excellent dining options and as the only wet spot in an essentially entirely dry region, Bowling Green makes a great base for those looking to sample the area. From Bowling Green, you can easily travel north to the caves and east to the Barren River Lake area. Other possible excursions include a visit to the Shaker Museum at South Union or a drive through Allen County's Mennonite community.

How long you want to spend in the cave area depends on how deep your affection is for caves. Spelunkers and other fans of going down under Kentucky-style can easily fill an entire week simply touring caves. Those who think a cave is a cave is a cave, although wrong, can opt to visit one or two of the region's caves and round out a weekend escape with other attractions in Horse Cave, Cave City, and Park City. These three towns are so close together that it doesn't particularly matter which you choose as a base.

If you're thinking lakes, you're going to have to get a bit more specific. If you're looking to cast a line and reel in a couple of keepers, consider Barren River Lake or Green River Lake. Although recreational boaters also enjoy these waters, there are plenty of quiet coves for fishing. If, instead, you're thinking houseboat, if you associate the lake with partying, and if sliding, swimming, and skiing are more your style than fishing, then make no doubt about it, Lake Cumberland is your destination. Dale Hollow comes in somewhere in between, offering both peaceful fishing areas and popular houseboat areas. While a day at the lake is undoubtedly a nice escape, a weekend or longer is even better, and many houseboat rentals are for a minimum three-night weekend or four-night weekday period.

In terms of when to visit, summer reigns. All attractions are open and keep longer hours than they do the rest of the year, but you'll have to deal with crowds, and reservations will be critical for such activities as touring Mammoth Cave or snagging a houseboat rental. It will also be hot (at least above ground), so don't forget the sunscreen and the water. Spring and fall offer the most pleasant temperatures, and it's a lovely time to travel through the more rural areas of the region. Most visitor sites will be open, although hours will be more limited than in summer and may even be restricted to weekends. In winter, most of the region is pretty quiet, although students at WKU keep Bowling Green bustling.

Travelers to this region should keep a few things in mind. First, the majority of the region is on what people in Kentucky call "slow time" and the rest of the world refers to as Central Standard Time, meaning it's one hour behind Louisville and the eastern United States. Exceptions include the Green River Lake area and the Burnside area of Lake Cumberland. Second, every county in this region is a dry county, meaning the sale of alcohol is prohibited. Bowling Green, however, is a wet city, meaning both package and by-the-drink sales are allowed. A few other towns, such as Burnside on Lake Cumberland, are moist, meaning you can purchase alcohol by the drink in certain restaurants. In dry counties, possession of alcohol is allowed only if the alcohol is for personal consumption on private property. While at the lake, if you are drinking in open view—meaning on the shore, in the water, or on the deck of a boat—you are in violation of the law. For all intents and purposes, you are legally allowed to drink only while inside the cabin of a boat. Many people break this law (although koozies are, at minimum, a good idea), and enforcement can be lax, but law enforcement is within their right to cite or arrest you for drinking or being intoxicated in public at the lake. And remember, drinking and driving (yes, of boats, as well) is always illegal, and alcohol and water can be a deadly mix. So please, be smart.

Bowling Green

Home to the Hilltoppers of Western Kentucky University, Bowling Green is a college town that has grown to be the third most populated city in the state, maintaining an air of casual familiarity while offering all the city amenities you need. Despite the city's growth in all directions, downtown has maintained its liveliness, with restaurants and shops centered around Fountain Square. The minor league ballpark is also downtown, and WKU perches on a hill right in the city center. Located just an hour north of Nashville on I-65, Bowling Green has a strong Southern feel and, in fact, was declared the capital of the Confederate government of Kentucky (the state itself was Union) during the Civil War. Today, the city takes great pride in being the only place in the world where Corvettes are made, and a tour of the museum and/or the plant is a must for Bowling Green first-timers. An anomaly in this region, Bowling Green is a wet city that knows how to have a good time but, like any good Southerner, never forgets its manners.

SIGHTS
◖ National Corvette Museum

As the only museum in the world dedicated solely to one specific model of car, the **National Corvette Museum** (350 Corvette Dr., 270/781-7973, www.corvettemuseum.com, 8am-5pm daily, last ticket at 4:30pm, $10 adults, $8 seniors, $5 youth 6-16, $25 family rate) is all about the Corvette, but you don't have to be an enthusiast to enjoy the museum. Well-designed exhibits trace the history of the Corvette, place it into context in American history, discuss its role in performance sports, and celebrate the Corvette lifestyle. Most impressive is the collection of 60-75 Corvettes on display in the various exhibits. The Corvettes, which cover all seven generations from the first Corvette in 1953 to current models, have either been donated to the museum or are on loan. Because loans last for a one-year period, the cars on display are constantly changing, meaning each time you visit, you'll find different Corvettes to admire, ogle, and desire. The museum made headlines in early 2014 when a sinkhole within the museum collapsed, affecting eight cars, but

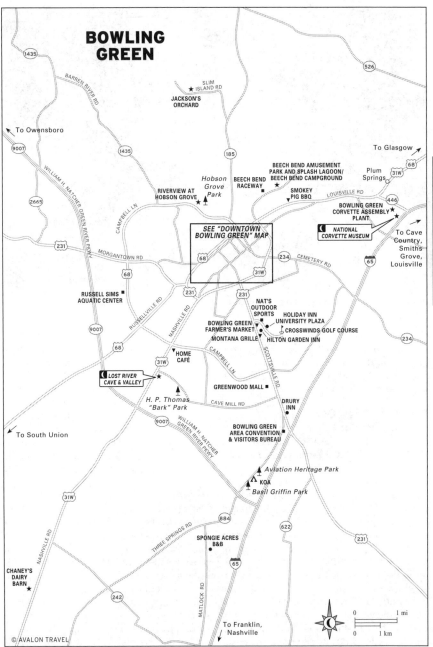

BOWLING GREEN

To Owensboro

To Glasgow

To Cave Country, Smiths Grove, Louisville

To South Union

To Franklin, Nashville

SLIM ISLAND RD

JACKSON'S ORCHARD

BARREN RIVER RD

RIVERVIEW AT HOBSON GROVE

Hobson Grove Park

BEECH BEND AMUSEMENT PARK AND SPLASH LAGOON/ BEECH BEND CAMPGROUND

BEECH BEND RACEWAY

SMOKEY PIG BBQ

Plum Springs

LOUISVILLE RD

BOWLING GREEN CORVETTE ASSEMBLY PLANT

NATIONAL CORVETTE MUSEUM

SEE "DOWNTOWN BOWLING GREEN" MAP

CEMETERY RD

WILLIAM H. NATCHER GREEN RIVER PKWY

CAMPBELL LN

MORGANTOWN RD

RUSSELL SIMS AQUATIC CENTER

RUSSELLVILLE RD

NASHVILLE RD

NAT'S OUTDOOR SPORTS

HOLIDAY INN UNIVERSITY PLAZA

BOWLING GREEN FARMER'S MARKET

CROSSWINDS GOLF COURSE

MONTANA GRILLE

HILTON GARDEN INN

HOME CAFÉ

CAMPBELL LN

SCOTTSVILLE RD

LOST RIVER CAVE & VALLEY

H. P. Thomas "Bark" Park

GREENWOOD MALL

DRURY INN

CAVE MILL RD

WILLIAM H. NATCHER GREEN RIVER PKWY

BOWLING GREEN AREA CONVENTION & VISITORS BUREAU

Aviation Heritage Park

KOA

Basil Griffin Park

NASHVILLE RD

THREE SPRINGS RD

SPONGIE ACRES B&B

MATLOCK RD

CHANEY'S DAIRY BARN

© AVALON TRAVEL

0   1 mi
0   1 km

1435
526
9007
1435
185
2665
231
68
446
65
234
9007
68
31W
9007
884
622
231
31W
242
65
68
31W
68
231
231
234
31W

BOWLING GREEN

© THERESA DOWELL BLACKINTON

different models of Corvettes on display at the National Corvette Museum

the museum recovered quickly. Your admission bracelet lets you come and go all day as you please, and the entrance fee allows visitors 16 and older to sign up for a 15-minute block on an educational driving simulator.

Bowling Green Corvette Assembly Plant

Witness the birth of America's sports car at the **Bowling Green Corvette Assembly Plant** (600 Corvette Dr., 270/745-8019, www. bowlinggreenassemblyplant.com, $7), the one and only place in the world where Corvettes are produced. The tour, which lasts a minimum of one hour and can last as long as two depending on the level of interest of those on the tour, allows participants to watch multiple steps of production, from the kitting out of the interiors to the marriage of the body with the chassis to the final testing process as the cars are driven off the line. For those with a passion for Corvettes or cars in general, the tour is a must. Others are likely to find it interesting, but it can get a little bit technical if you're not

a car geek. Tours, which take place at 8:30am, 11:30am, and 2pm Monday-Thursday, can be scheduled online or by phone up to a year in advance. Walk-ins are also welcome, although you should arrive about 45 minutes ahead of the tour time to get a ticket. Because this is a factory tour, you must wear flat-soled, closed-toe, closed-heel shoes and are not allowed to bring cameras, phones, backpacks, purses, or bags of any type on the tour. Children must be at least seven years old to participate.

Riverview at Hobson Grove

Dating back to the Civil War era, **Riverview at Hobson Grove** (1100 W. Main Ave., 270/843-5565, www.bgky.org/riverview, 10am-4pm Tues.-Sat., 1pm-4pm Sun., last tour at 3:15pm, closed Jan., $7 adults, $2.50 students, $14 family rate) is a glorious Italianate mansion open to the public for tours. Begun in 1850, completed in 1872, and occupied by the Hobson family until 1950, Riverview is decorated with original family pieces as well as other period furniture. Be sure to check out the parlor ceilings, which

BOWLING GREEN

Riverview at Hobson Grove

are beautifully painted. For the Christmas holidays, the house is decorated and tours are conducted by candlelight.

Corsair Artisan Distillery

Part of the Kentucky Bourbon Trail Craft Tour, **Corsair Artisan Distillery** (400 E. Main St., 270/904-2021, www.corsairartisan.com) handcrafts and bottles small batches of premium whiskey, gin, vodka, and absinthe right on the main square in downtown Bowling Green. Complimentary tours (on the hour 11am-3pm Tues.-Fri. and 10am-5pm Sat.) include a visit to the production area of the distillery and a tasting of two of the spirits.

Historic Railpark and Train Museum

Bowling Green's 1925 L&N Depot, which lost its purpose when passenger train service went out of style, has been given a new chance at life as the **Historic Railpark and Train Museum** (401 Kentucky St., 270/745-7317, www.historicrailpark.com, 9am-5pm Mon.-Sat., 1pm-4pm Sun., $12 adults, $10 seniors, $6 youth 5-12). The museum, which is housed in the lovingly restored depot, has exhibits that focus on the train experience, the various types of trains, and African American railroad history. Kids, especially, will enjoy the model train, which runs through a miniature Bowling Green, as well as the "ask a conductor/chef/engineer" interactive exhibits. The highlight of a visit to the museum is a tour of the five cars on-site (last tour at 3:30pm): a post office car, dining car, passenger sleeping car, presidential car, and caboose. When you exit the trains, you can't help but wonder why this wonderful way of travel has nearly gone extinct in America.

Western Kentucky University

Home of the Hilltoppers, Western Kentucky University is a bustling public university in the heart of Bowling Green. Of primary interest to visitors is the **Kentucky Library & Museum** (1444 Kentucky St., 270/745-2592, www.wku.edu/kentuckymuseum, 9am-4pm

BOWLING GREEN

© THERESA DOWELL BLACKINTON

entrance to Lost River Cave

Mon.-Sat., 1pm-4pm Sun., $10 adults, $5 seniors and youth 6-16, $20 family rate), which houses an 1815 log house as well as exhibits on the Civil War, arts and crafts, and local famous man Duncan Hines. Hines may now be best known as the name on cake mix boxes, but his fame originally came from the travel books he wrote recommending restaurants and hotels. Back in his day, "Recommended by Duncan Hines" was the equivalent of a Michelin rating. The museum is especially kid-friendly with lots of hands-on activities, including costumes that can be tried on and a Civil War tent that can be entered and explored. Adults won't want to miss the decorative arts exhibit on the third floor.

Other campus attractions worth checking out are the **Hardin Planetarium** (1501 State St., 270/745-4044, www.wku.edu/hardinplanetarium, shows at 2pm Sun., 7pm Tues. and Thurs., free) and the remains of **Fort Lytle,** a Civil War fort that was located atop the hill where WKU now sits. The fort offers the best view of Bowling Green.

◖ Lost River Cave & Valley

Lost River Cave & Valley (2818 Nashville Rd., 270/393-0077, www.lostrivercave.com, 9am-6pm daily Memorial Day-mid-Oct., 10am-4pm daily, mid-Oct.-Memorial Day, $15.95 adults, $10.95 youth 4-11, $3.95 youth 1-3) offers the only opportunity in the state to take a boat tour of a cave. The tour, which lasts about 45 minutes, begins with a walk along the river to the enormous cave entrance, where the boat tour departs. On the tour, participants will learn about cave formation as well as cave history and folklore. Lost River Cave's story is unique, with the cave having been used at various times in history as a mill site, a Civil War resting spot, a possible hideout for the likes of Jesse James, and, most interestingly, as a nightclub from the early 1930s to the early 1960s. The dance floor and bandstand still remain and are, in fact, used today for fundraising events, weddings, and local proms. In peak season, visitors may have to wait an hour or more for a tour, but the site offers many wonderful ways to occupy your time. You can hike the more than two miles of trails on the property, visit the butterfly habitat (late May-mid-Sept.), search for wildlife in the wetlands, borrow binoculars to try to spot as many of the park's 120 bird species as possible, sluice for fossils and gemstones, or borrow the site's GPS unit and give geocaching a go. All activities except the cave tour and sluicing are free, and it's easy to pass a few hours enjoying this natural oasis right in the city.

Aviation Heritage Park

The Phantom II plane that is the focus of **Aviation Heritage Park** (1825 Three Springs Rd., www.aviationheritagepark.com) is more than just a remarkable aircraft; it's the centerpiece of the story of two men from two different countries who fought on two different sides in one terrible war, and who, against all odds, became friends. Bowling Green native Dan Cherry flew Phantom II 550 in the Vietnam War, shooting down enemy aircraft. When he found the plane decades after the war in Ohio, he arranged to have it brought to Bowling Green and then set out on a quest to find out what happened to the pilot of a plane he vividly recalls destroying. Eventually, he found and met the Vietnamese pilot, and a surprising friendship ensued, bringing both men to each other's countries and catching the attention of the *CBS Evening News*. A Panther plane joined the Phantom in 2010 as a tribute to local Johnny Magda, who was commander of the Blue Angels, and it has since been joined by a Shooting Star and an Aardvark. While visiting the park, tune your radio to 89.3 FM for more information on the planes.

Beech Bend Amusement Park and Splash Lagoon

Belonging to the old school of family-run amusement parks, **Beech Bend** (798 Beech Bend Rd., 270/781-7634, www.beechbend. com, 10am-7pm Mon.-Fri., 10am-8pm Sat., 11am-7pm Sun., Memorial Day-July, weekends and select weekdays only, May and Aug.-Sept., $31.99 adults, $27.99 seniors and youth under 54 inches, season passes available) is

home to dozens of rides, including the wooden Kentucky Rumbler roller coaster and the Vortex, a high-swinging, 240-degree revolving pendulum ride new in 2013. In addition to standard amusement park rides, Beech Bend has a petting zoo, go-kart track, and mini-golf course, all of which are available at no additional cost. The Splash Lagoon Water Park, which is included with admission, features a wave pool and leisure pool, lazy river, and multiple water slides.

Walking Tours

The **ShakeRag Walking Tour** is a 15-stop tour of a neighborhood placed on the National Register of Historic Places for its significance to African American history. One of the stops on the tour is the State Street Baptist Church, home to the oldest African American congregation in Bowling Green. A free guide is available at the visitors bureau (352 Three Springs Rd., 800/326-7465, www.visitbgky.com).

The **Historic Fountain Square** brochure traces a walking route around the downtown square and provides historical and architectural information on many of the buildings on the square. Pick up a free copy of the brochure at the visitors bureau.

Agritourism

In response to low milk prices in the early 2000s, **Chaney's Dairy Barn** (9191 Nashville Rd., 270/843-5567, www.chaneysdairybarn. com, 11am-9pm Mon.-Sat., noon-8pm Sun.) evolved from a strictly commercial operation, a dairy farm run since 1940 by the Chaney family, to an agritourism destination, where the dairy's milk is turned into delicious ice cream (now famous enough to have been featured in an April 2011 episode of *Justified*). At 1pm on Monday and Fridays in June and July, individuals are invited to take a tour of the farm ($8) and learn about dairy cows and even try their hand at milking. The farm also hosts multiple events throughout the year, including an Easter egg hunt, a May Kentucky Proud Festival, and a fall corn maze. One of the most popular events is Ice Cream and a

Mooovie, a free summertime event in which family-friendly movies are projected onto the barn. Although the more than 30 flavors of rich ice cream are the main dish at Chaney's, the Dairy Barn also serves a selection of tasty homemade sandwiches and soups.

Handpick your own produce at **Jackson's Orchard** (1280 Slim Island Rd., 270/781-5303, www.jacksonsorchard.com, 8am-6pm Mon.-Sat., mid-Apr.-mid-Nov., also 1pm-6pm Sun. in fall), a popular family destination for decades. Peaches peak around Independence Day, Labor Day brings apples, and October is pumpkin season.

ENTERTAINMENT AND EVENTS
Bars and Clubs

Young professionals flock to **Micki's on Main** (440 E. Main St., 270/793-0450, www.440main.com, 11am-10pm Sun.-Thurs., 11am-midnight Fri.-Sat.), a lively bar with a New Orleans influence. The patio, which is right on the main town square, is packed on warm summer nights, and live music draws crowds on Friday and Saturday. Be sure to check out the food and drink specials during happy hour (4pm-6pm Mon.-Fri.).

Tidball's (522 Morris Alley, 270/793-9955, 9pm-2am Mon.-Sat.) plays host to great live music, which is accompanied by well-priced drink specials and a fun-loving crowd. This somewhat dive-ish bar, which has a stage on the bottom floor and a pool table area upstairs, can get loud and crowded, but that's kind of the point.

Performing Arts

In September 2012, the glass-fronted and light-filled **Southern Kentucky Performing Arts Center** (612 College St., 274/904-1880, www.theskypac.com), known as SKyPAC, opened, bringing an 1,800-seat main theatre, a 200-seat studio theatre, two visual art galleries, and an 800-seat outdoor amphitheatre to Bowling Green. The center hosts a Broadway series, concerts by big-name musicians, and performances by touring comedians and other national and international acts. SKyPAC is also the new home of **Orchestra Kentucky of Bowling Green** (www.orchestrakentucky. com), which has been bringing orchestra performances to Bowling Green since 2000. Going beyond the classic orchestral arrangements, Orchestra Kentucky pairs up with pop stars, performs retro hits, and presents children and family concerts. Tickets for all SKyPAC shows can be purchased online, over the phone, or in person.

The **Symphony at WKU** (270/745-7681, www.bgwso.org), which is composed of Western Kentucky University students and professional musicians, presents both a symphony series and a chamber music series each year. Performances take place on the WKU campus at Van Meter Auditorium. Tickets can be purchased online, over the phone, or in person on the day of the performance.

For theatre buffs, two community theatre companies offer an array of acts each year. The **Fountain Square Players** (313 State St. 270/782-3119, www.fountainsquareplayers. com) puts on four plays and one musical each year, while the **Public Theatre of Kentucky** (545 Morris Alley, 270/781-6233, www.ptkbg. org) presents four adult productions and two youth productions. Tickets for both theatres can be purchased online.

Festivals and Events

Every **Second Saturday** from April through September, downtown's Fountain Square is the place to be. From 10am to 5pm, the square plays host to arts and crafts vendors, food concessionaires, and live music. The event also features kids' activities and horse and carriage rides.

SHOPPING

Fountain Square Park is the heart of downtown, and the streets that make up the square are home to a number of fun shops. Arts and craft lovers will want to check out **Candle Makers on the Square** (417 Park Row, 270/843-3001, http://candlemakersbg.com, 10am-6pm Mon.-Thurs. and Sat., 10am-8pm Fri., noon-5pm

KENTUCKY'S YARD SALE EXTRAVAGANZAS

Who doesn't love a good yard sale? Amid dusty knickknacks, ugly lamps, and outgrown clothing, who knows what else you might find? Mickey Mantle's rookie baseball card? Ansel Adams's long-lost photos? A pair of perfectly worn-in cowboy boots? There's just something alluring about digging through someone else's discards. Here in Kentucky, there are plenty of opportunities to yard-sale shop on an enormous scale.

Yard sale season kicks off during the first week of June with the **400 Mile Sale** (www.400mile.com), which is held Thursday-Sunday along U.S. 68. U.S. 68 begins in the west just outside of Paducah and heads east across the state, passing through Land Between the Lakes, Hopkinsville, Bowling Green, and Glasgow before making a northern turn and continuing through Lebanon, Harrodsburg, Nicholasville, Paris, and Maysville. More than 60 communities along the route take part in the four-day event.

Next up on the schedule is the **World's Largest Yard Sale** (www.127sale.com), held annually for four days in August beginning on the first Thursday of the month. This over-the-top yard sale runs 690 miles along U.S. 127

from Gadsden, Alabama, to Hudson, Michigan. In Kentucky, the route begins to the east of Dale Hollow Lake; runs along the western shore of Lake Cumberland; continues north through Danville, Harrodsburg, Lawrenceburg, and Frankfort; cuts through Northern Kentucky; and ends at the Ohio River in Covington. With more than 200 miles of yard sale activity in Kentucky, you're bound to find something you just have to have.

If you haven't had enough shopping by the time fall rolls around, the **Rollercoaster Yard Sale** (www.rollercoasterfair.com) is a three-day, 150-mile yard sale held in south-central Kentucky and northern Tennessee on the first weekend of October. The looping route begins near Mammoth Cave, follows KY 90 through Glasgow and on to Burkesville on Dale Hollow Lake, circles around Dale Hollow Lake in Tennessee on TN 111 and TN 52, and then returns to Glasgow on KY 163 and KY 63.

In addition to the expected yard sale booths, you'll also find food vendors, live entertainment, and antique stores offering special sales. Even if you're not a big shopper, the yard sales provide a fun way to tour the state and meet lots of local folks.

Sun.) and **The Pots Place** (428 E. Main St., 270/904-0599, 10am-2pm Mon., Wed., and Sat., 4pm-7pm Fri.). Nearby **Gallery 916** (601 State St., 270/843-5511, www.gallery916.net, noon-6pm Tues.-Fri., 11am-2pm Sat.) is also worth a visit for its collection of fine art.

Greenwood Mall (2625 Scottsville Rd., 270/782-9047, www.greenwoodmall.com, 10am-9pm Mon.-Sat., 12:30pm-6pm Sun.) has four department stores, including a Macy's, and more than 100 other stores to satisfy any need you might have for mall shopping.

SPORTS AND RECREATION
Parks
Skaters will want to check out the bowls, moguls, and rails at the **Bowling Green Skate Park** (200 6th Ave., 270/393-3249, www.

bgky.org, 7am-11pm daily), which is well lit so that the many skate fans who gather at the park every day can practice and play well into the night.

Dog lovers can let their canines run free at **H.P. Thomas "Bark" Park** (850 Cave Mill Rd., 270/393-3249), which has two fenced-in areas, dog water fountains, and playground and picnic equipment for dog's best friend.

Biking
Bicyclists unfamiliar with the area or looking for group fun will want to get in touch with the **Bowling Green League of Bicyclists** (www.bglob.com), a group of cycling enthusiasts who regularly ride together. Check the online calendar for information on upcoming group rides as well as maps of favorite local routes. The group

sponsors the annual **Tour de Cave** in June, which has routes of 8, 16, 45, and 70 miles.

Golf

Named the best public golf course in Bowling Green, **CrossWinds Golf Course** (1031 Wilkinson Trace, 270/393-3550, www.bgky. org) is an 18-hole course set on 122 acres. Golfers will be challenged by the very large bunkers and will enjoy the well-manicured tees, fairways, and greens.

Disc Golf

Bowling Green is home to seven public disc golf courses and has hosted many national events. Two of the most centrally located courses are at **Hobson Grove Park** (1200 W. Main St.) and **Basil Griffin Park** (2055 Three Springs Rd.). If you didn't bring your disc, **Nat's Outdoor Sports** (1121 Wilkinson Trace, 800/327-1731, www.natsoutdoor.com, 9:30am-8pm Mon.-Sat., noon-5pm Sun.) will take care of you. In addition to a wide array of discs, they sell gear for most any other outdoor pursuit.

Swimming

The **Russell Sims Aquatic Center** (2303 Tomblinson Ln., 270/393-3271, www.bgky. org, 10:30am-6:30pm Mon.-Thurs. and Sat., 10:30am-8pm Fri., 1pm-6:30pm Sun., Memorial Day-early Aug., weekends only, mid-Aug.-Labor Day, $8 adults, $6 college students, $5 seniors and youth 6-15, $4 children 3-5, $2 babies 2 and under, half-price after 4pm) is not your average public pool. In addition to a 50-meter pool, the center features two diving boards, multiple water slides, and a splash park.

Spectator Sports

There's hardly a better way to pass a summer afternoon or evening than at a **Bowling Green Hot Rods** baseball game (300 8th Ave., 270/901-2121, www.bghotrods.com). The team, which is the Single-A affiliate of the Tampa Bay Rays, plays at an attractive stadium that opened in 2009 without a bad seat in the house. The games are very family friendly, with plenty of between-inning action, and the

stadium features two grassy berms, where kids are welcome to run around, as well as an enclosed children's play area. Lawn tickets are only $7, and box tickets can be had for $10.

Beech Bend Raceway (598 Beech Bend Rd., 270/781-7634, www.beechbend.com), which has both a drag strip and an oval track, attracts those with a need for speed. The NHRA (National Hot Rod Association) events on the schedule bring big names in drag racing to Big Bend, while fun racing events draw enthusiasts. The oval track is set up for stock car racing, with most major events taking place on Friday evenings. Races run on the oval track April-September, while drag racing runs March-November. Visit the Beech Bend website for a full schedule of races and ticket information. General admission tickets for Sunday NHRA races and Friday stock car races tend to be $10.

Fans of college sports should check to see what's going on with the **Western Kentucky University Athletics** (www.wkusports.com, 800/524-4733) program. The Hilltoppers compete in the Sunbelt Conference in eight men's sports and nine women's sports. The men's football team, which is bowl eligible, plays home games at 23,500-seat Houchens Industries-L. T. Smith Stadium, while both basketball teams play at E. A. Diddle Arena. Tickets for athletic events can be purchased online or in person at the ticket office inside Diddle Arena. Both venues are located on University Boulevard on WKU's campus.

ACCOMMODATIONS

Chain hotels are abundant in Bowling Green. The densest population of these hotels and motels can be found off of Exit 22. Most of these options are in the budget to mid-range price class. Right off the interstate, you'll find a Hampton Inn, Days Inn, La Quinta Inn, Ramada Inn, and many others. The rooms at the **Drury Inn** (3250 Scottsville Rd., 270/842-7100, www.druryhotels.com, $112.99) are standard, but in addition to a free hot breakfast, the hotel also offers a complimentary happy hour, where the hot snacks are plentiful enough to

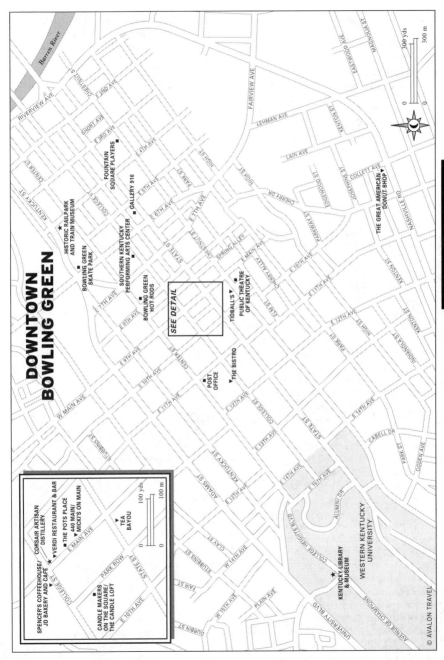

BOWLING GREEN

DOWNTOWN BOWLING GREEN

- HISTORIC RAILPARK AND TRAIN MUSEUM
- BOWLING GREEN SKATE PARK
- FOUNTAIN SQUARE PLAYERS
- GALLERY 916
- SOUTHERN KENTUCKY PERFORMING ARTS CENTER
- BOWLING GREEN HOT RODS
- TIDBALL'S
- PUBLIC THEATRE OF KENTUCKY
- THE BISTRO
- POST OFFICE
- THE GREAT AMERICAN DONUT SHOP
- KENTUCKY LIBRARY & MUSEUM
- WESTERN KENTUCKY UNIVERSITY

SEE DETAIL

Barren River

0 300 yds
0 300 m

Detail inset

- SPENCER'S COFFEEHOUSE/ JD BAKERY AND CAFE
- CORSAIR ARTISAN DISTILLERY
- VERDI RESTAURANT & BAR
- THE POTS PLACE
- 440 MAIN/ MICKI'S ON MAIN
- TEA BAYOU
- CANDLE MAKERS ON THE SQUARE/ THE CANDLE LOFT

0 100 yds
0 100 m

© AVALON TRAVEL

constitute a meal and alcoholic drinks can be purchased for $0.53 each.

The nicest of the chain hotels are located near the Convention Center, meaning they are often busy with businesspeople. Consider staying at the **Hilton Garden Inn** (1020 Wilkinson Trace, 270/781-6778, www.hiltongardeninn.hilton.com, $99) or the **Holiday Inn University Plaza Hotel** (1021 Wilkinson Trace, 270/745-0088, www.holidayinnbowlinggreen.com, $99).

Bed & Breakfasts

Zoning laws have, unfortunately, made it hard for bed-and-breakfasts to operate in Bowling Green, but there are a few worth noting just outside of town and an easy drive to area attractions. **◖ Spongie Acres Bed & Breakfast** (610 Matlock Rd., 855/752-1061, www.spongieacresbedandbreakfast.com, $129-169) sits on 14 acres near the intersection of I-65 and I-66 and has six spacious rooms, each with one comfy and finely suited king or queen bed. Owners and active cyclists Clint and Jaunnie rent bicycles to guests and can help you plan a cycling route. Car aficionados will appreciate the large garage where you can keep your prized ride. The B&B offers a lot of well-equipped public space, including a game room, an exercise room, a movie room, a back deck, and a front porch, allowing guests to easily socialize. In addition to a country breakfast, guests are also treated to afternoon cookies.

Another option is **1869 Homestead Bed & Breakfast** (212 Mizpah Rd., 270/842-0510, www.1869homestead.com, $99-129), which sits on 55 acres about 4.5 miles north of Exit 28. The B&B has two queen rooms and one suite, each with private bath, decorated in Civil War-era antiques and reproductions. Original features include the house's many fireplaces and a gorgeous circular staircase.

A little further outside of Bowling Green in Smiths Grove, a small town known for its antique shops just off Exit 38, is the **Victorian House Bed and Breakfast** (110 N. Main St., Smiths Grove, 270/563-9403, www.bbonline.com, $99-139), which has five rooms with private baths. A full country breakfast is served each day, and the large porch with a view of Main Street is a great place to wind down each evening.

For an in-town option, see whether **The Candle Loft** (417 Park Row, 270/843-3001, http://thecandleloft.net, $179), a two-room suite located on Fountain Square, has availability. The suite has a king bed, a queen bed, a full kitchen, a seating area, a dining area, and a den. For breakfast, you receive a voucher to be used at one of four area restaurants.

Campgrounds

Beech Bend (798 Beech Bend Rd., 270/781-7634, www.beechbend.com, $30-40) has a large campground with more than 500 spaces, half of which have full hookups. The campground is especially popular on race weekends. If you don't have your own RV but want to be part of the party, you can rent an RV that sleeps six from the campground ($200).

Bowling Green's **KOA** (1960 Three Springs Rd., 270/843-1919, www.bgkoa.com) has full hookup sites for RVs ($28-48), tent camping areas ($28), and one- and two-bedroom cabins ($66-110). The campground also has a fishing lake, mini-golf course, and a full schedule of summer events.

FOOD
Bowling Green Farmers Markets

Get a taste of what local farmers are producing at any of three **farmers markets** held April-October (1751 Scottsville Rd., 6am-1pm, Tues., Thurs., and Sat.; corner of 5th St. and High St., 7am-noon Sat., 7am-1pm Tues.; Nashville Rd. and Campbellsville Ln. parking lot, 8am-1pm Sat., 3pm-7pm Tues.).

Breakfast

Open 24 hours and charging rock-bottom prices, **◖ The Great American Donut Shop** (901 U.S. 31W Bypass, 270/842-7155) feeds your doughnut craving no matter when it hits and no matter what kind you prefer—cake, yeast, glazed, iced, filled, as a traditional doughnut or as a Long John or doughnut hole.

No choice—from the blueberry cake doughnut to the chocolate chip Long John—is a bad choice at this local institution. **JD Bakery and Café** (937 College St., 270/846-7890, 7am-6pm Tues.-Fri., 7am-2pm Sat.) will help you start your day right with such specials as Nutella-stuffed French toast, red velvet pancakes, and farm fresh omelets. Soup, salad, sandwiches, and daily hot specials are available at lunch.

Cafés and Coffeehouses

Home Café (2440 Nashville Rd., 270/846-1272, www.homecafebg.com, 10:30am-8pm Tues.-Fri., 8am-8pm Sat., 10am-2pm Sun., $4.49-8.99) focuses on in-season items, much of them locally sourced, which means their menu of pizzas, sandwiches, soups, and salads is always changing, but might include a charred peach salad, a Cajun crawfish pizza, or a roasted turkey sandwich with orange-cranberry relish.

As the name suggests, **Tea Bayou** (906 State St., 270/904-3889, 9am-6pm Mon.-Fri., 9am-3pm Sat.) specializes in teas ($1.95-3.25), with an enormous selection of black, green, white, and herbal tree, and Cajun food, serving such favorites as muffulettas and po'boys ($5.95). With free Wi-Fi, lots of sweet treats, and a cozy atmosphere, it's a great place to while away some hours.

Set right on the town square, **Spencer's Coffeehouse** (915 College St., 270/393-7060, 7am-8pm Mon.-Fri., 8am-8pm Sat.) is a favorite place to grab a cup of joe or a smoothie ($1.75-4.95) and settle in for some people-watching. Sandwiches, soups, and salads ($4.00-7.75) as well as breakfast sandwiches ($3-3.50) are also available, and wireless Internet is free for customers.

Barbecue

Follow the smoke to **Smokey Pig BBQ** (2520 Louisville Rd., 270/781-1712, 10:30am-7pm Tues.-Sat., $4.75-7.80). It's not much to look at, but the Smokey Pig delivers when it comes to mouthwatering deliciousness. Choose a sandwich or a plate of pork (shoulder, chop, or shredded), chicken, or ribs. Plates come with your choice of two sides, which include macaroni and cheese, baked beans, potato salad, and both vinegar and mayo slaw.

Contemporary American

Bowling Green's **Montana Grille** (1740 Scottsville Rd., 270/746-9746, www.montanagrille.com, 4pm-10pm Mon.-Thurs., 4pm-11pm Fri., 3pm-11pm Sat., noon-10pm Sun., $8.99-18.99), which is not part of the same-name chain owned by Ted Turner, draws consistent crowds with its warm, lodge-like atmosphere and its tasty food. The Tillamook cheese and pico de gallo appetizer can't be good for you, but it's so good it doesn't matter. For your entrée, try one of the thick cuts of steak or the rotisserie chicken, though really, everything on the menu is good. Portions are large, so go easy on the complimentary jalapeño corn bread.

440 Main (440 E. Main St., 270/793-0450, www.440main.com, 5pm-10pm Mon.-Sat., $13.95-27.95) is a white-tablecloth restaurant with an upscale New Orleans vibe that serves favorites like bourbon salmon, filet mignon, and jambalaya. Order a plate of Cajun spring rolls to share before settling on a main course. 440 Main is connected to Micki's on Main, where you can have a drink after dinner or while you wait for your table.

C The Bistro (1129 College St., 270/781-9646, www.thebistrobg.com, lunch 11am-4pm Mon.-Fri., dinner 5pm-9pm Mon.-Thurs., 5pm-10pm Fri.-Sat., brunch 10:30am-3pm Sun., $12-20) serves artisan pizzas, pastas, and such entrées as black truffle pork tenderloin in the lovely setting of a restored 1893 home. Pizzas and sandwiches ($8-13) are available at lunch.

European

The menu at **Verdi Restaurant & Bar** (410 E. Main Ave., 270/781-9817, www.verdibg.com, 11am-8pm Mon., 11am-9pm Tues.-Thurs., 11am-9:30pm Fri., noon-9:30pm Sat., $9-21), a Bosnian-run favorite in Bowling Green, is so long that you can't help but wonder if so many dishes can be that good. Set your anxieties aside. Whether you opt for schnitzel or souvlaki, you'll find yourself smacking your lips. The menu pulls from the cuisines around which Bosnian food is based— German, Greek, and Italian—but also shows some Kentucky influence. At lunch ($7-14), you can opt for smaller portions of popular entrées or choose from a long list of panini, wraps, and sandwiches.

INFORMATION AND SERVICES

The **Bowling Green Area Convention & Visitors Bureau** (352 Three Springs Rd., 800/326-7465, www.visitbgky.com) welcomes visitors to stop in their information center to find out about area attractions, hotels, and restaurants. If you contact them in advance, they'll gladly send you a visitor's guide that will help you plan your trip.

A **post office** is located downtown at 311 East 11th Avenue and is open 8am-5pm Monday-Friday and 8am-2pm Saturday.

GETTING THERE

Bowling Green is located along I-65, about 110 miles (two hours) south of Louisville and 70 miles (one hour) north of Nashville. From Lexington, the 150-mile trip (2.5 hours) is via westbound KY 9002 to Elizabethtown, then southbound I-65. Bowling Green is about 280 miles (4.5 hours) from St. Louis, 210 miles (3.5 hours) from Cincinnati, and 230 miles (3.5) hours from Indianapolis.

Bowling Green's downtown is located off of Exit 26, while most hotels are located at Exit 22. The Corvette Assembly Plant and the National Corvette Museum are located in the northern part of Bowling Green at Exit 28.

The nearest airports supporting commercial airlines are in Nashville and Louisville.

GETTING AROUND
Driving Tours

The **Duncan Hines Scenic Byway Tour** is an 82-mile route that begins and ends at the former home of Duncan Hines and winds through scenic Warren and Edmonson Counties. The driving tour passes through the colorful towns of Sunfish, Pig, and Bee Spring, approaches Nolin Lake, crosses the Green River via ferry, and cuts across Mammoth Cave National Park. The Duncan Hines brochure available at the visitors bureau (352 Three Springs Rd., 800/326-7465, www.visitbgky.com) and at attractions around the city gives detailed directions, or you can download information on the route from www.visitbgky.com.

Vicinity of Bowling Green

A former Shaker village and a gateway town offer additional sites and activities if you're in the Bowling Green area. South Union is worth seeking out for its Shaker Museum, while folks passing into or out of Tennessee on I-65 would do well to take a break in Franklin, which offers historic sites as well as recreational activities.

SOUTH UNION

South Union, which is located in rural Logan County, was founded by a community of Shakers in the early 19th century. Today the crossroads community lives on as a ghost town of sorts, where the buildings and traditions of the Shakers are preserved as Shaker Village at South Union.

Shaker Village

Established in 1807 and dissolved in 1922, **Shaker Village at South Union** (850 Shaker Museum Rd., 270/542-4167, www.shakermuseum.com, 9am-5pm Tues.-Sat., 1pm-5pm Sun. Mar.-Nov., 10am-4pm Tues.-Sat. Dec.-Feb., $8 adults, $4 youth 6-12) was the last of the western Shaker communities to close. Today, the Shaker Museum, which is located in the 40-room Centre House, preserves the remaining vestiges of that Shaker community.

Take a self-guided tour of the house, which is furnished with relics that demonstrate how the Shakers lived. Text panels provide just the right amount of information for each room. Fans of Shaker design should note that South Union is home to the largest collection of authentic southern Shaker furniture in the world. In addition to Centre House, five additional buildings—the well shed, smoke and milk house, ministry shop, steam house, and grain barn—are open to the public.

Accommodations

Built in 1869 as a restaurant and hotel for "people of the world," the **Shaker Tavern** (396 South Union Rd., 270/542-6801, www.shakermuseum.com, $70-80) has been brought back to life as a bed-and-breakfast. The tavern has six rooms, some with private bath, others with shared bath. A full breakfast is served each morning.

Getting There and Around

Shaker Village at South Union is about 25 minutes (15 miles) southwest of downtown Bowling Green and can be reached via U.S. 68. The museum is one mile south of U.S. 68 on KY 1466.

FRANKLIN

Friendly little Franklin sits on the Tennessee doorstep, with locals crossing back and forth between the two states without even noticing. Millions of others pass through, too, driving to destinations farther north or south on I-65. But Franklin's not just a gas station stop. It's the home of champion golfer Kenny Perry, who still lives here and shares the course he built with the public, and the location of the **Methodist church** (107 N. College St.) where Johnny Cash married June Carter on March 1, 1968, not to mention a few other sights worth a look.

Octagon Hall Museum

Constructed just prior to the Civil War by Andrew Jackson Caldwell, a Confederate sympathizer and man with a taste for the unusual,

© THERESA DOWELL BLACKINTON

Methodist church where Johnny Cash married June Carter

Octagon Hall (6040 Bowling Green Rd., 270/586-9343, www.octagonhall.com, 9am-11am and 1pm-3:30pm Wed.-Sat., $5 adults, $1 youth 6-12) served as a hospital and hiding place for Confederate soldiers during the war. Today, the only octagonal house in Kentucky has been preserved as a museum that displays various aspects of the house's history. Visitors can take a self-guided tour of the main floor, second floor, and basement of the house, and are also welcome to stop at the slave quarters, slave cemetery, summer kitchen, and the state champion dogwood tree on a walk around the grounds. Keep your eyes wide open on your tour as the house is said to be haunted. Ask the staff for stories and photos.

The Old Jail and Jailer's Quarters at the Simpson County Archives & Museum

As unbelievable as it may seem, **Simpson County's Old Stone Jail** (206 N. College St., 270/586-4228, www.simpsoncountykyarchives.com, 9am-4pm Mon.-Fri., 10am-2pm Sat., free), which was built in 1879 from huge limestone blocks, was used until 1986. Peek in the restored cell and just try to imagine it being used in the late 20th century; modern jails will seem downright luxurious in comparison. Right next door, the Jailer's Quarters is now used as a local history museum, with exhibits related to music, the military, agriculture, and pioneer life.

African American Heritage Center

The **African American Heritage Center** (500 Jefferson St., 270/598-9986, www.aahconline.org, 9am-6pm Mon., 9am-4pm Tues.-Fri., 9am-11am Sat., free) preserves and celebrates African American culture and achievements, with specific focus on Simpson County. Different rooms in the center host exhibits on genealogy, African American contributions to the military, the town's segregated Lincoln School, African American heroes, and African American fashion. The center has also rescued the first African American school

in Franklin, which they are restoring and opening to the public.

Shopping

Franklin is home to a slew of antiques shops. **Bright's Antique World** (281 Steele Rd., 270/598-9901, www.brightsantiqueworld.com, 9am-8pm Mon.-Sat., 10am-6pm Sun.) is a great place to start a quest for old treasures. The 35,000-square-foot facility is home to multiple dealers who specialize in everything from furniture to glassware to vintage toys to memorabilia.

For arts and crafts fans, **Gallery on the Square** (110 N. Main St., 270/586-8055, www.galleryonthesquare.org, 10am-4pm Tues.-Fri., 10am-1pm Sat.) is a must-stop. The nonprofit gallery represents the work of juried artists with talent that is decidedly not small-town. A selection of Kentucky Crafted products is also available, and one wall of the gallery is dedicated to rotating exhibits. Gallery on the Square conducts art classes for youth and adults, and goes beyond visual arts to present spoken word and music as well. After you make your purchases, be sure to check out the other shops located along the iconic town square.

Horse Racing

In September of each year, horses come to **Kentucky Downs Race Course** (5629 Nashville Rd., 270/586-7778, www.kentuckydowns.com, free) to compete on the only European-style turf racetrack in North America. The track first opened in 1990 as a steeplechase track called Dueling Grounds Race Course, but now focuses on flat racing. The original name references the many duels that took place in the 1800s on this piece of land right at the Kentucky-Tennessee border, including a duel involving Sam Houston. Outside the live racing season, Kentucky Downs simulcasts races and offers off-site betting. The property also hosts concerts and has a restaurant, The Clubhouse Bar & Grill, which serves a long list of appetizers and sandwiches as well as a selection of entrées.

Golf

PGA golfer Kenny Perry may have won millions of dollars on tour, but he's never forgotten his roots, remaining an involved and well-loved resident of Franklin. In fact, you can often find the famous golfer out on the links at **Kenny Perry's Country Creek** (1075 Kenny Perry Dr., 270/586-9373, www.kpcountrycreek.com), the course he designed and his family runs in Franklin. The 18-hole course is open to the public, and reasonable costs make it accessible to any golf lover. It's best to call for a tee time, although no reservations are taken for weekday afternoons, so show up then if you didn't plan in advance. If you spot Kenny, don't hesitate to say hello. He's about the most down-to-earth millionaire you'll ever meet.

Accommodations

Thanks to its location on I-65 at the Kentucky-Tennessee border, Franklin abounds with chain hotels. At Exit 2, the best option is the **Holiday Inn Express** (85 Neha Dr., 270/586-7626, www.hiexpress.com, $99), which opened in 2009 and has nice rooms, a hot breakfast, a large pool and hot tub, and a fitness room. At Exit 6, the **Comfort Inn & Suites** (105 Trotter Ln., 270/586-3832, www.comfortinn.com, $65), which opened in 2010 and features fresh rooms as well as an indoor pool, fitness room, and hot breakfast, is the top choice. Families should inquire about the rooms with attached extra bedrooms, which provide an economical alternative to booking separate rooms.

Food

Even if you're just passing through Franklin on your way elsewhere, it's more than worth it to get off the interstate for a meal at **Brickyard Café** (205 W. Cedar St., 270/586-9080, www.brickyardcafe.net, 11am-9pm Mon.-Thurs., 11am-10pm Fri., 5pm-10pm Sat., $8-22), which is located in a beautifully restored historic building on the town square. Run by a Croatian immigrant who started with a restaurant in Bowling Green before opening this location in Franklin, Brickyard Café serves up a tasty menu of Mediterranean- and Italian-influenced dishes, with everything from the bread to the salad dressings to the desserts made on-site. The café has a bar with an extensive wine and liquor list.

Information and Services

Located in a little log cabin off of Exit 2 on I-65, the **Simpson County Tourism Commission** (81 Steele Rd., 270/586-3040, www.franklinky.info) can set you up with all the information you need to enjoy your visit.

Getting There and Around

Franklin is the first place you'll hit when you cross into Kentucky from Tennessee on I-65. Located along this busy route just 20 miles (30 minutes) south of Bowling Green and 45 miles (45 minutes) north of Nashville, Franklin sees a lot of traffic.

Cave Country

Just beneath the surface of the rolling hills of south-central Kentucky, you'll find some of the state's most exciting geologic features. Hundreds of miles of caves wind their way through subterranean Kentucky thanks to the area's unique limestone and sandstone geology. Mammoth Cave, which is protected as a national park, is at the heart of this system, but many other caves are clustered around it. From north to south, the towns of Horse Cave, Cave City, and Park City act as the gateways to the caves.

HORSE CAVE AND VICINITY

Horse Cave is home to Hart County's major attractions, but despite attracting busloads of tourists, the town maintains its small-town charm. Part of this is due to a successful Main

BOWLING GREEN

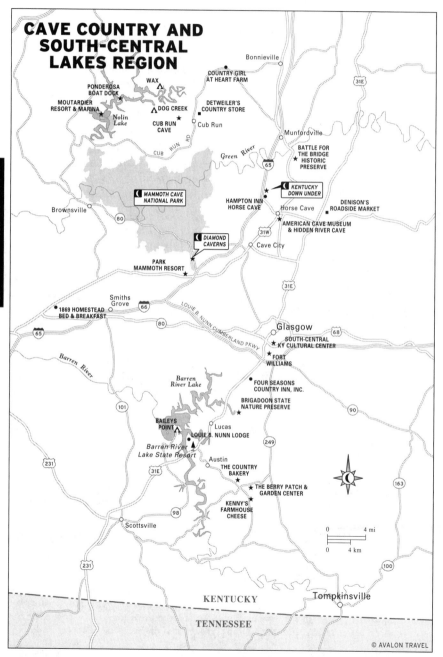

CAVE COUNTRY AND SOUTH-CENTRAL LAKES REGION

THINGS TO KNOW BEFORE YOU GO CAVING

Exploring one of Kentucky's caves should be on everyone's itinerary. Before you show up for a cave tour, however, there are a few things you should know.

First, do your research in order to choose the tour that's right for you. Are you interested in a history-based tour or a geology-based tour? Do you want to see enormous cave rooms or passageways thick with formations? Read the descriptions of the caves closely, and call the individual caves if you have questions about what you will see on a tour. More important than picking the right cave based on your interests, however, is picking the right cave based on your abilities. Are you able to handle stairs, some of which might be slippery due to the constant dampness of the caves? Are you claustrophobic? Will you, physically or mentally, have trouble fitting through small spaces? Are you afraid of heights? Are you afraid of the dark? Do you have difficulty stooping over or crawling? Answer honestly, because it's no fun for anyone if you get into a cave only to realize you can't handle it. But don't think that because you answered yes to one (or even all) of these questions, you have to rule out caving. With the variety of caves and tours in this area, you'll find one that fits your style with just a bit of research.

Second, come prepared. Wear closed-toe, closed-heel shoes with good traction. A few caves have boardwalks, but in the majority of caves you'll be walking on hard-packed dirt that can be rough and uneven. On spe-

lunking-style tours, boots are required. Also remember that caves maintain a year-round temperature of 50-60°F. You'll want to wear long pants and bring a light sweater or jacket with you regardless of the season. Leave bags and other accessories in the car. You're allowed to bring your camera into Kentucky's caves, but not camera bags or tripods. Finally, due to the threat of White Nose Syndrome, a disease that is wiping out entire populations of bats and that was found to have spread to Kentucky in 2011, do not wear into the caves anything that you might have worn into another cave. If you do, you could introduce the disease to the cave. This means that if you plan to tour multiple caves in the area, you need multiple changes of clothes (shoes can be decontaminated at stations set up at the caves). Although there's no way for a cave to know that you are complying with this commandment, please, please do so. The lives of bats are at risk, and failure to comply could result in their deaths as well as caves being closed to the public.

Finally, never enter a cave on your own. Sinkholes and unmarked caves are located all across this region, which is part of what makes it such a neat place. You should not, however, explore one of these caves without a trained and knowledgeable guide and without permission of the landowner. Caves can be very dangerous and aren't for casual exploration. To safely experience a cave, join a tour at one of the region's many established sites.

Street program, which has revitalized downtown. The facades of historic buildings have been spruced up and the buildings themselves renovated to attract restaurants and stores. It doesn't hurt that one of the town's primary attractions, Hidden River Cave, is located on Main Street. Just north of Horse Cave is Munfordville, which boasts some lovely 19th-century homes as well as a rich Civil War history. Surrounding these two towns, which have populations of around 2,200 and 1,500,

respectively, is a whole lot of scenic farmland, much of which is owned by Amish families.

American Cave Museum and Hidden River Cave

Once the most polluted cave in the United States due to groundwater contamination, **Hidden River Cave** (119 E. Main St., Horse Cave, 270/786-1466, www.cavern.org, 9am-5pm daily, until 7pm weekends Memorial Day-Labor Day, $15 adults, $10 youth 6-15,

BOWLING GREEN

© THERESA DOWELL BLACKINTON

sheep roundup at Kentucky Down Under

free youth 5 and under) is now considered a model show cave thanks to the hard work of local activists whose recovery efforts were so successful that delicate organisms like blind fish are again at home in the cave. Though not long, Hidden River Cave is deep and is entered through a dramatic, large opening. The one-hour walking tour proceeds via a walkway that runs over the river and requires participants to descend and ascend 230 stairs. (A modified tour is available for those unable to navigate stairs.) Those looking for a more adventurous visit should sign up for the Wild Cave Tour, a three-hour ($40) or five-hour ($55) trip that involves getting down and dirty as you wiggle through crawlways and explore parts of the cave most people never see. Admission to the cave also includes admission to the American Cave Museum, which has exhibits on cave formation, the historical uses of caves, cave ecosystems, and groundwater science and conservation. Those uninterested in touring the cave may purchase tickets for the museum only ($6).

◖ Kentucky Down Under

Kentucky might seem an unlikely place to find kangaroos and emus, but when Australian native Judy Austin married a Kentucky native and settled in Horse Cave, she decided to ease her homesickness by bringing a bit of Australia to the Bluegrass State. Now visitors to **Kentucky Down Under** (3700 L&N Turnpike Rd., Horse Cave, 270/786-1010, www.kdu.com, $19.95 adults, $17.95 seniors and high school and college students, $14.95 youth 4-13) are invited to feed budgies and lories in their aviaries, laugh along with a kookaburra, learn about aboriginal culture at Camp Corroboree, meet reptiles at a Scales & Tails presentation, watch a sheep roundup at the woolshed, and take an Outback Walkabout that includes a chance to pet a kangaroo. Guests can also literally go down under on a 45-minute guided tour of **Mammoth Onyx Cave,** a cave that features colorful natural formations. Kentucky Down Under opens daily at 9am. It closes at 4pm November-March, at 6pm April-May and September-October, and at 8pm June-August.

© THERESA DOWELL BLACKINTON

cave bacon, one of many interesting features of Cub Run Cave

Cub Run Cave

Though it's been described as being located at the back end of nowhere, **Cub Run Cave** (15101 Cub Run Hwy., Cub Run, 270/524-1444, www.cubruncave.net, $14 adults, $12 seniors, $9 youth 5-12) is worth the effort it takes to reach it. Vying for the title of the most beautiful cave in the region, Cub Run Cave features magnificent stalagmite, stalactite, and column formations, as well as "cave bacon" and boxwork speleothems, a rare honeycomb-like formation found in only three caves in the United States. Discovered in 1950, at which time it was open for tours for one short year, the cave reopened to the public in 2006. A sturdy boardwalk leads visitors 0.75 mile into the cave, with guides providing information on the cave and its many impressive formations. Thanks to the fact that there are no steps on the slow-paced, 1.5-hour tour, Cub Run Cave is friendly to those with mobility issues, although not entirely accessible. May-September, tours are offered at 9:30am,

noon, 1:30pm, 3pm, and 4:30pm. October-April, tours start at 10:30am, 12:30pm, 2pm, and 3:30pm.

Battle for the Bridge Historic Preserve

Three Civil War battles took place in the vicinity of Munfordville, which was considered a strategic site because it was the location of a railroad bridge crossing the Green River. Civil War buffs will want to carve out time for the **Battle for the Bridge Historic Preserve** (1309 U.S. 31W, Munfordville, 270/774-2098, www.battleforthebridge.org), where visitors can follow a two-mile interpretive trail around the battleground, which still retains its rural nature. The grounds are privately held, so visitors are asked to stay on the trails.

On the second weekend in September, Munfordville hosts Civil War Days, which features a battle reenactment as well as living history camps, period music, period dance lessons, an arts and crafts fair, and a parade.

Horse Cave Stories Walking Tour

On this 20-stop tour (www.horsecavestories.com), discover the history of Horse Cave, a designated Kentucky Cultural District. At each stop, you can use your cell phone to hear local citizens tell the story of that place and learn about the cave wars that once dominated this town and the growth and history of the area. The tour begins at 100 E. Main Street.

Old Munfordville Walking Tour

Take a 13-stop walking tour (www.visitmunfordville.com) that encompasses the central blocks of downtown Munfordville to gain a better understanding of the history of this small town. Many of the sites on the tour have connections to the Civil War, including the Wood House, where boyhood friends who would become opposing generals grew up, and the Presbyterian Church, which served as a Union hospital during the war. The tour begins at the **Hart County Historical Museum** (109 Main St., Munfordville, 270/524-0101, www.hartcountymuseum.org, 9am-4pm Mon.-Fri.,

BOWLING GREEN

BOWLING GREEN

8am-4pm Sat., free), which is heavy on Civil War artifacts.

Shopping

Once the fifth-largest burley tobacco market in the world, post-buyout Hart County no longer produces a single leaf of tobacco for commercial sale. As a result, farmers have had to find other ways of producing income. **Dennison's Roadside Market** (5824 U.S. 31E, Horse Cave, 270/786-1663, 8am-5pm Mon.-Sat., noon-5pm Sun., mid-Apr.-Dec.), which sells produce and greenhouse plants grown on-site—as well as Penn's hams, Kenny's cheeses, Chaney's ice cream, Amish baskets, local crafts, and agricultural products packaged specifically for the market—is one of the best examples of a successful tobacco diversification project. Stop by to stock up on farm goods, pick your own strawberries in the spring, or visit the petting zoo.

Hart County is home to the largest number of Amish family groups in the state, and resultantly Amish stores are scattered throughout the region, selling handmade furniture, jams, and all sorts of other products. Most of the stores, however, are not easily identifiable as Amish from the outside. The only real clue is the lack of electricity lines running to them. Although the stores were not established with tourists in mind, they do welcome visitors, so feel free to stop and browse at any store that catches your attention. **Detweiler's Country Store** (12825 Priceville Rd., Cub Run, 270/524-7967, 8am-5pm Mon.-Fri., 8am-4pm Sat.) is a wonderful one-stop shop. You'll find Amish staffing the store as well as shopping for fabric, handmade clothes, food, dry goods, farm products, and more. The store also has a small deli that serves sandwiches on homemade bread that you can enjoy at a picnic table outside.

Recreation

Visit **Green River Park & Arboretum** (100 River Rd., Munfordville, dawn-dusk) to enjoy the river landscape. Park amenities include playgrounds, playing fields, picnic shelters, a boat ramp, and a walking trail. In the summer, concerts and other events are often held at the park.

Choose from day trips of 4, 6, 8, or 12 miles or overnight trips of 21, 24, 29, or 39 miles on a canoe or kayak trip with **Big Buffalo Crossing Canoe & Kayak** (100 River Rd., Green River Park, Munfordville, 270/774-7883, www.bigbuffalocrossing.com). The outfitter will set you up with everything you need for a scenic trip down the Green River. With nearly all the riverside land in Hart County privately owned, this is the best way to see the many beautiful springs along the river. Some of the overnight trips enter Mammoth Cave National Park and allow paddlers the opportunity to explore side caves via boat.

Accommodations

The five rooms at █ **Country Girl at Heart Farm Bed and Breakfast** (6230 Priceville Rd., Munfordville, 270/531-5276, www.bedandbreakfastkentucky.net, $109-139) are meticulously furnished and decorated to reflect the groups of people for which they are named: farmers, pioneers, patriots, artists, and gentry. Each room is spacious and inviting, and each has its own large, private bathroom, many of which feature whirlpool tubs and one of which has a bath unlike any you've probably ever seen before—a horse trough converted into a soaking tub. The Farmers room on the first floor is completely wheelchair-accessible, including the shower, and two rooms have suite options suitable for families. In addition to a living room, where guests often gather along with host Darlene, the former Amish home-turned-B&B (gas lights still hang from the walls, although an environmentally friendly renovation means it boasts all modern amenities) also features a game room, movie room, and play area. Guests are encouraged to seek tranquility on explorations of the farm and are even invited to help gather eggs after the included full country breakfast. Located about 12 miles from downtown Munfordville on a country road, Country Girl at Heart makes for a perfect escape.

Just off of I-65 and close to Kentucky

© THERESA DOWELL BLACKINTON

BOWLING GREEN

barn at Country Girl at Heart Farm Bed and Breakfast

Down Under and other area attractions, **Hampton Inn** (750 Flint Ridge Rd., Horse Cave, 270/786-5000, www.hamptoninn.com, $109) offers clean rooms, friendly service, a hot breakfast, an indoor pool, and a fitness center. It's the best option for those looking for a reliable chain hotel.

In addition to RV campsites with full hookups and tent sites, **Horse Cave KOA** (489 Flint Ridge Rd., Horse Cave, 270/786-2819, www. koa.com, $27-36 for RVs, $22-27 tents) also rents eight cabins ($45-69). The campground has a lake, pool, playground, and mini-golf course and is convenient to the interstate and tourist sites.

Food

The menu at **Turtlini's** (formerly Snappy's Pizza & Pasta) (103 S. Dixie St., Horse Cave, 270/786-8686, 10:30am-9pm Mon.-Thurs., 10:30am-10pm Fri.-Sat., 11am-8pm Sun., $4.99-7.99) presents a selection of pastas, pizzas (specialty, signature, or make your own), calzones, and hot subs. At lunch, an all-you-can-eat buffet ($6.99) features pizzas, breadsticks, cheesesticks, and cinnamon sticks and is accompanied by a salad bar. On Sundays, an entrée is added to the buffet.

El Mazatlan (1512 Main St., Munfordville, 270/524-4874, www.elmazatlanrestaurant. com, 11am-9pm daily, $5.99-12.99) is a successful local chain that that serves Mexican favorites like burritos, enchiladas, and fajitas both here and at additional locations in Cave City, Bowling Green, and Glasgow. A long list of combo plates satisfies those who can't decide on just one thing. Lunch is a great value, with taco, enchilada, and tamale plates priced from $2.99. Plates are big, and service is fast and friendly. They'll be calling you *amigo* in no time.

For barbecue, head to **Big Bubba Buck's Belly Bustin' BBQ Bliss** (1802 Main St., Munfordville, 270/307-8309, 11am-8pm Tues.-Sat., $3.99-26.99). With a name like that, how can you resist? This tiny dive, which truckers claim is one of the best in the nation, serves raved-about ribs straight from the smoker.

You'll want to order the fried green tomatoes as one of your sides.

Information and Services

The northbound and southbound rest areas at mile marker 60 on I-65 are good for more than just a bathroom break and a snack. The two rest areas also contain **tourist information centers** (270/218-0386, www.kygetaway.com), which provide maps and brochures on Horse Cave and Munfordville, as well as other sites along Kentucky's I-65 corridor. The centers are staffed daily March-December and on weekends January-February.

Right in downtown Munfordville, you'll find the **Welcome Center** (113 Main St., Munfordville, 270/524-4752, www.visitmunfordville.com), which can help you find your way around the small town and surrounding areas. The friendly staff is quick to offer recommendations.

Getting There and Around

Horse Cave and Munfordville sit just off of I-65, about 40 miles (45 minutes) north of Bowling Green, 100 miles (1.5 hours) north of Nashville, and 75 miles (1 hour 10 minutes) south of Louisville. The two towns are separated by seven miles on the interstate, with the Munfordville interchange (Exit 65) north of the Horse Cave interchange (Exit 58). Most locals, however, choose to get between the two using U.S. 31W, which parallels the interstate to the east.

NOLIN LAKE

In this lake-heavy region, lovely Nolin Lake, which sits just north of Mammoth Cave, is often overlooked. The 5,800-acre lake is a great fishing spot, however—one of the top lakes in the state for bass, crappie, catfish, and walleye. Its clear, turquoise waters also make it a wonderful destination for skiing, swimming, and other water sports. Managed by the Army Corps of Engineers, Nolin Lake has seven recreational areas. Activities and amenities at the recreational areas vary, but may include hiking trails, beaches, picnic areas, and marinas.

Campgrounds are located at Dog Creek, Moutardier, and Wax recreational areas. The marina at Moutardier stocks groceries and offers some hot food, but you may want to consider packing a cooler at home and bringing it with you.

Nolin Lake State Park

On the southeastern shores of the lake, **Nolin Lake State Park** (2988 Briar Creek Rd., Mammoth Cave, 270/286-4240, http://parks.ky.gov, free) is a simple park that lets the natural world shine. A boat launch area allows those with their own watercraft to set out on the waters, and a sandy beach invites summertime swimmers. A 1.6-mile trail leads to a small seasonal waterfall.

Marinas

Ponderosa Boat Dock (865 Ponderosa Rd., Clarkson, 270/242-7215, www.ponderosaboatdock.com) rents ski and pontoon boats. **Moutardier Resort & Marina** (1990 Moutardier Rd., Leitchfield, 270/286-4069, www.moutardiermarina.com) rents pontoons, runabouts, and personal watercraft. **Wax Marina** (14008 Peonia Way, Clarkson, 270/242-7205, www.waxmarina.com), which is across from a campground run by the Army Corps of Engineers, rents pontoons that range in size 15-30 feet and can hold 4-12 people.

Accommodations

Ponderosa Boat Dock (865 Ponderosa Rd., Clarkson, 270/242-7215, www.ponderosaboatdock.com) has an inexpensive motel ($55). Rooms have lake views and full kitchens and can accommodate two adults and two children. Rustic cabins at **Moutardier Resort & Marina** (1990 Moutardier Rd., Leitchfield, 270/286-0471, www.moutardiermarina.com, $99-170) sleep 4-12 people and provide easy access to the lake.

Three of the recreational areas run by the Army Corps of Engineers have campgrounds. **Moutardier Campground** (1343 Moutardier Rd., Leitchfield, Apr.-Oct.) is the largest of the three with 167 sites, 81 of which have hookups.

A marina is nearby, and the campground has showers and flush toilets. **Wax Campground** (14069 Peonia Way, Clarkson, May-Sept.) has 110 sites, 56 of which have hookups. The campground is across from a marina with rentals and has showers and flush toilets. **Dog Creek Campground** (890 Dog Creek Rd., Cub Run, May-Sept.) has 70 sites, 24 of which have hookups, a boat ramp, beach, and playground. The campground has showers and flush toilets. Reservations for these campsites ($15-22) should be made a minimum of three days in advance at www.recreation.gov.

Nolin Lake State Park (2988 Briar Creek Rd., Mammoth Cave, 270/286-4240, http://parks.ky.gov) has a campground (Apr.-Oct., $12-28) that is popular with anglers and has 32 sites with hookups and 60 primitive sites. The campground has showers, flush toilets, and laundry facilities.

Getting There and Around

Nolin Lake takes up parts of three different counties—Hart, Edmondson, and Grayson—and isn't directly accessible from the interstate or any other major thoroughfare. The easiest directions are probably from Munfordville, which is east of the park. From Munfordville, westbound KY 88 will take you through Cub Run to the Dog Creek recreational area and then on to the Wax recreational area. To reach the state park, turn left off of KY 88 at Cub Run onto KY 1827 and follow it to the park entrance. Many back roads lead to various areas of the park, and other routes will be better depending on where you're coming from, so if you can, map your route in advance or see what your GPS suggests.

CAVE CITY

The dinosaur on the side of the interstate is what attracts the attention of most people who weren't intending to come to Cave City. The most popular entryway to Mammoth Cave National Park, Cave City seems to exist on tourism upon first glance. The road to Mammoth Cave is lined with attraction after attraction, seeking to capitalize on the national park's popularity. Some are interesting and educational, others border on hokey. Cave City does have a nice historical center. Unfortunately, most people never make it there, as the road to Mammoth Cave takes you in the opposite direction.

◖ Mammoth Cave National Park

Upon entering **Mammoth Cave National Park** (1 Mammoth Cave Pkwy., 270/758-2180, www.nps.gov/maca, free), visitors first see dense stands of eastern hardwood forest that is home to large populations of deer and wild turkey. Beneath this lies the park's main attraction: the most extensive cave system in the world. With nearly 400 miles of mapped passageways and perhaps hundreds of miles of undiscovered routes, Mammoth Cave is so big that no known cave in the world is even half as long as Mammoth. It's also incredibly diverse, supporting about 130 life-forms. Evidence indicates that humans explored Mammoth Cave 4,000 years ago, although it wasn't until 1798 that the cave was rediscovered. Established as a national park in 1941, Mammoth Cave was a tourist attraction as early as 1816, making it the second-oldest tourist site in the United States behind Niagara Falls.

To explore the cave, sign up for one of the many tours ($5-24 adults, $2.50-12 seniors, $3.50-11 youth 6-12) offered each day. Tours range in distance from 0.25 mile to 5.5 miles and in time from 1.25 hours to 6.5 hours. In addition to a selection of introductory and general tours, which give an overview of the cave, its history, and its formation, Mammoth Cave also offers specialty tours, which range from lantern-lit tours to photography tours to geology-focused tours. Those wanting a real spelunking adventure will want to sign up for the **Wild Cave Tour** ($48 adults, $24 seniors), which takes participants to rarely visited areas of the cave and can require crawling, slithering, duck walking, and other physical challenges. Tours can be reserved by phone (877/444-6777) or online (www.recreation.gov), and reservations are highly recommended in the summer when tours are often fully booked.

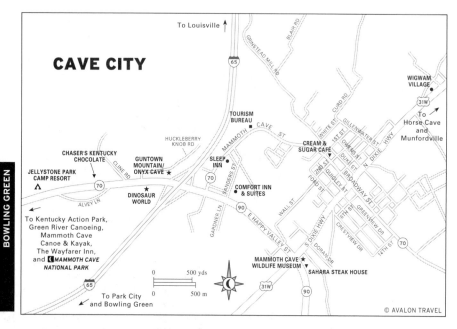

The NPS tries to accommodate guests by adding tours, and when that is not possible, they offer a self-guided tour.

Above ground, Mammoth Cave National Park is also worth exploring. More than 60 miles of trails are open to hikers, with designated trails also open to mountain bikers and horseback riders. Additionally, three trails are wheelchair-accessible. Trail maps are available at the visitors center (8:15am-6:30pm daily, Memorial Day-Labor Day, 8:30am-5:15pm daily, September-October and mid-Mar.-Memorial Day, 8:30am-4:30pm daily, November-mid-Mar.), and rangers can suggest hikes based on your ability level and interests. Anglers can toss a line into the Green and Nolin Rivers, which are also open to kayaks and canoes. Check with the visitors center for information on the day's ranger-led programs, which are always interesting as well as informative, and the Junior Ranger Program.

An on-site hotel, campgrounds, and restaurants make the park a convenient base in the area.

Dinosaur World

Visitors are invited to walk among prehistoric creatures at **Dinosaur World** (711 Mammoth Cave Rd., 270/773-4345, www.dinoworld.net, 8:30am-4:30pm daily, $12.75 adults, $10.75 seniors, $9.75 youth 3-12), an educational park that features more than 150 life-size fiberglass dinosaur models positioned outside in natural surroundings along a one-mile paved path. After completing the Dinosaur Walk, visitors will also want to visit the Prehistoric Museum, which provides information on dinosaurs; the Boneyard, where kids can act as paleontologists while unearthing a buried dinosaur; and the Fossil Dig, where kids are welcome to sift through sand for fossils, three of which they are allowed to take home.

Guntown Mountain

With its schedule of Wild West gunfights, cancan shows, magic shows, and country music performances, **Guntown Mountain** (101 Huckleberry Knob Rd., 270/773-3530, http://guntownmountain.net, 10am-6pm

THE LEGEND OF FLOYD COLLINS

Born in 1887, Floyd Collins became known as the region's greatest cave explorer. He scouted multiple caves in central Kentucky and discovered **Crystal Cave,** which his family ran as a tourist attraction. With the main entrance to the cave too far off the road to attract a good crowd, Collins set about to locate another access point and was hopeful that he could find a way to connect his cave with the larger Mammoth Cave system. On January 30, 1925, while searching, Collins became trapped in a narrow passageway about 55 feet below the surface, his leg pinned by a boulder. He was found the next day, and a rescue mission began immediately. Food, water, and a heat source were lowered down to Collins, while rescuers tried to excavate a way to him. Unfortunately, on February 4, a cave-in occurred that impeded any further supplies from getting to him. The rescuers continued to work feverishly, and in the meantime, the media caught hold of the story. Soon Floyd Collins was on the front page of newspapers across the country. Reporters flocked to the scene, and thousands of people gathered to watch the events unfold. It was one of the biggest media events of the era. The rescue shaft finally reached Collins on February 17, but it was too late. He had already died. Because of the instability of the cave, his body was not recovered until late April.

The legend of Floyd Collins grew with his death. In 1927, after the Collins family had sold Crystal Cave, the new owner disinterred the body of Floyd Collins and had it displayed in a glass coffin in the cave. The body was stolen in 1929. When it was recovered shortly after its theft, one leg was missing. The body remained on display until 1961 when the National Park Service purchased the cave and closed it to the public. The body of Floyd Collins was reinterred in 1989 at the request of his family.

Despite the tragic nature of the event, the media coverage helped draw attention to Kentucky's caves and garner support for the creation of Mammoth Cave National Park. Louisville's *Courier-Journal* won a Pulitzer Prize for its coverage of the event. Multiple books, a musical, and a folk song have all been written about the legend of Floyd Collins. Curious travelers can learn more at the **Floyd Collins Museum** (1240 Old Mammoth Cave Rd., 270/773-3366) located in the Wayfarer Inn in Cave City.

daily, June-mid-Aug., weekends only, May and Sept.-mid-Oct., $16.95 adults, $10.95 youth 5-11) offers the kind of old-fashioned entertainment that used to be found all along the interstate system. All shows are family-friendly and are heavy on audience participation. The theme park is a bit hokey but can be a good time for those willing to let loose. The view from the top of the mountain, which can be reached by chairlift or shuttle bus, is undoubtedly the best in town.

Also located on Guntown Mountain is **Onyx Cave** (onyxcave.com, 9am-4pm daily, Mar.-mid-Dec., $7.95 adults, $4.95 youth 5-11), the most recent of the area's show caves to be discovered. Thirty-minute guided tours take visitors into the formation-rich cave, which has an impressive amount of cave coral.

Kentucky Action Park

The **Kentucky Action Park** (3057 Mammoth Cave Rd., 270/773-2560, www.kentuckyactionpark.com, 10am-6pm daily, Apr.-Labor Day, noon-6pm weekends, Mar. and Sept.-Nov.) offers a range of active pursuits that will have the whole family worn out at day's end. A park favorite is the 0.25-mile alpine slide, which is reached by chairlift and allows the brave to zoom back down the hill. Other thrills can be had on go-karts, bumper boats, a trampoline, a climbing wall, and a mini-golf course. Horse lovers can opt for a 30-minute ($14), one-hour ($18), or two-hour ride ($34) through some of the park's 500 acres aboard one of the park's 50 horses, and those who just can't get enough of caves should sign up for the 30-minute tour of chilly **Outlaw Cave,** which

© THERESA DOWELL BLACKINTON

Dinosaur World

is wheelchair-accessible. Individual ride tickets can be purchased for $4-5, though an all-you-can-ride pass for $24.95, which includes the cave but not horseback riding, is the best deal.

Mammoth Cave Wildlife Museum

More than 1,600 specimens of wildlife from around the globe are stuffed and on display at **Mammoth Cave Wildlife Museum** (409 E. Happy Valley St., 270/773-2255, http://mammothcavewildlifemuseum.webs.com, 9am-5pm daily, Mar.-Oct., weekends only, Nov.-Feb., $7.95 adults, $4.95 youth 3-11). The buffalo and grizzly bear wow with their size, while the snow leopard provides a close-up look at an animal very few of us would ever see otherwise.

Recreation

Either of two outfitters, **Mammoth Cave Canoe & Kayak** (1240 Old Mammoth Cave Rd., 270/773-3366, www.mammothcavecanoe-k.com) or **Green River Canoeing** (3057 Mammoth Cave Rd., Cave City, 270/773-5712, www.mammothcavecanoe.com), can

outfit you for an enjoyable paddling trip down the Green River in either a canoe (from $50 for a half-day trip) or kayak (from $45 for a half-day trip). Beginners are encouraged to try the 8-mile trip from Dennison Ferry to Green River Ferry, while more intermediate paddlers can choose from a 12-mile day trip or a number of overnight trips. Those who can't get enough of the water may want to dare to do the 136-mile trip from Campbellsville, north of Green River Lake, to Houchins Ferry near Mammoth Cave, which can take anywhere from a week to 10 days depending on the water level. Paddlers are encouraged to enjoy the scenery and take time to picnic, swim, and fish, with the duration of all trips up to those in the boat.

Get a bird's-eye view of Kentucky on a zip-line canopy tour with **Mammoth Cave Adventures** (1994 Roy Hunter Rd., 270/773-6087, www.mammothcave-adventures.com, $55). The route, which takes 1.5 hours to complete, includes five zip lines and two sky bridges. In fall, the ride is particularly scenic as you soar over brightly colored trees. Mammoth Cave Adventures also offers hour-long horseback riding trips ($25) through forested terrain.

Accommodations

Those wishing to overnight in **Mammoth Cave National Park** (1 Mammoth Cave Pkwy., 270/758-2180, www.nps.gov/maca) can book a room at the **Mammoth Cave Hotel** (270/758-2225, www.mammothcavehotel.com, $95-105). Rooms are typical of much national park lodging, small and dated but clean and with a location that can't be beat. Request a room on the ravine side, where the view can be enjoyed from your balcony. Quaint **cottages and cabins** ($61-80) offer a more private retreat. Campers will find 105 sites at the **Mammoth Cave Campground** ($17), which has restrooms and showers, and 12 primitive (tent-only) sites at the **Houchin Ferry Campground** ($12). For a real retreat, establish camp at a primitive backcountry site (free).

Located right at the park boundary, **The Wayfarer Inn** (1240 Old Mammoth Cave Rd., 270/773-3366, www.bbonline.com, $75-115)

BOWLING GREEN

CAVE CITY'S WIGWAM VILLAGE

Ever wanted to sleep in a wigwam? How about not a real wigwam, but a concrete building shaped like a wigwam? Well then, you're in luck, because **Wigwam Village Inn #2** (601 N. Dixie Hwy., Cave City, 270/773-3381, www.wigwamvillage.com, $60-70) offers you the opportunity. Built in 1937, Cave City's Wigwam Village was the second of seven of such villages built around the country and is one of only three that remain today. The village is made of up 15 wigwams arranged in a semicircle and an ad-ditional enormous wigwam acting as the office. Each wigwam is outfitted with air-conditioning and heat, cable television, private bathroom, and either one or two double beds. Furnishings are original pieces that date to the 1930s. You and your fellow tribe members can congregate in the grassy area outside the wigwams, complete with playground and deck. Although not a luxurious hotel experience, it is certainly an original hotel experience, ideal for the adventurous traveler.

© THERESA DOWELL BLACKINTON

Wigwam Village

is well located for those looking to spend a few days exploring Mammoth Cave and nearby attractions. Each of the three rooms has a queen bed and private bath. The residence has a bit of a lodge feel thanks to wood-paneled walls. Next door to the main house is the Hanson Cottage ($125), a cozy rental with queen bedroom, a kitchen, a living area, and a patio.

Among the chain hotels located in Cave City,

Sleep Inn (801 Mammoth Cave St., 270/773-2030, www.sleepinn.com, $109-129), which opened in 2010, and **Comfort Inn & Suites** (819 Sanders St., 270/773-3335, www.comfortinn.com, $109-129), are the best options, both delivering clean, comfortable rooms in a convenient location.

The place to camp in Cave City, **Jellystone Park Camp Resort** (1002 Mammoth Cave Rd.,

270/773-3840, www.jellystonemammothcave. com) offers 137 campsites with hookups ($47-55), 20 primitive campsites ($30), and 56 cabins ($65-242), which can accommodate 4-16 people. On-site amenities include a mini-golf course, lake, pool, waterslide, basketball court, volleyball court, playground, pet playground, bathhouse, and camp store. Summer weekends have a two-night minimum, with Memorial Day, Independence Day, and Labor Day weekends having a three-night minimum. Although large, the campground regularly fills up in high season, so it's wise to reserve in advance.

Food

Three restaurants are located in the national park's **Mammoth Cave Hotel** (270/758-2225, www.mammothcavehotel.com), offering to-go fare, café fare, and fine dining options, none of which is particularly inspired.

Make lunch a panino at **Cream & Sugar Café** (105 Broadway, 270/773-2822, 6:30am-2:30pm Tues.-Sat., 8:30am-2:30pm Sun., $4.85-6.15) or choose from the list of traditional sandwiches, which includes reubens, grilled cheese, BLTs, and other favorites. Save room for a slice of pie for dessert. Cream & Sugar Café also serves breakfast, with options including omelettes, waffles, pancakes, French toast, and biscuits and gravy.

For dinner, options are limited. **Sahara Steak House** (413 E. Happy Valley St., 270/773-3450, $4.95-21.95) serves steaks, chicken, fried shrimp, and hamburgers, and all dinners include a trip to the soup and salad bar as well as a choice of side. The atmosphere is small-town casual (more of a family restaurant than a steakhouse), and the TV is often tuned to Fox News when sports aren't on.

If your sweet tooth needs satisfying, seek out **Chasers' Kentucky Chocolate** (812 Mammoth Cave Rd., 270/773-8766, www.chaserskentuckychocolate.com, 10am-7pm Thurs.-Tues.). They're known for their liquor crèmes, which are crafted with a unique sweet dark chocolate. In addition to a traditional bourbon ball, Chasers also makes an Irish cream ball that isn't quite as intense. Other sweet treats include

fudge, turtles, nut clusters, peanut butter cups, and candy suckers, all of which are made by the husband-and-wife owners.

Information and Services

The **Cave City Tourism Bureau** has a visitors center in front of the Convention Center (502 Mammoth Cave St., 270/773-5159) and a website (www.cavecity.com) with information on the area's attractions, restaurants, and hotels.

Getting There and Around

Located just off of I-65 at Exit 53, Cave City is 30 miles (35 minutes) north of Bowling Green, 90 miles (1.5 hours) north of Nashville, and 85 miles (1 hour 20 minutes) south of Louisville. Cave City is the gateway to Mammoth Cave National Park, and most attractions are along Mammoth Cave Road, which leads to the park.

PARK CITY

Park City developed thanks to the fact that three major roads—Louisville and Nashville Turnpike, Glasgow Road, and Bardstown Road—came together here, the railroad passed through, and the route to Mammoth Cave began here. What made travelers stop here was not the junction, however, but Bell's Tavern. Nineteenth-century tourists, especially those traveling via stagecoach to Mammoth Cave, would overnight and eat at Bell's Tavern, which was also a popular gathering spot for politicians. The tavern burned in 1859, and the Civil War kept it from being rebuilt. Today, the ruins remain, with local activists working to turn the site into a heritage park. Unfortunately, Park City has never again been as popular as it was then. Although once the main route to Mammoth Cave, Cave City has taken over that role, and today's Park City is a sleepy place with a population that barely numbers more than 500.

◖ Diamond Caverns

Diamond Caverns (1900 Mammoth Cave Pkwy., 270/749-2233, www.diamondcaverns. com, 9am-5pm daily, Mar. 15-Labor Day, 9am-4pm daily, Labor Day-Oct., 10am-4pm daily,

Nov.-Mar. 14, $17 adults, $8 youth 4-12) is the most visually stunning cave in the region, with amazing formations everywhere you look. State-of-the-art lighting accents the cave's natural beauty, highlighting the most outstanding drapes, cascades, stalactites, stalagmites, and other formations. Tours, which last one hour and cover 0.5 mile, are kept to a maximum of 25 people, making it easy to ask questions of the guide and see the cave in detail. The 348 steps on the tour are the only difficulty, although, fortunately, there are never more than 50 steps at a time.

Park Mammoth Resort

Park Mammoth Resort (22850 Louisville Rd., 270/749-4101, www.parkmammothresort.us), originally a golf resort and still luring golfers with its 18 holes and golf packages, has evolved to become a premier sport shooting venue. The Rockcastle Shooting Center features a 15-station sporting clays course, an archery range, and a pistol and rifle range, and offers weapon training and education courses. Since opening in 2009, the resort has become the home to many well-known shooting events, including the 2013 Pan American Shotgun Championships, and was a primary site for the filming of the Military Channel's *Ultimate Weapon*.

Accommodations and Food

At Park Mammoth Resort, those uninterested in golf or guns may still enjoy a meal at **Lookout Restaurant** (22850 Louisville Rd., 270/749-4101, www.parkmammothresort. us, $5.99-14.99), which serves Southern favorites in a dining room with a magnificent view of the Mammoth Cave sinkhole basin. The restaurant is open for breakfast, lunch, and dinner daily March-October; November-February, the restaurant serves dinner on Friday, all three meals on Saturday, and breakfast and lunch on Sunday.

Park Mammoth Resort has a 100-room lodge that has a lot of potential, but is currently outdated and in need of renovation. For accommodations and food, visitors to Park City would be best served staying in Cave City.

Information and Services

The **Cave City Tourism Bureau** (502 Mammoth Cave St., Cave City, 270/773-8834, www.cavecity.com) also covers Park City.

Getting There and Around

Park City, like the other towns in this region, lies right on I-65, 25 miles (30 minutes) north of Bowling Green, 85 miles (1 hour 20 minutes) north of Nashville, and 90 miles (1.5 hours) south of Louisville. It's just six miles south of Cave City, with U.S. 31W the most direct route between the towns. Although most people reach Mammoth Cave National Park via Cave City's Mammoth Cave Road, Park City's Mammoth Cave Parkway provides a more direct route, especially if you're coming from the south.

BOWLING GREEN

South-Central Lakes Region

Load up the cooler, throw on your bathing suit, and pack the fishing pole. The south-central section of Kentucky is essentially a water lover's paradise. Four major manmade lakes attract anglers, boaters, swimmers, and other adventure seekers, especially in summer, when Kentucky is uniformly hot and humid. Winter and the cooler ends of spring and fall might keep pleasure boaters at home, but anglers consider the lakes year-round destinations. On dry land, you'll find lakeside state parks, a couple of charming small towns, Civil War and other historic sites, and a few agritourism destinations scattered among acres and acres of farmland.

GLASGOW AND BARREN COUNTY

Glasgow, which is the county seat of Barren, is all charm. A red brick courthouse with white clock tower sits in the middle of a downtown square that's in the midst of a revitalization, with restaurants, art galleries, and shops taking up residence in once-abandoned historic storefronts. Named by a Scottish man for his hometown, Glasgow celebrates its ties to Scotland with the annual Highland Games, which draw kilt-wearing, battle-ax-throwing visitors from around the globe. Just north of Barren River Lake, Glasgow is the portal to the recreational areas and agritourism sites of Barren County, which was named the best place to live in rural America by *Progressive Farmer* magazine.

South Central Kentucky Cultural Center

Although many area history museums hold little interest to outsiders, the **South Central Kentucky Cultural Center** (200 W. Water St., Glasgow, 270/651-9792, www.kyculturalcenter.org, 9am-4pm Mon.-Fri., 9am-2pm Sat., free) manages to create broad appeal while focusing on life in the Barrens region of Kentucky. The 30,000-square-foot museum is full of well-presented exhibits that tell the story of the natural, social, cultural, and military history of the region and, in turn, the country through artifacts, photos, and stories. Be sure to step inside the re-created General Store, check out the one-room schoolhouse, and poke around the authentic log cabin.

Fort Williams

On a hilltop that now overlooks a cemetery on one side and a shopping center on the other stands the remains of **Fort Williams** (off U.S. 31E, just south of Main St., Glasgow, dawn-dusk, free), a Civil War fort that was attacked by Confederates in October 1863. Although the small force of Confederates was able to defeat the larger Union force, the Union quickly regained the fort and maintained hold of Glasgow through the war. The fort was built in response to a January 1862 raid by John Hunt Morgan, during which he held control of Glasgow for three days while destroying railways and communication facilities.

Agritourism

The tiny town of Austin, which is southwest of Glasgow off of U.S. 31E and just across from Barren River Lake State Resort Park, packs an agritourism punch. Make your first stop **The Country Bakery** (6190 KY 87, Austin, 270/434-2253, 6am-6pm Tues.-Sat., $0.75-1.89), where you'll have a hard time choosing among the better-than-Krispy-Kreme doughnuts, the kolaches, the ham and cheese pinwheels, and the caramel pecan rolls. If you're looking for more than a snack, the bakery also serves pizzas ($10) made to order.

Continue your agritourism field trip at **The Berry Patch & Garden Center** (3069 Thomerson Park Rd., Austin, 270/670-5917, 7:30am-5pm Tues.-Sat.), where you can pick your own strawberries in early summer and blackberries and raspberries in late summer. Once sufficiently loaded up with berries, make your way to **Kenny's Farmhouse Cheese** (2033 Thomerson Park Rd., Austin, 888/571-4029, www.kennyscheese.com, 9am-3pm Mon.-Fri., 9am-1pm Sat.), where the Mattingly family makes more than 30 types of artisan cheese using the old-world European style and milk from their own cows. A huge sample plate lets you try before you buy. If you call in advance, they may be able to give you a tour. Once you're aware of Kenny's cheeses, you'll start noticing them all over the state, from fine restaurants to tiny country stores.

Entertainment

Built little by little during the Depression, the **Plaza Theatre** (115 E. Main St., Glasgow, 270/361-2101, www.plaza.org) originally showed movies, which were later complemented by live shows. Among the performers to take the stage during the Plaza Theatre's heyday were Loretta Lynn, the Carter family, Porter Wagoner, Dolly Parton, Roy Rogers, and Gene Autry. Closed in 1970, the theater languished as a rental property until 2001, when the city bought it and set to work bringing the theater back to its former glory. Today concerts and comedy performances draw crowds. Tickets can be purchased online or in person. If there's no show on the schedule, see if you can find someone to let you in for a peek at the magnificent theater, which has balconies that might make you think of *Romeo and Juliet*.

Events

The annual **Glasgow Highland Games** (www.glasgowhighlandgames.com), which are held at Barren River State Park on the first weekend of June, celebrate the region's Scottish heritage through three full days of events. On the schedule are competitive events like battle-ax throwing and clan tug-of-war, sheepdog demonstrations, Celtic music and dance performances and competitions, a rock concert, and plenty of other Scot-inspired activities. The festival draws Celtic fans from around the world, but you don't need to know a thing about kilts or cèilidhs to have a good time.

Hiking

Preserving a tract of forest that includes old-growth stands of beech and tulip poplar, **Brigadoon State Nature Preserve** (Mutter Rd., Glasgow, 270/651-3161, www.naturepreserves.ky.gov, sunrise-sunset, free) is home to a one-mile hiking trail that leads through the forest, down into ravines, and up onto ridges. Birds and spring wildflowers are the main attraction, although you may also spot deer, turkey, and other forest wildlife. On most days, you probably won't see another person while hiking at this preserve that, although very close to Barren River Lake, is off the radar. To reach the preserve, travel southbound on U.S. 31E for 6.5 miles from downtown Glasgow, turn left onto Browning School Road, and then turn left again after 1.5 miles onto Mutter Road. The unmarked parking area is on your left after about 0.5 mile. Walk down the mown path for about 25 yards to reach the trailhead sign.

Accommodations

Located just off the town square, **Hall Place Bed and Breakfast** (313 S. Green St., Glasgow, 270/651-3176, www.bbonline.com, $85-125) is an 1852 home that has four large guest rooms, each filled with period furniture, antiques, and decor. A full breakfast is served in the library, while an upstairs game room provides a place to relax or mingle with other guests. All rooms have private baths, small TVs with cable, microwaves, refrigerators, and wireless Internet access. Owners Karin and Gary are active in the community and are working to restore a couple of Glasgow's beautiful old storefronts; ask them for the home's story, which, aside from being interesting historically, might also make you wonder if there is such a thing as fate.

Main Street Bed and Breakfast (208 E. Main St., Glasgow, 270/590-1410, www.bbonline.com, $79-99) is a sister property of Hall Place under the same ownership. This 1818 home, which was first owned by Abraham Lincoln's law partner, offers five spacious rooms, each with queen bed and private bath. The home has been renovated and furnished with an eye to its history as well as to

BOWLING GREEN

© THERESA DOWELL BLACKINTON

wildflowers at Brigadoon State Nature Preserve

guests' comfort. A full breakfast is served every morning.

Between Glasgow and Barren River Lake, **Four Seasons Country Inn** (4107 Scottsville Rd., Glasgow, 270/678-1000, www.fourseasonscountryinn.com, $79-130) has 21 rooms, each of which is decorated in a unique style. Choose from double, queen, king, and executive king rooms or the honeymoon suite. Rooms have TVs with HBO and wireless Internet access. The continental breakfast is disappointing, but will get you started. During the summer, an outdoor pool is open to guests.

Food

When the Lanes moved back to Glasgow after 25 years in Houston, Texas, they brought with them a slew of recipes, which they now serve to a consistently full house at **A Little Taste of Texas** (303 S. Broadway, Glasgow, 270/659-2441, www.glasgow-ky.com/littletasteoftexas, 11am-2pm and 4:30pm-8:30pm Mon.-Fri., dinner only on Sat., $6-24). You'll find the likes of barbecue chicken, fried catfish, rib eye steaks, and Mexican hamburgers on the menu. Plates are huge and served with a salad and your choice of fries or baked potato. The restaurant is small and fills up as soon as it opens, but service is quick, so any wait will be short.

Although Mexican food might not be the first thing that springs to mind in central Kentucky, Glasgow has more than its share of Mexican restaurants, with **Garcia's Grill** (516 N. Race St., 270/361-2900, 11am-9pm Mon.-Thurs., 11am-10pm Fri.-Sat., 11am-8pm Sun., $8-18) the best of the bunch. Their use of fresh ingredients is obvious in their salsa, fajitas, fish tacos, and other tasty dishes. Portions are large, and the margaritas are generous.

Information and Services

While taking the required trip around the Glasgow town square, pop in at the **Glasgow-Barren County Tourist & Convention Commission** (118 E. Public Sq., 800/264-3161, www.visitglasgowbarren.com) to stock up on information about the area.

Getting There and Around

Glasgow is located southeast of Cave Country in an area known as the Barrens because of the fact that this area, unlike most of Kentucky, was covered by a savannah instead of forests when pioneers first arrived. The lack of trees in the area gave it its name. To reach Glasgow, take Exit 43 off of I-65 and merge onto eastbound Louie B. Nunn Parkway-Cumberland Parkway. After 11 miles on the parkway, take Exit 11 to northbound U.S. 31E. After 0.3 mile, you'll want to turn left on Green Street, which will lead to downtown Glasgow. Glasgow is about 30 miles (40 minutes) from Bowling Green, 12 miles (20 minutes) from Cave City, and 95 miles (1 hour 40 minutes) from Louisville.

U.S. 31E is the main north-south thoroughfare in the Glasgow area, and traveling south on it will take you to Barren River Lake's eastern shores and the state park. The Louie B. Nunn-Cumberland Parkway is the main east-west route across this region of the state. If you travel east from Glasgow, the parkway provides access to the Green River Lake and Lake Cumberland areas.

BARREN RIVER LAKE

Created in 1964 by the Army Corps of Engineers, 10,100-acre Barren River Lake stretches through three counties, although the most common access points are in Barren County, with Glasgow the nearest town of note. The lake is popular with anglers who cast for bass and crappie, as well as with water-sports enthusiasts. Barren River Lake is surrounded by private property, so, aside from the state park, there are no lakeside resort areas. There are, however, eight Corps-run recreational areas. **Beaver Creek** (Beaver Creek Rd., Glasgow) and **The Narrows** (1880 Narrows Rd., Glasgow), both of which are on the east side of the lake, and **Baileys Point** (3147 Baileys Point Rd., Scottsville) and **Tailwater** (1055 Tailwater Rd., Scottsville), both of which are on the west side of the lake, are the most popular recreational areas. The Narrows and Tailwater have campgrounds, boat ramps, picnic areas, hiking trails, and playgrounds. Baileys Point has all of that plus a beach. Beaver Creek doesn't have the hiking trails and playgrounds, but it does have a beach.

Barren River Lake State Resort Park

Those looking for mixed recreational opportunities while at the lake should head for **Barren River Lake State Resort Park** (1149 State Park Rd., Lucas, 270/646-2151, http://parks.ky.gov, dawn-dusk daily, free). The park has a boat launch and slips for those with their own boats; those without can rent fishing boats, pontoons, deck boats, and jon boats for a cruise around the lake. Off the lake, options also abound. There's an 18-hole golf course, a horse stable that offers 45-minute guided trail rides (Memorial Day-Labor Day, $18), a public beach (Memorial Day-Labor Day), a 2.5-mile paved mixed-use trail, 4 miles of wooded hiking trails, a full array of naturalist-led educational programs, a campground, a lodge, and a restaurant. Barren River Lake is a popular nesting spot for migrating birds, including the sandhill crane, and bird-watching programs are held in January and February when the cranes pass through Kentucky.

Accommodations

Barren River Lake State Resort Park (1149 State Park Rd., Lucas, 270/646-2151, http://parks.ky.gov) offers a choice of overnight accommodations. Tent and RV campers can pick one of the 99 spots at the **campground** (Apr.-Oct., $29), which has showers, restrooms, and laundry facilities. Those looking for a less rugged stay can opt for a room at the **Louie B. Nunn Lodge** ($99.95), which is set above the lake. Each of the 51 rooms has two queen beds and a balcony with either a lake view or view of the woods. Larger groups should inquire about the two-bedroom, two-bath **cottages** ($199.95-249.95), which can sleep eight. The beach cottages have lovely lake views from their back decks, while other cottages are situated in wooded areas near the lodge. A pool is open to both lodge and cottage guests.

BOWLING GREEN

ALLEN COUNTY'S MENNONITE COMMUNITY

In rural Allen County, between the towns of Franklin and Scottsville, you'll find a significant Mennonite community. These Mennonites live simply, shunning electricity, traveling by horse and buggy, and working in primarily agricultural pursuits. They happily interact with outsiders, however, so there's no need to be shy. In fact, a number of Mennonite businesses welcome visitors.

When traveling through the area, drive carefully. The roads are narrow and winding, and you may quickly come upon a horse and buggy. If you do, slow down, then pass when it's safe to do so. Go ahead and wave as you go past; they'll be waving at you. Leave your camera in its bag, however. The Mennonite people do not like to be photographed, and you should respect their wishes.

Take note of the following Mennonite businesses, all of which have addresses in Scottsville. For more information and a listing of additional Mennonite businesses, contact the Scottsville-Allen County Chamber of Commerce (110 S. Court St., 270/237-4782, www.scottsvilleky.info).

· **Habegger's Amish Market** (415 Perrytown Rd.): This market sells homemade jams, relishes, pickles, and sweets, along with dried goods and other groceries. A deli counter serves sandwiches and ice cream.

· **Countryside Jam House & Lawn Furniture** (987 Perrytown Rd.): Purchase expertly made wooden lawn furniture as well as homemade jams.

· **Spring Valley Sorghum Mill** (269 Strawberry Ln.): Watch as sorghum molasses are made in the fall.

· **Tim and Susie Hen House** (1597 Squire Lyles Rd., http://timandsusiehenhouse.com): Although the owners of the hen house aren't Mennonite, they host a small animal swap meet on the third Saturday of each month, which draws large numbers of Mennonite families and is simply a wonderful taste of rural life.

· **Southern Kentucky Horse Drawn Machinery Auction** (Scottsville): Held annually on the first Saturday in April, this auction attracts not only local Mennonites, but also Mennonites from all over the eastern United States.

© THERESA DOWELL BLACKINTON

Be alert for horse-and-buggies.

Reservations for the Army Corps of Engineers campgrounds at **The Narrows** (1880 Narrows Rd., Glasgow), **Baileys Point** (3147 Baileys Point Rd., Scottsville), and **Tailwater** (1055 Tailwater Rd., Scottsville) can be made through www.recreation.gov. The campground at **Beaver Creek** (Beaver Creek Rd., Glasgow) is first-come, first-served. All campgrounds have showers, flush toilets, and water and electricity hookups.

A range of vacation rental properties for Barren River Lake is listed on **VRBO** (www.vrbo.com). One option for a cabin rental is **Harston Hideaways** (13020 Scottsville Rd., Lucas, 270/646-3199, www.barrenlake.com/harston, $125-195). The hand-built log cabins are rustic in style but complete with modern amenities. Each lakefront cabin can sleep up to six (adults only) and features a fireplace, front porch with swing, and full kitchen.

Food

Driftwood Restaurant (breakfast 7am-10am daily, lunch 11am-2pm Mon.-Sat., 11am-3pm Sun., dinner 5pm-9pm daily, $5.95-13.95), which is located inside the lodge at Barren River Lake State Resort Park, focuses on fish, which is apt for a park set on the lake, but also serves other Kentucky favorites in a casual atmosphere.

Getting There and Around

Barren River Lake is located between Glasgow and Scottsville along U.S. 31E. The state park is most easily reached by driving south on U.S. 31E for 13 miles from Glasgow. The Narrows and Beaver Creek recreational areas, both of which are north of the state park, are also accessed from U.S. 31E, with signed turnoff points leading to them. Baileys Point and Tailwater recreational areas, which are on the western shore of the lake, can be accessed by taking southbound KY 101 (Exit 38) or southbound KY 234 (Exit 26) from I-65 to KY 1533. Turn left onto KY 1533, which will dead-end at Barren River Dam Road. To reach Tailwater, turn left; to reach Baileys Point, turn right.

GREEN RIVER LAKE AREA

The 8,000-plus-acre Green River Lake is a popular fishing spot thanks to its premier muskie fishery as well as its bass and crappie populations. Like many Kentucky lakes, Green River Lake is under the management of the Army Corps of Engineers. The corps runs 4 of the lake's 10 boat ramps—Holmes Bend (69 Corps Rd., Columbia), Smith Ridge (35 County Park Rd., Campbellsville), Pikes Ridge (4725 Pikes Ridge Rd., Columbia), and the Dam Area (544 Lake Rd., Campbellsville).

First-time visitors to Green River Lake would be well advised to stop at the **Green River Lake Visitor Center** (544 Lake Rd., Campbellsville, 270/465-4463), which has exhibitions about Native American artifacts and water safety along with a large aquarium. A log house used as a Civil War hospital is located on the grounds. The visitors center can provide information on lake recreation as well as nearby attractions. It's also the place to get maps of the many hiking trails surrounding the lake and information on hunting in the Green River Wildlife Management Area.

Green River Lake State Park

On the western shore of the lake, **Green River Lake State Park** (179 Park Office Rd., Campbellsville, 270/465-8255, http://parks.ky.gov, dawn-dusk daily, free) is primarily focused on water recreation. The marina rents fishing, pontoon, jet, and ski boats, as well as houseboats and personal watercraft, so you can get out on the lake and swim, ski, tube, and fish. The park also boasts a beach where you can sun and swim or play a game of sand volleyball. A mini-golf course, basketball court, and picnic and playground areas are nearby. Green River Lake State Park has a noteworthy 28 miles of hiking, equestrian, and mountain biking trails. Three main trails—Windy Ridge, North Trail, and Marina Main Trail—lead to multiple spur trails.

If you want to see the park by horseback and don't have your own mount, neighboring **Green**

© THERESA DOWELL BLACKINTON

BOWLING GREEN

Tubing is one of many popular pursuits at Kentucky's lakes.

River Stables (592 Robin Rd., Campbellsville, 270/789-4525, www.greenriverstables.com) can outfit you for a ride.

Other Marinas

Three marinas are located on Green River Lake. **Green River Marina Resort** (2892 Lone Valley Rd., Campbellsville, 270/465-2512, www.greenrivermarina.com) rents houseboats as well as pontoons and fishing boats, and provides overnight accommodations in floating cabins with space for up to eight people (three-day min., $600-1,400). **Holmes Bend Marina Resort** (5380 Holmes Bend Rd., Columbia, 800/801-8154, www.holmesbendresort.com) offers houseboats that range in size from 46-72 feet, along with fishing, pontoon, and ski boats. Those who like to sleep on dry land can book a two- or three-bedroom cabin ($165-195). **Emerald Isle Resort** (1500 County Park Rd., Campbellsville, 270/465-3412, www.emeraldisleresort.com) rents pontoon and fishing

boats, offers two- and three-bedroom condo rentals ($159-225), and has an on-site restaurant serving breakfast and lunch.

Sights

The 11 stops along the three-mile driving tour of the **Tebbs Bend Battlefield** (Tebbs Bend Rd., Campbellsville, 270/465-8726) commemorate the Union's repulsion of General John Hunt Morgan and his raiders on Independence Day in 1863. Text panels describe locations of importance, such as military campgrounds, field hospitals, and the main battleground.

Recreation

The 50-mile **Green River Paddle Trail** (www.greensburgonline.com) runs from the tailwaters of Green River Lake to Lynn Creek Camp, and you can paddle as much or as little of it as you want. Those with their own canoes and kayaks can download a map of the trail and access points from the website and go solo. Paddle fanatics can continue the trip beyond the county line, passing through Munfordville and into Mammoth Cave National Park. If you're looking to rent a canoe or kayak and arrange for shuttles, call Mike Daugherty at 270/789-2956.

Accommodations

Those wishing to stay overnight at **Green River Lake State Park** (179 Park Office Rd., Campbellsville, 270/465-8255, http://parks.ky.gov) can reserve a spot at the lakeside **campground** (Mar.-Nov., $15-31), which has showers, restrooms, laundry facilities, and a grocery. The campground has 157 sites with utility hookups and 72 dedicated tent camping sites.

The Army Corps of Engineers manages campgrounds with both primitive and RV sites at Holmes Bend (69 Corps Rd., Columbia), Smith Ridge (35 County Park Rd., Campbellsville), and Pikes Ridge (4725 Pikes Ridge Rd., Columbia). Reservations are available at www.recreation.gov.

If you don't want to stay at a campground, in a cabin at one of the marinas, or on a houseboat, nearby Campbellsville is home to multiple chain hotels and motels, including a **Holiday Inn Express** (102 Plantation Dr., 270/465-2727, www.holidayinnexpress.com, $92-110).

Food
For meals, browse the selections on Campbellsville Bypass (KY 210) and on Broadway in Campbellsville. You'll find a wide range of fast-food choices, Mexican restaurants, and barbecue joints, as well as **Colton's Steakhouse & Grill** (399 Campbellsville Bypass, Campbellsville, 270/789-4745, www.coltonssteakhouse.com, 11am-9:30pm Sun.-Thurs., 11am-10:30pm Fri.-Sat., $7.29-23.99).

Information and Services
The **Taylor County Tourist Commission** (325 E. Main St., Campbellsville, 270/465-3786, www.campbellsvilleky.com, 9am-5pm Mon.-Sat., 1pm-5pm Sun.) distributes information about Green River Lake and the surrounding area.

Getting There and Around
Green River Lake sits in the north-central section of this region, and from most everywhere else in this chapter, it is most easily accessed

ON THE TRAIL OF GENERAL JOHN HUNT MORGAN AND HIS RAIDERS

General John Hunt Morgan served in the Confederate Army during the Civil War and led multiple raids through Kentucky in various attempts to attack Union troops, divert attention from other battles, disrupt Union supply lines, and convince people to his cause. Born in Alabama, Morgan moved to Kentucky at age six and spent his adult life in the Lexington area. Though not immediately a secessionist, Morgan was a supporter of slavery and, having been a militiaman since the Mexican-American War, was quick to raise a regiment after the war began in hopes of winning Kentucky for the Confederacy.

Morgan is known in particular for three raids, although he entered and terrorized Kentucky on many occasions. On his first raid, in July 1862, Morgan crossed into Kentucky from Tennessee at the Cumberland River, just east of what is now Dale Hollow Lake. He passed through Tompkinsville, Glasgow, and Horse Cave before proceeding up to the Lexington area and then retreating south to Tennessee. On his Christmas Raid of 1862, Morgan and his raiders again entered Kentucky near Tompkinsville and proceeded to Glasgow, where they captured the Union Army troops stationed there. Continuing north, they burned railroad bridges, took

more Union troops hostage, and destroyed train lines before turning around north of Bardstown and returning to Tennessee. Morgan's Great Raid took place in July 1863. On this raid, he entered Kentucky a bit to the east at Burkesville, then proceeded through Columbia, Campbellsville, Lebanon, and Springfield before turning west and eventually entering Indiana at Brandenburg. He continued into Ohio, where nearly 700 of his men were captured and he was forced to surrender. He did escape, however, and through the help of friends in Kentucky, made it safely back to the south. While in Kentucky on this raid, he set fire to Lebanon, suffered 71 casualties at Tebbs Bend, and took part in multiple skirmishes. Morgan would lead a few more raids into Kentucky, although none of any major consequence to the war, before being killed in September 1864 during a Union raid in Tennessee. He is buried in Lexington.

Those with an interest in Civil War history can trace Morgan's routes through Kentucky on the **John Hunt Morgan Heritage Trail** (http://trailsrus.com/morgan). Sixty wayside exhibits provide information on Morgan and his men and point out locations of interest. Maps and additional information can be found on the trail's website.

via the Louie B. Nunn-Cumberland Parkway. From Bowling Green, which is about 1.5 hours away, take I-65 north to eastbound Cumberland Parkway (Exit 43). Then follow the parkway past Glasgow to Columbia (Exit 49), where you exit the parkway and turn onto northbound KY 55, which leads to the park. From the Lake Cumberland area, which is about an hour away, you would take the parkway westbound and then follow the same directions.

If you are approaching from Louisville, which is about 1 hour 45 minutes north, take southbound I-65 to eastbound KY 61 (Exit 91). When KY 61 ends at KY 210 after 12 miles, turn right and drive for 27 miles until KY 210 becomes KY 55, which will lead to the state park.

Campbellsville, which lies directly north of the lake, about seven miles (15 minutes) from the state park, is the nearest major city. U.S. 68 is the main thoroughfare in Campbellsville, and you can follow it 90 miles northeast to Lexington (1 hour 45 minutes) and then on to Maysville (148 miles; 3 hours) or take it southwest through Hopkinsville, across Land Between the Lakes, to Paducah (211 miles; 3 hours 20 minutes). KY 210, which is known locally as the bypass, is home to the usual assortment of box stores and chain restaurants.

◖ DALE HOLLOW LAKE

The waters of Dale Hollow Lake are a magnificent turquoise green, clear enough that they attract scuba divers in addition to the usual water-sports enthusiasts. The lake's islands, which allow primitive camping, add a hint of allure to this inland body of water. The majority of 27,700-acre Dale Hollow Lake lies in Tennessee, but a portion of the lake pokes up into Kentucky. The premier destination on the Kentucky side is Dale Hollow Lake State Resort Park, but a few other marinas are also located on the Bluegrass section of the lake.

Dale Hollow Lake State Resort Park

As you might expect, the biggest draw at **Dale Hollow Lake State Resort Park** (5970 State

Park Rd., Burkesville, 270/433-7431, http://parks.ky.gov, dawn-dusk daily, free) is the lake itself. Dale Hollow is a great fishing lake, holding the state records for smallmouth bass and muskie and also stocking crappie, bream, walleye, trout, catfish, and four other species of bass. Launch your own boat from the park's marina, built new in 2008, or reserve a rental pontoon, fishing boat, runabout, or personal watercraft at **Dale Hollow Rentals** (270/433-6600, www.dalehollowrentalsllc.com). Aside from anglers and pleasure boaters, the clear waters of Dale Hollow also draw scuba divers and spear fishers. You must have your own gear, but the park supports these pursuits and will help you determine the best way to go about them.

Beyond the lake, the forest and hill landscape of the park provides opportunities for other active pursuits. Particularly noteworthy are the 15 miles of multipurpose trails that follow old logging roads up and along park ridges. The 1.8-mile, one-way Eagle Point Trail leads to a vista-rich overlook, while those looking to cover some real distance should check out the 8.3-mile Boom Ridge Trail and its many spurs. While horses and bikes are welcome on the trails, there are no rental facilities for either in the park, so come prepared. Other recreational options include a long and hilly 18-hole golf course, a mini-golf course, a pool, and a cave that can be explored via guided tour or on your own by signing in and renting equipment at the lodge. During the months of January and February, bald eagles nest at Dale Hollow and the park runs eagle-watching weekends that include educational programs and boat and hiking trips to see the birds. Wild turkeys are present year-round in large numbers. In fact, it's practically impossible not to spot one—or 20—on a walk or drive through the park.

Other Marinas

Sulphur Creek Resort (3622 Sulphur Creek Rd., Burkesville, 270/433-7272, www.sulphurcreek.com), located along one of the lake's many arms, has a marina that rents

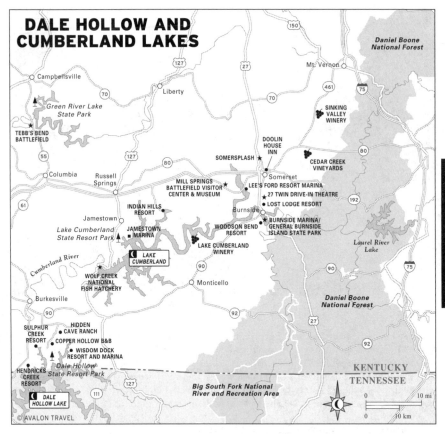

DALE HOLLOW AND CUMBERLAND LAKES

Daniel Boone National Forest

Campbellsville

Liberty

Green River Lake State Park

TEBB'S BEND BATTLEFIELD

Columbia

Russell Springs

Jamestown

Lake Cumberland State Resort Park

Cumberland River

Burkesville

SULPHUR CREEK RESORT

HIDDEN CAVE RANCH

COPPER HOLLOW B&B

WISDOM DOCK RESORT AND MARINA

Dale Hollow State Resort Park

HENDRICKS CREEK RESORT

DALE HOLLOW LAKE

© AVALON TRAVEL

Mt. Vernon

SINKING VALLEY WINERY

DOOLIN HOUSE INN

SOMERSPLASH

SOMERSET

MILL SPRINGS BATTLEFIELD VISITOR CENTER & MUSEUM

LEE'S FORD RESORT MARINA

27 TWIN DRIVE-IN THEATRE

LOST LODGE RESORT

Burnside

INDIAN HILLS RESORT

JAMESTOWN MARINA

WOODSON BEND RESORT

BURNSIDE MARINA/ GENERAL BURNSIDE ISLAND STATE PARK

CEDAR CREEK VINEYARDS

LAKE CUMBERLAND WINERY

LAKE CUMBERLAND

WOLF CREEK NATIONAL FISH HATCHERY

Monticello

Laurel River Lake

Daniel Boone National Forest

KENTUCKY
TENNESSEE

Big South Fork National River and Recreation Area

0   10 mi
0   10 km

BOWLING GREEN

fishing boats, pontoon boats, and houseboats and has a ramp for those with their own watercraft. Sulphur Creek Resort also features cabins ($75-189), a campground ($35), and a floating restaurant serving catfish, burgers, chicken fingers, and the like (11am-8pm daily).

Other Kentucky-side marinas include **Wisdom Dock Resort and Marina** (7613 Wisdom Dock Rd., Albany, 606/387-5821, www.wisdomresort.com), which offers cabins ($75-129), a floating restaurant, and fishing, pontoon, and houseboat rentals; and **Hendricks Creek Resort** (945 Hendricks Creek Rd., Burkesville, 270/433-7172, www.hendrickscreekresort.com), which offers boat and cottage rentals (three-night min., $455-645).

Accommodations

At **Dale Hollow Lake State Resort Park** (5970 State Park Rd., Burkesville, 270/433-7431, http://parks.ky.gov) guests are invited to stay overnight at the **Mary Ray Oaken Lodge** ($119.95-139.95). The lodge, which is located on a bluff above the lake, has 60 well-maintained motel-style rooms with balconies. Pay the extra bit for a lake-view room if one is available. A **campground** (Apr.-Oct., $26) with 145 spaces can accommodate tents, RVs, and horse campers. Six basic **cabins** ($58) with bunks are also available for rental in the campground.

Those who like more luxury than that afforded by campgrounds, cabins, and park hotels should reserve a room at **Copper Hollow**

BOWLING GREEN

© THERESA DOWELL BLACKINTON

marina at Dale Hollow Lake

Country Inn (3462 State Park Rd., Burkesville, 866/334-7100, http://.copperhollowcountry-inn.com, $129-139), which sits just outside the state park. The B&B has five bedrooms, each with whirlpool tub and comfy bed. In addition to a full breakfast, guests are also treated to evening snacks.

At **Hidden Cave Ranch** (877 Thrasher Rd., Burkesville, 270/433-3225, www.hiddencaver-anch.com, $69-119), a recreational ranch run by a transplanted Dutch couple, guests can choose from five rooms, all decorated in lodge style with log beds. Three of the rooms have private baths. The other two share a bath and can only be reserved in conjunction with the adjoining room. The 156-acre ranch, which is about seven miles north of the state park, is home to a stable of American Bashkir Curly horses that guests are invited to ride ($27 for one hour, $60 for three).

Food

At Dale Hollow Lake State Resort Park, the **Island View Restaurant** (5970 State Park Rd., Burkesville, 270/433-7431, http://parks.ky.gov, breakfast 6:30am-10am, lunch 11:30am-4pm, dinner 5pm-9pm daily, $5.95-14.95) serves standard Kentucky favorites like Hot Browns, fried chicken, and a fisherman's platter. The dining room has three glass walls, allowing for panoramic views of the lake.

Getting There and Around

Dale Hollow Lake is located right on the border with Tennessee about smack in the middle of Kentucky's southern border, not particularly close to anything. The nearest major road is the Cumberland Parkway, with the town of Columbia about 35 miles north via KY 90 and KY 61. Those coming from the I-65 corridor will want to head to Glasgow. From there, access to Dale Hollow is straightforward, since it's a direct 45-mile (one hour) drive on eastbound KY 90 from Glasgow to KY 449, which turns into State Park Road. To make the 35-mile (one hour) drive to Lake Cumberland, take KY 449 to KY 90, and follow it east to northbound U.S.

© THERESA DOWELL BLACKINTON

BOWLING GREEN

dam at Lake Cumberland

127, which leads right to Lake Cumberland State Resort Park.

█ LAKE CUMBERLAND

Lake Cumberland is houseboat heaven. Although the lake, which covers more than 65,000 acres, provides great fishing opportunities for those pursuing trout, bass, sturgeon, and walleye, Lake Cumberland is most known for its houseboat lifestyle. At 101 miles long, Lake Cumberland is a long, narrow lake with many creeks and coves shooting off in all directions. These coves invite houseboats to tie up and establish camp. People throw out rafts and go for a float or a swim, and then return to the houseboat to take a ride down the slide or jump in the hot tub. Those in the know, including members of the "Ohio Navy"—Ohioans who basically call Lake Cumberland home during the summer—come with coolers of adult beverages. It's the only way you'll get alcohol out on the lake, because the entire area surrounding it is dry. The lake's biggest party spot used to be 76 Falls, but lower lake levels in recent

years have made it impossible to access, thus the party has moved to Harmon Creek, which is on the south side of the lake, east of State Dock Marina and west of Camp Earl Wallace. For those launching from the eastern side of the lake, near Burnside, the gathering spot, known aptly as Party Cove, is on the south fork of the lake. A lone cove on the western side of the fork, Party Cove is about 1.5-2 miles past the Woodson Bend Community Dock. Entertainment at these party coves can be decidedly not family-friendly, so those with children in tow should bypass them and look for a quieter spot, of which there are plenty.

Two state parks and multiple private resorts and marinas line the shores of Lake Cumberland, offering options for renting boats and providing places to sleep for those who don't like to overnight on the water. The lake has two main activity areas. The Jamestown area, which is on the northwest section of the lake, is home to Cumberland Lake State Resort Park and many of the most popular marinas. The Burnside area, at the far eastern end of the lake and close to the city of Somerset, is where you'll find the quieter General Burnside State Park and a handful of other marinas.

Jamestown Area

Due to the popularity of Lake Cumberland State Resort Park, which is located on the northwestern shores of Lake Cumberland, the Jamestown area bustles, especially in summertime. It's the place to go if you want to rent a houseboat, thanks to the large inventories at State Dock and Jamestown Marina. The towns of Jamestown and Russell Springs serve lake visitors with food and shopping options.

LAKE CUMBERLAND STATE RESORT PARK

Lake Cumberland State Resort Park (5465 State Park Rd., Jamestown, 270/343-3111, http://parks.ky.gov, dawn-dusk daily, free) offers recreational activities away from the lake for those who've had all the water they can stand. There's a disc golf course, a mini-golf course, a horse riding stable (9am-5pm daily, Memorial Day-Labor Day, $18 for 45-minute ride), daily naturalist programs, and two hiking trails, one a four-mile loop and the other a 1.5-mile, one-way trail. Those who prefer chlorinated water to lake water can make use of the public outdoor swimming pool during the summer. A game room with pool tables, table tennis, and foosball tables provides entertainment should you find yourself at the park on a rainy day.

Most people come to Lake Cumberland to enjoy the lake itself, however. **State Dock** (888/782-8336, www.statedock.com), a large marina, can set you up with a fishing, ski, or pontoon boat, or send you out in style on a houseboat for three-, four-, or seven-night vacations. The economy-range houseboats have four private bedrooms plus a sofa bed, 1.5 bathrooms, a galley kitchen, open-top deck, and waterslide, while the top-of-the-line Mega Cat has eight private bedrooms plus a sofa bed, 3.5 bathrooms, a gourmet kitchen, third-level sundeck, 15-person hot tub, and

a two-story tube slide. Whatever your style, State Dock can accommodate you. Reserve your houseboat as far in advance as possible. However, last-minute vacationers may find a houseboat available at short notice, although rarely on weekends.

OTHER MARINAS

Just across from State Dock is **Jamestown Marina** (3677 KY 92, Jamestown, 270/343-5253, www.jamestown-marina.com), another popular place to rent a houseboat. Jamestown Marina rents three different styles of houseboats, which can accommodate up to 12 adults. Pontoons are also available.

Indian Hills Resort (2108 KY 1383, Russell Springs, 270/866-6616, www.indianhillsresort.com) is another place to inquire about houseboat rentals. They also rent pontoon and fishing boats.

For listings of other marinas in the area, visit www.lakecumberlandvacation.com.

SIGHTS

Although it might not sound exciting, a tour of **Wolf Creek National Fish Hatchery** (50 Kendall Rd., Jamestown, 270/343-3797, www.fws.gov, 8am-5pm daily, free) is really quite interesting. The hatchery provides all of the stocked trout in Kentucky, and the tours show how the trout are raised from egg to stockable size. Visitors can feed the trout and fish for them in the creek outside the hatchery. The attached Environmental Education Center has aquariums, geology displays, and other hands-on exhibits.

ACCOMMODATIONS

If you didn't reserve a houseboat in time or just aren't interested in sleeping on the water, **Lake Cumberland State Resort Park** (5465 State Park Rd., Jamestown, 270/343-3111, http://parks.ky.gov) has lodge, cottage, and campground accommodations. The 63 rooms at **Lure Lodge** ($129.95-134.95) all have lakeside balconies and are filled with bright, natural light. **Pumpkin Creek Lodge** ($114.95-119.95) is a smaller, simpler facility with only 13 rooms. Walls are a bit thin, but the rooms are comfortable and offer standard motel amenities. One- and two-bedroom hillside **cottages** ($149.95-209.95) are also available. Although from the outside they look a bit like standard ranch houses, the cottages have a rustic cabin feel inside, thanks to an abundance of wood. They are equipped with modern amenities. An indoor pool is open to both lodge and cottage guests. The park's **campground** (Apr.-Oct., $15-22) has 129 sites, most of which are back-in sites with hookups, although a handful are reserved for tents only.

Jamestown Marina (3677 KY 92, Jamestown, 888/656-7622, www.jamestownmarina.com) offers landlubbers lakeside lodge suites ($179.95), chalet-style condos ($199.95) perched on a hill with views of the lake, bargain fishing cabins ($89.95-109.95), and modern log cabins ($159.95).

There's a KOA at **Indian Hills Resort** (2108 KY 1383, Russell Springs, 270/866-5616, www.indianhillsresort.com, $20-29) with a swimming pool, tennis court, mini-golf course, trails, and other recreational facilities.

FOOD

Lake dining isn't really much to get excited about. Most people tend to self-cater with picnic lunches or meals cooked in cabins or on houseboats. Most marinas have a restaurant serving casual fare like hamburgers and fried fish. **Rowena Landing Restaurant** (Lake Cumberland State Resort Park, 5465 State Park Rd., Jamestown, 270/343-3111, http://parks.ky.gov, breakfast 7am-10:30am daily, lunch 11:30am-4pm daily, dinner 5pm-8pm daily, $5.95-13.95) boasts panoramic views of Lake Cumberland. It's known for its high-season seafood buffets ($24.95), which are offered on the third Friday of the month. With all-you-can-eat crab legs, shrimp, catfish, salmon, and more, the buffet draws park guests as well as folks from the nearby community. Kentucky favorites and comfort foods make up the regular menu.

For fast-food options, Chinese buffets, and the like, head to Jamestown or Russell Springs.

INFORMATION AND SERVICES

The western section of Lake Cumberland is located in Russell County, and their tourist commission runs a website, www.lakecumberlandvacation.com, with information about the lake, accommodations, restaurants, and activities.

GETTING THERE AND AROUND

Jamestown is just south of the Cumberland Parkway on U.S. 127 (Exit 62). From Bowling Green, which is 95 miles (1.75 hours) to the west, and the I-65 corridor, eastbound Cumberland Parkway is the best way to go. From Louisville, which is 130 miles (2.5 hours) northwest, instead of going all the way south to the parkway, exit I-65 at southbound KY 61 (Exit 91). Follow KY 61 for 56 miles to Columbia, where you'll transfer to southbound KY 55. After 19 miles, KY 55 will become U.S. 127, which leads to the state park. From Lexington, it's a straight 100-mile (2.5-hour) drive south on U.S. 127.

Russell Springs, which offers additional food options, is located just north of Jamestown on the other side of the Cumberland Parkway. From Jamestown, drive four miles north on U.S. 127, then turn left on Lake Way Drive and continue just over a mile into town.

To get to the Burnside area of the lake from the Jamestown area, travel east on Cumberland Parkway for 26 miles to southbound U.S. 27, which leads through Somerset to Burnside. The drive from one end to the other takes more than an hour.

Burnside Area

On the eastern end of Lake Cumberland, the Burnside area encompasses a small state park, the tiny (but wet!) town of Burnside, and the city of Somerset. For those who want something to do after they dock the boat, this area delivers, with nearby wineries, a Civil

War site, a drive-in theater, and a noteworthy bed-and-breakfast.

GENERAL BURNSIDE ISLAND STATE PARK

Located at the eastern end of Lake Cumberland, **General Burnside Island State Park** (8801 S. U.S. 27, Burnside, 606/561-4104, http://parks.ky.gov, dawn-dusk daily, free) is a small park that has boat ramps for those with their own watercraft, an 18-hole golf course, picnic tables, shelters, and a campground.

MARINAS

Conveniently located to General Burnside Island State Park, **Burnside Marina** (680 W. Lakeshore Dr., Burnside, 606/561-4223, www.burnsidemarina.com) is one of the easiest places to rent a houseboat if you want to base yourself on the eastern side of the lake. The marina also rents ski, fishing, and pontoon boats and personal watercraft.

Lee's Ford Resort Marina (451 Lees Ford Dock Rd., Nancy, 606/636-6426, www.leesfordmarina.com) is a comprehensive resort with boat rentals (house, pontoon, fishing, ski, personal watercraft), cottages, and a restaurant.

SIGHTS

The North and South met each other in battle in January 1862 in the Lake Cumberland area, and important sites from this Civil War battle are now preserved as part of the Mill Springs Battlefield Driving Tour. Those wishing to travel the route should begin their trip at the **Mill Springs Battlefield Visitor Center & Museum** (9020 W. KY 80, Nancy, 606/636-4045, www.millsprings.net, 10am-4pm Wed.-Thurs., 10am-6pm Fri.-Sat., 1pm-4pm Sun., free), which is located next to Mill Springs National Cemetery. Most of the other interpretive stops on the driving tour are located on nearby KY 235.

Three wineries are located in the vicinity of Lake Cumberland, offering visitors the rare opportunity to imbibe an alcoholic drink in this very dry region of the state. **Sinking Valley Winery** (6515 KY 461, Plato, 606/274-0223, www.sinkingvalleywinery.com, 10am-6pm Mon.-Sat., free) invites visitors to try some of their 14 wines, including some barrel-fermented white wines, in their tasting room, which was once the Plato general store and post office. At a second location (3610 S. KY 27, Somerset, noon-8pm Mon.-Sat., 1pm-6pm Sun.), they offer craft beer tasting in addition to wine tasting. If you get a chance to talk to owner Zane Burton, ask to hear just how this former tobacco farmer and the son of teetotalers came to be a vintner.

Cedar Creek Vineyards (294 Cedar Creek Ln., Somerset, 606/875-3296, www.cedarcreekvineyards.net, 1pm-6pm Tues.-Sat.), which strives to be a good steward of the earth, produces a variety of wines, up to six of which may be tasted for $3 on a visit to the facility. The vineyard also hosts a number of unique events.

The newest addition to the local wine scene, **Lake Cumberland Winery** (122 Cedar Lane Farm, Monticello, 606/348-5253, www.lakecumberlandwinery.com, 11am-6pm Thurs.-Sat.) is unique in that it offers samples and bottles of both their own wines and the wines of other Kentucky wineries. They have a long list of reds, whites, and fruit wines to choose from. Check their website for information on summer concerts and other events.

RECREATION

Those who just can't get enough of the water might want to put **Somersplash** (1030 KY 2227, Somerset, 606/679-7946, www.somersplash.com, 10am-7pm Mon.-Sat., 1pm-7pm Sun., Memorial Day-Labor Day, $14.95) on the agenda. The water park features tube and body slides, a wave pool, a lazy river, and a kids' play area.

ENTERTAINMENT AND EVENTS

The **27 Twin Drive-In Theatre** (5270 S. U.S. 27, Somerset, 606/679-4738, www.27drivein.com, $6 adults, $2 youth) still shows a double feature every Friday, Saturday, and Sunday during the summer season. For some throwback fun, load up the car and enjoy the show.

On the fourth Saturday of the month,

April-October, downtown Somerset hosts the **Somernites Cruise Car Show** (www.somernitescruise.org). Classic car owners and fans from all over the region converge in Somerset to show off their rides. It's a fun family outing off the water.

ACCOMMODATIONS

If you're not interested in staying on a houseboat, don't worry. There are plenty of other options. **General Burnside Island State Park** (8801 U.S. 27, Burnside, 606/561-4104, http://parks.ky.gov, Apr.-Oct., $22) offers a 94-site campground, while **Lee's Ford Resort Marina** (451 Lees Ford Dock Rd., Nancy, 606/636-6872, www.leesfordmarina.com) offers cottage rentals ($750-1,300 per week) or basic hotel accommodations ($80).

Two popular resorts are **Lost Lodge Resort** (265 Lost Lodge Rd., Somerset, 606/561-4451, www.lostlodge.com, $94-179) and **Woodson Bend Resort** (14 Woodson Bend, Bronston, 800/872-9825, www.woodsonbendresort.com, two-night min., $200-500). Lost Lodge is more rustic, with activities centered around the lake, while Woodson Bend boasts a swimming pool, tennis courts, and an 18-hole golf course.

For a luxurious getaway, try 🅒 **Doolin House Inn** (502 N. Main St., Somerset, 606/678-9494, www.doolinhouse.com, $94-144), a gorgeous bed-and-breakfast located in the Somerset historic district. The five rooms, which are named for Kentucky Derby winners, are large and sumptuous with elegant but comfortable furnishings and decor. You won't lack for amenities. Mounted flat-screen TVs and wireless Internet are standard, and rooms may feature enormous whirlpool tubs as well as gas fireplaces. One room is entirely wheelchair-accessible. You definitely won't want to skip breakfast here. Owners Charles and Alison are both professional chefs who run a very popular catering business, and they'll personally whip up the breakfast you choose from a short menu.

FOOD

Somerset has your usual selection of fast-food, Chinese, Mexican, and family restaurants.

Drive down U.S. 27, and you're sure to find something that will satisfy although probably not thrill you. Another option is to check out the restaurants at the area's lodges and marinas, such as **Sully's Lakeside Grill** (680 W. Lakeshore Dr., Burnside, 606/561-4223, www.burnsidemarina.com, 11am-8pm Thurs.-Sun., $3.95-7.95) at Burnside Marina, which serves quick bites like hamburgers and chicken salad sandwiches.

Your best bet is probably **Harbor Restaurant** at Lee's Ford Marina (451 Lees Ford Dock Rd., Nancy, 606/636-4587, www.leesfordmarina.com, 11am-10pm Mon.-Thurs., 11am-midnight Fri.-Sat., 11am-8pm Sun., $8.99-24.99), especially if you're after a cold beer. Through a feat of legal maneuvering, Harbor Restaurant managed to incorporate in Burnside, the only moist town in the entire area, so the restaurant is allowed to serve alcoholic beverages. The large decks with lake views make it an excellent place to kick back and relax after a day on the water. The menu features pastas, pork, seafood, steaks, and sandwiches. If you're hungry, go for the grouper.

INFORMATION AND SERVICES

The eastern half of Lake Cumberland falls in Pulaski County, and their visitors bureau provides information on the lake, the city of Somerset, and the surrounding area. Visit them in person (522 Ogden St., Somerset, 606/679-6394) or on the web (www.lakecumberlandtourism.com). The tiny town of Burnside, which advertises itself as the only town actually on the lake, has its own tourism bureau, which runs www.burnsidetourism.com.

GETTING THERE AND AROUND

The eastern portion of Lake Cumberland is at the far end of this region, butting up against the Daniel Boone National Forest and Eastern Kentucky. The town of Somerset, which is the gateway to this part of the lake, is almost directly 75 miles (1.5 hours) south of Lexington. To reach Somerset and Lake Cumberland from Lexington, travel south on I-75 for about 40 miles to southbound KY 461 (Exit 62), which will lead into Somerset after 18 miles. From Bowling Green, which is 110 miles (1.75 hours) to the west, and the I-65 corridor, take the Cumberland Parkway for 88 miles to southbound U.S. 27, which is one of the major thoroughfares running through Somerset and on to Burnside. From Louisville, which is 130 miles (2.5 hours) northwest, rather than following I-65 and the Cumberland Parkway, it's faster to take eastbound I-64 to U.S. 127 (Exit 48), then follow it 32 miles to U.S. 150, which intersects with U.S. 27 after 10 miles. Turn right onto U.S. 27, and drive another 38 miles to Somerset.

To get from the Burnside area of the lake to the Jamestown area, drive 26 miles on westbound Cumberland Parkway to southbound U.S. 127 (Exit 62), which leads into the state park. It's more than an hour's drive between the two state parks.

OWENSBORO, PADUCAH, AND LAND BETWEEN THE LAKES

Kentucky's far western region is a land that gets progressively smaller as the Ohio River, its northern boundary, twists and turns its way south. It's a fertile area, with much of the acreage given over to farmland. Kentucky's dark leaf tobacco is grown here, and it's also where the western coalfields are located. For visitors to the area, however, those things are incidental. The draws of this region are its musical tradition, its emphasis on art, its talent for barbecue, and its amazing recreational opportunities.

Owensboro, which is located in the northeastern part of this region, is Kentucky's fourth-largest city, but it's not an urban area. You don't come here for the typical city attractions. Instead, Owensboro draws tourists with its bluegrass heritage, its mutton and burgoo (which are types of barbecue, for the uninitiated), and its penchant for throwing a party. Owensboro is the gateway to Rosine, the birthplace of bluegrass music, and is home to a top-notch museum dedicated to the genre and an important bluegrass music festival. True bluegrass fans must leave town, however, and travel to Rosine to see where Bill Monroe was born and to experience the Rosine Barn Jamboree. Before you go, you'd better have some Owensboro barbecue. This ubiquitous dish gets unique treatment in Owensboro, with pulled and chopped mutton and the stew-like burgoo the dishes of choice.

Bluegrass isn't the only music with roots in the area. Blues have a strong connection to the city of Henderson, which is worth a visit as you travel from Owensboro farther west. On the way to Paducah, one of Kentucky's

© THERESA DOWELL BLACKINTON

HIGHLIGHTS

◖ International Bluegrass Music Museum: Learn what makes bluegrass bluegrass at this museum dedicated to the popular style of music that has its roots here (page 356).

◖ Rosine Barn Jamboree: This honest-to-God barn jams every Friday night, when bluegrass fans from near and far gather to pick and sing in the town where bluegrass was born (page 363).

◖ Jerusalem Ridge Festival: Though you could fill a calendar with bluegrass festivals in Kentucky, this four-day event held at the birthplace of bluegrass should top the list (page 364).

◖ The National Quilt Museum: You'll never look at quilts the same way after you see the masterpieces on display here (page 370).

◖ Lower Town Fine Arts District: Visit studios and galleries on a stroll through this art-focused community in Paducah (page 374).

◖ Land Between the Lakes National Recreation Area: Get in touch with the great outdoors at one of Kentucky's favorite playgrounds by taking to the area's two gorgeous lakes or exploring the shoreline on foot, by bike, or by horse (page 382).

LOOK FOR ◖ TO FIND RECOMMENDED SIGHTS, ACTIVITIES, DINING, AND LODGING.

most charming cities, you can also explore Kentucky's largest Amish community, located in Union County. In the far west, Paducah is a lively place where art plays a major role. Between the National Quilt Museum and the Lower Town Arts District, there's art everywhere.

This region's biggest attraction isn't a city, however. In fact, it's basically the opposite. Western Kentucky's most popular destination is the Land Between the Lakes region. With two enormous lakes and a national recreational area, Land Between the Lakes is where you go to get away from it all. Fish, swim, sail, hike, bike, or just sit on the shore and enjoy the breeze—Land Between the Lakes is an outdoor lover's paradise.

PLANNING YOUR TIME

This region, which most people broadly refer to as Western Kentucky, can be divided into three distinct areas: Owensboro and the northeastern part of Western Kentucky, Paducah and the southwestern part of Western Kentucky, and Land Between the Lakes. Additionally, you have the region that sits just east of Land Between the Lakes, which is geographically large but has limited attractions. Trying to combine all of this into one trip would make for quite the eclectic vacation and would also add up to lots of hours in the car. Your best bet is to tackle it piece by piece.

Although Owensboro is Kentucky's fourth-largest city, on its own it's probably just a one-day destination. Throw in trips to Henderson and Rosine, a must for any music fan, however, and you're looking at a weekend's worth of things to do. Try to plan your trip to coincide with a festival, such as the Handy Blues and Barbecue Festival in Henderson, River of Music Party in Owensboro, or the Jerusalem Ridge Festival in Rosine. If that's not possible, try to make it to the area on a Friday evening so you can experience the Rosine Barn Jamboree. Of course, hotel rooms become scarce during the biggest festivals, so advance planning is recommended.

Paducah is a much smaller town (population just over 25,000), but it too has a whole lot going on. A weekend is definitely recommended in order to visit the museums and gallery-hop in Lower Town. If, in the summer, you can stay overnight on a Saturday, you'll get to enjoy Live on Broadway, which will give you the opportunity to mingle with locals and see how much fun the city is. Paducah is also the best base for exploring Wickliffe Mounds and Columbus-Belmont State Parks in the far

western reaches of the state. It's also possible to make a day trip from Paducah to Land Between the Lakes, which is less than an hour away.

Most people consider the Land Between the Lakes area to be at minimum a weekend destination. Visiting the sites in Land Between the Lakes National Recreation Area will fill an entire day, leaving you another day to get out on the waters of either Kentucky Lake or Lake Barkley. Four days would be a better amount of time if you have it, allowing for the type of relaxation that a lake vacation practically demands and giving you time to add in outdoor activities like hiking, biking, horseback riding, and maybe even a round of golf. A week, for many, is not too much time.

When to go depends heavily on what you want to do. Summer is peak season for the Land Between the Lakes area. Prices will be higher for accommodations, and you'll definitely want to book in advance, but the lakes themselves are so big that they never feel crowded. Outside of summer, a lot of nearby attractions dramatically cut their hours, although the shoulder season of May and September—before school lets out and after it begins again—are perfect for those without kids in tow, as prices drop but the weather is still nice and attractions still have reasonable hours. Music fans might want to consider June, when both Owensboro's River of Music Party and Henderson's Handy Blues and Barbecue Festival take place. October is also lovely in this part of the state, and that's when the Jerusalem Ridge Festival happens in bluegrass's hometown.

Owensboro

Although you probably wouldn't guess it if you arrived without knowing, Owensboro is Kentucky's fourth-largest city. It's distinctly different from Kentucky's other big cities, offering much more of a small-town feel, which probably has a lot to do with the fact that it's a bit geographically isolated. Instead

of a cityscape, there's a downtown of historic buildings undergoing revitalization. Where big name hotels or million-dollar homes crowd the waterfront in other cities, Owensboro is creating open park space where everyone can get an equal share of Ohio River views.

No, Owensboro isn't cosmopolitan, but

OWENSBORO

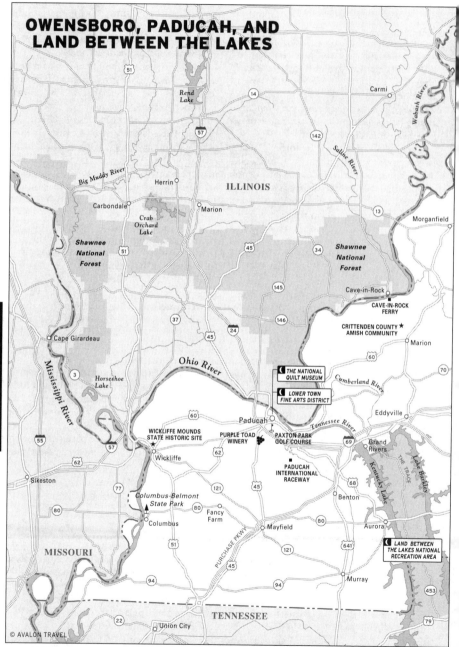

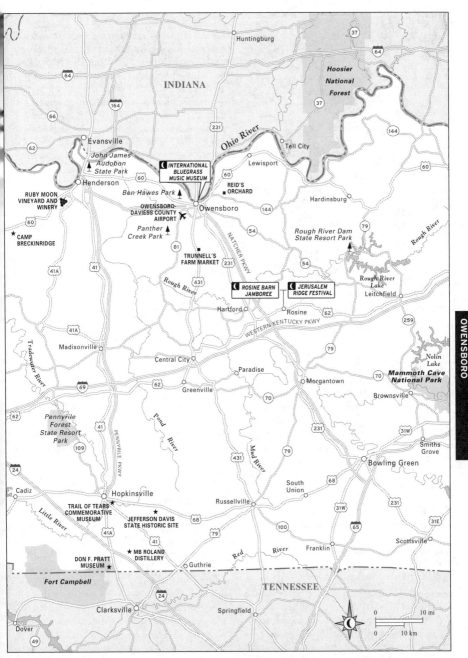

© THERESA DOWELL BLACKINTON

International Bluegrass Music Museum

OWENSBORO

that's not of concern to the city's residents. They'd rather be known as friendly. And that they are. They also like to have a good time. Nicknamed Festival City, Owensboro throws bash after bash, averaging nearly two festivals each month. The biggest revolve around barbecue, especially the mutton kind popular in these parts, and bluegrass music, which was born just down the road. Fans of either will definitely want to make plans to visit Owensboro, which deals in these two specialties all year-round.

SIGHTS
◖ International Bluegrass Music Museum
The **International Bluegrass Music Museum** (117 Daviess St., 270/926-7891, www.bluegrassmuseum.org, 10am-5pm Tues.-Sat., 1pm-4pm Sun., $5 adults, $2 students) celebrates the tradition of bluegrass music, which got its start right here in this region before becoming popular around the globe. The displays in the permanent exhibit trace the history of bluegrass,

focusing on pioneers of the genre, the music that influenced bluegrass, and the way in which bluegrass has grown, changed, and spread. Artifacts, such as outfits from Bill Monroe, the father of bluegrass, and instruments that belonged to the Blue Grass Boys, accompany text panels, photographs, and lots of listening stations. Rotating exhibits, which are located on the second floor, complement the permanent exhibit. Be sure to schedule some time at the first floor stage area, where you can watch remarkable oral histories documenting the lives and careers of first-generation bluegrass musicians such as banjo great and Blue Grass Boy Earl Scruggs. The museum offers music lessons on Saturday mornings, and hosts jams at 6pm on the first Thursday of the month.

Owensboro Area Museum of Science & History
The excellent Government Education Center, which educates visitors on the American political system and honors former senator Wendell H. Ford, is the highlight of the **Owensboro Area Museum of Science & History** (122 E. 2nd St., 270/687-2732, www.owensboromuseum.org, 10am-5pm Tues.-Sat., 1pm-5pm Sun., $3). A Columbian mammoth and the Speedzeum, which focuses on different types of motor racing, are also popular, but other exhibits can feel a little slapdash. Kids, however, will definitely have a good time at this inexpensive museum with a play area and hands-on experiment zone.

Owensboro Museum of Fine Arts
Fifteen galleries display classic and contemporary art at the **Owensboro Museum of Fine Arts** (901 Frederica St., 270/685-3181, www.omfa.us, 10am-4pm Tues.-Thurs., 10am-7pm Fri., 1pm-4pm Sat.-Sun., $2 adults, $1 youth under 13), which consists of two historic buildings—a former Carnegie library and a pre-Civil War house—connected by a postmodern atrium. Highlights of the permanent collection include a sculpture by Degas, a portrait by Sir Thomas Lawrence, and the stained-glass gallery, which hosts a beautiful display of

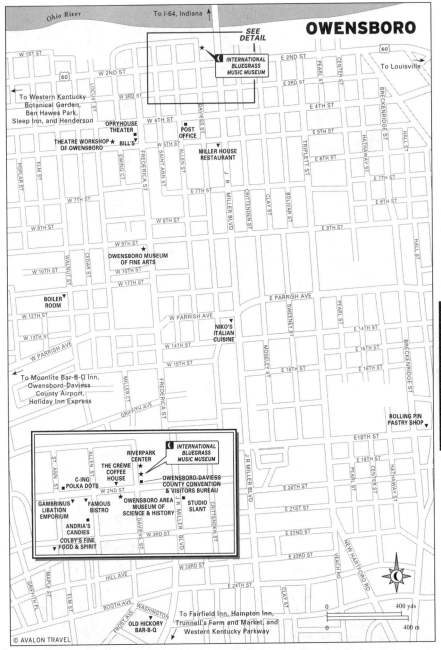

OWENSBORO

OWENSBORO

Ohio River

To I-64, Indiana

SEE DETAIL

★ INTERNATIONAL BLUEGRASS MUSIC MUSEUM

To Louisville

W 1ST ST
W 2ND ST
W 3RD ST

To Western Kentucky Botanical Garden, Ben Hawes Park, Sleep Inn, and Henderson

OPRYHOUSE THEATER

THEATRE WORKSHOP ★ BILL'S
OF OWENSBORO

POST OFFICE

MILLER HOUSE RESTAURANT

W 4TH ST
W 5TH ST
W 7TH ST
W 8TH ST
W 9TH ST

OWENSBORO MUSEUM ★
OF FINE ARTS

W 10TH ST
W 11TH ST

BOILER ROOM

W 12TH ST
W 13TH ST
W PARRISH AVE

E PARRISH AVE
W PARRISH AVE

NIKO'S ITALIAN CUISINE

W 14TH ST
W 15TH ST

To Moonlite Bar-B-Q Inn, Owensboro-Daviess County Airport, Holiday Inn Express

ROLLING PIN PASTRY SHOP

E 2ND ST
E 3RD ST
E 4TH ST
E 5TH ST
E 6TH ST
E 7TH ST
E 8TH ST
E 9TH ST
E 14TH ST
E 15TH ST
E 16TH ST
E 18TH ST
E 19TH ST
E 20TH ST
E 21ST ST
E 22ND ST
E 23RD ST
E 24TH ST
W 23RD ST

INTERNATIONAL BLUEGRASS MUSIC MUSEUM

RIVERPARK CENTER ★

THE CRÈME COFFEE HOUSE

C-ING POLKA DOTS

OWENSBORO-DAVIESS COUNTY CONVENTION & VISITORS BUREAU

GAMBRINUS LIBATION EMPORIUM

FAMOUS BISTRO

OWENSBORO AREA ★ MUSEUM OF SCIENCE & HISTORY

STUDIO SLANT

ANDRIA'S CANDIES

COLBY'S FINE FOOD & SPIRIT

HILL AVE

BOOTH AVE

WASHINGTON

OLD HICKORY BAR-B-Q

To Fairfield Inn, Hampton Inn, Trunnell's Farm and Market, and Western Kentucky Parkway

0   400 yds
0   400 m

© AVALON TRAVEL

OWENSBORO

© THERESA DOWELL BLACKINTON

flowers in bloom at the Western Kentucky Botanical Garden

16 former church windows crafted in the late 19th century. Nationally touring exhibits are hosted at the museum and change every 6-8 weeks. Check the website for special events at the museum.

Western Kentucky Botanical Garden

Immerse yourself in beauty at the **Western Kentucky Botanical Garden** (25 Carter Rd., 270/852-8925, www.wkbg.org, 9am-3pm daily, Mar.-mid-Nov., 9am-3pm Mon.-Fri., mid-Nov.-Feb., $5 adults, $3 seniors, $1 students), where you can follow a half-mile path through 10 themed gardens, including a rose garden, Japanese garden, iris garden, herb garden, and children's garden. The daylily garden, which has more than 350 plants, has received national recognition, and the colorful blossoms of this plant species are celebrated in late June at the Dazzling Daylily Festival. Different plants peak at different times of the year, making this all-volunteer garden a year-round destination and place to return to time and again.

Agritourism

Trunnell's Farm Market (9255 U.S. 431, Utica, 270/733-2222, www.trunnellsfarmmarket. com, 10am-6pm Mon.-Sat., noon-5pm Sun.) is known for its sweet corn and other fresh produce, but don't try telling that to the kids. They favor the Family Fun Acre, which allows them to work out a bit of their energy in rope and straw mazes and on the straw pyramid and 80-foot tunnel slide. During the spring/summer season (May-July), admission costs $3 and the Family Fun Acre is open 11am-5pm Monday-Saturday and noon-5pm Sunday. During the fall season (mid-Sept.-early Nov.), admission, which includes a hayride to the pumpkin patch and additional fall-only activities, costs $9 and the Family Fun Acre is open 3pm-6pm Friday, 10am-6pm Saturday, and noon-5pm Sunday.

Get your fill of freshness at **Reid's Orchard** (4812 KY 144, 270/685-2444, www.reidorchard.com, 8am-7pm Mon.-Sat., 10am-5pm Sun.), where delicious apples, strawberries, peaches, blackberries, and vegetables are available seasonally. The orchard's **Apple Festival,** held annually on the third weekend of October, is a favorite event, featuring food and craft booths along with lots and lots of apples.

ENTERTAINMENT AND EVENTS
Bars and Clubs
Gambrinus Libation Emporium (116 W. 2nd St., 270/663-5464, www.kinggambrinus.com, 6pm-midnight Mon., 4pm-midnight Tues.-Fri., 5pm-midnight Sat.) offers premium beer, wine, and cocktails in an updated downtown building. The rich fabric booths, studded leather chairs, chandeliers, and long marble-top bar in an open layout make Gambrinus a fun place to catch up with friends or meet and mingle.

The college-age crowd congregates at the **Boiler Room** (1100 N. Walnut St., 270/684-4999, 2pm-2am Mon.-Fri., 11am-2am Sat.), where live music fills the bar on weekends.

Performing Arts
RiverPark Center (101 Daviess St., 270/687-2787, www.riverparkcenter.org) is a regional performing arts center that hosts both a Broadway series as well as the **Owensboro Symphony Orchestra** (270/684-0661, www.owensborosymphony.org) in its Cannon Hall. RiverPark also acts as a civic center, and is home to the **Friday After 5** (www.fridayafter5.com) free summer concert series, a free summer movie series, and annual events such as Taste of Owensboro and the International Mystery Writers' Festival. Located on the banks of the Ohio River, RiverPark's patio provides nice views of river traffic.

Theatre Workshop of Owensboro (TWO) (407 W. 5th St., 270/683-5333, www.theatreworkshop.org) brings a full schedule of plays to Owensboro through community theater performances at Trinity Centre, an 1875 gothic-style former church turned into an intimate theater. TWO stages five shows each year and also sponsors concerts, which take place at either Trinity Centre or the Opryhouse Theatre (418 Frederica St.). Tickets can be purchased online or at the box office (10am-2pm Mon.-Fri. and one hour before shows) for all shows.

Festivals and Events
Connoisseurs of Owensboro-style barbecue, which revolves around mutton and burgoo, converge on the city every second weekend of May for the **International Bar-B-Q Festival** (www.bbqfest.com). While barbecue, and tons of it, is the focus of the festival, eating isn't the only thing on the agenda. Earn your plate of barbecue by taking part in the 5K run, or walk up an appetite while touring the classic car show or shopping at the arts and crafts festival.

Sponsored by the Bluegrass Museum, the **River of Music Party** (http://rompfest.com) is a four-day toast to bluegrass music held annually in late June at Yellow Creek Park (5710 KY 144). From morning until night, big names in bluegrass show off their high harmonies in performance after performance. Dance bands keep things going at an after-party for the young and young at heart. A slew of workshops, given by some of the best in the business, are scheduled throughout the festival, and a jam camp is held in the days preceding it. Whether you're just becoming acquainted with bluegrass or are a veteran of more jam sessions than you can remember, ROMP is a delightful way to immerse yourself in the music, enjoying some of the best bluegrass music in the world right in its homeland. On-site camping is available.

There's good reason behind Owensboro's moniker of Festival City. It's nearly impossible to find a weekend without a festival. Apples and pumpkins, bluegrass and gospel, Independence Day and Halloween, daylilies and dogwoods, and crafts and cultures are all good reasons for a celebration, according to Owensboro. A full listing of each year's events is located at http://visitowensboro.com.

SHOPPING
Revitalization has come to downtown Owensboro, and many of the historic storefronts are once again home to shops. The compact size of downtown makes it easy to stroll about, poking your head in whenever a

window display catches your eye. Be sure to pop in at **C-Ing Polka Dots** (115 W. 2nd St., 270/240-4394, www.c-ingpolkadots.com, 11am-6pm Mon.-Fri., 10am-5pm Sat.), which carries original art, jewelry, and furniture, and **Studio Slant** (412 E. 2nd St., 270/684-3570, 10am-5:30pm Tues.-Sat.), an art gallery and handmade boutique. For a treat, make a stop at **Andria's Candies** (217 Allen St., 270/684-3733, www.chocolate-candy.com), which specializes in chocolate treats, such as bourbon balls, truffles, and creams, as well as brittles.

SPORTS AND RECREATION
Parks
The prime attractions at **Ben Hawes Park** (400 Booth Field Rd., 270/687-7134, www.owensboroparks.org, dawn-dusk daily) are the 18-hole regulation golf course and the 9-hole par-three course, but the park also has an archery range, four miles of mountain biking trails, softball fields, basketball courts, and playground and picnic areas. The remains of an early 20th-century deep coal mining operation are located on the park grounds and can be reached via a hiking trail.

Panther Creek Park (5160 Wayne Bridge Rd., www.daviesscountyparks.com, 8am-11pm daily, Apr.-Oct., 8am-5pm daily, Nov.-Mar.) offers multiple recreational options, including a stocked six-acre lake, baseball diamonds, a nine-hole disc golf course, volleyball and basketball courts, and playgrounds. The park also has seven hiking trails ranging in distance from 0.25 to 4 miles, some of which are wheelchair-accessible. Be sure to stroll out onto the swinging bridge over Panther Creek and climb the fire tower for a view of the surrounding countryside.

ACCOMMODATIONS
Chain hotels are the rule in Owensboro. The majority of these hotels are clustered along the Wendell Ford Bypass, close to where it intersects with Frederica Street. Although this intersection allows for easy access to downtown, the hotels aren't within walking distance of the city center. Your best options in this cluster are the

Hampton Inn (615 Salem Dr., 270/926-2006, www.hamptoninn.com, $119) and the **Fairfield Inn** (800 Salem Dr., 270/688-8887, www.marriott.com, $99), both of which offer standard clean rooms, wireless Internet, and complimentary breakfast.

To the west of the city are two other properties that rank highest among the chains in Owensboro. The **Sleep Inn** (51 Bon Harbor Hills, 270/691-6200, www.sleepinn.com, $99), which is located between the Botanical Gardens and Ben Hawes Park, has large, clean rooms with flat-screen TVs and wireless Internet, friendly staff, and complimentary breakfast. The **Holiday Inn Express** (3220 W. Parrish Ave., 270/685-2433, www.hiexpress.com, $105) has fresh rooms with all the expected amenities, including complimentary breakfast and free cookies in the evening.

During large festivals, hotel rooms can be hard to come by in Owensboro. Book as far in advance as possible. It can also be difficult to find a room in Owensboro during the girls' state softball championship in early June, which is almost always held in Owensboro.

FOOD
Bakeries
If you need a doughnut fix, **Rolling Pin Pastry Shop** (1129 E. 18th St., 270/683-8363, www.rollingpinpastryshop.com, 4am-5:30pm Mon.-Fri., 4am-2pm Sat., 5am-12:30pm Sun.) has got you covered. Each day, they make more than 20 types of fresh doughnuts, of both the yeast and cake varieties, although the chocolate Long John holds the title as the locals' favorite. Cakes and pastries are also available.

Coffeehouses
The Crème Coffee House (109 E. 2nd St., 270/683-7787, http://cremecoffeehouse.com, 7:30am-8pm Mon.-Thurs., 7:30am-10pm Fri., 9am-9pm Sat., $2.25-4.95) feels like a cool, urban coffeehouse although it's set in the relatively quiet downtown of Owensboro. The inside goes for fun and funky, while the back garden is a peaceful oasis. Drinks include

a selection of coffees and hot drinks, along with Italian sodas, smoothies, and more. The brownies are delicious and other pastries tempting. Bring a book, your laptop, or a friend and relax with a drink or nibble.

Barbecue

Everyone who comes to Owensboro must try the barbecue for at least one meal. It's not local law, per se, but it might as well be. Just as Kansas City, Texas, Carolina, and Memphis all have their own special styles and recipes, so does Owensboro. Here mutton—not beef, chicken, or pork—is the specialty, and it's served chopped or sliced after being cooked over an open-pit hickory fire for 12 hours or longer. Burgoo, a stew-like concoction of meat (often mutton, beef, and pork) and vegetables simmered all day, is another menu mainstay at Owensboro's barbecue joints.

Moonlite Bar-B-Q Inn (2840 W. Parrish Ave., 270/684-8143, www.moonlite.com, 9am-9pm Mon.-Thurs., 9am-9:30pm Fri.-Sat., 9am-3pm Sun.) is an Owensboro institution, famous for its buffet ($10.49 lunch Mon.-Sat., $13.99 dinner Mon.-Thurs. and lunch Sun., $17.79 dinner Fri.-Sat.), which features a full salad bar; nearly 10 side dishes; burgoo; a selection of chopped and sliced barbecue beef, pork, and mutton; and a dessert bar. Dinner plates are also available, but nearly everyone who visits Moonlite opts for the buffet. The large and very casual restaurant is consistently busy, and waits are common at prime meal times.

Although Moonlite is the most well known of Owensboro's barbecue restaurants, the local vote for best barbecue goes to **(Old Hickory Bar-B-Q** (338 Washington Ave., 270/926-9000, http://oldhickorybar-b-q.com, 9am-9pm Sun.-Thurs., 9am-10pm Fri.-Sat., $5.50-13.75). The sauce, which is smoky, tangy, and a little bit sweet, provides a distinctive taste to the pit-smoked barbecue. Although the pork, beef, and chicken are all excellent, the mutton is the go-to dish. In addition to the plates, which come with two sides, you can also order sandwiches ($2.50-4.20) and burgoo.

Contemporary American

Colby's Fine Food & Spirits (204 W. 3rd St., 270/685-4239, www.colbysfinefoodandspirits.com, 11am-9:30pm Mon.-Thurs., 11am-10:30pm Fri.-Sat., $7.99-20.99) serves up excellent portions of American food in a lovely atmosphere. Large arched windows and a checkerboard floor add ambience to the historic building, but the high-ceilinged restaurant can get noisy when busy. Menu favorites include gumbo, pork chops, prime rib, and a roast beef Manhattan. The separate bar area is a popular place to grab a drink and socialize. Those who beat the dinner rush by dining 4pm-6pm are rewarded with early bird specials.

Located in an exquisitely restored historic home, with multiple rooms upstairs and down serving as dining space, the **(Miller House Restaurant** (301 E. 5th St., 270/685-5878, www.themillerhouserestaurant.com, 11am-2pm and 5pm-10pm Tues.-Fri., 5pm-10pm Sat., 10am-2pm Sun., $7.99-27.99) is Owensboro's destination for special occasion dinners thanks to its ambience as well as its food. It is, however, just as welcoming to those looking for a tasty lunch or a dinner with friends. Sandwiches, such as the turkey and avocado or fried green tomato BLT, make for a great lunch and come with your choice of fruit, coleslaw, homemade chips, or hand-cut fries. Entrées range from jumbo lump crab cakes to pork chop with bourbon peach chutney to herb grilled chicken with squash casserole. The menu changes seasonally but is consistently delicious.

One of the newest restaurants in Owensboro, **Bill's** (420 Frederica St., 270/852-8120, www.atbills.com, lunch 11am-2pm Tues.-Fri., dinner 5pm-9pm Tues.-Thurs., 5pm-10pm Fri.-Sat., $17.50-23.50) is a chef-owned restaurant that has won over locals with such dinner options as grilled sea bass smothered with crawfish étouffée and duck fettuccini Bolognese. The lunch ($8-10) choices, which include a crab cake sandwich, a Thai chicken salad, and a daily special, make it a popular midday option as well. Service is excellent, and the decor understated, allowing the food to shine.

Italian

Niko's Italian Cuisine (220 E. Parrish Ave., 270/852-1618, www.nikositalian.com, 11am-9pm Mon.-Fri., 4pm-9pm Sat., $12.99-26.99) is a small, upscale Italian restaurant popular for date nights as well as business dinners. A wide choice of pastas, hand-cut and aged steaks, and extremely fresh and well-prepared seafood are the highlights of the menu, which also includes chicken, chops, and pizzas. Service is good, and the ambience is warm and intimate. The small bar area is usually bustling, and the restaurant can get a little bit loud when full. The lunch menu ($8.99-13.99) features pizzas and pastas, along with calzones, panini, signature sandwiches, and smaller portions of entrées.

Mediterranean

Classic Greek dishes like moussaka, spanikopita, and *youvetsi* (baked shrimp) are at the heart of the menu at **Famous Bistro** (102 W. 2nd St., 270/686-8202, www.famousbistro.com, 11am-9pm Mon.-Thurs., 11am-10pm Fri.-Sat., $17-28), a casual eatery located in a historic downtown building. Glass-topped tables are covered in snapshots, while the walls of the long, narrow restaurant are packed with photos and paintings. In addition to Greek specialties, the dinner menu also includes pastas and homemade pizzas, as well as fish, steak, and chicken dishes. At lunch ($5-12), a wide variety of hoagies, grinders, and pita sandwiches are offered along with pizzas, pastas, and Greek favorites.

INFORMATION AND SERVICES

Located downtown near RiverPark and the International Bluegrass Music Museum, the **Owensboro-Daviess County Convention & Visitors Bureau** (215 E. 2nd St., 270/926-1100, www.visitowensboro.com) can offer advice on how to make the most of your stay in Owensboro, so pop in and say hello or contact them in advance for help with planning.

The downtown **post office** (118 E. 4th St.) can take care of all your mailing needs 8am-4:30pm Monday-Friday.

GETTING THERE

Car

Looking at a map, you might find it hard to believe that Owensboro is one of Kentucky's largest cities, because it's not located on any major transportation aside from the Ohio River. Fortunately, a couple of major state and national highways mean most routes, although not necessarily fast, are fairly straightforward.

From Louisville, you have two options. You can take I-64 east through Indiana for 72 miles to southbound U.S. 231 (Exit 57A), which you'll follow for 33 miles to Owensboro (1.75 hours). Another option is to follow U.S. 60 the entire way from Louisville to Owensboro, a total of about 115 miles (2.25 hours). From Lexington, the most straightforward route is to take I-64 to U.S. 231, as you would do if you were coming from Louisville. This 186-mile trip takes about three hours.

To get from Paducah to Owensboro (2.5 miles), you'll again want to take U.S. 60, in this case traveling eastbound for 120 miles. On this route, you'll pass through Henderson, which is about 30 miles west of Owensboro on U.S. 60.

To travel from the Land Between the Lakes area to Owensboro (two hours), take the Wendell H. Ford Western Kentucky Parkway east to Exit 58, where you'll transfer to northbound U.S. 431. After about 35 miles, U.S. 431 will become downtown Owensboro's Frederica Street.

The Bowling Green to Owensboro route (1.25 hours) is another easy drive. Just drive north on KY 9007 for 75 miles, and you'll find yourself in Owensboro.

From Nashville (130 miles; two hours), take northbound I-65 to Bowling Green and proceed from there. From St. Louis (224 miles; 3.5 hours), take eastbound I-64 to southbound U.S. 231 (Exit 57 A). From Indianapolis (210 miles; 3 hours 20 minutes), take southbound I-65 to Louisville and proceed from there. From Cincinnati (205 miles; 3 hours 20 minutes), take southbound I-71 to Louisville and proceed from there.

Air

The nearest major airport is in Louisville. The small **Owensboro-Daviess County Airport** (Airport Rd., 270/685-4179, www. owb.net) does, however, offer a limited number of direct flights to Daytona and Orlando on Allegiant Airlines and to St. Louis on Cape Air.

GETTING AROUND

Many of Owensboro's major attractions are clustered together downtown and are easily accessed by foot. Free two-hour parking is available on most downtown streets, and it's not hard to find a spot.

For $0.50, the **River City Trolley** (270/687-8570, 9am-4pm Tues.-Sat., 1pm-4pm Sun.) will take you through downtown Owensboro and then take you south to the shopping centers. A trolley begins the route about every hour, and signs are posted at the many trolley stops around town providing estimated times of departure.

Vicinity of Owensboro

Owensboro is conducive to a number of day trips. The most popular one is to the small community of Rosine, birthplace of bluegrass music. Those looking for relaxation and fun in the sun can make a short drive southeast to Rough River Lake, a popular water sports destination.

ROSINE

On a farm ridge in Rosine, Bill Monroe took the music of generations, did something special to it, and became the father of bluegrass. If it weren't for him, Rosine might not make the map. As it stands, this tiny town is a mecca for bluegrass lovers. They come to pay tribute to Monroe at the house where he was raised and to hear the legacy of his music as it lives on at the weekly Rosine Barn Jamboree. There's not much here for those without an interest in bluegrass, but if you come, you just might find you had an interest you didn't know about. The beauty of bluegrass is not hard to find.

Jerusalem Ridge

Enter the white clapboard house on the farm known as **Jerusalem Ridge** (6210 U.S. 62E, 270/274-9183, 9am-5pm Mon.-Sat., 1pm-5pm Sun., free), and you might swear that you hear music. This house is where Bill Monroe, the

father of bluegrass, grew up. Here Monroe learned to play first the mandolin and then other instruments from his Uncle Pen and other family and neighbor musicians. Here he turned both the joys and the tribulations of his life into lyrics. Here bluegrass music was born. Tours of the house are given daily, the five rooms of the restored home filled with family heirlooms and memorabilia from Monroe. It's not unusual to find a Monroe devotee pickin' on the porch.

◖ Rosine Barn Jamboree

Every Friday night, a handful of bluegrass bands take to the stage at the **Rosine Barn Jamboree** (8205 U.S. 62E, 270/274-5552), the heart and soul of Rosine. By 5pm, folks begin to gather at the barn, claiming seats inside or setting up lawn chairs outside when the weather's nice and the doors are rolled open. If you've got an instrument, bring it, as there are always informal jam sessions going on and you might learn a new song or two. The feature entertainment starts at 7pm and rolls on late into the night. The jamboree is literally held in a weathered old barn, plain except for a painted sign and a bronze plaque honoring Bill Monroe, who made one of his last appearances here. Admission is free,

OWENSBORO

© THERESA DOWELL BLACKINTON

Jerusalem Ridge, the birthplace of bluegrass

though a plate is passed for donations during the show.

Bill Monroe's Gravesite

Bill Monroe's grave is marked with an obelisk, a marker outlining his many accomplishments, and a bench that lets you reflect on it all at the small Rosine cemetery, located near the Rosine Barn Jamboree on KY 1544. Other Monroe family members, including his legendary Uncle Pen, are buried nearby.

◖ Jerusalem Ridge Festival

For four days in early October, the **Jerusalem Ridge Festival** (www.jerusalemridgefestival.org) brings upwards of 40 bluegrass bands to Bill Monroe's homeplace for some amazing music. The main stage is located in a valley that forms a natural amphitheater just a few hundred yards from the homeplace. Bring your own lawn chairs and blankets, as there is no seating at this old-fashioned, family-friendly event. The festival goes 10am-10pm daily, with on-site food

vendors meaning you don't have to miss a song. Tickets are available for individual days or as three- or four-day passes and allow attendees to camp on the grounds and take a free tour of the home. As with any good bluegrass festival, impromptu jam sessions occur all the time. For honest-to-god bluegrass fans, the Jerusalem Ridge Festival is a must.

Accommodations

Being the tiny town that it is, Rosine doesn't have accommodation options to speak of. Many people opt to sleep in Owensboro and make the 45-minute trip to Rosine for the day.

Food

Sharing a parking lot with the jamboree is the **Rosine General Store** (8205 U.S. 62E, 270/274-7570, 6am-3pm Mon.-Sat., $2.95-5.95), where you can have a seat at one of the mismatched tables and enjoy a hamburger or other simple fare. You'll find lots of locals happy to chew the fat here at the town's meeting place.

Getting There and Around

Rosine is located about 35 miles (45 minutes) southeast of Owensboro. To get there from Owensboro, drive south on U.S. 231 for 25 miles, then turn left on U.S. 62, which will lead into Rosine and past all of the town's attractions. The road up to Jerusalem Ridge is a bit rough and winding, but unless you're driving a Corvette, you should be fine. Just take it slow and easy and be alert for oncoming traffic on the narrow road.

ROUGH RIVER LAKE

Rough River Lake, a 5,100-acre manmade reservoir, is a playground for anglers and recreational boaters. Managed by the U.S. Army Corps of Engineers, the lake is surrounded by recreational areas that allow camping and offer access to the water via boat ramps. A few also have beaches. The state park is at the center of the lake's action.

Rough River Dam State Resort Park

Located on the waterfront in the area surrounding the dam, **Rough River Dam State Resort Park** (450 Lodge Rd., Falls of Rough, 270/257-2311, http://parks.ky.gov, dawn-dusk daily, free) focuses on helping visitors enjoy the water. A marina invites guests to get out on the lake through use of their ramp or through the rental of a pontoon boat. Boat tours of Rough River Lake are also offered daily during peak season on the *Lady of the Lake* ($8 adults, $3 youth). The lake can be enjoyed from the shore thanks to a public beach and plenty of great places for casting a line.

A mini-golf course and tennis, volleyball, and shuffleboard courts provide additional recreational opportunities. Hikers will want to check out the one-mile Lake Ridge Trail, which offers lake views and bird-watching opportunities, as well as the 0.7-mile looping Folklore Trail, which goes past a pioneer cabin.

Accommodations

At Rough River Dam State Resort Park (450 Lodge Rd., Falls of Rough, 270/257-2311,

http://parks.ky.gov), **Rough River Dam Lodge** ($119.95) offers 40 rooms, all of which have double beds and private balconies or patios with views of the river. For more privacy or if you have a bigger group, consider renting one of the 17 two-bedroom **cottages** ($149.95-229.95) located near the lake in wooded surroundings. Both the lodge and the cabins are clean, but furnishings and decor are dated. The **campground** (Apr.-Oct., $15-23) has 51 tent sites and 34 sites with hookups. Showers, restrooms, laundry facilities, and playground areas are also located at the campground.

For those looking for a more upscale experience, consider the options at **The Falls Resort and Golf Club** (57 Jennie Green Rd., Falls of Rough, 800/504-0906, www.thefallsresortandgolfclub.com). Mahogany beds and baroque-style furnishings give character to the nine luxurious rooms in the Green Mansion, an exactingly restored home from the early 1800s. A full breakfast is served daily, and baked goods are offered in the afternoon. The resort also offers cabins that have a rustic appearance but are very well equipped with a master bedroom with queen bed, loft with two double beds, living room, kitchen, bathroom, and a porch with lake views.

Food

Grayson's Landing Restaurant (Rough River Dam State Resort Park, 450 Lodge Rd., Falls of Rough, 270/257-2311, http://parks.ky.gov, 7am-10am, 11:30am-3pm, and 4:30pm-8pm daily, $5.95-13.95), located in the Rough River Dam Lodge, serves three meals a day in a dining room with views of the lake. The specialty is catfish, although a buffet is offered daily along with a menu of Southern-style entrées.

Getting There and Around

Rough River Lake is located about 40 miles (one hour) southeast of Owensboro. To reach the state park from Owensboro, drive 30 miles on eastbound KY 54. Turn left on KY 110, and drive eight miles to the intersection with KY 79, where you'll turn left. After 1.5 miles, you'll reach the park entrance.

Henderson

Almost directly west of Owensboro on another bend of the Ohio River, Henderson is a growing city with sights and events that attract travelers in their own right, although many choose to visit the city on a combined trip with Owensboro. Some of the city's biggest draws revolve around famous names that have called Henderson home, including renowned naturalist John James Audubon and father of the blues, W. C. Handy.

SIGHTS
John James Audubon State Park
Built by the Civilian Conservation Corps, **John James Audubon State Park** (3100 U.S. 41, 270/826-2247, http://parks.ky.gov, dawn-dusk daily, free) honors the famous naturalist and artist who called Henderson home from 1810-1819. A museum (10am-5pm daily, mid-Mar.-Dec., Thurs.-Sun., Jan.-mid-Mar., $4 adults, $2.50 youth 6-12, $10 family) chronicling

Audubon's life and work is the centerpiece of the park and contains many spectacular pieces, including original works by Audubon, a four-volume edition of *Birds of America,* and one of only three known lithograph stones from *Quadrupeds of North America.* The attached Nature Center keeps the focus on birds, offering an observation room for birders and exhibitions about bird behavior. The park also offers a nine-hole golf course, tennis courts, a fishing lake, multiple picnic and playground areas, and a nature preserve crisscrossed by over six miles of hiking trails.

Ruby Moon Vineyard & Winery
Since opening its doors to the public in 2006, **Ruby Moon Vineyard & Winery** (9566 U.S. 41, 270/830-7660, www.rubymoonwinery.com, 11am-6pm Tues.-Sat.) has continued to grow. From their eight varieties of grapes grown on three acres as well as some other local fruit,

museum at John James Audubon State Park

© THERESA DOWELL BLACKINTON

Ruby Moon produces a selection of red, white, and fruit wines. Visitors to the vineyard are treated to an intimate experience, with tastings ($2 or free with purchase) served by the owners themselves and the vineyards open for strolls. An inviting patio overlooking the vines is a perfect place to enjoy a bottle of wine, and you're welcome to bring a picnic. During harvest season (five to eight weeks starting in early August), volunteers are welcome to join in the work. A breakfast is served between 6 and 6:30am, with harvesting commencing afterward.

Walking Tours

The city of Henderson has created two walking tours that allow for a closer look at the city. The **Audubon Sculpture Walking Tour** leads participants around downtown on a tour of 13 bronze sculptures depicting birds as painted by John James Audubon. The **Historic Walking Tour** highlights 36 buildings in downtown Henderson, with a brochure providing information about each building's history and architecture. Free brochures for each tour can be picked up at the welcome center (101 N. Water St., 270/826-3128, www.hendersonky.org, 10am-5pm Mon.-Fri.) or downloaded from www.hendersonky.org.

FESTIVALS AND EVENTS
W. C. Handy Blues & Barbecue Festival

The **W. C. Handy Blues & Barbecue Festival** (www.handyblues.org) celebrates the Father of the Blues, who spent a decade in Henderson and wrote in his autobiography that he found his inspiration for writing blues songs while living there. The weeklong festival in mid-June is packed with free blues concerts, with headliners as well as fans coming from around the country. Local barbecue masters serve up their goods, fueling the festival with ribs, pork, chicken, and more.

Bluegrass in the Park Folklife Festival

Enjoy two days of music set against the backdrop of the Ohio River at the free **Bluegrass in the Park Folklife Festival** (www.bluegrassintheparkfestival.com), held in mid-August. On Saturday, the folklife part of the festival occurs, celebrating local cultures with displays and events. Also accompanying the music festival are a disc golf tournament, tennis tournament, pole vault event, 5k run/walk, and the Pickin' and Pedalin' Bicycle Tour.

SPORTS AND RECREATION
Parks

Located on the riverfront at the former site of John James Audubon's grist mill, **Audubon Mill Park** (Water and 2nd Sts.) is a great place to have a picnic lunch, go for a stroll, or relax and catch a breath of fresh air. The neighboring **Riverfront Fountains** are the place to be when the mercury rises. Children, teens, and even a few adults love to splash about in the fountains, which vary in size and strength, but are consistently refreshing.

Biking

Cyclists will want to check out the four bike routes detailed at www.hendersonky.org. The routes range in distance 12-62 miles. The **Pickin' and Pedalin' Bicycle Tour** (www.pickinandpedalin.com), held in conjunction with the Bluegrass in the Park Folklife Festival, is a fun day of cycling through the countryside of Henderson County, with supported routes of 12, 22, 40, or 65 miles available.

Spectator Sports

Ellis Park (3300 U.S. 41, 270/826-0608, www.ellisparkracing.com) offers live thoroughbred racing Friday-Sunday July-Labor Day on the longest dirt and turf tracks in the state. General admission is free, although those who can't take the heat can upgrade to air-conditioned clubhouse or sky theater seats. Races are simulcast at Ellis Park year-round with off-site wagering available.

ACCOMMODATIONS
$50-100

An 1895 Victorian mansion, the **L&N Bed and**

OWENSBORO

OWENSBORO

Breakfast (319 N. Main St., 270/831-1100, www.lnbbky.com, $85), which is located next to a railroad bridge, originally housed railroad employees. Its dozen rooms now host guests, who can stay in one of four bedrooms, each with private bath, TV, and wireless Internet access. Choose from queen, double, or twin beds. Family heirlooms, antiques, and railroad memorabilia decorate the house. Hosts Norris and Mary Elizabeth live next door, giving guests full run of the B&B.

Outfitted with authentic 19th-century furniture, **Victorian Quarters Bed and Breakfast** (109 Clay St., 270/831-2778, www.victorianquartersbb.com, $85-95) transports guests to the home's mid-1800s heyday. The Italianate mansion overlooks the Ohio River and has wonderful window views. Choose from four large rooms, each with private bath, kitchen area, and sitting room.

For a romantic getaway, consider the Sunset Suite at **Ruby Moon Vineyard & Winery** (9566 U.S. 41, 270/830-7660, www.rubymoonwinery.com, $89), which features a private deck overlooking the vineyards. The suite is well-equipped with a queen bedroom, living room with flat-screen TV and satellite service, a kitchenette area, and bathroom. Continental breakfast is provided.

John James Audubon State Park (3100 U.S. 41, 270/826-2247, http://parks.ky.gov, $80-160) rents five one-bedroom cottages and one two-bedroom cottage. The cottages are located near the lake and open year-round.

Campgrounds

The **John James Audubon State Park campground** (3100 U.S. 41, 270/826-2247, http://parks.ky.gov, $21-27), which is very green and natural, is open spring through fall. The campground has 66 sites with utility hookups and 17 sites specifically for tents. Showers and restrooms are available.

FOOD
Barbecue

Locals pack the handful of tables and booths at **J&B Barbecue** (48 S. Holloway St.,

270/830-0033, 10:30am-6pm Tues.-Fri., 10:30am-1pm Sat.), run by two once-retired Henderson men with a passion for barbecue. The chicken gets rave reviews, but the ribs and pork are also excellent. Plates ($6.50) are enormous, overflowing with your meat of choice and two sides. (Try the potato salad.) Barbecue sandwiches are also available. Service is fast and friendly in this small, casual favorite.

Contemporary American

◖ **Commonwealth Kitchen + Bar** (108 2nd St., 270/212-2133, www.ckbhenderson.com, 11am-10pm Mon.-Sat., $5.95-12.95) is a unique addition to the Henderson dining scene, serving contemporary American dishes tapas style. You'll want to order a number of plates to share; consider the lamb meatballs, the pork belly hash, and the Brussels sprouts. An impressive list of signature cocktails, beers, and wines complements the food.

INFORMATION AND SERVICES

Located next to Audubon Mill Park on the waterfront, the **Henderson Welcome Center** (101 N. Water St., 270/830-9707, www.hendersonky.org, 10am-5pm Mon.-Fri.) can set you up with all the information you need for a visit to the area.

GETTING THERE AND AROUND

Henderson is located along the Ohio River, just south of Evansville, Indiana, and directly west of Owensboro. To reach Henderson from Owensboro, drive east on U.S. 60 for 30 miles (45 minutes). The Pennyrile Parkway provides the most direct access to areas south of Henderson. Hopkinsville is 75 miles (1 hour 10 minutes) directly south on the parkway, while the Land Between the Lakes area (1.25 hours) can be reached by taking the Pennyrile Parkway 44 miles to southbound I-69, which you'll take for an additional 40 miles to the top of the lakes. U.S. 60 provides the most direct route to Paducah, which is nearly 100 miles (two hours) southwest.

STOP THAT CAR! HIGHLIGHTS OF UNION AND CRITTENDEN COUNTIES

Primarily rural, Union and Crittenden Counties are located in between Henderson and Paducah on the banks of the Ohio River. Although most people drive right through, there are a couple of unique offerings in these counties that are worth stopping for.

CAMP BRECKINRIDGE

Few Americans are aware of the fact that Axis POWs were held throughout the United States during World War II, but **Camp Breckinridge** (1116 N. Village Rd., Morganfield, 270/389-4420, www.breckinridge-arts.org, 10am-3pm Tues.-Fri., 10am-4pm Sat., 1pm-4pm Sun., $3 adults, $1 youth) is doing its best to bring that part of history to light. Home to 4,000 POWs from 1942 to 1945, Camp Breckinridge now displays memorabilia related to this era and allows visitors to view a stunning collection of murals painted by the prisoners onto the walls of the NCO club. Additionally, the museum hosts a wide variety of other military artifacts because the camp was also used as an infantry training site during World War II and the Korean War. Anyone with an interest in history will find a visit to Camp Breckinridge to be utterly fascinating.

CRITTENDEN COUNTY AMISH COMMUNITY

More than 500 Amish call the hills of Crittenden County home. The majority of them live and work in the area north of Marion and south of the river, between KY 91 and KY 645. Drive through the country roads in this region, and you might come across them riding in their horse-and-buggies or working on their farms. Some of the local Amish make and sell cabinetry, furniture, and baked goods at small stores or roadside stands that you're welcome to stop at. Signs direct you to these businesses as you travel down the various back roads, or you can download a map from **www.marionkentucky.org** if you want to hit as many as you can. Please respect Amish beliefs and do not take photos of Amish people's faces. Avoid visiting on Sunday, their day of worship.

CAVE-IN-ROCK FERRY

While touring the Amish area of Crittenden County, a fun detour is to go north from Marion on KY 91 to the river. Here, the **Cave-In-Rock ferry** (618/289-4599, 6am-9:30pm), an old-fashioned ferry that accommodates around 10 cars, transports people and automobiles across the river free of charge. Take the short ride just for the nostalgic fun of it.

© THERESA DOWELL BLACKINTON

the Cave-in-Rock ferry

OWENSBORO

OWENSBORO

Paducah

The most western of Kentucky's cities, Paducah deceives people into thinking it's bigger than it is. Although the population of Paducah is just over 25,000, this city has a lot going on. It's home to top-notch museums, including a quilt museum that draws art lovers from around the nation and even some international visitors, a revitalized downtown that always seems to have something going on, an inspiring art scene, and a fine selection of restaurants serving good food. Physically, Paducah is centered around the Ohio River, with barges and riverboats never far from sight. Lying near Kentucky's western border and not all that far from its southern border, Paducah is close to Illinois, Missouri, and Tennessee, but despite this proximity maintains a distinctly Kentucky identity. A unique place, Paducah is a city on the rise, and despite the fact that it's a long way from much of the state, it's a city worth seeking out.

SIGHTS
◖ The National Quilt Museum

Think of quilts and you probably think of a bedcover at grandma's house. Visit the **National Quilt Museum** (215 Jefferson St., 270/442-8856, www.quiltmuseum.org, 10am-5pm Mon.-Sat., year-round, also 1pm-5pm Sun., Mar.-Nov., $11 adults, $10 seniors, $5 students, free youth 12 and under), however, and your ideas will be turned upside-down. In more than 30,000 square feet of gallery space, contemporary quilts of competition quality demonstrating cutting-edge techniques are on display. The main gallery displays about 30 quilts from the museum's collection at a time as well as a selection of miniatures, while the two side galleries host rotating exhibits that change frequently. One of the most popular annual exhibitions displays the winners and finalists from the museum's New Quilts from an Old

The National Quilt Museum

© THERESA DOWELL BLACKINTON

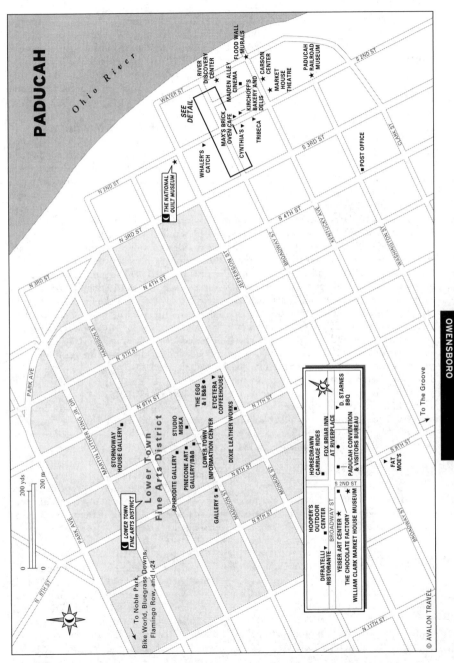

PADUCAH

Ohio River

WATER ST

SEE DETAIL

RIVER DISCOVERY CENTER
MAIDEN ALLEY CINEMA
FLOOD WALL MURALS
KIRCHOFF'S BAKERY AND DELIS
CARSON CENTER
MARKET HOUSE THEATRE
PADUCAH RAILROAD MUSEUM
MAX'S BRICK OVEN CAFE
CYNTHIA'S
TRIBECA
WHALER'S CATCH

THE NATIONAL QUILT MUSEUM

N 2ND ST
N 3RD ST
N 4TH ST
S 2ND ST
S 3RD ST
S 4TH ST
CLARK ST

POST OFFICE

JEFFERSON ST
BROADWAY ST
KENTUCKY AVE
WASHINGTON ST

PARK AVE

N 3RD ST
HARRISON ST
N 5TH ST
N 6TH ST

Lower Town Fine Arts District

LOWER TOWN FINE ARTS DISTRICT

STORNOWAY HOUSE GALLERY
STUDIO MISKA
THE EGG & I B&B
ETCETERA COFFEEHOUSE
APHRODITE GALLERY
PINECONE ART GALLERY/B&B
LOWER TOWN INFORMATION CENTER
DIXIE LEATHER WORKS
GALLERY 5

MARTIN LUTHER KING JR. DR
MADISON ST
MONROE ST
N 7TH ST
N 8TH ST
N 9TH ST

To Noble Park, Bike World, Bluegrass Downs, Flamingo Row, and I-24

200 yds
200 m

HORSEDRAWN CARRIAGE RIDES
FOX BRIAR INN AT RIVERPLACE
D. STARNES BBQ
PADUCAH CONVENTION & VISITORS BUREAU

HOOPER'S OUTDOOR CENTER
DIFRATELLI RISTORANTE
YEISER ART CENTER
THE CHOCOLATE FACTORY
WILLIAM CLARK MARKET HOUSE MUSEUM

BROADWAY ST
S 2ND ST

FAT MOE'S

To The Groove

S 9TH ST
BROADWAY ST
N 11TH ST
WASHINGTON ST
N 8TH ST

OWENSBORO

© AVALON TRAVEL

Favorite contest. For this contest, quilt artists reinterpret a traditional quilt pattern. You'll be blown away by what they come up with, and I promise you'll never again look at quilts as old-fashioned or boring. Before you leave, be sure to seek out the wood quilt. If you don't believe it's made of wood (it's that good), peek behind it for confirmation.

River Discovery Center

The highly interactive **River Discovery Center** (117 S. Water St., 270/575-9958, www.river-discoverycenter.org, 9:30am-5pm Mon.-Sat., year-round, also 1pm-5pm Sun., Apr.-Nov., $7 adults, $6.50 seniors, $5 youth 3-12) relays the story of rivers, focusing on the four rivers—the Ohio, Tennessee, Mississippi, and Cumberland—that shape life in Paducah. The center features models of boats, a scale-model reenactment of a flood, and displays that demonstrate how hydroelectric dams and locks work, along with lots of audio stations and other exhibits. A 17-minute film titled *Rivers: Heart of Our Nation* discusses the importance of rivers both then and now. Be sure to check out the simulator, which allows you to captain a tugboat, Coast Guard boat, or pleasure boat down the river, and the camera footage that shows the most recent 24 hours of life on the river. The center also pays homage to the fact that it's located in downtown's oldest building with an upstairs furnished to look the way it would have when lived in by a banker in 1843.

William Clark Market House Museum

Located in the 1905 market house where butchers used to sell their meats, the **Market House Museum** (121 S. 2nd St., 270/443-7759, www.markethousemuseum.com, noon-4pm Tues.-Sat., $4 adults, $1 youth 6-11) is packed with artifacts that relay the history of Paducah and the surrounding region. Among the more interesting exhibits are a display of original linen and elderberry ink maps of the city drawn by William Clark (of Lewis & Clark), who founded the city; a collection of personal belongings from Paducah resident and Vice President Alben Barkley; and furniture used by the Lincolns in the White House and General Grant when he stayed in Paducah during the Civil War. The gingerbread woodwork on the first floor was taken from the closed List Drug Store and is regarded as one of the best examples of this handcraft in the South.

Paducah Railroad Museum

Run by the local chapter of the National Railway Historical Society, the **Paducah Railroad Museum** (2nd and Washington Sts., 270/519-7377, http://paducahrr.org, 1pm-4pm Wed.-Fri., 10am-4pm Sat., $5 adults, $2 youth 12 and under) shares the joy of trains with visitors. Inside the museum, you'll find a re-created depot waiting room, freight office, and centralized traffic control office, all set up using authentic pieces from closed railroad offices. The museum also contains a number of railroad repair vehicles, but the real highlight of a visit is the chance to observe the model train layout that takes up an entire room. Club members are almost always on-site working on the layout and are happy to talk to visitors about the model and let them take the train for a run down the tracks.

Flood Wall Murals

A series of more than 50 murals decorate Paducah's **flood wall** (Water St., between Jefferson and Washington Sts.) depicting important events in the city's history. Murals portray Native American life, the Lewis and Clark expedition, the steamboat and river industry, African American heritage, the opening of the city's uranium enrichment plant, and other significant events. A plaque in front of each mural describes the image.

Yeiser Art Center

Located at one end of the Market House, the **Yeiser Art Center** (200 Broadway, 270/442-2453. www.theyeiser.org, 10am-5pm Tues.-Sat., free) hosts visual art exhibitions that change every six weeks. Exhibitions are produced by the center and are also received on loan from museums and traveling shows.

LOWER TOWN'S ART STUDIOS

The most rewarding part of visiting Paducah's Lower Town is interacting with the artists who call the neighborhood home. While not all studios have galleries, many do, and to make the most of your tour, you should plan to visit during peak gallery hours. The following galleries are among the most consistently open, and the artists behind these establishments are eager to engage with customers, so don't be shy. Although art buyers are always appreciated, browsers are greeted just as warmly.

The hours for each gallery are not set in stone. Most galleries have no staff beyond the artist, so if the artist is out of town or otherwise occupied, the gallery may be closed. Additionally, many galleries welcome visitors outside of set hours, opening their doors whenever the artist is around. If you're dead set on visiting a specific gallery, you should call in advance to confirm opening hours.

- **Aphrodite Gallery** (503 N. 7th St., 270/444-6871, noon-5pm Fri.-Sat.): Jeweler Julie Shaw creates wearable art that is built around semiprecious stones and metals with remarkable patinas. Her work has been included in some of the nation's most exclusive jewelry shows. In addition to displaying and selling Shaw's jewelry, Aphrodite Gallery also sells jewelry made from other artists as well as some photography, paintings, and ceramics.

- **Dixie Leather Works** (306 N. 7th St., 270/442-1058, www.dlwleathers.com, 10am-5pm Mon.-Sat.): Famed for their authentic historical leather reproductions, Dixie Leather Works has produced artwork for movies, museums, and reenactments. They don't limit themselves to reproductions, however, but also make unique trunks and luggage, belts, bags, and other accessories and decorative items.

- **Gallery 5** (803 Madison St., 270/444-2020, www.renzulliart.com, 11am-5pm Fri.-Sat.): Artist Bill Renzulli specializes in architectural landscapes, painting them using watercolors, pastels, and acrylics, depicting them through clay mono printing, and constructing them in three-dimensional shadowboxes. Cityscapes, barns and other rural architecture, and images from his ancestral homeland of Italy are popular subjects. Visitors are welcome to check out the studio and see any works in progress.

- **Pinecone Art Gallery** (421 N. 7th St., 270/443-1433, www.char-downs.com, 2pm-6pm Fri.): Char Downs, artist and gallery owner, exudes energy and creativity, welcoming visitors to explore the gallery that is also her studio. Much of her art is in the form of mixed media on paper, but she also works in photography, canvas, wood sculpture, ceramic tile, mural, and print. Her gallery often hosts exhibitions from other artists, and Char also teaches art classes.

- **Stornoway House Gallery** (513 N. 6th St., 270/444-9446, noon-5pm Wed.-Sat., 1pm-4pm Sun.): Husband-and-wife team Wil and Carolyn MacKay use their gallery to display their own artwork as well as to sell the fine art, crafts, and decorative items of others. Wil specializes in oil painting, with many of his works depicting coastal scenes from Cape Ann, Massachusetts, or pastoral scenes from Wisconsin, both places he lived before relocating to Paducah.

- **Studio Miska** (627 Madison St., 270/442-5266, www.fredafairchild.com, noon-5pm Fri.-Sat.): A former costume designer, artist Freda Fairchild now focuses primarily on printmaking, although she occasionally ventures into textile art and other mediums. For those unfamiliar with printmaking, she'll happily teach you about the process and explain how she makes her art, although she leaves its interpretation up to you. Her work is often layered and full of arresting images.

OWENSBORO

OWENSBORO

© THERESA DOWELL BLACKINTON

art studio in Lower Town

Subject and genre vary greatly, and shows can range from solo exhibitions to juried shows. Annual events include a fiber show during Quilt Week and the Photo Paducah competition, which draws entries from around the globe and is one of the most prestigious photo contests in the south-central United States.

Downtown Walking Tour

Get acquainted with downtown on a cell phone walking tour. The free tour brochure, which can be picked up at the tourism office or downloaded from their website, has a map of sites and instructions on how to use your cell phone to get information on each site. All you have to do is dial a phone number and enter the audio stop number of the site you're at, and you'll be treated to a brief history of the site.

Other free walking tour brochures available at the visitors center include a tour of Civil War sites, a tour of historic churches, and a tour of Upper Town, a historic African American area.

Lower Town Fine Arts District

The **Lower Town Fine Arts District** (www.paducahalliance.org/lowertown-arts-district) is an ongoing experiment that was begun in 2000 as an attempt to turn Paducah's oldest neighborhood into an artist haven and to drive economic growth through the arts. Through the Artist Relocation Program, artists from around the nation are invited and encouraged through financial and cultural incentives to move to Paducah to live and work surrounded by other artists. Despite some growing pains as the community tries to really figure out who it is and how it best works, Lower Town is still a remarkable idea and a visit to the neighborhood is highly recommended. Not all artists have galleries open to the public, and not all galleries are open at all times, but on any trip, you should be able to see a variety of work and interact with multiple artists. Look for flags outside the galleries that indicate they are open. To see as much art as possible, visit on the second Saturday of the month, when many galleries are open until 8pm. For more information, check with the **Lower Town information center** (402 N. 7th St., 270/408-4030, noon-4pm Thurs.-Sat.), housed in an old Texaco station.

Purple Toad Winery

One of Kentucky's youngest wineries, **Purple Toad Winery** (4275 Old U.S. 45, 270/554-0010, www.purpletoadwinery.net, 10:30am-6:30pm Mon.-Thurs., 10:30am-8pm Fri.-Sat., free) opened in summer 2009 and immediately set about winning awards for their wine. The Paducah Blue made with Concord grapes is particularly popular. The winery invites visitors to wander through the vineyard and then savor the goods in the tasting room.

ENTERTAINMENT AND EVENTS
Bars

Nightclubs and dedicated bars have often struggled in Paducah, with many people opting to drink and socialize at restaurants instead, but there are a few places worth checking out. One popular spot that is more bar than restaurant is **Fat Moe's** (902 Broadway, 270/442-6637, 11am-1am Sun.-Thurs., 11am-3am Fri.-Sat.). The live bands and dance floor make Fat Moe's a happening weekend spot. If you want to dance to the latest music, head to **The Groove** (2223 Bridge St., 270/443-4117, 7pm-3am Thurs.-Sat., $5 cover), where the DJ spins hip-hop tunes for a party crowd.

Movie Theaters

Maiden Alley Cinema (112 Maiden Alley, 270/441-7007, www.maidenalleycinema.com) brings independent, foreign, and classic films to Paducah, showing them on the big screen in a modern, stadium-seating theater. Films are shown on Friday at 7pm and 9pm; Saturday at 4pm, 7pm, and 9pm; and Sunday at 4pm and 7pm. The theater also hosts a children's film series, a chick flick series, and other regularly occurring events.

Performing Arts

Opened in 2004, the **Carson Center** (100 Kentucky Ave., 270/450-4444, www.

thecarsoncenter.org) is the main performing arts center for the surrounding area. The center hosts a Broadway series as well as concerts, ballets, comedy acts, and other performances. Tickets can be purchased through the box office (10am-5pm Mon.-Fri. and two hours before performances). Additionally, the **Paducah Symphony Orchestra** (270/444-0065, www.paducahsymphony.org) calls the Carson Center home, playing a full season of concerts at the center each year. Tickets for the orchestra can be purchased at the door or in advance at the box office (2101 Broadway, 9am-5pm Mon.-Fri., 10am-2pm day of performance).

Passion for and support of local arts is not restricted to visual art; it also encompasses performing arts, as witnessed by the success of **Market House Theatre** (141 Kentucky Ave., 270/444-6828, www.mhtplay.com). This community theater, which has been filling the house for productions of its plays and musicals since the 1960s, has received national recognition. Although the actors are not professional, many have voice and theater

OWENSBORO

© THERESA DOWELL BLACKINTON

Market House Theatre

backgrounds, and the performances are always enjoyable. Attending a performance is a great way to get a taste for the community. Tickets can be purchased online, over the phone, or from the box office (132 Market House Sq., noon-5pm Tues.-Fri. or beginning 1.5 hours before a show).

Festivals and Events

Held annually in late April, the **American Quilter's Society Quilt Week** (www.americanquilter.com) brings so many quilt enthusiasts to Paducah that it effectively doubles the city's population. Quilt artists from around the nation and world enter their best works in one of the most prestigious competitions of its type, and festival attendees are invited to view the hundreds of quilts on display, attend workshops, and shop for quilting supplies from a vendor mall. Beyond the festival, the entire city gets in on the event, with textile exhibits at many galleries and special events and demonstrations at the National Quilt Museum.

The **Lower Town Arts and Music Festival** (www.lowertownamf.com) celebrates the cultural wealth of the region with a juried art show and music festival over three days in mid-May. It's a great time to explore Lower Town and to witness its unique character.

More than 50 barbecue teams converge on Paducah in late September for the chance to be named grand champion of **Barbecue on the River** (www.bbqontheriver.org). The three-day festival offers attendees the invitation to indulge in as much barbecue as they can handle while enjoying live blues, jazz, bluegrass, and rock music.

The **River's Edge International Film Festival** (www.riversedgefilmfestival.com) is a four-day festival celebrating independent films entered for judging in the categories of narrative, documentary, animation, and experimental film. The early November festival allows moviegoers to enjoy the films at a variety of venues and also to meet and mingle with filmmakers.

On summer Saturday evenings, Paducah invites residents and guests alike to enjoy the outdoors at **Live on Broadway** (6pm-9pm Sat., Memorial Day-Labor Day). Broadway between Water and 5th Streets is closed to traffic while bands play, live performers entertain, and people mingle, dance, take carriage rides, and enjoy the evening. Many nearby businesses stay open late to allow for shopping and dining.

SHOPPING

Paducah's bustling downtown is a great place to get in a bit of retail therapy, especially if it's antiques you're after. The 200 block of Broadway is full of great stores to peruse, with antiques store neighboring antiques store. A non-antiques 200 block favorite is **Hooper's Outdoor Center** (219 Broadway, 270/443-0019, www.hoopers.net, 10am-8pm Mon.-Sat.), a sporting and outdoor gear store helping to bring retail shopping back downtown.

Second Street offers another excellent set of stores to browse, including gift shops, arts and crafts stores, and antiques stores. Fuel your bargain hunting with a treat from **The Chocolate Factory** (109 S. 2nd St., 270/442-5222, www.chocolatefactoryky.com, 9am-5pm Mon.-Fri., 10am-4pm Sat.), where you'll have a hard time choosing between the fudges and the many varieties of gourmet chocolates.

Art lovers will, of course, want to head to Lower Town, where art can be purchased at each of the individual galleries open to the public.

SPORTS AND RECREATION
Parks

Noble Park (2801 Park Ave.) supports just about any recreational activity you can think of. Visitors to the park can play basketball, baseball, or tennis; throw a round of horseshoes; go for a dip in the outdoor pool; cast a line in the stocked five-acre lake; show off their skills at the skate park; or enjoy a picnic and time on the playground. The **Greenway Trail,** a 10-foot-wide, multi-use trail that will link five of Paducah's parks when finished, has a trailhead here. A one-mile section currently links Noble Park with Stuart Nelson Park, which features a disc golf course.

OWENSBORO

Biking

Bike World (809 Joe Clifton Dr., 270/442-0751, www.bikeworldky.com, 10am-8pm Mon.-Fri., 10am-4:30pm Sat.) is a great place to get information on the local biking scene, as well as to purchase any gear you might need. The shop organizes both morning and evening weekday rides. Bike World also sponsors the Mis-Aligned Minds Bike Tour in late September, which features 20-, 45-, 60-, and 100-mile routes through the countryside around Paducah, and a free, minimally supported 108-mile round-trip ride across Kentucky held in August.

Golf

If you're looking for a good walk spoiled, as Mark Twain once described the game of golf, **Paxton Park Golf Course** (841 Berger Rd., 270/444-9514, www.paxtonpark.com) was recognized by *Golf Digest* as one of its best places to play. The par-71 course is built around mature trees and winding creeks.

Water Sports

Access to the Ohio River is available downtown, with a boat ramp at the foot of Broadway. This area of the river sees a lot of barge traffic, so boaters should be experienced with river navigation before putting in.

Spectator Sports

Bluegrass Downs (150 Downs Dr., 270/444-7117, www.caesars.com/bluegrassdowns, free) hosts harness racing starting at 2pm Friday-Sunday in June. Simulcast racing is offered at Bluegrass Downs during the rest of the year.

The 0.375-mile high-banked oval dirt track at **Paducah International Raceway** (4445 Shemwell Ln., 270/898-7469, www.paducahracing.net, $10 adults, free youth 12 and under) hosts late-model stock car and sprint car races on Friday nights April-October. Races at Paducah International Raceway, which is co-owned by NASCAR stars Dale Earnhardt Jr., Kenny Schrader, and Tony Perry, take place at 7pm, but the grandstands open at 5pm and the pit gates open at 3pm, and fans like to gather

early. The track's most prestigious race is the USA World 50, which is held in late August.

ACCOMMODATIONS

In addition to the local accommodations listed in this book, more than 30 chain hotels are located in the Paducah area, primarily off of I-24 at Exits 3 and 4. Better choices include the **Drury Suites** (2930 James Sanders Blvd., 270/441-0024, www.druryhotels.com, $109.99), **Holiday Inn Express** (3994 Hinkleville Rd., 270/442-8874, www.hiexpress.com, $95), **Residence Inn** (3900 Coleman Crossing Cir., 270/444-3966, www.marriott.com, $139), and **Hampton Inn** (3901 Coleman Crossing Cir., 270/442-0200, www.hamptoninn.com, $109).

Lower Town Arts District

Artists and art lovers will want to consider staying in the Lower Town Arts District. A number of artists offer a room or two in their homes/studios, and standalone accommodation is also available.

 The Egg & I Bed and Breakfast (335 N. 6th St., 270/443-6323, www.eggandiarts.com, $95) offers a 1,200-square-foot suite with a living area and bedroom separated from each other by a fireplace, as well as an additional bedroom. In total, the suite has a queen bed, double bed, and double sofa bed. The two bedrooms share a bathroom with large walk-in shower. Cable television and wireless Internet are available in the suite, which is decorated with artwork, of course, and antiques.

Artist Char Downs, owner of Pinecone Art Studio, offers a room right off of her studio. The room, which is fully accessible, has a double bed, private bathroom, microwave and refrigerator, and private entrance, which opens onto a peaceful patio garden with koi pond. Guests of **Pinecone Bed and Breakfast** (421 N. 7th St., 270/443-1433, www.chardowns.com, $85) can arrange for art classes with Char.

Downtown

Set yourself up in the heart of the action with a

OWENSBORO

suite at ◖ **Fox Briar Inn at Riverplace** (100C Broadway, 270/443-7004, www.foxbriarinn. com, $145-350), located in a historic building on downtown's most popular street and just a block from the river. Each of the suites is set up like an individual apartment with living room, full kitchen, bathroom, and washer/dryer. The smallest has 950 square feet of space, while others boast well more than 1,000 square feet, and the grandest is a whopping 4,000 square feet. Styles vary, but exposed brick walls, hardwood floors, and river views are offered in many of the rooms.

Nearby Countryside

If you're looking for a true escape, check into **Fox Briar Farm Inn** (515 Schmidt Rd., 270/554-1774, www.foxbriarinn.com, $200-275), which is located on 100 acres and overlooks a lake. The seven guest rooms and one suite are decorated in unique themed styles and have private bathrooms. Two common area fireplaces and an enormous covered porch offer relaxation and an opportunity to mingle with other guests. A formal breakfast is served each morning in the dining room, where guests are given their own private table with view of the lake. Located just west of I-24, Fox Briar Farm Inn is a 15-20-minute drive from downtown Paducah.

FOOD
Bakeries

With five generations of experience under its belt, ◖ **Kirchhoff's Bakery & Deli** (118 Market House Sq., 270/442-7117, www.kirchhoffsbakery.net, 7am-5pm Mon.-Fri., 8am-5pm Sat., $3-5.95) knows how to make bread. Slices of the artisan loaves bookend sandwiches, of which there are nearly 30 to choose from. You can get anything from a tuna melt to a muffuletta to a Cuban to a veggie hummus sandwich. Salads, sides, soups, and a plate of the day are also on offer. Sandwiches are large, but you'll want to save room for a cookie or pastry from the bakery, where you can also purchase bread by the loaf.

Coffeehouses

If you need a break while wandering Lower Town, find your way to **Etcetera Coffeehouse** (320 N. 6th St., 270/443-7760, http://etc-coffee.com, 7:30am-5:30pm Mon.-Thurs., 7:30am-10:30pm Fri., 8am-9:30pm Sat., 8am-5:30pm Sun., $1.30-4.50), the neighborhood gathering spot. The hip joint specializes in organic, fair-trade coffee, but also offers teas, bubble teas, smoothies, and specialty sodas. If you need a nibble with your drink, homemade treats, Kirchhoff's bagels, yogurt bowls, and brownie sundaes are available. The coffeehouse also does homemade quiche on the weekends. Supporting the art scene, Etcetera invites local students and up-and-coming artists to display their works.

Barbecue

Barbecue is a competitive sport in Western Kentucky, and in Paducah, **d. Starnes BBQ** (108 Broadway, 270/442-2122, 11am-3pm Mon.-Sat.) is the reigning king of 'cue. Order your meat (pork, ham, or turkey), which comes dry, mild, medium, or spicy, and then top it with as much of their famous sauce as you wish. Sandwiches ($3.75) come on toasted white or rye bread, or you can order a plate with two sides ($8). The mustard-based potato salad is very good. Other menu options include ribs, burgers, and soups. Save room for dessert—the meringue pies are awesome.

Contemporary American

Although a white-tablecloth restaurant, ◖ **Max's Brick Oven Café** (112 Market House Sq., 270/575-3473, www.maxsbrickoven.com, 5pm-11pm Mon.-Thurs., 10pm-midnight Fri.-Sat., $10-23.50) welcomes guests for both casual dinners out as well as special occasion evenings. Diners can choose from a wide variety of dishes that range from crisp and delicious wood-fired pizzas to hearty pastas to such mouthwatering entrées as Brazilian-style steak, Asian-style grilled tuna, or a spicy shrimp Creole. Portions are filling, service is friendly, and the atmosphere is upscale casual. The long, narrow, brick-walled dining area is filled with two- and four-top tables that can be arranged to accommodate larger groups. Beware that it can get noisy when the restaurant is full. On nice nights, opt for a table on the large patio.

Caribbean

Located away from downtown near Paducah's main shopping area, **Flamingo Row** (2640 Perkins Creek Dr., 270/442-0460, www.flamingorow.com, 10:30am-9pm Mon.-Thurs., 10:30am-10pm Fri.-Sat., 11am-9pm Sun., $6.95-14.95) is worth a visit if you're looking for the flavors of the Caribbean. The menu is extensive, offering salads, pastas, burgers, sandwiches, and fish, all prepared with an island twist. The cheese dip appetizer is a favorite, and the stuffed breads win for most popular dish. With bright colors and a neon sign reminiscent of the strip at the beach, Flamingo Row is a fun, casual spot with a beachy atmosphere, even though it's near the Home Depot and not the ocean.

Italian

The most recommended restaurant in town for a nice evening out, **Cynthia's** (125 Market House Sq., 270/443-3319, www.cynthiasristorante.com, 5pm-10pm Tues.-Sat., $16.50-28) serves a selection of California Italian cuisine that uses local ingredients and changes weekly. You may find goat cheese truffles and smoked trout crepes on the appetizer menu, while entrée choices might include seafood risotto, bacon-wrapped Angus beef, or pan-seared duck. An extensive wine and specialty drink list complement the menu. The candlelit antique tables create an aura of romance, while the tile-topped bar and stained-glass windows add an artistic feel to the restaurant. Reservations are highly recommended.

The menu at **DiFratelli Ristorante** (211 Broadway, 270/442-7054, www.difratelli.net, 5pm-10pm Tues.-Sat., $12-26), which changes seasonally, offers a choice of five pastas as well as a selection of steak and seafood entrées. Warm, yellow walls, a tile floor, and bold artwork create a welcoming, upscale atmosphere.

Latin American

Tribeca (127 Market House Sq., 270/444-3960, www.tribecarestaurant.net, 11am-3pm and 5pm-9pm Tues.-Fri., noon-9pm Sun., $8.75-14.95) can handle any hankering you might have for Mexican food, serving up tasty takes on favorites like tacos, burritos, enchiladas, and fajitas. Chips are homemade and the salsa is excellent. Rotating exhibitions of local artwork add flavor to the decor at this casual restaurant. Sidewalk seating is available for those who prefer to dine al fresco.

Seafood

Locals and visitors alike love to grab a seat on the multi-level deck at **Whaler's Catch** (123 N. 2nd St., 270/444-7701, www.whalerscatch.net, 11am-9pm Mon.-Thurs., 11am-10pm Fri., 2pm-10pm Sat., $12.99-26.99) and enjoy a view of downtown with their meal. A huge selection of seafood—shrimp, oysters, scallops, clams, crab, lobster, fish, and more—is at the heart of menu and is served most any way you like it. For non-seafood eaters, there are also plenty of pasta, beef, pork, and chicken options, although you ought to try the red beans and rice. The inside dining room, anchored by a long 19th-century mahogany bar, has a Southern casual feel.

INFORMATION AND SERVICES

In the heart of downtown, the **Paducah Convention & Visitors Bureau** (128 Broadway, 270/443-8783, www.paducah.travel, 9am-5pm Mon.-Fri.) welcomes visitors to come in and ask questions, pick up brochures, or just say hello. Although the office is closed on weekends, during festivals, tourism ambassadors are prominently situated to answer any inquiries and direct visitors.

The most centrally located **post office** is at 300 South 4th Street. It is open 8:30am-5pm Monday-Friday.

OWENSBORO

GETTING THERE

Paducah is located on the northern border of the far western section of the state, where the Ohio and Kentucky Rivers come together. Southern Illinois is directly across the river, and Tennessee is only an hour to the south.

From Owensboro (150 miles; 2 hours 20 minutes), travel west on KY 56 to the Pennyrile Parkway, which you'll take south for 43 miles to southbound I-69 (Exit 34B). Take that 38 miles to westbound I-24 (Exit 68B) and drive another 37 miles to eastbound U.S. 60 (Exit 16), which will lead you into Paducah. From there, you'll follow U.S. 68 to U.S. 62, which will lead into and around Paducah. From Henderson, the route is more direct as you simply have to stay on U.S. 60 for almost 100 miles (two hours).

The Land Between the Lakes area is very close to Paducah, and easily reached via eastbound I-24, which runs across the top of the lakes, providing access to Grand Rivers (30 miles; 35 minutes), Land Between the Lakes National Recreation Area (50 miles; one hour), Kuttawa (35 miles; 45 minutes), Eddyville (37 miles; 40 minutes), and Cadiz (60 miles; one hour). Those going south to Kenlake State Park (40 miles; 50 minutes) and other areas along Kentucky Lake should take eastbound U.S. 68 instead, as it provides a more direct route.

Louisville is 215 miles (3.25 hours) from Paducah. The best way to travel from Louisville to Paducah is to take southbound I-65 to Exit 91, where you'll merge onto southbound I-69 and then follow the same directions as from Owensboro. Lexington is 265 miles (four hours) from Paducah. You'll want to take the westbound Blue Grass Parkway to southbound I-65 and then follow the direction from Louisville.

Nashville is 135 miles (two hours) southeast of Paducah and can be reached via a straight shot on eastbound I-24. The nearest airport to Paducah is located in Nashville. St. Louis is 175 miles (2.75 hours) from Paducah via eastbound I-64, southbound I-57, and eastbound I-24.

GETTING AROUND

Most of Paducah is easily explored on foot. Attractions are within easy distance of each other, and the city is built for pedestrians. Lower Town, although distinct from downtown, is only a couple of blocks away and perfectly walkable. Free parking is available on the street in both downtown and Lower Town, and a large parking lot on Broadway at Water Street provides additional free options.

Public Transportation

If it's too hot or you're too tired to walk, catch the Paducah Area Transit System's **trolley** (www.paducahtransit.com, 8am-4pm Mon.-Fri., 9am-4pm Sat., free), which runs from Lower Town, along the downtown Riverfront, and to the Quilt Museum and the Expo Center.

Horsedrawn Carriage Rides

Take a 20-minute ride along the waterfront and through downtown with **John's Pass Carriage Service** (2nd St. and Broadway, 270/210-6095, www.kyshoresfun.com, $10 per person). Rides depart from the gazebo at Broadway and 2nd Street between 4pm and 9pm on Friday and Saturdays.

Vicinity of Paducah

The very western tip of Kentucky, south from Paducah and west from Kentucky Lake, is primarily agricultural, with a few small towns breaking up the landscape here and there. Along the Ohio River, which forms Kentucky's border with Missouri, two state parks provide recreational opportunities while also offering history lessons.

WICKLIFFE MOUNDS STATE HISTORIC SITE

Wickliffe Mounds State Historic Site (94 Green St., Wickliffe, 270/335-3681, http://parks.ky.gov, 10am-4pm Thurs.-Sun. Apr.-Oct., $5 adults, $4 seniors and youth 5-15) preserves the remains of a Mississippian village occupied from approximately 1100 to 1350. The Mississippians were a mound-building people who farmed, hunted, and gathered in this region where the Ohio and Mississippi Rivers converge. They left no written records, so knowledge of these people, who were most likely the ancestors of such southeastern Native American tribes as the Chickasaw, is limited to what can be discovered through archaeological excavations. The site, which has been a state park since only 2004 but has been a tourist attraction since the 1930s, encompasses three excavation sites. Each site is covered by a wood building, which also contains artifacts, reproductions, and interpretive panels. The first building, which covers former village homes, focuses on the lifestyle of the Mississippians, including their food, tools, and arts. The second building, which covers a burial ground, interprets their beliefs about death. The third, which encloses what was likely the site of the chief's home, contains displays about architecture as well as images of the excavations done here. A ceremonial mound that was partially excavated and then rebuilt is also located at Wickliffe Mounds.

COLUMBUS-BELMONT STATE PARK

During the Civil War, the area that is now **Columbus-Belmont State Park** (350 Park Rd., Columbus, 270/677-2327, http://parks.ky.gov, dawn-dusk daily, free) was considered of critical importance to the Confederates, who built a fort on the site in 1861, then stretched a chain from there across the Mississippi River to Illinois in what would be a failed attempt to blockade the river. The park pays homage to this history through the preservation of trenches and groundwork fortifications and with the display of cannons as well as the remarkable chain and anchor. A **museum** (9am-4:30pm daily, Apr.-Sept., $4 adults, $3 seniors and youth 6-12), which is housed in a building that was used as a Civil War hospital, contains artifacts from the Civil War and tells the story of the fort and the 1861 Battle of Belmont. Every year on the second weekend of October, Civil War Days are held at the park, with events ranging from battle reenactments to a Civil War-era ball. The park is more than a Civil War site, however; it's also a very popular spot for picnics, with four shelters and multiple picnic tables as well as a nice playground, lots of green space, and panoramic river views.

ACCOMMODATIONS AND FOOD

Accommodations and food are both scarce in this part of the state. Unless you're looking to camp at **Columbus-Belmont State Park** (350 Park Rd., Columbus, 270/677-2327, http://parks.ky.gov, $20-22), there's really no reason to stay overnight in the area. The 38-site campground is located on the riverside cliffs, is open year-round, and has utility hookups and a bathhouse.

As for food, pack a picnic or be on the lookout for a roadside barbecue shack. Most are completely unadvertised, and some don't even

POLITICKING KENTUCKY STYLE

In the days before politicians competed to see how many "friends" they could accumulate on Facebook or sent out campaign updates over Twitter, before politicians even appeared on television, politics was all about pressing the flesh, with politicians attempting to win over crowds with speeches given from decorated flatbed trucks. In Kentucky, that still happens.

Although the **Fancy Farm Picnic** (www. fancyfarm.net) began in 1880 as nothing more than a community gathering with opportunities to dance, play horseshoes, and picnic with neighbors, it has become the unofficial kickoff to the fall campaign season. Ever since lieutenant gubernatorial candidate A. B. "Happy" Chandler appeared at the picnic in 1931, those seeking state and federal positions have made it a point to attend the picnic, which is held in the tiny community of Fancy Farm in Graves County (population 900). Even national figures like Vice President Alben Barkley, a Western Kentucky resident, and Vice President Al Gore have made appearances at the picnic. Although the politicians who appear at Fancy Farm will go on to use every means possible of getting their message out, they don't underestimate the importance of the picnic. More than 15,000 people attend the Fancy Farm Picnic annually, more in important election years, and people take note of the politicians who don't show up.

Held on the first Saturday in August, the picnic gets underway at 10am with carnival games and live bluegrass and country music. Stump-style speeches by candidates begin at 2pm and last until 4pm, when picnic-goers return to the games and good times. The picnic officially ends at 11pm with the raffling off of a new car. Admission to the picnic is free.

have a name, but the food is darn good and cheap to boot. One such joint, with carry-out and a couple of picnic tables, is located directly across the street from Wickliffe Mounds State Historic Site.

GETTING THERE AND AROUND

The nearest city of note to Wickliffe Mounds State Historic Site and Columbus-Belmont State Park is Paducah. Reaching Wickliffe is straightforward; simply follow westbound U.S. 62 to KY 286 for a total of 30 miles (45 minutes). Signs will direct you to the park. To reach Columbus, take U.S. 62 from Paducah to KY 123, which will take you to the park (40 miles; one hour). To get between the two parks (18 miles; 30 minutes), take U.S. 51 from Wickliffe for 8 miles, and then turn right onto KY 123 and travel an additional 10 miles.

Land Between the Lakes Region

The Land Between the Lakes region is one of the state's premier recreation areas, especially for water-sports enthusiasts. Encompassing two large lakes—Kentucky Lake and Lake Barkley—and the national recreation area that separates them, the Land Between the Lakes area offers excellent waters for fishing as well as lots of wide open space for sailing, skiing, tubing, swimming, and simply cruising. Despite the immense popularity of the lakes, they never feel crowded. On land, recreational opportunities are just as abundant. Hiking, camping, biking, and wildlife-watching are among the most popular pursuits off the water.

◀ LAND BETWEEN THE LAKES NATIONAL RECREATION AREA

Before it became a national recreational area under the management of the U.S. Forest

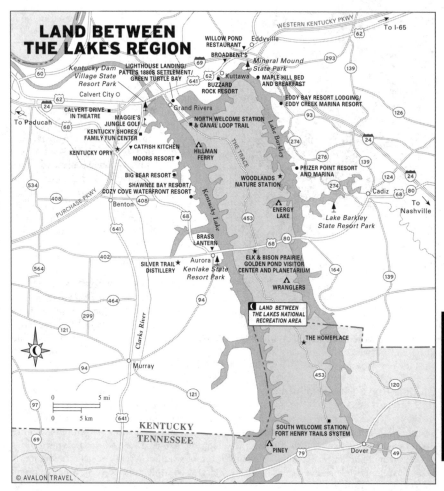

LAND BETWEEN THE LAKES REGION

WESTERN KENTUCKY PKWY

To I-65

62

Eddyville

WILLOW POND RESTAURANT
BROADBENT'S

Mineral Mound State Park

293

139

Kentucky Dam Village State Resort Park

LIGHTHOUSE LANDING/
PATTI'S 1880S SETTLEMENT/
GREEN TURTLE BAY

60

69

62

Kuttawa

MAPLE HILL BED AND BREAKFAST

641

BUZZARD ROCK RESORT

Calvert City

62

EDDY BAY RESORT LODGING/
EDDY CREEK MARINA RESORT

126

24

Grand Rivers

CALVERT DRIVE-IN THEATRE

68

To Paducah

MAGGIE'S JUNGLE GOLF

KENTUCKY SHORES FAMILY FUN CENTER

NORTH WELCOME STATION & CANAL LOOP TRAIL

93

Lake Barkley

274

276

24

139

KENTUCKY OPRY

CATFISH KITCHEN

MOORS RESORT

HILLMAN FERRY

THE TRACE

PRIZER POINT RESORT AND MARINA

124

24

BIG BEAR RESORT

WOODLANDS NATURE STATION

274

Cadiz

68

80

534

SHAWNEE BAY RESORT/
COZY COVE WATERFRONT RESORT

408

To Nashville

408

Benton

Kentucky Lake

ENERGY LAKE

Lake Barkley State Resort Park

641

68

453

BRASS LANTERN

80

402

68

564

464

SILVER TRAIL DISTILLERY

Aurora

Kenlake State Resort Park

ELK & BISON PRAIRIE/
GOLDEN POND VISITOR CENTER AND PLANETARIUM

164

139

94

WRANGLERS

299

121

LAND BETWEEN THE LAKES NATIONAL RECREATION AREA

Clarks River

94

Murray

THE HOMEPLACE

453

120

121

97

0   5 mi

0   5 km

641

69

KENTUCKY

TENNESSEE

SOUTH WELCOME STATION/
FORT HENRY TRAILS SYSTEM

PINEY

79

Dover

49

© AVALON TRAVEL

OWENSBORO

Service, **Land Between the Lakes** (www.lbl.org) was home to one of the most isolated communities in the state. Called Between the Rivers, this community was accessible only by ferry, and the people here lived in their own way and by their own rules. After the impoundment of Lake Barkley in 1964, the government saw the potential of the area for recreation, and by 1969 had, through the Tennessee Valley Authority, acquired all of the land and relocated the former residents. Today the last remaining vestiges of the former communities are the tiny cemeteries dotted throughout the recreational area and the Homeplace, a preserved farmstead.

In place of homes and farms, you'll now find visitor sites focused on the natural world and environmental education as well as thousands of acres of land set aside for hiking, biking, camping, and other outdoor pursuits. Go ahead and enjoy the many recreational opportunities, but don't forget to take

© THERESA DOWELL BLACKINTON

The Homeplace, Land Between the Lakes

OWENSBORO

so you can decide when to go based on your taste in tunes.

Elk and Bison Prairie

The **Elk and Bison Prairie** (dawn-dusk daily, $5 per car) provides a home for about 50 buffalo and 30 elk, animals that were once native to the region. A 3.5-mile paved road with three interpretive stops loops through the prairie, allowing opportunities for visitors to observe the animals. Although the area is enclosed, this is not a zoo. At 700 acres, there is plenty of space for the animals to roam—and to hide, should they choose. Sightings are not guaranteed. To increase your chances of seeing the elk and buffalo, aim to arrive at dawn or dusk. The route is one-way, but you're welcome to make as many loops you like. The prairie is located one mile north of the visitors center on The Trace.

Woodlands Nature Station

Take a loop through the backyard at the **Woodlands Nature Station** (10am-5pm daily, Apr.-Oct., Wed.-Sun. only in Mar. and Nov., $5 adults, $3 youth 5-12) to encounter wildlife native to the region. Among the animals that live here are deer, coyotes, red wolves, bobcats, groundhogs, wild turkeys, vultures, bald eagles, owls, and hawks. Accompanying the backyard is an indoor learning center with exhibits on plants, reptiles, amphibians, and habitats. A number of hiking trails depart from the Nature Station, allowing for additional opportunities to spot wildlife. Woodlands Nature Station is located on Mulberry Flat Road, which connects to The Trace about eight miles north of the visitors center.

The Homeplace

Experience life on an 1850s farm on a visit to **The Homeplace** (10am-5pm daily, Apr.-Oct., Wed.-Sun. only in Mar. and Nov., $5 adults, $3 youth 5-12), which is located just across the Tennessee border. Sixteen log structures make up the farm, which was built on a Revolutionary War land grant. At the farm, you'll find animals such as horses, oxen, pigs, and chickens that would have been on such a

a moment to remember those who lost everything so that we could have this wonderful outdoor playground.

Golden Pond Planetarium and Observatory

Images of space are projected onto the 40-foot-diameter dome at the **Golden Pond Planetarium and Observatory** (intersection of U.S. 68 and The Trace, $5 adults, $3 youth 5-12) during multiple shows each day. There are usually four different shows available each day, with topics covering everything from the extreme reaches of our galaxy to the night sky as seen from your own backyard, and including images from the world's most powerful telescopes. Shows are at 10am, noon, 1pm, 2pm, 3pm, and 4pm weekdays, with an extra show added at 11am on weekends.

The planetarium also hosts laser light music shows ($7) on Tuesdays, Fridays, and Saturdays ($10) at 5:30pm and 7pm June-August. Music selections run the gamut from the Beatles to U2 to country, but the schedule is set in advance, farm, as well as a vegetable garden, tobacco barn, tool barn, wood shed, smoke house, and family home. Costumed interpreters demonstrate farm tasks from the mid-19th century and help bring the farm to life. The last tickets are sold at 4pm. The Homeplace is located 12 miles south of Golden Pond Visitors Center on The Trace.

Hiking

Hiking trails are plentiful in Land Between the Lakes, with distances and difficulty levels to suit any taste. The granddaddy of trails is the **North/South Trail,** a 58-mile trail that runs the entire length of Land Between the Lakes. The trail is divided into two halves. The northern half (31 miles, from Northern Welcome Station to Golden Pond Visitors Center) stays close to the shore of Kentucky Lake, although it also runs through the forest and up ridges, and is primarily single track. Eight springs and three backcountry shelters are located along this stretch of trail. The southern half (27 miles, from Golden Pond Visitors Center to Southern Welcome Station) remains inland for most of its length, traveling through mature forest and wildlife clearings, and is primarily old logging roads, 11 miles of which are shared with equestrians. An additional eight springs can be accessed on this portion of the trail, and there are two backcountry shelters. Those wishing to do the length of the trail on a multi-day trip need to purchase a backcountry camping permit.

The **Fort Henry Trails System,** located in southwestern Land Between the Lakes (in Tennessee) offers nearly 30 miles of hiking that can easily be broken down into smaller loops perfect for day hikes. The Devils Backbone Trail, a 1.5-mile stretch that can be accessed from the Telegraph Trail, makes for a popular hike, with the trail following a ridge between two hollows. The 2.2-mile Pickett Loop is a good choice for a short outing, with the trail passing historic home sites and running, in parts, along the shores of Kentucky Lake. History buffs may want to hike the 3.2-mile Artillery Trail, which follows the route General Grant and his Union troops took on his way to Fort Donelson.

The most recent trail to be added to the collection is the **Central Hardwoods Scenic Trail,** an 11-mile trail spanning the width of Land Between the Lakes, connecting Kentucky Lake with Lake Barkley. It runs just south of U.S. 68. Access is in Fenton on the Kentucky Lake side and in Cumberland on the Lake Barkley side, with multiple other access points on Land Between the Lakes.

Five hiking trails are located in the vicinity of the Nature Station, ranging in distance 0.2-4.5 miles. The 2.2-mile Hematite Trail and the 4.5-mile Honker Trail both circle lakes, allowing for multiple opportunities to spot wildlife, especially waterfowl. The 0.3-mile Center Furnace Trail is an interpretive trail that leads to an old iron furnace. The 0.2-mile Long Creek Trail and the 1-mile Woodland Walk Trail focus on forest habitats.

Biking

Although the **Canal Loop Trail** is also open to hikers, it is mostly known as a mountain biking trail. The trail system is made up of one 11-mile loop and four connector trails ranging in distance 0.5-0.8 mile, allowing bikers to create many different routes. A trailhead is located at the North Welcome Station. Mountain bikers are also welcome to travel the northern 31 miles of the North/South Trail, between the North Welcome Station and the Golden Pond Visitors Center, and the entirety of the Central Hardwoods Scenic Trail.

Road bikers are a common site along The Trace, the main paved road that runs the length of Land Between the Lakes and from which multiple side roads lead to campgrounds, picnic areas, beaches, and scenic viewpoints.

Adult and youth mountain bikes, hybrid bikes, and cruisers can be rented at the Hillman Ferry and Piney Campgrounds.

Horseback Riding

Equestrians love Land Between the Lakes thanks to its Wranglers Campground, a beautiful camp designed especially for horses and

OWENSBORO

saddled up and ready to ride

© THERESA DOWELL BLACKINTON

their riders. More than 70 miles of riding trails radiate out from the campground. The trails run along the shore and through meadows and forest, leading past beautiful wild areas and to historic sites. If you don't have your own trusty steed, **Rocking U Riding Stables** (270/924-2211, 9am-4pm daily Apr.-Oct.), which is located at the campground, offers 45- ($18) or 90-minute ($30) guided trail rides that leave on the hour. Wranglers Campground is just south of the visitors center and can be accessed by a five-mile road that runs right from the center. An additional access road is located right at the Kentucky-Tennessee border.

Boating

Boat ramps are located up and down Land Between the Lakes, providing access to both Kentucky Lake and Lake Barkley. You must, however, have your own boat, as there are no marinas or rental facilities for motorboats in the area. You can, however, rent a canoe or kayak ($10 per hour) from the Nature Station or at Energy Lake Campground.

Accommodations

As a national recreation area, Land Between the Lakes does not have any lodges, hotels, or other forms of indoor accommodation. It does, however, have a multitude of campgrounds. To begin with, there are four major **developed campgrounds:** Hillman Ferry, Piney, Energy Lake, and Wranglers. Wranglers is specifically intended for horse camping with stalls, hitching posts, and watering troughs. Hillman Ferry is located right on Kentucky Lake at the northern end, while Piney is located on the southern end of Kentucky Lake in Tennessee, and Energy Lake is located on a secluded inlet of Lake Barkley. Piney is especially popular with RVs, and Energy Lake often hosts groups. All the developed campgrounds have modern shower and toilet facilities, camp stores, recreational offerings, and sites for tents and RVs. Piney and Wranglers also offer simple cabins that sleep four ($40) or eight ($60). Campsites range in cost from $12 for a basic site to $40 for a full-hookup, 50-amp site. Shelters cost $35. The campgrounds are open March-November, except Wranglers, which is open year-round.

In addition to the four major campgrounds, Land Between the Lakes also has three **self-service shoreline campgrounds** ($9). These campgrounds have designated campsites, picnic tables, grills, drinking water, and boat ramps, but have no showers or flush toilets (pit only).

Finally, Land Between the Lakes also offers the option of **backcountry camping,** of which there are two varieties. The first is camping at one of 12 designated backcountry areas, each of which is located on the shore and has a boat ramp. Most of them also have pit toilets, and some are hardly different from the self-service campgrounds with picnic tables and fire rings. The views from these sites are achingly beautiful, and although they can and do accommodate RVs, they're ideal for tent camping. Tent campers may also wish to opt to overnight in true backcountry style. Campers are allowed to set up tents nearly anywhere they wish on Land Between the Lakes, so long as they are at least 200 yards from any major road or public day-use facility. You can go for a hike and find a trailside spot that suits your fancy or steer your boat onto shore and camp next to it. Backcountry permits ($7 for 1-3 days, $30 for an annual permit) are required for both designated and non-designated spots and can be purchased at the visitors center, welcome stations, and the four major campgrounds.

Food

Aside from camp stores, no food is available for purchase on Land Between the Lakes. Bring your own food with you and make use of the picnic areas.

Information and Services

The **Golden Pond Visitors Center** (100 Van Morgan Dr., Golden Pond, 270/924-2000, www.lbl.org, 9am-5pm daily), which is home to the planetarium and observatory, is centrally located on Land Between the Lakes, near the intersection of The Trace with U.S. 68. Staff here can provide permits for backcountry camping and access tokens for the Elk and Bison Prairie, arm you with maps, and inform you about what's going on that week. Also located inside the visitors center are museum-style displays that tell the story of the impoundment of the lakes and the establishment of Land Between the Lakes as a recreation area.

Welcome stations are located at both the north and south entrances to Land Between the Lakes, providing both information and maps as well as camping permits.

Visitors to Land Between the Lakes should be aware that there are no gas stations in the recreational area, so you should fill your tank before entering.

Getting There and Around

There are only two access roads to Land Between the Lakes, one running north-south and the other running east-west. The northern entrance, which puts you on the road known as The Trace, is through Grand Rivers, which is at the tip of Kentucky Lake, just off of I-24. U.S. 68 provides the east-west access to LBL. From the west, the entrance is at Kenlake State Resort Park in Aurora, while the east entrance sits to the southwest of Lake Barkley State Resort Park in Cadiz. All campgrounds, boat ramps, trailheads, and attractions are located either directly off The Trace or off of side roads running from The Trace.

KENTUCKY LAKE

Kentucky Lake is my idea of heaven on earth. The smell of the pines that line the shore, the refreshing chill of the water, the feel of the wind in your hair as you cruise the lake, and the sight of barge lights blinking in the night define Kentucky Lake. It's a water lover's paradise, with opportunities to do everything from ski and swim to canoe and cruise to sail and windsurf. The fishing is particularly good, with the lake holding the state records for white bass, buffalo carp, and yellow perch. Created in 1944 by the impoundment of the Tennessee River, Kentucky Lake is the largest lake east of the Mississippi River, covering more than 160,000 acres and stretching 185 miles with 2,380 miles of shoreline. It is connected to Lake Barkley on

OWENSBORO

the east side of Land Between the Lakes by a canal at the top of the lake, making it possible to go back and forth between the lakes without ever having to set foot on dry land. Two state parks as well as multiple resorts provide accommodations for visitors to the area.

Kenlake State Resort Park

The first modern resort park in the Kentucky state park system, **Kenlake State Resort Park** (542 Kenlake Rd., Hardin, 270/474-2211, http://parks.ky.gov, 24 hours daily, free) is ideally located on the western shore of Kentucky Lake, about midway down the lake, at one of only three entry points to Land Between the Lakes. Recreation opportunities are abundant. The park is the only one to have a tennis center (Nov.-mid-Apr.), with indoor courts providing top-level playing surfaces ideal for winter workouts. During the summer, outdoor courts are available. Those wishing to hike can opt for the 0.7-mile Cherokee Trail or the 1-mile Chickasaw Trail. In the summer, check at the hotel for a list of daily recreational activities. Of course, the lake is the primary draw at the resort, and a marina with boat ramp and dock allows those with or without their own watercraft to get out on the water. Fish, ski, bass, and pontoon boats as well as personal watercraft are available for rent. You don't have to have a boat to fish, however, as you're welcome to cast a line from shore. The Bay View area is a popular place to cast a line.

Special events are held at Kenlake through the year. The most popular events are the Hot August Blues Festival, which brings big-name blues bands to the park amphitheater on the last weekend of August, and the Visit with Eagles program, which takes place in February and allows visitors to view wintering bald eagles.

Kentucky Dam Village State Resort Park

Before becoming a state park, the area that is now **Kentucky Dam Village State Resort Park** (113 Administration Dr., Gilbertsville, 270/362-4271, http://parks.ky.gov, 24 hours daily, free) was used to house the TVA workers

who built Kentucky Dam between 1938 and 1945. That dam, which created Kentucky Lake, is now in view from almost all of the park, which is conveniently located near the north entrance to Land Between the Lakes. The sprawling park offers multiple recreational activities. There's a beach; a marina with ramp, docks, and ski, fish, bass, pontoon, and houseboat rentals; a very highly ranked 18-hole golf course; and a stable that offers 45-minute guided horseback rides (Memorial Day-Labor Day, $18). Daily recreational activities are scheduled for the summer season, with eagle-watching weekends in the winter.

Silver Trail Distillery

Although local laws prevent you from tasting the goods at the **Silver Trail Distillery** (136 Palestine Rd., Hardin, 270/354-6209, http://lblmoonshine.com), it's still interesting to stop by to learn how they make their LBL Moonshine, winner of the 2012 SIP award for best moonshine. Be sure to ask about the family history of moonshining, which is fascinating. Because this is a small, family-run operation, you should call to arrange a visit.

Recreation

Most activities in this area center around the two lakes and Land Between the Lakes. A couple of family adventure centers provide a break from the lake. **Kentucky Shores Family Fun Center** (6251 U.S. 641, Gilbertsville, 270/362-4774, www.kyshoresfun.com, 10am-9pm Sun.-Thurs., 10am-10pm Fri.-Sat., Memorial Day-Labor Day, weekends only in Mar., Apr., Sept., Oct.) offers laser tag, a rock-climbing wall, go-karts, bumper boats, mini-golf, and zip lines. You can purchase tickets for individual activities or a combination pass.

The most popular mini-golf course is located at **Maggie's Jungle Golf** (7301 U.S. 641, Gilbertsville, 270/362-8933, www.maggiesjunglegolf.com, 10am-9pm Mon.-Thurs., 10am-10pm Fri.-Sun., Memorial Day-Labor Day, 5pm-8pm Fri., 10am-8pm Sat.-Sun., Apr., May, and Sept., $4), where you'll also find a petting zoo ($2).

Entertainment

Few people have much energy left after a day on the lake under the hot Kentucky sun, but if you're not ready to retire right after dinner, you have a couple of options for evening entertainment. The **Kentucky Opry** (88 Chilton Ln., Draffenville, 270/527-3869, www.kentuckyopry.com, 7:30pm Sat. year-round, 7:30pm Fri., June-Aug. and Dec., $16 adults, $15 seniors, $10 student, $7.50 youth 12 and under) puts on an old-fashioned country music and comedy show that will take you back to the era of variety shows. For a different type of old-school entertainment, park your car at the **Calvert Drive-In Theater** (111 Drive In Ln., Calvert City, 270/395-4660, www.calvertdrivein.com, $7, free youth under 12), which shows a double feature every night in the summer and on weekends in spring and fall. Showtimes vary based on sunset.

Resorts

Most Kentucky Lake vacationers like to set themselves up at one of the many resorts that line the shores of the lake, primarily between Grand Rivers in the north and Aurora in the south. Those new to the area should be aware that the term "resort" is used loosely, indicating only that in addition to accommodation options, the properties also have some recreational facilities. Although the resorts each have distinct personalities, they have much in common. They are universally family friendly and casual, not necessarily rustic, but not fancy either. Many of the resorts feel a bit like they're stuck in the 1950s, and although some updates wouldn't hurt, most resorts are completely full every summer. Many vacationers return year after year to the same resort, and resorts are known to take reservations up to five years in advance. This isn't to say they book up that far in advance, but they are almost without fail at full occupancy for the entire summer season (June-mid-Aug.), so it's wise to reserve as far in advance as possible. The listing that follows is not comprehensive, but represents a selection of the best Kentucky Lake resorts. Information on many more resorts can be found at www.kentuckylake.org.

[**Lighthouse Landing** (320 W. Commerce Ave., Grand Rivers, 270/362-8201, www.lighthouselanding.com, $130-250) offers a selection of cozy cottages that are fully equipped and nicely furnished. Each one-, two-, or three-bedroom cottage has a view of the lake and a deck from which to enjoy it. Lighthouse Landing has a marina with slips for those with their own boats and also rents sailboats and runs a sailing school. A public beach is located in the Lighthouse Landing complex along with a jetty from which you can fish as well as watch the sunset. The Grand Rivers location is ideal, because it allows for easy access to both Kentucky Lake and Lake Barkley via boat and Land Between the Lakes via car.

Green Turtle Bay (263 Green Turtle Bay Dr., Grand Rivers, 270/362-8364, www.greenturtlebay.com, $145-440) is one of the more upscale resorts, featuring townhouse-style condominiums that are individually owned but available for rent through the resort. The condos range in size from one to four bedrooms. Additional resort amenities include a fitness center, tennis courts, one indoor and two outdoor pools, and a beach. A marina is available for those with their own boat, while the on-site Waterway Adventures rents fishing boats, ski boats, pontoons, houseboats, personal watercraft, kayaks, and paddleboats. If you've got a bit of extra cash in your pocket, you can also buy a yacht on-site. **Dockers Bayside Grill** (7am-2pm daily Mar.-Sept., $3.99-8.99) serves quick breakfast and lunch daily, and guests of the resort are welcome to have dinner at the Commonwealth Yacht Club, which is about as fancy as lake dining gets (you can leave your suit at home).

In business since 1951, **Moors Resort** (570 Moors Rd., Gilbertsville, 270/362-8361, www.moorsresort.com) retains the old-fashioned, family-friendly feel of that era. Guests can choose to stay in one of the hotel-style rooms at the log cabin lodge ($94) or opt for one of the fully equipped cottages ($105-325). The cottages vary greatly in style and size, and not all are located on the waterfront. The website provides very honest information on each option, noting the new ones as well as the old ones, and providing floor plans and images, so you can choose the lodging that best fits you. A marina rents boats as well as fun equipment like tubes, wakeboards, kneeboards, and skis. The resort also has a beach, a pool, and a mini-golf course. **Ralph's Harborview Grill** (early Mar.-late Oct., sunrise-9pm daily, $3.99-16.99) serves three meals a day. Breakfasts are filling, and the burgers, served with home-made chips (ask for the spicy version), are big and tasty. Moors Resort is particularly popular with families.

The first resort on Kentucky Lake, **Big Bear Resort** (30 Big Bear Resort Rd., Benton, 270/354-6414, www.bigbearkentuckylake.com, $120-400) still pays homage to its fishing camp roots while also offering modern facilities. The accommodation options are extensive. On the budget end, you can choose from basic one- and two-bedroom Fisherman's Cottages, a room at the Fisherman's Motel, a one-bedroom Fisherman's Apartment, or a Fisherman's Duplex that can sleep up to six. Good group options include the townhouses, which can sleep 8-10 people, and the chalets, which can sleep up to 9. At the luxury end are the privately owned condos, which can typically accommodate eight people. Large parties should check out the historic log cabin, which dates to 1812, but in its fully renovated and modern condition can sleep 15. Resort amenities include a pool, beach, volleyball and basketball courts, and a full-service marina that rents boats and all the fun equipment that goes with them.

C Cozy Cove Waterfront Resort (1917 Reed Rd., Benton, 270/354-8168, www.cozycovewaterfront.com) lives up to its name, with only 16 cottages located on 12 waterfront acres. The cottages, which are named after species of fish you can catch in Kentucky Lake, range in size from the studio-style Minnow, which can sleep two, to the luxurious five-bedroom KY Spotted Bass, which can sleep 16. From the beach, you can swim out to a dock with slide, or you can just choose to sunbathe in the sand.

Fishing, ski, and pontoon boats are available for rental. For those who want a quiet getaway, Cozy Cove is an excellent option. During the peak summer months of June-August, all rentals are by the week ($429-2,339).

The 15 guest cottages at **Shawnee Bay Resort** (1297 Shawnee Bay Rd., Benton, 270/354-8360, www.shawneebayresort.com) range in size from one to five bedrooms and can accommodate up to 10 people. Each unit is fully equipped and arranged along the treed shoreline with sundecks or screened porches offering views of the lake. A quiet beach is backed with trees and lined with umbrellas and deck chairs for those looking to relax, while a 2.5-mile walking trail caters to the active. The private marina provides slips for guests with their own boats and rents fishing and pontoon boats to those without. During the summer months of June-August, rentals are by the week only ($1,020-2,799).

Other Accommodations

Kenlake State Resort Park (542 Kenlake Rd., Hardin, 270/474-2211, http://parks.ky.gov) offers multiple popular accommodation options. Built in 1952, **Kenlake Lodge** ($109.95) has 48 comfortable rooms fitted out in standard mid-range hotel decor. Walls are a bit thin, but this isn't a party place, so you won't be kept up late. You could, however, be woken up by an angler heading out early. Some rooms have partial views of the lake. If you want more privacy, opt for one of the park's **cottages** ($149.95-209.95). You can choose from one-, two-, or three-bedroom and one- or two-bathroom layouts and wood or lake views. The cabins feature screened porches, decks, and are fully equipped. My vote for best view goes to Cottage 269, which has a great angle on the lake. A nice pool, which overlooks the lake, is located at the lodge and is open to both lodge and cottage guests. Those who don't want anything between them and the great outdoors can reserve one of the 87 spots at the **campground** (Apr.-Oct., $21), a few of which have lake views. Restrooms and showers are available at the campground.

Kentucky Dam Village (113 Administration Dr., Gilbertsville, 270/362-4271, http://parks.ky.gov) boasts the most accommodation options in the state park system. The 72 motel-style rooms at the **Village Inn Lodge** ($124.95) are bright and airy thanks to renovations in 2006-2007 and have nice, freshly tiled bathrooms along with private patios or decks, some of which have views of the lake. The park also has an impressive 68 **cottages** ($129.95-309.95), in one-, two-, and three-bedroom configurations. The majority of the cottages are located off the water, across KY 641 from the lodge. These one-story, fully renovated cottages once housed the dam workers and are arranged in a neighborhood-like setting. An additional set of cottages, which are more modern and have lovely wraparound porches, overlook the golf course, while a handful of two-story executive cottages are located in the wooded area near the park dock. A pool at the lodge is open to both lodge and cottage guests. The enormous **campground** (Apr.-Oct., $17-24) has 205 sites with paved camp pads and utility hookups and nine dedicated tent sites. Four comfort stations with restrooms and showers mean you never have to wait long to use the facilities.

Food

Food options are surprisingly limited for the area being such a popular vacation destination. Many people opt to self-cater, especially because resort accommodations usually have full kitchens. A number of resorts also have restaurants, which are open to both guests and the general public. Benton has a selection of fast-food outlets, while nearby Murray is home to most national chains. For a special dinner out, your best option may be to head to Paducah. A few good options are available in lakeside towns, especially if you like catfish and Southern specialties.

At Kentucky Dam Village, **Harbor Lights Restaurant** (113 Administration Dr., Gilbertsville, 270/362-4271, http://parks.ky.gov, 7am-9pm daily, $6.49-12.49) features a casual dining room overlooking the dam. Specialties include a catfish filet and a Kentucky hot brown.

At Kenlake State Resort Park, **Aurora Landing Restaurant** (542 Kenlake Rd., Hardin, 270/474-2211, http://parks.ky.gov, 7am-8pm daily, $5.95-13.95) is located in the lower level of Kenlake Lodge, overlooking colorful flower gardens, the pool, and the lake. The menu offers the same southern favorites as the restaurant at Kentucky Dam Village.

The nicest restaurant in the area, **Brass Lantern** (16593 U.S. 68 E., Aurora, 800/474-2773, www.brasslanternrestaurant.com, 5pm-9pm Tues.-Sat., $13.99-34.99) specializes in charbroiled steaks, but also offers other traditional fine-dining staples, including lobster tail, daily fish specials, and prime rib au jus. The restaurant is divided into five themed rooms, with the Garden Room and Fireplace Room holding the most diners. Although the food is very good and reservations are recommended, the atmosphere is decidedly casual and service friendly and familiar.

Diners at **C Catfish Kitchen** (136 Teal Run Cir., Benton, 270/362-7306, 4pm-8pm Wed.-Thurs., 4pm-9pm Fri.-Sat., 11am-8pm Sun., $5.99-9.99) are greeted with a basket of delicious hush puppies. Enormous portions of perfectly fried catfish follow. Very casual, this fish shack fills quickly with locals and visitors craving some of the best catfish you'll ever have. Come early or be prepared to wait, although service is quick.

Patti's 1880's Settlement (1759 JH O'Bryan Ave., Grand Rivers, 888/736-2525, www.pattis-settlement.com, 10:30am-8pm daily Jan.-Mar., 10:30am-9pm daily Apr.-Dec., $16.95-32.95) is an experience. Some love it. Others find it at once overwhelming and underwhelming. The restaurant is packed to the gills with kitsch, and employees are dressed in pioneer-style clothing. Portions are ridiculously large—the two-inch-thick pork chop is their signature dish—but the food is average in quality and rather expensive. The cream pies are worth a taste, however. The restaurant, which is situated amid an entire village of tourist attractions, is consistently packed, so obviously a lot of people enjoy the restaurant. If you're in the area, stop in and see if it's your cup of tea. Different strokes for different folks. Reservations are recommended.

Information and Services

If you're planning a trip to Kentucky Lake, your best sources of information are www.kentuckylake.org, which covers the area along the western shore of Kentucky Lake, and www.grandrivers.org, which covers the town at the top of Kentucky Lake. You'll find listings of accommodations, restaurants, attractions, and more on each website.

Getting There and Around

Towns along Kentucky Lake include Grand Rivers, at the top of the lake at the canal; Gilbertsville, also on the top near the dam; Draffenville and Benton, on the northern portion of the lake; and Aurora, about halfway down the Kentucky portion of lake at the eastern entrance to Land Between the Lakes. Murray, which is southwest of Aurora, is a bit off the lake, but is the biggest city in the immediate area.

To travel the length of Kentucky Lake, U.S. 641 is the main route, with multiple east-west roads branching off of it. U.S. 641 is off the lake, but because of the lake's many long coves, it's the only non-interrupted north-south road. U.S. 68 provides a direct route from Kentucky Lake to Lake Barkley via Land Between the Lakes. U.S. 62 and I-24 run across the top of both lakes.

Kentucky Lake is about 25 miles (35 minutes) southeast of Paducah, 120 (2 hours) miles southwest of Owensboro, 200 miles (3 hours) southwest of Louisville, and 230 miles (3.5 hours) southwest of Lexington. To reach Land Between the Lakes from Paducah, take eastbound I-24 if you're trying to reach Grand Rivers or Kentucky Dam Village State Resort Park. If you're going south along the shore, take eastbound U.S. 68. From Owensboro, take southbound KY 9007 to westbound KY 9001 to southbound I-69 to westbound I-24. From Louisville and points east, take I-65 to

U.S. 31 (Exit 91) and then immediately merge onto the Western Kentucky Parkway, which leads to I-69 and I-24. From Lexington, take the westbound Blue Grass Parkway to southbound I-65 and then follow the directions from Louisville.

From Nashville, it's a 115-mile (1.75-hour) trip on westbound I-24. From St. Louis, it's a 200-mile (three-hour) trip via eastbound I-64, southbound I-57, and eastbound I-24. From Indianapolis, it's a 300-mile (4.5-hour) trip via southbound I-65 to Louisville, from where you'd then follow the above directions. From Cincinnati, it's also a 300-mile (4.5 hour) trip, although you'll take southbound I-71 to Louisville and then proceed from there.

LAKE BARKLEY

At 58,000 acres, Lake Barkley is significantly smaller than Kentucky Lake, but is still a very large body of water with ample opportunity for all water pursuits. Named for the 35th vice president of the United States and Western Kentucky resident Alben Barkley, Lake Barkley was created in 1964 by impounding the Cumberland River. Lake Barkley is located on the eastern side of Land Between the Lakes, and like its counterpoint on the western side is lined with waterfront resorts offering access to the lake as well as other family-friendly activities.

Lake Barkley State Resort Park

Lake Barkley State Resort Park (3500 State Park Rd., Cadiz, 270/924-1131, http://parks.ky.gov, 24 hours daily, free) has the most prime location of the three state parks in the area, perfectly perched on the shore of Lake Barkley.

To get out on the water, visit the marina, where you can rent fishing, ski, and pontoon boats, as well as launch your own watercraft. Largemouth, white, and spotted bass, along with bluegill, channel catfish, and crappie, are the most frequent catches. If you're looking to swim, the park has a beach with volleyball court and bathhouse. Other park amenities include an 18-hole golf course, a fitness center, a game room, tennis courts, a trap range, and nine miles of hiking trails, seven of which are also open to mountain bikers.

Recreation

Golfers will find another area course to play at **Mineral Mound State Park** (48 Finch Ln., Eddyville, 270/388-3673, http://parks.ky.gov). The park's 18-hole course offers challenging holes in the woods and along the lake.

Resorts

The resorts on Lake Barkley are similar to those on Kentucky Lake, with most offering both freestanding cottage units and motel-style units. Located right on the waterfront, the resorts are perfect for those who plan to spend most of their time out on the lake, but also like having the option of other activities. The majority of Lake Barkley resorts are located at the north end of the lake or in Cadiz by the state park.

Buzzard Rock Resort (985 Buzzard Rock Rd., Kuttawa, 270/388-7925, www.buzzardrock.com, $99-189) has rustic cabins that can accommodate eight people in two bedrooms and a sleeping loft. The cabins are basic, but they do have large decks with great lake views that are furnished for outdoor dining. Efficiency-style motel units with kitchens and access to a deck are also available. The resort has a marina that rents fishing and pontoon boats, a café (9am-9pm Sun.-Thurs., 8am-10:30pm Fri.-Sat.) with good burgers and two bars, and play areas. Overnight guests receive access to a complimentary boat slip.

Although **Eddy Bay Resort Lodging** (75 Forest Glen Dr., Eddyville, 800/324-8807, www.eddybaylodging.com) does not have a marina, it does have a dock and slips for those with their own boat and a variety of resort-based activities. Visitors to Eddy Bay will find a swimming area with water trampoline, volleyball court, horseshoe pit, campfire area, and playground. You have a variety of accommodation options to choose from. There's a very nice five-bedroom waterfront house with covered deck ($1,525 per week), cozy one- or two-bedroom suites ($400-860

per week) with kitchens in a lodge close to the lake or a lodge farther up the hill, or standard motel rooms ($350 per week).

Eddy Creek Marina Resort (7612 KY 93, Eddyville, 270/388-2271, www.eddycreek.com) offers motel rooms ($82) with two queen beds or log cabins ($195) that can sleep 10. The resort has a beach, pool, playground, waterside restaurant, and a marina with boat rentals. The resort also has an RV park with spacious shady sites and access to the resort's amenities.

Prizer Point Marina and Resort (1777 Prizer Point Rd., Cadiz, 270/522-3762, www.prizerpoint.com, $85-340) covers all the bases, in regard to both accommodation and activities. For overnight stays, you can choose from cabins, cottages, condos, or bungalows, which sleep between 4 and 12 people, or you can grab a spot in the KOA campground ($35-93). All accommodations are in wood buildings with easy access to the lake. Decor is lake-standard—nothing fancy but clean and comfortable. A marina with rentals and a restaurant is on-site. For entertainment, choose among outdoor movies, a pool, a giant chessboard, volleyball and basketball courts, a soccer field, hiking and biking trails, paddleboats, pedal carts, a mini-golf course, and playgrounds.

Other Accommodations

If you'd like something a bit posher than a rustic waterfront cabin, consider a B&B. **Maple Hill Bed and Breakfast** (13 Maple Hill Dr., Eddyville, 270/388-4963, www.maplehillbb.com, $129-199) has four elegant rooms perfect for a romantic escape or relaxing getaway. Rooms have king beds, plush mattresses, clawfoot tubs, fireplaces, TVs with DVD players and movies, and wireless Internet. On the shores of Lake Barkley, this 1850s home offers the best of both worlds.

The wings of the 120-room **Lake Barkley Lodge** ($129.95) at **Lake Barkley State Resort Park** (3500 State Park Rd., Cadiz, 270/924-1131, http://parks.ky.gov) are built of Western cedar and Douglas fir and blend perfectly into the surroundings. The wings curve away from each side of the pool, which seems to hover just

OWENSBORO

OWENSBORO

over the lake, the bright blue of the pool and the dark blue of the lake mingling beautifully. Unfortunately, beyond the lovely setting, the lodge doesn't have a lot to recommend it. What was once a fantastic property has been, because of budgetary or other reasons, let go, so that it badly needs updating. Four rustic two-bedroom log **cabins** nestled in the woods and nine two-bedroom executive **cottages** ($249.95) near the water are also available. Completing the checklist of accommodation options at the park is a 78-site **campground** ($14-22) with utility hookups, restrooms, and showers.

Food

The Lake Barkley side of Land Between the Lakes doesn't have any more to offer than the Kentucky Lake side with regard to food. You can check out the restaurants at the various resorts and marinas or the state park. Cadiz has the biggest selection of chains and family restaurants.

Stunning views of the lake unfold for diners in the aptly named **Windows on the Water Restaurant** (Lake Barkley State Resort Park, 3500 State Park Rd., Cadiz, 270/924-1131, http://parks.ky.gov, 7am-9pm daily, $5.95-13.95), which serves the typical park menu of sandwiches, fried catfish, and country-style favorites.

Catfish—fried, baked, grilled, or blackened—is the main focus at **Willow Pond Restaurant** (124 U.S. 62, Eddyville, 270/388-4354, www.willowpondcatfishrestaurant.com, 4pm-9pm Mon.-Sat., 11am-9pm Sun., $6.99-13.99), but you can also order shrimp, tilapia, frog legs, chicken, sandwiches, burgers, salads, and steak. Dishes are served with white beans, slaw, potato, and hush puppies. Country casual, Willow Pond has more of a restaurant atmosphere than Kentucky Lake's Catfish Kitchen,

although, in my book, Catfish Kitchen wins on flavor.

Broadbent's (257 Mary Blue Rd., Kuttawa, 800/841-2202, www.broadbenthams.com, under $5) is known for their country hams, having produced 14 state fair grand champion hams. In fact, their 2010 winner sold at a charity auction for $1.6 million. For a quick lunch, stop into their store and get a country ham sandwich. Dessert options include ice cream, cookies, and Kentucky silk pie. There are a few tables in the shop where you can sit and eat, and you can purchase all sorts of packaged products to take with you when you go.

Information and Services

For information about Lake Barkley and the surrounding area, visit www.lakebarkley.org, where you'll find listings of lodging, restaurants, and attractions in Eddyville, Kuttawa, and the northern stretches of the lake. For information about the southern part of the lake in the area near Cadiz, visit www.gocadiz.com.

Getting There and Around

Towns along Lake Barkley include Kuttawa and Eddyville, at the top of the lake at the canal, and Cadiz, on an arm of the lake about halfway down the Kentucky portion of the lake.

There is no one single road that runs the length of the lake. To travel south from Eddyville, start out on KY 93, and then transfer to KY 274, which continues south to Lake Barkley State Resort Park. U.S. 68 provides a direct route between Kentucky Lake and Lake Barkley via Land Between the Lakes. It then intersects with I-24 east of Cadiz.

The northern access to Lake Barkley is at Exit 40 on I-24. To get to the area, use the same directions as given for Kentucky Lake.

East of Land Between the Lakes

The region east of Land Between the Lakes is large but is primarily rural, with only a smattering of small towns interrupting farmland. Hopkinsville is the only city of note in this area, a lively and diverse place made even more so by its close proximity to Fort Campbell Army Base, which is among the largest bases in the United States. For those seeking outdoor recreation, Pennyrile Forest State Resort Park delivers.

HOPKINSVILLE AND CHRISTIAN COUNTY

Known informally as Hoptown, Hopkinsville is the seat of Christian County. Although one of Kentucky's bigger cities, Hopkinsville maintains a small-town feel, with a historic downtown that contains an old-fashioned hardware store, museums celebrating local history, and restaurants filled with regulars. The energy from nearby Fort Campbell Army Base helps keep it all hopping. Outside of Hopkinsville, much of Christian County is rural, which is beneficial to MB Roland, a new microdistillery turning locally grown corn into bourbon and other spirits. History buffs will want to visit the birthplace of Jefferson Davis, president of the Confederate States of America, as well as the Trail of Tears Commemorative Park.

Trail of Tears Commemorative Park

When the Cherokees were forced, despite a Supreme Court ruling in their favor, to move off their lands in the eastern United States to a reservation in Oklahoma, they passed through Hopkinsville on what came to be known as the Trail of Tears. Today, the **Trail of Tears Commemorative Park** (Skyline Dr. and U.S. 41, Hopkinsville, www.trailoftears.org, free) marks the spot of a camp where 10 detachments stayed on their trip westward. Tragically, Clan Chief Fly Smith and Warrior Chief White Path both died while at this camp, and their remains

are still buried here. A statue of the two men and a poem pay tribute to them. A Heritage Center (10am-5pm Tues.-Sat.) is located inside an 1830s log cabin similar in style to what the Cherokee would have lived in. The center is divided into an intertribal side and a Cherokee side, with artifacts such as clan masks, weapons, tools, a copy of their written alphabet, quilts, and an 1800s bible on display.

An intertribal powwow is held at the park annually on the weekend following Labor Day. Native Americans from around the nation convene at the park, performing in dance competitions, offering crafts for sale, and presenting the public with information on their unique heritage and traditions.

Pennyroyal Area Museum

Located in the former post office, the **Pennyroyal Area Museum** (217 E. 9th St., Hopkinsville, 270/887-4270, 9am-5pm Mon.-Fri., 10am-3pm Sat., $2 adults, $1 seniors and youth 4-12) is chock-full of artifacts related to local history. Of particular interest is the exhibit on renowned clairvoyant and local resident Edgar Cayce, information about "the little green men" said to have sieged the nearby town of Kelly in 1955, and the display on the Night Riders and the Tobacco War. Be sure to hop across the street to the Woody Winfree Fire-Transportation Museum, which is part of the Pennyrile Area Museum and houses antique fire trucks, cars, and other means of transportation. Those curious about the past will be captivated by the complete collection of recorded fire calls that date all the way back through Hopkinsville history.

Jefferson Davis State Historic Site

The **Jefferson Davis State Historic Site** (258 Pembroke-Fairview Rd., Fairview, 270/889-6100, http://parks.ky.gov, 9am-5pm Fri.-Mon.) pays tribute to the man best known as president

GREENVILLE: A SMALL TOWN REVITALIZED

Much of Kentucky is made of small towns that grew up around agriculture and industry. As economies have changed and the state, like the nation, has become increasingly migratory, with people moving from small towns to big cities, these small towns have been hit with the challenge of redefining themselves. The Western Kentucky town of Greenville (population 4,300), which is located almost smack between Land Between the Lakes and Mammoth Cave and just south of the Western Kentucky Parkway, is one such town. The seat of a county known for its coal and dark tobacco production, Greenville is a standout example of how a small town can rejuvenate itself when the people who live there care enough to invest in their hometown. All the more stunning is that Greenville's transformation took place through the depths of the recession and through three federally declared natural disasters. While traveling through Western Kentucky, stop in at Greenville to see what's going on there, being sure to check make time for the following:

DOWNTOWN WALKING TOUR

Take a stroll through downtown along the newly repaired sidewalks, music filling the air from speakers on the historic-style lampposts, and past once-vacant buildings that have been freshly painted and restored to their original colors and designs and now host restaurants and shops. See what the **Muhlenberg Community Theatre** (www.mctiky.org) has going on at the **Palace Theatre** (119 N. Main

St.), which has been updated with a neon marquee that is a replica of the original, then pop into the beautiful beaux arts **Muhlenberg County Courthouse** (100 S. Main St., 8am-4pm Mon.-Fri.), whose dome was completely rebuilt in 2011. When hunger hits, enjoy the diner classics (plus a root beer float) and old-fashioned atmosphere at **My Friends Place** (129 S. Main St., 270/338-5962, 10am-8pm Mon.-Sat., 10am-2pm Sun.).

BRIZENDENE BROTHERS NATURE PARK

Not far from downtown, the 12-acre **Brizendene Brothers Nature Park** (Pritchett Dr., 270/338-2966, dawn-dusk daily) lets you get back to nature with a half-mile trail through wooded areas and open meadow, picnic tables, and a stream with a manmade waterfall. It's not uncommon to see deer, turkeys, and other wildlife, as well as plenty of birds.

SATURDAYS ON THE SQUARE

On Saturday nights in July and August at 8pm, the square outside the courthouse fills as Greenville residents and people from further afield gather for free music from live bands in a wide range of genres. It's a family-friendly way to enjoy the weekend and the beauty of summer nights.

For more information on what's happening in Greenville, contact the **Greenville Tourism Commission** (112 N. Main St., 270/338-1895, www.tourgreenville.com).

---

of the Confederacy, but who was also a congressman, senator, and secretary of war under Franklin Pierce. A 351-foot concrete obelisk, reminiscent of the DC monument that honors the first president of the United States, marks the site where Davis was born in 1808, while a one-room museum contains exhibits about Davis's life and career. Tours of the monument are given every 30 minutes 9:30am-4:30pm, with participants ascending to the top of the obelisk, where you can take in panoramic

views of the countryside from three sides. Combination tickets for the museum and monument cost $5 for adults and $4 for seniors and youth 4-12. Museum-only or monument-only tickets are available for $2 for adults and $2 for seniors and youth 4-12. Jefferson Davis's birthday is celebrated every year on the first weekend of June. The celebration includes a battle reenactment as well as a Miss Confederacy pageant, in which contestants dress as Southern belles and display their knowledge of the customs of

view from the Jefferson Davis monument

OWENSBORO

the era. Seeing that it is a birthday celebration, there's also cake.

MB Roland Distillery

MB Roland Distillery (137 Barkers Mill Rd., Pembroke, 270/640-7744, http://mbrdistillery. com, 10am-6pm Tues.-Sat.) is a true craft distillery, where a handful of employees do everything from cook the mash to run the still to bottle the barrel-proof bourbon and whiskey and the variety of moonshines. MB Roland also uses all local corn for their production. Learn about the distillery and their products on a complimentary tour, which departs on the hour and includes a tasting. On select Saturdays May-November, the distillery hosts pickin' on the porch from 5pm-9pm, to which visitors are invited to bring picnics to accompany the free music.

Don F. Pratt Museum

Fort Campbell Army Base, which straddles the Kentucky-Tennessee border, is home to the 101st Airborne, the only Air Assault Division in the world, as well as a number of other units. It's basically a self-contained city, with a population of approximately 30,000. Located on base is the **Don F. Pratt Museum** (5702 Tennessee Ave., Fort Campbell, 270/798-3215, www.campbell.army.mil, 9:30am-4:30pm Mon.-Sat., free), which serves as the division museum for the 101st. Through well-crafted exhibits, the museum tells the story of the 101st and the many engagements in which it has been involved from World War II to the present day. In addition to photos, uniforms, and other artifacts, a plane and a tank are located within the museum, and additional planes and helicopters are located on the grounds. To access the museum, enter Fort Campbell through Gate 4 and stop at the visitors center, where everyone must provide identification and the owner of the vehicle must also provide the car's registration and proof of insurance.

Pennyrile Forest State Resort Park

Pennyrile Lake, surrounded by forest, is at the

OWENSBORO

heart of **Pennyrile Forest State Resort Park** (20781 Pennyrile Lodge Rd., Dawson Springs, 270/797-3421, http://parks.ky.gov, 24 hours daily, free). The small lake, where you can fish for bass, crappie, bluegill, and catfish, does not allow large motorboats, which means that those who take out one of the dock's rental pedal boats, rowboats, or canoes have run of the lake. Another way to enjoy the lake is at the public beach, which is deep and sandy and has a volleyball court. On-shore recreational options include playing a round of golf at the 18-hole regulation course or on the mini-golf course, challenging friends to a game of basketball or a tennis match, or hiking on one of the seven trails that range in distance from a few tenths of a mile to 13.5 miles. Pennyrile Forest State Resort Park is a great back-to-nature park with a true wilderness feel that appeals to those looking for a break from the developed world.

Agritourism

Much of the area surrounding Hopkinsville is agricultural, with corn and wheat fields painting the landscape. Enjoy a taste of rural life on a visit to one of the area's agritourism destinations. Plant lovers will want to stop in at **Hosta Haven** (1710 Long Pond Rd., Pembroke, 270/885-4000, www.hosta-haven.com, 8am-6pm daily), which has more types of hosta than you could possibly have known existed. The hostas landscape a gorgeous yard, providing ideas for gardeners, who can then buy the plants they like. An on-site gift shop also sells Amish quilts, antique glassware, and many other forms of locally made arts and crafts.

Family-run **Bravard Vineyards & Winery** (15000 Overton Rd., Hopkinsville, 270/269-2583, 10am-5pm Sat.) welcomes visitors to tour the six-acre vineyard, take a peek at the wine cellar, and enjoy a complimentary tasting.

Recreation

Scuba diving might be the last sport you'd think would be practiced in a city in southwestern Kentucky, but you'd be wrong. **Pennyroyal Scuba Blue Springs Resort** (602 Christian Quarry Rd., Hopkinsville, 270/887-2585, www.pennyroyalscuba.com) offers dives for beginners to advanced divers in a quarry filled with shimmering turquoise water. The 22-acre quarry ranges 5-120 feet in depth. Divers can view fish as well as more than 40 sunken treasures. The resort offers classes and rents equipment to qualified divers.

Accommodations

At **Pennyrile Forest State Resort Park** (20781 Pennyrile Lodge Rd., Dawson Springs, 270/797-3421, http://parks.ky.gov), the **Pennyrile Lodge** ($119.95) offers 24 standard double rooms with gorgeous lake views. The lodge has a rustic feel and is perched on a cliff above the lake. Additionally, 13 one- and two-bedroom **cottages** ($139.95-159.95) are available for rent. Some cottages have lake views (as well as private docks), while others are situated in wooded areas. Campers can choose from 36 sites with hookups in the state park's nicely wooded **campground** ($22) with restrooms, showers, and laundry facilities.

Multiple chain hotels are located along Fort Campbell Boulevard. The best of the bunch are the **Comfort Suites** (210 Harvey Way, 270/985-5484, www.comfortsuites.com, $109-119) and the **Fairfield Inn** (345 Griffin Bell Dr., 270/886-5151, www.marriott.com, $114). The Comfort Suites is newer, but both have clean rooms, friendly staff, wireless Internet access, and complimentary breakfast.

Food

The best food in Hopkinsville is at downtown's ◖ **Harper House** (914 S. Main St., 270/874-2858, www.harperhouseky.com, 5pm-10pm Wed.-Thurs., 5pm-11pm Fri.-Sat., $13.99-23.99), where regional favorites from around the United States are given the chef's personal touch. Get dinner started with ahi tuna tacos or Wisconsin cheese curds. Choosing an entrée is difficult, but the shrimp and grits, served in a rich gravy with bacon and mushrooms, is a favorite; you also can't go wrong with the margarita-braised short ribs, the chicken pot pie, or any of the steaks. Located in a restored

HOW A TOWN NAMED PARADISE TURNED INTO HELL

If you've ever listened to John Denver's *Rocky Mountain High* album, you've heard the song "Paradise" by John Prine, about a town that was destroyed by strip mining done by the Peabody Coal Company. The Paradise in that song was a town in Muhlenberg County, located, as John Denver sings, in Muhlenberg County, down by the Green River. If you look at a map, you'll find Paradise just south of the Western Kentucky Parkway to the east of Greenville. There's really no need to locate it, however, because Paradise no longer exists.

Although the song implies that Mr. Peabody and his coal train were responsible for the destruction of Paradise, that's not the whole story. While the strip mining done in Muhlenberg County and the Paradise area by the Peabody Coal Company and other companies like the Pittsburg & Midway Coal Mining Company certainly made Paradise a less desirable place to live, it didn't do it in completely. What made Paradise completely unlivable was the construction of the Paradise Fossil Plant by the Tennessee Valley Authority, one of the biggest consumers of the area's strip-mined coal. The plant rained ash on the town, creating major health concerns.

In 1969, the Tennessee Valley Authority bought out what was left of Paradise, destroying it completely, and expanding the plant, which, in the years since, has come under fire for noncompliance with the Clean Air Act. What remains of Paradise is one lone cemetery atop a hill and the receding memories of those who lived there before Paradise became hell.

100-year-old building, Harper House manages to feel sleek and contemporary and warm and welcoming at the same time. The booths at the bar, which offers an extensive list of drinks, are fun. Service is friendly, and the atmosphere is upscale casual.

Step back in time at **Ferrell's Snappy Service** (1001 S. Main St., Hopkinsville, 270/886-1445, 24 hours, $2.95-5.95), where waitresses still make hamburgers right in front of you by throwing a ball of beef on the grill, smashing it down into the sizzling grease, and then handing it to you piping hot. A Hopkinsville institution since 1929, Ferrell's also does breakfast, the menu dictated by what can be cooked on the grill.

Information and Services

Arm yourself with information on Hopkinsville and Christian County with help from the **Hopkinsville-Christian County Convention and Visitors Bureau** (2800 Fort Campbell Blvd., Hopkinsville, 270/885-9096, www.visithopkinsville.com, 8am-5pm Mon.-Fri.).

Getting There and Around

Hopkinsville is located east of Land Between the Lakes at the intersection of U.S. 68 and U.S. 41. From Cadiz, travel 20 miles (30 minutes) on U.S. 68 to reach Hopkinsville. Hopkinsville is also easily reachable from Henderson, which is directly 72 miles (1 hour 10 minutes) north of it by way of the Pennyrile Parkway.

Pennyrile State Forest Resort Park is northwest of Hopkinsville and can be reached by driving 21 miles (35 minutes) on northbound KY 109. Fort Campbell is to the south of Hopkinsville and can be reached by driving 16 miles (30 minutes) on southbound Fort Campbell Blvd. The Jefferson Davis State Historic Site is 10 miles (17 minutes) east of Hopkinsville on U.S. 68.

OWENSBORO

BACKGROUND

The Land

When the western United States was just a dream, a land visited by only a few intrepid men, Kentucky was known as the Gateway to the West. Now that the United States stretches from the Atlantic Ocean to the Pacific Ocean, Kentucky is best described as being located about smack in the middle of the eastern United States. Beyond that, Kentucky is a bit hard to define. It borders seven states (Missouri, Illinois, Indiana, Ohio, West Virginia, Virginia, and Tennessee), some of which are decidedly Midwestern and some of which are wholeheartedly Southern. Kentucky falls somewhere in between, with different areas leaning different ways. As for the official word, the Census Bureau groups Kentucky with the Southern states.

GEOGRAPHY

At 40,411 square miles (39,669 of which are land), Kentucky ranks 37th in size among the states, although the broad diversity of landscape belies the moderate size. As you move eastward across the state, from the peaks and valleys of the Appalachians to the lowland along the Mississippi River, you'll encounter two national parks, two national recreational areas, two national forests, 49 state

© THERESA DOWELL BLACKINTON

parks, nearly 40,000 acres of state forest, and 82 wildlife management areas. Among the developed land, there are only three truly urban areas (Louisville, Lexington, and Northern Kentucky). Geographically, the state is divided into five different regions: the Cumberland Plateau, the Bluegrass, the Pennyroyal, the Western Coalfield, and the Jackson Purchase.

Cumberland Plateau

A subsection of the Appalachian Plateau, the Cumberland Plateau runs through Eastern Kentucky, encompassing the Cumberland and Pine Mountain Ranges. The land here is composed of mountains, plateaus, and valleys. In the northwest corner, the hills are small, rising only a few hundred feet, but the hills grow as the Cumberland Plateau stretches southeast, with Black Mountain, Kentucky's highest peak, rising 4,139 feet above sea level. The Eastern Coalfields are contained within the Cumberland Plateau, hence the reason the region is often locally referred to as the Eastern Mountains and Coalfields. This region also hosts large (but threatened) stretches of hardwood forest. The Cumberland Plateau transitions to the Bluegrass and Pennyroyal regions at the Pottsville Escarpment, which is located in Daniel Boone National Forest. Here a sandstone belt creates cliffs, gorges, natural bridges, waterfalls, and other remarkable geologic formations.

Bluegrass

Encompassing the north-central section of the state, the Bluegrass is a land of rolling meadows. When most people think Kentucky, this is the geography that first comes to mind. Underlying layers of limestone, dolostone, and shale make the water pure and the land fertile, good for growing tobacco, breeding thoroughbreds, and making bourbon. The outer Bluegrass is marked by sandstone knobs, which encircle the inner meadows. The knobs are actually monadnocks, or freestanding hills created by the erosion of the land around them. The Kentucky River, a tributary of the Ohio River, cuts across the Bluegrass, creating a deep canyon called the Kentucky River Palisades. Here, you can find the most forested area in the Bluegrass, providing habitat for a variety of wildlife, including Kentucky's endangered bats, as well as hosting brilliant displays of wildflowers. Sinkholes, caves, and streams that disappear underground are commonly found near the Palisades.

Centered on Lexington, the Bluegrass region also encompasses Louisville and Northern Kentucky, making it the most populated region in the state. The Bluegrass region is bordered on the east by the Cumberland Plateau and on the south and west by the Pennyroyal.

Pennyroyal

Named for a small herb common to the region, the Pennyroyal (sometimes spelled as Pennyrile) stretches across southern Kentucky from the Cumberland Plateau to Kentucky Lake. The southern part of the Pennyroyal is mainly composed of flat land with few hills and is used primarily as farmland. It's also where you will find many of Kentucky's most popular man-made lakes. Limestone bedrock is prominent throughout the region. Its propensity to form caves, especially when capped with sandstone, helped establish the world's most extensive cave system, Mammoth Cave. As you move north across the Pennyroyal, the land transitions from flat farmland to the limestone ridges overtop the caves to an area of hard siltstone knobs that form the Muldraugh Hill escarpment where the Bluegrass meets the Pennyroyal.

Western Coalfield

Carved out of the Pennyroyal, with the Ohio River as its northern border, the Western Coalfield is home to large coal deposits that make it Kentucky's second coal-producing region. The land closer to the river is used for farming, with Kentucky's dark leaf tobacco grown here. Owensboro, the fourth-largest city in the state, is located in the Western Coalfield region.

Jackson Purchase

Comprising the most westward section of the

state, the Jackson Purchase was not purchased from the Chickasaw Indians until 1818. The purchase was negotiated by Isaac Shelby, first governor of Kentucky, and Andrew Jackson, who would go on to be the seventh president of the United States, hence the region's name. The region is bordered on the west by the Mississippi River, on the north by the Ohio River, on the east by Kentucky Lake, and on the south by Tennessee. Part of the Gulf Plains Region, it is characterized by floodplains and is the lowest-lying region in Kentucky. The Madrid Fault runs under this region, placing it in a high-risk category for earthquakes. In fact, major earthquakes in 1811 and 1812 reversed the course of the Mississippi and created Reelfoot Lake, which Kentucky shares with Tennessee.

Waterways

The fact that Kentucky has the greatest length of navigable waterways in the continental United States surprises many, but if you look at a map, this statistic makes sense. Kentucky's southern border is its only land border. The Ohio River forms the northern border, the Mississippi the western border, and the Big Sandy and Tug Fork the eastern border. These four rivers, along with the internal Kentucky, Green, Cumberland, and Tennessee Rivers, combine for a total of 1,070 miles of navigable waterway.

In addition to rivers, Kentucky boasts more than 45 noteworthy lakes and hundreds of smaller lakes and ponds, almost all of which are manmade. Kentucky Lake ranks as the largest manmade lake east of the Mississippi by surface area, covering 160,300 acres, while Lake Cumberland ranks as the largest manmade lake east of the Mississippi by water volume, with 6.1 million acre-feet of water, enough to cover the entire state with three inches of water. The profusion of lakes makes Kentucky a popular place for anglers and water-sports enthusiasts.

CLIMATE

Kentucky enjoys/suffers through (choose your verb depending on time of year) a moderate, relatively humid climate influenced by the Gulf of Mexico. Spring brings warm temperatures that average in the 60s and low 70s, although nights can still be chilly, and a colder day here and there is not unheard of. Variable is the best word to describe the season; just check out a decade's worth of Derby Day weather to see how much it can change. Your chances of needing a scarf or needing SPF 30 sunscreen on the first Saturday of May are about equal. Spring is the wettest season in Kentucky, although the state's biggest floods have occurred in winter. Tornadoes—which tend to occur most often between March and May, although they have touched down in Kentucky during every month of the year—are the biggest spring weather threat.

Summer weather in Kentucky can be summed up with two words: *hot* and *humid*. Temperatures generally reside in the 80s and often stretch into the 90s and even up to 100°F, with July the hottest month, although don't tell that to August. Nighttime lows hover around

A barge loaded with coal chugs down the Ohio River.

© THERESA DOWELL BLACKINTON

70°F in most of the state. Thunderstorms are fairly common, although they're usually quite short, with actual rainy days quite rare. Unfortunately, droughts affect the state with regularity and are especially difficult for Kentucky's many farmers.

Fall is mild in Kentucky and is the favorite season of many residents. Temperatures begin to fall in mid-September, although it's usually October before real relief from the heat sets in. As we move toward winter, temperatures fall through the 70s, pause for a while in the 60s and high 50s, and then head toward cold. Days are usually clear and sunny and are definitely crisp by most Halloweens. In mid- to late October, the trees really burst into color, with the Daniel Boone National Forest and Appalachian Mountains the best leaf-peeking locations.

Winter in Kentucky is cool to cold, depending on whether you're comparing the state to regions south of it or regions north of it. High temperatures average in the 40s, although there are plenty of days where the mercury doesn't rise past the 30s, and lows average in the 20s, although temperatures can plummet to the teens and single digits. Snowfall is unpredictable, although at least a few flurries fall every year. Large snows do occur but are fairly infrequent, with years of minor snow falling in between. In recent history, a late-season March snow in 1993 brought over 18 and up to 30 inches to many parts of the state, and in 2004 a snowstorm just before Christmas brought record snowfall to western and central parts of the state. Most recently, a severe ice storm hit the state in January 2009, killing 35 people and leaving 500,000 homes without power, some for over a week. Winter 2010 was also a rough one for Kentucky with repeated snows of six inches or more and bitter cold temperatures. More recent winters have been on the mild side.

Winter has also brought the worst floods to Kentucky. In January and February 1937, during the Great Depression, the Ohio River flooded its bank, severely affecting cities and towns along the length of it. In Paducah, which received 18 inches of rain in 16 days, the river crested at 60.8 feet. In Louisville, which received 15 inches of rain in 12 days and 19 inches over the course of the month, the river crested at 85.4 feet, 30 feet over flood stage, submerging more than 70 percent of the city. In March 1997, the river again rose to dangerous levels (up to 20 feet over flood stage), beating 1937 records in some areas. In many areas, the flooding lasted for more than two weeks and caused major damage and 19 deaths. In Louisville, both I-64 and I-65 were shut down.

ENVIRONMENTAL ISSUES

Far and away, Kentucky's most pressing environmental issues are related to mining. Two types of mining take place in Kentucky, underground and surface (also known as strip or mountaintop removal), with surface mining being the most environmentally devastating. Although a recent uptick in regulations has dramatically cut the number of surface mines in Kentucky, surface mining is far from extinct. In surface mining, mountaintop blasting is used to remove the sometimes hundreds of feet of rock and soil that exist overtop a mine seam. Before the blast, the mountains are usually completely logged. In the past, the overburden (or what remained of the mountain after the blast) was deposited in valleys, creating valley fills. In the process, much of the overburden ended up dumped into headwater mountain streams, polluting the water and even sometimes stopping it up. An EPA report estimates that between 1985 and 2001, 724 miles of Appalachian streams were covered by overburden. Current regulations require that mines be covered with the overburden and the mountain reclaimed once the mine's resources are exhausted. How well that is done is a matter of debate. Proponents of coal mines point to the many successful restoration projects. In Eastern Kentucky, for example, many people credit the mines with providing them flatland for development, a rare commodity. Golf courses, parks, government buildings, office complexes, and wildlife management areas have all been located on reclaimed surface mines. Opponents often argue that the

© THERESA DOWELL BLACKINTON

the now-closed Blue Heron Mine

plants used to reclaim surface mine sites are non-native and invasive.

Another environmental danger introduced by coal mines are slurry ponds, storage sites for the billions of gallons of toxic waste created by mining. In October 2000, a 2.2-billion-gallon slurry pond that belonged to Massey Energy failed and sent 300 million gallons of coal sludge into Coldwater and Wolf Creeks. This spill was 25 times larger than the Exxon-Valdez oil spill.

Kentucky's waterways are threatened by more than the coal industry. Elevated levels of mercury and PCBs (polycarbonate biphenyls) have been regularly found in Kentucky lakes and rivers, with the Ohio River one of the worst affected. Point source discharge, agricultural runoff, inappropriate waste disposal, urban runoff, resource extraction, and habitat modifications all lead to contamination. Some bodies of water also suffer from fecal coliform pollution caused by the illegal straight pipe discharge of sewage. The Division of Water provides updates on safe fish consumption as well as swimming warnings. There is some good news, however, especially for those who hate to add to our waste problem through the consumption of bottled water. In 2013, Louisville's drinking water was named the best-tasting water in the country by the American Water Works Association.

According to the Air Quality Index, Kentucky's overall air quality is good, although people with respiratory illnesses should be aware that Louisville and other Ohio Valley cities and towns can be hard on the lungs in the peak of summer. Industry emissions, car emissions, and other air pollutants can become trapped in the valley, leading to high ozone levels. News reports as well as electronic interstate signs display ozone alerts on days when air pollution is bad. Louisville also regularly shows up on lists of the worst cities for allergies, especially spring allergies.

Flora and Fauna

TREES

A remarkable 48 percent of Kentucky land is forested. Oak/hickory forests account for most of this acreage (72 percent), while beech/maple forests account for most of the rest. Also spreading their canopies in Kentucky are four species of magnolias, tulip poplars (the state tree), eastern hemlocks, white pines, birches, buckeyes, paw paws, dogwoods, beeches, hollies, and ashes. In the Jackson Purchase region, coastal tree species more common to southeastern states, such as the bald cypress, willow oak, pecan, and sweet gum, are routinely found, while the Bluegrass region showcases old species of the coffee tree, black walnut, bur oak, and blue ash. Blanton Forest on Pine Mountain in Eastern Kentucky's Harlan County is home to the largest old-growth forest in Kentucky. Trees here are over 100 feet tall and date back to the 1600s. With so much land dedicated to forests, it's not surprising that Kentucky ranks second nationally in lumber production, with white oak, yellow poplar, and red oak the lead lumber producers.

FLOWERS, SHRUBS, AND GRASSES

Among the many wildflowers that brighten Kentucky parks and roadways in the spring and fall are Virginia bluebells, trilliums, stonecrops, star chickweeds, squirrel corns, May apples, larkspurs, Jacob's ladders, poppies, and catchflies. Standing tall among these flowers is the goldenrod, the state flower. Thirty species of goldenrod can be found throughout Kentucky; its abundance was one of the reasons it was chosen as state flower in 1926.

Much more than goldenrod, bluegrass is the plant most commonly associated with Kentucky. The association is so strong that it comes as a surprise to most people to learn that bluegrass is not native to Kentucky or to anywhere in the United States. Europe, northern Asia, and the mountains of Algeria and Morocco are bluegrass's native habitats. Biologists speculate that this popular grass was brought to North America by early settlers and then began to thrive in Kentucky. A hearty species, Kentucky bluegrass is a popular choice for baseball fields and other turf playing surfaces. As for the name, it comes from the flower heads that develop and appear blue if the grass is allowed to grow to its full height of nearly two feet.

MAMMALS

Among Kentucky's mammals you'll find many of the usual suspects for the region. White-tailed deer are everywhere, making up the highest per-capita population in the United States. In wooded areas, gray and red fox, raccoons, skunks, and woodchucks make their homes. Near water, you'll find beavers, river otters, mink, and muskrats. But Kentucky

© THERESA DOWELL BLACKINTON

a bear cub climbing a tree

© THERESA DOWELL BLACKINTON

the gray squirrel, Kentucky's state animal

has a few surprises up its sleeve too. Coyotes are abundant, often living much closer to humans than you'd suppose. Bobcats are widespread, although they prefer heavy forest and hunt at sunrise and sunset, making spotting them difficult. Pumas (also known as cougars and mountain lions) have been reported but not confirmed. In the mountains of Eastern Kentucky and in Daniel Boone National Forest, black bears can be found. Perhaps the least expected of Kentucky's wildlife, however, is the elk. Reintroduced to Kentucky's eastern counties in 1997, the elk population now numbers more than 10,000, making Kentucky's herd the largest east of the Rocky Mountains. Perhaps not as exciting as elk and bear, but vitally important to the ecosystem, are bats, of which Kentucky has several species, including the endangered gray, Indiana, and Virginia big-eared species. Also in the category of unappreciated animals is the squirrel, which, for reasons unknown to me or any other Kentuckian I know, is the state animal. To be more specific, it's the gray squirrel that holds the title.

BIRDS

Kentucky has a healthy avian population of songbirds, raptors, waterfowl, and game birds. Cardinals (the state bird), blue jays, robins, bluebirds, chickadees, swallows, sparrows, finches, warblers, wrens, and vireos, as well as woodpeckers and hummingbirds, are easily spotted throughout the state. Head to the lake and you'll find many species of heron, duck, and geese. As for raptors, hawks, vultures, and owls are the most common. Peregrine falcons and eagles (bald and golden) are less common but present. You're most likely to spot bald eagles near waterways in the colder months. They're regularly seen along the Ohio River, and some state parks—including Dale Hollow Lake and the parks at Land Between the Lakes—offer eagle watches and walks. If you're a hunter, set your sights on quail, pheasant, and wild turkeys. Restocked in the state in the 1950s, wild turkeys have successfully established residence, and Kentucky now has the highest per capita population of wild turkeys in the United States.

FISH, AMPHIBIANS, AND REPTILES

Thanks to the many rivers, streams, and lakes in Kentucky, fishing is a popular pastime, and anglers face no shortage of fish. Cast a line, and you could reel in a number of species of bass (including largemouth, smallmouth, and striped), crappie, carp, catfish, perch, sunfish, trout, and walleye. Also found in Kentucky is the muskie, a relatively uncommon fish that is favored by anglers who like a challenge. Muskie regularly grow to four feet or longer, but despite their size, manage to remain hard to catch and even harder to land, and are often referred to as "the fish of ten thousand casts." Cave Run Lake, known as the muskie capital of the South, is the place to give muskie fishing a go.

In addition to fish, Kentucky's waterways are home to salamanders, newts, toads, and numerous types of frogs. The deep bellow of a bullfrog is summertime music to many nature lovers.

Among the reptiles that call the Bluegrass

which are very rare, also prefer forests. All four of these snakes avoid human contact whenever possible. You're much more likely to encounter a black rat snake, garter snake, milk snake, cotton snake, king snake, or other non-venomous snake. If you are bitten, however, you should seek immediate medical attention.

INSECTS

More than 10,000 species of bugs can be found in Kentucky. Winning the award for least popular is the mosquito, which has been known to ruin more than one summer night. In recent years, they've also acted as carriers of the West Nile Virus. Another particularly detested creature, though actually a mite and not an insect, is the tick, which is common in wooded areas. Though known Lyme disease-carrying ticks have not been found in Kentucky, multiple cases of Lyme disease are reported every year. Additionally, ticks carrying the potentially more dangerous Rocky Mountain Spotted Fever are found in Kentucky.

Not all insects are pests, of course, and many perform the important job of pollination. Some of the more beloved Kentucky insects are butterflies, dragonflies, and damselflies. Everyone's childhood favorite is the firefly, or lightning bug, a type of flying beetle with a luminescent abdomen that flashes during the summer mating season. Fireflies are found in lawns, meadows, and woodlands across the state, and no childhood in Kentucky is complete without evenings spent catching lightning bugs and keeping them in Mason jars. Another notable summer insect is the cicada, a fairly large (usually longer than an inch) bug usually found on trees, at least until they shed their skin and take flight. What makes cicadas really stand out is the high-pitched droning noise they make as part of their courtship ritual. Many people find the noise extremely irritating, and when cicada numbers are high, the noise can be overwhelmingly loud. Two kinds of cicadas are common in Kentucky: the annual cicada and the periodical cicada. Periodical cicadas emerge only every 13 or 17 years, so they're not often seen or heard, but you'd better believe that when they do come out, you'll know it.

© THERESA DOWELL BLACKINTON

Eagles visit Kentucky in winter.

State home are a few species of skinks, multiple species of turtles, and 32 species of snakes. Of these snakes, four are venomous: the copperhead, water moccasin (also called cottonmouth), timber rattlesnake, and Western pygmy rattlesnake. All four of these snakes belong to the pit viper family and thus have similar characteristics. Three shared characteristics allow you to distinguish these four venomous species from Kentucky's 28 non-venomous species: pupil shape (venomous snakes have elliptical, cat-like pupils in contrast to the round pupils of non-venomous snakes), the presence of a pit (venomous snakes have a sensory area on the side of the head that looks like a nostril), and scale arrangement (venomous snakes have only a single row of scales on their underside, whereas non-venomous snakes have a double row). Copperheads prefer deciduous forest and mixed woodlands; water moccasins prefer swamps, shallow lakes, and sluggish streams (not deep, clear, or moving water); timber rattlesnakes prefer rugged terrain in deciduous forests; and western pygmy rattlesnakes,

History

NATIVE AMERICANS

Although Kentucky was frequented by several Native American tribes who used the land as a hunting ground, very few Native American settlements existed. The Cherokee frequented southeastern Kentucky, while the Shawnee would cross into Kentucky from the north. The most lasting claim to the land was made by the Chickasaw, who established a permanent settlement in the very western area of Kentucky along the Tennessee border. The Chickasaws maintained claims to this area until it was purchased from them by Andrew Jackson and Isaac Shelby in 1818. The name Kentucky traces its origin back to the Iroquois word *Ken-tah-ten,* meaning "land of tomorrow."

EARLY SETTLEMENT

In 1750, Dr. Thomas Walker led the first documented exploration into Kentucky, building the first non-Native American house in the state while surveying for the Loyal Land Company. Prior to his visit, other Europeans had certainly passed through, but none had left witness, and other settlers would follow despite a 1763 royal proclamation forbidding settlement west of the Appalachians. The most notable of settlers, famous frontiersman Daniel Boone, first entered Kentucky in 1767, returning in 1769 to conduct two years of intensive surveying. In 1774, James Harrod established the first permanent settlement in Kentucky, Harrodsburg, which quickly came under attack by Native Americans, was abandoned, and was resettled in 1775. Boone, who spent 1775 blazing the Wilderness Trail into Kentucky through the Cumberland Gap, then founded Boonesborough as Kentucky's second settlement. In 1776, Kentucky became a county of Virginia, and in the following years, the population grew rapidly as settlers entered the state via the Cumberland Gap or the Ohio River. During the Revolutionary War, a number of skirmishes took place in Kentucky, including the 1782 Battle of Blue Lick, one of the last battles of the war, in which 50 British rangers and 300 Indians ambushed 182 Kentucky militiamen, including Daniel Boone and his son Israel, who was killed. Economic restrictions imposed by Virginia as well as a perceived lack of protection from Virginia led to a series of conventions held in Danville from 1784 to 1791 with the goal of independence. This goal was achieved on June 1, 1792, when the Commonwealth of Kentucky was admitted to the union as the 15th state.

ANTEBELLUM KENTUCKY

Kentucky grew rapidly in the late 1700s and early 1800s as river traffic began to crowd the Ohio and Mississippi Rivers. Louisville emerged as the state's largest city, a transportation hub and commercial center, while Lexington became a cultural center, dubbed the Athens of the West. The War of 1812 brought economic prosperity, as manufacturing boomed due to trade restrictions with Britain, but it also brought great loss of life. Kentucky suffered more casualties than all other states combined.

In addition to an influx of settlers from other states, Kentucky also experienced emigration from other countries, with large numbers of German and Irish settling in the Bluegrass State. By the mid-1850s, German immigrants made up one-third of Louisville's population. This swift change in demographics led to growing prejudice and the formation of the Know-Nothing Party, an anti-immigrant, anti-Catholic party whose name came from the secretive nature of the party with members claiming to "know nothing" when questioned. In Louisville, racial tension peaked on August 6, 1855, which came to be known as Bloody Monday, when rumors that foreigners and Catholics had interfered in the day's elections

© THERESA DOWELL BLACKINTON

a Civil War cemetery

led to violence. Estimates of the death toll reach above 100, with many others injured and much property destroyed by fire. In the years leading up to the Civil War, more than 10,000 immigrants would leave the state, striking out for Chicago, St. Louis, and Milwaukee, but many more would stay and make a profound impact on Kentucky.

Throughout most of Kentucky, small-scale agriculture ruled during the first half of the 1800s, and as a result there was little use for slaves. In fact, it was illegal to import slaves into the state from 1833 to 1850. That law was overturned, however, and Kentucky soon became the site of a huge slave market, thanks to its location along the Ohio River. Opinions on slavery were split in the state, with proponents of the institution and staunch abolitionists clashing frequently on the issue. Kentucky played a large role in establishing national policy on slavery thanks to Congressman Henry Clay, who authored both the Missouri Compromise and the Compromise of 1850, earning the nickname the Great Compromiser.

CIVIL WAR

When the Civil War broke out, Kentucky decided not to choose sides, declaring itself neutral in May 1861. For a short period, that neutrality was respected as Union troops set up camp just across the border in Indiana, while Confederate troops established their camps in Tennessee. In September 1861, however, the Confederates occupied Columbus, Kentucky, stretching a chain across the Mississippi River to prevent Union boats from moving south. General Grant retaliated by entering Paducah with his Union troops. State elections in the fall of 1861 had changed the constituency of the Kentucky government to a majority of Unionists, so in response to the violation of neutrality, the General Assembly demanded that the Confederates withdraw and raised the Union flag over the capital. Not all of Kentucky agreed with this move, and in December a Confederate provisional government was set up in Bowling Green, with this government entering the Confederacy on December 10. Kentucky thus became the only state to have a star on both the Union and the Confederate flags.

The Civil War in Kentucky was very much brother against brother. In fact, both the president of the Union, Abraham Lincoln, and the president of the Confederacy, Jefferson Davis, hailed from Kentucky. The two men were born in log cabins less than 100 miles from each other within the span of one year. As a slave state, with slaves accounting for nearly 20 percent of the population at the start of the war, and a border state, Kentucky was of great value to both sides. Lincoln, recognizing the state's importance, said, "I hope to have God on my side, but I must have Kentucky." He followed this with the proclamation, "I think to lose Kentucky is nearly the same as to lose the whole game."

Major battles that took place in the Bluegrass State include the Battle of Mill Springs in January 1862 and the Battle of Perryville in October 1862. That year also brought the first of John Hunt Morgan's famous raids, which would eventually extend into Indiana and Ohio and mark the northernmost penetration of Confederate forces.

Underground Railroad

Although itself a slave state, Kentucky played an important role in the Underground Railroad thanks to the fact that it shared 700 miles of border with free states. Cincinnati, which was home to a free black population a few hundred strong and large populations of anti-slavery Quakers, Presbyterians, and Methodists, was an important station on the Underground Railroad. As a result, many slaves passed through the state as they attempted to reach freedom. Kentucky was actually one of the last states to free its slaves. As a slave state in the Union, Kentucky was an anomaly, and because the Emancipation Proclamation freed slaves in the Confederate States, Kentucky's slaves did not benefit.

EARLY 20TH CENTURY

The early 20th century was a tumultuous, but also lucrative, time for two of Kentucky's main industries: coal and tobacco. Coal mines proliferated at the start of the century, with coal companies sprouting up all over the coal regions of eastern and western Kentucky. Production boomed through World War I, but the postwar years were difficult, with decreased demand leading to unrest. In the 1930s, attempts were made to organize the coal industry, resulting in often bloody riots between miners and mining companies and a 1937 investigation into allegations that miners' civil rights were being violated. Finally, in 1939, United Mine Workers of America was recognized as the bargaining agent for Kentucky miners. Demand for coal surged again with World War II and has remained strong in the decades since.

For tobacco, the dawn of the 20th century brought depressed tobacco prices due to monopolistic practices put in place by buyers. A gathering of more than 1,000 farmers in tiny Guthrie, Kentucky, led to the formation of the Planters Protective Association, which sought to protect the interests of the growers. Some farmers refused to join, and as a result were paid higher prices by the buyers trust. In retaliation, members of the association became night riders, burning the barns and fields of those who sold independently to the buyers and intimidating thousands of more farmers into joining their association. This outbreak of lawlessness, known as the Black Patch War or the Tobacco War, lasted from 1904 to 1909, when the state militia bargained a truce, breaking the monopoly and instituting tobacco auctions, which remained the primary way of selling tobacco until the buyout of 2004.

The Great Depression left many in Kentucky without work, although many were later employed in relief jobs that brought improvements to the state. The Tennessee Valley Authority (TVA) was one of the biggest employers, putting Kentuckians to work building dams, improving highways, and creating recreational areas. The Civilian Conservation Corp (CCC) was also active in Kentucky, and many state parks still retain evidence of CCC work. World War II, which helped lift the United States out of the Depression, brought jobs to the state. Many men enlisted in or were drafted into the military, while other Kentuckians, including many women, went to work manufacturing supplies needed for the war effort. Additionally, Kentucky's coal and agricultural products were again in high demand.

CIVIL RIGHTS MOVEMENT

Although most people associate the Civil Rights Movement with the 1960s, efforts in Kentucky date back to the Civil War era. In fact, in 1870, members of the A.M.E. church in Louisville organized a protest of the city's segregated streetcars, beginning the practice of churches being heavily involved in civil rights efforts. The protests were mainly unsuccessful, with the 1904 Supreme Court case *Plessy v. Ferguson* institutionalizing Jim Crow and the concept of "separate but equal." Kentucky would use this ruling to enact the Day Law in 1908, segregating schools. Although later appealed to the Supreme Court, it was upheld. In both this case and *Plessy v. Ferguson,* Justice John Marshall Harlan, a Kentuckian, would dissent, arguing in the favor of civil liberties for all.

Notable changes to racial policies began to take hold in Kentucky in the 1940s, with Louisville taking some of the first steps. The main branch of the Louisville Free Public Library and Louisville-area hospitals were desegregated in 1948. In 1950, the Day Law was amended to allow universities to admit black students if Kentucky State, the state's African American college, did not offer the program they were interested in. That year, Bellarmine, Ursuline, Nazareth, and the University of Louisville admitted black students, as did Berea, which had admitted blacks since the college's founding, but had been forced to stop by the Day Law. The University of Kentucky, however, did not admit African American undergraduates until *Brown v. Board of Education* ruled segregation of schools illegal in 1954. By 1955, all Kentucky universities were desegregated, and the integration of public schools began in 1956. Although many schools desegregated reluctantly, they mainly did so peacefully. An exception, however, was Sturgis High School in Union County, where Governor Chandler had to send in the state police and the National Guard to protect the black students who had enrolled and were trying to attend class.

The highlight of the 1960s was the passing of the Kentucky Civil Rights Act in 1966, which Martin Luther King Jr. hailed as "the strongest and most comprehensive civil rights bill passed by a Southern state." Among other provisions, the law prevented discrimination in employment and public accommodations and repealed all old segregation laws. An amendment to protect against housing discrimination was added in 1968.

KENTUCKY TODAY

Twenty-first century Kentucky is a state in the midst of great change. Traditional jobs are leaving the state as well as the nation, and the government and citizens are having to rethink the economy and how best to be equipped for today's marketplace. The population, although still overwhelmingly white, is growing more diverse, keeping racial issues (though now much more broadly defined) in the foreground. Reworking the education system has been a long-term project and remains so. For now, the challenge for Kentucky is to keep pace with the rapidly changing world while staying true to the culture and values that make the Bluegrass State unique.

Government and Economy

GOVERNMENT

As with the national government, Kentucky's state government is composed of an executive branch, a legislative branch, and a judicial branch. Officially named the Commonwealth of Kentucky, the Bluegrass State joins Virginia, Pennsylvania, and Massachusetts as the nation's only commonwealths. It also belongs to the small group of five states that holds elections in odd-numbered years. Kentucky governors of note include A. B. "Happy" Chandler, who went on to become the second commissioner of Major League Baseball and oversaw the integration that brought Jackie Robinson and other African American players into the league, and Martha Layne Collins, the first and (so far) only female governor.

Historically Kentucky has been a Democratic state with more than 50 percent of the population registered Democrat and less than 40 percent registered Republican. Kentucky Democrats have always been more conservative, especially socially, than their counterparts on the coasts. For many years, Kentucky was somewhat of a swing state, going to both Republican and Democrat presidential nominees. In fact, from 1964 to 2004, Kentucky's vote always went to the man who would become president. Only in 2008, when the state went to John McCain (who won the state by a 16 percent margin) and the country went to Barack Obama did Kentucky lose its status as a bellwether state. In the 2008 election, only eight of Kentucky's 120 counties went to Obama—four in Eastern Kentucky, two in Western Kentucky (near Owensboro), the county containing Louisville, and the county containing Lexington. In a troubling turn for Democrats, a number of union-stronghold counties in the southeast went Republican for

Kentucky State Capitol

© THERESA DOWELL BLACKINTON

the first time since 1984. This trend held in 2012. Interestingly, while voting Republicans to national office, Kentucky continues to send Democrats to Frankfort. Only eight Republicans have held the post of governor.

At the federal level, Kentucky is represented by two voices in the Senate and six in the House of Representatives. At the time of research, the only Democrat of the bunch was Representative John Yarmuth of the Third Congressional District, which covers Louisville. The two senators, Mitch McConnell and Rand Paul, carry what many might consider outsized influence in the Republican Party and the Senate in general.

ECONOMY

With a 2011 per capita personal income of $23,033, Kentucky ranks nearly at the bottom, in position 46 among the 50 states. The economic crisis that hit in 2009 further damaged an already weak economy, and the recovery has been slow, with unemployment lingering at 8.1 percent as of May 2013. Additionally, the poverty rate in 2011 (the last year for which data are available) was 18.1 percent, 4 percentage points higher than the national average, and again placing Kentucky near the bottom. Most disturbing, perhaps, is how concentrated the poverty is in Eastern Kentucky. Thirty of Kentucky's 120 counties have poverty rates above 25 percent; all but four of these are in Eastern Kentucky. Wolfe County, with a 42.2 percent poverty rate and a median income of only $20,910, is Kentucky's poorest. Only four of Kentucky's counties can boast of a poverty rate of less than 10 percent; three surround Louisville, and one is in Northern Kentucky. Oldham County, with a median income of $79,417, is the wealthiest. It isn't all bad news for Kentucky, however. The state's big cities continue to attract jobs, and health and education, two of the only fields to see continued growth even during the recession, have taken over as Kentucky's biggest employers. The major challenge for Kentucky, in addition to maintaining and growing jobs, is to find a way to spread opportunity throughout the state.

© THERESA DOWELL BLACKINTON

Horses are big money in Kentucky.

AGRITOURISM

With tobacco sales in a state of decline and the ability to make a living from traditional farming becoming increasingly difficult, Kentucky farmers are looking for new ways to maintain their livelihood as well as their traditions. For many of these farmers, agritourism is the path to the future. It allows them to keep their farms and the lifestyle they love, while allowing city folk to get back to their roots, or at least to get a better idea of where their food comes from. As Kentucky's agritourism website (www.kentuckyfarmsarefun.com) so plainly puts it, farms are fun. Check out these agritourism ventures, and you're sure to agree.

BOYD'S ORCHARD

From the first strawberries of the spring to the last pumpkins of the fall, **Boyd's Orchard** (www.boydorchards.com) in Versailles grows and sells some awfully fine produce. You can venture out into the fields to pick your own or choose from the selection in the farm market. Fall is celebrated with festivals that feature hayrides, a petting zoo, pony rides, and a giant kids' play area. You'll want to stay for lunch, the creative café menu making the most out of what's fresh.

CHANEY'S DAIRY BARN

Chaney's Dairy Barn (www.chaneysdairybarn.com) is the place to get ice cream in Bowling Green. Each of the rich flavors, from straight-up vanilla to Wow Now Brownie Cow, is made on-site with milk from the farm's cows.

Take a tour of the farm to meet and even milk the cows. Special events like Ice Cream and a Mooovie are family favorites.

KENNY'S FARMHOUSE CHEESE

For another delicious dairy product, try some of **Kenny's Farmhouse Cheese** (www.kennyscountrycheese.com). Some of the finest restaurants in the state serve these delicious cheeses, which come in a variety of styles. Try the Kentucky Rose, a creamy light blue cheese. The cheese is made in the old-world style with the farm's own milk. Call ahead to arrange a tour when you're in the Barren River area.

LAVENDER HILLS OF KENTUCKY

The first lavender farm in the state, **Lavender Hills of Kentucky** (www.lavenderhillsofkentucky.com) brightens up the Northern Kentucky countryside with its gorgeous fields of flowers. Enjoy the scent and the sight, and then browse the gift shop to see the many ways in which lavender can be used.

LOVERS LEAP VINEYARDS & WINERY

Located in Lawrenceburg, **Lovers Leap Vineyards & Winery** (www.loversleapwine.com) is a fun alternative to all the nearby bourbon distilleries. Visitors are welcome to wander the 20-acre vineyard and sit for a tasting. If you're interested in the process, don't be shy about asking for a peek at the machinery.

Agriculture

While other states have moved away from agricultural-based economies, Kentucky maintains a strong tie to its roots, with more farms per square mile than any other state and more than half of the state's land used for agriculture. Overall, Kentucky ranks fifth in number of farms, the majority of which are small, family-run outfits.

Kentucky's farms are divided between livestock and crop farms. Horses are the largest moneymakers in the livestock category. In fact, Kentucky accounts for 82 percent of horse and mule production in the United States. Thoroughbred horses are Kentucky's specialty, and sale and stud fees bring in big bucks, although the horse industry was hit hard by the recession. Other livestock commodities that contribute to Kentucky's economy are beef cattle, dairy products, hogs, and chickens.

Of Kentucky's cash crops, the biggest are corn, soybeans, wheat, hay, fruit, greenhouse products, and, of course, tobacco. Kentucky farms produce more than 170 million pounds of tobacco annually. Only North Carolina produces more tobacco than Kentucky. Two main types of tobacco are grown in Kentucky: burley, which is used in cigarettes, and dark leaf tobacco, which is used in snuff. Burley tobacco farms are found in 110 of Kentucky's 120 counties, while dark leaf tobacco farms are concentrated in 20 counties in Western Kentucky. A national buyout in 2004 ended price supports, quotas, and geographic limitations and provided $2.5 billion to Kentucky farmers over a 10-year period to help them move from tobacco to other crops. As a result, the number of tobacco farms in Kentucky has dropped dramatically, and nearly all remaining tobacco farmers work under contract to a buyer. Declines in domestic sales and increases in worldwide tobacco production have contributed to lower demand.

Overall, farming is becoming a much more difficult means of making a living. While net farm income has continually gone up, family living expenses have surpassed any gains. Agritourism (www.kentuckyfarmsarefun.com) is a bright spot in agriculture, with more people becoming interested in visiting farms to learn firsthand where their food comes from. To support Kentucky farmers, look for the Kentucky Proud label wherever you shop. A directory of farmers markets can be found on the Kentucky Department of Agriculture webpage (www.kyagr.com).

Coal Mining

Coal mining in Kentucky dates back to 1820 when the first commercial mine opened in Western Kentucky's Muhlenberg County. It didn't take long for the field to take off. In 1843, 100,000 tons of coal were mined. In 1879, that number reached one million, and in 1963, it topped 100 million. In 2000, production peaked at 150 million tons, and in the years since then has remained around 120 million tons. This remarkable tonnage places Kentucky third on the list of most productive coal-mining states, falling in line behind Wyoming and West Virginia.

Kentucky's coal comes from two distinct fields, the Eastern Coal Field, which is the most productive in the nation, and the Western Coal Field. Kentucky uses two types of mining to extract coal: surface (also known as strip or mountaintop removal) and underground. Of the 108.8 million tons of coal produced in 2011, 65.3 million tons came from underground mines and 43.5 million tons came from surface mines. In total, 400 mines are located in Kentucky, with 375 of them in the Eastern Coal Field. The mines are located in 32 counties, 24 in the east and 8 in the west.

Coal that is mined in Kentucky is put to a variety of purposes. At home, it is used for power, with more than 90 percent of Kentucky's electricity coming from coal. Because coal is locally sourced, Kentucky's power costs rank among the lowest in the nation. That doesn't mean it comes without a price, however. Setting aside environmental and philosophical thoughts, coal mining does bring much needed revenue to the state. Kentucky earns more than $3.5 billion from the sale of coal to 30 states and four countries, with coal company taxes bringing in an additional $220 million. About 18,000 Kentuckians are employed directly in the mines, with an additional 54,000 indirectly employed by coal mining. Many coal miners earn upwards of $1,000 a week, making it a very well-paying job for the state.

Since commercial coal mining began in Kentucky, more than 7,000 miners have died. From 2000 to mid-2013, 104 miners lost their lives in Kentucky. The most recent mine disaster (defined as an incident killing five or more people) was an explosion in the Darby Mine in Holmes in 2006, resulting in the death of five miners. Additionally, thousands of other Kentucky miners have died as a result of black lung disease. Nationwide, more than 20,000 miners died from the disease between 1990 and 2007, and despite regulations regarding coal dust and the development of better equipment, black lung deaths rose 38 percent from 1998 to 2004. In a study conducted from 2005 to 2009, 9 percent of participating coal miners in Eastern Kentucky had black lung.

WHAT'S THAT YOU SAY?

As you travel across Kentucky, you may notice a broad array of dialects. You'll find people who speak with Midwestern accents and people who speak with Southern accents. You'll find people with no noticeable accent, and you'll find people with accents that are simply unidentifiable to the untrained ear. The most distinct and delightful of Kentucky's dialects is the Appalachian dialect, which can be traced back to Scotch-Irish immigration, and which has maintained its peculiarities thanks to the isolated nature of the region. (You really do have to get off the beaten path to find the communities that have preserved this dialect more than on a superficial level.) For lovers of language, a conversation with someone with deep roots in Appalachia is a treat. Unfortunately, for many in this area, their unique language has often been deemed a sign of ignorance or stupidity, although it's no more a reflection of their intelligence than the Bostonian need to call a car a "cah" is a reflection of theirs.

The following "glossary" reveals some of the most interesting idiosyncrasies you may hear as you travel throughout Kentucky.

UNUSUAL PRONUNCIATIONS

- **liberry:** library
- **pacific:** specific
- **nekkid:** naked
- **crick:** creek
- **holler:** hollow
- **worsh:** wash
- **worter:** water
- Additionally, many Kentuckians tend to stress the first syllable of words that are more commonly stressed on the second syllable. For instance: UM-brell-a, DE-troit, IN-sur-ance.

UNIQUE VOCABULARY

- **Coke:** any and all types of soda
- **pocketbook:** purse
- **gully washer:** torrential rain
- **poke:** bag
- **stove eye:** burner
- **your people:** relatives, kin
- **Papaw and Mamaw or Peepaw and Meemaw:** Grandpa and Grandma

Healthcare

Although Kentucky has been slow to leave behind or transform traditional industries that are unable to keep pace in today's world, the state has at the same time been making leaps and bounds in the health field, one of few occupational areas that has continued to grow both nationally and within the state during tough economic times. Humana, which is headquartered in Louisville, is Kentucky's third-biggest private employer, while Norton, a Kentucky-based hospital chain, employs thousands of others. Other healthcare workers find jobs in the state's many hospitals as well as at corporations in the health field. Lexington's University of Kentucky hospital and multiple hospitals in Louisville, including Kosair Children's Hospital, University of Louisville Hospital, Jewish Hospital, Baptist Health Louisville, and Norton Hospital, have received national recognition. Jewish Hospital was the site of the nation's first hand transplants as well as the first and second transplants of the AbioCor artificial heart.

Manufacturing and Other Industry

Manufacturing has long played a vital role in the Kentucky economy, coming in behind health and education services in the number of workers employed. Ford, Toyota, and GE employ the largest numbers of workers in the field. Unfortunately, for Kentucky workers, the majority of whom lack a college education,

- **Monday a week:** next Monday
- **over yonder:** over there
- **plainspoken:** honest
- **put out:** angry or upset
- **funny turned:** unusual
- **learned me:** taught
- **ought not:** shouldn't
- **fixin':** preparing

UNFAMILIAR PHRASES

- **Give someone down the road:** to tell someone off
- **Bless your heart:** A means of softening an insult. Example: "That girl of yours sure does have big ears, bless her heart."

UNCOMMON GRAMMAR

- **Use of "done" as a modifying verb:** I done told you.
- **Use of past participle in place of past simple:** I seen her last night.
- **Nonstandard past tenses:** "knowed" in place of "knew," "choosed" in place of "chose," "brung" in place of "brought"

- **Use of "was" in place of "were":** You was sitting by the fireplace.
- **Use of "been" instead of "have been":** I been living here since I graduated.
- **Use of double modals:** I might could eat a second dessert.
- **Use of "got" in place of "have":** I got a fishing pole.
- **Use of "got to" for "started":** I got to drinking with my friends at the bar and didn't get home until morning.
- **Irregular use of contractions:** He don't like me none. When I weren't looking, he took my pen.
- **Use of "real" instead of "really":** Our neighbor's real nice.
- **Use of "right" instead of "quite":** I'm right tired.
- **Use of "this here" and "that there":** This here is my plate. That there is your dog.
- **Use of "them" instead of "those":** Them's irises.
- **Use of the "a-" prefix:** I'm a-going. I'm a-learning. I'm a-fixin.'

manufacturing is an industry in decline. Shortly after the North American Free Trade Act was signed into law in 1993, an exodus of manufacturing jobs occurred. In the most recent economic recession, the auto industry was particularly hard-hit, and thousands of employees were laid off, some for only short periods, but many permanently. In the one-year period from February 2009 to February 2010, more than 16,000 jobs were lost in the manufacturing sector. These jobs are unlikely to be replaced, making it vital that Kentucky look to other fields.

Other important employers in Kentucky include Brown-Forman, producer of wines and spirits; Papa John's Pizza, the third-largest pizza chain in the country; UPS, the world's largest package delivery company; Yum! Brands, the world's largest restaurant company; and Zappos, everyone's favorite online shoe shop. All of these corporations have headquarters or major facilities in Kentucky and together employ thousands of Kentuckians.

The Brain Drain

Kentucky, like many other states as well as some countries, suffers from what has come to be called "brain drain," or the net loss of college-educated people to other locations. Statistics show that more Kentuckians with a college degree are leaving the state than people from other states with a college degree are moving to Kentucky. Recognizing the need to stem the brain drain, Kentucky has put together initiatives to encourage the college-educated citizenry to consider calling the Bluegrass State home. Scholarship programs have been created to keep top high school students in-state for college, and some cities have made a concerted effort to woo businesses that attract college-degree holders and the creative class. Additionally, Kentucky is working hard to improve marketing of the state, touting its low cost of living, friendly citizens, unique cultural heritage, and natural beauty. Only time will tell if the campaigns work and if Kentucky is able to attract the type of jobs that talent follows.

People and Culture

DEMOGRAPHY

With a population of nearly 4.4 million people, Kentucky ranks 26th among the states. More than 41 percent of Kentucky's population, or more than 1.8 million people, live in rural areas, although trends indicate an overall move from rural to urban areas. The biggest cities in the Bluegrass State by population are Louisville, Lexington, Bowling Green, Owensboro, and Covington.

Although Kentucky's biggest cities are diverse, home to people of many ethnicities, the state population is overwhelmingly white, with nearly 86 percent claiming white race. An additional 3 percent of Kentuckians declare themselves to be white and of Hispanic descent, 8 percent identify as black, and the remaining 3 percent are of Asian, Native American, or mixed race. Of Kentucky's total population, only 3 percent of the people are foreign-born and only 5 percent speak a language other than English at home. The most commonly claimed ancestries in the Bluegrass State are American (20 percent), German (16 percent), Irish (13 percent), and English (11 percent).

Of Kentucky's black population, nearly 50 percent live in the Louisville metropolitan area. The big cities in general are the most diverse, although all still have a white majority: 68 percent of the Louisville population is non-Hispanic white, 73 percent of the Lexington population is non-Hispanic white, 73 percent of the Bowling Green population is non-Hispanic white, 86 percent of the Owensboro population is non-Hispanic white, and 81 percent of the Covington population is non-Hispanic white. Lexington boasts the largest percentage of foreign-born residents, with 8.5 percent of the population born outside the United States. Magoffin County, in Eastern Kentucky, is not only one of the least diverse counties in the state, with 97.9 percent of people claiming white descent, but is also one of the least diverse in the nation.

By sex, Kentucky is divided almost evenly, with 51 percent of the population female and 49 percent male. By age, 23 percent of Kentuckians are under 18, 14 percent are over 65, and the remaining 63 percent fall in between. Education-wise, Kentucky trails national averages, although progress has been made. Whereas 85 percent of the overall U.S. population has a high school diploma, 82 percent of Kentuckians do, and whereas 28 percent of the overall U.S. population has a bachelor's degree or higher, 21 percent of Kentuckians do. Lexington has the most educated populace, with 88 percent of its people holding high school diplomas and 39 percent having a bachelor's degree or higher.

RELIGION

Religion plays a large role in the lives of many Kentuckians, with Christianity the dominant religion in the state. The largest portion of people, 49 percent, identify as evangelical Protestants, with the majority of these people belonging to the Southern Baptist denomination. Southern Baptists dominate the southern portion of the state, which lies in the Bible

© THERESA DOWELL BLACKINTON

Religion is a significant presence in Kentucky communities.

Belt. Fourteen percent of people, a very high amount for a Southern state, identify as Roman Catholics. Louisville, Lexington, Owensboro, and Covington, in particular, have large Catholic populations. Seventeen percent of the population identify as mainline Protestant, with the majority belonging to the Methodist church. Twelve percent claim no church affiliation, and the remaining 8 percent claim other theologies.

Louisville boasts the most religious diversity with a sizeable Jewish population, a notable Muslim population, and the state's only Hindu temple. Louisville is also home to the Roman Catholic Archdiocese of Louisville, which covers 24 counties and has more than 135,000 members, and Southeast Christian Church, Kentucky's largest church and the fifth-largest church in the United States with more than 30,000 members. The Southern Baptist Theological Seminary and the headquarters of the Presbyterian Church are also located in Louisville.

The Arts

LITERATURE

Kentucky has a solid tradition of turning out major literary voices, many of whom draw on their experiences living in Kentucky to create their works. Robert Penn Warren, who was born in Guthrie, became the first (and only) person to win the Pulitzer Prize for both prose and poetry. In 1947 he won for his novel *All the King's Men,* in 1957 he won for his collection *Promises: Poems 1945-1956,* and in 1979 he won again for his collection *Now and Then: Poems 1978-1979.* Warren also served as the Poet Laureate of the United States and was a cofounder of the *Southern Review.* Jesse Stuart, born in Eastern Kentucky's W-Hollow, wrote many short stories, poems, and novels about Southern Appalachia and served as Kentucky's Poet Laureate in 1954. Among Kentucky's contemporary writers, the most well-known are Wendell Berry, a poet, novelist, essayist, and

outspoken environmentalist who also works as a teacher and farms the 125-acre farm in Henry County that has been in his family since the early 1800s; Bobbie Ann Mason, who grew up on a farm outside Mayfield, graduated from the University of Kentucky, and now writes fiction about Western Kentucky's working class; Sue Grafton, Louisville native and University of Louisville grad famous for her "alphabet series" of crime novels featuring detective Kinsey Millhone; Barbara Kingsolver, who grew up near Carlisle and who, since her first novel, *The Bean Trees,* has gone on to write numerous bestselling and award-winning novels, essay collections, and nonfiction works, most of which deal with issues of social justice; Tania James, a Louisville native, who has published a highly regarded novel and short story collection; and Holly Goddard Jones, who grew up in Western Kentucky, graduated from the University of

© THERESA DOWELL BLACKINTON

Guitars and dulcimers are common instruments in Kentucky.

provide accompaniment. To many, bluegrass is as much about the feel as it is about the music. In Bill Monroe's words, bluegrass is "Scotch bagpipes and ole-time fiddlin.' It's Methodist and Holiness and Baptist. It's blues and jazz, and it has a high lonesome sound. It's plain music that tells a good story. It's played from my heart to your heart, and it will touch you. Bluegrass is music that matters."

In the 1960s, bluegrass really came into its own as bluegrass festivals sprang up across the nation. It was then that the genre actually took the name bluegrass, in tribute to the founding father's band. In recent years, instruments like the accordion, harmonica, electric guitar, and drum have been added to traditional bluegrass music, creating a subgenre that many refer to as Newgrass. Its founding is credited to another Kentuckian, Sam Bush. In Kentucky, Rosine and the nearby Owensboro area remain a center for bluegrass music, although you'll find jam sessions, pickin' on the porch, and bluegrass festivals at locations all over the state.

Kentucky, and has set both her short story collection and novel in a fictional Kentucky town named Roma.

MUSIC
Bluegrass

Many people think bluegrass music is as old as the hills themselves, and although its influences are, the genre itself is not. Bluegrass actually only dates back to 1939, when Bill Monroe, a native of Western Kentucky's Rosine, put together a band called the Blue Grass Boys, which he named in honor of his home state. His band featured mandolin, fiddle, guitar, banjo, and bass, and the toe-tapping sound that these instruments produced soon caught on around the country. Bluegrass takes its influence from many sources, can be accompanied by lyrics sung in two-, three-, or four-part vocal harmony, usually with one high voice referred to as the "high lonesome sound," and characteristically features one instrument taking a turn playing the melody (with improvisations as the musician sees fit) while the other instruments

Country

Nashville might be the home of country music, but Kentucky's influence on the genre cannot be overlooked. Long before country music was a commercial success, Kentuckians, especially those in Eastern Kentucky, were composing songs and ruminating about love, loss, and life while keeping tune on the guitar. Some claim there must be something in the water in Eastern Kentucky because a plethora of stars have come from this section of the state. In honor of these musicians, the section of U.S. 23 that runs through the Bluegrass State is named the Country Music Highway, and a road trip down it will take you into the heart of country music. Among the stars that were born in Eastern Kentucky and elsewhere in the state are Billy Ray Cyrus, Naomi and Wynonna Judd, Loretta Lynn, Crystal Gayle, John Michael Montgomery, Eddie Montgomery, Troy Gentry, Ricky Skaggs, Dwight Yoakam, Patty Loveless, and Keith Whitley. Numerous venues in Kentucky feature country music. Renfro Valley is Kentucky's country music capital, and it's a great place to catch a show.

Other Genres

Beyond bluegrass and country, old-time American, folk, and gospel music also have strong Kentucky roots, particularly in the mountains and other rural areas. A key component of old-time American music is the Appalachian dulcimer, also called the mountain dulcimer, which is native to Appalachia and has been played by generations of mountain folk. The dulcimer also played a role in folk music and was used by such artists as Joni Mitchell in the 1960s.

Benton, a town near Land Between the Lakes, is famous for its Big Singing, which has taken place on the fourth Sunday in May at the Marshall County Courthouse since 1884. Considered to be the oldest music tradition in the United States, the Big Singing brings together shape-note singers who perform songs from the *Southern Harmony*, a Southern tune book containing more than 300 songs and dating back to the early 1800s.

Kentucky musicians who have made a name for themselves on the popular charts include alternative Southern rappers Nappy Roots, who got their start in Bowling Green, and rock band My Morning Jacket, which was formed in Louisville.

FOLK ART

Folk art refers to the works of self-taught visual artists. It is sometimes referred to as "primitive art" or "outsider art," terms that are not meant to be derogatory, but instead reference the way in which the art is created by artists without training who are outside of the art establishment. Folk art is often utilitarian or decorative, and religious themes as well as images taken from daily life appear frequently. In Kentucky, this form of expression thrives in Appalachia, but can be found throughout the state. Wood carver Edgar Tolson is considered to be the most influential Kentucky folk artist, and his works center around the theme of temptation, which has both religious and personal overtures. Other artists of note include Junior Lewis, Lillian Barker, and Minnie and Garland Adkins, all wood carvers from

Isonville; Charley and Noah Kinney, painters and carvers from Toller Hollow; Minnie Black, a sculptor from East Bernstadt; and Marvin Finn, a sculptor from Louisville. The Kentucky Folk Art Center in Morehead, the Kentucky Museum of Art & Craft in Louisville, and the entire town of Berea are musts for those interested in folk art.

TELEVISION AND FILM

Kentucky doesn't show up on television or in films too often, but it hasn't been completely ignored by Hollywood. Film titles featuring the Bluegrass State include *Secretariat, Elizabethtown, Dreamer, Coal Miner's Daughter, Sea Biscuit,* and *The Insider.* Additionally, the 1964 James Bond flick *Goldfinger* featured Fort Knox, and the 1976 documentary film *Harlan County USA* won an Academy Award for its depiction of a coal miners' strike against Duke Power Company.

Harlan also has made its way onto TV screens as the setting for FX's *Justified.* Although the image it casts of the area is not exactly flattering, it does manage to get a number of details right, like the bottles of Ale-8 the characters can be seen drinking.

Hollywood stars who can trace their roots back to Kentucky include Rosemary Clooney, who was born in Maysville; George Clooney, who grew up in Lexington and whose parents still live in Augusta; Ashley Judd, who was raised in Eastern Kentucky and is still a passionate UK basketball fan; Johnny Depp, who was born in Owensboro; Molly Sims, a product of Murray; Rebecca Gayheart, who grew up in Hazard; and Ned Beatty, Maggie Lawson, Jennifer Lawrence, and Jennifer Carpenter, all of whom got their start in Louisville.

Fans of the Coen brothers' film *The Big Lebowski* will be interested to know that the Lebowski Fest, an annual tribute to the movie, was begun in Louisville in 2002. Although the festival has now spread to other cities, the annual event still draws big crowds to Louisville every summer. The main event is a bowling party that incorporates costume, trivia, and other contests.

ESSENTIALS

Getting There

BY AIR

The **Cincinnati/Northern Kentucky International Airport** (www.cvgairport.com), which is physically located in Northern Kentucky, is Kentucky's largest airport. It offers 70 direct connections to domestic and international destinations on Air Canada, American, Delta, Frontier, United, and US Airways. **Louisville International Airport** (www.flylouisville.com) is served by AirTran, American, Delta, Southwest, United, and US Airways. Most direct connections are to the East Coast or to nearby regional hubs, although with Southwest you can fly as far as Phoenix and Las Vegas, and you can hop straight to Denver on United. Lexington's **Blue Grass Airport** (www.bluegrassairport.com) is the most centrally located option. It's smaller and usually more expensive, but you do find deals on occasion. Allegiant, American Eagle, Delta, United, and US Airways serve Lexington.

BY CAR

For those arriving by car from the east or west, I-64 is the main thoroughfare, entering Kentucky from West Virginia at Ashland, then passing through Lexington before exiting into Indiana at Louisville. For travelers from the north and south, I-65 and I-75

© THERESA DOWELL BLACKINTON

are the major roadways. I-65 leads up from Nashville, passes through Bowling Green, and then exits into Indiana at Louisville. I-75 heads north into Kentucky from Knoxville, Tennessee, parallels the Daniel Boone National Forest, then shoots up to Lexington, exiting into Ohio at Covington. I-71, I-69, and I-24 also pass through Kentucky. I-71 runs between Louisville and Covington, I-69 runs diagonally from the western border with Tennessee to Land Between the Lakes, and I-24 runs from Paducah, around Land Between the Lakes, and then south toward Nashville.

BY BUS

Greyhound (www.greyhound.com) has stations in Ashland, Berea, Bowling Green, Lexington, London, Louisville, Madisonville, Morganfield, and Paducah. Although not the quickest or most comfortable way to travel, Greyhound will get you there.

BY TRAIN

Amtrak (800/872-7245, www.amtrak.com) has four stations in Kentucky, none of which are in major metropolitan areas. Stations in Ashland, Maysville, and South Shore are served by the Cardinal three times per week as it travels between Chicago and New York City. The station in Fulton is served by the City of New Orleans as it travels from Chicago to New Orleans daily. All four stations are unstaffed, so you must reserve tickets over the phone or via the website.

Getting Around

BY CAR

To explore Kentucky, you need to have a car. Rental car companies have desks at all airports as well as at in-city locations. Most companies require that drivers be a minimum of 25 years old. Those wishing to rent a car must also have a valid driver's license and credit card. Car insurance is required by law in Kentucky; see if your personal auto policy or your credit card provides rental insurance.

Roadways

Roadways in Kentucky, whether interstates, state highways, or city streets, are generally well maintained, although potholes can be a problem after a rough winter. Interstate speed limits reach up to 70 miles per hour in rural areas, although sometimes drop to 60 or 65, and when passing through urban areas drop all the way to 55 miles per hour. Divided highways generally have speed limits between 45 and 55 miles per hour, while the speed limits in residential and urban areas range 25-35 miles per hour. School zones typically limit drivers to a speed of 25 miles per hour.

Traffic is not bad in Kentucky, although you'll find heavier (but still moving) traffic during rush hours in and around the major cities. Rush hours are, fortunately, rather short in the state, lasting from about 7:30am-9am and 4:30pm-6pm. The I-64/I-65/I-71 exchange in Louisville, known as Spaghetti Junction, can cause headaches at rush hours, as can the bridge crossings between Louisville and southern Indiana, which have been under continual construction in recent years. In Lexington, New Circle Road as well as downtown city streets can experience delays, and the interstates and bridges between Northern Kentucky and Cincinnati see heavy traffic during rush hours or during Reds and Browns games. Outside of rush hours, traffic snarls are limited to major events, accidents, and construction. For traffic, construction, and other road condition information, call 511 or visit http://511.ky.gov.

Most dangerous driving situations are related to weather, especially during the winter. If you don't have experience driving in the snow or you don't have to go anywhere, it's best to keep your car parked. Snow usually doesn't linger too long in Kentucky, at least in the cities. Interstates and major roads are cleared first by

You never know what you'll find yourself behind on Kentucky's roads.

© THERESA DOWELL BLACKINTON

the state. How fast other roadways are cleared depends on local government. If you do have to drive in the snow, lower your speed, maintain your distance, and be alert for black ice—highly transparent ice that freezes on roadways and can be extremely dangerous. Be extra cautious when driving in the rain as well. Roads are most slippery immediately after it starts raining, so don't wait until it's pouring to slow down. In intense storms, flash floods can occur. Never drive your car into water. Cars can be swept away by only a couple of inches of running water.

In rural areas, be alert for farm machinery on the road as well as livestock. In the mountains and on Kentucky's many country roads, drive slowly and carefully as you navigate the many twists and turns. If you're slowing up traffic, pull over and let others pass before continuing on, but never feel that you have to increase your speed to an uncomfortable pace. Also never stop in the road to take a photo, no matter how lovely the scenery. Find a safe place to pull over even if you don't see

another car anywhere nearby. Deer present a danger to motorists throughout the state, especially at dawn and dusk. If you see a deer, proceed cautiously, as there will usually be other deer nearby, and they often dart into the road without warning. For a roadway emergency in Kentucky, call 911.

Kentucky law requires that all drivers and passengers wear a seatbelt at all times. Children under 40 inches must be secured in a child seat, and children who are 40-50 inches but under seven years old must be in a booster seat. Texting while driving is illegal in Kentucky (although common sense ought to tell you that's a terrible idea), and those under 18 are not allowed to use cell phones while driving.

BY FERRY

Although you might not expect it, considering Kentucky is not on the coast and bridges seem to span nearly every body of water these days, Kentucky has 10 ferries currently in operation. Seven of the ferries are state-funded operations, two are federally funded, and one is privately run. The Augusta and Anderson ferries ply the Ohio River between Kentucky and Ohio. The Cave-in-Rock ferry also makes runs across the Ohio River but transports passengers to Illinois. The Dorena-Hickman ferry in Western Kentucky traverses the Mississippi River between Kentucky and Missouri. Of the remaining six ferries, four cross the Green River, one crosses the Cumberland River, and the other crosses the Kentucky River, all transporting passengers in-state. All of Kentucky's ferries are simple affairs, able to hold just a couple of cars each per crossing. The only ferries to charge a fee are the Augusta ($5 cars, free for foot passengers), Anderson ($5 cars, $0.50 for foot passengers), and Dorena-Hickman ferries ($14 cars, $1 for foot passengers). Information about the ferries, including schedules, can be found on the Department of Transportation's website (http://transportation.ky.gov).

Sports and Recreation

Kentucky is an outdoor lover's paradise. An excellent state park system, thousands of acres of forests, the most miles of waterway in the continental United States, some of the region's largest lakes, and an unbeatable cave system mean there are opportunities for a wide range of pursuits.

PARKS

The **Kentucky State Parks** (http://parks.ky.gov) system includes 49 parks, 17 of which are resort parks, meaning they offer overnight accommodations in a lodge. The other parks are recreational parks, which may offer camping but no other accommodation options, and historic parks. In many cases, parks fall under multiple headings. Admission to all of Kentucky's state parks is free, although there may be charges for activities, such as boat rental, golf and mini-golf courses, horseback riding, and museum or historic home tours.

City and county parks are also abundant, with Louisville's Olmsted Park System nationally renowned. Louisville is home to the largest urban park system in North America.

HIKING

The number one destination for hiking in Kentucky is Red River Gorge, which is located in the **Daniel Boone National Forest** (www.fs.fed.us). This impossibly beautiful area offers more than 40 different trails of varying lengths and difficulty. Other sections of the Daniel Boone National Forest are also excellent for hiking. In total, more than 600 miles of trails lie within the forest. Long-distance hikers will want to add the forest's Sheltowee Trace National Recreation Trail to their life list. This 260-mile backcountry trail runs the length of the forest.

State parks offer additional hiking opportunities, with trails generally on the shorter and easier side, although determined hikers can often link them for a more challenging route. The **Pine Mountain Trail** (www.pinemountaintrail.com), although only partially complete as of 2013, will connect Breaks Interstate Park with Cumberland Gap National Historical, spanning about 120 miles along Pine Mountain and passing through some truly wild terrain. Nature preserves (www.nature.org) are also good places to seek out hiking trails.

BIKING

More than 600 miles of the **TransAmerica Bike Trail** (www.adventurecycling.org) pass through Kentucky. From the west, the trail enters Kentucky via the Cave-In-Rock ferry. It then passes through Marion, the Rough River Lake area, Hodgenville, Bardstown, Harrodsburg, Berea, the Red River Gorge area, Hazard, and the Southern Appalachians before exiting into Virginia at Breaks Interstate Park. Other multistate trails that pass through

© THERESA DOWELL BLACKINTON

pedaling along the Louisville waterfront

Kentucky include the **Mississippi River Trail** (www.mississippirivertrail.org) and the **Underground Railroad Bike Route** (www.adventurecycling.org). The **Department of Transportation** (502/564-7433, http://transportation.ky.gov) puts out a brochure called Kentucky Bicycle Tours with information on routes as well as biking events, cycling clubs, and more.

The individual tourism bureaus can provide information on biking routes in their area. On the web, www.kybikerides.org offers cue sheets for rides mainly in the Louisville area, and www.mapmyride.com can help you find routes and events as well as bike rentals.

WATER SPORTS

The state's many rivers and lakes make Kentucky heaven for water lovers. Fishing and recreational boating are popular activities, especially in summertime. The state's most visited lakes are Kentucky Lake, Lake Barkley, Lake Cumberland, Dale Hollow Lake, Green River Lake, Barren River Lake, Taylorsville Lake, Rough River Lake, and Nolin Lake, although there are many other great spots throughout the state.

If you wish to cast a line in Kentucky, you must have a valid state fishing license. Licenses are issued by the **Kentucky Department of Fish and Wildlife** and can be purchased online (http://fw.ky.gov), over the phone (877/598-2401), or from license agents. Most marinas, bait and tackle shops, and convenience stores near the lakes are license agents, or if they're not, can direct you to one. Kentucky residents can purchase a one-day license, an annual license, or a husband-wife license. Reduced-price passes are valid for seniors and those with disabilities. Out-of-state visitors can choose from a 1-day license, 7-day license, 15-day license, or an annual license. A special permit is required to fish for trout. Youth under the age of 16 do not need a fishing license.

Kentucky has many species of fish for the angler to pursue. In Kentucky's lakes and rivers, you'll find redear sunfish, walleye, muskie, chain pickerel, northern pike, crappie, rainbow trout, brown trout, brook trout, and many types of bass—largemouth, smallmouth, spotted, Coosa, rock, white, yellow, and striped. All fish, except brook trout, which are catch-and-release only, may be kept, although there are minimum size limits and maximum possession limits for most species. Limits are posted on the Fish and Wildlife website and at the launch ramps of many lakes. For more information about fishing in Kentucky, contact the Department of Fish and Wildlife.

Paddlers are well served by the state's many waterways. The Green River, which runs through Cave Country; the Elkhorn River, which is near Frankfort; the Licking River, which runs through Northern Kentucky; and the Red River, which runs through Red River Gorge, are good spots for beginner paddlers as well as those looking for a relaxing outing. Those looking for a thrill should look to the Cumberland River system in Daniel Boone National Forest, which offers whitewater

© THERESA DOWELL BLACKINTON

canoeing on one of Kentucky's many waterways

recreation, and to the Russell Fork River in Pike County, which is especially good in October when water is released from the dam.

HORSEBACK RIDING

Most people assume that horseback riding opportunities must abound in Kentucky, but that's not exactly true. Kentucky is known for thoroughbreds, which you have no place riding unless you're a highly trained jockey. That doesn't mean it's impossible to go for a ride; you just need to do a little advance research. The state park system is one of the best places to seek out horseback riding. Guided horseback rides are offered at Barren River, Carter Caves, Cumberland Falls, Lake Barkley, Lake Cumberland, and Kentucky Dam Village. Private outfitters also offer rides, although you must almost always reserve a trip in advance. If you have your own horse, you'll find plenty of trails that are equestrian-friendly. Land Between the Lakes, which has a dedicated equestrian campground, is a very popular place to ride.

ROCK CLIMBING

Red River Gorge is one of the best rock climbing destinations in the eastern United States, thanks to an abundance of sandstone cliffs and arches. The online guidebook at www.redriverclimbing.com is a great resource for scouting routes; e-book versions are available. The **Red River Gorge Climbing Coalition** (http://rrgcc. org) is also an excellent source of information for potential climbers.

HUNTING

Game animals in Kentucky include deer, rabbit, squirrel, turkey, grouse, quail, and waterfowl, as well as elk and bear. You must have a license to hunt in Kentucky. A hunting license allows you to use gun, bow, dog, or falconry to take game species. Resident, nonresident, and junior hunting licenses are offered. Sportsman licenses, which allow for both fishing and hunting, are also available. Additional permits are needed for all animals except small game. To hunt elk, you must enter a special lottery, which is held annually in May for hunting dates between October and December. Only 800 permits are issued, and the permits are specifically for a bull, cow, or spike elk. There is no lottery for bear hunting permits, but bear hunting is limited to two days in December, and if the very strict quota is met on the first day, the second day is cancelled. For more information on hunting in Kentucky or to purchase a license or permit, contact the **Kentucky Department of Fish and Wildlife** (877/598-3401, http://fw.ky.gov).

SPECTATOR SPORTS

You can't come to Kentucky and not spend a day at the track watching thoroughbred horse racing. The state's premier venues are Louisville's Churchill Downs, home to the Kentucky Derby, and Lexington's Keeneland, the prettiest of all the tracks. Churchill Downs has a spring meet, which runs from the last weekend in April through July 4 weekend; a September Homecoming meet; and a fall meet, which runs from late October through Thanksgiving weekend. Keeneland offers a spring meet in April and a fall meet in October. Other horse racing venues include Turfway Park in Florence, which has a holiday meet and a winter/spring meet; Ellis Park in Henderson, which offers live racing July-Labor Day weekend; and Kentucky Downs in Franklin, which has a short meet in September.

College basketball is Kentucky's other passion. If you can, try to make it to a Kentucky Wildcats game at Rupp Arena or a Louisville Cardinals game at the KFC Yum! Center. Even better, try to get your hands on tickets to the UK-U of L game, where you'll learn what rivalry really means.

Accommodations and Food

ACCOMMODATIONS

Accommodation options in Kentucky run the gamut. You've got mom-and-pop motels, immediately recognizable chain hotels covering a range of budgets, independent and boutique hotels and inns, and bed-and-breakfasts located in everything from Victorian mansions to working farmhouses to retired schools. At Kentucky's lakes, rental properties provide a popular alternative to parks, resorts, and campgrounds. Check www.vrbo.com for house and cabin rentals throughout the state.

Rates and Reservations

Rates listed in this book are for double occupancy during peak season (and are subject to change). In major hotels in the state's urban areas, you can often find better prices on weekends, when business travelers return home, than on weekdays. In popular tourist spots, weekend rates tend to be higher. At Derby time, prices for hotels in Louisville and the immediate surrounding area soar, and reservations can be very hard to get. Plan as far in advance as possible. In Lexington, hotels definitely see an upsurge in business during the two Keeneland meets (April and October). The lodges and cabins at the state parks are busiest in summer, especially on weekends, and during the peak of fall. For most hotels, the best way to make a reservation is directly through the property. Don't forget to ask for discounts based on membership in organizations such as AAA and AARP or your status as active military.

Camping

Those looking to park an RV or pitch a tent will find myriad options in Kentucky. The state park system is home to many campgrounds, which offer anywhere from around 20 sites to a couple hundred. Most sites are equipped with water and electricity hookups, although some sites are designated as tent only, and a few parks have specific primitive camping areas. The **U.S. Army Corps of Engineers** (www.usace.army.mil) also runs multiple campgrounds in Kentucky, specifically at the lakes that they manage. Land Between the Lakes

© THERESA DOWELL BLACKINTON

LEED-certified Boone Tavern Hotel combines modernity with Southern charm.

National Recreation Area and the Daniel Boone National Forest are other camping hot spots, offering both full-service campgrounds as well as backcountry camping opportunities. Some campgrounds are year-round, but many are closed during the winter, so call ahead to make sure facilities are open.

FOOD

A wide diversity of food can be found in Kentucky, especially in Louisville, Lexington, and Northern Kentucky. These areas have broad ethnic offerings as well as restaurants that specialize in Southern, contemporary and traditional American, and continental cuisine. Restaurants range from casual budget places to formal affairs, with prices and styles to meet any demand. The nationwide trend of emphasizing local food is alive and well in Kentucky, with multiple restaurants offering farm-to-table menus. Named by *Bon Appétit* magazine as one of the country's foodiest cities, Louisville has James Beard award-winning chefs and restaurants that are doing creative things with

food and receiving national recognition for it. Don't assume you'll only find good food in the state's biggest cities, however. Although country cooking does tend to dominate once you move away from the urban areas, restaurant gems are scattered all over the state.

Vegetarians should have no problem finding something to satisfy them in Kentucky's metropolitan areas, but they may have trouble in smaller towns and rural areas, where lard is a common oil and vegetables are often cooked with meat. Ask carefully about ingredients and how things are cooked to be sure there are no misunderstandings. Gluten-free menus are becoming more common, but again, you'll have better luck in the bigger cities.

Regional Food

Thanks to the Colonel, Kentucky and fried chicken are practically inseparable. KFC, however, doesn't have a stranglehold on chicken around here. Fried chicken is found on many Kentucky menus, and most often it's way better than KFC, the best of it pan-fried

KENTUCKY'S VINEYARDS AND WINERIES

In 1798, America's first commercial winery was opened in the Bluegrass region of Kentucky, in what is now Jessamine County, and throughout the 1800s, Kentucky's wine industry thrived. Prohibition, however, destroyed the industry and led farmers to plow under their vines and plant tobacco instead. Throughout most of the 20th century, Kentucky had little to do with wine, although a few small vineyards began to open in the latter part of the century. With the declining market for tobacco that marked the start of the 21st century, Kentucky saw a revitalized interest in growing grapes and producing wines, and as of 2013, 62 wineries were operating in Kentucky. The wineries tend to be small, family-run operations, but the wines they produce have won awards at competitions across the nation. No matter what region of the state you're in, you'll find wineries that welcome you in for a walk through the vineyards and a tasting. Some wineries are specifically listed in the relevant chapters; for a full listing of Kentucky's wineries, visit www.kentucky-wine.com.

© THERESA DOWELL BLACKINTON

grape vines at a vineyard

in a blazing hot skillet of lard. Southern home cooking is probably the most popular style of food in the state. Favorites other than fried chicken include country ham, fried catfish, and pork chops. In the veggie department, you've got the fried type (green tomatoes, okra), the cooked with bacon type (green beans, lima beans), the covered in butter type (corn), and the not-even-veggies type (mac and cheese). In Appalachia especially, pinto beans, also known as soup beans, and cornbread is a standard meal.

Barbecue is another Kentucky specialty, with Western Kentucky being the focal point of this flavor. Here, mutton, either chopped or sliced, is the barbecue of choice. Burgoo, a barbecue-style stew of meats and vegetables, is served right alongside it.

On the must-sample list of anyone wishing to taste Kentucky originals are a Hot Brown, Benedictine, beer cheese, Kenny's cheeses, Penn's ham, goetta, Cincinnati-style chili, spoonbread, bourbon balls, and Chaney's ice cream. If you like to buy local, look for the Kentucky Proud label on your food products, which signifies they were grown and produced in the state.

Drinks

In regard to drink, bourbon, obviously, is a must. Any true Kentuckian knows that the only way to drink it is neat or with just a bit of water, but those who balk at that can sample the spirit in a mint julep or a Kentucky Manhattan. If you prefer beer to bourbon, check out the microbreweries in Louisville and Lexington. If you're looking for a nonalcoholic drink, try Ale-8-One, a ginger ale made in Winchester since 1926.

Visitors to Kentucky should be aware that despite the fact that Kentucky is the birthplace of bourbon, only 32 of Kentucky's 120 counties are wet. The rest are dry, which means you can't buy a drink anywhere, or limited (aka "moist"), which means you can't buy packaged liquor, but may be able to buy a drink by the glass at certain restaurants.

Meals and Mealtimes

Breakfast in Kentucky is often big, featuring such favorites as grits, biscuits and gravy, eggs, and pancakes. Lunch is most typically a small meal, although in many parts of the state, Sunday lunch (called Sunday dinner) is the biggest meal of the week. Dinner, which is often called supper, is generally the day's most sizable meal, and is often eaten between 5pm and 7pm. Although restaurants in Kentucky's urban areas stay open until late in the evening, it's not uncommon for restaurants in less populated areas to close by 8pm on weekdays and 9pm on weekends, so don't wait too long to eat. In the cities, Monday is a common day for restaurants to be closed, while Sunday is a more common off-day in rural areas.

© THERESA DOWELL BLACKINTON

a mint julep and an Oaks lily, the official drinks of the Kentucky Derby and Kentucky Oaks

Tips for Travelers

WHAT TO TAKE

Kentucky is uniformly casual, where comfort, for the most part, reigns. Some restaurants offer suggestions on appropriate attire, but very few have strict requirements. Some bars and night-clubs, especially in the cities, may restrict flip-flops, sneakers, baggy pants, and tank tops, but this isn't New York City, and you don't have to wear designer duds to gain admission. For the Derby, you'll want to pack your finest attire if you have seats in the grandstands, and items you don't mind getting muddy if the infield is your destination.

Don't forget to pack sunscreen in the summer, although it doesn't hurt to wear it year-round, and bug spray is a good idea for those with outdoor activities on the agenda. In the spring and fall, you'll want to have a jacket on standby, while those packing for a winter visit shouldn't forget gloves, hat, and a coat.

TRAVELERS WITH DISABILITIES

Thanks to Title III of the Americans with Disabilities Act (ADA), all new construction (including renovations) since 1992 must be accessible to those with disabilities. Additionally, existing buildings were required to remove barriers to access where possible. This means that there are few sights, attractions, hotels, restaurants, or other facilities unable to accommodate those with special needs. The few exceptions are historic properties, where such updates are not feasible. In Kentucky, this means many bed-and-breakfasts and historic homes are only partially accessible, or in some cases, completely inaccessible. Persons with disabilities interested in visiting or staying at a facility that does not seem accessible should inquire about options before ruling the establishment out, as many of the facilities may be able to accommodate guests with disabilities if given advance notice.

As required by Title II of the ADA, all public transportation in Kentucky is accessible. Buses feature wheelchair lifts or ramps as well as reserved seating for those with disabilities. Some buses also kneel to assist those who have trouble with steps. Additionally, some cities offer special door-to-door bus services for those with severe disabilities. Contact the individual provider for more information or to arrange services.

TRAVELING WITH CHILDREN

From museums to state and national parks to farms to festivals, Kentucky is a kid-friendly state. Feel free to bring your children with you nearly everywhere you go, but do use good judgment when picking restaurants and hotels. Some are certainly more child-friendly than others. Please respect the wishes of bed-and-breakfasts with adult-only policies; everyone will enjoy their stay more if you pick a place that welcomes children.

SENIOR TRAVELERS

Discounted rates are available for seniors at attractions throughout the state, as well as on public transportation. Be sure to inquire, even when posted rates don't indicate a discount. Additionally, members of AARP (www.aarp.com) are often eligible for additional hotel, auto, and travel discounts.

GAY AND LESBIAN TRAVELERS

Unfortunately, Kentucky is not leading the way in equal rights for gays and lesbians, but like the rest of the country, it is starting to move in the right direction on this issue. Cities like Louisville, Lexington, Bowling Green, Owensboro, and Covington/Newport are more diverse than rural areas and have active GLBQT communities. That's not to say that rural areas are unwelcoming, however. In fact, the tiny town of Vicco in eastern Kentucky made national headlines in January 2013 for its gay-rights ordinance. In general, it's unlikely that gays and lesbians will encounter outright discrimination, but they may be the recipients of inappropriate looks, gestures, or comments that create discomfort. Throughout much of rural Kentucky, public displays of affection, whether between homosexual or heterosexual couples, are frowned upon. A number of Kentucky B&Bs make a point of advertising themselves as gay-friendly; you can find a listing at www.purpleroofs.com.

INTERNATIONAL TRAVELERS

All international travelers wishing to enter the United States must abide by U.S. visa requirements. Although nationals of the 37 countries that currently participate in the Visa Waiver Program do not need visas, they must still receive authorization to travel to the U.S. through the Electronic System for Travel Authorization. Visa processing can be a slow process, so apply well in advance of your intended travel dates. Visit the State Department website (http://travel.state.gov) for specific requirements.

Travelers should be aware that few people in Kentucky speak a language other than English, especially outside the cities. Within the cities, it's likely that you can find someone who knows Spanish, but speakers of other languages will not be as fortunate. Hone your English skills before visiting or carry a good translator.

CONDUCT AND CUSTOMS

One way in which Kentucky is indubitably Southern is in regard to hospitality. Politeness, friendliness, and respectfulness are ingrained traits. Expect people you pass on the sidewalk, wait in line with, or share an elevator with to greet you, usually in the form of a simple "hi," "good morning/afternoon/evening," or "how ya doin.'" It doesn't matter if they know you or not, so there's no need to look over your shoulder to see if the stranger greeting you is actually talking to someone behind you. They're not. Returning the greeting with a smile is expected. Expect personnel in retail, restaurants, hotels, and other industries to be just as friendly, so bring a little patience with you. It might take longer to check out, check in, or order, but Kentuckians find the trade-off to be in their favor.

In addressing people you don't know, begin by addressing them as "Mr." or "Ms." If they would like you to use their first name, they'll ask you to. In some parts of the state, you'll find that people use the title Mr. or Ms. with a person's first name (e.g., Ms. Sarah or Mr. John). Many folks still appreciate the use of "ma'am" and "sir," so don't be offended if someone refers to you that way. They're not implying you're old; they're just being polite.

Health and Safety

WEATHER-RELATED ISSUES
Heat

The combination of heat and humidity that marks a Kentucky summer can be killer—literally. The elderly, young children, pregnant women, and those with heart and respiratory conditions are at the highest risk of heat-related illness, but even healthy people in their prime can fall victim to the heat. During summer, increase consumption of water and other liquids, avoid activity during peak heat, and wear sunscreen whenever you are outside. Never leave children or pets waiting in a car. It takes only a very short time for the temperature inside a car to reach unsafe levels.

Know the signs of heat exhaustion and heat stroke, and seek treatment immediately if you notice any. Heat exhaustion is marked by weakness; dizziness; pale, moist skin; and nausea and vomiting. To treat, move the victim immediately to a cooler place (preferably to an air-conditioned area, but to a shaded area if none

KID-FRIENDLY KENTUCKY

Kentucky loves kids, inviting them almost everywhere to do almost everything. But let's face it, there are certain activities kids prefer more than others. Although they can tour a distillery, they're probably not going to enjoy it. Although they're welcome at horse farms, they're probably not particularly interested in how horses are bred. They will, however, most likely love petting sharks, observing gorillas, riding a boat through a cave, and meeting Daniel Boone. We all know that happy kids make for happy parents, so if you have the young 'uns in tow, consider the following itinerary for your travels through the Bluegrass State. Alternatively, consider Kentucky's **state parks,** which are among the most family-friendly destinations in the state.

DAY 1

Louisville can keep kids busy for days, but if you have a schedule to keep, plan for two days in Kentucky's biggest city. Spend day one downtown. Head first to the **Louisville Slugger Museum & Factory** to witness bats being made and get your free souvenir mini-bat. Grab lunch at **Dish on Market,** and then proceed to the **Louisville Science Center,** where your kids will have no idea they're learning new things because they're so busy having hands-on fun. If your kids are into the performing arts, see what's playing at **Stage One,** Louisville's children's theater, grabbing an early dinner of gourmet pizza that will please the whole family at **Garage Bar** before the show. **Old Louisville's Aleksander House Bed and Breakfast** welcomes children, and the suites are ideal for four to six people.

DAY 2

On day two, head to the **Louisville Zoo**

first thing in the morning when the animals are more likely to be active. Giggle at the penguins, observe the gorillas, and watch the polar bears play. You might want to pack the kids' bathing suits, because the zoo has a water play area perfect for hot days. At lunchtime, drive a few miles to Bardstown Road and grab a gyro at **Zaytun** or a Vietnamese sandwich at **Banh Mi Hero,** with a treat from **Homemade Ice Cream and Pie Kitchen** for dessert. In the afternoon, head to **Waterfront Park** to take a walk across the Big 4 Bridge or rent a surrey and pedal around. For dinner, head east to **Captain's Quarters** to eat on the deck and watch the boats pass by on the river.

DAY 3

Head south toward Bowling Green on day three, but don't plan to arrive until the evening because you have a few detours to make along the way. Your first stop is **Bernheim Arboretum** in **Clermont,** where kids and adults alike can burn off some energy in beautiful surroundings. See how many frogs you can spot at the kingfisher pond, venture out onto the canopy tree walk for a view of the forest from above, and say hello to the deer. Bring a picnic for a peaceful lunch. After lunch, drive to **New Haven** in time for an afternoon train ride, departing from the **Kentucky Railway Museum.** Once in **Bowling Green,** try **Montana Grille** for dinner, and then choose your favorite of the city's chain hotels.

DAY 4

Bowling Green has a lot to offer the whole family. First on the agenda is a visit to **Lost River Cave and Valley** for a boat ride through a cave. Have lunch and an ice cream

is available), remove the person's clothes, and have the person drink fluids. If the victim isn't breathing, cannot follow commands, or is vomiting, call 911. Heat stroke is a very serious condition in which the body's cooling system fails completely. Symptoms include hot, dry skin; a

lack of sweating; a very fast pulse; confusion; and in extreme cases, seizures and comas. Call 911 immediately if you suspect heat stroke, and try to cool the victim through moving them to a cooler place, removing their clothes, and wrapping them in cold, wet sheets or placing at **Chaney's Dairy Barn,** and then head to the campus of Western Kentucky University to the **Kentucky Museum.** The kids will have fun playing with period costumes, climbing inside a Civil War tent, and seeing the Duncan Hines test kitchen. If you enjoyed the train ride in New Haven, then visit Bowling Green's **Historic Railpark and Train Museum,** where you can step aboard a mail car, a dining car, and a car used for presidential travel. End the night at a **Hot Rods** baseball game, Class A fun for everyone.

DAY 5
Lexington is your next overnight stop, but you'll first want to detour to **Richmond** for a living history lesson at **Fort Boonesborough State Park.** Say hi to Daniel Boone and interact with interpreters performing the same tasks that Kentucky's earliest pioneers would have done. The home-cooking at **Jackson's** will make for a filling lunch. Once in Lexington, let the kids run off any extra energy at the **UK Arboretum** before having dinner at **Ramsey's Diner** and then settling into a family-size room at **SpringHill Suites.**

DAY 6
After doughnuts from **Spalding's Bakery,** start your day at the **Kentucky Horse Park,** where kids will have fun riding the horse-drawn trolley and viewing the horses. Chow down on some authentic Cuban food at **Old San Juan** before continuing the day's adventure at the **Explorium,** Kentucky's only dedicated children's museum. It's tailored more to the younger set with water play tables, giant bubble stations, and other hands-on fun. For dinner, continue the ethnic food trend with a meal at **Asian Wind.**

DAY 7
From Lexington, drive north to **Newport** to spend the day at the **Newport Aquarium,** where you can pet sharks and be amazed by all sorts of sea life. With **Dewey's Pizza** located in the Levee right by the aquarium, it's the obvious lunch choice. If the aquarium doesn't take your entire day, kids seem to love **Ride the Ducks Newport,** although parents might want to bring earplugs. End the day with dinner at **Hofbräuhaus Newport,** where parents can down a well-deserved beer while kids enjoy the pretzels and unique German atmosphere. Save room for ice cream at **Graeter's** before passing out on the pillows at the **Comfort Suites.**

© THERESA DOWELL BLACKINTON

penguins at the Newport Aquarium

ice packs at their neck, groin, and armpits while you wait for help to arrive.

Tornadoes, Earthquakes, and Floods
Tornadoes are the most common of Kentucky's natural dangers, although warning systems make deaths rare. Tornado warnings are issued via television and radio, and blaring sirens alert communities to the danger. If a warning is issued, immediately seek shelter in a basement or in a windowless room on the lowest level of

a building. If outside, seek out a ditch or other low-lying area.

The New Madrid Fault runs under Western Kentucky, which means that although Kentucky is rarely affected by earthquakes, it is at risk. If the ground should start shaking while you are indoors, drop to the ground and protect yourself by taking cover under a solid piece of furniture. If outdoors, move to an open area away from buildings, trees, and power lines.

In case of heavy rain, flash floods or even more severe flooding can occur. During heavy rain and floods, seek higher ground immediately. Do not wait to see if the water will stop or recede, because it can rise quickly, making evacuation impossible. Never drive through water.

Animal Threats

On an absolute scale, Kentucky's most dangerous animals are black bears and the four species of venomous snakes—copperhead, water moccasin, timber rattlesnake, and pygmy rattlesnake—that call Kentucky home. It's unlikely that you'll encounter any of these, however, so on a relative scale, they're practically harmless. In fact, only one bear attack has happened in recorded Kentucky history. Should you come face-to-face with one of Kentucky's black bears, slowly back away from the animal while talking loudly (but not shrilly) to it. Should the bear act aggressive, stop (never run or climb a tree), make yourself as big as possible (by huddling together with others, raising your pack over your head, etc.) and stand your ground. Most likely the bear will leave at this point. If it should attack, then fight back with everything you have. Avoid encounters by making noise as you hike through bear country, and never, ever keeping food or other scented products in your tent. In case of snakebite, seek medical attention immediately.

The most dangerous creatures you're likely to encounter in Kentucky are mosquitoes, which are not just annoying but can also carry West Nile Virus and encephalitis, and ticks, which can carry Lyme disease and Rocky Mountain Spotted Fever. To avoid bites, wear long pants and long sleeves, especially in wooded areas, and use insect repellent with DEET. If a tick should attach itself to you, grab the tick by its head with tweezers, and pull slowly and steadily. Dab antiseptic on the site of the bite. Should you experience a strange rash, especially in a bull's-eye pattern, or flu-like symptoms over the next several weeks, contact your doctor and alert him to the bite so that proper testing can be done.

Some animals in Kentucky, such as bats, skunks, raccoons, and even dogs, are known to be carriers of rabies, so be aware of animals acting strangely. If you are bitten by a wild animal, contact local authorities and seek medical attention immediately. Never feed wild animals.

Smoking

Perhaps unsurprising when you consider the role of tobacco in the Kentucky economy and the fact that Kentucky is third in the nation in percentage of the adult population that smokes (over 25 percent), no statewide smoking ban exists in the Bluegrass State. A number of cities and counties, however, have enacted bans, including Lexington, Louisville, Frankfort, Paducah, Ashland, Henderson, Bowling Green, and Daviess County (Owensboro). Bans vary by location, but range from forbidding smoking in restaurants, retail locations, and offices to forbidding smoking in all buildings and some outdoor spaces. Smokers should familiarize themselves with local laws before lighting up. Additionally, all state buildings, including those on universities, are smoke-free.

HOSPITALS AND PHARMACIES

With more than 100 hospitals spread throughout the state, medical care is never far away. Most hospitals are equipped to deal with the majority of illnesses and injuries, although only Louisville and Lexington have Level 1 trauma centers. If you need medical care, seek the nearest available hospital. Hospital staff will provide any immediate care necessary, evaluate future needs, and handle transfers if necessary. In most medical emergencies, the best practice is to call 911 and allow professionals to transfer you to the hospital. The **Kentucky Hospital Association** (www.kyha.com) provides a listing of all hospitals in the state.

Pharmacies are easily found throughout the state and carry both prescription drugs and over-the-counter medicines. **Rite-Aid** (www.riteaid.com), **Walgreens** (www.walgreens.com), and **CVS** (www.cvs.com) are widespread, with some stores offering 24-hour pharmacies. Big box stores, such as Target, K-Mart, and Walmart, as well as many grocery stores, also have pharmacies.

As is true throughout the nation, medical care in Kentucky is expensive. International travelers should purchase travel health insurance before visiting the United States. Health clinics and immediate care centers often offer lower priced services than hospitals, but those with life-threatening medical conditions should proceed immediately to a hospital, regardless of insurance coverage.

SAFETY

Kentucky is primarily a safe place, and visitors to the state are unlikely to be the victim of a crime, but it pays to be aware. As with most places, crime rates tend to be higher in the cities, and there are certainly areas that are best avoided. As a visitor, it's unlikely you'll end up in any of these areas, since they aren't known for their attractions, but if you do find yourself in an area that feels unsafe, just pass through as quickly as possible. It's unlikely that anything will happen. In regard to vehicle safety, park in well-lit areas, lock your car doors at all times, and don't hesitate to ask for an escort to your car if you feel uncomfortable. In hotels, keep the door to your room locked, secure valuable items in the safe, and don't open your door to unexpected guests, even if they claim to be hotel staff.

Women travelers, in particular, should avoid walking alone at night in areas that aren't well lit or highly trafficked. In bars and nightclubs, be cautious with your drinks. It's best to order for yourself. If you lose sight of your drink, throw it away. Ruffies are not common, but it's always better to err on the side of caution. Finally, if you need a ride, call for a cab instead of flagging one down on the street.

If you should be the victim of a crime or feel threatened in any way, dial 911. This number will immediately connect you with police, fire, and EMT services, regardless of where you are in the state. Be aware, however, that cell phone coverage is limited or unavailable in some sections of the state, particularly the mountains of Eastern Kentucky.

Information and Services

MONEY

ATMs are ubiquitous in most of the state, and can be found in banks, convenience stores, and grocery stores. Most banks are closed on Sunday and in the evenings, although some grocery store branches offer extended hours seven days a week. When heading into small towns, especially in the mountains, it's wise to make a stop at the ATM first as not every town has a bank or ATM.

Credit Cards

Although most places take credit cards, smaller mom-and-pop shops are often cash only, and other businesses may have a minimum charge ($5 or $10) for credit card purchases, so try to have a bit of cash on hand at all times.

Tipping

Tipping is common and expected in the service industry. Waiters and waitresses, in particular, are highly dependent on tips. For average service, it is customary to leave a 15 percent tip. Good service deserves a tip of 20 percent or more. If you suffer from poor service, you can leave less of a tip or no tip at all, but you should request to talk to the manager and explain your situation. If you use coupons, you should calculate your tip based on what the meal would have cost without the coupon. Often, for large parties, a tip is already included on the bill, so be sure to check.

Other people you should tip for services provided include taxi drivers (10-15 percent), hairdressers (15-20 percent), hotel cleaning staff (a couple of dollars left in the room), and bartenders (a dollar on a mixed drink or a couple of beers). In Kentucky, it is also customary to tip the groom or other farm representative who shows you around on a horse farm tour. A tip of $5-10 is average, depending on how long and in-depth the tour was.

Sales Tax
State sales tax in Kentucky is 6 percent and is added to the price of all goods, except groceries and prescription drugs. Hotel taxes vary by area. In Louisville, the hotel tax is 15.01 percent, while it is 13.4 percent in Lexington and 11.24 percent in Northern Kentucky.

MAPS AND TOURIST INFORMATION
The **Kentucky Department of Tourism** (800/225-8747, www.kentuckytourism. com) maintains an informative website that contains information on attractions, restaurants, hotels, and festivals and also provides suggested itineraries based on location or interest. The department also produces multiple brochures, which may be downloaded from the website or requested via phone. Additional tourist bureaus are run by cities and counties throughout the state. Contact information for each is provided in the relevant chapters.

For those traveling by car, Kentucky runs eight interstate welcome centers, each of which is stocked with maps, brochures, and has on-site staff ready to answer questions. The welcome centers are Bullitt County (Louisville area, I-65 S), Christian County (southwestern Kentucky, I-24 W), Franklin (Frankfort area, I-65 N), Berea (central Kentucky,

I-75), Grayson (Western Kentucky, I-64 W), Shelby (Louisville area, I-64 E), Whitehaven (Paducah, I-24 E), and Williamsburg (southeastern KY, I-75 N).

AAA members can get maps and tour books from their local office for free. Additionally, almost all hotels offer state maps and other brochures.

COMMUNICATIONS AND MEDIA
Internet Access
Those looking to hop online while in Kentucky shouldn't have to search too hard for a connection, especially if you have your own computer. Many hotels, cafés, and restaurants offer wireless access to patrons. For those with or without a computer, Kentucky's public libraries offer online access through both wireless service and publicly accessible computers. For a listing of wireless access points throughout the state, visit www.wififreespot.com/ky.html.

Area Codes
Kentucky has four area codes: 270, covering Paducah, Owensboro, Bowling Green, and most of Western and southwestern Kentucky; 502, covering Louisville, Bardstown, Frankfort, and surrounding areas; 606, covering Ashland, most of Eastern Kentucky, and northeastern Kentucky; and 859, covering Lexington, Covington, and surrounding areas.

Cell Phones
Cell phones have taken over Kentucky, with much of the state getting reliable cell phone reception. Dead zones do exist, however, especially in Appalachia and very rural areas. AT&T customers seem to report the most problems and Verizon customers the least, although no company is exempt from complaints, dropped calls, or areas with poor or no reception.

Newspapers and Magazines
Kentucky's major newspapers, covering local, state, national, and international news are

Louisville's *Courier-Journal* (www.courier-journal.com) and the *Lexington Herald-Leader* (www.kentucky.com). All cities and nearly every town support a newspaper, many offering intensely local coverage.

Kentucky Monthly (www.kentuckymonthly.com) is a magazine celebrating the Bluegrass State and its people. *Louisville Magazine* (www.loumag.com) focuses specifically on the largest city in the Commonwealth while also covering topics of statewide interest. The annual dining guide provides a wealth of information on the city's many restaurants. For the sports fan, multiple magazines are devoted to Kentucky sports including *Cats' Pause* (www.kentucky.rivals.com), which focuses on UK basketball and football; *Inside the Ville* (http://louisville.scout.com), a resource for UL fans; and *Kentucky Game and Fish* (www.kentuckygameandfish.com), for the avid hunter and angler.

TIME ZONES

Kentucky is divided into two time zones, Eastern and Central. All of the sites within the Louisville; Lexington and Horse Country; Bardstown, the Bourbon Trail, and Frankfort; Northern Kentucky; and Appalachia chapters fall within the Eastern Time Zone. All of the sites within the Owensboro, Paducah, and Land Between the Lakes chapter and the majority of the sites within the Bowling Green, Cave Country, and South-Central Lakes chapter fall within the Central Time Zone (sometimes referred to as "slow time" by Kentuckians). If you're uncertain of the time zone, call and confirm with the visitors bureau or the attraction you wish to visit. The entire state observes Daylight Savings Time, advancing clocks one hour in the spring (at 2am on the second Sunday in March), and turning them back one hour in the fall (at 2am on the first Sunday in November).

RESOURCES

Suggested Reading

GENERAL INFORMATION

Kleber, John E. *The Kentucky Encyclopedia.* University Press of Kentucky, 1992. If you have a question about the Bluegrass State, you can probably find the answer somewhere within this book's 1,080 pages and more than 2,000 entries. Completed for the state's bicentennial, *The Kentucky Encyclopedia* covers all things Kentucky.

LITERATURE

Berry, Wendell. *Collected Poems.* North Point Press, 1985. Drawing together nearly 200 poems from eight collections, this work contains some of Berry's most notable poems, the type that sear themselves into your memory and stay with you long after you've closed the book.

Grubbs, Morris Allen, ed. *Home and Beyond: An Anthology of Kentucky Short Stories.* University Press of Kentucky, 2001. With stories from 40 Kentucky authors, this collection celebrates the best short fiction to come out of the Bluegrass State between 1945 and 2000. The stories, which range broadly in theme and location, will take readers across time and space. Each story is fronted by a brief autobiography of the author. Familiar names include Robert Penn Warren, Jesse Stuart, Barbara Kingsolver, Bobbie Ann Mason, and Wendell Berry.

Jones, Holly Goddard. *Girl Trouble.* Harper, 2009. The eight stories in this debut collection are set in the fictional town of Roma, located in Western Kentucky. Through well-developed characters, Jones turns an unsentimental eye on life in this small town.

Kingsolver, Barbara. *The Bean Trees.* Harper, 1998. Kingsolver's debut novel tells the story of Kentucky girl Taylor Greer as she sets out from her small town and heads west, eventually landing in Phoenix, Arizona. It's the type of book that makes you laugh and cry at the same time, and one that I never get tired of reading.

Mason, Bobbie Ann. *Spence + Lila.* Ecco, 1998. Although it seems a simple love story, *Spence + Lila* is also an honest depiction of working-class life in Western Kentucky and the profound changes this region of the country has undergone in recent decades.

Stuart, Jesse. *The Thread that Runs so True.* Touchstone, 1950. This autobiographical book by one of Kentucky's poet laureates tells the story of his teaching career in Eastern Kentucky, where he started out in a one-room schoolhouse.

HISTORY AND CULTURE

Clark, Thomas D. *A History of Kentucky.* J. Stuart Foundation, 1992. First published in 1937, this book by Kentucky's most noted historian is considered the authoritative history on the Bluegrass State.

Harrison, Lowell H., and James C. Klotter. *A New History of Kentucky.* University of Kentucky Press, 1997. This book from two contemporary Kentucky historians is considered to be the most comprehensive look at Kentucky history since Clark's *A History of Kentucky.* The investigation of history is in-depth, and although not a light read, the book is a must for any scholar of the Bluegrass State.

Pearce, John Ed. *Days of Darkness: The Feuds of Eastern Kentucky.* University Press of Kentucky, 1994. Journalist John Pearce answers the who, what, and why in relation to six of Eastern Kentucky's most famous feuds in this compelling and extensively researched book.

Wheeler, Lonnie. *Blue Yonder: Kentucky, The United State of Basketball.* Orange Frazer Press, 1998. For many Kentuckians, UK basketball is a religion and a deeply important part of local culture. This book relates the history of the most successful men's basketball program in the nation in a way that will appeal to both Wildcat fans and those who (mistakenly) believe that it's just a game.

ARCHITECTURE, MUSIC, AND PHOTOGRAPHY

Barnes, Thomas G. *Kentucky's Last Great Places.* University Press of Kentucky, 2002. Kentucky's bounteous beauty is documented in more than 100 photographs showcasing the many natural environments in the state. The accompanying essays provide context.

Domer, Dennis, Gregory A. Luhan, and David Mohney. *The Louisville Guide.* Princeton Architectural Press, 2004. Louisville is a city rich in important architecture and is a leader in the field of historic preservation. This book takes readers on a tour of the city's most significant buildings, providing background and history that is accessible to architectural scholars as well as the general public.

Titon, Jeff Todd. *Old-Time Kentucky Fiddle Tunes.* University Press of Kentucky, 2001. Fiddlers will love the transcriptions of favorite tunes from Kentucky, while aficionados who aren't musicians will enjoy reading about the history of these songs and the people who played them as well as listening to the accompanying CD.

Wolfe, Charles K. *Kentucky Country: Folk and Country Music of Kentucky.* University Press of Kentucky, 2009. Music lovers keen to learn more about Kentucky's tradition of folk and country music will want to get a hold of this book, which takes readers on a tour of sites important to the development and history of the genres and introduces readers to both music stars and the behind-the-scenes movers and shakers.

OUTDOORS

Brown, Michael H. *Hiking Kentucky.* Falcon, 2007. For those looking to explore Kentucky by foot, this book offers descriptions of 79 hikes, which range from easy family outings to multi-day backpacking trips.

Lander Jr., Arthur B. *A Fishing Guide to Kentucky's Major Lakes.* University Press of Kentucky, 1998. With information on 22 of Kentucky's most popular fishing lakes, this book provides all the details an angler needs to land the big one.

Molloy, Johnny. *The Best in Tent Camping: Kentucky.* Menasha Ridge Press, 2006. Highlighting 50 campgrounds that cater to the tent camper, this guide will appeal to the camping purist looking to pitch a tent in Kentucky.

Reigler, Susan. *The Complete Guide to Kentucky State Parks.* University of Kentucky Press, 2009. Those wishing to get better acquainted with Kentucky's state parks will want to pick up a copy of this book, which provides details on each of the parks, including the various activities and amenities offered at the parks.

Sehlinger, Bob and Johnny Molloy. *A Canoeing & Kayaking Guide to Kentucky*. Menasha Ridge Press, 2004. With descriptions of 77 waterways, this book offers suggested kayaking and canoeing trips for water lovers of all skill and ability levels.

TRAVEL

Berry, Wes. *The Kentucky Barbecue Book*. University Press of Kentucky, 2013. Wes Berry set out on a mission to try every barbecue joint in Kentucky. In this book, he documents not only the places he visits and the food he eats at them, but also all the interesting characters he meets along the way.

Holland, Jeffrey Scott, Mark Moran, and Mark Sceurman. *Weird Kentucky: Your Travel Guide to Kentucky's Local Legends and Best Kept Secrets*. Sterling, 2008. If strange, unusual, and downright weird describes your favorite type of attraction, pick up this book.

Kappele, William. *Kentucky Scenic Driving*. Falcon, 2000. Featuring 37 drives, this book highlights road trips with the best scenery in the state.

West, Gary. *Eating Your Way Across Kentucky: 101 Must Places to Eat*. Acclaim Press, 2006. Although the 2006 publication date means this book doesn't include the latest of the greatest, it does give readers a good idea of the variety of cuisine that you can find in Kentucky and makes suggestions about the best places to try Kentucky favorites.

COOKBOOKS

Lundy, Jonathan. *Jonathan's Bluegrass Table*. Butler Books, 2009. The chef at Jonathan's at Gratz Park, a Lexington favorite known for its redefined Kentucky cuisine, reveals 147 of his favorite recipes, most of which are accompanied by a mouthwatering photo, in this book.

Schmid, Albert W. A. *The Kentucky Bourbon Cookbook*. University Press of Kentucky, 2010. Build all your meals around bourbon with recipes from this cookbook, which covers breakfast, lunch, dinner, and dessert.

Internet Resources

GENERAL INFORMATION

State of Kentucky
http://kentucky.gov
The official website of Kentucky contains information on government, education, employment, and tourism. It's most useful for residents or those considering moving to Kentucky.

Kentucky Tourism
www.kentuckytourism.com
With information on all the regions in Kentucky, as well as listings of events and festivals, this should be your first online stop for travel planning.

OUTDOORS

Kentucky State Parks
http://parks.ky.gov
This comprehensive site provides details on all of Kentucky's state parks. Find out what there is to do at each park and reserve lodge or campground accommodations.

Kentucky Department of Fish and Wildlife
http://fw.ky.gov
Visit this website to apply for hunting and fishing licenses, download guides to wildlife management areas and lakes, and sign up for outdoor education courses.

Trails-R-Us
http://trailsrus.com
Covering Kentucky, Tennessee, West Virginia, Virginia, and South Carolina, this site covers a full range of outdoor offerings from ATV trails to paddleways.

Kentucky Farms Are Fun
www.kentuckyfarmsarefun.com
This one-stop shop contains listings for agritourism destinations all over Kentucky. You can find farmers markets, wineries, orchards, distilleries, livestock farms, and more.

OFFBEAT SITES
Roadside America
www.roadsideamerica.com
If you're a collector of roadside oddities, visit this website to get information on places like the Mother Goose House or the world's longest go-kart track, both located in Kentucky.

Index

XYZ

List of Maps

MAP SYMBOLS

▨ Expressway	◖	Highlight	✗	Airfield	⚲	Golf Course
Primary Road	○	City/Town	✈	Airport	🅿	Parking Area
Secondary Road	◉	State Capital	▲	Mountain	⬗	Archaeological Site
Unpaved Road	⊛	National Capital	✛	Unique Natural Feature	⚑	Church
Trail	★	Point of Interest			⛽	Gas Station
Ferry	•	Accommodation	🦑	Waterfall	Glacier
Railroad	▾	Restaurant/Bar	▲	Park	Mangrove
Pedestrian Walkway	▪	Other Location	🚩	Trailhead	Reef
Stairs	⋀	Campground	⛷	Skiing Area	Swamp

CONVERSION TABLES

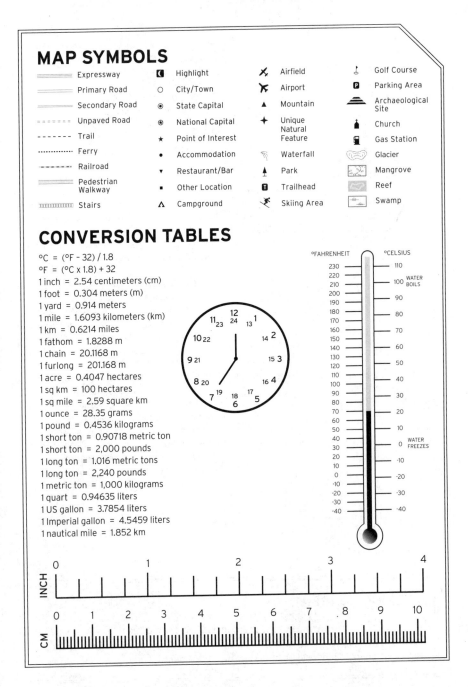

$°C = (°F - 32) / 1.8$
$°F = (°C \times 1.8) + 32$
1 inch = 2.54 centimeters (cm)
1 foot = 0.304 meters (m)
1 yard = 0.914 meters
1 mile = 1.6093 kilometers (km)
1 km = 0.6214 miles
1 fathom = 1.8288 m
1 chain = 20.1168 m
1 furlong = 201.168 m
1 acre = 0.4047 hectares
1 sq km = 100 hectares
1 sq mile = 2.59 square km
1 ounce = 28.35 grams
1 pound = 0.4536 kilograms
1 short ton = 0.90718 metric ton
1 short ton = 2,000 pounds
1 long ton = 1.016 metric tons
1 long ton = 2,240 pounds
1 metric ton = 1,000 kilograms
1 quart = 0.94635 liters
1 US gallon = 3.7854 liters
1 Imperial gallon = 4.5459 liters
1 nautical mile = 1.852 km

MOON KENTUCKY

Avalon Travel
a member of the Perseus Books Group
1700 Fourth Street
Berkeley, CA 94710, USA
www.moon.com

Editor: Nikki Ioakimedes
Series Manager: Kathryn Ettinger
Copy Editor: Melissa Brandzel
Graphics and Production Coordinator: Lucie Ericksen
Cover Designer: Faceout Studios, Charles Brock
Moon logo: Tim McGrath
Map Editor: Kat Bennett
Cartographers: Stephanie Poulain, Brian Shotwell
Indexer: Rachel Kuhn

ISBN-13: 978-1-61238-740-6
ISSN: 2159-872X

Printing History
1st Edition – 2011
2nd Edition – May 2014
5 4 3 2 1

Text © 2014 by Theresa Dowell Blackinton.
Maps © 2014 by Avalon Travel.
All rights reserved.

Some photos and illustrations are used by permission and are the property of the original copyright owners.

Front cover photo: Cumberland Falls State Park near Corbin, Kentucky © Danita Delimont/GettyImages
Title page photo: A bridge reflected in water © Theresa Dowell Blackinton
Interior color photos: pages 4-12, 14-23: © Theresa Dowell Blackinton; page 13: © dndavis/123RF
Back cover photo: © Theresa Dowell Blackinton

Printed in Canada by Friesens

Moon Handbooks and the Moon logo are the property of Avalon Travel. All other marks and logos depicted are the property of the original owners. All rights reserved. No part of this book may be translated or reproduced in any form, except brief extracts by a reviewer for the purpose of a review, without written permission of the copyright owner.

All recommendations, including those for sights, activities, hotels, restaurants, and shops, are based on each author's individual judgment. We do not accept payment for inclusion in our travel guides, and our authors don't accept free goods or services in exchange for positive coverage.

Although every effort was made to ensure that the information was correct at the time of going to press, the author and publisher do not assume and hereby disclaim any liability to any party for any loss or damage caused by errors, omissions, or any potential travel disruption due to labor or financial difficulty, whether such errors or omissions result from negligence, accident, or any other cause.

KEEPING CURRENT

If you have a favorite gem you'd like to see included in the next edition, or see anything that needs updating, clarification, or correction, please drop us a line. Send your comments via email to feedback@moon.com, or use the address above.